THE PRESIDENCY OF
DONALD J. TRUMP

# The Presidency of Donald J. Trump

## A First Historical Assessment

Julian E. Zelizer, Editor

PRINCETON UNIVERSITY PRESS
PRINCETON AND OXFORD

Published by Princeton University Press
41 William Street, Princeton, New Jersey 08540
99 Banbury Road, Oxford OX2 6JX

press.princeton.edu



Library of Congress Cataloging-in-Publication Data

Names: Zelizer, Julian E., editor.
Title: The presidency of Donald J. Trump : a first historical assessment / edited by Julian Zelizer.
Description: Princeton : Princeton University Press, [2022] | Includes bibliographical references and index.
Identifiers: LCCN 2021032764 (print) | LCCN 2021032765 (ebook) | ISBN 9780691228945 (paperback) | ISBN 9780691228938 (hardback) | ISBN 9780691228952 (ebook)
Subjects: LCSH: Trump, Donald, 1946– | United States—Politics and government—2017– | Political culture—United States—History—21st century. | Presidents—United States.
Classification: LCC E912 .P74 2022 (print) | LCC E912 (ebook) | DDC 973.933092—dc23
LC record available at https://lccn.loc.gov/2021032764
LC ebook record available at https://lccn.loc.gov/2021032765

British Library Cataloging-in-Publication Data is available

Editorial: Bridget Flannery-McCoy, Alena Chekanov
Jacket/Cover Design: Karl Spurzem
Production: Erin Suydam
Publicity: James Schneider, Kate Farquhar-Thomson
Copyeditor: Elizabeth Schueler
Jacket/Cover Credit: Shutterstock

This book has been composed in Adobe Text Pro

Printed on acid-free paper. ∞

Printed in the United States of America

10 9 8 7 6 5 4 3 2 1

*In honor of all the people whose lives were lost during the COVID-19 pandemic. May their memory be for a blessing.*

# CONTENTS

# ABOUT THE CONTRIBUTORS

**KATHLEEN BELEW** is author of *Bring the War Home: The White Power Movement and Paramilitary America.* She has appeared as a CNN contributor and on *The Rachel Maddow Show*, *Frontline*, *Fresh Air*, and *All Things Considered*. She is assistant professor of history at the University of Chicago.

**ANGUS BURGIN** is associate professor of history at Johns Hopkins University. He is the author of *The Great Persuasion: Reinventing Free Markets since the Depression*, which won awards from the Organization of American Historians and the History of Economics Society, and serves as a coeditor of *Modern Intellectual History*.

**GERALDO CADAVA** is the Wender-Lewis Teaching and Research professor at Northwestern University. He has written two books: *The Hispanic Republican: The Shaping of an American Political Identity, from Nixon to Trump* and *Standing on Common Ground: The Making of a Sunbelt Borderland*.

**MERLIN CHOWKWANYUN** is the Donald Gemson Assistant Professor of Sociomedical Sciences at Columbia University's Mailman School of Health. He is the author of *All Health Politics Is Local: Community Battles for Medical Care and Environmental Health*. He is the principal investigator for ToxicDocs.org, a National Science Foundation–funded repository of millions of once-secret documents on industrial poisons, and he recently served on the *Lancet* Commission on Public Policy and Health in the Trump Era.

**BATHSHEBA DEMUTH** is assistant professor of history and environment and society at Brown University, where she specializes in the lands and seas of the Russian and North American Arctic. Her multiple-prize–winning first book, *Floating Coast: An Environmental History of the Bering Strait*, was named a *Nature* Top Ten Book of 2019 and Best Book of 2019 by *NPR*, *Kirkus Reviews*, and *Library Journal*, among others. Demuth holds a BA and MA from Brown University, and an MA and PhD from the University of California, Berkeley. Her writing has appeared in publications including the *American Historical Review* and the *New Yorker*.

**GREGORY P. DOWNS** is professor of history at University of California, Davis, and the author of three books about emancipation and Reconstruction, as well as a prize-winning short story collection. With Kate Masur, he authored the National Park Service's Reconstruction theme study that helped lead to the creation of the first National Park site devoted to Reconstruction, at Beaufort, South Carolina. He and Masur coedit the *Journal of the Civil War Era*. With Scott Nesbit, he created Mapping Occupation, a digital history of Reconstruction. With Masur, Hilary Green, and Scott Hancock, he runs the #wewantmorehistory campaign for creative public history.

**JEFFREY A. ENGEL** is the founding director of the Center for Presidential History at Southern Methodist University. He is the author or editor of thirteen books on American foreign policy and presidential politics; his latest is *When the World Seemed New: George H.W. Bush and the End of the Cold War*. In 2019, SMU Residential Life students named him their campus-wide HOPE Professor of the Year.

**BEVERLY GAGE** is professor of history and American studies at Yale University, specializing in twentieth-century U.S. political history. She is the author of *The Day Wall Street Exploded: A Story of America in Its First Age of Terror*, which examines the history of terrorism in the late nineteenth and early twentieth centuries, focusing on the 1920 Wall Street bombing. Her latest project, *G-Man: J. Edgar Hoover and the American Century*, is a biography of former FBI director J. Edgar Hoover. In addition to her teaching and research, Gage has written for numerous journals and magazines and is currently a contributing writer at the *New York Times Magazine*.

**NICOLE HEMMER** is an associate research scholar with the Obama Presidency Oral History Project at Columbia University and author of *Messengers of the Right: Conservative Media and the Transformation of American Politics* and *Partisans: The Conservative Revolutionaries Who Remade American Politics in the 1990s*. She is the founding editor of Made by History, the historical analysis section of the *Washington Post*, and a columnist at CNN Opinion. She also cohosts the podcasts *Past Present* and *This Day in Esoteric Political History*.

**MICHAEL KAZIN** teaches history at Georgetown University and is emeritus editor of *Dissent*. He is the author of seven books of U.S. history on topics ranging from the language of populism and the life of William Jennings Bryan to the American left and the movement that opposed World War I. His newest book is *What It Took to Win: A History of the Democratic Party*.

**DANIEL C. KURTZER** is the S. Daniel Abraham Professor of Middle East Policy Studies at Princeton University's School of Public and International Affairs. A twenty-nine-year veteran of the U.S. Foreign Service, Kurtzer served as the U.S. ambassador to Egypt and the U.S. ambassador to Israel. He is the coauthor most recently of *The Peace Puzzle: America's Quest for Arab-Israeli Peace*. He received his PhD from Columbia University.

**JAMES MANN** is the author of two books about the foreign policy of Trump's immediate predecessors: *Rise of the Vulcans* and *The Obamians*. He has also written three books about America's ties with China. He was formerly a Washington and Beijing correspondent for the *Los Angeles Times*.

**MAE NGAI** is Lung Family Professor of Asian American Studies, professor of history, and codirector of the Center for the Study of Ethnicity and Race at Columbia University. She is author of *Impossible Subjects: Illegal Aliens and the Making of Modern America*; *The Lucky Ones: One Family and the Invention of Chinese America*; and *The Chinese Question: The Gold Rushes and Global Politics*. She writes on immigration history and policy for the *New York Times*, *Washington Post*, *The Atlantic*, and other publications.

**MARGARET O'MARA** is the Howard and Frances Keller Endowed Professor of History at the University of Washington and author of several books on modern U.S. political and economic history, including *The Code: Silicon Valley and the Remaking of America.*

**JASON SCOTT SMITH** is professor of history at the University of New Mexico. He has published widely on aspects of American political history and political economy. He is the author of *Building New Deal Liberalism: The Political Economy of Public Works, 1933–1956* and *A Concise History of the New Deal.* In 2017–2018, he held the Mary Ball Washington Chair in American History at University College Dublin, Ireland, a U.S. Fulbright Scholar Award.

**KEEANGA-YAMAHTTA TAYLOR** is a professor in the Department of African-American Studies at Princeton University. She is author of *Race for Profit: How Banks and the Real Estate Industry Undermined Black Homeownership*, longlisted for a National Book Award for nonfiction and a 2020 finalist for the Pulitzer in History. Taylor's book *From #BlackLivesMatter to Black Liberation* won the Lannan Cultural Freedom Award for an Especially Notable Book in 2016. She is also editor of *How We Get Free: Black Feminism and the Combahee River Collective*, which won the Lambda Literary Award for LGBTQ nonfiction in 2018.

**LEANDRA ZARNOW** is an associate professor in the Department of History and affiliated faculty in Women, Gender, and Sexuality Studies and Jewish Studies at the University of Houston. Her first book was *Battling Bella: The Protest Politics of Bella Abzug* and she coedited with Stacie Taranto the collection *Suffrage at 100: Women in American Politics since 1920*. Her commentary on women in politics has appeared in outlets including *Time*, the *Washington Post, Axios, NPR*, and the *Houston Chronicle.*

**JULIAN E. ZELIZER** is the Malcolm Stevenson Forbes, Class of 1941 Professor of History and Public Affairs at Princeton University, a CNN political analyst, and a regular guest on NPR's *Here and Now.* He is the author or editor of twenty-one books, including *Burning Down the House: Newt Gingrich, the Fall of a Speaker, and the Rise of the New Republican Party*. The *New York Times* named the book as an Editor's Choice and one of the 100 Notable Books in 2020. His most recent book is *Abraham Joshua Heschel: A Life of Radical Amazement*. Zelizer, who has published over one thousand op-eds, has received fellowships from the Brookings Institution, the Guggenheim Foundation, the Russell Sage Foundation, the New York Historical Society, and New America.

# THE PRESIDENCY OF DONALD J. TRUMP

# 1

# Introduction

## THE MOST PREDICTABLE, UNCONVENTIONAL PRESIDENCY

*Julian E. Zelizer*

I knew this project would differ from the others in my series about the modern American presidency. President Donald J. Trump's four-year administration had been unlike anything else American democracy had experienced in recent decades, if ever. But I had not anticipated what would happen after the authors of this volume gathered for two days—on Zoom, given that we were still in the throes of a devastating global pandemic—to spend almost eight hours discussing early drafts of the chapters. The *New York Times* published a lengthy story by culture reporter Jennifer Schuessler about our conference.[1] When the piece appeared in print, I received an email from Jason Miller, who had been the chief spokesman for Trump's 2016 campaign and a senior adviser on his reelection campaign in 2020. Miller, whose White House career had been sidetracked by a sex scandal, was advising the former president as he decided what to do next.

Miller wrote to say that Trump had read the article and that the former president was very interested in speaking with all of us. He was happy to answer any questions we might have. According to Miller, Trump wanted to give us his side of the story. Miller sent, along with correspondence from Trump's assistant Molly Michael, several backgrounders highlighting the accomplishments of the administration. Trump desired, Miller explained, to help my colleagues "tighten up some of the research" we were conducting.[2]

Former presidents George W. Bush and Barack Obama never contacted me. Though the *New York Times* had published an article about the conference I convened for the book on the Obama presidency,[3] we never heard from the former president or his staff. This time was different. Trump, with potential ambitions for seeking a second term, seemed eager to influence how historians saw the past. Given the enormous energy he expended during his presidency attempting to influence how Americans understood the events they were witnessing, this wasn't a total surprise. His term had even ended with his promoting a pointed narrative, an effort to sell to his supporters, and to some extent the history books, that he was not an unpopular one-term president like Herbert Hoover or Jimmy Carter whose record had been rejected by the public. Rather, Joe Biden won the election, Trump said, only because he had stolen it.

The authors' responses to the invitation were mixed, which was itself revealing of how different this presidency had been. Whereas some contributors were interested to listen to the president, though skeptical that he would be honest with us, others weren't sure about the value of hearing from a leader likely to repeat the talking points in the documents. More important, a number of people who are not contributors to the book, including some who had worked in Washington, urged us to proceed with caution because the former president, they said, had a record of misconstruing the nature of these conversations. If he ran for reelection, one person feared, we could suddenly be described as historical advisers.

I agreed to set up a Zoom meeting where the president could speak to us. Miller responded that he was excited and would set something up soon. Over the following weeks, the tumult continued. After my call with Miller, both he and the former president were involved in several explosive stories. Miller himself was in a widely publicized legal struggle, ordered by a federal judge to pay $42,000 in legal fees for a failed defamation suit. The former president's business was under a criminal investigation by the attorney general of New York. He was also deciding what his role should be in the 2022 midterm elections and how to reestablish his visibility in the media.

Although I wasn't sure that the meeting would really happen, the event took place on July 1. This was one of over twenty-two interviews, according to Axios, that Trump had given for books being written after his term ended.[4] The preparation for the Zoom event was more haphazard than I had imagined. Trump's team allowed me to set up the video link on my own—and to record the event—without any kind of preconditions or even much of a discussion about how it would be structured. His staff did ask me if the meeting would be in a grid or two-person format and whether I would moderate. Though it is impossible to imagine any former commander in chief handling almost any meeting in this loose of a fashion, it wasn't a total surprise for a president who took pride in doing so many things in broad daylight.

At 4:15 in the afternoon, I signed into Zoom so that his team could check the visuals on their end. I was sitting in the family living room, with a bookcase behind me, the same makeshift "studio" that I used for television, classes, and talks since the start of the pandemic. As his production team prepared to go live, I could see that Trump would be sitting at a wooden desk in his Bedminster Golf Club with an American flag on the side. It almost looked like a set from a bare-bones television show about the presidency. He would be positioned in between two windows, each with the blinds drawn down. At 4:20, the contributors gradually started to sign in, all remaining on mute as I had asked them to do. Trump's box went dark once his staff was ready to go, with the video and audio temporarily muted. The screen read "Donald J. Trump." With seconds to go, I took a deep breath, imagining what his debate opponents must have felt like before going on stage, though in this case my job was just to listen and to moderate.

Right at 4:30, Trump's Zoom screen turned on. There was the forty-fifth president of the United States. He was dressed in a standard black suit, wearing a blue tie. As our meeting got under way, the first thought that ran through my head was that this could only happen with this particular president and in the year 2021. Everything about it felt surreal. "Welcome Mr. President, how are you?" I said. "How are you, thank you Julian," he responded. I introduced the president and we began.[5]

This meeting, which happened one day after C-SPAN released a poll of historians who ranked him as fortieth (beating out only Franklin Pierce, Andrew Johnson, and James Buchanan),[6] was an opportunity for him to tell us how he had strengthened the nation's standing. He spoke in a relatively calm voice, with a single piece of white paper in front of him on the desk, devoid of much of the explosive rhetoric that had become familiar to Americans. Not wanting to waste a second, Trump launched into a fervent defense of his record. He said that he had seen the *New York Times* article about our conference and wanted to make sure that we were accurate. "I read a piece . . . and I said that I'd like to see accuracy. I think that we had a great presidency. . . . We did things in foreign affairs that nobody thought even possible, the Abraham Accords, and other things. . . . It's an honor to be with you. . . . If you are doing a book, I would like you to be able to talk about the success of the Trump, the Trump administration. We've had some great people, we've had some people that weren't so great. That's understandable. That's true with, I guess, every administration. But overall, we had tremendous, tremendous success."

In the surreal modern communications format that resembles the old *Hollywood Squares* television show, on the same day that the Trump Organization was charged with a "scheme to defraud" the government, Trump reiterated a number of claims that he had been making about his term. The consummate showman, Trump knew his audience. Building on documents that Miller had shared with our group, which presented him as a rather conventional and moderate president with a long list of achievements, Trump focused primarily on what he believed to be the most important components of his record on the economy, foreign policy, trade, and the pandemic.

Before the pandemic, Trump said, the economy was breaking all records. And Trump deserved credit. "We got rid of NAFTA, the worst trade deal ever made," he stated as an example. Trump became especially animated when outlining his trade deal with China that had a "tremendous impact" for U.S. farmers, which he admitted to have spoken about very "braggadociously," before having to pull back as a result of COVID-19 ("the plague," he said, "or whatever you want to call it") since it "eviscerated everything we had to do with China." Most people said the COVID-19 vaccine would take a long time to make, if it ever came to fruition (three to five years), but Trump boasted to us that the United States finished work on the cure in less than a year. He wanted credit since his administration "made, maybe, one of the best bets in history" by buying billions and billions of dollars in vaccines "long prior to knowing" whether they would work. Though the Federal Drug Administration didn't like his style, Trump said, the pressure that he put on the agency proved successful: "They were very bureaucratic, they were very slow." He added that he also managed to contain costs for the vaccine and other relevant medicines, as well as for other pharmaceutical drugs before the pandemic started.

On foreign policy, Trump moved in rapid-fire fashion through a succession of issues, eager to squeeze in as much as he could before our time ended. When turning to Russia, he reiterated how tough he was with the country, despite getting along with Vladimir Putin. The North Atlantic Treaty Organization (NATO) received a substantial amount of time as Trump wanted to explain to us his success in compelling member countries to pay higher dues. "It was a rollercoaster downward" while we were a "rocketship upward" he said of a twenty-year period during which the United States paid a disproportionate amount. Trump told us of a meeting with NATO leaders that didn't get "picked up by the press" in which he made demands to our allies to do better. He recounted a speech in which he said that the United States was protecting everyone from "Russia, was the Soviet Union, now Russia, very similar, as you understand, better than anybody." When one leader at the meeting had asked him directly if he would pull out of NATO should they not pay more, Trump said yes. If he had not done that, Trump argued to our group, the negotiations would not have worked. The "other presidents that you write about, in some cases glowingly, they would go to NATO, they wouldn't even mention it, they'd make a speech and say good luck." In contrast, Trump wanted us to understand that he delivered. At another point in his presentation, the former president went into considerable detail about a deal that he worked out with South Korea despite its leader's energetic protestation (the opposite of former Florida governor Jeb Bush, he noted in a side quip). He also vented about governors from blue states who would praise him in private strategy meetings about COVID but then go in front of a press conference one or two days later and "knock the hell out of me." It was "so unfair," he remarked. The previous "administrations," had been unprepared, he claimed. Trump made sure to take a few swipes at President Joe Biden before he was done, including offering us a Buzzfeed-style list of countries that were happy about the 2020 election: China, Iran, Russia, and South Korea.

Toward the end of his half-hour presentation, the president made sure to come back to the place where he started.

> I just thought that I would speak to you people, and I respect you. . . . And I thought if you are writing a book, it would really be nice if we had an accurate book. We've had some good ones, we've had some bad ones. We have books written that bear no relationship to the facts, but they want to write them because, you know, they just want to write them. . . . I've gone a little bit out of my way, Julian, to speak to people. They are going to write a book, it's history. Your book is a very important book. . . . I'm looking at the list, it's a tremendous group of people. And I think rather than being critical I'd love to have you hear me out, which is what we are doing now, and I appreciate it.

Trump concluded with an unexpected foray into the construction of the navy's $13 billion supercarrier, "the stupidest thing that I've ever seen," the USS *Gerald R. Ford*. The press had been reporting on the technical difficulties that the navy had been experiencing. Trump recalled his visit to the carrier during which he had allegedly warned "Mr. Architect," who was in charge of the technologically cutting-edge project, that they were making big mistakes. Trump remembered meeting with one of the "catapulters," who had been there for twenty-one years, who didn't understand why they put the tower in the back of the ship and used electric rather than steam. None of them agreed with what the higher-ups were doing with the design. All the new technology, the worker had told then president Trump, didn't make sense to anyone who had experience in aerial military operations and you had to be "Albert Einstein" to fix things that in older eras would have been easy to repair; steam was simpler than electric. Though the puzzled faces in the Zoom boxes of our contributors suggested to me they were not quite sure what Trump was trying to tell us, the point of the story seemed to be that he knew how to build things and that even the best and brightest—perhaps a not so subtle jab at all of us—without "common sense" often didn't know what they were doing in contrast to average, hardworking people who didn't get any respect.

Over the second half hour of our event, Trump took the questions in stride, repeatedly saying that everything was "fair" and answering every query in a relatively constrained tone. To be sure, there were moments of classic Trumpism, such as his criticism of James Comey as a "sick person" whom liberals had hated until he fired him or describing January 6 as a peaceful rally, with "way over" a million people, that was ruined by a small group, infiltrated by Antifa and Black Lives Matter activists, who were not contained as a result of poor decisions by Speaker Nancy Pelosi and the U.S. Capitol Police. He spoke about why the standard press releases that he had been using since being banned from Twitter were "far more elegant" forms of communication than 140-character missives, sounding almost as if he were the one to have discovered the format that presidents have been using for decades.

But Trump did not become confrontational. This was not the proper setting. When Jeffrey Engel asked if he could really have imagined not coming to the defense of a member of NATO should one of them have been attacked, he acknowledged the importance of alliances and that there was a "good thing" to unity and the organization, but returned to the point that he wanted every member to pay its fair share. Michael Kazin asked if he thought of himself as part of the conservative tradition or whether he had remade conservatism. Trump said that, though he was a conservative, he preferred to think of himself as a "common sense person," wherever that mentality led him—"I believe we have to have borders, I believe in good education, I believe in a strong military, I believe in law and order. . . . I think they are mostly conservative," and he believed in "fair" trade, devoid of the bad agreements that had been negotiated by "stupid people" on Capitol Hill. Trump pushed back on the perception that he was antiexpertise, instead coming back to the idea that he was motivated by common sense, listening to many voices for whom he had "tremendous respect," including Anthony Fauci (who, he explained, liked to say, "Call me Tony, sir"), but then using his own instincts to decide what was the best path forward for the nation.

Trump had a few seemingly candid moments. He admitted, for instance, that he should have been more careful with whom he retweeted, since some of the individuals whose messages he blasted out "fairly quickly" were not "the best person to retweet." He suggested understanding why so many people were taken aback by the language he used in his infamous "rocket man" tweets about North Korea's Kim Jong-un but believed the bluster helped check the dangerous nation and prevent any sort of war. When Beverly Gage began her question by explaining that she was writing the chapter on Trump's relationship to the FBI and intelligence communities, he flashed a bit of humor by predicting that "it's going to be a beauty."

As we reached the end of our time, I brought the discussion to a close. After I thanked him, he thanked us as well for the opportunity and said, "I hope it's going to be a number one best seller!"

Then, as is the case in the world of Zoom, I clicked the red "leave meeting" button and the event ended. The meeting was over, the president and my contributors were gone. Within minutes I received a thank-you note from him, via one of his assistants, that said, "Julian, So interesting—thank you very much. Please feel free to call if I can be of further assistance. President Donald J. Trump."

Two days later, Trump was back on the campaign trail. Announcing that he had already made his decision about whether to run again in 2024, Trump delivered a blistering speech at a "Save America" rally in rainy Sarasota, Florida. Going after "prosecutorial misconduct" by the Manhattan District Attorney's office, a "rigged" election system, and the "fake media," he promised that "together we will take back the House and we will take back the Senate, and we will take back America." On July 9, as a final coda to the story, Trump announced to the press that doing so many interviews with authors writing books about him had been a "total waste of time." He added: "These writers are often bad people who write whatever comes to their mind or fits their agenda. It has nothing to do with facts or reality."[7]

The entire interaction immediately suggested the unique challenges that any historian faces when trying to write about the recent past. Whether dealing with a living subject as unpredictable as President Trump or tackling more staid questions, the challenge of contemporary history is formidable. This is a subject that historians have debated many times over the centuries.

In 1967, writing in *The Atlantic*, the historian Arthur Schlesinger Jr. took on the bias against historians (like himself) who sought to interpret the times in which they lived. Schlesinger, who had famously been an adviser to President John F. Kennedy, published one of the classic texts on the administration after being inside the closed doors of decision-making.[8] Contemporary history was not only legitimate, Schlesinger argued, but more vital than ever before. The accelerating pace of change in modern times, he claimed, meant that "the 'present' becomes the 'past' more swiftly than ever before." Schlesinger offered a robust defense of this kind of writing, claiming that it was no longer "a personal whim or passing fashion. It is now a necessity—a psychic necessity to counter the pressures of life in a high velocity age and a technical necessity to rescue and preserve evidence for future historians."[9]

The premise of my series with Princeton University Press has always been that the first draft of history matters. Though incomplete and part of an ongoing conversation, it is an important first step. My exploration of presidents when they finish their term attempts to offer a template for undertaking this kind of work. Knowing that interpretations of any presidency will continue to evolve in perpetuity, and that historians who are themselves part of an era have a firsthand feel for the political atmosphere and key actors who shaped a moment, the initial historiography can offer important interventions. Too often, however, it is not done in the most useful fashion. Indeed, I launched this project in response to fielding questions from journalists who believe that the major contribution we can offer them is to rank different presidencies or to state with certainty what their "legacy" will be. Because I felt that neither question was especially pertinent or even answerable, my goal has always been to let professional historians do what they do best: contextualize a political leader within the long-term institutional, organizational, social, and cultural forces shaping the nation.

With each volume in this series, I have hoped to offer a foundation for thinking about what happened within a four- to eight-year period by turning to historians with expertise in relevant issues. I have searched for scholars whose work sits outside the cluster of "presidential historians" frequently seen and quoted in the press (though some of those presidential-centered scholars, whose writing retains a firm footing in the academy, have been included as well). Rather than exploring how a president "did" relative to his predecessors on some illusory scale, we seek to understand how the commander in chief operated in relation to what he inherited upon stepping into the Oval Office.

Although this series has dealt with divisive presidents before, never has the challenge felt as complicated as with President Donald Trump. Trump is one of the most unconventional presidents in American history. For any historian, the question instantly emerges: How does one write the history of a tumultuous period such as this? How does a scholar capture the events of this era with words that are direct and accurate but that will inevitably suggest normative assessments? What kind of language should one use? How does one write about a president who uttered words appealing to white nationalists in 2020 and incited a violent insurrection against the U.S. Congress, but do so in the analytical language that one might use to describe tax policy? Is that even the correct way to evaluate the period? How can we write about continuities and familiar political dynamics without "normalizing" behavior that must be understood to be a massive departure from political tradition?

The authors of this book, who are among the best historians in the country, have taken up the challenge with gusto. Unlike the work of journalists and writers whose focus has been on telling the behind-the-scenes, day-to-day events that consume any White House—the "fire and fury" of the moment, as the journalist Michael Wolff called it[10]—these essays are all about putting events into a long-term perspective. They use the knowledge and data currently available, and vast bodies of scholarly literature about the relevant pillars of the past leading to this moment, to examine what parts of this epoch can be understood as continuity—and thus a reflection of the troubled state of democracy toward the end of the 2010s—and what elements constituted sharp breaks, revealing how this administration pushed the country in new directions. They look beyond narratives of Trump as an out-of-control lone ranger maneuvering, as different advisors either tried to support or subvert him, to instead offer readers a bigger canvas to understand the moment.[11]

Whereas first-rate journalistic accounts of President Trump's immigration policies start their narrative with a cadre of America First hardliners, such as Stephen Miller and Stephen Bannon,[12] who discovered in Trump someone who could champion their vision for a winning candidate in 2016, the historians in this book begin back in the 1990s with the broader shift away from the 1965 immigration paradigm as a result of changes in political economy and partisan alignment. Reporters highlight Trump's personal fury at China to explain his willingness to break with the free-trade axioms of his party; this book looks at the gradual, multidecade breakdown of the accord that Richard Nixon reached with China in 1972 as part of his foreign policy of détente. The debate over racism and policing exploded, the pundits would write, after horrendous acts of violence against African Americans were captured on smartphones. The historian goes back to the urban rebellions of the 1960s,[13] at a minimum, to trace the ongoing struggle against institutional racism in our criminal justice system.

---

At the center of each chapter is Donald John Trump, a man who came to Washington from the world of New York real estate and reality television. Born on June 14, 1946, in Queens, New York, Trump was one of five children (the second youngest) of a real estate developer from the Bronx named Fred Trump and his wife, Mary Anne MacLeod Trump. The family raised the kids in Queens. Donald attended the Kew-Forest School until seventh grade and then, because of misbehavior, went to the New York Military Academy at age thirteen. He studied for two years as an undergraduate at Fordham University before transferring to the University of Pennsylvania, where he earned a degree from the Wharton School of Business in May 1968. Though Trump finished college while the United States was fighting in Vietnam, he avoided service five times, first through student draft deferments and then through medical exemptions.

Trump worked for his father's real estate company, Trump Management, starting when he was in college. His father had amassed more than twenty-seven thousand pieces of real estate in the outer boroughs of New York. The company bought rental properties around the city.

When Donald's older brother died from alcoholism at age forty-two, Fred decided that Donald would be the heir to his business. Just three years after graduating from college, Donald moved into the position of president and grew the operation into the Trump Organization. His father provided him with the money he needed to make investments. He had been receiving hundreds of thousands a year from his father since he was a child. Transfers of money and shell corporations amounting to more than $413 million in his lifetime revolved around elaborate schemes by which his family could avoid taxes.[14] Trump made a name for himself in the city by purchasing the beat-up Commodore Hotel and transforming it into the Grand Hyatt, which officially opened in Midtown in 1980. He developed Trump Tower and purchased the Plaza Hotel in 1988. Meanwhile, Trump started to invest in other properties. In Palm Beach, Florida, he purchased the Mar-a-Lago estate. In Atlantic City, New Jersey, he opened the Harrah's at Trump Plaza in 1984 and the Trump Taj Mahal in 1990.

Besides procuring real estate, Trump focused much of his attention on branding. He licensed his name for clothing, food, and buildings that his company did not run. He bought the New York Generals in 1983, a football team in the upstart United States Football League, and sponsored boxing matches. In 1988, Trump acquired Eastern Air Lines Shuttle and turned it into the Trump Shuttle. Like most of his ventures, this business lasted for just four years, failing to produce any profit. Within two years, the company wasn't earning enough to cover the mortgage payment for the $245 million loan he used to buy the planes. He depended on family partnerships to bail himself out of these ventures.

During the 1980s and 1990s, Trump emerged as a well-known figure in the New York media, a constant presence on the gossipy Page Six of the *New York Post.* One reporter wrote in 1984, "Donald J. Trump is the man of the hour. Turn on the television or open the newspaper almost any day of the week and there he is, snatching some star from the National Football League, announcing some preposterously lavish project he wants to build."[15] Always focusing his attention on the brand name, Trump relished his reputation as a brash, straight-talking real estate mogul who took part in the city's colorful nightlife. "Trump seemed an ideal subject for us," one reporter from the *Post* recalled, "as apt a symbol of the gaudy 1980s as the Christian Lacroix pouf skirt—and just as shiny and inflated."[16] Though he never found acceptance within New York's elite social circles, with many of the city's prominent figures seeing him as too brash—more Long Island than Upper East Side—and untrustworthy, the media soaked him up. He reveled in the image of being a tough, say-it-like-it-is guy, a man of the people who had done well. His father's wealth and money didn't make it into the narrative. Never hesitant to provide provocative statements to reporters, Trump emerged as a go-to guest on radio and television shows. "He is tall, lean and blond, with dazzling white teeth," noted an early *New York Times* profile, "and he looks ever so much like Robert Redford. He rides around town in a chauffeured silver Cadillac with his initials, DJT, on the plates. He dates slinky fashion models, belongs to the most elegant clubs and, at only 30 years of age, estimates that he is worth 'more than $200 million.'"[17] His love life continued to fascinate, first his 1977 marriage to the Czech model Ivana Zelníčková (with whom he had Donald Jr., Ivanka, and Eric), and then his affair with Marla Maples, whom he married in 1993 after divorcing Ivana (they had a daughter, Tiffany). He and Marla divorced in 1999, and Trump married Melania Knauss, a Slovenian model, in 2005 (they had a son named Baron). As of this writing, twenty-six women have accused Trump of sexual misconduct, including rape, since the 1970s. The allegations didn't stifle his growing presence. In 1987, his best-selling book *The Art of the Deal*, ghostwritten by Tony Schwartz, burnished his image as a master deal maker unrivaled in negotiations. The public started to perceive him as a brilliant entrepreneur. "Mr. Trump makes one believe for a moment in the American dream again. It's like a fairy tale," one reviewer noted.[18] Trump's appearances on professional wrestling and the *Howard Stern Show* made him a known voice. *Trump: The Game* came out two years after the book. Milton Bradley sold just eight hundred thousand of the two million game units produced.

On numerous occasions, he dipped his toes into the political waters. When five Black and Latino teenage men were (wrongly) arrested in 1989 for raping a woman jogging in Central Park, Trump purchased an advertisement in the city newspapers, including the *New York Times*, demanding the death penalty. "I want to hate these murderers and I always will," Trump stated in the ad. "I am not looking to psychoanalyze or understand them, I am looking to punish them . . . BRING BACK THE DEATH PENALTY AND BRING BACK OUR POLICE!" In a different light, he published an advertisement calling for peace in Central America and for President Ronald Reagan to pursue arms negotiations with Soviet leader Mikhail Gorbachev. Trump frequently switched party affiliations. He registered as a Republican in 1987, with the Independence Party in 1999, as a Democrat in 2001, as a Republican in 2009, with no party in 2011, and then again with the GOP in 2012.

Notwithstanding the image of himself that he promoted, Trump's business career was always problematic. Starting in 1973, when he hired former senator Joseph McCarthy's chief counsel, Roy Cohn, to advise him, the U.S. Department of Justice sued the Trump Management Corporation for racially discriminatory practices, violating the Fair Housing Act of 1968 in thirty-nine properties. Cohn, who would remain a close adviser for many years, helped Trump Management countersue the government for $100 million for making the charges. The company's discriminatory practices were well known. The folk singer Woody Guthrie, who had lived in one of Trump's properties, penned lyrics for a song called "Old Man Trump" about the elder: "Old Man Trump knows just how much racial hate he stirred up in that bloodpot of human hearts when he drawed that color line here at his Beach Haven family project." The Department of Justice found that the company refused to rent property to African Americans and lied about availability. The government and the Trumps reached a settlement in June 1975. Trump's company was required to provide the New York Urban League with a list of available apartments every week, and, in turn, the league could share the list with potential applicants. Besides race relations and labor practices, his business track record also caused deep concerns in the financial community. After the 1980s, most banks refused to do business with him because he had defaulted on hundreds of millions of dollars in loans; only Deutsche Bank was willing to lend him funds. During the 1990s and early 2000s, his organization filed for bankruptcy six times. He used the bankruptcies and other techniques to avoid paying income taxes for almost eighteen years.

His road into presidential politics happened gradually. Trump had run in some primaries as the Reform Party candidate in 1999 (he attacked his opponent, Patrick Buchanan, as a "Hitler Lover"). He roared back into the political spotlight in 2011 when he spoke to the Conservative Political Action Committee conference. Standing at the podium, Trump spoke for fourteen minutes, warning that the United States was becoming the "laughingstock" and "whipping post" for the world because its leaders were "weak and ineffective." He argued that China was a grave threat to the nation and dismissed Republicans like Ron Paul. "I like Ron Paul," Trump said as Paul's supporters started calling out his name. "I think he's a good guy—but honestly, he has just zero chance of getting elected."[19] That year, and in 2012, Trump emerged as a major figure in the birther movement, a campaign that stemmed from fringe right-wing organizations claiming that Barack Obama had not been born in Hawaii. Because of his public standing, he brought the effort to challenge the legitimacy of the first African American president to a bigger stage. "I'm starting to think he was not born here," he told the *Today* show. With newfound notoriety, he used the social media platform Twitter, while it was still relatively unknown, to continue blasting the president and to keep attention on himself. "How amazing," he wrote in one tweet in 2013, "the State Health Director who verified copies of Obama's 'birth certificate' died in plane crash today. All others lived." In another tweet, he called on hackers, who were "hacking everything else," to obtain Obama's college records and determine his place of birth.

Reality television, however, constituted his main path to political power. The producer Mark Burnett, a successful Briton who had pioneered this art form with the show *Survivor*, decided to launch a series about business. The premise of the show, which premiered on January 8, 2004, was that a successful tycoon would judge contestants who were competing in different tasks, from advertising to selling goods. Burnett thought that Trump would be the perfect person for the job. His brash, larger-than-life personality was the exact character he was searching for. And the formula worked. *The Apprentice* was a smash hit for fifteen seasons, attracting millions of viewers per episode; there was also a spin-off, *Celebrity Apprentice*, that featured B-level entertainers competing for Trump's affection. With the tagline "You're Fired!" the shows promoted Trump's reputation as the tough-as-nails, brutally honest business mogul who was the only person willing to tell it like it is. New Yorkers were more than familiar with him, but *The Apprentice* brought Trump to massive audiences around the country. As Frank Rich wrote, "The ritualistic weekly firing on 'The Apprentice' is an instant TV classic—right up there with Rod Serling beckoning us into the Twilight Zone."[20] Many came to perceive him as one of the savviest and most skillful entrepreneurs around—even as his actual business dealings were suffering. "For millions of Americans," one profile explained, "this became their image of Trump: in the boardroom, in control, firing people who didn't measure up to his standards. Trump lived in grand style, flew in a Trump-emblazoned jet or helicopter, and traveled from Trump Tower on Fifth Avenue to Mar-a-Lago in Palm Beach, Florida."[21] At the 2016 Emmy Awards, seven weeks before the election, the comedian Jimmy Kimmel looked at Burnett, who was sitting in the audience, and said, "Television brings people together, but television can also tear us apart. I mean, if it wasn't for television, would Donald Trump be running for President? . . . Thanks to Mark Burnett, we don't have to watch reality shows anymore, because we're living in one."[22]

When he officially decided to run for president, Trump was forced by NBC to step down from the show. Some speculated that he had toyed with running for the presidency in order to negotiate a better contract. But by the time his role on the show ended, Trump had the name recognition and image he wanted. On June 16, 2015, Trump came down the escalator of the glitzy Trump Tower in New York City—where *The Apprentice* had been filmed and where he lived—to announce before a hallway packed with reporters that he would "make America great again," warning of the undocumented Mexicans and Chinese officials who, he said, were threatening the United States. "Our country is in serious trouble," he said. "We don't have victories anymore."[23]

During the 2016 Republican primaries, Trump squared off against a number of formidable opponents, including Florida governor Jeb Bush, Florida senator Marco Rubio, Texas senator Ted Cruz, New Jersey governor Chris Christie, Ohio governor John Kasich, and many others in a crowded field. He turned his rallies into a central promotional instrument. Drawing passionate crowds, Trump stoked division and rage by railing against the multiple threats he claimed were undermining the country. After violence erupted at these events, such as when an African American protester was physically punched and kicked, he appeared to egg it on from the stage. The campaign used the events to collect data about supporters, while endless national media coverage of these spectacles provided the kind of free airtime that was impossible for other candidates to obtain. As a product and fan of television, Trump understood the medium. He knew that making provocative statements on air, as well as on social media platforms such as Twitter and Facebook, would generate greater attention for what he was trying to do. At the same time, he capitalized on the fact that the press seemed to bend over backward to demonstrate that they were being "fair and balanced" in covering him, inviting surrogates from the campaign to appear on air as "political analysts."

Politics, as Finley Peter Dunne's character Mr. Dooley proclaimed, was never "beanbag." But Trump took things to an entirely different level. In early January 2016, he attacked Republican senator John McCain, a well-respected Vietnam War veteran, by saying that he preferred war heroes "who weren't captured." He mocked other Republicans in the primaries, giving them nicknames like "Lyin' Ted" Cruz and "Liddle Marco." At one point, Trump compared Ben Carson's "pathological temper" to "child molesting" and insulted the physical appearance of the businesswoman Carly Fiorina.[24] Coming in just behind Cruz in Iowa, Trump went on to win the primaries in New Hampshire, South Carolina, and Nevada. He relished being the underdog, pitting himself against the political establishment and using each victory to show that the conventional analysts had no idea what they were talking about. He took seven out of eleven states on Super Tuesday. In May, he secured the nomination. To shore up support with evangelical Republicans, Trump promised to appoint conservative-leaning judges drawn from lists crafted by the Right through the Federalist Society. To be sure, there were Republicans who opposed the nomination. President George W. Bush and his father refused to attend the Republican Convention. Former Republican nominee Mitt Romney delivered a blistering speech calling Trump a "phony and fraud," mocking failed ventures such as Trump Steaks, and imploring the party to reject him before it was too late. Senator Ben Sasse of Nebraska announced that he would not attend his own party's convention, explaining that he would rather take his kids to "watch some dumpster fires across the state, all of which enjoy more popularity than the current frontrunner."[25]

Despite her impressive résumé, the Democratic nominee Hillary Clinton struggled as much of the media focused on Trump. Nor could she contain the endless email scandal stories that dogged her campaign. During the spring of 2016, Russian hackers infiltrated the emails of John Podesta, the head of the Democratic National Committee, and leaked them onto the internet through WikiLeaks in July. The data dump offered some embarrassing, though routine, private exchanges that stoked divisions among Democrats, particularly the lingering tensions between supporters of Senator Bernie Sanders, who had done better than expected in the primaries, and Clinton. The press discovered that when Clinton had been secretary of state, she had maintained a private email server, which was sometimes used for official business. Alleging that this had posed a national security threat, Republicans claimed that the emails were at the center of what was her worst criminal activity. The story triggered an FBI investigation. "Hillary's emails" turned into a major talking point for the GOP. There were also stories coming from the press that her decisions as secretary of state had been influenced by donors to the Clinton Foundation. The attacks constantly raised suspicions that somehow Clinton was corrupt while diverting attention from the major policy issues that the candidate wanted to discuss. Even when FBI director James Comey announced on July 5 that "no reasonable prosecutor" would bring a case against Clinton, recommending that no charges be made, the Republican attacks against Clinton on this issue continued.

The 2016 Republican Convention in Cleveland didn't disappoint. It was as if the world of professional wrestling, on whose shows Trump had appeared, choreographed the proceedings. Ignoring critics within his party, Trump and fellow Republicans put on a blistering show where every speaker threw red meat to the crowd. In the Quicken Arena, the speakers offered a gloomy assessment of the nation. They went after Clinton—former First Lady, U.S. senator, and secretary of state—by portraying her as a criminal. One night of the celebration showcased mothers who were in mourning after their kids had been killed by undocumented Latinos. "A vote for Hillary," one mother said, "is putting all of our children's lives at risk." New Jersey governor Chris Christie, as "former federal prosecutor" (he told the delegates), made a case against Clinton. General Michael Flynn stole the show when he galvanized the delegates with the chant "Lock her up! Lock her up!" In his acceptance speech, Trump said, "The attacks on our police, and the terrorism in our cities, threaten our very way of life." Trump promised that he alone "can fix it."

Clinton and the Democrats still felt good about their chances. It was hard for many Democrats to believe that Trump wouldn't cause many Republicans to defect from the party ticket—some made predictions of a landslide akin to 1964, when reaction against the extremist senator Barry Goldwater's nomination caused a massive victory for President Lyndon Johnson—and that Democrats wouldn't flock to the polls. It was also difficult for many in the press to see how a majority of Americans could cast their ballots for such a divisive figure as Trump, who lacked any experience in government and made a mockery of the election process. When data in October showed a close race in key states, analysts tended to assume that those competitions would inevitably end up in Clinton's favor.

The general election didn't get any prettier. Trump replaced his manager, the seasoned campaign operative Paul Manafort, with a team that included Roger Ailes, the creator of Fox News, who had been fired because of sexual harassment charges; the chairman of Breitbart News, Stephen Bannon; and a small group of other close advisers who pushed Trump to embrace his America First, conservative populist, antiestablishment message. The connection with the Far Right troubled some Republicans, but not enough for them to announce their support for Clinton. Trump played to core themes of white resentment, attacking China for robbing American workers of their jobs and continuing to paint immigration as a dire threat to the nation. There were frequent retweets of antisemitic, Islamophobic, and xenophobic messages. When CNN's Jake Tapper questioned Trump about the fact that Ku Klux Klan grand wizard David Duke had endorsed him, the Republican nominee refused to disavow the endorsement and would not acknowledge that he knew who Duke was or even what Tapper meant by "white nationalism." "I don't know anything about David Duke. I don't know what you're even talking about with white supremacy and white supremacist," he said.[26] When these kinds of statements led Clinton to state at a fund-raiser, "You know, just to be grossly generalistic, you could put half of Trump's supporters into what I call the basket of deplorables, right? The racist, sexist, homophobic, xenophobic, Islamophobic—you name it. And he has lifted them up," Trump supporters lit into the Democrats and embraced the term as their own. "DEPLORABLE LIVES MATTER," one banner said.

Trump dodged scandal after scandal. Moments that would have brought down many other campaigns didn't seem to affect him. He made Teflon seem sticky. In early October, the media reported on an audio recording from 2005 during an interview with the entertainment program *Access Hollywood*. While speaking off-camera, without knowing that he was on tape, Trump recounted his sexual conquests to the host Billy Bush and boasted of having sexually assaulted women. "I'm automatically attracted to beautiful women—I just start kissing them. It's like a magnet. Just kiss. I don't even wait. When you're a star, they let you do it. You can do anything." When Bush said, "Whatever you want," Trump replied, "Grab 'em by the pussy. You can do anything." Some Republicans feared that this would be the end of the campaign. The head of the Republican National Committee, Reince Priebus, urged the candidate to drop out to save the party. But Trump would have none of it. And he was right. The tape wasn't a turning point. It barely dented his support. And he survived. Dismissing the recorded conversation as "locker room talk," Trump and his supporters used this scandal as another example of "politically correct" Democrats coming after him and "real" American men. The *Access Hollywood* story drowned out coverage of a major public announcement by the U.S. intelligence community that Russia was meddling in the election to help bolster Trump.

The televised debates were a spectacle. While Clinton attempted to offer substantive answers to the questions about policy and leadership, while warning the nation of the dangers that would come from her opponent winning, Trump conducted these events like a reality show. He blasted insults at his opponent and physically lurked behind her as she spoke. He repeatedly uttered false statements and did little to engage the questions asked. At one encounter, he brought into the audience three women who had accused Bill Clinton of sexual assault; two hours before the debate, he appeared with them at a press conference.

Clinton was jolted one last time when FBI director James Comey, who in the summer had announced that the investigation into Clinton's emails was closed, told the press on October 28 that it was being revived in light of new evidence. With eleven days left until the election, Comey's announcement swung the coverage back to the Clinton scandals in the final days of the campaign, chipping away at her narrow lead. A few days later, Comey would tell reporters that the investigation was closed again and that there was nothing there. It was too late. The damage had been done. At the same time, the Clinton campaign failed to pay sufficient attention to what was going on in states like Michigan or Pennsylvania, where they were convinced that victory was at hand.[27] The events on the ground were inadequate, as was the daily polling, to turn out voters to support her.

On Election Day, the seventy-year-old Trump was victorious. Clinton won the popular vote with three million more than Trump, but she lost the Electoral College by 227 to 304. While Clinton did well in blue states, Trump retained Republican support in the red states and even did better than Romney had in 2012 in three key battleground states—Wisconsin, Michigan, and Pennsylvania—where Trump won by razor-thin margins. During his inauguration speech, Trump promised a nation still stunned by the outcome, "This American carnage stops right here and right now."

Trump's opponents had greatly underestimated how much desire there was among voters for a businessman and celebrity to win the highest office in the land. They could have observed how celebrities had successfully transitioned into politics, such as the former professional wrestler Jesse Ventura (governor of Minnesota) and the former bodybuilder Arnold Schwarzenegger (governor of California). Ross Perot, a Texas businessman, didn't win but did run two successful third-party candidacies for the presidency. The nation's celebrity culture had elevated the stature of figures who succeeded in the world of entertainment and business, sometimes granting them greater standing than experienced career politicians who knew the ropes of Capitol Hill and the federal bureaucracy. Since the 1970s, the "anti-politician" had also gained strength in presidential campaigns. In the aftermath of the Vietnam War and the Watergate scandal, a number of politicians (with more political experience than Trump) won office by positioning themselves as emanating from outside of Washington. In 1976, former Georgia governor Jimmy Carter made his lack of experience in Washington a virtue as he promised voters that they could trust him. Ronald Reagan never shied away from making the federal government—and everyone who worked in it—the foil of his attacks.[28] He was not part of the city, and that, he said, is what would make him a great leader. Except for George H. W. Bush, career officials like Lyndon Johnson were increasingly rare; successful candidates ran against the nation's capital rather than based on their experience of working within it. Trump was perfectly situated to take on this persona.

Nor had his opponents come to terms with how much the deep partisan polarization of the nation gave room for a candidate who played to the most extreme elements of the electorate. Many politicians still adhered to the conventional wisdom that presidential candidates needed to play to the center if they wanted to win. Trump had absorbed the fact that America had become a deeply polarized nation. Centrists were no longer a major presence in the electorate and almost nonexistent within the GOP. Whereas other presidential candidates, such as George W. Bush and Obama, pushed back against partisan division, Trump relished it. There was a red America and a blue America; he would put all his attention on the red. And the strategy worked. Trump likewise had a keen feel for how the Republican Party had moved far to the right over the previous decade, with a formidable media infrastructure to broadcast right-wing messaging. Politics was polarized; Republicans were radicalized. From attacking Mexican immigrants to railing against a corrupt, biased media, Trump played directly into this modern reality. The real key to Trump's Electoral College victory against Hillary Clinton was that in the final weeks of the campaign Trump whipped up Republican energy behind the ticket. The red states did not turn blue. This was essential, or his seventy-eight-thousand-vote margin in swing states would not have mattered. Faced with a choice between Trump and Clinton on Election Day, Republicans came home.

Whether or not Trump was self-conscious about his sensibility of the national political culture, he understood the illiberal traditions deeply embedded in the fabric of America. His version of conservative populism played into the nativism, racism, sexism, insular xenophobic nationalism, and white rage that all had deep histories in this country.

Not only were these uglier values part of the American political tradition, but in varying degrees they had served as a foundation of the strategies used by politicians who championed white working- and middle-class Americans. Trump just took it to another level and did so without any sense of hesitation or shame.[29]

Once Trump had political power, he shook this country to the core. Very few Americans remained indifferent to his words or deeds. For his opponents, Trump was doing nothing less than threatening the very foundations of the nation's democratic institutions—some argued planting the seeds of authoritarianism—and leaving everyone in the United States in a permanently weakened condition. For supporters, he was virtually a messiah, fighting against elements of the country that were gradually undermining what they saw as our traditions and our social fabric. By the time his four years were over, an ending that Trump never accepted and insisted to his supporters was a fraudulent outcome, the United States was torn apart.

---

The following pages take a deep dive into the four turbulent years between 2017 and 2021. Most historians in this collection simultaneously understand Trump to be a product of the era, not the cause but someone who had the capacity to break with our politics in fundamental ways. The authors all seek to explain the Trump presidency by grounding these years in much longer time frames, a product of developments reshaping democratic politics since the 1960s, some dating back all the way to our founding. Their chapters reveal a president who could sometimes generate immense heat while failing to actually redirect policy, and at other times push through deep changes to the substance of the administrative state.

Several themes loom over these chapters as they move into the heart of this presidency. How healthy are U.S. democratic institutions in the twenty-first century? Often, we hear that despite all the division and tumult, citizens can have confidence that the democracy still works. The nation's constitutional system of checks and balances, as well as the separation of powers, is enduring enough to survive the most tumultuous periods in our nation's history. This was the refrain sometimes uttered after Richard Nixon's disgraceful fall from power. Yet during the Trump presidency, some observers wondered whether this was really the case. More than any recent president, Trump tested the constraints on power, willing to do things in broad daylight that most presidents would have avoided or done secretly, thereby exposing massive vulnerabilities and broken elements of our political processes. Partisanship protected him twice from being convicted in the Senate after the House voted to impeach him. The following chapters consider what the different elements of the Trump presidency reveal about the condition of our polity.

The authors also reconsider the nature of political polarization since the 1970s. After many years when historians and political scientists focused on the growing division between Democrats and Republicans, more recently attention has shifted to the different ways each party has developed. Polarization has not been equal. Republicans have moved further to the extremes than Democrats. The Trump presidency offers a path to understand the state of the modern Republican Party in terms of its issue agenda, its political tactics and organization, and its relationship to governance. Some of the contributors see in his presidency a notable drift toward authoritarianism. Others characterize his regime as the culmination of a radicalized party that champions policies that are far off center and embraces a form of smashmouth partisan warfare where there are no guardrails.

This asymmetric history of partisanship connects to the state of the conservative movement in the 2010s. Historians, including myself, have examined the long history of this movement, starting from the decades when it took form in the 1960s and 1970s, to its entrance into the halls of power between Reagan's and George W. Bush's presidencies. Although frequently described as a lone wolf, Trump instead must be seen to be at the center of conservatism in the current era. His policy agenda and his strategies—from immigration restrictionism to conservative court appointees to tax cuts to deployment of the right-wing media—are grounded in this stage of modern conservative politics. While there were important variations within conservativism, he drew on strands of the movement that were there from the start.

Under Trump, this style of Republican partisanship converged with the vast expanse of presidential power that had occurred in the twentieth and twenty-first centuries. The power, staff, and regulatory authority accorded to the president vastly increased. In the age of the Cold War and then the war on terror, the growth of the national security apparatus handed the inhabitant of the Oval Office unprecedented resources to act without congressional oversight. Even the elevation of the bully pulpit meant that the president, through his words, could affect the public agenda in dramatic fashion. As I argued in my volume about George W. Bush, conservatives came to love presidential power as much as liberals, creating a bipartisan consensus around a muscular executive branch.[30] Even after the fallout from Vietnam and Watergate in the 1970s, which included a burst of reforms that strengthened the legislative branch, presidential power remained robust. Trump used this authority in aggressive fashion to pursue his goals with or without the consent of Congress. His presidency twice tested the capacity of a polarized Congress to execute the impeachment process when legislators believed that power had been abused.

All of this also points our attention to the state of what one group of historians called the "New Deal Order."[31] The systematic attack on the policies, ideas, and interests that coalesced during the decades between the 1930s and the 1970s has been at the center of the conservative movement. The decades since Reagan ended his presidency have witnessed a fierce and ongoing battle over key elements of that older order that have endured, ranging from social safety-net programs like Social Security and voting rights, to defining ideals such as pluralism, racial justice, and liberal internationalism, to institutions such as unions, the administrative state, and the United Nations. Even after the Cold War ended in the early 1990s, much of this order survived. Through his efforts to dismantle the legacies of twentieth-century politics, Trump allows us to gain insight into their condition as we approach the middle part of the twenty-first century. In certain cases, Trump deployed executive power and his rhetoric to make deep cuts into policies and guiding principles. In other cases, the persistence and expansion of liberalism was far more robust than he or other Republicans had imagined.[32]

The historians in this book agree that these were the most serious of times. They don't tend to concur with what might be called the "aberration school of thought." The presidency was not some one-off that will automatically result in a course correction, but a period of deep-seated conflict that profoundly wounded our polity. Some of the chapters focus on the institutional and coalitional foundations upon which the Trump presidency was built (Zelizer, Hemmer, Burgin, Belew, Cadava, Zarnow). Others explore the roots and impact of President Trump's domestic policies (Ngai, Smith, Demuth, Taylor, O'Mara) and foreign policies (Engel, Mann, Kurtzer). Finally, the rest of the authors look at the political and policy forces that checked and weakened the presidency of Donald Trump and ultimately brought it to an end (Gage, Chowkwanyun, Kazin, Downs).

When his term was done, the Trump presidency cemented some of the biggest fault lines in the nation. We exited the Trump years in a different place than we started. In many respects, no one could see the presidency, or the country, in the same light as they did when the Trump presidency began.

# 2

# Reckoning with the Trumpian GOP

*Julian E. Zelizer*

The turbulent presidency of Donald J. Trump shone a spotlight on the state of the Republican Party in the twenty-first century. For some political observers, including a handful of prominent Republicans, the years between 2017 and 2021 were a rude awakening. Trump's election and the fiercely loyal support he received from the GOP—even when stoking a violent insurrection against the U.S. Congress in the final days of his term—exposed how one of the nation's major political parties had been radicalized. Top leaders were willing to go to extraordinary lengths to preserve their party's power. As Stuart Stevens, a major Republican campaign operative who had managed Mitt Romney's presidential campaign in 2012, argued in his book *It Was All a Lie*, "In the end, the Republican Party rallied behind Donald Trump because if that was the deal needed to regain power, what was the problem? The rest? The principles? The values? It was all a lie."[1] In May 2021, GOP House caucus chair Liz Cheney of Wyoming, the daughter of the vice president under George W. Bush, and one of the Republicans who had voted in favor of Trump's second impeachment, tweeted, "The 2020 presidential election was not stolen. Anyone who claims it was is spreading THE BIG

LIE, turning their back on the rule of law, and poisoning our democratic system."[2] During an interview with the podcast *The Dispatch*, former Republican president George W. Bush warned that "if the GOP stands for 'White Anglo-Saxon Protestantism,' then it's not going to win anything."[3] In other words, the considerations that have traditionally guided the political behavior of elected officials—concerns about governing and the health of our democratic institutions—had fallen by the wayside or become secondary. The party's own tradition of government activism and racial egalitarianism was vanquished.[4]

The chaos and dysfunction stemming from the White House led many observers to ask how the "Party of Lincoln" had become the "Party of Trump." The key to answering the question is to grasp that the Trump presidency was not an aberration but the culmination of more than three decades in the GOP's evolution. The party had radicalized in its ideology as well as in its approach to partisan warfare long before Trump came to town. The transformation occurred when increasingly conservative voices tied to a grassroots movement pushed their way to the top of the party, insisting that the GOP embrace its rightward character if it ever hoped to pose a genuine challenge to the New Deal coalition that had dominated politics since the 1930s. As politicians and activists from the conservative movement nudged their leaders away from ideological centrism, they simultaneously championed an aggressive vision of partisanship that did not adhere to traditional guardrails and observed almost no limits on what was considered permissible in battling against Democrats. For young conservative renegades like Congressman Newt Gingrich of Georgia, smashmouth partisan politics was the only way to defeat the opposition. Senior party officials kept entering into alliances with Gingrich and future generations of renegades, confident they could contain them, only to be swept out of their way.

In tracing the history of the modern Republican Party, it is useful to draw on the concept of "asymmetric polarization."[5] Born out of the social sciences and political journalism, this theory posits that partisan polarization—which stemmed from a number of factors including the sorting of the electorate and rules that strengthened centralized party leadership—since the 1970s has not played out the same way among Democrats as among Republicans. Although both parties have moved further away from the center, with moderates gradually diminishing as a political force, the parties have come to operate by different rules. As a whole, Republicans have moved much further to the right than Democrats have moved to the left.[6]

Democrats remained more internally divided while the GOP tended to act in unison on positions far from the center of the political spectrum. Studies showed that the way members of each party consumed their news reflected this reality. For instance, Republican voters were generally more willing to believe what they heard from conservative media outlets than Democratic voters were from liberal platforms. In partisan politics, Republican leaders were comfortable acting more aggressively than Democrats. Republican leaders regularly stressed and even broke core processes and norms.[7]

Democrats prepared for pillow fights, Trump's onetime adviser Steve Bannon quipped in an interview with documentarian Michael Moore, whereas Republicans came ready to deliver a head wound. As the political scientists Thomas Mann and Norman Ornstein wrote in 2012, "If our democracy is to regain its health and vitality, the culture and ideological center of the Republican Party must change. . . . We understand the values of mainstream journalists, including the effort to report both sides of a story. But a balanced treatment of an unbalanced phenomenon distorts reality."[8]

There were several false starts in this evolution. For a moment, it seemed as if a breakthrough had occurred in the 1964 presidential election. At the height of the Cold War and the civil rights movement, Arizona senator Barry Goldwater secured the GOP nomination to challenge President Lyndon Johnson. Goldwater emanated from what was called the "Radical Right" in a period when the center held. In the 1950s and 1960s, the Republican Party was deeply divided between a midwestern wing that held strong antigovernment views and liberal Republicans from the northern states, such as New York's senator Jacob Javits and governor Nelson Rockefeller, as well as Michigan governor George Romney, who often aligned with liberal Democrats on issues such as civil rights. The conventional wisdom was that the safest bet for the GOP was to veer toward the middle. Goldwater refused to acknowledge the pragmatic bias toward moderation. The senator challenged key figures in his party, such as Rockefeller, who insisted on appealing to a broad base. Goldwater's campaign revolved around a full embrace of conservatism. He voted against the Civil Rights Act of 1964, and later stood by his vote. He opposed Social Security, the proposed Medicare program, the Tennessee Valley Authority, and other core elements of the welfare state. He took on moderates such as Rockefeller, whom Goldwater's delegates booed at the convention. "Extremism in defense of liberty is no vice. Moderation in pursuit of justice is no virtue!" he told the Republican convention in San Francisco. Goldwater called for a hawkish approach to fighting communism. His candidacy, noted the historian William Henry Chamberlin in the *Wall Street Journal*, "was an interesting test of the drawing power of conservatism, a decisive rollcall for conservatives." Unlike many other members of his party, the senator had "firmly nailed the conservative colors to his masthead."[9]

Goldwater's success shocked much of the Republican establishment. Unlike Wisconsin senator Joe McCarthy in the 1950s, who also roiled the waters with this anticommunist crusading conservative populism, Goldwater shattered the conventional wisdom that it was impossible for someone of his perspective to be nominated as a presidential candidate without nodding to the liberal consensus.[10] There were Republicans who feared that the genie could not be put back into the bottle. George Gilder and Bruce Chapman, the editors of the liberal Republican *Journal Advance*, wrote after the election fallout, "Most of the supposed moderate leaders, such as Richard Nixon, who failed the party from 1960 to 1964, fail it still and the right wing is eager for the party to perform yet another self-immolation."[11]

Yet the power of Republican moderation survived Goldwater.[12] His overwhelming defeat by President Johnson, which produced massive Democratic majorities in the House (295) and Senate (68), led most in the GOP to conclude that the electorate was not ready for the kind of conservatism he promoted. Republicans spent the rest of the decade running away from Goldwater's legacy for fear of being labeled extreme.[13]

Richard Nixon, a hard-line Cold Warrior, shied away from his predecessor's positions during his 1968 campaign against Vice President Humbert Humphrey. Nixon played to the safe center on a large number of domestic issues (barely mentioning the Great Society, for instance) and promised to bring peace in Southeast Asia. The former vice president championed the policy of détente, easing relations with the Soviet Union through arms negotiations, which was anathema to conservatives like Goldwater or California governor Ronald Reagan. Although Nixon certainly held his share of hard-line positions, including capitalizing on the white backlash to civil rights by calling for "law and order" in the cities, he put the brakes on the swing to the right that Goldwater had started. Nixon also continued to govern, even with the scandals revealed during Watergate, within many of the traditional political processes that had guided Washington politics for almost a century. The Watergate scandal destroyed any plans that Nixon had to move harder to the right after winning his landslide reelection in 1972 against Senator George McGovern. Instead, his term ended in investigation and disgrace with his resignation in August 1974. Nixon was succeeded by Vice President Gerald Ford, who, though a staunch midwestern conservative, also believed that his party could not afford to veer toward extremes. Ford, a Washington insider's insider, entered the White House as an institutionalist who had spent almost his entire life working in government. When Reagan challenged Ford in the 1976 Republican primaries, almost pulling off an upset, the president was nonetheless able to secure the nomination with the help of the political operative Paul Manafort.

Meanwhile, important electoral changes were altering the internally divided state of the parties. For much of the twentieth century, Democrats and Republicans had been factionalized. Democratic politicians courted liberal northern voters and conservative southerners. Republicans depended on a complex coalition of liberal northeasterners and staunch antigovernment conservatives from the Midwest. These fault lines ensured that bipartisan coalitions were essential to any legislative breakthrough.

During the 1970s, conditions started to change. The southern electorate joined the Republicans. Years of efforts to build the party at the local level began to pay off.[14] The southern opposition to Lyndon Johnson's civil rights legislation in 1964 and 1965 had generated growing regional support for a rebranded GOP that promised to contain the use of federal power to mediate race relations. In 1972, Nixon had become the first Republican to sweep the South. The southernization of the party intensified the social and cultural pull of a staunchly conservative electorate, creating stronger incentives for candidates to stand on the right if they wanted to secure positions of power. The process took several decades to complete. Democratic candidate Jimmy Carter proved in 1976 that he still had the support of his region. But the change would be nearly finished by the 1990s. Some northern ethnic voters, angered by Johnson's open housing bill in 1968 that prohibited discrimination in the sale or rental of property and by the Democratic Party's move against a muscular national security posture after Vietnam, had also weakened their ties to the Democrats.

The 1980s were the turning point for the party. Facing off against President Carter in 1980, Ronald Reagan pulled off what Barry Goldwater had failed to achieve. The former actor turned conservative spokesman turned governor turned presidential candidate brought conservative Republicans into the halls of power when he won the presidency with 489 Electoral College votes. Confronted with the multiple crises of Americans being held captive in Iran, economic stagflation, and an energy crisis—along with the Soviet invasion of Afghanistan—Carter lost the presidential election. Reagan's antigovernment platform moved the GOP sharply to the right. He railed against federal regulations and taxes and called for cutting down the social safety net and allocating more money to defense. Rejecting the notion that the lesson of Vietnam was that America had to be cautious overseas, Reagan championed a militaristic and adversarial stance toward the Soviet Union. His vision of supply-side economics, the argument behind a major tax cut in 1981, favored wealthier Americans on the basis of the claim that economic benefits would eventually "trickle down" to the rest of the population. Reagan handcuffed federal agencies by putting them under the control of figures who disagreed with their primary responsibilities. At the Equal Employment Opportunity Commission, for example, chairman Clarence Thomas didn't hide his opposition to affirmative action, refusing to file lawsuits in response to discrimination complaints against companies. Reagan gave voice to conservative Christians who wanted to limit reproductive rights and turn back American culture while appointing conservative justices to the federal courts. With his savvy mastery of how to speak when the television cameras were rolling, Reagan presented many of the same ideas as Goldwater but with much greater effect.

Reagan's political success rested on an immense grassroots movement that had coalesced over the previous decade. The conservative movement, which included evangelical Christians, neoconservative Democrats, Wall Street and business Republicans, and northern working-class voters disaffected with the party of FDR, constituted his base of support. The movement had constructed a formidable infrastructure of think tanks, interest groups, fund-raisers, and political tactics, such as direct mail. Though Reagan would fail to achieve many of his policy objectives over the course of two terms owing to the persistent power of liberalism, the president recast public debate.[15] "Government is not the solution to our problem," he said in his first inaugural address; "government is the problem." He even survived the political fallout from negotiating a major arms agreement with the Soviets, the Intermediate-Range Nuclear Forces Treaty, by selling the deal as a product of his tough defense policies rather than a triumph of diplomacy. The breakthrough also helped Reagan survive the Iran-Contra scandal, which revealed how high-level officials in the executive branch had sold arms to Iran (considered a terrorist state) and then used the revenue to finance the Nicaraguan Contras (which Congress had prohibited). As his second term ended in 1989 with Reagan enjoying strong approval ratings, Republicans had become more comfortable embracing this kind of conservatism than running away from it. Since he had helped win acceptance of the Right, Republicans across the board became more comfortable taking conservative stands; a new generation of Democrats started to drop core principles for fear of being tagged as radical.

Reagan's ideological accomplishments, as well as concrete measures like conservative judicial confirmations, tax cuts, and executive-ordered deregulation, would not be sufficient for movement activists. They wanted more and now had the organization to keep fighting. Republicans learned that, for all of Reagan's appeal, there were limits to what their party could achieve without gaining power in Congress. Democrats continued to enjoy power on Capitol Hill. Republicans were unable to recapture control of the House of Representatives during the Reagan era and gained control of the Senate only from 1981 to 1987. To complete a genuine conservative revolution, a growing number of younger members of the GOP argued, the party would need to be much more forceful in its tactics.

This was the basic insight of Congressman Newt Gingrich, a former history professor elected to represent Georgia's Sixth District in 1978. Gingrich was a revolutionary figure in the history of the GOP. From the moment he set foot in Washington, Gingrich urged his caucus to mount a no-holds-barred attack to dislodge Democrats from their positions of power.[16] He believed that Reagan's ideological vision could be fulfilled only if the party was prepared to be far more combative. Within the course of a decade, he legitimated his ruthless partisanship at the highest levels of power. He argued that senior Republicans had become too ensconced in a status quo that left them marginalized. Even with Reagan in the White House, most party leaders in the GOP, Gingrich lamented, continued to believe that bipartisanship and civility mattered. They abided by norms and processes that kept Democrats in charge, he said. To obtain power, those would have to be blown up or the status quo would endure. Republican minority leader Robert Michael of Illinois, who had served in Congress only when Democrats controlled the House (since 1954), was emblematic of the kind of senior member who, Gingrich thought, had to be brought down. As Gingrich had told a group of young Republicans in 1978, "One of the great problems we have in the Republican Party is that we don't encourage you to be nasty. We encourage you to be neat, obedient, and loyal and faithful and all those Boy Scout words, which would be great around the campfire but are lousy in politics."[17] Although many colleagues continued to fear that he was a modern incarnation of Joe McCarthy, someone who could destabilize the functionality of government and create an atmosphere in which interparty negotiation was impossible, Gingrich gradually persuaded the rest of his party to deploy a full-throated style of partisanship in which almost any tactic was permissible.

Gingrich understood politics to be akin to military warfare. When he had first run for the House in 1974, unsuccessfully, he told supporters that "the Congress is a kind of club. I intend to go up there and kick the system over, not try to change it."[18] By the 1980s, Gingrich was doing just that. As a junior member, he urged Republicans to deploy toxic rhetoric about their opponents and to weaponize every procedure available to them. Smearing reputations, grinding the legislative process to a halt, and taking whatever steps were necessary to destroy opponents were all fair game. He organized a group of like-minded

Republicans in the Conservative Opportunity Society (COS), a small caucus modeled after the liberal Democratic Study Group (created in 1959 to combat southern conservatives in the party). Even as colleagues warned Gingrich that his tactics would undermine their ability to solve the nation's problems and to govern, he moved forward without hesitation or regret. The news media was his central arena of combat, television in particular. Gingrich understood that in the emerging era of cable television, sensational and provocative rhetoric would always attract attention. "You don't get on TV with cars that get home safely," Gingrich liked to say.[19] Simple one-minute speeches at the end of the day, traditionally reserved to grant any legislator the opportunity to make statements that would appeal to the district (praising notable constituents or announcing named post offices, for example), became televised spectacles deployed to eviscerate Democrats. Capitalizing on congressional reforms that allowed cameras to film House proceedings and gavel-to-gavel televised coverage by the cable station C-SPAN—reforms intended to let sunlight into the political process—Gingrich and his COS allies went on the airwaves every day to make vicious insinuations about the national security beliefs of Democrats. Gingrich used the House ethics rules created after Watergate to make legislators more accountable to the public as an instrument with which to pressure Speaker of the House Jim Wright to resign in 1989. Whereas Wright urged both parties to "bring this period of mindless cannibalism to an end" upon stepping down, Gingrich smelled blood.[20] He wanted more.

Rather than distancing themselves from Gingrich's tactics, Republicans were seduced by them. Given that they had been part of a "permanent minority" on Capitol Hill, senior Republicans were willing to open the doors to Gingrich and his allies, sensing that his fervor could be politically valuable and believing that in the long run they could always contain him. In 1989, House Republicans elected Gingrich to the position of minority whip. Though a moderate, Maine representative Olympia Snowe cast her vote for the Georgia bomb-thrower. In 1990, GOP candidates eagerly read a memo from Gingrich's political action committee, GOPAC, teaching them how to "Speak Like Newt," which meant using words such as "traitors," "pathetic," "cheat," and "steal" when talking about their opponents in campaigns. After the 1994 midterm elections, when Republicans took control of Congress for the first time since 1954, the party selected Gingrich to be Speaker of the House. His smashmouth partisanship became the operating norm for Republicans. Within four years, the party forced two major government shutdowns. "There had been federal funding lapses before," wrote the journalist McKay Coppins, "but they tended to be minor affairs that lasted only a day or two. Gingrich's shutdown, by contrast, furloughed hundreds of thousands of workers for several weeks at Christmastime, so Republicans could use their paychecks as a bartering chip in negotiations with the White House."[21]

Before and after the government closures, Gingrich headed his caucus as they spent endless time investigating every element of President Clinton's administration, culminating with their vote to impeach him for perjury about his affair with White House intern Monica Lewinsky. Gingrich didn't survive to enjoy the fruits of his success, however, since young Republicans persuaded him to step down after their poor showing in the 1998 midterms and because he was having an extramarital relationship at the same time the GOP was going after Clinton for doing the same. In a private conference call with fellow Republicans, Gingrich denounced his opponents, saying that "we need to purge the poisons from the system." Using the same language as Speaker Jim Wright in his resignation speech almost ten years earlier, Gingrich added that many Republicans were just using him as a scapegoat for their poor showing in the midterms: "The ones you see on TV are hateful. I am willing to lead, but I won't allow cannibalism."[22]

Gingrich had found a kindred spirit in Republican campaign politics with South Carolinian Lee Atwater, who likened campaigns to professional wrestling—with the goal being to destroy how the audience thought of your opponent. He understood the dynamics of backlash politics and was happy to embrace the strategy, which he described in 1981 during a disturbing off-the-record interview with the political scientist Alexander Lamis that was littered with racial slurs [23]

In the 1988 presidential campaign, Atwater, often called the "Babe Ruth of Negative Politics," had brought his blistering style to Vice President George H. W. Bush's campaign. Bush, who was not naturally predisposed to political ruthlessness, concluded that it was necessary for victory. His campaign destroyed the reputation of the technocratic, centrist Massachusetts Democrat Michael Dukakis with television spots that depicted him as a far-left lover of the American Civil Liberties Union who supported burning American flags and opposed the death penalty. Even as Reagan was engaged in diplomatic negotiations with the Soviets, Bush's campaign went retro by blasting Democrats as weak on defense in the war against communism; they used a picture of Dukakis in a tank to convey the impression he would be meek militarily. The most notorious element of the Bush campaign appealed directly to the white backlash by focusing on an African American named Willie Horton; Horton, who had been allowed out on a weekend furlough program, raped a woman and killed her boyfriend.[24] "Let's face it," New York representative Charles Rangel said, "you don't have to be a Democrat to know that is an appeal along racial lines."[25] Atwater's game plan was considered a low point in the history of modern campaign politics but one that set the GOP's template for decades to come.

The modern Republican Party depended on conservative media as much as on the formal party apparatus. The GOP used right-wing media outlets as a mechanism to promote its agenda and launch attacks on Democrats.[26] Talk radio was Republicans' first weapon of choice as the number of programs vastly expanded in 1987, when the Federal Communications Commission abandoned the fairness doctrine, the rule that shows give equal time to both sides of a political issue. National talk radio stars emerged, such as Rush Limbaugh, who warned callers of the dangers of "feminazis" and "political correctness." In 1996, Rupert Murdoch launched the cable television network Fox News, a station that would jettison norms of objective journalism and present stories from a conservative point of view, with an eye toward sensationalism and commercial appeal. The expansion of the internet would offer many more types of conservative media platforms from which Republicans could launch attacks.

The rightward transformation of the party was still not complete, however. Formidable forces within the GOP didn't subscribe to the emerging vision of their party even though they were willing to enter into alliances of convenience. While Reagan, Gingrich, and others had pushed the GOP to the right, traditional centrist voices claimed a place at the table. Indeed, President George H. W. Bush had demonstrated the enduring power of moderation when he supported a tax increase in 1990—despite his "No New Taxes" pledge in the campaign—and strong environmental protections. Republicans also crafted the Americans with Disabilities Act, a major expansion of civil rights regulations. Bush believed in the liberal international order put in place after World War II, and he staffed his administration with insiders such as Lawrence Eagleburger and James Baker, who had no interest in tearing down political systems. As the Soviet Union collapsed, Bush avoided the confrontational and nationalistic rhetoric that Reagan had deployed. Bush's administration generally worked within mainstream policy frameworks inherited from earlier decades and believed in the imperative of governance—even while fighting to win power. They were products of Washington, not its enemy. In the 1992 Republican primaries, Bush handily defeated former speechwriter Patrick Buchanan, who ran as a far-right conservative populist. Though Buchanan generated headlines by delivering his blistering "culture wars" address, claiming that "the agenda Clinton and Clinton would impose on America—abortion on demand, a litmus test for the Supreme Court, homosexual rights, discrimination against religious schools, women in combat—that's change, all right. But it is not the kind of change America wants. And it's not the kind of change we can abide in a nation that we still call God's country,"[27] Bush won the nomination.

By the late 1990s, the sort of institutional centrism President Bush embraced stood on thin ice. Red-state constituencies were far more conservative than ever before. A new generation of Republicans who had come of age when Gingrich was an overpowering force were in no mood to compromise. They welcomed extremist elements to help whip the vote. An entire infrastructure of conservatism, from interest groups that pressed legislators on issues such as gun rights to the rightward twenty-four-hour news media, made sure that there was little space for Republican dissenters to survive. Funders like Richard Mellon Scaife poured enormous resources into these causes. "Our funding," he said, "is based on our support of ideas like limited government, individual rights and a strong defense."[28]

Powerful Democrats facilitated this rightward drift by redefining their agenda within the parameters Reagan had set. President Clinton, for instance, accepted certain ideas from his Republican predecessor, such as the primacy of markets over government, unregulated free trade, and welfare reform. When Clinton declared that the "era of big government is over" in his 1996 State of the Union address, he delivered a rhetorical blow to fellow Democrats who continued to believe a robust federal government was essential. "No presidential utterance has come to me as a more unpleasant surprise," noted Massachusetts congressman Barney Frank in his memoirs.[29] The first Democrat to win the presidency since Ronald Reagan had given official credence to a core argument of Republicans.

The election of Texas governor George W. Bush in 2000 portended to some observers the possibility that the GOP could move in a different direction. The son of the former president, and his top adviser Karl Rove, had ambitions to build a new coalition comparable to those assembled by the GOP in 1896 and FDR in 1932. Bush ran against Vice President Al Gore on a platform of "compassionate conservatism" that aimed to broaden the Republican base of support, softening some of the harsh edges of the Reagan Revolution.

Yet the election process itself turned into a display of how far Republicans were willing to go in pursuit of power. Election night ended with uncertainty of the results in Florida because of faulty ballots and reports of voter suppression. The state undertook a recount in select counties. While Gore's team put together a first-rate legal group that focused on defending the legal processes of the recount, Bush's team, led by James Baker, handled the matter like a political campaign. Surrogates flooded the airwaves, warning that Gore was trying to fish for votes. The team went so far as to organize a boisterous protest, called the Brooks Brothers Riot, filled with congressional staffers acting as if they were a spontaneous mob to pressure the people working on the recount. The election ended when the Supreme Court on December 12 stopped the process, giving Bush the victory. Gore went on television to concede and to tell his followers to accept the results.

After taking office, President Bush did follow through on certain initiatives meant to attract Democratic support, such as the No Child Left Behind Act, legislation cosponsored with Massachusetts Democrat Ted Kennedy expanding the role of the federal government in maintaining school standards.

But much of the 2000 campaign rhetoric about compassion and bipartisanship quickly fell by the wayside. Gingrich's party was now in power. On domestic policy, Bush generally stuck to a traditional script of supply-side tax cuts and deregulation that appealed to the corporate base of the party. In 2001, the administration secured support for a massive supply-side tax cut that relieved wealthier Americans of the highest burdens. He withdrew from the Kyoto Protocol, an international agreement on climate change, and used executive authority to dismantle regulations that the Clinton administration had put in place to curb carbon emissions. The president shocked the scientific community by limiting stem-cell lines for research to appease antiabortion activists. He and his cabinet launched an attack on all kinds of accepted expertise to justify changes supported by the corporate community. As the historian David Greenberg wrote about the Bush administration in his essay for this series, "Although the taunts of Bush's critics frequently descended into glibness, the president's denigration of independent expertise was real, and it marked one of the more significant and all-encompassing features of his administration. . . . As never before, administration officials and their allies in politics and the news media openly disregarded the empirically grounded evidence, open-minded inquiry, and expert authority that had long underpinned governmental policymaking."[30]

Following the tragic terrorist attacks on September 11, 2001, that destroyed the World Trade Center, damaged the Pentagon, and killed more than three thousand people, Bush pursued a hawkish national security program by deploying executive power and spreading misleading information. For instance, the president used "signing statements" to ignore limitations that Congress placed on his ability to pursue potential threats. He built a massive surveillance program on American citizens that lacked oversight. Bush's advisers, such as John Yoo of the Office of Legal Counsel, developed a theory of the "unitary executive" to claim that the president possessed nearly total control over his branch of government. These arguments were used to justify "enhanced interrogation," otherwise known as torture, of suspected terrorists.[31] Guantanamo Bay became a facility to detain suspected terrorists without any legal rights or protection. In March 2003, Bush launched a war against Iraq on the basis of inaccurate claims that President Saddam Hussein possessed a cache of weapons of mass destruction and that his regime had direct connections to the 9/11 al-Qaeda terrorists.

Bush's reelection campaign in 2004 dove right into the trenches of the contentious culture wars. As part of the strategy to increase evangelical turnout, the president took on the issue of same-sex marriage, a hot-button topic as numerous states and courts were taking dramatic steps to legalize these unions. Originally, President Bush had expressed his support for same-sex civil unions; Vice President Richard Cheney, whose daughter Mary is gay, had publicly argued that the states should decide this issue. But with two weeks left before the Democratic convention, Bush veered hard to the right by proclaiming his support for a constitutional amendment to ban same-sex marriage: "The union of a man and a woman is the most enduring human institution, honored and encouraged by every religious faith. Marriage cannot be severed from its cultural, religious and natural roots without weakening the influence of the good society."[32]

On the rare occasions when the president tried to push Washington in a bipartisan direction, he encountered fierce resistance from Republicans in Congress. Following his reelection victory, the president turned to a bipartisan coalition in the Senate interested in sweeping immigration reform. Though the GOP had moved to a hard-line position on immigration since the 1990s, Bush valued the benefits that immigration offered the nation's cultural and economic fabric. The administration supported a "Grand Bargain" whereby more than eleven million undocumented immigrants would be granted a path to citizenship in exchange for stricter deportation and border policies. House Republicans slammed on the brakes. There was no support for granting citizenship and the caucus scuttled the bill. The same thing happened when President Bush pushed for a major economic stimulus program after the markets crashed in September 2008. The administration ended up working with Speaker Nancy Pelosi and House Democrats, since members of the president's own party refused to vote for the bill.

The temperature heated up in the 2008 campaign when Arizona senator John McCain, the Republican nominee, selected Alaska governor Sarah Palin as his running mate. If there was hope that McCain signaled the endurance of independent voices in the GOP, Palin dispelled it. McCain had already dropped many of his "independent" views to secure the nomination. Palin did not shy away from the new character of the party. Instead, she reveled in it. During her rallies, Palin blasted the "lamestream media" and attacked coastal elites. The people in New York and California just mocked her supporters; they were people who, she said, believed "that they're—I guess—better than anyone else."[33] When critics ridiculed her interviews with CBS anchor Katie Couric, arguing that her answers demonstrated a lack of intelligence, she counterpunched, claiming her critics were out of touch with average Americans. She didn't have a problem when supporters at her gatherings called Barack Obama a terrorist and waved racist images as she spoke. The fervor seeped into McCain's rallies as well, and his supporters started yelling "terrorist" and questioning Obama's religion.[34] At one event in Clearwater, Florida, the crowd waved sticks and shouted obscenities at the press area; one told an African American soundman, "Sit down, boy."[35] "Through Palin," Obama wrote in his memoirs, "it seemed as if the dark spirits that had long been lurking on the edges of the modern Republican Party—xenophobia, anti-intellectualism, paranoid conspiracy theories, an antipathy toward Black and brown folks—were finding their way to center stage. She had no idea what the hell she was talking about."[36]

Within months of starting his presidency, Obama was confronting the full force of the radicalized GOP. Senate minority leader Mitch McConnell (R-KY) vowed to make Obama a one-term president. Even when the administration was dealing with economic programs in the middle of a severe crisis, only a handful of Republicans agreed to support Obama's legislation. Obama kept reaching out to the GOP, compromising on his plans before proposing them, only to have them vote against his bills. In the 2010 midterm elections, Tea Party Republicans helped the GOP take control of the House. They were prepared to undertake dramatic action to fight the administration. In their struggle against the administration's spending proposals in 2011, for instance, Republicans threatened to vote against raising the federal debt ceiling—a move that would send the government into default. They were comfortable going on Fox News to spread disinformation and they used Congress as a platform to investigate scandal.[37] The organization Keep America Safe, launched by Liz Cheney, released an advertisement criticizing Obama's Department of Justice, showcasing a headline that asked, "DOJ: Department of Jihad?"[38] Speaker John Boehner, himself part of the Gingrich revolution and someone who had helped the Tea Party win its campaigns, later called young Republicans like Jim Jordan "legislative terrorists."[39] Like so many Republicans before him, he opened the door to the renegades only to see that they could not be stopped.[40] When former Massachusetts governor Mitt Romney unsuccessfully ran against Obama in the 2012 election, he shed his well-known proclivity toward moderation by embracing the Right. He criticized Obama's Affordable Care Act, a landmark health-care program modeled after the policy that Romney himself put into effect in his own blue state. "We don't know what's causing climate change on this planet," quipped the Republican who had fashioned himself as an advocate of environmentalism.[41] Romney, the son of the late Michigan governor who embodied the tradition of Republican moderation more than anyone other than Rockefeller, held a controversial meeting with the notorious Lt. General Jerry Boykin, the vice president of the Family Research Council who had made controversial statements about Islam.[42]

The birther movement in 2013 and 2014 brought conservative forces together to question the legitimacy of the first African American president. Although Obama had posted a copy of his birth certificate on a website during the campaign to rebut charges that he had not been born in the United States, conservatives were unrelenting. The birthers claimed that the certificate was forged. The accusations circulated in the conservative media ecosystem. Gingrich told Fox News that Obama's policies could be understood only by those who grasped "Kenyan, anticolonial behavior." Louisiana senator David Vitter told one crowd, "I know all the information I've been able to get my hands on through the media. But obviously with the mainstream media as a filter, that's not a whole lot. I personally don't have standing to bring litigation to court." When asked about the matter, Sarah Palin replied, "I think the public rightfully is still making it an issue." Though he would dismiss birtherism years later, at the time Speaker Boehner argued that "it's not my job to tell the American people what to think." With polls showing that more than half the party believed Obama was born overseas, their responses were not much of a surprise.[43]

Reality television star Donald Trump burst onto the national political scene by taking on the issue. Trump took the birther issue from the conservative into the mainstream media. He went on *Good Morning America*, where he admitted to being "skeptical" about whether Obama had been born in Hawaii. On ABC's *The View*, Trump demanded that Obama show his certificate. "I want him to show his birth certificate," he told the hosts. "There's something on that birth certificate he doesn't like." Though Karl Rove warned that Trump was "off there in the nutty right,"[44] many Republicans were right there with him.

Republicans, whose electoral base was shrinking as it centered on rural, white, male, and undereducated constituencies, were depending on hardball, and sometimes antidemocratic, mechanisms to retain power. After Republicans took back control of the House in the 2010 midterms, the party launched Operation RedMap, which poured money into legislative races with the goal of controlling state houses so that Republicans could dominate the redistricting process.[45]

Republicans also pushed for tougher voting restrictions, on the basis of unsubstantiated claims of significant voting fraud. Most experts agree that the Republican Party has benefited more from lower turnout than have Democrats.[46] The party received judicial support on this issue from the Supreme Court in 2013 with the *Shelby v. Holder* decision striking down the Voting Rights Act's preclearance formula and requirement that the federal government approve of changes to election law in municipalities with records of voting discrimination. Praising the decision, Alabama senator Jeff Sessions called it "good news, I think, for the South, in that [there was] not sufficient evidence to justify treating them disproportionately than, say, Philadelphia or Boston or Los Angeles or Chicago." Justice Ruth Bader Ginsburg saw things differently: "Hubris is a fit word for today's demolition of the VRA."[47] In 2014, fifteen states enacted tougher voting restrictions.

A radicalized Republican Party was now fighting against the legacy of the Reconstruction-era "Radical Republicans" who had fought for a robust federal program to achieve racial, political, and economic equality. Not only had the party dropped the agenda of Republicans such as Congressman Thaddeus Stevens (PA), but leaders engaged in efforts to actively undermine a social justice program.

Decades of party change culminated with the Republican primaries in 2016. Trump's strength against opponents like Florida governor Jeb Bush and Texas senator Ted Cruz caught some observers by surprise, but it shouldn't have. The pundits continued to speak about a "divided" party, where the so-called establishment was trying to hold off Trump's candidacy. "Trump Forces Didn't Just Beat the Establishment, They Overran It," proclaimed a headline for NBC News.[48]

But the popular narrative masked the deep-seated changes that had already taken place. The radicalization of the GOP had led the party to embrace a smashmouth approach to partisan politics, opened the door to extremist organizations at the highest levels of power, and settled on an agenda far to the right of the mainstream. Before 2016, Gingrich and COS were already doing Trumpism, as was the Tea Party. Republicans were more than comfortable working in a media environment where disinformation and smear were commonplace. In many respects, notwithstanding his eccentricities, Trump fit perfectly in the Republican establishment circa 2016.

When Trump ran a campaign that aimed to divide and polarize, undertaking devastating character attacks and not even feigning concern for governing—in fact, Trump went so far as to act in mocking fashion before reporters to show what being presidential "boring" looked like—many Republican voters were elated. Except for his attacks on free trade, Trump echoed key themes that by then were familiar to the GOP. He took a staunch line against immigration, called for the deregulation of markets and passage of more supply-side tax cuts, railed against European allies' not paying their fair share for international institutions, appealed to the Religious Right, and promised to appoint conservative judges, publishing a list drawn up by the head of the Federalist Society. Trump's abrasive and theatrical quality may have made Republicans uncomfortable, but it worked because he and the GOP were one and the same.

Despite predictions of a 2016 landslide victory by the Democratic nominee Hillary Clinton, with speculation that states such as Texas or Georgia might shift to the Democratic column because Trump was so extreme, Republican voters had come home. Trump secured the vote of most of the traditional Republican coalition and expanded his reach into narrow slivers of the Democratic electorate. During his presidency, his approval ratings would remain extremely strong within the GOP. Congressional Republicans, other than a few exceptions—such as Senator John McCain, who voted against the administration's

FIGURE 1. Senate Majority Leader Mitch McConnell (*left*) walks with President-Elect Donald Trump for a meeting on November 10, 2016. Photo by Susan Walsh via AP.

bill to repeal and replace the Affordable Care Act, and Senator Mitt Romney, who voted in favor of indicting the impeached president—usually came to the president's defense and lent their support to his bills. There was no oversight to speak of. During both impeachment trials, most Republicans stood firm. Even Romney, who had defined the #NeverTrump movement with his speech in 2016, voted with the president more than 80 percent of the time.

Republicans such as Senator McConnell were pleased with the results. Because of Trump's tenure in office, the party was able to deliver on huge corporate and upper-income tax cuts with the Tax Cuts and Jobs Act of 2017, reverse measures to protect the environment, and appoint a historic number of conservative judges to the federal courts (more than two hundred judges to the federal bench, which included almost as many federal appeal court judges as Obama appointed in two terms).[49] Access to abortion services continued to decline. It wasn't surprising that by the end of his term almost 80 percent of white evangelical voters supported him.[50] The president's alliance with the party's conservative religious voters remained strong since he continued to deploy rhetoric about people of faith being under constant attack from the left. Besides the conservative court appointments, this constituency cheered when the president railed against the "Johnson Amendment," which prohibited non-profit organizations from endorsing specific candidates. Trump had also staffed key agencies with officials who were not interested in fulfilling the missions of the agencies,[51] a hallmark of conservative governance since the Reagan years, leaving huge organizational voids in places like the State Department. Voting restrictions gained traction in a greater number of red states with the president's imprimatur. The president's term ended with the confirmation of Associate Justice Amy Coney Barrett, solidifying a 6–3 conservative majority on the Supreme Court that was a huge victory for the Right. Despite a devastating pandemic that left more than a half million people dead, former New Jersey governor Chris Christie reflected the sentiment of many in his party when he went on national television in May 2021 to say he would give Trump an "A."

To be sure, there had been a few moments of bipartisanship. In 2018, for instance, the president moved forward with major criminal justice reform legislation that received praise from both sides of the aisle. The First Step Act, signed into law on December 21, reduced certain kinds of long federal sentencing and reformed conditions in federal prisons. Trump, as James Mann and Margaret O'Mara recount in this volume, also took tough steps against China that had broad support in the foreign policy establishment and business community. But, overall, this was not how Trump governed. Bipartisan appeals were the exception, not the norm. Trump preferred to play to the political and policy interests of his own party.

In 2020, even in defeat the president's vote total increased over his total in the 2016 election to more than seventy-one million. The Republicans did well in the Senate and expanded their numbers in the House. Overall, the party, as polls continued to show, seemed quite comfortable with Trump despite all the Sturm und Drang. The predicted exodus of Republican voters from the party did not come to fruition.[52]

None of this should have come as a surprise. The radicalization of the Republican Party had been taking place over decades, not over a few months. By 2016, the GOP was primed for a leader like Trump. To be sure, some were unwilling to accept what the party had become, while others imagined that it was something very different. Most Republicans, however, were all in.

The party leaders sat back, occasionally shrugging their shoulders at Trump's latest Twitter storms or his most controversial rally statements. And even when the president aggressively challenged the legitimate results of the 2020 election based on the "Big Lie" of massive voting fraud, his support remained firm. He represented the party establishment, so what else was there to do?

The GOP was Trump's party, not because Trump had seized control but because he fit so perfectly into what some observers were still nostalgically calling the Party of Lincoln.

# 3

# Remade in His Image

## HOW TRUMP TRANSFORMED RIGHT-WING MEDIA

*Nicole Hemmer*

Donald Trump was furious.

Fox News had just called Arizona for Democratic presidential nominee Joe Biden, a call that, if it held, would almost certainly mean that Trump had lost his reelection bid. Just as important, the Arizona call, coming relatively early on election night, robbed him of his plan to leverage a "red mirage"—the appearance of a Republican lead caused by the unusual distribution of ballot counts owing to pandemic-driven changes in voting patterns—to claim victory early and lob accusations of fraud when vote counts shifted toward Biden. But the Arizona call seriously damaged that strategy. And it came from the network that he expected to stand by him in his effort to throw the election into doubt.

Members of the Trump team immediately hopped on the phone to begin lobbying Fox News to reverse the call. It did not. As a result, Trump instructed his supporters to abandon the conservative cable news outlet for friendlier, fringier outlets like One America News (OAN) and Newsmax, both of which rushed to demonstrate their loyalty to Trump. For a few fevered months after the election, ratings for Fox News cratered while Newsmax saw its audience numbers spike. Trump supporters hoisted protest signs denouncing liberal media, in which they lumped Fox News in with cable news rivals CNN and MSNBC.

It was not the first time Trump had taken out his anger on Fox News. He had been alternately bashing and praising the channel since his campaign began in 2015. The network, aware that his wrath could cost it not only viewers but legitimacy and influence within the party, had carefully molded itself around his politics and personality during his four years in office. It was not the only right-wing media outlet to do so. Over the course of his time in office, Trump bent conservative media to his will, shifting and fracturing the right-wing media ecosystem. Turning the tactics once used against nonconservative outlets toward Fox News, Trump helped solidify the notion that there was not only a liberal media establishment that the Right should rail against but also a conservative media establishment that needed to be brought to heel as well.

Heel they did, with destructive, even deadly, consequences.

By the time Trump entered the presidential race in 2015, the conservative media industry had fully matured. Born in the 1940s and 1950s, the first generation of conservative media had been developed by right-wing activists eager to change the course of American politics. The founders of publications such as *National Review* and *Human Events* and radio shows such as *The Manion Forum* and *The Dan Smoot Report* were convinced that the path to political power ran not through the ballot box but through media. In the early 1950s, William F. Buckley Jr. explained that *National Review*'s purpose was "to change the nation's intellectual and political climate." The media they constructed were devotedly conservative and, importantly, self-consciously separate. As Manion insisted about his radio program, "Every speaker over our network has been 100 per cent Right Wing. You may rest assured, no Left Winger, no International Socialist, no One-Worlder, no Communist will ever be heard."[1]

That first generation of activists had entered the field not as entertainers or journalists but as ideologues interested in using media to build a movement and amass political power. The second generation, heralded by Rush Limbaugh's nationally syndicated radio show that launched in 1988, created a world of political entertainment media that was far more popular, far more profitable, and far more connected with the Republican Party. Limbaugh in particular commanded extraordinary deference from Republican politicians: in 1992 George H. W. Bush invited him to an overnight stay at the White House; in 1994 he was dubbed "the Majority Maker" and made an honorary member of the Republican House caucus. By 2009, when he topped polls asking who led the Republican Party, he had become untouchable. In a sign of how much stronger Limbaugh was than the party, Republican National Committee chair Michael Steele was forced to apologize in 2009 after calling Limbaugh an entertainer engaged in "incendiary rhetoric."[2]

That experience of the Republican Party infrastructure bending around a singular media figure reflected the new power of right-wing media in the world of electoral politics. It would be a power Limbaugh soon shared with Fox News, which launched in 1996. Within a decade, Fox had become a necessary campaign stop for any Republican politician running for president. As Dick Morris noted as he sat on the sprawling red couch on *Fox & Friends* just before the 2012 Iowa caucuses, in a moment that was as much promotion as analysis, "You don't win Iowa in Iowa. You win it on this couch. You win it on Fox News."[3] And indeed, that year's Iowa caucus was won by one of the two candidates that had to quit Fox News before running for president: Rick Santorum. Of course, Santorum had also spent months in the state doing retail politics, but his win became part of the mythology around Fox News's power.

The idea of "Fox News: Kingmaker" had taken root in political circles in the years after the 2008 campaign. But there were signs of weakness as well: Santorum, along with Newt Gingrich, had been a Fox News commentator in the lead-up to 2012. Both men were also some of the first to criticize Fox during the primary campaign, arguing that the network was too cozy with the Republican political establishment and pulling hard for that establishment's candidate, Mitt Romney. Gingrich denounced Fox News for "bias" and "distortion," while Santorum grumbled that Romney was the front-runner because "he has Fox News shilling for him every day."[4]

Donald Trump's path to the presidency ran through Fox News, but it also ran through this insider-turned-critic framework that Gingrich and Santorum deployed. In 2011, Trump began appearing as a regular commenter on *Fox & Friends*, popping up on the morning show every Monday to weigh in on the latest news about the Obama administration.[5] That turn to politics began by flogging the long-debunked racist conspiracy theory that Barack Obama had been born outside the United States, which Trump took up in March 2011. Trump's fame as a reality-television star meant his conspiracy mongering garnered outsized media attention, making him the loudest voice advocating for birtherism at the time.[6]

Within a year, Trump had accrued enough political credibility through his Fox News appearances that Romney, as the Republican nominee, traveled to the Trump casino in Las Vegas to receive his endorsement.

When Trump began his own presidential bid in 2015, he quickly demonstrated that he had grown far more powerful than the political media ecosystem that had boosted his right-wing bona fides. Asked about his long history of sexist statements by Fox News host Megyn Kelly at a primary debate, Trump dismissed her question as an excess of "political correctness," then added, "I've been very nice to you, although I could probably maybe not be based on the way you've treated me, but I wouldn't do that." But he would: after the debate, he not only attacked her repeatedly in interviews and online—including the infamous statement to CNN's Don Lemon that "you could see there was blood coming out of her eyes, blood coming out of her wherever"—but also immediately called up Roger Ailes to complain: "I thought you were my friend, Roger."[7]

It was the start of months of tension between the network and the candidate, during which Trump, who had led polls since July 2015, encouraged his followers to turn away from the network. And they did. Network analysis shows that in the spring of 2016, as the Fox feud reached its peak, Fox News held diminished sway in conservative media, replaced by the online site Breitbart. Researchers at Harvard and the Massachusetts Institute of Technology mapped the emergence of a new "right-wing media network anchored around Breitbart" and showed how these outlets used social media "as a backbone to transmit a hyper-partisan perspective to the world." Not only did the pro-Trump media attack Fox News, but they displaced it as the center of the right-wing media ecosystem.[8]

The emergence of Breitbart as the hub of the right-wing media industry marked an unexpected but telling shift. The website, founded in 2007 by Andrew Breitbart, had drawn inspiration from the Drudge Report, the aggregation site that became popular after breaking the story of President Bill Clinton's affair with White House intern Monica Lewinsky. Breitbart populated his site with stories that reflected his populist-right politics. After his death in 2012, the site fell into the hands of Steve Bannon, who in the following years would transform it, as he put it in 2016, into "the platform of the alt-right."[9]

The alt-right, a term coined by white supremacist Richard Spencer and paleoconservative Paul Gottfried in 2008, was a strain of conservatism that put overt white-power policies at the heart of its politics. Discussing this group before the H. L. Mencken Society, Gottfried lamented that the mainstream conservative movement had failed for two reasons: it had opened the door, through its immigration policies, to white Americans "being physically displaced by the entire Third World," and it had abandoned any interest in "the cognitive, hereditary preconditions for intellectual and cultural achievements."[10] In other words, it had become too open to nonwhite immigration and too closed to racist IQ theories.

Through his technology writer Milo Yiannopoulos, Bannon helped cultivate this community and other white supremacist groups as part of Breitbart's core audience. As he was providing space for these groups, he was also cultivating a relationship with Donald Trump. The two men met in 2011, when Trump adviser David Bossie brought Bannon to Trump Tower to game out what a presidential bid might look like. Bannon would continue crafting Trump's political strategy behind the scenes, staging events like Trump's 2012 pledge to pay $5 million if President Obama released his passport application and college records.[11] Bannon also armed Trump with something like a cohesive political platform, one built on anti-immigrant, anti-Black, anti-Muslim, and antiliberal politics—the same agenda Breitbart.com was promoting. And sure enough, Trump's Twitter feed during the campaign linked to Breitbart more than any other news site.[12]

By putting Breitbart's politics and newsfeed at the center of Republican politics in 2016, Donald Trump already showed how his candidacy could reshape conservative media, just as it was reshaping the Republican Party. Aware that a war with Trump could kneecap the network, Roger Ailes stayed silent, and Fox executive Bill Shine told on-air anchors not to come to Kelly's defense.[13]

Once Trump emerged as the presumptive nominee, right-wing media outlets coalesced around him, with a few notable exceptions. Radio and television host Glenn Beck remained an open critic, as did a group of "Never Trumpers," who tended to be most visible at places like *National Review* and the *Weekly Standard*. They had various reasons for not supporting Trump: Beck, a Mormon, reflected the religious group's revulsion toward Trump's libertine lifestyle and grotesque rhetoric. *Weekly Standard* writers, who tended to support neoconservative foreign policy, were repelled by Trump's protectionism and professed desire to withdraw from the international order. And there were still stalwarts at *National Review* who believed in an ideological and programmatic conservatism untainted by populism, something Trump had little interest in. But despite these holdouts, just as most of the Republican Party shifted to support Trump in the general election, so too did most conservative outlets.

Figuring out how full-throated that support should be was a more difficult question. With Trump lagging in the polls, right-wing outlets had a tricky set of incentives to balance. They worried that Trump would lose, and lose big, and take the party down with him. Hugging Trump close meant that if he went down in flames, the fire would consume them as well. But audiences were starting to insist that outlets back Trump, and at least some were willing to abandon their favorite sites if they seemed insufficiently supportive of the candidate.

Then there was the worry that Trump was not just poised to destroy the Republican Party in the 2016 election but well placed to become part of the right-wing media industry himself after his failed run. Rumors about "Trump TV" began circulating in the summer, picking up traction in October as his poll numbers cratered and news broke that his son-in-law, Jared Kushner, had been meeting with media dealmakers about the idea.[14]

The campaign seemed to be trying out the idea on its Facebook live broadcasts, which featured Trump family members and media figures such as Tomi Lahren, a young conservative who had gotten her start on OAN, a small right-wing cable network, before hopping over to Glenn Beck's BlazeTV. The rickety livestreams even featured Fox News–like chyrons and news scrolls.[15] In the closing months of the campaign, commentators had convinced themselves that this was the real purpose of Trump's run: to build up his political bona fides and his base to launch a television network.

The boundaries between right-wing media and the Republican Party had never been as blurred as they were in that moment. That Trump might have conceived of the presidential nomination as a path to a right-wing television network as much as he saw his time at Fox News as a path to the presidency suggested that the two worlds had largely merged. After his election, they would become almost indistinguishable.

---

When Trump won the primary, and then the presidency, right-wing media began to shift to meet the movement's new loyalty requirements. Fox News remade its evening opinion lineup to fit the Trump administration. A few days after Trump's election, Tucker Carlson, the network personality most in line with Trump's America First politics and anti-Black racism, was given his own show, *Tucker Carlson Tonight*, at seven o'clock weeknights. When Megyn Kelly announced she was leaving Fox in early January, Carlson was given her primetime slot, and when Bill O'Reilly was fired for sexual harassment in April, Carlson was moved to eight o'clock, the network's most prized hour.

That left Carlson and Trump confidant Sean Hannity as the tentpoles of Fox News's primetime lineup, but the rapid departures of Kelly and O'Reilly left a hole in primetime. Fox announced the person who would join Carlson and Hannity in September: Laura Ingraham. Ingraham, a right-wing personality with a strong anti-immigrant bent, had spoken in support of Trump at the 2016 Republican National Convention and had just written a book, *Billionaire at the Barricades*, that argued Trump's victory was a "populist revolution" and the fulfillment of the Reagan Revolution.

With Ingraham's hire, the transformation of the primetime lineup into three hours of Trump cheerleading was complete. Two years into the Trump presidency, the network had become perhaps the closest thing the United States had seen to a powerful state media outlet. True, other presidents had developed questionably close ties to journalists. Ben Bradlee, a *Newsweek* reporter covering U.S. politics, developed a close relationship with John Kennedy, first while a senator then as president. Other White House personnel would go on to become straight-news journalists, like Pierre Salinger and George Stephanopoulos, both of whom moved to ABC News after working for their respective Democratic administrations.

But the relationship between Fox News and Donald Trump was different. For one, he developed relationships not just with individual on-air personalities but with people throughout the network, influencing everything from primetime programs to the morning show to the behind-the-scenes decision-making. More than that, though, the idea of Fox News as state TV reflects the way Fox News bent itself to please the preferences of Donald Trump and the close personnel ties connecting the network and the White House.

The on-air content reflected the Trump administration's agenda, with a keen awareness that the president was watching. (Trump often live-tweeted *Fox & Friends* while he watched from the White House.) Programming wasn't entirely aimed at an audience of one, but Fox was so attuned to Trump's watchful attention that it became a running joke on *Fox & Friends*. One morning in late January 2017, the hosts joked that they were speaking directly to the president through the cameras, and that Trump should flick the lights in the residence off and on to show he was watching. On-screen, a shot of the White House showed a window lighting and dimming, though the hosts were quick to assure their audience that the video editors were just having some fun.[16]

But while Trump wasn't flickering the lights, he was quite often picking up the phone. His aimless calls into *Fox & Friends*, often running upward of an hour and blowing the show's commercial breaks, were a regular feature of the first years of the administration. That he so often turned to Fox News was a sign that, though he regularly criticized the network for being insufficiently pro-Trump, he also needed it in order to address his base through a friendly set of hosts.

Nor was it just the network's airtime that he wanted. Donald Trump's primary form of media consumption, along with Twitter, was television. He reportedly watched between four and eight hours of cable news each day as president.[17] And as someone whose path to the White House ran through Fox News, Trump saw television and politics as inseparable. Appearance, narrative, airtime, and headlines were more important to him than policy and governance. So it is no wonder that when he looked to staff his campaign and his administration, he was heavily influenced by Fox News. After Roger Ailes, the CEO of Fox News, was forced out in 2016 after years of sexual harassment, accusations he became an adviser to the Trump campaign. When Bill Shine, who replaced Ailes as a copresident of Fox News, was fired for harassment in May 2017, he was hired by the Trump administration as White House communications director. Other administration hires came from the on-air side of Fox, including Heather Nauert (spokesperson for the State Department), Anthony Scaramucci (White House communications director for ten days), Sebastian Gorka (deputy assistant to the president), and Monica Crowley (spokesperson for Treasury).

Just as important as these personnel choices was the informal network of advising and communications happening between Fox News personalities and the White House. The most prominent of these advisers was Sean Hannity, who regularly spoke with Trump after wrapping his nine o'clock show. Likewise, Pete Hegseth, a weekend host of *Fox & Friends*, lobbied Trump both on-air and behind the scenes for pardons of military personnel convicted of war crimes, pardons that Trump granted in December 2020.[18]

Other parts of right-wing media also had a role to play, most notably Steve Bannon. Hired in August 2016 to serve as the campaign's CEO, Bannon served as the most direct connection between the alt-right and the Trump campaign (the other major contender for that connection, Stephen Miller, worked closely with Bannon on Trump's early immigration policies, including the Muslim ban). Bannon served as chief strategist and senior counselor to the president, bringing Breitbart into the White House, until he was fired a week after the white-power rally in Charlottesville, Virginia. From there, he returned to Breitbart.

Though Fox and Breitbart were the center of the Trump-media ecosystem, the rest of right-wing media changed as well over the course of the administration. Once part of the Never Trump rump of the movement, the website RedState purged most of the site's Trump critics in 2018. The site's founder, Erik Erickson, called Trump "a racist" and "a fascist" during the 2016 campaign and said he would never vote for him, but by 2019 he was firmly aboard the Trump train. Likewise, Glenn Beck, who compared Trump to Hitler the day after the election and made a very public mea culpa for his attacks on President Obama in early 2017, traded his sackcloth and ashes for a Make America Great Again (MAGA) hat in 2018.[19] Though Beck blamed the media's "Trump Derangement Syndrome" for forcing him to become a Trump supporter, business incentives were likely at play as well; in June 2017, his media company the Blaze laid off 20 percent of its employees. Not long after Beck's MAGA-fication, the Blaze merged with CRTV, the television outlet run by avidly pro-Trump radio host Mark Levin.[20] As Charlie Sykes, a former right-wing radio host in Wisconsin, put it, "There's really not a business model for conservative media to be anti-Trump, and perhaps Glenn Beck is just simply acknowledging that."[21]

Those who didn't bend, broke. Sykes lost his radio show. The *Weekly Standard*, founded in 1995 by Rupert Murdoch as the leading voice of neoconservatism, folded. RedState Trump critics lost their jobs. Shep Smith, one of the few remaining Trump skeptics on Fox, finally quit in 2019.

The reshuffling of existing properties was not the only change afoot in right-wing media. Two other sectors were on the rise: an even further-right pro-Trump media, embodied in such outlets as Newsmax, OAN, the *Epoch Times,* and *Just the News,* and the Never Trump media, found in new outlets such as *The Bulwark* and *The Dispatch.* The young pro-Trump media outlets, though mostly founded before Trump took office, gained traction in part because they served as useful foils as Trump tried to keep other right-wing media outlets, especially Fox News, in line. Whenever his frustration with Fox peaked, he would both castigate the network and then promote its competitor, OAN.

OAN may have been a useful foil, but it also showed the limits of Trump's boosterism. Founded in 2013 by media and technology executive Robert Herring Sr., OAN grew out of a partnership with the right-wing newspaper the *Washington Times* and accrued a moderate amount of recognition as host Tomi Lahren gained social media notoriety. But even as Trump promoted the network as an alternative to Fox, it did not appear to have sizable audience growth. Nor did Trump appear to watch it often, still preferring the slick graphics and familiar faces on Fox.

The Never Trump outlets also demonstrated the range of Trump's reach. *The Bulwark*, founded in December 2018 by Charlie Sykes and Bill Kristol after the *Weekly Standard* folded, sought to be a voice of "rational, principled, fact-based center-right voices who were not cowed by Trumpism."[22] But while it primarily published neoconservative and libertarian writers, it also hired liberal writers like Molly Jong-Fast to round out its roster, showing that its Never Trump identity mattered more than an exclusively conservative one. *The Dispatch*, a subscription-based online magazine founded in December 2019, drew in refugees from the *Weekly Standard* and *National Review*, which had become overwhelmingly anti-anti-Trump in the Trump era. Writers at the foundational conservative magazine found that explicitly anti-Trump pieces drew complaints not only from readers but also from donors, slowly closing the door to such criticisms. Both are quite small magazines with relatively little capital, a reflection of how small the audience for anti-Trump right-wing media remains.

As right-wing media became almost uniformly pro-Trump, nonconservative outlets were changing as well. Trump's attacks on journalism, so over-the-top and unrelenting, fed this sense of danger and led to a noticeable shift in liberal news consumers. First, there was a new intensity to liberals' criticism of media outlets, both for the amount of airtime they had given Donald Trump during the campaign, which many believe had helped him win the presidency, and for the tendency to introduce a false sense of balance to issues that liberals felt had clear-cut moral stakes or were the result of asymmetrical political actions. These critiques were not only more frequent but more visible thanks to their proliferation on social media.

At the same time, many liberals—and many journalists—valorized journalism in the Trump era, cheering on a fact-based media that counterbalanced the pro-Trump media of the right. As the president slammed the press as "enemies of the people" and encouraged violence against them, the image of journalists as noble defenders of truth took hold. In February 2017, the *Washington Post* changed its tagline to "democracy dies in darkness," a nod to its readers' belief that democracy was imperiled by the Trump presidency and that the paper had a role to play not only in informing the public but also in defending liberal democracy. These tensions between the sense that journalists were failing and that they were the last line of defense for democracy brought intense attention not only to the stories coming out of professional journalistic organizations but also to the process of reporting and editing as well. And while some journalists and outlets went through a period of soul-searching over the purpose of their work, they also profited handsomely from the turmoil. Subscriptions to the *New York Times* and *Washington Post* soared during the Trump era, as did ratings at CNN and MSNBC.

—

By the end of March 2020, the United States had functionally shut down. The uncontrolled spread of COVID-19 across the country had shuttered major sectors of the U.S. economy, shedding millions of jobs in just a few weeks' time. Deaths mounted rapidly in New York, New Jersey, and Washington State, while uncertainty around the nature of the virus and public-health protocols created a public hungry for reliable information and reassurance. Neither were services the Trump administration had the capacity or the will to deliver. It quickly became clear that Trump would continue to be a source of misinformation throughout the pandemic and that his misinformation would have deadly consequences.

For conservative media outlets, this presented a conundrum. The claims of the president directly contradicted much of the early public health information. And while information would sometimes find its way onto the networks, more often they would parrot the president's misinformation—and, because conservative outlets were his primary source of news, he would parrot theirs. That led to a situation where, for instance, the Fox News medical contributor told Hannity viewers on March 6, 2020, that "the virus should be compared to the flu," calling flu-level illness the "worst-case scenario." Misinformation spread about masks, lockdowns, and even death totals, which pundits on Fox News, Newsmax, talk radio, and social media falsely argued were much lower than reported.[23]

There were moments when personalities on right-wing outlets showed some resistance to Trump's misinformation. Tucker Carlson took the virus far more seriously than most on the right in the early days of its spread (that would change by April).[24] After Trump revealed he had secretly been taking the drug hydroxychloroquine, a wide-eyed Neil Cavuto told his audience not to take the drug simply on the word of the president.[25] And in September, facing potential exposure to the virus after moderating a debate between Trump and former Vice President Joe Biden, Chris Wallace told viewers not to listen to doctors like Trump favorite Scott Atlas but "to people like Anthony Fauci and people like Deborah Birx who have been largely cut off, listen to the independent people who don't have a political ax to grind." He later told *Fox & Friends* viewers to "wear the damn mask and follow the science," to the chagrin of the morning-show hosts.[26]

The misinformation that swirled through conservative media had serious consequences. A study conducted in New Hampshire in July 2020 showed that people who consumed conservative media were less likely to wear masks and more likely to ignore lockdown restrictions.[27] A national survey from April 2020 showed that people who relied on right-wing outlets like Fox News and Rush Limbaugh were more likely to believe conspiracy theories and misinformation about the pandemic, including the notion that Vitamin C could effectively prevent transmission of the virus and that the pandemic's threat had been exaggerated in order to damage Donald Trump.[28]

The second crisis of 2020, the murder of George Floyd, also strained right-wing media in unusual ways. Hosts who had routinely downplayed the threat of police violence and ridiculed the Black Lives Matter movement seemed stunned by the video of Floyd's murder. "I just can't justify it," Limbaugh told his audience.[29] On his radio show, Hannity criticized the police and seemed overwhelmed by the video. "The tape, to me, is devastating," he said on his radio show. "I watch it, I get angrier every time."[30] Perhaps the strangest moment came when Rush Limbaugh chose to do a crossover episode with *The Breakfast Club*, a nationally syndicated radio show on progressive politics and Black culture. Predictably, it was not a productive conversation, with Limbaugh declaring that "white supremacy or white privilege is a construct of today's Democratic Party" and denying that people are treated unequally on the basis of race. Limbaugh later touted the interview as evidence of his openness, even if the conversation demonstrated how unwilling he was to consider the experience of Black Americans.[31]

Other right-wing outlets quickly reverted to form as well. As protests spread across the country, hosts adopted a law-and-order framework, denouncing the peaceful gatherings as "criminal mobs" and encouraging vigilante groups to confront the protesters.[32] Portland, Oregon, where protesters clashed with police and right-wing extremists as part of a years-long conflict in the city, became the focus of most conservative outlets, which used the images and sounds from the conflict to present the protests as uniformly chaotic and violent.[33]

The primary right-wing conspiracies emerging from the protests centered on billionaire philanthropist George Soros and Antifa. Soros has long been a bogeyman on the right, used both to suggest a global conspiracy and to denigrate mass protests as Astroturf. The Antifa conspiracies are newer, growing out of the prominence the movement gained after the deadly white-power rally in Charlottesville, Virginia, in 2017. Since then, right-wing outlets, along with Trump, have falsely presented Antifa as a terroristic threat, in an effort to counter an uncomfortable reality: the growing threat of right-wing violence. (Even under the Trump administration, the Department of Homeland Security named far-right and white-supremacist violence as "the most persistent and lethal terroristic threat" in the United States.)

Then there was the third crisis of 2020: the election and its aftermath. Conservative outlets served as part of the campaign's communications team, their power amplified by their unity around Trump. The efforts of right-wing media to spread misinformation around the election began early, as they helped construct a conspiracy theory around Biden's son Hunter. The primary source for this conspiracy could be found in *Secret Empires*, a book written by Breitbart contributor Peter Schweizer, who had also authored *Clinton Cash* a few years before the 2016 election. In *Secret Empires* and at Breitbart, Schweizer detailed his theory of Hunter Biden's—and by extension, Joe Biden's—corruption.

That book held the seeds of the Ukraine conspiracy: that Joe Biden had used his power as vice president to protect his son from prosecution. That conspiracy was picked up by John Solomon, an investigative reporter who marched steadily right during the Trump years. Solomon wrote a series of articles for the newspaper *The Hill* that promoted the

Ukraine story. His accusations and Schweizer's swirled through conservative media throughout 2018 and 2019—and through the White House as well. The conspiracy they created about Biden led to the phone call Trump made to Ukraine in July 2019, for which he was impeached in January 2020.[34]

Though he was not convicted, the impeachment hearings helped show how the Trump campaign sought to use misinformation developed in right-wing circles to influence the outcome of the 2020 election. That proved useful to nonconservative outlets, which responded with skepticism when a new Hunter Biden story, based on the contents of a suspiciously located laptop, appeared in the closing weeks of the election. Published by the *New York Post*, then blocked on social media, the story received wall-to-wall coverage in right-wing media. But outside that industry, journalists treated it as a potential component of a misinformation campaign, and though they investigated the story, they ran relatively little coverage because of their inability to confirm the authenticity of the laptop's contents or its source.[35]

Thwarted in these efforts to tarnish Biden with misinformation and struggling in the polls, the Trump campaign began to push the narrative that Democrats and the media were angling to steal the 2020 election. At an August rally, Trump claimed that the changes to make voting safer during the pandemic were a plot by Democrats to turn the election into "the greatest scam in the history of politics." Right-wing media amplified and expanded on that idea, arguing that Democrats were engaging in an electoral coup against Trump. For months before the election, that conspiracy found a home in nearly every right-wing outlet, from Fox to The Federalist to Breitbart to Glenn Beck.[36]

The chaos of election night helped right-wing media spread even more election conspiracies. The 2020 election results defied the polls, with the race far closer than preelection polling suggested. Live results reporting was also presented in a confusing way, with wild swings caused by the partisan difference in voting methods. Even as the Trump campaign was exploiting those differences to spread confusion about the outcome, something happened on Fox News that would upend right-wing media over the coming months: the network called Arizona for Joe Biden, a call that, if confirmed, would make it nearly impossible for Trump to win.

The culture of the Fox News Decision Desk played a major role in how the night unfolded. In 2000, the Fox team included John Ellis, cousin to George W. Bush, the Republican candidate that year. Fox called Florida, and the election, for Bush that night, setting the narrative that Bush had won and aiding the campaign through the weeks of recounting and court cases that followed. That understandably created the impression that the Decision Desk was as partisan as the network, which undermined its election night credibility.[37]

Over the following years, there were concerted efforts to wall off the Decision Desk from network influence. That was on full display on election night 2012, when the desk called Ohio for Barack Obama. Karl Rove, the Bush adviser offering commentary that night, insisted that the desk revoke the call, saying Republican Mitt Romney was still poised to win the state. Despite Rove's tantrum, the call stood—and the Decision Desk got a moment in the spotlight when anchor Megyn Kelly put them on camera to explain the call.

Arnon Mishkin, the Decision Desk head who replaced Ellis and had been interviewed by Kelly in 2012, was back on camera again on election night 2020 to explain why the network had called Arizona for Joe Biden. Behind the scenes, the network was facing far more pressure than an irate Karl Rove. The Trump team was outraged. Campaign adviser Jason Miller quickly called the network and asked it to retract the call. Kushner went directly to Fox News owner Rupert Murdoch. When Fox refused to change the call in the days that followed, Trump went to war.[38]

By making Fox News the target of his ire, Trump set up a new loyalty test: to call the election for Biden was to betray Trump. For many right-wing outlets, this was a test they were happy to take. Newsmax and OAN made clear to viewers they had no intention of calling the race. And talk-radio outlets, even though they were not in direct competition with Fox, took the opportunity to ensure their listeners that *they* would never cow to liberal pressure to call the election. Even Sean Hannity, who had to toe the line on his nightly television show, told his radio audience that he was one of the few true believers left on Fox. Once networks finally called the election for Biden a few days later, most right-wing personalities refused to refer to him as president-elect.[39]

The campaign against Fox had an effect. At rallies, signs started to appear lumping Fox in with "liberal media" and "fake news." The chant "Fox News sucks" began to replace the old standby "CNN sucks." As Newsmax's ratings rose, Fox's fell. And while Newsmax was not positioned to directly challenge Fox News's ratings dominance, its ability to siphon off significant numbers of Fox viewers meant that, for the first time in nearly two decades, Fox News slipped to third behind CNN and MSNBC.[40]

On-air personalities could not undo the damage of that election night call, but they could help shore up the president's claim that the election had been stolen. That claim was repeatedly bolstered and expanded in right-wing media in the months after the election. No matter where you looked or listened, you could find a right-wing outlet promoting increasingly arcane theories for how Trump would ultimately win. Sidney Powell, one of the more conspiratorial lawyers associated with the campaign's legal-slash-propaganda efforts to contest the election, became a mainstay of conservative media. And while at times Beck or Limbaugh would use hedge statements—"It's a long shot," Limbaugh repeatedly told his audience before promoting the latest theory for how Trump could stay in office—no outlet wanted to be the first to say it was over. Instead, they competed to see who could be the most faithful.

As these outlets promoted election-theft conspiracies and convoluted mechanisms for keeping Trump in power, they began to sound increasingly like the QAnon conspiracy. QAnon, a far-right conspiracy that claimed a ring of Satan-worshipping pedophiles was conspiring against Trump, was built on the idea of Trump's ultimate victory. QAnon devotees believed Trump was in fact several steps ahead of his enemies and had a plan to both expose them and retain power. And while only a few fringe outlets openly pedaled QAnon content, more established right-wing outlets were inching closer and closer to a shared belief about a last-minute procedural trick that would keep Trump in the White House.

The consequence of these conspiracies became manifest on January 6, 2021, when hundreds of Trump supporters, encouraged by right-wing media and Donald Trump, stormed the U.S. Capitol in a deadly insurrection aimed at overturning the election.

There was a time in the United States that such startling violence would have bought at least a few days of unity. But with blood still drying on the Capitol floor, more than one hundred Republican members of Congress voted to overturn the election and spread conspiracies about a "false-flag" operation that had already begun to circulate within right-wing media. Over the next twenty-four hours, hosts went on air to denounce the violence, then immediately began to argue, falsely, that left-wing agitators and Antifa were responsible for the insurrection.

The characteristics of right-wing media on display in the weeks after the election and the insurrection—slavish loyalty, reflexive antiliberalism, conspiracism, and a growing skepticism about democracy itself—were not new features of the industry. They had, however, metastasized under Trump, becoming even more entangled in governing and even more divorced from the reality feedback loop. And while Trump himself is no longer in the White House, his effect on right-wing media will be a lasting one, with serious consequences not just for political media but for U.S. democracy.

# 4

# The Crisis of Truth in the Age of Trump

*Angus Burgin*

How can we account for Donald Trump's extraordinary record of lies? From the outset of his campaign to the closing weeks of his presidency, he unleashed an unprecedented torrent of false claims and misinformation. The lies themselves are now so familiar as to have become clichés. He regaled audiences at his rallies with stories of a fictitious past: as the child of a German immigrant, who graduated first in his class at Wharton, and benefited only from a modest inheritance, before enjoying a sustained string of business successes, building a TV show that stayed at the top of the ratings for a number of years, ascending to the presidency with a majority of the popular vote, and celebrating before record-breaking inaugural crowds.[1] He promised from the outset to deal with a slew of fictitious problems: a wrecked economy (after ninety-one consecutive months of economic expansion), a slew of "criminals, drug dealers, rapists" streaming over borders (after a nearly decade-long decline in rates of unauthorized immigration, and much research suggesting that the correlation between unauthorized immigration and crime was, if anything, negative), and a catastrophic rise in the murder rate (which was still hovering near fifty-year lows).[2] And he promised his audiences a fictitious future: he would unveil precisely how Mexico would pay for a border wall, he would share his tax records for all to see, he would introduce a new health-care plan that had all the benefits of Obamacare with none of its flaws, and he would make COVID-19 disappear weeks after it had reached American shores.[3] Even his administration's most obvious successes were leavened with hyperbole until they too grew into lies. His tax cut was the biggest ever, his administration had built "the greatest economy in the history of the world," he enjoyed 95 percent approval from the Republican Party, and he'd been featured on more *Time* magazine covers than anyone else.[4] Few rays of truth emerged undisturbed after passing through the prism of Trump's words.

The leading news organizations—already wrestling with challenging market conditions amid cord cutting and the overabundance of free media—struggled to arrive at a coherent strategy to account for a major-party candidacy, and later a presidency, that showed such blithe disregard for facts. Was it appropriate to grant cable news airtime to someone who exploits it, repeatedly, to spread easily documented falsehoods? How could news organizations preserve their putative commitment to "balance" in covering candidates whose arguments were founded in deception? In wrestling with the latter question during the 2016 campaign, the public editor for the *New York Times* captured the pathos of a profession in crisis. The word "lie" is "loaded" and "feels partisan," she wrote—but sometimes, as in Trump's "unequivocally false" claims about Barack Obama's birth certificate, it was nonetheless "time to call a lie a lie."[5] Journalists increasingly worried that their attempts to appear evenhanded were being exploited in the service of false and misleading claims, but also that observing their falsehood would play into Trump's narrative that their reporting was untrustworthy, "fake," and distorted by liberal bias.[6] His willful defiance of convention had left them in a double bind.

Many aspects of the Trump administration's dishonesty, of course, weren't entirely new. The cliché, after all, transcends time and place: politicians, by and large, tend to lie.[7] Anyone who has dipped into the Nixon tapes knows that even presidents can be surprisingly candid about their craven interest in distorting the truth. Bill Clinton was prosecuted for perjury while still in office. And Stephen Colbert had coined the word "truthiness," in a mockery of those who bought into the distorted claims used to justify the Iraq War, a decade before Trump formally entered the political scene.[8] Populist anti-intellectualism and a corresponding suspicion of expert knowledge had animated American political movements since the early Republic, and its propagators were no strangers to the White House.[9] And new media technologies had been used to spread falsehoods since the emergence of console radios or the rise of the printing press.

But Trump was less cautious than these predecessors. Instead of merely disparaging "eggheads," as was common among McCarthyites in the midcentury years, Trump claimed that his own knowledge exceeded that of experts and scientific authorities. "We are smarter than they are," he told the attendees of one rally. "They say the elite. We are the elite. You are the elite."[10] And the scale and openness of Trump's lies struck many observers as novel, inspiring journalists—eager as ever to deflect accusations of bias with hard numbers—to quantify them. The *Washington Post*, especially, was dogged in its early efforts to translate Trump's lies into easy-to-digest statistical and graphical form. Its journalists kept a running tally of Trump's lies, charting them neatly by month and in aggregate, in graphs that told a story of acceleration rather than chastened recalibration. They noted that Trump's statements received "four Pinocchios"—their score for the most egregious lies—65 percent of the time, more than twice the rate recorded for any politician other than Michele Bachmann.[11] Later they added a new category, the "bottomless Pinocchio," to account for Trump's propensity to repeat some debunked lies more than twenty times.[12]

Another quality that seemed to set the Trump administration apart from precedents was its officials' curious willingness to nod winkingly at the instability of truth itself. Two conversations with the NBC political correspondent Chuck Todd were exemplary. The first came shortly after the inauguration, when Todd asked Trump adviser Kellyanne Conway about Sean Spicer's transparently erroneous claims about the relative size of the assembled crowds. Conway disagreed, describing Spicer's account as based on "alternative facts." Todd did a double take: "Wait a minute—Alternative facts? . . . Four of the five facts he uttered were just not true. Look, alternative facts are not facts. They're falsehoods."[13] The phrase "alternative facts" was quickly adopted by critics as a symbol of the new president's epistemological nihilism. And two years later, in explaining Trump's refusal to testify under oath before special counsel Robert Mueller, Trump's lawyer Rudolph Giuliani told Todd that any account he was asked to provide would merely be "somebody's version of the truth. Not the truth." The following exchange ensued:

TODD: Truth is truth.
GIULIANI: No, no, it isn't truth . . .
TODD: Truth isn't truth?
GIULIANI: No, no, no.
TODD: This is going to become a bad meme.[14]

When combined with the sheer number of lies recorded by nonpartisan fact-checkers, such statements left little doubt that something novel was afoot.

More controversial has been the question of what caused these departures from even the most pro forma commitments to the truth. As will become clear, many commentators have rooted their answers in the very idea of truth itself, suggesting that our politics began to go awry when postmodern philosophers and critics called it into doubt. The acids of these postmodern theorists' critiques, according to such accounts, have proved an extraordinarily powerful solvent for discursive realism and social consensus. But in the end, I will argue, this argument relies more on easy inferences than identifiable causes—and thus reveals more about those who wield it than about those who have embraced and disseminated the falsehoods propounded by Trump. A more persuasive account roots the spread of these falsehoods in shifts in the flow of information, ranging from the rise of talk radio and cable news in the 1990s to the explosive growth of social media in the new millennium. The American population, such accounts emphasize, is increasingly self-sorting itself into political communities that reward adherence to shared dogma and diminish incentives and capacities for consensual reasoning.

Even those who find this latter narrative compelling, however, are left with a dispiriting predicament. Combatting lies and propaganda spread by citizens on subreddits and social media, or by talk show hosts with broad popular audiences, is more complicated than the efforts of earlier generations to combat lies and propaganda spread by the state. Putative solutions present themselves as a tangle of paradoxes. In the wake of the Trump presidency, does the unprecedented ease of online expression really necessitate the implementation of unprecedented restraints? Must we conclude that the pursuit and preservation of intersubjective truth require the ongoing restriction of intersubjective expression? Will the truth now set us free only if we first agree to be bound?

---

From its outset, the Trump administration provoked a panic of unprecedented scope about the nature and status of truth. What had been an esoteric concern burst onto the shelves of mainstream bookstores with titles that spoke to mounting public anxiety. We were confronting, they proclaimed, a "war on science," a "new war on truth," an "assault on truth," or an "assault on reason."[15] This epochal battle had created a "misinformation age," a "fake news nation," or a "post-truth world order."[16] It was characterized by a "new conspiracism" and "weaponized lies" and heralded the "death of expertise."[17] We needed journalists and scholars to set about "mapping the politics of falsehood," explaining "why we love it when Trump lies to us," or (punningly) revealing "when feelings and opinions trump facts and evidence."[18] The root question, as one journalist bluntly put it, was "how bullshit conquered the world."[19]

According to a number of commentators, the answer could perhaps be found in the migration from the humanities departments of a prior generation to the conservative politicians of the new millennium. Their story goes roughly as follows. First, postmodernists under the influence of French theory disavowed the idea of objective reality. "The flight from facts began in the 1960s and 1970s with writers on the far left," the Kennedy School scholar Thomas Patterson wrote in *How America Lost Its Mind*. "Rebelling against 'the establishment,' they argued that reality is a social construction used by elites to manipulate the masses." Then, in a twist that critics found delicious with irony, these ideas were discovered and deployed by unscrupulous conservative politicians and their enablers.[20] Although Trump was not the first conservative who seemed to draw on the suspicion of objective reality fostered in the seminars of left-leaning professors, many commentators came to see him as the "perfect manifestation" of the trend: a "right-wing postmodern antihero," or a "simulacra businessman" who embodied the very "culmination of late capitalism."[21]

The moral of this story was captured in a quote from George Orwell, invoked by the philosopher of science Lee McIntyre in his book *Post-Truth*: "So much of left-wing thought is a kind of playing with fire by people who don't even know that fire is hot." In this case, postmodern theorists had destabilized the idea of truth in the service of critique, only to make the "embarrassing" discovery that these insights could be added to the toolkit of those in positions of power.[22] As Casey Williams—a doctoral student in literature at Duke University, one of the great centers of postmodern theory—acknowledged in the *New York Times*, "It often feels like Trump has stolen our ideas and weaponized them."[23] Such commentaries suggested that, regardless of its theoretical merits, the political implications of postmodernism were proving disastrous. "This is the post-truth paradox," the political scientist Colin Wight concluded. "The more educated societies have become, the more dysfunctional democracy seems to be."[24]

The most prominent exponent of this story about Trumpism was the venerable *New York Times* critic Michiko Kakutani, whose 2018 book *The Death of Truth* unfolded as an extended screed against the cultural implications of postmodernism. In Kakutani's telling, postmodernism was best captured through the turn toward deconstruction in literary criticism—a method that she found "deeply nihilistic" in suggesting that "reason is an outdated value" and "that language is not a tool for communication but an unstable and deceptive interface that is constantly subverting itself." Over the past four decades, she wrote, such ideas had migrated "from academia to the political mainstream," clearing "the way for today's anti-vaxxers and global warming deniers." Those who abetted Trump's rise, she continued, now drew on "dumbed-down corollaries" of postmodern ideas to explain away his lies and to undermine faith in any scientific consensus.[25] His ascendance to the presidency was a predictable, if ironic, conclusion to a decades-long academic endeavor to undermine faith in the very idea of truth.

The story Kakutani relayed, in conjunction with the many less prominent journalists and scholars who made similar claims, had a certain compelling logic. Phrases like "truth isn't truth" might carry a ring of familiarity to those who have taken college courses on postmodern social theory. A few Trumpian para-intellectuals proudly displayed their knowledge of postmodernism in justifying their suspicions of expert consensus.[26] And some of the most prominent critics of the idea of objectivity had been warning of the potential subversion of postmodern social theory since early in the new millennium. The historian of science Bruno Latour had experienced just such a crisis in faith in 2004, after the Iraq War and the consequences of a warming climate had brought the perils of sowing doubt into stark relief. Perhaps now, he suggested, the primary "danger would no longer be coming from an excessive confidence in ideological arguments posturing as matters of fact—as we have learned to combat so efficiently in the past—but from an excessive *distrust* of good matters of fact disguised as bad ideological biases!" In a world in which dangerous extremists sometimes appropriated the idea of social construction, he wondered if the task of critical theory was reversing. "While we spent years trying to detect the real prejudices hidden behind the appearance of objective statements, do we now have to reveal the real objective and incontrovertible facts hidden behind the *illusion* of prejudices?"[27] Even if Latour's anxious questions left more room for uncertainty than Kakutani's confident assertions, they shared a common inference: the political crises of our era may well derive from an epistemological wrong turn.

Those making these inferences, however, have yet to assemble a convincing story of *how* postmodern ideas migrated across the political spectrum. Too often, loose threads of correlation are woven into tight claims of causation, without the difficult work that any such history would require. With the gentlest of probing, such associations begin to unravel. Even a cursory reading of many of the theorists most often associated with postmodernism—whether Jean-François Lyotard or Michel Foucault or Clifford Geertz or Thomas Kuhn or Richard Rorty—reveals belabored efforts to disassociate their views from the epistemological "nihilism" of the sort Kakutani decried. And while the effects of their work have transformed the postgraduate study of the humanities, they have only reverberated faintly in the context of the academic social sciences and can be difficult to trace in contexts beyond the leading literary reviews. Indeed, scholars in related fields have spent two generations debating why the public shows ever less interest in their insights.[28] Further, those most drawn to Trumpism—older, white, working-class Americans without a college degree—are among the demographic groups least likely to have been exposed to the writings of postmodern theorists. Attempts to blame Trumpism's disregard for the truth on a postmodern turn, in short, rely on inferences about a cultural osmosis that seems to affect people in inverse proportion to their degrees of exposure.[29]

As a general rule, moral panics tend to reveal more about their propagators than their prey—and the recent alarm about the epistemological implications of postmodernism is no exception. While it has done little to explain the historical development of the Trumpian right, it tells us much about the current predicament of the center left. Liberal institutionalists, seeking simple truths to wield in counteracting Trump's simple lies, have found little solace in the complex ironies offered by postmodern social theory. Wanting to combat falsehoods with facts, or emotion with reason, or demagoguery with deliberation, they have grown increasingly frustrated by political theories that render all such distinctions problematic. In scapegoating the postmodern turn, they often evince a nostalgia for the more confident knowledge claims of earlier generations, without providing new grounds for such confidence. Approaching philosophy as a search for means rather than a search for meaning, they reject postmodernism for its failure to provide a cudgel against Trump.

While such instrumentalist approaches are unlikely to achieve much traction in the world of social theory, they do reveal a renewed search for certainty on the center Left. Perhaps the most lasting legacy of Trump's disregard for the concept of truth will be the creation and mobilization of a new constituency for it.

---

Early in the morning on Tuesday, May 26, 2020, Donald Trump fired off another Twitter salvo in his ongoing war against voting by mail. "There is NO WAY (ZERO!) that Mail-In ballots will be anything less than substantially fraudulent," he wrote. Ballots would be "forged," mailboxes would be "robbed," and experts would instruct people "how, and for whom, to vote," leading to a "Rigged Election." However, as journalists and fact-checkers had long observed, there were very few documented cases of fraud associated with mail-in ballots.[30] What, then, was Twitter to do about such assertions? The platform had long exempted Trump from many of its rules, indicating that it was in the "public interest" to keep his words freely available, even in cases of evident malfeasance, owing to his status as a "world leader." But it had tightened its policy on misinformation amid the early spread of the pandemic, and executives now found themselves under public pressure to forestall Trump's ability to spread falsehoods to his eighty million followers on their platform.

They decided that in casting unfounded aspersions on the democratic process, he had crossed a line. The tweet was flagged with an addendum imploring readers to "get the facts about mail-in ballots" by following a link that told them that "these claims are unsubstantiated" and that "experts say mail-in ballots are very rarely linked to voter fraud." Trump immediately fired back, saying that "Twitter is completely stifling FREE SPEECH, and I, as President, will not allow it to happen!" But it was the first of many Trump tweets that the platform would seek to counterbalance—peaking in the weeks after Election Day, when over a third of his tweets were so flagged.

This digital skirmish followed a template characteristic of the Trump presidency: the use of social media to amplify falsehoods among millions of followers, the dissemination of those messages across sympathetic audiences on conservative talk radio and cable news, the countervailing outrage among fact-checkers, leftists, and liberals, and the hapless attempts of a technology corporation to navigate between preserving free speech and preventing the spread of misinformation in matters of broad public concern. And its pattern foregrounds a second story about the fate of truth in the era of Trump, less focused on high theories of epistemology than the channels through which information flows. According to this narrative, the rise of political misinformation was attributable to what the journalist Bill Bishop described as the "Big Sort": the siloing of a media landscape along political lines. Shorn of legal requirements to maintain "balance," and abetted by social media networks that amplified partisan sensibilities, news had increasingly become identified with competing perspectives rather than consensual truths.[31]

In contrast to those who blame the crisis of truth in the age of Trump on postmodern social theory, those who foreground the changing media environment have established a detailed causal narrative, focused on both systematic efforts to erode the foundations of social consensus and the contingent (and unanticipated) effects of online communication. The story of deliberate efforts to counteract social consensus follows on Naomi Oreskes and Erik Conway's book *Merchants of Doubt*, which shows how cigarette manufacturers sought for decades to cast doubt on the scientific evidence that connected smoking to lung cancer, and how tactics associated with this "tobacco strategy" were subsequently deployed in efforts to muddle established science on acid rain, the ozone layer, and most recently climate change.[32] The historian of science Robert Proctor has memorably designated such efforts as subjects for "agnotology," or "the study of ignorance making."[33] Proctor and his colleagues argued that much like knowledge, ignorance could be produced and disseminated. And they assiduously cataloged the characteristic parameters of such efforts: cultivate, fund, and draw attention to dissenters from a scientific consensus; use them to raise questions about issues that most researchers consider largely settled; exploit journalistic ethics to ensure that this outlier perspective is accorded equal weight in a manufactured "debate"; and then ensure that it's repeated ad nauseum within an "echo chamber" of sympathetic media outlets and politicians. Trump did not share the tobacco strategy's emphasis on the importance of a veneer of scientific authority, instead expressing an open hostility to claims of scientific expertise.[34] But he nevertheless trafficked in its characteristic deceptions, as in his periodic suggestions that climate change was "mythical," "nonexistent," or "an expensive hoax."[35]

Such claims were rendered far more effective when repeated and amplified through sympathetic channels. In this regard, two developments proved especially crucial in facilitating and rewarding lies told by politicians. The first was the Reagan administration's decision in 1987 to revoke the postwar Federal Communications Commission rule that had become known as the "fairness doctrine." This rule had required media outlets, as a condition of their access to the public airwaves, to offer a balanced lineup of left- and right-leaning programming. The decade after its repeal witnessed the national syndication of programs such as *The Rush Limbaugh Show* and the founding of cable news outlets—for example, Fox News and MSNBC—that curated a more explicitly partisan lineup and often served to reaffirm the perspectives of their self-selected audiences.

By the first decade of the new millennium a range of commentators were already expressing concerns that this new media landscape was eroding Americans' capacity for rational debate on the basis of a shared empirical reality. Even David Foster Wallace, who had risen to prominence through postmodern fictions wrought from an exuberant collision of perspectives, worried that the proliferation of partisan information networks was simply too much. "The ever increasing number of ideological news outlets creates precisely the kind of relativism that cultural conservatives decry," he observed in the *Atlantic Monthly* in 2005. The result was an "epistemic free-for-all in which 'the truth' is wholly a matter of perspective or agenda."[36] The following year a *Washington Post* journalist and a Stanford communications professor conducted an experiment showing that—even when the title and content of the articles were randomized—Republicans overwhelmingly chose to read news material attributed to Fox News, while Democrats opted for NPR and CNN.[37] The result of such perspectival fragmentation was, as *Slate* technology reporter Farhad Manjoo wrote in 2008, a media environment that fostered "*selective exposure*, in which we indulge information that pleases us and cocoon ourselves among others who think as we do," and "*selective perception*, in which we interpret documentary proof according to our long-held beliefs." We were entering, in short, a "Rashomon world, where the very idea of objective reality is under attack."[38] While Barack Obama had risen to office on calls to transcend the red/blue divide, Trump presented himself from the outset as an unapologetic creature of this new media age. His Twitter feed became a record of his feedback loop with Fox News, lifting its hosts' takes and narratives as often as he fed his own back to them.

But if the "tobacco strategy" dated back to the 1960s, and the fairness doctrine was withdrawn in the closing years of the Reagan presidency, and Fox News was founded before the new millennium, why did political falsehoods accelerate so dramatically in and after the 2016 campaign? The most significant shift in the flow of information over the decade preceding the Trump campaign was the dramatic rise of social media. Its ascendance created an extraordinarily powerful mechanism for him to bypass media filters altogether in communicating with his supporters, and for those supporters to create thick networks that amplified and affirmed one another's beliefs.

As far back as the mid-1990s, scholars had begun to realize that the capacity for information exchange and social connection unleashed by the internet might, ironically, lead to a narrowing rather than an expansion of its users' worldviews. This phenomenon, labeled "cyberbalkanization" by the MIT professor Erik Brynjolfsson and his then student Marshall Van Alstyne, was made possible by the geographic dispersal of the internet. The resulting erosion of the link between social and geographic proximity, they hypothesized, would make it easier than ever for people to establish and maintain networks with others whose views aligned with their own.[39] In the early years of the internet, such communities were fostered on message boards and facilitated by the rise of news aggregators with a partisan slant. But their scope expanded dramatically with the steep ascent of social media in the decade between 2005 and 2015, which turned such online connections into tightly knit communities often centered on the exchange of information, news, and opinions. By the 2016 election, it was easier than ever for those affiliated with both the political Left and Right to create carefully curated media environments, in which they primarily encountered news that validated their opinions, filtered and affirmed by friends whose perspectives largely aligned with their own. In such an atmosphere the (already tenuous) capacity to arrive at consensus about even the most basic elements of complex issues, such as climate change, immigration policy, or election security, evaporated.

The elective and communal aspects of online communication provided a much subtler and more dynamic venue for the dissemination of propaganda than the clumsier state organs that accompanied the rise of mass media eight decades earlier. In promoting their views, twenty-first-century politicians could benefit from news conglomerates run by sympathetic media barons, think tanks and lobbyists well versed in sowing uncertainty, networks of supporters ready to amplify and reaffirm their messages, and even foreign actors trained to tip the social media scales. As social psychologists observed, the resulting feedback loops were leading even highly engaged citizens to develop more insular and dogmatic worldviews.[40] Trump's genius was to recognize that in these novel conditions, it was no longer necessary to play the cautious game that politicians and their handlers had refined in an earlier media age. New circumstances made it possible for some followers' understandings of reality to be not just periodically reframed but continually remade.

It's no coincidence that sales of *1984* skyrocketed during the Trump administration, even topping the best-seller list in the weeks after Kellyanne Conway's reference to "alternative facts."[41] A host of commentators drew close parallels between Trump's propagandistic manipulation of self-evident truths and the machinations of an Orwellian state.[42] But the characteristic propaganda of the new millennium had been transformed since the era when Orwell wrote. *1984* was set in a paradigmatic totalitarian government, modeled on those of the era of the Second World War: people were treated as a collective by an omnipotent state, and messages were projected to them from above via oversize screens. If Orwellian propaganda emerged in consonance with the tools of mass media, Trumpian propaganda was a product of the internet: fractured and dispersive rather than aggregative and totalizing. Instead of fostering a shared misapprehension of reality, overseen by a dictatorial state, the internet was generating discrete subcommunities that viewed reality in entirely different ways. The collapse of a shared political "truth" that Trump embodied, therefore, was not the product of dangerous ideas in seminar rooms but rather the very tools that we use to communicate and the choices we make in doing so. The search for a scapegoat loses some of its luster when the enemy turns out to be us.

---

After his supporters' assault on the U.S. Capitol on January 6, 2021, Trump's ability to leverage the major social media platforms collapsed. Facebook barred Trump indefinitely from posting on its platform, pending eventual review from its Oversight Board; Twitter temporarily suspended his account, then reinstated it, then banned it permanently. Platforms associated with Trump's followers, too, came under heavy pressure: the social networking service Parler was cast into disarray as Microsoft and Google removed its app from their stores, and Amazon Web Services ceased hosting its content. Trump's supporters responded with outrage, viewing the bans as a restriction on open public discourse and freedom of speech. "We are living Orwell's *1984*," Donald Trump Jr. told his followers. "Free-speech no longer exists in America. It died with big tech."[43] Many commentators, however, reacted to the ban with evident relief. After nearly four years of around-the-clock monitoring of the frenetic postings of the commander in chief, an uncanny calm descended on Twitter. One research organization announced, to much public notice, that in the brief period after his ban the online spread of misinformation had declined by 73 percent.[44] "I am starting to realize that Trump's Twitter was far more menacing to society than I'd suspected," the columnist Farhad Manjoo wrote in the *New York Times*, "and the ban quite a bit more successful at stifling his style of trolly propaganda than I'd guessed."[45] Columnists on other major platforms called the ban long overdue, suggesting that "social media companies need to act far more swiftly in the future."[46] But others worried that the dramatic effects of Trump's muzzling were a sign that a small number of technology platforms had become a commons, policed under unclear standards by executives who had not been democratically chosen to serve as mediators of political discourse.[47] What pathology was leading us to plead with corporations to serve as the arbiters between truth and falsehood, or speech and incitement, in the primary venues of public debate?

Having anticipated just such a moment throughout the Trump presidency, scholars worked to develop justifications for the regulation of online speech. Some defended corporate restrictions on postings on narrow constitutional grounds. "There's no right to free speech on Twitter," the Harvard Law School scholar Noah Feldman told *Wired* in 2017. "The only rule is that Twitter Inc. gets to decide who speaks and listens—which is its right under the First Amendment."[48] The logic of such arguments was clear enough: Trump had many other potential venues for public speech, so on what grounds could Twitter be obligated to publish his musings or misinformation? Others in the legal academy, however, went further, suggesting that the First Amendment itself was due for a reassessment. The Columbia law professor Tim Wu argued in 2017 that new conditions had made speech overabundant and attention scarce, and had thereby enabled new means of manipulating public discourse—such as "flooding" information channels with fake news and propaganda, or unleashing "troll armies" on disfavored speakers. In his view the main threat to political speech was no longer the use of the levers of government to suppress dissident opinion, but rather the mobilization of online mobs and the capacity to drown online discourse in a sea of misinformation. (Trump himself, as Wu recounted, was a pioneer in the use of both of these tools.) In such an atmosphere, he suggested, it was reasonable to consider whether protecting certain kinds of speech was counterproductive, and whether the government should again be allowed to regulate the boundaries of political discourse. "It could mean that the First Amendment must step slightly to the side and allow different legal tools . . . to do the lion's share of the work needed to promote a healthy speech environment," he wrote. For instance, he continued, "the elected branches should be allowed, within reasonable limits, to try returning the country to the kind of media environment that prevailed in the 1950s."[49] Perhaps, such an argument implied, nearly every major media development of the past half century had demonstrated troubling effects—and our elected representatives would be justified to circumscribe the First Amendment in their efforts to put the toothpaste back in the tube.

Concerns about the implications of an "overabundance" of speech were not merely the province of the legal academy—in the wake of Trump's rise, even one of our wisest philosophical historians suggested that democratic politics, and the pursuit of truth, may now be hindered more than helped by the freedom of speech. "It can also seem as if the basic tenets of the democratic imaginary, starting with the idea of a 'free market' approach to speech, are not necessarily suited to the social and cultural conditions of today or that traditional ideals can no longer work in the way they were once intended," Sophia Rosenfeld wrote. "One might even be tempted to conclude that some of these traditions are exacerbating our current problems, particularly as they relate to maintaining the delicate balance between popular knowledge and expertise."[50] The unease of these questions is evident in Rosenfeld's dissociative prose, but the connotations are clear. By making it easier for politicians to spread misinformation, and for citizens to cocoon themselves from opposing views, the internet might now require regulations on political speech that previous generations would have dismissed out of hand.

In this sense, the central concern raised by the crisis of truth in the age of Trump was not—despite his obvious admiration for those in positions of despotic power—about an excess of authoritarianism but rather about a possible excess of democracy. By making it ever easier for people to watch what they want to watch, read what they want to read, and publish what they want to publish, had the evolution of our media environment created a need for heavier-handed regulation? Were we conceding that freedom of speech led to a functional politics only when channeled within certain bounds? Did we need to exhume century-old arguments for granting special privileges and protections to those in positions of expertise? Or did all such calls rely on a gauzy nostalgia for the media landscape of the midcentury years, in which we encountered *just enough* opposing views and *just the right* level of difficulty in trying to make public our own?

We should perhaps be encouraged that the most distinguished critic of the midcentury media landscape, the philosopher Jürgen Habermas, sees some cause for optimism now. Habermas had argued in the 1960s that organs of mass media like radio and television were depriving society of the venues for rational-critical debate that were essential to a functioning polity.[51] From its earliest phases, the rise of the internet had promised an escape from all the potential threats associated with such unilinear channels of communication, and the possibility of a new era of decentralized and democratic forms of deliberation. Yes, Donald Trump's tweets suggested that this vision had gone awry. "You can't even say that this individual is below the political cultural level of his country," Habermas stated in an interview. "Trump is permanently destroying that level." But he was skeptical that the failures of this moment were inherent to the relatively frictionless communications environment opened by the internet world. In contrast to the pessimism of many journalists and academics, he expressed an enduring faith in the prospects for reasoned debate in an age of information abundance. "It's only a couple of decades old," he emphasized. "Perhaps with time we will learn to manage the social networks in a civilized manner."[52]

But how? The relative calm that followed Trump's removal from Twitter has begun to draw attention away from that question, even as the answer remains as unclear as ever. In the absence thereof, historians will have cause to approach Trump more as exemplar than anomaly, and his lies as enactments of an ongoing epistemological crisis rather than as inspirations for its end.

# 5

# Militant Whiteness in the Age of Trump

*Kathleen Belew*

In August 2017, a group of young white men wearing polo shirts and bearing torches paraded through the streets of Charlottesville, Virginia, menacing people in a chorus of "You Will Not Replace Us / Jews Will Not Replace Us." Over the following several days, the organized white power movement stormed into the limelight as members marched, chanted, beat counterprotesters, and killed a young woman by driving a car into a crowd of people. The movement remained present for the duration of Donald J. Trump's tenure in the Oval Office, at some moments less visible and at others directly called to action by the president himself. On January 6, 2021, we watched as white power activists joined Trump supporters and QAnon conspiracy theorists to storm the U.S. Capitol, a show of force meant to recruit and radicalize still more people. When Trump left office, facing a second impeachment trial, the white power movement didn't give up and go home but, in fact, regrouped. An enduring legacy of the Trump administration is that it flung open the gates for far-right extremism to enter mainstream American politics. This legacy includes changes to law, political norms, speech, and rules of behavior, both written and unwritten. But it also includes a casualty count—one still mounting.

This is a history that calls attention to the relationship among street-level white power action, political rhetoric, and policy making—a relationship that is not yet borne out in our traditional archives and that historians have only just begun to examine. A full history of both the Trump administration and the broad alliance of fringe groups it was able to mobilize for its own purposes will require time and distance, yet some of this story is apparent even in the immediate aftermath of the Trump presidency.

The white power movement is a groundswell of groups and activists that has, since the late 1970s, united Klansmen, neo-Nazis, radical tax resisters, skinheads, militiamen, and followers of white power theologies in every region of the country. It is a social movement joined by close ties and common purpose, by ideology and alliances. It is comparatively small, but profoundly diverse in every way but race, bringing together people across regions, classes, genders, and more.[1]

The white power movement is decades, if not generations, old. It is not simply an incarnation of Trumpism. Nor is it the same thing as the nativist and often white supremacist rhetoric and policy making that issued from the White House and its allies during the Trump administration. But a look at the white power movement shows us the ground game, one that is instructive in understanding how policy makers used these activists for their own purposes. It also allows us to examine white power activism as it compares with white nationalist policy making, and how white supremacy ran central to both and thus remains a live wire in our national politics.

*White power* refers to a branch of the larger militant Right, a coalition that also includes some violent conservatives who say they are not motivated by race. White power is both white supremacist and committed to violence.

*White nationalism*, on the other hand, can refer in common usage to two very different things. One is the idea that there is something about America that is, and should be, intrinsically white, and that people pursuing policy making should ensure that this remains so. This kind of white nationalism includes inhumane anti-immigration policies targeting communities of color, disenfranchisement of voters of color, defense of purportedly "white" cultural forms and whitewashed versions of American history, and more. The second use of the term refers to people seeking a white homeland (also sometimes called *white separatism*). America is sometimes imagined as one such terrain, but others seek a different kind of white homeland—one that is fundamentally antidemocratic and that rejects the United States. For white power movement activists, the "nation" in white nationalism is not the United States but the Aryan nation, a transnational body of white people they believe to be superior to others. Many consider themselves the only true humans in a world populated by nonhuman others.

In other words, the Trump years featured both a white nationalist policy project helmed by people in the administration *and* a white power social movement that believed many of the same claims about whiteness but wished for a white ethnostate, ideally through the overthrow of the country. Although these goals have often aligned, they may not remain so.

White power and white nationalism both fall under a broader category: *white supremacy*. This refers not only to people who have racist belief systems (overtly or covertly) but also to a broad array of systems, histories, and infrastructures that continue to contribute to racial inequality even when individual racism is absent. Here, we might consider differential outcomes in hospitals, schools, prisons, water resources, courts, and more: white supremacy is a matter of a long and complex historical legacy of racial capitalism. White nationalism and white power make up only one facet of its workings. Even overt white supremacy is a mainstream political position: historians have shown that ordinary Americans over the past century have been deeply invested in maintaining inequality. They redlined neighborhoods to keep out Black residents, resisted integration and interracial marriage, and sought out majority-white communities through flight from urban areas into suburbs.[2] The persistence of white supremacy, both systemic and at the level of personal belief, is a marker of the great unfinished work of American democracy. But during the Trump years, these problems manifested as deep wounds, with both white nationalism and white power proponents on the steady march.

A panoply of Trump administration officials aided in creating policies concordant with white nationalist goals. Trump himself spurred much attention along these lines, beginning with his rhetoric on the campaign trail. Speculation about his own beliefs about whiteness followed him into the presidential race, including a racial discrimination suit brought against him in the 1970s and his call for the execution of the Central Park Five—a group of Black and Latino young men who were coerced by police into confessing to and were later exonerated of the assault of a woman jogger in the park in 1989.[3] He did not move to deny either instance of racially motivated action.[4] So, too, did rumors fly that Trump's father, Fred Trump, was a Klansman. Fred Trump had been detained at a Klan parade that became a "near-riot" in 1927, but the article reporting this at the time did not specify whether he was a member of that organization.[5]

In many ways, these early concerns paled in comparison with the escalating series of statements and policy decisions that, taken together, reflected deeply rooted nativism, white supremacy, and white nationalist policy making within the Trump administration. Donald Trump announced his presidential candidacy in June 2015 with astonishing anti-immigrant rhetoric, commenting, "When Mexico sends its people, they're not sending their best. They're not sending you. . . . They're sending people that have lots of problems, and they're bringing those problems with us. They're bringing drugs. They're bringing crime. They're rapists. And some, I assume, are good people."[6] Here and through his attempts to "Build That Wall" at the southern border, he presented immigration not just as a political issue but as a threat to white people. At campaign events, he made clear that the people endangered by this threat were primarily white women, who joined him onstage as "Angel Moms," clad in white, to mourn their children who had been killed by undocumented immigrants.[7] This piece of performative activism called directly to white power activists who had long considered maintenance of the white birth rate to be the center point of their politics, and who viewed white women's reproduction as a contribution to an ongoing race war.[8]

Islamophobia was also a prominent feature of the campaign, and of several people appointed to staff positions in the White House after Trump's victory. Hires of Stephen Bannon, Sebastian Gorka, and Stephen Miller all set off warnings among watchdog groups, which pointed out long records of antisemitic, anti-Islamic, and nativist activity.[9] Bannon's Breitbart News had become a platform for the "alt-right," the name many white power activists briefly adopted from 2015 to

2017.[10] Soon enough, the Trump administration delivered policy to match its rhetoric. In January 2017, Trump signed Executive Order 1376, effectively banning, with a few exceptions, travel to the United States from several predominantly Muslim countries. This led to hundreds of travelers being detained en route, often without recourse or legal representation. The order was widely decried as unfairly stigmatizing all Muslim travelers as terrorists or potential terrorists, leading to weeks of protests at airports. As judges blocked enforcement of the law, the administration countered with new versions. The Supreme Court upheld a version of the travel ban in June 2018.[11]

Dehumanization of immigrants ran through Trump's remarks and policy decisions about immigration across the southern border as well, ranging from attempts to construct a border wall, to the very real separation of migrant children from their family members, to the detention of undocumented migrants in cages and substandard facilities without potable water or access to basic hygiene. "The cruelty [was] the point" of many of these policies, as Trump administration officials remarked. They were meant to deter immigrants.[12] Trump surrogates used mass crossings, like a caravan of people making the journey from Central America to the border in fall 2018, to gin up fear among supporters (Fox News has kept migrant caravans in its regular headlines ever since).[13] Trump himself also expressed hatred and animosity toward migrants. As the *New York Times* reported of conversations around March 2018, "Privately, the president had often talked about fortifying a border wall with a water-filled trench, stocked with snakes or alligators, prompting aides to seek a cost estimate. He wanted the wall electrified, with spikes on top that could pierce human flesh. After publicly suggesting that soldiers shoot migrants if they threw rocks, the president backed off when his staff told him that was illegal. But later in a meeting, aides recalled, he suggested that they shoot migrants in the legs to slow them down. That's not allowed either, they told him."[14]

What the Trump administration *did* implement imposed the same degree of cruelty. Between April and June 2018, nearly four thousand children crossing the border were forcibly separated from their parents and guardians, who faced prosecution as the children disappeared into foster care and other arrangements. The Trump administration made no provision to reunite these families, failing to recognize the most basic degree of humanity in its treatment of the migrants. Although the policy ended, first by executive order signed under mounting pressure and then under injunction, the damage had already been done. Many families would not be reunited, and still others had endured unspeakable trauma.[15]

This policy, too, connected directly to white power movement rhetoric, and this time there was a clear and direct link with a substantive paper trail between white power ideology and Stephen Miller, the Trump aide widely credited with designing the family separation policy. Emails between Katie McHugh and Miller, both of whom worked at Breitbart News in 2015–16, show Miller exhorting her over and over to read the white power novel *Camp of the Saints* and use it to frame present-day issues. To be sure, there is a reasonable chance that Miller didn't believe the book's message himself. Although *Camp of the Saints* is more Islamophobic than antisemitic, Miller's Jewish roots caused many people to wonder what home, if any, he could find in white power circles. Perhaps, too, he was merely using white power material opportunistically to connect Trump with a pool of recruitable supporters. But there is irrefutable evidence that Miller, the architect of family separation, wanted to position immigration in political discourse as the sort of threat it presents in *Camp of the Saints*, in which immigrants appear as a mass horde intent on the destruction of Western culture.[16]

This fear is not new, although it has been reemphasized in recent white nationalist, white power, and militant Right rhetoric. In the twentieth century alone, as historians have documented, nativists have repeatedly used language that depicts immigrants as a horde or a swarm, or as a flood, a wave, or a tide, to emphasize threat and inexorability. Often these fears, too, connect to discourses about the reproductive capacity of immigrant populations of color compared with stagnant or falling white birth rates. The white power movement, from the 1970s forward, mobilized against Vietnamese refugees with tropes about communism, disease, and accusations of eating rats. It mobilized ideas about hyperfertile Mexican women, and about immigrant rapists in their printed materials, going so far as to refer to extralegal Ku Klux Klan border patrols as "Operation Hemline" in the 1980s, implying that migrants presented a sexual threat to the nation even by crossing the border. This set of ideas moved easily from fringe to mainstream, where they mapped onto general concerns about population growth and the demographic shift of the United States away from a white majority.[17]

Miller's engagement with white power activists and discourse was substantial and prolonged. He directly engaged white power thinking and movement activity on other occasions, including reading and reposting content from white power website VDARE. That site, named for Virginia Dare—supposedly the first white baby born in colonial America—was built on and named for this same discourse about white reproduction as an inherent part of the American body politic. Miller also read and circulated content from Jared Taylor, head of the longtime white power website and sometimes-publication *American Renaissance*. He defended the sale and flying of the Confederate flag, which, in the case of a Jewish man who grew up in California, can hardly be claimed as a heritage symbol related to the Civil War. Miller also had contact with neo-Nazi and alt-right leader Richard Spencer, perhaps the most prominent white power activist at the time of the Unite the Right rally in Charlottesville. How much of Miller's activity was opportunistic and how much of it reflected sincerely held belief is impossible to say, but also largely irrelevant: someone so conversant in white power ideology, symbols, and rhetoric would and could only be tasked with a policy-making role if the Trump administration sought white nationalist policy goals, at least in some areas.[18]

This nativism did not necessarily prioritize "America First" as neatly as Trump's "Make America Great Again" slogan might imply. For Bannon and Gorka, and for many in violent white power groups, a transnational conception of whiteness sometimes or always outweighed obligations to the nation. This was clear in transnational speaking gigs and communications at the high level, but even more stark in the street-level white power movement, where activists understood their nation not as the United States but as whiteness itself, and their countrymen as white people the world over. This opened the door to transnational organizing amplified by social media.

Together with the extremist ideology that played a role in conceiving of nativist policy, Trump himself continued to sound the rhetorical alarms that appealed to the white power faithful, as well as white supremacists more broadly. At a roundtable about immigration in California in 2018, even as family separation drew enormous opposition,

Trump remarked, "We have people coming into the country or trying to come in—and we're stopping a lot of them—but we're taking people out of the country. You wouldn't believe how bad these people are. These aren't people. These are animals."[19] Here, Trump followed centuries of anti-immigrant rhetoric that compared migrants to animals to intentionally dehumanize them, making it easier to enact violence through policy later.[20] The consequences were immediate for too many children and parents, and they framed a series of events that would follow.

## White Power Is in the Streets

In 2018, a gunman killed eleven people and wounded six at the Tree of Life Synagogue in Pittsburgh. In 2019, a gunman opened fire on two mosques in Christchurch, New Zealand, killing fifty-one people. A few months later, in an El Paso, Texas, Wal-Mart, another gunman killed twenty-three and wounded that many more. These events have usually been described as individual acts of antisemitic, anti-Islamic, and anti-immigrant violence—and they certainly were. But they were also carried out by white power activists, all of whom shared the same ideology. Each of the gunmen in these shootings referred to the same tropes and symbols; all of them worried about the white birth rate and swelling tides of immigrants. The Trump rally Angel Moms looked very much like the white-clad women in the photo montage that ended one of the gunman's manifestos: a collage of white women and children meant to underscore their endangerment at the hands of swelling populations of nonwhite others.[21]

It would be a mistake to think about this part of the story as a series of "lone wolf" attacks—indeed, use of that phrase was a deliberate white power movement strategy implemented in the 1980s to direct our attention away from its social organization and to distract the public from several decades of illegal activity that followed.[22] It would also be a mistake to think of these events as simply a series of tragedies disconnected from a larger political landscape. Instead, white power must be understood as a groundswell of different groups and actors who vary in commitment, organization, and intensity but who share a motivating ideology and unifying strategy. This groundswell not only produced mass shooters during this period, but also gave rise to several other alarming markers of violent activity.

The history of white power activism shows that the movement has typically operated at two registers: public-facing, performative activism; and paramilitary, underground work that paves the way to future violence. These are knit together by social ties, and often the same people and groups engage at both registers. But because the underground activity is kept secret, we don't often take its full measure in real time. Indeed, the underground we can document in the earlier period (1968–1995) owes to a huge archive of materials accessible only decades later, such as declassified documents, trial testimony, and autobiographical accounts of people who left the movement. This is why this history is so important: without it, we would have no mechanism to connect the seemingly disparate parts of this groundswell. When taking the earlier history into account, however, a clear pattern emerges that has raised alarm among historians, watchdog organizations, government personnel, and others.[23]

This pattern is evident in a rising tide of white power activity. The three mass shootings (alongside which we might also consider the shooting of Black Bible study worshippers in Charleston and the shooting of children at a summer camp in Norway and several similar events in Germany) are only one part of the story. We should also notice recent arrests of members of Atomwaffen Division, a transnational organization that has attempted to start a race war through acts of terrorism. We should look at the activities of The Base, a group that similarly uses paramilitary training camps to prepare for war. We have to watch the Oath Keepers, which recruits veterans, active-duty troops, and police; the Three Percenters, which claim to be enforcing the Constitution through extralegal militia activity; and the Proud Boys, who have flashed white power hand signs and referenced movement texts even as they deny their commitment to the ideology. All of these groups are part of the same movement. Indeed, we know from its earlier history that activists frequently move among these groups and belief systems, seeing all of them as interlocking parts of the same desperate battle to save the white nation from extinction.[24]

Indeed, this sense of apocalyptic threat tangled white reproduction with a host of other issues like anti-immigration, Islamophobia,

"Western chauvinism," antifeminism, misogyny, anti-LGBTQ action, and white supremacy. Each of these issues also runs, in one way or another, through the mainstream Republican platform. But for white power activists and many white nationalists, all of them threatened by the lower white birth rate, leading—as they saw it—not to peaceful demographic transformation but to a future annihilation of the white race. This end, they believed, could not be peaceful. It would be an extinction event that could only be resisted through war on the state. It's worth noting here that even visions for white separatism are inextricable from this violent worldview and are often considered by activists to be incremental steps to the overthrow of the country, and perhaps the eventual establishment of an all-white world. Such beliefs call for race war. Many of the activists in this movement have called for, prepared for, and even attempted to wage an antidemocratic race war for decades.

The white power movement of the 1980s found a home within the antigovernment militia movement of the 1990s. After the Oklahoma City bombing in 1995—an act of domestic terror that represented a crescendo of white power activism—militia groups swelled even as the nation seemed to think the problem was resolved. False narratives about "lone wolf" attackers disconnected from social networks persist into the present moment, leaving us largely hamstrung in confronting the militant Right. Indeed, white power persists not because of one failure but because of manifold failures across different scales of social response: over and over again, historical research has shown that public misperception, journalistic misdescription, bias in the legal system, surveillance agency resource allocation issues, problems keeping active-duty military personnel out of groups attempting to overthrow the country, and lack of executive will have *all* contributed to the continued activity of the white power movement.

The major problem in the Trump years, however, went beyond the combination of public ignorance of the movement and inattention that characterized earlier periods. Instead, some Republicans actively directed attention away from it. In the wake of the El Paso shooting, a GOP talking points memo suggested steering "the conversation away from white nationalism to an argument that implies both sides are to blame."[25] Similarly, in the spring of 2020, when officials at the Department of Homeland Security attempted to publish a new threat assessment—one that would name white extremist violence as the greatest terrorist threat to the homeland, outstripping both leftist activity and radical jihadism—the Trump administration delayed its release. The country, quarantined and tuned to a different crisis, hardly noticed.

## Coronavirus and Black Lives Matter

Racial animus unsurprisingly shaped the Trump administration's response to the novel coronavirus, which locked the country into rolling quarantines beginning in March 2020. Trump routinely called COVID-19 the "Kung Flu" or the "China Virus," referring to its origins in Wuhan, China, but effectively racializing the virus itself. These remarks have contributed to an increase in anti-Asian hate crimes.[26]

Trump's dismissal of the virus dovetailed with rising frustrations about quarantine and masking ordinances, creating an opportunity for white power activists. They were among the heavily armed people who stormed the Michigan state capitol on April 15, 2020, and regularly thereafter, targeting Governor Gretchen Whitmer. They bore Confederate flags and nooses and carried signs like "Tyrants Get the Rope." Michigan legislators came to work in bulletproof vests.[27] Similar antimasking protests focused on state capitol buildings nationwide, with a pattern of white power and militant Right involvement. Proud Boys, the Michigan Militia, and Michigan United for Liberty organized actions at the state house in Lansing. Proud Boys were involved in actions in Las Vegas, in Carson City, and in Oregon, often alongside other groups like Patriot Prayer, the Lightfoot Militia, and Boogaloo Boys. Patriot Muster, which organized an event in Denver, had ties with the Colorado GOP. Proud Boys organized more than fifty "Freedom March" events nationwide. Monitors noted the emergence of some 513 new far-right Facebook groups dedicated to protesting coronavirus restrictions, reaching more than 1.9 million group members. These spaces connected white power and militant Right extremists with new recruitment opportunities.[28]

After the brutal murder of George Floyd at the hands of police officer Derek Chauvin in May 2020, Black Lives Matter (BLM) and other social justice groups flooded the streets in unprecedented racial justice actions, including as many as twenty-six million protesters of varying race, class, and gender identities.[29] These uprisings were met with police violence, and, in some cases to be sure, clashes resulted in violence to structures and property that served in many media outlets as a distraction from widespread police assaults against protesters.[30] Wildly inflated damage and fatality estimates on the part of BLM protesters have largely been discredited.[31] Yet Trump invoked centuries-old ideas of Black criminality to decry the protests and threatened retaliatory violence, calling demonstrators "thugs" and tweeting, "When the looting starts, the shooting starts."[32] It's impossible to argue that he had no awareness of the meaning of such invective; just a month later, the president retweeted a video of his supporters featuring one of them shouting "white power."[33] A white couple in St. Louis who threatened BLM protesters with weapons even became featured speakers at Trump's nominating convention, emphasizing the continued interweaving of street-level white power action, political rhetoric, and policy making.[34]

Trump and the GOP maintained that the protests had been violent and costly even as they ignored a disturbing trend: white power activists and others on the militant Right were using the BLM protests as an opportunity to incite violence, aiming to increase social instability and engineer bad press for racial justice activists. To outline just a few examples, in Pennsylvania in June, white agitators with *molon labe* tattoos—meaning those opposing firearms should "come and take them," and signifying Second Amendment and militant Right activism—infiltrated a peaceful protest to instigate violence. Hundreds of extralegal militiamen outfitted with AR-15s and other weapons showed up to BLM protests in Coeur d'Alene, Idaho, a longtime white power movement epicenter. Neo-Nazis and other white power activists, marked by neo-Nazi patches and tattoos, crashed a BLM protest in Boise, shouting "white power" and "heil Hitler." In Richmond, white supremacists posing as BLM activists incited riots. Proud Boys clashed with protesters in multiple states. In Kenosha, Wisconsin, a militia action against BLM resulted in a teenager, Kyle Rittenhouse, allegedly shooting and killing two people. And in Oakland, California, Boogaloo-affiliated Steven Carrillo allegedly assassinated a white police officer, using peaceful BLM protests as a cover.[35]

Because of the collision of coronavirus and the racial justice protests, large groups of people on the right used one or both of these mobilizations to express broad frustrations with the nation and its governance, joining fringe ideologies that called for revolution. To be clear, the phenomenon I refer to here is distinct from BLM or even Defund the Police, both of which used public protest with aims for democratic reform. I'm calling attention instead to people who sought to exploit this moment to bring about social unrest or civil war. The most prominent moniker for these activists was the Boogaloo Boys, in some cases more of a phenomenon than an organized group.[36] Wearing Hawaiian shirts and patches featuring plays on the name like "Big Igloo," Boogaloo Boys nevertheless represented a fundamentally violent and antidemocratic position, advocating for the instigation of violence to bring about a collapse of society. This brought together apolitical reasons for wishing an end to social structure (frustration and rage at the pandemic or the economy, for example), as well as political reasons tied to white supremacy. To be sure, other ideologies may have been present in Boogaloo groups. But many of them, and the most organized, were white power activists who wanted the collapse of society to lead to a long-awaited race war.[37]

Boogaloo's presentation was carefully calculated to distract from its violent intent, just as the khakis and polo shirts had been at Unite the Right in Charlottesville. Here, too, activists drew from a century-long playbook in which white power and Klan groups had tacked to the prevailing cultural winds. In the 1980s they had worn camouflage fatigues in part for tactical readiness, but also because that uniform had wide cultural appeal in the era of paintball and war movies.

As usual, white power activists were above all opportunistic, looking for any available window for recruitment and radicalization—and, in 2020, the window was thrown open both by circumstance and at the hands of the Trump administration.

Far from decrying this record of violence, the Trump administration zeroed in on "antifa and the left" as the main threat to the nation. Antifa, to be clear, represents an ideology rather than a movement, and one that does not share the extensive infrastructure, weaponry, organizing, and casualty counts of the white power movement and militant Right.[38] As the *New York Times* later reported,

> In late spring and early summer, as the racial justice demonstrations intensified, Justice Department officials began shifting federal prosecutors and F.B.I. agents from investigations into violent white supremacists to focus on cases involving rioters or anarchists, including those who might be associated with the antifa movement. . . . Federal prosecutors and agents felt pressure to uncover a left-wing extremist criminal conspiracy that never materialized. . . . They were told to do so even though the F.B.I., in particular, had increasingly expressed concern about the threat from white supremacists, long the top domestic terrorism threat, and well-organized far-right extremist groups that had allied themselves with the president.

Meanwhile, the White House and Trump faithful at the Justice Department "stifled internal efforts to publicly promote concerns about the far-right threat, with aides to Mr. Trump seeking to suppress the phrase 'domestic terrorism' in internal discussions." They also denied requests for additional analysts to monitor social media for threats by white power and militant Right groups.[39]

In the first presidential debate between Trump and Democratic nominee Joseph Biden on September 29, Trump took this position one step further. When asked to condemn "white supremacists and militia groups," he attempted to misdirect attention to leftist violence before saying "Proud Boys, stand back and stand by." The day after the debate, Trump claimed not to know who the Proud Boys were and that he had told them to "stand down." But the Proud Boys were prominently involved in the Charlottesville rally and Trump should have known who they were. Even in the most generous interpretation of this comment, if one assumes that he simply meant to say "stand down," the damage had already been done. Rather than condemn white power groups, Trump had instead issued a call to arms.

At that point, of course, analysts debated how to classify the Proud Boys, whose members publicly claimed not to be white supremacists. In the following months, their position became less ambiguous as they were labeled a terrorist group in Canada, flashed "white power" hand signs in photographs, and directed journalists to read the white power novel *The Turner Diaries*. Proud Boys ideology was always openly white supremacist, even as law enforcement underestimated the threat posed by the group.[40]

Before the debate, Trump's use of white power movement activists as foot soldiers in a war on democracy itself might not have been fully clear. But afterward, it was glaringly evident. Perhaps the most discussed "dog whistle" for white power violence was Trump's infamous comment about there being "fine people on both sides" in Charlottesville—that one was taken out of context. He meant not that the Klansmen and neo-Nazis were fine people, but that other "fine people" were the main participants in the Unite the Right rally. But Charlottesville was only one of several moments when Trump and his administration did things that were perceived by militant Right groups as green lights for further activity. "Stand back and stand by" was far more damaging, and it escalated militant Right momentum not just among the Proud Boys but across the whole groundswell.

Before the night was over, the Proud Boys had incorporated "Stand Back, Stand By" into a badge logo and tweeted their readiness to the president. Other groups aligned with the white power movement also took his words as a call to action.[41] A few days later, on October 8, the FBI stopped a white power plot to kidnap Michigan governor Gretchen Whitmer and burn down the state capitol; part of the plan was to remove her "for trial." In militia movement history, this plan has often involved violence—in this case, they had bombs—and usually referred not to a court trial but to trial by hanging. It's very likely that Whitmer faced death if the plot had succeeded. This plot, too, indicated strategy that would shape movement action going forward, particularly in the terrorist attack on the Capitol on January 6.[42]

After months of delay from the Trump administration, the Department of Homeland Security finally published its Threat Assessment in October 2020. Its findings were stark: white extremism represented the single greatest terror threat to the nation.[43]

## Insurrection

Donald Trump embarked on a campaign to cast doubt on the results of the 2020 election even before it began, issuing repeated statements that if he lost, it would owe to massive fraud. When he did lose, he mounted a host of "Stop the Steal" legal challenges, rallies, and protests in every possible arena. White power activists, perhaps not acting in true devotion to Trump so much as capitalizing on a window of opportunity, used this moment strategically. They had stayed away from poll violence on Election Day, talking among themselves of the danger of arrest, and had instead planned ahead. On January 6, 2021, they joined two other streams of far-right mobilization: die-hard members of the Trump base mobilized around "Stop the Steal" and recently radicalized QAnon conspiracy theorists.

Information about how the insurrection happened is still unfolding, with charges issued against hundreds; at the time of writing, it was not yet clear whether these charges might in some cases rise to the level of criminal conspiracy. But much of the event unfolded in plain view on our television screens. Before January 6, Trump officials helped organize a "Stop the Steal" rally. Militant Right and white power activists prepared to inflame this event into a confrontation, coordinating their communication channels, weaponry, and more. Someone not yet known planted pipe bombs at both Republican and Democratic party headquarters near the Capitol, perhaps to draw police response away from protesters. Some individuals came armed with Molotov cocktails and military-grade weapons. Some even discussed bringing weapons across the Potomac River by boat. Photographers documented protesters in paramilitary uniforms and carrying heavy-duty restraints, indicating organization and a plan to detain and most likely harm legislators.[44]

On January 6, Trump addressed a crowd near the White House, saying, "If you don't fight like hell, you won't have a country anymore," and invited his audience to march to the Capitol. They marched, and many followed the crowd into radical action in storming the building. Some organized members of the militant Right had left the speech early to encircle the Capitol, targeting vulnerable entrances. Trump had called the media crooked; protesters scrawled "Murder the Media" on a Capitol door.[45]

Notably, the mob used strategies directly out of white power novel *The Turner Diaries*, a movement text that imagines a successful coup by white power activists who take over a homeland, then the United States, and then the world. Several of the methods used in the book appeared in the insurrection. One is the "Day of the Rope," in which "traitors" (including members of Congress, people in interracial relationships, journalists, and more) are publicly hanged. On January 6, the mob erected a gallows and people took selfies in front of it. There is good reason to believe that, had the mob found legislators, they would have done much worse.

*The Turner Diaries* also prominently features an attack on the U.S. Capitol, though somewhat different from the one we witnessed. In the book, it's an attack with mortars—a shelling from outside the Capitol building. But significantly, it is imagined not as a mass casualty—in a book brimming with them—but rather as a show of force designed to demonstrate that a small group of people can strike at the heart of power. It's meant to "awaken" other white people to the cause and to draft them into an evolving race war.

To be clear, the plan outlined in the *Turner Diaries* is profoundly genocidal, antidemocratic, and anti-American, envisioning the violent overthrow of the United States and the annihilation of all nonwhite people throughout the world with chemical, nuclear, and biological weapons. The book has been enormously important to white power, militant Right, and accelerationist activists (those seeking to provoke race war) not because it's a good novel, but because it explains how a small number of people might overthrow the United States.[46]

It is, indeed, a novel with unbroken utility by the militant Right. *The Turner Diaries* appeared at the training camps and recruitment events of white power activists in the 1980s. As those groups found a home within the broader antigovernment militia movement of the 1990s, Oklahoma City bomber Timothy McVeigh read and distributed the novel, and found a blueprint there for carrying out the 1995 bombing of the Alfred P. Murrah Federal Building.[47]

The presence of *Turner Diaries* imagery and the fact that Proud Boys are talking about it are important. It reveals that at least some of the people who stormed the Capitol come from the same movement that has been threatening democracy and killing civilians for decades, if not generations. As new as QAnon was, it wielded some old, familiar tropes that had appeared in the white power movement and even earlier: the idea that white women and children were in danger of sexual violence from a cabal of elite outsiders was a reiteration of the fiction that fueled New World Order ideas in the 1990s and the Zionist Occupational Government white power conspiracy theory that came before.

So, too, did QAnon mobilize the same paramilitarism: Ashli Babbitt, a QAnon believer and a multitour veteran who was killed as she stormed the Capitol, referred to the protesters as "boots on the ground," thus comparing them to a military force. And her death would fit into an idea of endangered white women, and women's martyrdom at the hands of a cruel state, that connected her to Vicki Weaver's death at Ruby Ridge in 1992. That event inflamed an earlier militia movement just as Babbitt's death became a new instrument of radicalization after January 6.[48]

At the end of the Trump presidency, militant whiteness was in the streets in greater numbers and with greater fervor than at any time in the recent past. Americans could no longer ignore the militant white power activists who proclaimed open racism and called for violence, whether they were wearing polo shirts and khakis at Charlottesville or dressed in militia gear and carrying yellow-and-black flags on January 6. Polls reported that more and more people were prepared to use violence to defend their political beliefs.[49] By April 2021, more than half of Republicans, according to a Reuters poll, said they believed the January 6 insurrection was a "non-violent protest or was the handiwork of left-wing activists trying to 'make Trump look bad.'" And only three in ten thought Trump was responsible.[50] Meanwhile, Republican lawmakers almost uniformly stalled efforts to examine the events of the day, saying that a commission—like the one instituted after the terror attacks of September 11, 2001—was unnecessary. Even as body camera footage revealed stark and terrifying images of the day, Representative Andrew Clyde (R-GA) described the storming of the Capitol as "a normal tourist visit."[51]

Such misrepresentations of white power terrorism are not new. But the speed of these distortions, the disregard for norms of factual proof and civil discourse: these are the legacies of the Trump years and the harbingers of our political future if we do not find a better path.

## References

### ARCHIVES

Elinor Langer Research Collection, Special Collections, University of Oregon, Eugene, Oregon

Gordon Hall and Grace Hoag Collection of Dissenting and Extremist Printed Propaganda, Ms. 76, Brown University Library, Providence, Rhode Island

Greensboro Public Library, Greensboro, North Carolina (Clipping File: Greensboro Shooting, November 3, 1979)

Intelligence Project Holdings, Southern Poverty Law Center, Montgomery, Alabama (Clipping Files, Database, Photographs, Unpublished Materials, Court Records)

Keith Stimely Collection on Revisionist History and Neo-Fascist Movements, Special Collections, University of Oregon, Eugene, Oregon

Western History Collection, Denver Public Library, Denver, Colorado (Biography Clipping Files: Berg, Alan, 1934–1984)

Wilcox Collection of Contemporary Political Movements, Kenneth Spencer Research Library, University of Kansas, Lawrence, Kansas

## SELECTED NEWSPAPERS, NEWSLETTERS, AND PERIODICALS (WHITE POWER MOVEMENT AND AFFILIATE GROUPS)

*America's Promise Newsletter*
*Aryan Crusaders for Christ Newsletter*
*Aryan Women's League Newsletter*
*Battle Flag*
*Calling Our Nation*
*Christian Patriot Women*
*Confederate Leader*
*Crusader*
*Fiery Cross*
*Focus Fourteen*
*From the Mountain*
*Inter-Klan Newsletter and Survival Alert*
*Jubilee*
*Klansman*
*National Vanguard*
*New Order*
*Oklahoma Separatist*
*Patriot Matchmaker*
*Patriot Report*
*Patriot Review*
*Right as Reina*
*Scriptures for America Worldwide*
*Seditionist*
*Teutonic Unity*
*Thunderbolt*
*True Israelite*
*White Aryan Resistance / White American Resistance (WAR)*
*White Carolinian*

*White Patriot* (Metairie, Louisiana, and Tuscumbia, Alabama)
*White Power*
*White Sisters*

## SELECTED MOVING IMAGE SOURCES

Greensboro Truth and Reconciliation Commission Testimony News footage of the Greensboro shooting, WTVD-TV, WFMY-TV Race and Reason (public access)
*Sally Jessy Raphael*
*Saturday Night Live*
Video recordings of speeches
Government documents

## DOCUMENTS OBTAINED THROUGH THE FREEDOM OF INFORMATION AND PRIVACY ACT

Bureau of Alcohol, Tobacco, and Firearms
Central Intelligence Agency
Department of Justice
Federal Bureau of Investigation (Correspondence, Reports, Clippings, Files)
U.S. Marshals Service

## TRIAL TESTIMONY AND COURT DOCUMENTS

Consent Decree, Brown v. Invisible Empire Knights of the Ku Klux Klan, no. 80-NM-1449-S, S.D. Ala., Nov. 21 (1989).
Vietnamese Fishermen's Association, et al., v. The Knights of the Ku Klux Klan, et al., no. H-81-895, 518 F. Supp. 198 (1982); 34 Fed. R. Serv. 2d (Callaghan) 875; June 3, 1982.
United States of America v. Bruce Carroll Pierce et al., CR-85-0001M (W. D. Wash, 1985), Accession 21-95-0078, Location 823306, Seattle, WA.
United States of America v. Miles et al., no. 87-20008 (W. D. Ark, 1988), Center for Research Libraries, Chicago, IL F-7424.

## WATCHDOG GROUPS

Anti-Defamation League
Center for Democratic Renewal (Anti-Klan Network) John Brown Anti-Klan Committee
Southern Poverty Law Center, Montgomery, Alabama
Klanwatch Intelligence Project

# 6

# Latinos for Trump

*Geraldo Cadava*

The Trump administration's outreach to Latinos was perhaps the most ordinary part of an extraordinary presidency. It relied on a playbook that Republicans have used for at least four decades, ever since Ronald Reagan's 1980 presidential campaign. The Reagan campaign hired three advertising and media executives—Alex Armendariz, Fernando Oaxaca, and Lionel Sosa, all Mexican Americans from California and Texas—to launch the first-ever national television, radio, and print campaigns targeting Latino voters. As part of the "Viva Reagan" campaign, Armendariz, Oaxaca, and Sosa held strategy meetings where they tried to articulate the core characteristics of the Hispanic Republican. They settled on religious devotion, a tireless work ethic, anticommunism, and the related belief in free-market capitalism as the best path to prosperity.[1] Whether the Trump administration was aware of the similarity or not, it used the same script.

Certainly, there were differences between Reagan and Trump, especially when it came to the U.S.-Mexico border and immigration. As a candidate, Reagan said he would work with Mexican president José López Portillo to "make the border something other than a locale for a nine-foot fence." Meanwhile, a central feature of Trump's campaign rallies was his and his supporters' chants of "Build the Wall," and the wall Trump built was thirty feet tall. As for immigration, during Reagan's second term in office he signed a bill—the Immigration Reform and Control Act of 1986—that granted amnesty to millions of undocumented immigrants. Trump and his adviser Stephen Miller, on the other hand, did everything they could to criminalize undocumented immigration and impose rules that made it much more difficult to enter the United States.

In the sweep of the history of the Republican Party over the past forty years, George H. W. Bush and his son George W. Bush were more like Reagan on immigration because of their support for laws that would include immigrants from Latin America, whereas Trump's immigration restrictions were meant to exclude them. Trump's positions were more like those of Republican candidates Pat Buchanan, Bob Dole, John McCain, Mitt Romney, and Herman Cain (Cain at one point argued for an electrified border wall to electrocute migrants). Indeed, Reagan and both Bushes were Republican outliers when it came to immigration and border enforcement, while Trump's anti-immigrant policies were in line with the Republican mainstream.

Despite the differences between Trump and Reagan, Trump's Latino supporters have argued that Trump found success among Latinos for the same reason that Reagan did: he appealed to their ideological conservatism, which, they claim, stood in contrast with what they have called the "Republican-lite" approach that defined the careers of both Bushes. The theory of the Bushes, they say, was that Republicans had to appeal to Latinos through messages of inclusion and moderation on immigration. This amounted to kowtowing to the Democrats. But what Trump proved, just as Reagan had before him, was that Republicans could win Latino support by appealing to their conservatism.[2]

For Trump's Latino supporters, this was the main lesson of the 2020 election, when Trump increased his support among Latinos despite the widespread assumption that they would turn out en masse to vote against him because of his four years of assaults against them. Latinos did in fact help vote him out of office, especially in key states like Arizona and Nevada and Pennsylvania, but even in these places the percentage of Latinos who voted for Trump in 2020 compared with 2016 increased. Even though Trump lost, his marginal gains among Latinos gave Hispanic Republicans hope that the conservative movement they had worked for decades to build was once again on the rise. Ironically, they believed they had Trump to thank for it.[3]

How could it be that Trump increased his support among Latinos, when to all appearances, both as a candidate and during his four years in office, he seemed to do everything he could to alienate them? In order to understand this conundrum, it is important to view the split-screen reality that defined Trump's four years in office; his administration's persistent efforts to court Latino support from his first days in the White House; and the inflammatory, violent, and damaging rhetoric, along with exclusionary and divisive policies, that many Americans believed would lead Latinos to reject him by a historic margin. As was the case with other issues, the understandable and justified media coverage of the outrages of the Trump era obscured the more mundane but effective ways that Trump built Latino support with his persistent focus on immigration, the economy, religious freedom, and the supposed rise of socialism within the Democratic Party. Paying attention to one side of the split screen can illuminate an important part of the story of Latino politics during the Trump era, but only viewing both sides simultaneously can help us see the bigger picture.

Both sides of the screen were on full display from the earliest weeks of Trump's campaign in the early summer of 2015. In June, Trump infamously rode down his golden escalator and declared himself a candidate for president, then went on to give a speech that decried Mexican immigrants as murderers, rapists, and thieves. Only some of them were good people, he said. The next month, he proclaimed that he would "win the Latino vote," after saying that he had a "great relationship with the Mexican people." He had "many legal immigrants" working with him, and "they love me, I love them."[4] The dissonance between his statements only a month apart struck many as the hyperbolic and baseless bluster of a showman of little substance, and to be sure, Trump, like most Republicans before him, did not come close to winning the Latino vote in 2016. He won 28 percent, which was on the lower end of the quarter to a third of the Latino vote that Republicans have usually won since the early 1970s.

Between 2016 and 2020, though, the rapists, murderers, and thieves slander got repeated over and over again, in many ways defining for many Americans his view of all Latinos. Yet Trump's back-to-back

TABLE 1. Republican Share of the Latino Vote

| Year | Candidate | Vote, according to exit polls |
|---|---|---|
| 1980 | Reagan | 35% |
| 1984 | Reagan | 37% |
| 1988 | G. Bush | 30% |
| 1992 | G. Bush | 25% |
| 1996 | Dole | 21% |
| 2000 | G.W. Bush | 35% |
| 2004 | G.W. Bush | 40% |
| 2008 | McCain | 31% |
| 2012 | Romney | 27% |
| 2016 | Trump | 28% |

*Source:* Pew Research

remarks against Mexican immigrants and courting Latino voters made a certain kind of sense. They appealed to his nationalist, xenophobic, white supremacist base at the same time that they appealed to Latinos who did not prioritize immigration as an issue, or whose views of immigration were, in fact, aligned with Trump's.

In opinion surveys over the years, Latinos have repeatedly said that they care about jobs, education, and health care more than immigration, yet scholars have argued that immigration is nevertheless a gateway issue for them: if a candidate's position on immigration is at odds with what Latinos believe, then they won't listen to the candidate's positions on other issues. There is some truth to that, even for Trump's Latino supporters. In August 2016, Trump spoke in Phoenix, Arizona, supposedly to offer a detailed policy proposal for how he planned to stop the "illegal flow of drugs, cash, guns, and people across our border, and to put the cartels out of business." But instead of a policy speech, he delivered another diatribe about the "gang members," "sanctuary cities," and "open borders" that were responsible for untold American deaths. At the end of the speech, he brought onstage with him mothers whose daughters and sons allegedly were killed by "illegal immigrants."[5] The speech drew criticism from a wide range of Latino advocates, and as a result, several members of his Hispanic Advisory Council resigned, including immigration attorney Jacob Monty, pastor Ramiro Peña, and former George W. Bush administration official Alfonso Aguilar.[6] They were not the only ones. Even before Trump's immigration speech, Lionel Sosa, the advertising executive who worked on Reagan's Hispanic campaign, and Linda Chavez, who worked for the Reagan administration in the Office of Public Liaison, rebuked Trump and said that they would vote for Hillary Clinton.[7] Largely because of Trump's positions on immigration and border enforcement, many longtime Republicans vowed to leave the party.

But not all of them. The Hispanic Republicans who stuck with Trump supported him because of his immigration and border policies, not despite them. An outsider to politics, Trump, they said, would defy the bipartisan consensus within Washington to ignore U.S. immigration laws. Some had relatives who had immigrated to the United States, or they themselves had immigrated, but had done so legally. Others had lived in the United States their whole lives, or their families had been in the United States for generations and were therefore disconnected from, and largely unsympathetic with, the immigrant experience. More claimed that immigration mattered to them, but other issues were more important, above all making sure that their own families had food on the table and roofs over their heads. But one last group of Latino Trump supporters flat out supported President Trump's immigration and border policies because they, like Trump, believed that immigrants stole jobs from Americans and were responsible for the challenges faced by their communities. El Paso native Raymundo Baca, the founder of Border Hispanics for Trump, for example, said Trump stood for "border security."[8] Another Texan, Monica De La Cruz, who ran for a seat in the U.S. Congress to represent her native Edinburg, in the Rio Grande Valley, said that the residents of her community were terrified by the "caravans" of Central American migrants trying to enter the United States.[9]

Trump's most loyal Hispanic supporters—Baca and De La Cruz among them—went even further, arguing that Democrats had misrepresented Trump's immigration and border policies and, in their obsession with "identity politics" and immigration as the key to unlocking the Latino vote, had misread the ambitions of the Latin Americans who immigrated to the United States. In an interview with *CNN*, Baca pushed back on a reporter who asked him about Trump's racist immigration policies, saying he did not believe that Trump was racist. Trump's policies targeted immigrants who broke the law and therefore deserved to be punished, and had nothing to do with Latinos as an ethnic or racial group, Baca said. For her part, De La Cruz said that liberal media got the migrant detention and family separation stories wrong. The border patrol detained migrants and separated migrant families in order to protect them, she said, since many were being trafficked by criminals seeking to enter the United States illegally, who attached themselves to migrant children and falsely claimed to be their relatives in order to ease their passage.

Alfonso Aguilar, the former Bush administration official who abandoned Trump in 2016 but then once again lent Trump his support in 2020, noted that the migrant detention centers that were notorious during the Trump years were in fact built and used by Barack Obama when he was president. Before Trump, Obama had been the "deporter in chief," expelling some five million migrants from the country during his eight years in office.[10] Democrats were therefore hypocrites, he argued, for criticizing Trump for something Obama himself had done, and also for politicizing immigration in a way that ran contrary to how Latin American migrants saw themselves. Migrants, he said, came to the United States because they wanted to get ahead and because they believed that the United States was a functional democracy, not because they wanted to get lumped together with other Latinos as part of an American minority group. They also did not like seeing statues being torn down in U.S. cities during the summer of 2020, Aguilar said, because it reminded them of the sort of chaos they saw in Caracas, Venezuela, Managua, Nicaragua, or wherever they had come from.[11]

All of these ideas about Trump's immigration policies—expressed by Baca, De La Cruz, Aguilar, and many other Hispanic Republicans—were meant to answer the question they were asked over and over again: How could they support a president who was so anti-immigrant, and maybe even anti-Latino? For the askers of the question, it had a moral undertone and no justifiable answer. For the Latinos being questioned, they rationalized, contextualized, and upheld Trump's words and policies as characteristic of a president who cared only about what was best for the United States, just as they did. By and large, Trump's Latino supporters rejected the premise that Trump was either anti-immigrant or anti-Latino, but without a doubt they felt themselves to be on firmer ground when talking about their support for Trump because of his economic policies, his defense of religious freedom, and his strong statements against socialism.

---

One of Trump's main appeals for Latinos and all of his supporters was his self-presentation as a businessman who could deliver prosperity to individuals and to the nation as a whole. The truth was more complicated, yet Latinos praised him as a billionaire real-estate developer, someone who understood their aspirations to establish and grow their own businesses, and whose policies would help them join the middle and maybe even the upper class. The Latino surrogates Trump surrounded himself with were curated carefully in order to reinforce this impression. Men like Goya Foods CEO Roberto Unanue, or the owner of the Los Angeles Angels, Arte Moreno, stood beside Trump and told (exaggerated) stories of their own modest upbringings and how they had grown rich only through hard work, determination, and the blessings of American capitalism. They were meant to inspire other Latinos to become like them.

Until the very end of his presidency, many months into a pandemic that had devastated Latino workers, families, and even business owners who had to lay off workers or shutter their stores, restaurants, and companies, Trump still received high marks from Latinos as a steward of the economy and the candidate who would bring the economy back quicker than his opponent Joe Biden. As the *New York Times* reporter Jennifer Medina put it, Latino men in particular "want to support the party they believe will allow them to work and become wealthy." One of the men she interviewed, Sergio Arellano of Phoenix, Arizona, told her, "I didn't want to be poor, I wanted to be rich, so I chose Republican," because Republicans promised lower taxes and fewer regulations.[12]

The Tax Cuts and Jobs Act of 2017, one of Trump's few legislative victories, disproportionately benefited white over Black and Latino Americans, but during his years in office Trump nevertheless used it as a cornerstone of his appeal to Latinos. According to an analysis of the effects of the tax cut by race, Black Americans received 5 percent of its benefits even though they earned 6 percent of the national income, while Latino Americans received 7 percent of its benefits even though they earned 8 percent of the national income. White Americans received $218 billion in tax cuts in the year after the law was enacted, while Black and Latino Americans received a combined $32 billion in tax cuts.[13]

Another analysis by the Center for American Progress concluded that the tax cut had "left the Latino community behind" in three ways: many Latino families were unable to benefit from the child tax credit, the bill refused benefits to taxpayers with an Individual Taxpayer Identification Number instead of a Social Security Number, and its estate tax exemptions overwhelmingly benefited the 30 percent of white households that received an inheritance rather than the 7 percent of Latino households that did.[14] None of this stopped Trump from proclaiming throughout his presidency that his tax cuts and financial deregulations had made it possible for Latinos to profit from "the booming Trump economy."[15]

The appeal of economic uplift during the Trump years was nothing new for a Republican president. During Richard Nixon's first term, he appointed the first Hispanic head of the Office of Economic Opportunity, Phillip Sánchez, and the first Hispanic treasurer of the United States, the owner of a Mexican food distribution company in Southern California named Romana Acosta Bañuelos. He also established the Office of Minority Business Enterprise and the National Economic Development Agency, headed by an economist named Benjamin Fernandez, who would go on to become the first Hispanic to run for president, in 1980, as a Republican. Nixon considered economic uplift for Black and Latino Americans—black and brown capitalism, as he called it—to be a third plank of the civil rights movement. Economic uplift did not get the attention that social and political protests did, Nixon argued, but was every bit as important to Latino progress.[16]

Republican presidents from Nixon to Trump have made the same argument, even though the benefits of their economic policies have been distributed unequally. Even at the beginning of the pandemic, Trump's version of the story was that, during his presidency, six hundred thousand Latinos had been lifted from poverty, their median household incomes surpassed $50,000 a year for the first time ever, and a record share of Latino households earned more than $200,000 a year. Four out of five Latino-owned businesses, Trump said, anticipated increased revenues and planned to hire more workers. Because of the new United States–Mexico–Canada Agreement, which replaced the North American Free Trade Agreement, Latino-owned businesses would gain even greater access to North American markets. These improved economic figures for Latinos in fact began during Obama's presidency, after a slow recovery in the years after the Great Recession of 2008, but Trump was more than happy to take credit for them.

Throughout his presidency, Trump had the support of allegedly nonpartisan but in fact Republican-aligned Latino organizations. The Latino Coalition, the Job Creators Network, and the LIBRE Initiative, for example, helped Trump convince Latinos of his administration's successes. The Latino Coalition is headed by Hector Barreto Jr., the son of the founder of the national Hispanic Chamber of Commerce and former head of the Small Business Administration during the second Bush presidency. It advocates for Latino business owners—the fastest-growing group of business owners in the United States over the past couple of decades—and helps match them with public and private lenders that can help them grow their businesses. The Job Creators Network is headed by president and CEO Alfredo Ortiz, who said that his mission is to lead "the defense of small businesses from the onslaught of bad government policies." When the Latinos for Trump campaign launched to help reelect Trump, Ortiz became a member of its advisory board, and Trump appointed him as one of the commissioners of his Hispanic Prosperity Initiative. Finally, the LIBRE initiative is headed by Daniel Garza, who served during the second Bush presidency in the Department of the Interior and the Office of Public Liaison. Funded by the Koch Foundation's Americans for Prosperity political advocacy group, the LIBRE Initiative calls itself a nonprofit grassroots organization that "advances the principles and values of a free and open society to empower the U.S. Hispanic community."[17]

Trump supporters like Barreto, Ortiz, and Garza fought an uphill battle to promote the successes of the Trump economy after the pandemic struck. Almost a quarter of Latino-owned businesses applied for funds from the Paycheck Protection Program, and a survey of five hundred Latino business owners found that less than 20 percent of Latino applicants received money. According to a report by the Stanford Latino Entrepreneurship Initiative, 86 percent of Latino-owned businesses experienced "immediate negative effects" caused by COVID-19, including "loss of revenue, complete closure, loss of clients and client engagement (including contractors and employee furloughs), and project delays or postponement." Two-thirds of Latino business owners said their businesses would not survive more than six months, and by the late spring of 2020, only a couple of months into the pandemic, more than half of Latino business owners said they had already begun to lay off employees, many of them fellow Latinos who worked on the front lines of the health-care and food service industries.[18]

In concert with the Latina head of the Small Business Administration, Jovita Carranza, Barreto's Latino Coalition hosted conference calls with hundreds of Latino business owners, as part of an effort to allay their fears. They said that the Trump administration was doing everything it could to help them, argued that the pandemic was a once-in-a-century phenomenon that Trump had no control over, and suggested that in any event Trump would help Latino business owners and ordinary workers more than Biden would.[19] He would help businesses stay afloat and get Americans back to work quicker than a Democratic president would. Their hope was that Trump's prosperity gospel would be more powerful than the difficult realities Latinos were facing.

---

If Trump's prosperity gospel made sense—if only because the Republican Party had preached it for so long—so Latino conservatives would adhere to it blindly, utterly perplexing was the idea that a twice-divorced, marital infidel, accused sexual abuser, spokesperson for whatever the opposite of personal responsibility was, could somehow be the pious defender of religious freedom. Yet that was exactly the argument that Trump's faithful Latino supporters made during his four years in office. Even if Trump was not the best personal representative of morality, his Latino supporters whose politics were guided by their faith concluded that Trump was the candidate who best supported their interests, especially by pushing the Supreme Court far enough to the right that *Roe v. Wade* might be overturned.

The religiosity of conservative Latinos has long been assumed to be the main driver of their Republican partisan identities. President Nixon focused on economic uplift rather than faith, but Republican presidents from Reagan forward, largely because of the rise of the religious Right, based their appeal to Latinos on their so-called traditional values such as pro-life views and frequent church attendance, but also, some have argued, homophobia and patriarchal family structures. When Reagan chose his Mexican American treasurer of the United States, Katherine Ortega, as the keynote speaker at the 1984 Republican National Convention, she told reporters that her affiliation with the Republican Party stemmed from the fact that her mother, after whom she was named, was "very religious, a strong Catholic."[20]

Hispanic Heritage Month, which takes place from September 15 to October 15 every year, has been another opportunity for Republican presidents to argue that their faith drives their conservatism. During the commemorations for one Hispanic Heritage Month, George W. Bush praised Hispanics' "faith in God, and a deep love of family."[21] Trump echoed Bush in his Hispanic Heritage Month speeches, saying in 2018 that "Hispanic Americans embody American values" including "devotion to faith and family."[22] Even if Trump admired religious leaders mainly for the media empires they had built—that is what spoke to him as a businessman—and privately called their religious practices "bullshit," he nevertheless understood the importance of reciting a script handed down to him by previous Republican presidents.[23]

Early in his reelection campaign, Trump said his administration "would never stop fighting for Americans of faith." He claimed to be the defender of their religious liberties and the "sanctity of life." At a speech in Ohio, he claimed that his opponent Biden, who was pro-choice despite being a lifelong Catholic, was "against God."[24] Such language appealed to many Latinos, but their support for religious freedom went beyond their pro-life views. It also had to do with their support for prayer in schools, charter schools with religious affiliations, and a general desire to blur the lines between religious and public life. Aspiring politicians like Gerson Hernandez, whose parents emigrated from El Salvador to Texas in the 1980s, saw every political issue, from community service to gun rights, through the lens of scripture. With his father, a mechanic and evangelical pastor, Hernandez founded Agape Connect, a nonprofit linked to his father's church, Templo Cristiano Agape, that has fed and outfitted thousands of Texas families in need. Evangelicals like Hernandez were critical to Trump's support from Latinos.

From his first year in office, Trump visited with evangelical leaders and deputized his vice president, Mike Pence, to visit evangelical churches, including the megachurches whose parishioners were Latinos. While most Latinos were Catholic, the fastest-growing religion among them was evangelical Christianity. There was still a Catholics for Trump group with Latino leaders embedded in the Trump campaign, but Latino evangelicals received more attention and had greater influence with his administration. One of Trump's closest Latino advisers was Samuel Rodriguez, a Puerto Rican who was the senior pastor at the New Season Christian Worship Center in Sacramento, California, as well as president of the National Hispanic Christian Leadership Conference. Other evangelical leaders close to Trump included the Cuban American pastor from Miami, Mario Bramnick, who believed that Trump was "anointed by God"; the Mexican American pastor from Las Vegas, Pasqual Urrabazo; and the Mexican American pastor from Waco, Ramiro Peña.[25] They were members of Trump's National Hispanic Advisory Council for the 2016 campaign, served on Trump's Evangelical Advisory Board, and were part of the Latinos for Trump campaign in 2020.

It is not that all Latino evangelicals were politically conservative. The Latino Religions and Politics National Survey, overseen by the historian Gastón Espinosa, found that Latino evangelicals were evenly divided in their support for Biden and Trump—46 percent supported Biden, while 48 percent supported Trump.[26] Gabriel Salguero, a pastor in Orlando and president of the National Latino Evangelical Coalition, said that Latino evangelicals are classic swing voters, and Jose Rivera, a pastor in Phoenix, called them "politically homeless."[27] Yet the near 50-50 split between Latino evangelicals who support Republicans and those who support Democrats was, for Republicans, better odds than the 25–75 percent, or 33–67 percent, split between Latino support for Republicans and Democrats in general. Moreover, Latino evangelicalism in the United States was a religion practiced by many recent immigrants from Latin America, and Republicans have known that in order to win elections in the future, they will have to reach out to youth and new Americans instead of continuing to rely on their aging base of white voters.

For the Latinos for Trump campaign, Florida was a key site of organizing among Latino evangelicals. Mike Pence and Trump's Latino surrogates visited evangelical churches in Orlando early and often, which helped Trump win more than a third of the Puerto Rican vote in Central Florida's Orange and Osceola Counties, where Puerto Ricans began settling in the 1970s, and where many thousands more moved after Hurricane María in 2017. In a blitz of Hispanic outreach in January 2020, Trump visited Miami and met with evangelical Venezuelans. At a church in the city, he said, "America was not built by religion-hating socialists" but, rather, "by churchgoing, God-worshipping, freedom-loving patriots."[28] He combined two of the themes—religion and socialism—that helped him grow his support among Latinos between 2020 and 2016.

---

In fact, socialism was not a separate issue but rather was deeply intertwined with issues such as Trump's economic policies and his support for religious freedom. His tax cuts and financial deregulations, Republicans argued, were the opposite of socialism. Likewise, his support for school prayer, they claimed, defied big government's encroachments on the religious freedoms of faithful Americans. The connection between socialism and other issues is significant because it helps us see that invoking fears of socialism had to do with more than the Latin American leftists—for example, Fidel Castro, Daniel Ortega, Hugo Chavez—who have loomed large in the minds of exiles and refugees from Cuba, Nicaragua, and Venezuela, especially in South Florida.

At the same time, though, it was a misconception to believe that Latin American leftists were bogeymen only in the minds of Cubans, Nicaraguans, and Venezuelans in South Florida. Conservative Latinos from all national backgrounds had their own antisocialist narratives. Conservative Mexicans whose families immigrated to the United States in the 1920s, in the wake of the Mexican Revolution, called Mexico's 1917 Constitution a socialist document because it expropriated privately owned lands and diminished the power of the Catholic Church. Conservative

Puerto Ricans have called independence activists—like the followers of Puerto Rican nationalist Pedro Albizu Campos, or Lolita Lebrón and her accomplices, who in 1954 fired bullets in the U.S. Congress—socialists. As an issue, socialism resonated beyond Florida and was polarizing even for Latino Democratic primary voters, who split their votes between Biden and the democratic socialist candidate Bernie Sanders.

While the smear of socialism was certainly a carryover from the Cold War, during Trump's years in office, Republicans also used it to warn against what they described as the growing radicalism of the Democratic Party. In a speech at the Latino Coalition's annual Legislative Summit, held in Washington, DC, in the spring of 2019, Ted Cruz, in a single sentence, named Castro, Maduro, and Congresswoman Alexandria Ocasio-Cortez of New York as equally dangerous threats to the United States. Socialists were taking over the Democratic Party, he argued, foreshadowing the argument in the summer of 2020—articulated at the Republican National Convention and several stump speeches that further fanned the flames of unrest—that Biden was a "trojan horse" for socialism. Biden himself may not have been a socialist, but, as president, he would do the bidding of the left wing of his party. As Trump himself put it in an August 2020 speech in Oshkosh, Wisconsin, Biden may have "no clue, but the people around him are tough, and they're very smart."[29]

For all of Trump's bluster about socialism, some conservative Cubans and Venezuelans in Florida argued that he had not done anything to help Cuba or Venezuela beyond performative gestures such as inviting the conservative opposition leader of Venezuela, Juan Guaidó, to attend his State of the Union Address in February 2020. He took the opportunity to proclaim Guaidó the "true and legitimate president of Venezuela" and asked him to take the message back to his country that "all Americans are united with the Venezuelan people in their struggle for freedom."[30] But he did not follow through on the policies he announced and promises he made.[31] It was reminiscent of the frustration that some Cuban Americans felt toward Reagan during his second administration, after he had promised but failed to rid the island of Castro. They also claimed that Reagan's trade embargo had been a "complete joke," since there were still economic ties between Miami and Havana.[32]

In the aftermath of the 2020 election, which Trump lost at the same time that he expanded his share of the Latino vote, there was much hand-wringing among Democrats who argued that they needed to figure out over the next several years how to answer the charge of socialism. An article in *New York Magazine*, based on interviews with half a dozen Democratic and Republican elected officials, concluded that "the biggest factor in the swing toward Republicans was that these voters had a negative response to the Democratic Party's shift to the left nationally and the rise of self-described democratic socialists such as Sanders and Ocasio-Cortez."[33] One of the Democratic congresswomen who lost their seats, Florida's Debbie Mucarsel-Powell, refuted the idea, tweeting ten days after the election that "it's not just about socialism." Instead, she argued that the Biden campaign needed to invest more in advertisements that targeted Latinos in English and Spanish, knock on doors, and focus on the economy, instead of just assuming that "racial identity is how we vote."[34] Nevertheless, Democrats argued over whether they needed to do a better job of explaining what democratic socialism meant, as Sanders had tried to do as a candidate, or whether they should ignore it entirely since it was a preposterous charge that Republicans had leveled against Democrats for many decades and thus did not deserve more airtime.

---

The months after the election were defined by two contending narratives about how Latinos voted. Democrats brushed aside the increase in support for Trump, arguing instead that we needed to pay attention to the fact that Latino organizing in states like Arizona helped clinch the election for Biden. Republicans, meanwhile, argued that Trump's strong performance in South Florida, South Texas, and even in urban areas such as Los Angeles County, Harris County in Texas (which includes Houston), Cook County in Illinois (which includes Chicago), and Bronx County offered a glimpse at the future of the Republican Party. These different positions felt more like posturing by two opposed camps of advocates, trying to convince whoever would listen that their side knew what the political future will look like for Latinos. In fact, if early reports are true that Latinos today may be more like swing voters than a lock for any one party, then the future seems less certain than ever.

On the one hand, the history of the past half century could lead us to conclude that between a quarter and a third of Latinos will continue to support Republican presidential candidates in the future. On the other hand, history as a story of change over time teaches all of us that just because things have been one way for a long time does not mean that they will be that way in perpetuity. Trump's relative success among Latinos in 2020 compared with 2016 could therefore be seen as within the predictable historical range, or it could be seen as the early warning of the Latino red wave to come. Only time will tell, but, regardless, 2020 has left us a lot to ponder.

In addition to the results in particular states such as Arizona, Florida, and Texas, the gender breakdown of Trump's Latino support also came as a surprise. In the months leading up to the election, reporters speculated that Latino males would provide the overwhelming share of Trump's Latino support overall, because of their machismo or the fact that they work in male-dominated industries such as border policing or construction. But an April 2021 report from EquisLabs found that conservative Latinas made the greatest shift toward Trump in 2020 compared with 2016. That it happened is undeniable, but experts will spend the next several years trying to determine why. Early theories hypothesize that women moved toward Trump because, as business owners themselves, they admired Trump's businessman persona and his direct way of talking, and perhaps even accepted "a dominant male hierarchy."[35]

Trump may not have been the second coming of George W. Bush, who to this day remains the Republican president with the greatest share of the Latino vote—about 40 percent in 2000 and 2004—but there are some things he did right. As odd as it may seem, Trump was committed to courting Latino voters ever since 2015, when he claimed that he would win the Latino vote just a month after he called Mexican immigrants rapists, murderers, and thieves. In 2016, he courted Black voters in Michigan by asking them, "What the hell do you have to lose?" by taking a chance on him.[36] He didn't win the Latino, Black, or Asian American vote that year or in his losing reelection bid. But he did diversify his appeal.

FIGURE 2. Latinos gathered at a Trump campaign rally in Orlando, Florida, on October 10, 2020. Photo by Paul Hennessy/NurPhoto via AP.

From 2016 to 2020, according to exit polls, Trump went from 28 to 32 percent among Latinos, 27 to 34 percent among Asian Americans, and 8 to 12 percent among Black voters.[37] He showed that Republicans can win diverse support because Democrats have, at times, taken voters of color for granted, failed to deliver on campaign promises, and reduced their interests to putatively ethnic-group-based concerns, instead of foregrounding how Democratic policy plans would improve their lives more than Republican initiatives would.

Trump's gains were incremental, and over 70 percent of nonwhite voters still chose the Democrat Joe Biden. But for a politician who often deployed xenophobic, sometimes race-baiting rhetoric, Trump's gains suggest that there's more room for Republicans to convert minority voters across the socioeconomic spectrum and around the country. As Senator Marco Rubio (R-Fla.) tweeted in November, Trump had mobilized "a multi-ethnic multi-racial coalition of working AMERICANS."[38]

At the moment, it remains difficult to imagine a repeat performance by Trump's multiethnic, multiracial coalition of working Americans.

The Republican Party has won only one popular vote in the twenty-first century, and consistently winning between a quarter and a third of the vote from a growing demographic is hardly a recipe for long-term success and hardly reason for somersaults. Yet Latino Republicans believe that Trump's improved performance signaled the growing conservatism of Latinos. That is only a theory, but it is one that Democrats should not ignore.

In the recent past—2008 and 2012 come to mind—political analysts praised Democrats for their success microtargeting the voters they needed to win elections. In 2020, the animosity toward Trump was enough to get Biden over the hump, but Biden himself did not necessarily have a compelling narrative of what the Democratic Party today stands for. In many ways, Trump's Republican Party had a clearer story—even if it was one that many, even most, Americans found horrifying—and they knew how to reach the voters who could help them keep the result close. Those voters included a fair number of Latinos, who will become even more important in future elections as their share of the U.S. population increases.

# 7

# "Send Her Back"

## TRUMP'S FEUD WITH FEMINISTS AND CONSERVATIVE WOMEN'S TRIUMPH

*Leandra Zarnow*

On January 21, 2017, the day after President Donald J. Trump's inauguration, an unexpected swell of nearly five million protesters streamed into the streets in over 650 locations around the nation and more than 260 worldwide. Women and men, young and old, marched together, some wearing Pussy Hat Project knitted caps and others carting homemade signs with slogans like "Proud Nasty Woman," "Love Trumps Hate," and "We Are the Resistance."[1] This Women's March—harking back to early suffrage parades and the 1970 Women's Strike for Equality—was the largest one-day demonstration in U.S. history.[2]

This stunning display began with a Facebook event posted by the most unlikely of activists. Teresa Shook, a grandmother of four girls, had packed up her Indianapolis legal practice and settled into a quiet retirement in Hawaii. She did not set out to call for a march. As she explained, "I wasn't that political." Yet, Secretary Hillary Clinton's presidential loss had been hard to take. Her friend had signed her up for the pro-Clinton group Pantsuit Nation on Facebook, and the conversations in this virtual space gave her a cathartic charge. "We have to march," Shook urged, but never expected the event page she created on a lark would take off nationally.[3] A handful of enthusiasts agreed to join her the evening she posted this call. By sunrise, the number had increased to over ten thousand. That it would expand into the millions "was just mind-boggling" for Shook, who recalled of the Washington, DC, march she attended, "It was an out-of-body experience, to look out and see that sea of pink bodies."[4]

Within a matter of weeks, a combination of first-time and seasoned organizers proved that a social media wildfire could kindle online and catch hold in America's vast and varied public squares, from suburban strip malls to the National Mall. The early critique that Shook and other first organizers had prioritized white liberal feminist interests quieted after the emergence of national cochairs Carmen Perez, Linda Sarsour, Tamika Mallory, and Bob Bland, who were Chicana, Arab American, Black, and white, respectively.[5] Their efforts helped secure over four hundred sponsors as diverse as local Young Women's Christian Associations, Code Pink, Occupy Wall Street, Human Rights Watch, the American Federation of Labor and Congress of Industrial Organizations, League of Women Voters, Greenpeace USA, American Indian Movement, Planned Parenthood, the National Association for the Advancement of Colored People, and the American Civil Liberties Union.

These wide-ranging partners coalesced around intersectional feminism, the concept that identities are multifarious and forces of oppression are interrelated. In doing so, the march helped popularize a worldview once restricted to activist circles and women's studies classrooms. As a first scholarly assessment notes, the Women's March "explicitly (and unapologetically) centered the experiences and knowledge and leadership of people of color, queer people, differently abled, immigrants, undocumented, and those with any other marginalized identity."[6] This historic march also further provoked an ongoing tug-of-war to define the acceptable terms of politics, with one side calling for wokeness and the other lamenting cancel culture. Gender has been at the center of this contest that boils down to who has the right to be empowered and in power, and President Donald J. Trump helped make it so.

## Redefining Empowerment

The idea of empowerment, and with it feminism, became the crucial pivot around which the 2016 presidential campaign revolved. Secretary Hillary Clinton's slogan "Making History" had primed her followers for a breakthrough presidency that celebrated, as CNN characterized, "the long journey from Seneca Falls to Hillary 2016."[7] In contrast, Trump flaunted his masculinity each time he encouraged followers to "lock her up." Winning the election, he suffered little setback during the campaign when an *Access Hollywood* tape from 2005 surfaced where he bragged he could "do anything" to women, including "grab 'em by the pussy."[8]

Any history of the Trump presidency will need to contend with his hypermasculinity, his history of womanizing, and his use of gender and sexuality as a means to belittle adversaries and deflect criticism. His frequent slights from "Crooked Hillary" to "Send Her Back" should be seen as more than rhetorical weaponry. These buzzwords delivered by Trump and repeated by followers at rallies and on Twitter were the most overt displays of the misogyny that drove his presidency. Less obvious, but essential to highlight, is how Trump oversaw an administrative challenge of feminist inroads in the executive and a focused reordering of the legal and material impact of feminist gains in the policy arena since the 1960s. Put simply, President Donald J. Trump sought to reaffirm that the United States was a patriarchal nation in the very moment women reasserted their place in politics as they looked toward the suffrage centennial in 2020.

And here is a great irony of the Trump presidency: as diverse women's numbers in electoral politics hit historic heights, the president took measures to restore the executive as a male domain, making tokenistic appointments of predominantly white women. Yet, these women were not just props. Rather, as his leading messengers, they helped shape and convey his rightward vision for America. Indeed, conservative women were among Trump's most ardent emissaries and executors of spin and strategy, his presidency their greatest shot at political influence and ultimate realization of their ideological purpose. No president since Ronald Reagan offered right-wing women more opportunity to be political insiders with a direct channel to the West Wing. For this personal success, they were grateful and devoted. "I've never felt anything but respected and empowered by him to do my job," professed Press Secretary Sarah Huckabee Sanders.[9]

The language of empowerment Sanders uses here, like color blindness, has been deployed by conservatives as a device to counter how much the mass feminist movement of the 1960s and 1970s successfully shifted the gender landscape in the United States. Since then, more Americans have embraced women's rights. In response, conservatives have been savvy in their deployment of empowerment speech when brushing aside sexist acts or repackaging antifeminist goals as good for women. "Engaging, Inspiring and Empowering Women to Make a Difference!" promises the Women for America First website, calling on MAGA (Make America Great Again) women to "come together in our 21st century suffrage movement." This group, which launched the "Stop the Steal" Facebook page after the 2020 election, defined any challenge to their ideas and actions as an attempt "to shut us up just because we are women."[10]

To be sure, many conservative women sincerely believe that feminism has something to offer them. Paying more than lip service to feminist terminology, they have adopted the individualist strain of feminism that encourages self-fulfillment and personal advancement. Nonetheless, the primary purpose of Trump women, from high-level advisers to the rank and file, during the president's time in office was to muddy the rhetorical waters and diminish support of feminist goals. This was especially important to accomplish because a reactive counterforce to Trump formed on day one of his presidency and the energized Women's March participants did not disperse. Rather, they became a sustained resistance force that not only protested but organized in historic numbers to get out the vote and move into politics from local offices to the U.S. Congress. For, conservatives' empowerment talk rang hollow to critical listeners as the Trump years brought into stark relief cultural undercurrents of misogyny, xenophobia, racism, and homophobia as well as class inequities that divided America.

## Creating Alternative Facts

Leading Trump adviser Kellyanne Conway anticipated this resolute counterforce when first responding to the Women's March. Most instrumental among Trump's spin doctors, she introduced a rhetorical strategy that gave Trump followers permission to ignore unwelcome developments as they unfolded and to deny uncomfortable truths in the nation's past. She introduced the concept of alternative facts, which became the central trope that defined the Trump presidency. Future historians will do well to remember the gendered beginning of this leading weapon in the conservative political arsenal.

News stations did not take long to broadcast split screens visually comparing the Women's March thickly filling in the mall and the previous day's noticeably smaller inauguration crowd. Speaking at the Central Intelligence Agency as the Women's March unfolded, Trump expressed frustration. "I get up this morning, I turn on one of the networks, and they show an empty field," he criticized, correcting, "I made a speech. I looked out. The field was—it looked like a million, a million and a half people."[11]

This was not the first time a presidential inauguration had been upstaged by women. In 1913, the National Woman's Party orchestrated a horse-led procession of around five thousand suffragists down Pennsylvania Avenue the day before President Woodrow Wilson's inauguration. When his train pulled up at Union Station, a "small but vociferous" crowd of five hundred greeted him before he made his way to the Shoreham Hotel "through practically a deserted city." The new president was not the attraction, for most Washingtonians had "taken themselves to the more alluring spectacle . . . where the suffragists were marching."[12] Wilson learned to live with the suffragists and ultimately got on board with their cause, framing suffrage as a wartime measure. Trump instead rewrote history as it was made to his liking, but he needed a master wordsmith's help to do so.

Enter acolyte Kellyanne Conway, a whiz Republican pollster who had long moved past her aisle-crossing moment in 2005 when she teamed up with Democratic counterpart Celinda Lake to write *What Women Really Want*.[13] Conway shared Lake's goal of activating women's civic engagement, for Republican and Democratic women alike since the ratification of the Nineteenth Amendment had been equally committed to translating their voting clout into political power. But there they parted ways.

Conway, the daughter of a single mother who worked in a Las Vegas casino, could get behind the feminist goal of economic independence, which squared with her free-market individualism.[14] Still, Conway's identity as a devout Italian Catholic fueled her faith-driven social conservatism and willingness to stay in women's traditional lane of family-focused politics. Conway could strike this difference because feminists' articulation of choice—such as the choice to pursue a career or stay at home—squared well with liberalist principles of free enterprise and personal responsibility. Broader structural goals espoused by progressive feminists such as eradicating systemic sex discrimination or legalizing universal child care, and moralistic hot-button issues such as transgender bathrooms or abortion, could be set aside.

Here, Conway drew on the example modeled by Republican leaders before her. Elizabeth Dole, who served in four administrations, ran for president in 2000, and held two terms in the Senate thereafter, paved a path for ambitious conservative women. Although childless, she crafted an identity as a dutiful defender of home and country as the wife of politician Bob Dole, who described her as practicing "sensible feminism." Defining this brand, Elizabeth Dole explained, "What we women fought for was the ability to make decisions as to what we feel is best for ourselves and our family." What she could not get behind were "prepackaged answers that are handed down by the political correctness club."[15] Making this distinction in the 1980s, Dole provided Republican women with a way forward in new terrain that included Title VII, Title IX, and the Equal Credit Opportunity Act, but also within a political party that no longer supported the Equal Rights Amendment (ERA) and now defined itself as antiabortion.

Dole was more comfortable wearing this skin than was Eagle Forum leader Phyllis Schlafly, an antifeminist conservative torchbearer who continued to be influential. Schlafly delivered a final consequential act before she died in September 2016: she endorsed Donald Trump for president at the Republican National Convention. In doing so, she linked the early days of family values politics to the showdown between Clinton and Trump. Once before, Schlafly had made the ERA "into a contest over the soul of the Republican Party."[16] She believed that the party was ripe to be remade again by Trump and women could be instrumental in getting him there. Conway ultimately came to the same conclusion.

"Thank you, Phyllis Schlafly, for your grace, strength, courage and impact. Always classy. Never shirked from a fight. God bless you,"

Conway tweeted the day of Schlafly's passing, one month after becoming Trump's campaign manager.[17] On the surface, Conway seemed like an improbable candidate for the job. She had crafted Senator Ted Cruz's attack on Trump during the Republican primary, calling him a "thrice-married, non-church-going billionaire." Then, she was willing to say out loud what she later told confidants in the White House discreetly: that she believed Trump was "a total fucking misogynist." Still, Conway was shrewd and ambitious, and like Schlafly, she saw the potential for conservative women to not only capitalize on but also build the growing Trump Nation. The Trump team brought her on board because they believed she could deliver women swing voters, and saw this support as essential to win. Equally so, as Trump backer and former governor Chris Christie observed, "Very few in political life . . . knew how to use language as effectively as Kellyanne."[18] Her fast-talking semantics aided Trump in clinching an Electoral College victory in which white women favored Trump by a small margin—47 percent to Clinton's 45 percent—as opposed to 98 percent of Black women and 67 percent of Hispanic women who voted for Clinton.[19]

Conway proved ever more useful as a counselor in the White House skilled at returning incoming fire on unfriendly Sunday morning talk shows. During her first Sunday tour on *Meet the Press*, host Chuck Todd asked Conway to explain a "provable falsehood." Press Secretary Sean Spicer, directed by President Trump, had exaggerated the size of the inauguration crowd compared with that of the Women's March. "You're saying it's a falsehood," Conway responded, "when rather we offered alternative facts."[20]

With this rejoinder, Conway gave permission to Trump followers to not simply ignore, but rewrite history in progress. Historical work has always been, in part, tied to nationalizing and partisan projects, but even more so during Trump's presidency. Thinking about legacy as events unfolded, Conway sought to direct attention to what should be loyally defended and remembered by Trump supporters even if it was not true. When asked on one mainstream media outlet if the Women's March was important, she replied that she "didn't see the point."[21] One week later, she addressed March for Life demonstrators who had gathered in the same spot as feminist protesters. "We hear you. We see you. We respect you. And we look forward to working with you," Conway encouraged. These words heartened Annette Saunders, who drove five hours to publicly exhibit her devotion to the new president, for as she enthused, "I felt like God told me to vote for Donald Trump."[22] Over the next four years, Trump's followers would become even more rapturous, encouraged along by his clergy of apostles.

## Dress like Women

With the exception of Sean Spicer and a few others working behind the scenes, women led Trump's communication team. This choice was both traditional and strategic, for women delivered what Senior Communications Director Mercedes Schlapp characterized as "a bit of softness" to take the edge off Trump's policy-by-Tweet.[23] Far from political neophytes, these women had decades of experience shaping campaign talking points for conservative Republicans. Schlapp's politics reflected her upbringing as the daughter of Cuban exiles. Her path from working on Republican campaigns to being a veteran of George W. Bush's administration, a Fox News commentator, cofounder of the lobbying firm Cove Strategies, and a board member of the National Rifle Association was not unlike those of other women on the White House staff.[24]

After Spicer, Sarah Huckabee Sanders, Stephanie Grisham, and Kayleigh McEnany successively served as press secretary. Sanders had managed her father Mike Huckabee's 2008 and 2016 presidential campaigns, the former pastor and Arkansas governor moving from opponent to loyal ambassador of Trump on his *Huckabee* show. Grisham, a self-taught politico, shifted gears from press relations work to spokesperson for Arizona politicians. She did a stint working for Mitt Romney for President before landing the opportunity of a lifetime serving as First Lady Melania Trump's press secretary. While a plagiarizing case marred Grisham's past, McEnany brought Ivy League pedigree to Trump's team. A deeply devout Baptist from Florida raised on Rush Limbaugh, McEnany quickly rose as a political commentator on CNN and producer of *Huckabee* to serve as spokesperson for the Republican National Committee before joining the White House staff.[25] Likewise, Communications Director Hope Hicks, who had worked for the Trump Organization, seamlessly transitioned to her role at the White House, then to Fox News in 2018, and back again to Pennsylvania Avenue in

2020. Her rehab mission amid the coronavirus crisis: to "position the president in a way he wants to be viewed as the man in charge, while guarding against the threat of overexposure."[26] All were great communicators who blurred the line between making the news and reporting on it in this period of information warfare.

Trump's communication team often used gender as a deflection device when performing rhetorical gymnastics. Sanders, for instance, dispelled questions about the administration's revolving door of staffers by responding, "If you want to see chaos, come to my house with three preschoolers."[27] Domesticity was disarming, but also the wedge into politics for many of these politicos. And one of this topsy-turvy administration's most constant features was its throwback, anti–affirmative action approach to personnel.

Trump's promise to drain the swamp reflected a long trajectory of concern over government's red tape, and often with it an unfounded anxiety that the U.S. government had become a feminized federal workforce.[28] A hiring freeze was announced during the president's first week in office to combat an exaggerated "dramatic expansion of the federal workforce in recent years."[29] In reality, this workforce had grown less than 1 percent between Presidents George W. Bush and Barack Obama; however, its demographic diversity had improved dramatically under Obama, who amassed the most racially diverse administration in U.S. history, in which 44 percent of administrative positions were occupied by women.[30]

The "very male Trump Administration" stood in stark contrast.[31] High-profile appointments from Secretary of Transportation Elaine Chao to CIA Director Gina Haspel made headlines. Even so, Trump's cabinet was overwhelmingly white and male, and George W. Bush's women A-Team had exceeded that of Trump by 4 percent. Inside the West Wing, women fell from roughly parity to 40 percent of the staff, and from being paid eighty-five to eighty-nine cents to sixty-nine cents for every dollar a male staffer made.[32] It was the capaciousness of Trump's house-cleaning of the administrative state—firing at will, freezing pay, and gutting of human resources in every agency—that hurt women civil servants most.

The greatest frontal attack was a failed attempt to dismantle the Office of Personnel Management, which its acting director Margaret

Weichert called a unit "fundamentally not set up for success, structurally."[33] This action, thwarted by Congress, did not stop Trump officials from subtly transferring powers to the General Services Administration. Meanwhile, the Office of Management and Budget responded to #MeToo and #BlackLivesMatter with a directive to discontinue diversity training at agencies. This systemic shakeup also undercut the legal gains of earlier rights movements and the ensuing expansion of human resources. Nothing made this clearer than Trump's appointment of former corporate lawyer Janet Dhillon in 2019 to head the Equal Employment Opportunity Commission (EEOC). This federal entity tasked with oversight of Title VII of the 1964 Civil Rights Act had been a channel through which workers could lodge complaints about race-based, sex-based, and other forms of discrimination they experienced on the job. Well aware of this history, Dhillon drastically slowed the pace of litigation forwarded by the EEOC, one of its key mechanisms to hold employers accountable.[34]

Alongside this attack on affirmative action, President Trump visibly returned the federal workforce to the sexpot midcentury standard on display in the hit show *Mad Men*. Perhaps this should not be surprising from the former owner of the Miss Universe Pageant who proudly paraded his model third wife, First Lady Melania Trump. *Axios* scooped that Trump's unofficial dress code for female staff was "to dress like women" in form-fitting dresses and stilettos, mirroring the unwritten standard for women employees at Fox News.[35] The social media response to this story was fierce, with #DressLikeAWoman portraits of women in scrubs to soccer uniforms taking off in the Twittersphere in February 2017.[36] This campaign highlighted how Trump women staffers' hyperfemininity visually weakened women's workplace gains, instead making the White House a highly sexualized space.

## Entrepreneurship over Human Rights

Daughter Ivanka Trump—about whom President Trump had once publicly asked, "She's hot, right?"—tried to counter this image blunder by rebranding her father as a champion of women.[37] The dutiful daughter did make some gains. She initially received an F from the Center for American Progress for not executing campaign promises of subsidized family leave and child care. By the end of her father's term, Ivanka had effectively lobbied for twelve weeks of paid family leave for federal employees. In 2018, Congress also expanded funding of the Child Care and Development Block Grant by $5.8 billion, an initiative she championed.[38] While these advances are notable, what is equally clear is how much the Trump administration took credit for policy change already in motion and trends under way, especially overstating women's job growth and dips in unemployment.

Ivanka Trump's Women's Global Development and Prosperity Initiative, created in 2019, provided microloans to over two thousand women-owned businesses internationally.[39] Yet, the program felt like a rehabilitative afterthought incongruous with the president's frenetic foreign policy that had one defining feature: an instinctive challenge to Secretary of State Hillary Clinton's women's rights as human rights doctrine. Clinton had first outlined this commitment in a speech she gave as First Lady at the United Nations (UN) Fourth World Conference on Women in Beijing in 1995. When heading the State Department, Clinton made this the centerpiece concern that undergirded a wider diplomacy-first, globalist posture.[40] In contrast, Trump enacted a military-first, isolationist, and nativist foreign policy that ran counter to America's postwar commitment to global human rights.

For his spokesperson on the international stage, Trump appointed Nikki Haley, a former South Carolina governor and daughter of Indian immigrants, as the U.S. ambassador to the UN. "Reince [Priebus], I don't even know what the United Nations does!" she recalled saying when offered the job. "All I know is everybody hates it."[41] Her political climb from state representative to Republican presidential hopeful had been "a tug-of-war between conscience and calculation."[42] Once mocking Trump when she was a Marco Rubio surrogate, Haley set aside her reservations about his treatment of people of color and women in exchange for a seat on the National Security Council. She made clear in her debut speech before the UN that she would not follow the leader, proclaiming, "I wear heels . . . because if I see something wrong, we're going to kick them every single time."[43] In her nearly two years at Turtle Bay, she emerged as a fierce defender of Israel and a more forceful challenger of Soviet and Syrian aggression than her boss. Upon her exit, she managed to remain in his good graces while also garnering praise from the *New York Times* for being "a practitioner of multilateral diplomacy" who left the UN "with her dignity largely intact."[44]

As Haley worked the UN, the Trump administration decisively curtailed global women's health. The Global Gag Rule, first adopted by President Ronald Reagan, was extended by the "Protecting Life in Global Health Assistance" policy, which curbed aid to nongovernmental organizations that offered abortion counseling as part of their family planning services. This elastic definition of support encompassed over $8.8 billion in assistance delivered by the State Department, United States Agency for International Development, and Department of Defense, as opposed to the previous figure of $600 million. Interviews with U.S. aid workers and beneficiaries have highlighted how this policy cut so deep it in effect provided a green light for global regimes to enact regressive policies, diminished protections from gender violence, and limited access to women's health services.[45] For antiabortion leaders in the United States, the policy about-face was a clear victory.

This form of reproductive gatekeeping abroad was a corollary to anti-immigrant calls to "build a wall" at home. Family reunification and offering asylum to refugees fleeing nondemocratic states once made sense to Cold War conservatives. Now, Schlafly's Eagle Forum was not alone in calling for "immediate border security" alongside defending religious liberty and pro-life interests.[46] Likewise, President Trump sounded the alarm that immigrant women produced anchor babies and immigrant men were potential rapists, feeding into enduring white supremacist discourse around guarding white women's sexual purity.[47]

The world looked on aghast as the United States turned away victims of domestic violence and separated children from their parents at the border. In the mid-1990s, immigrant rights and anti–domestic violence movements had successfully lobbied for domestic violence to be added as an asylum category. In 2018, the Department of Justice closed this channel, Attorney General Jeff Sessions explaining, "Asylum was never meant to alleviate all problems, even all serious problems, that people face every day all over the world."[48] Rights groups implored the Trump administration to rescind this policy, particularly when it was clear with the onset of the COVID-19 pandemic that there was a "horrifying global surge in domestic violence."[49] Trump remained unmoved. Similarly, in May 2018, the Trump administration enacted a family separation policy at the U.S.-Mexico border that Secretary of Homeland Security Kirstjen Nielsen described without irony as humane, noting, "We are a country of compassion. We are a country of heart."[50] Human rights watch groups and journalists onsite disagreed, observing that underage children caged in detention centers were "treated worse than dogs."[51] Critics of Trump calling out his xenophobia gained limited traction when challenging these policies, though they turned to the courts and Congress to try.

## #MeToo Reckoning

Frustrated feminists lamented that their nation had elected a misogynist-in-chief. With Trump seemingly untouchable in the Oval Office, women unsurprisingly reevaluated other workplaces around them and did not like what they saw. A cultural reckoning to publicly expose sexual harassers and acknowledge the pervasiveness of sexual assault naturally ensued. Consequently, the Trump years brought forward one of the greatest upsets in sexual politics in U.S. history. The #MeToo moment ultimately bore political results. For not unlike the Year of the Woman in 1992 following the Anita Hill–Clarence Thomas sexual harassment scandal, Democratic women set on cleaning up politics flipped the House in 2018 and reinstated Speaker Nancy Pelosi. At the same time, the remaking of the Supreme Court through the appointments of Justice Brett Kavanaugh and Justice Amy Coney Barrett exposed the #MeToo movement's limits.

On October 15, 2017, actress Alyssa Milano tweeted, "If you've been sexually harassed or assaulted write 'me too' as a reply to this tweet."[52] The #MeToo hashtag she reintroduced, first created a decade earlier by anti–sexual violence advocate Tarana Burke, went viral with millions coming forward with their survivor stories. Black women such as Burke have been the most influential Twitter activists of this era, and yet her role in #MeToo was initially overshadowed by a Hollywood purge.[53] Journalist Ronan Farrow helped expose an "open secret" that producer Harvey Weinstein was a habitual assaulter, encouraging a flood of women in entertainment to launch the #TimesUp movement.[54] Once Hollywood cleaned house, media outlets, business, higher education, and legislatures soon followed with high-profile firings gaining the most attention.

In November 2017, Brave New Films released a documentary interviewing sixteen female accusers of "the most powerful, and public, sexual harasser in America—the president," yet the man who survived the *Access Hollywood* leak remained unscathed.[55] Public discourse soon shifted from alarm and dismay over revelations that beloved figures such as comedian Bill Cosby and PBS host Charlie Rose were longtime predators to concern of "a witch hunt atmosphere" that assumed men were guilty-by-accusation.[56] Editorials delivered at rapid fire defended women's right to challenge "the smothering, delusional, galactic entitlement of powerful men" to the wrong of "nutballs who seek to turn #MeToo into a cultural frenzy that indicts American men in general instead of specific toxic individuals."[57]

Women in politics translated #MeToo into a campaign to dismantle the last vestiges of the old boys club in government. In California, nearly two hundred women legislators, aides, and lobbyists signed a letter "denouncing a culture of rampant sexual misconduct in and around state government"; this was the largest case impacting state capitols, with others brought to light in Illinois, Iowa, Nevada, Oklahoma, Oregon, and Rhode Island.[58] Congress too came under scrutiny. In December 2017, Senator Al Franken and Representative John Conyers Jr. resigned under considerable pressure when accused of sexual harassment. "You need to draw a line in the sand and say none of it is O.K. None of it is acceptable," Senator Kirsten Gillibrand argued, leading the call for Franken to resign.[59] A beloved progressive, Franken buckled under the pressure, leaving Congress after six women accused him of forcibly kissing or groping them when he was on tour as a comedian. Democrats' zero-tolerance approach was meant to strike a difference with the Republican Party, for its reprimand of Alabama gubernatorial candidate Republican Roy Moore, who allegedly stalked teenage girls at malls, had been tepid. In retrospect, Franken regretted his decision to resign, submitting that he should have pressed for a hearing before the Senate Ethics Committee. Subsequently, new rules on sexual harassment reporting and required training for members of Congress and Capitol Hill staff were put in place.[60]

When #MeToo came to Washington, the movement left an unintended and consequential imprint on the highest court. Justice Brett Kavanaugh's nomination went through despite the sexual assault allegation Christine Blassey Ford raised during his hearings in September 2018. For many watching, it felt like déjà vu. In 1991, law professor Anita Hill publicly accused Supreme Court nominee Clarence Thomas, her former boss at the EEOC, of sexual harassment. As television cameras rolled, she discussed her allegation before an all-white, all-male Senate Judiciary Committee chaired by Joe Biden, testimony Thomas equated to a "high-tech lynching."[61] Rather, watching Hill receive the brunt of invasive questioning about her sexuality and veracity enraged many women, a fury that motivated 218 to run for Congress in the 1992 primary.[62] Democratic women candidates benefited most in this election that moved women's representation in Congress forward more than any other to this point, but conservative women too responded. The Independent Women's Forum, founded in the aftermath of the Hill-Thomas controversy, called it a "sorry spectacle" and made light of the irony that Hill defended President Bill Clinton in 1998 when he was embroiled in the Monica Lewinsky scandal.[63]

The Ford-Kavanaugh exchange dredged up this buried history. It also proved equally motivating for Democratic women voters and candidates, many of whom had already joined the 2018 race before this late summer special. When Ford came forward, Hill urged senators to "get it right" this time. Afterward, she called the confirmation hearings a "disservice to the American public."[64] Ford recalled with pained precision the details of her high school encounter with Kavanaugh, which he dismissed as an alcohol-induced episode he could not recall. Former prosecutors turned senators Kamala Harris and Amy Klobuchar posed exacting questions to Kavanaugh, while conservative columnist Ann Coulter called into question "what the left pulls against a sweet nerd like Brett Kavanaugh."[65] And so it was the customary "he said, she said" that divided along party lines. Ford supporters camped out in solidarity during the hearings, with over two hundred forcibly removed and more tweeting #KavaNo. Republicans stood behind Kavanaugh, who wrote a mea culpa in the *Wall Street Journal* for publicly exhibiting his "deep distress at the unfairness of how this allegation has been handled."[66]

All of this posturing did not change the outcome, a foregone conclusion. The Republican-controlled Senate sped through the hearings and secured the votes needed to nominate Justice Kavanaugh. When Justice Ruth Bader Ginsburg died during the general election in 2020,

President Trump delivered a further blow by replacing the iconic Jewish liberal feminist with pro-life Catholic Justice Amy Coney Barrett. "My most fervent wish is that I will not be replaced until a new president is installed," Ginsburg relayed to her granddaughter.[67] Discarding this wish, Senate Majority Leader Mitch McConnell pushed through Barrett's nomination, for Republican leadership understood that overturning *Roe v. Wade* continued to motivate their base.

## Flipping the House

Republicans sought to inflict Kavanaugh's Revenge in the 2018 midterms, but swinging a few red-state Senate seats did not stave off a women-led blue wave.[68] The Kavanaugh nomination had simply been one more "moral shock" that began with the election of President Trump.[69] Media coverage aiming to predict if 2018 would be a Year of the Woman centered on the question: Would the Women's March effectively channel protest into politics? Women were determined to answer yes. One indicator: over forty thousand women reached out to the pro-choice political action committee (PAC) Emily's List to inquire about running in comparison with 920 the previous election cycle.[70] Groups fresh on the scene such as She Should Run, Indivisible, and Black Girls Vote expanded the web of training and fund-raising support for women candidates. Predicting a Trump effect before the election, political scientists Jennifer L. Lawless and Richard L. Fox confirmed afterward that his presidency had indeed been a supercharge for Democratic women, compelling at least one-quarter of new candidates to run.[71] As the *New York Times* pronounced the day the returns came in, "They marched, they ran, and on Election Day, they won."[72]

The 2018 congressional races tell a story that was replicated at every office level: in House races, 476 women competed in the primaries (compared with 273 in 2016), 234 moved forward to the general election, and 102 won; and in Senate races, 53 women ran in primaries (compared with 40 in 2016), 23 in the general election, and 14 won. Of the 116 women who ran and won, 100 were Democrats and 14 were women of color. As a result, Congress welcomed its most diverse freshman class, expanding women's overall presence from 20.5 to 23.7 percent.[73] With women still vastly underrepresented in electoral politics, the midterm outcomes also added to historic firsts. Texas sent its first two Latinas to Congress, Representatives Sylvia Garcia and Veronica Escobar, while New Mexico and Kansas elected their first Native American women, Representatives Deb Haaland and Sharice Davids.[74] The 2020 election would move the bar forward still.

This breakthrough election was significant for another reason: women delivered the House of Representatives to the Democratic Party. Yet, Democrats' postelection celebration minimized the fact that they enjoyed a slim margin of influence in the House and still did not have control of the Senate, limiting House activity to symbolic gestures of defiance. Likewise, women's foothold in representative government remained precarious, their numbers in Congress still hovering at one-quarter one hundred years after women gained the constitutional right to vote with nearly half of all women who had served elected since 1998. As former Colorado representative Patricia Schroeder assessed, "I was so excited to see the new women . . . but for all the great job they are doing, I think, 'Oh my God, it's 2019, and we are not even a full twenty-five percent of the House.' You need critical mass in an institution to change it."[75]

Democratic women indicated their new clout by appearing in suffrage white at the State of the Union speech in February 2019. To little avail, Nancy Pelosi tried to leverage her return to power by resurrecting feminist and gay rights campaigns straight from the 1970s playbook. In 2019, congressional Democrats reintroduced the Equality Act to expand the 1964 Civil Rights Act to include LGBT rights, a bill that Representative Bella Abzug had debuted in 1974. One year later, the House passed a bill to extend the Equal Rights Amendment's 1982 deadline after three final states needed to ratify the constitutional amendment—Nevada in 2017, Illinois in 2018, and Virginia in 2020—finally did so.[76] These bills were dead in the water owing to an unreceptive Republican-majority Senate.

President Trump impulsively responded to the 2018 midterm results by heightening his rhetorical assault on women politicians. Doing so stoked conspiratorial concern about a menacing matriarchal state on the far right, while ostracizing suburban white women voters he needed even more.[77] Speaker Pelosi confounded Trump, her demure presentation as a devout Catholic grandmother not squaring with her shrewd politicking and unwillingness to buckle to his will. All came to a head at a meeting on Syria in October 2019, when Trump stormed out after calling Pelosi a "third-grade politician"; they would not speak again during the remainder of his presidency. Pelosi frequently characterized Trump as a "master of distraction." When asked about their final interaction, she told reporters, "It shook him up, melted him down, and he behaved accordingly."[78] Unfettered, Trump revved crowds at his rallies with his rants about "Crazy Nancy."

## "Send Her Back" Backfire

President Trump believed he could exact even more damage with the catchphrase "Send Her Back," first introduced in July 2019. Instead, it further galvanized a counterresistance that helped ensure his reelection loss. Racist, sexist, and nativist, Send Her Back called into question women of color's rightful place in politics. Trump directed the slight initially toward Representative Ilhan Omar (D-MN), a Somali refugee and naturalized U.S. citizen who was part of a foursome of newly elected left-leaning congresswomen the media quickly dubbed the Squad. The others were Representatives Alexandria Ocasio-Cortez (D-NY), of Puerto Rican descent; Rashida Tlaib (D-MI), of Palestinian heritage; and Ayanna Pressley (D-MA), who is Black.

The Squad had highlighted the absence of women of color in centers of political power during their campaigns, vying for a seat at the table as they argued for racialized gender parity in politics. Ocasio-Cortez emerged as the breakout leader of the Squad in part because her takedown of ten-term incumbent and fourth-ranking House Democrat Joe Crowley in Queens's Fourteenth Congressional District was the most stunning race of 2018. Just twenty-eight at the time and working as a waitress, Ocasio-Cortez was gravely underestimated by Crowley. He overlooked her experience as a social-media-savvy field organizer fresh off Senator Bernie Sanders's 2016 presidential campaign. Ocasio-Cortez made light of her difference as a Democratic socialist running against a white man in a majority-minority district. "Women like me aren't supposed to run for office," she said in one campaign ad.[79] All Squad members won upset races that pundits had predicted would be unachievable, for women candidates historically have been directed toward safe seats. Yet, as Pressley rallied during her challenge of ten-term representative Michael Capuano, these women had effectively argued, "Change can't wait."[80]

Trump saw the Squad as a vulnerability he could exploit because they supported the Green New Deal and Medicare for All, but even more so because they were women of color. Trump's tweet—"Why don't they go back and help fix the totally broken and crime infested places from which they came"—immediately set off a frenzy of excitement on the right and indignation on the left.[81] Within three days, this tweet had morphed into the Trump rally chant "Send Her Back!" "We cannot be defined by this," Republican representative Mark Walker of North Carolina tweeted after attending one such rally.[82] The damage already done, Send Her Back was a glaring, irreversible indicator that the Republican Party was not a welcome home for women of color or new immigrants. "I am where I belong, at the people's house and you're just gonna have to deal!" Omar responded on Twitter.[83]

Not simply a xenophobic rant, the Send Her Back incident was also an anti-impeachment strategy. Omar, Pressley, Ocasio-Cortez, and Tlaib were among the earliest and most ardent members of Congress calling for Trump's exit. They followed the lead of California representative Maxine Waters, who beginning in February 2017 publicly declared, "He's someone that I'm committed to getting impeached!"[84] Uncoincidentally, President Trump delivered his July 2019 attack on the Squad just over a week before Special Prosecutor Robert Mueller testified before the House Judiciary and Intelligence Committees detailing his March report on Russian interference in the 2016 election. David Winston, former aide to Speaker Newt Gingrich, directly linked the Squad and their "obsession with impeachment" to Mueller's appearance, forewarning in an editorial that they would secure Republican wins in the "Forgotten 31" districts who both voted for Trump and sent Democrats to Congress.[85]

The greatest tipping point toward impeachment occurred two months later. Speaker Pelosi, "politely but firmly resisting" to strike, swiftly and methodically did so when news broke that the president had pressured the Ukrainian government to investigate likely Democratic presidential candidate Joe Biden's son Hunter.[86] What caught the most attention was an editorial in favor of impeachment penned by defense and intelligence agency veterans Representatives Gil Cisneros (D-CA), Jason Crow (D-CO), Chrissy Houlahan (D-PA), Elaine Luria (D-VA), Mikie Sherrill (D-NJ), Elissa Slotkin (D-MI), and Abigail Spanberger (D-VA).[87] The five white women in this group, who described themselves as "badasses," had flipped Republican-controlled seats in 2018. They encouraged moderate Democrats' turn toward impeachment, drawing on their military and intelligence credentials to make the case that President Trump remaining in office was a national security concern. In contrast, Upstate New York's Elise Stefanik, the Harvard-educated founder of the women-focused Elevate PAC first elected in 2015 at age thirty, emerged as one of President Trump's leading defenders during impeachment hearings. For this, Trump sanctified her as a "new Republican star" and assured her ascent in House leadership; Stefanik would be the biggest winner in the fallout after Wyoming representative Liz Cheney defiantly voted for Trump's second impeachment, replacing Cheney in 2021 as the third-ranking House Republican Conference chair.[88] However, it was Speaker Pelosi who proved most instrumental.

Pelosi expertly guided the nation through the third impeachment proceedings and the first run by a woman in U.S. history. After the House vote to impeach was cast on December 18, 2019, she declared, "He'll be impeached forever. No matter what the Senate does. He's impeached forever because he violated our constitution."[89] Forceful and succinct, Pelosi's message reflected her style of precision politics, slicing to the core of the matter, delivering the last blow—and unexpectedly once more when the House again impeached President Trump on January 13, 2021. In this role, Pelosi easily joined the ranks of the United States' most successful Speakers. It is unfortunate that she held this anticorruption cleanup role nevertheless, for doing so did not recast women outside their historic place in politics as moral guardians of the nation.

## All Eyes on Georgia

What happened outside Washington, more than within, ultimately sealed Trump's fate. The Trump administration's bumbling response to the COVID-19 pandemic that set in as the Democratic presidential primary heated up was most to blame for the president's plunging popularity. The pandemic adversely impacted women of color disproportionately, their role as essential workers brought their predominance in the public and service sectors into view and spurred discussion about the ongoing feminization of poverty. At the same time, school closures and inadequate public childcare led to a mass exodus of nearly three million women from the workforce, surpassing numbers reached during the Great Depression. Other losses will be more difficult to quantify, such as delayed career milestones, curtailed advancement, and salary freezes.[90] The disruption of work and family during the pandemic brought forward renewed attention to long-standing feminist goals of revaluing caregiving and expanding subsidized child care and family leave benefits. The economic and cultural shocks of this public health crisis further motivated women to exercise their voting power.

Women in Georgia worked at the forefront of a growing nationwide movement to preserve voting rights and shift the political terrain to enhance people of color's clout and representation. National media outlets slow to report on this organizing scrambled to catch up when Georgia undid Trump's chances to achieve an electoral win in 2020, and it became clear that women of color's door-to-door campaign to defeat the president made the difference.[91] This ground-game challenge delivered by thousands of grassroots workers in groups such as Turn It Blue and New Georgia Project had been building to this point for multiple election cycles. Get-out-the-vote efforts developed alongside those to rebuild the Democratic Party infrastructure and to recruit more women to run for office; in 2018, ninety-one women were on the ballot in Georgia.[92] Political organizing was a slow process, but one that women had mastered having long served as the ground troops of political parties and social movements. As Black Voters Matter cofounder LaTosha Brown explained, "All of it really boils down to the organizing. . . . The way that you win elections is organized power."[93]

Former Georgia State Speaker Stacey Abrams naturally emerged as the national face of a renewed voting rights struggle after she lost a razor-thin gubernatorial election to Brian Kemp and, "as a woman of conscience and faith," would not concede.[94] Abrams contended that Kemp's shady dealings overseeing state election procedures during the governor race in his capacity as secretary of state cost her the election.

These ran the gamut from unannounced polling sites closures to "use it or lose it" voter purges impacting at least 107,000 Georgians.[95] "Most of us understand voter suppression as the 1960s images of billy clubs and hoses and dogs barking—aggressive interference," she explained. "But in the 21st century, voter suppression looks like administrative errors. . . . But it is just as intentional and just as insidious."[96] This was especially the case after *Shelby v. Holder* (2013) stripped the 1965 Voting Rights Act of its regulatory muscle, eliminating the requirement for states with histories of discriminatory election laws to have new rules vetted by the Justice Department.

Despite widespread efforts to curb voting access, Americans turned out in record numbers to vote for and against President Trump with two-thirds of all eligible voters casting ballots. In the final months, pandemic woes motivated some voters, while the swell of #BlackLivesMatter protests responding to George Floyd's and Breonna Taylor's deaths at the hands of police spurred on others.[97] The outcome, fatefully, came down to the slim win former vice president Joe Biden squeezed out in Georgia. There, Republican state leaders preserved the integrity of the election, standing up to President Trump when he repeatedly claimed election fraud.

In 2020, once again, political discourse revolved around who was worthy to be in power, with Democrats discussing who had the best chance to defeat Trump and the connected concern of whether the nation was ready for a woman president. "May the best woman win," Senator Amy Klobuchar tweeted in July 2019, previewing Annie Leibovitz's portrait for *Vogue* that featured Democratic presidential contenders who were officeholders—Representative Tulsi Gabbard and Senators Klobuchar, Kamala Harris, Kirsten Gillibrand, and Elizabeth Warren.[98] This was a historic showing, but ultimately Biden—a noncontroversial moderate who looked like Trump but acted markedly different—emerged as the nominee. Biden understood these optics in the year of the suffrage centennial. He responded favorably when over one thousand prominent Black women urged him to "seize this historic opportunity to choose a Black woman running mate," and they reminded, "It is a fact that the road to the White House is powered by Black women."[99]

Biden selected as his running mate Senator Kamala Harris, who had abandoned her own bid for president in December 2019. Striking a clear difference between Democrats and Republicans, Harris offered a visual rebuke of Trump's Send Her Back rhetoric as a daughter of immigrants and biracial Black woman. She made light of the historic role she would play one heartbeat away from the presidency in her nomination speech, highlighting the shoulders she stood on and promising to "pick up the torch—and fight on."[100] And yet, the 2020 election that some predicted would widely rebalance a gender gap slightly favoring Democrats instead resulted in very little movement.[101]

Indeed, Trump did even better with white women voters in 2020 than four years prior, and Republican women enjoyed a breakout moment in Congress, electing thirty-five members, which topped the previous record of twenty-five in 2004.[102] Many of these first-timers had captured seats women Democrats gained in 2018, transferring power rather than greatly raising the overall count of congresswomen. Many were candidates whom Trump had backed, reflecting his continued hold on the party and his willingness to support women's political ambitions. Representatives Nicole Malliotakis (R-NY), Maria Elvira Salazar (R-FL), and Victoria Spartz (R-IN), all raised in antisocialist immigrant households, positioned to form "our own 'squad' . . . of new Republicans who love America."[103] And while Georgia gained the most attention for ousting Trump, the state also sent unabashed QAnon supporter Representative Marjorie Taylor Greene to Congress.[104] Thus, Republican women, though still a minority of a minority in Congress, highlighted in 2020 how women's political ambition cuts across party lines.

Vice President Kamala Harris will help Americans reimagine political leadership more expansively, but after the Trump years, where misogyny openly reared its ugly head, it is clear that there is not yet political will for a Madam President. As attorney Kim Foxx observed of her mentor Harris, "When you are the first, when you are cracking the glass ceiling, it's your scalp [that] ends up with the shards."[105] Ultimately, the Trump presidency will be remembered as the worst nightmare come true for progressive feminists and the greatest boon for conservative women. Not only did women on the right have an advocate in the White House, Trump provided them the opportunity to shape the MAGA Nation and in turn America.

# 8

# Immigration Policy and Politics under Trump

*Mae Ngai*

The immigration policies and practices of the Trump presidency were among the most extreme of his administration, brutally harming immigrants (both undocumented and legal residents), refugees, and asylum seekers. These harms were promised and enacted in order to cynically fuel a politics of nativism and racism that characterized Trump's popular base of support. In this chapter I consider immigration as ideology and politics, in one register, and as policy, in another; and the dynamics of their relationship. I am especially interested in the role that immigration politics played in the creeping authoritarian danger represented by the former president and his party. Because immigrants—including legal immigrants—lack most constitutional rights of due process, they were an easy target for summary exclusion and removal, and for laying the basis for broader and more sweeping anti-democratic measures.

Extreme racial nativism was a fundamental, defining ideological feature of Trumpism, encapsulated in its slogans "America First" and "Make America Great Again" (MAGA). Donald Trump famously began his presidential campaign in the summer of 2015 with an incendiary

FIGURE 3. Jacob Chansley at the U.S. Capitol on January 6, 2020, with the anti-immigrant "wall" tattooed on his arm. Photo by Amy Harris.

speech in which he claimed Mexico was sending "rapists" and "drug dealers" to the United States. By the time that Trump's supporters stormed the U.S. Capitol on January 6, 2021, the anti-immigrant worldview had become so subsumed into MAGA that it hardly needed explicit reference. Nativism appeared at the Capitol as the sublime, as tattoos of the wall on the arms of the insurrection's poster boy, Jacob Chansley, also known as Jake Angeli and Q-Shaman. "Take back our country," in the immediate context of the January 6 insurrection, referred to the liberals, communists, Democrats, and "fake" Republicans who, they alleged—wholly without evidence—"stole" the election from Trump. The underlying premise, of course, was that "the Left" and the "deep state" had stolen the election in order to allow the foreign born and Black people to "take" the country away from white Americans. This was always the fundamental racial grievance fueling MAGA.

Nativism was indeed the core political strategy for building and sustaining Trump's electoral and popular support. Nativism and, more generally, racism will undoubtedly remain key tenets of Republican and conservative politics, however they survive in the post-Trump era. Whether relatively muted or overt, nativism and racism will continue to generate opposition to legalizing the undocumented and support for voter suppression—both efforts aim to diminish democratic citizenship. In this context, Trump's immigration politics and policies may be understood as part of the authoritarian trend in the Republican Party.

As expected, upon assuming office, President Biden immediately overturned his predecessor's executive orders on immigration: the Muslim travel ban, "zero tolerance," and building the wall on the southern border. The new president is also proposing a far-reaching immigration reform bill.[1] It remains to be seen how much of it will survive the legislative process and, more broadly, whether the country reckons with the nativism inflamed by Trump and its political usefulness to conservative politics.

Nativism—virulent opposition to foreigners as dangers to the "American way of life" (however defined)—did not drop from the sky with Trump.[2] Nativism has been a staple of conservative politics since the 1980s, but during the last decades of the twentieth century Republican opinion was not monolithic. The GOP included both business interests, which wanted to exploit immigrants, and racial and cultural nationalists, who wished to expel them. But by 2016, "expel" triumphed over "exploit" in mainstream Republican politics, as Trump made "Build the Wall" the lead nativist slogan of his master MAGA trope.

To understand the ideological nature—and potency—of nativism we might begin with historian John Higham's classic work, *Strangers in the Land* (1955). Higham defined nativism as an "intense opposition to an internal minority on the ground of its foreign (i.e., 'un-American') connections," which translate "broader cultural antipathies and ethnocentric judgments . . . into a zeal to destroy the enemies of a distinctively American way of life." He identified three ideological traditions—religion, ideology, and race—that provided channels through which xenophobia flowed, acquired new meanings, and gained political force.[3] Higham's ideological trinity is useful because we can see its expression in contemporary hostility toward Muslims, "terrorists," and Latinos. His analysis shows that the construction of the "other" is historically contingent—not simply a "natural" human reaction to those who are "different"—although he did not use the language of social construction. Higham showed that nativism is necessarily reproduced according to changing conditions, including the adaptation of older ideas to new contexts.

In my opinion, though, Higham erred in his view that economic competition and unemployment were the material causes of anti-immigrant politics, which is in fact the conventional explanation for nativism. Rather, nativism emerges not in times of economic contraction but in periods of expansion associated with large structural transformation, or what economists call sectoral change. These shifts engender anxiety as opportunity looms simultaneously large and elusive for portions of the population. Immigrants generally do not "replace" native-born workers but work in new or expanding sectors and contribute to economic growth. Sectoral changes provide context for the major upsurges of nativism in American history: the Chinese exclusion movement during the opening of the West and consolidation of a national market after the Civil War, the restrictionist movement against southern and eastern Europeans amid industrialization and urbanization at the turn of the twentieth century, and deindustrialization and the rise of service and finance at the turn of the twenty-first century. Moreover, American nativism's various historical iterations have always been symbiotically linked—politically and structurally—to contemporaneous surges of racism and racial oppression of African Americans: the reversal of Reconstruction in the late nineteenth century, Jim Crow during the Progressive era, and the present era of mass policing and incarceration. This should not be a surprise: nativism is a form of white supremacy. But its specific ideological and political structures require specific analysis.[4]

---

During our own time, as in previous surges of nativism, the aggrieved are often workers from older industries. Domestic manufacturing jobs have been lost to automation and offshore production. But grievance also runs through the middle class, which has suffered from increased property-tax burdens resulting from tax breaks for the wealthy and shrinking federal and state budgets. A cult of celebrity surrounding billionaire entrepreneurs such as Jeff Bezos, Elon Musk, and Donald Trump (an ersatz billionaire) fueled a toxic mix of adulation and aspiration, on the one hand, and envy and resentment, on the other. White grievance is not limited to the working class: exit polls from the 2020 presidential election reported that Trump was the favored candidate not only among white voters but also among those earning more than $100,000 a year.[5]

Immigrants are not responsible for economic anxiety among whites. Nativism harnesses grievance via a theory of difference and in turn is weaponized by politicians. In our time, racism against immigrant communities of color, especially Latino communities, is the fundamental core of nativism. It breeds from economic precarity as well as white Americans' fears of demographic change and a perceived loss of social and political power. But open racism became impolitic in the post–civil rights era. It became dressed as a complaint against "illegal aliens." Of course, it is nothing new to associate immigrants with crime; but in the late twentieth century, nativism went further, making "illegality"—that is, crossing the border without a visa—a kind of racial condition. Popular opinion assumes that most, if not all, Latinos are undocumented and that illegal aliens make up a large share of the workforce. In fact, nearly 80 percent of Latinos living in the country are U.S. citizens, and undocumented workers make up 5 percent of the U.S. workforce.[6]

Nevertheless, focusing on "illegal immigration" and not directly on Latinos or race enabled conservative think tanks and policy organizations to promote a restrictionist agenda with a semblance of intellectual legitimacy. The website of the Federation for American Immigration Reform (FAIR), the most prominent anti-immigration group in the United States, states its aims without overtly racial language: "defend our borders, national self-determination and the American quality of life ensured by responsible immigration limits." But it also offers provocative links to "Check out President Trump's Immigration Accomplishments," "How Much Are You Paying for Illegal Immigration?," and "Stolen Lives: Victims of Illegal Alien Crime."[7] According to the Southern Poverty Law Center, FAIR's connections to white supremacist organizations are not exactly hidden either.[8]

The focus on illegal immigration appealed not only to conservatives but also to moderates, including mainstream Democrats, many of whom do not consider themselves racist but profess concern with "fairness" and "rule of law," values allegedly rejected by the undocumented because they cut in line and enter the country without authorization. It appealed even to more established Latino and Asian immigrants, especially in the 1980s and 1990s, who were anxious about the low wages of the newest immigrants undermining their own, often modest but hard won, gains.[9] Immigration-reform politics, focused on the problem of the undocumented, cut across partisan lines during the late twentieth and early twenty-first centuries. The last bipartisan reform bill to pass the Senate in 2013 was characterized by compromise and contradiction, a result of pressures from both the Right and the Left. For example, the 2013 Senate bill included legalization for the undocumented and a path to citizenship, but that path was thirteen years long, strewn with fines and tests, and contingent upon yet more border enforcement. But the far-right conservative caucus in the House thwarted it, a sign of what was to come.[10]

Donald Trump dramatically shifted the politics of immigration restriction. During the 2016 presidential campaign and throughout his presidency, Trump stoked a nativism that was unapologetically racist in order to excite his base of support among white supremacists. During the 2016 presidential campaign, Trump's advisers Stephen Bannon and Stephen Miller cannily chose immigration as the key issue to build an electoral base among white voters in the midwestern states, which they believed was key to an Electoral College victory. Both Bannon and Miller were committed hard-line restrictionists. Bannon was the provocative chief executive of Breitbart, the right-wing online news outlet known for sensationalism, conspiracy mongering, and disregard for facts. Miller, an iconoclastic figure obsessively opposed to immigration and civil rights since he was in high school, had worked for then representative Michele Bachmann (R-MN), a right-wing evangelical, and then senator Jeff Sessions (R-AL), also a far-right conservative committed to immigration restriction and white supremacy. Miller cultivated ties with conservative think tanks and media outlets and helped bring hard-line restrictionist politics into the mainstream of the Republican Party. Miller and Bannon forged a partnership while organizing Sessions's campaign against bipartisan immigration reform legislation in 2014 (they succeeded).

Miller joined the Trump campaign staff in January 2016 and rose quickly within the organization. He and Bannon jettisoned the Republican Party's recent strategy of courting Latino voters with a pro-immigration agenda that was previously promoted by mainstream Republicans, notably President George W. Bush. Instead, they made their singular priority white working-class voters, among whom election turnout had fallen. They counseled Trump to link unemployment to immigration and trade with China, two sides of the protectionist, America First coin. The strategy was taken straight from the nativism playbook: popular grievance explained by false theories and harnessed for partisan politics.

Bannon and Miller understood that Trump was not necessarily a reliable ideological partner when it came to immigration. To be sure, he was already known for racist provocation: recall his publicity campaign that demanded the death penalty for five young Black men convicted of raping a woman in Central Park in 1989—falsely accused and finally exonerated in 2002—and that he jumped into national politics in 2008 with the lie that Barack Obama was born in Africa. But Trump was always an opportunist who lacked political principles. His racism and antisemitism were base and instinctual, a common inflection among white entrepreneurs in New York's outer boroughs in the 1950s and 1960s. Trump did not have a history of nativism or an interest in immigration policy. Bannon suggested "Build the wall" as a memetic device to keep Trump on message during campaign rallies. Miller wrote the speeches; Trump added his own flourishes—Mexico would pay for the wall; it would be big and beautiful. "Build the wall" brewed with "Lock her up" (which cast his opponent Hillary Clinton as a criminal), a toxic mix of nativism and misogyny that drove Trump's popularity and his election victory.[11]

---

Within days of taking office in January 2017, Trump began implementing the nativist agenda. The first executive orders he issued as president were related to immigration: he instructed the government to build a wall on the U.S.-Mexico border, to round up undocumented immigrants en masse, and to ban Muslims from entering the United States.[12] He took full advantage of the president's executive authority and, perhaps more importantly, the so-called plenary power, the constitutional doctrine that deems federal regulation of immigration a matter of national security. This extraordinary authority dates to the U.S. Supreme Court's justification of Chinese exclusion in 1889: "To preserve its independence, and give security against foreign aggression and encroachment, is the highest duty of every nation. . . . It matters not in what form such aggression and encroachment come, whether from the foreign nation acting in its national character, or from vast hordes of its people crowding in upon us."[13] Before that ruling the court had held that the commerce clause of the Constitution authorized federal regulation of immigration. National security and the plenary power provided justification for racist legislation. They provide the foundation for nearly unlimited executive power over immigration to this day.[14]

The plenary power doctrine places noncitizens in matters of entry and removal beyond the reach of constitutional protection. Save for narrow exceptions, it excludes from judicial review both immigration legislation and individual immigration cases. The national security rationale is codified in Section 212(f) of the Immigration and Nationality Act, which gives the president authority to suspend entry or impose restrictions on noncitizens whenever he deems it "detrimental to the interests of the United States." Trump, generally unschooled in and indifferent to matters of law and the Constitution, loved the clause. He believed "section 2-something-something" gave his administration "magical authority . . . to keep anyone out."[15]

Almost. Section 212(f) cannot be used to override other federal laws. Litigation against the Muslim travel ban cited religious discrimination as violations of both the First Amendment's religious establishment clause and the nondiscrimination clause of the Immigration and Nationality Act. Over the course of eighteen months federal district and appellate judges enjoined the ban (including a second version that added a few non-Muslim countries and exempted people already holding permanent residency visas) in decisions that suggested a chink in the plenary power's armor.[16] In July 2018 the U.S. Supreme Court's Trump-friendly majority upheld a third version of the ban, based on a narrow, context-less reading of the order that ignored the public record of Trump's anti-Muslim rhetoric. *New York Times* columnist Linda Greenhouse called it "one of the sorriest excuses for a Supreme Court decision in recent years."[17]

Donald Trump pursued the nativist agenda through executive orders and administrative decisions in the Department of Homeland Security (DHS) and the Department of Justice. The executive orders (fifteen major orders in all) were just the tip of the iceberg. Altogether, some one thousand changes in immigration policy were made by rule modifications, directives, form changes, memos, certifications, executive orders, presidential proclamations, pending rule changes, and other bureaucratic actions.[18] Trump favored the expediency and publicity of proclamation. He did not bother to pursue legislation, which entails a more complex process but ultimately yields more durable results.

A few of Trump's initiatives faltered. The building of the border wall was slow. Mexico, of course, declined to foot the bill, and Congress approved only a fraction of his request for $5 billion. Trump attempted to divert $10 billion from the Pentagon budget for the wall but was rebuked by the Ninth Circuit. After four years in office, fifteen miles of new concrete "primary barrier" and a few hundred miles of replacement or secondary barrier made of steel-bollard fencing had been built.[19] The Supreme Court rejected a few orders, notably the rescission of the Deferred Action for Childhood Arrivals (DACA) program and the addition of birthplace and citizenship questions to the 2020 decennial population census. The Supreme Court did not rule on the substance of the orders but criticized them for being poorly written—arbitrary and capricious in the DACA case and nonsensical in the census case—and returned them to their respective agencies for revision. It's worth noting that the criticism of sloppy legal reasoning—also raised against the first two versions of the Muslim ban—was a recurring theme of the Trump years. It signaled both the political arrogance and the intellectual laziness of the administration.[20]

In the main, however, the administration proceeded aggressively against immigrants, both the undocumented and legal residents. It also drastically reduced refugee admissions, down to twelve thousand in 2020 (compared with eighty-five thousand in 2016), and virtually eliminated the country's asylum system in contravention of domestic and international law.[21] The pace and trajectory of these moves were breathtaking, deliberately cruel in intent, and surgical in precision. They were orchestrated by Stephen Miller, who became a special adviser to the president. Miller gained renown as the most skilled operative in the Trump White House. He already had a close relationship with his former boss, Jeff Sessions, whom Trump appointed attorney general, at the Department of Justice. It was a bigger challenge for Miller to bend the DHS to his will. He engineered the fealty of the agency by circumventing lines of authority within the department and cultivating direct ties to midlevel bureaucrats. At Miller's bidding, Trump purged those at the top who hesitated to support the White House's increasingly extreme plans, including Ronald Vitiello, head of Immigration and Customs Enforcement (ICE); Francis Cissna, director of Citizenship and Immigration Services; and even Kirstjen Nielsen, the secretary of homeland security.[22]

Trump's popular base required constant messaging and stoking. DHS's Citizenship and Immigration Services removed the phrase "nation of immigrants" from its home page.[23] The president opposed proposals to protect immigrants from Haiti, El Salvador, and African nations, calling them "shithole countries," and said Norway was the ideal source of immigrants—invoking the discredited national origins quota system enacted in 1924.[24] Trump pardoned Joe Arpaio, the notorious sheriff of Maricopa County, Arizona, after he was convicted of criminal contempt for disobeying a federal court ruling against racial profiling of immigrants.[25] Miller pursued increasingly brutal policies to demonstrate "toughness," orchestrating a dance of politics and policy that spiraled relentlessly downward. The most important of these concerned "zero tolerance" and maximum enforcement against unauthorized entry and presence, separation of families, refusal of asylum seekers, and efforts to limit legal immigration.

## Enforcement

Under Trump the DHS continued to implement the existing policy of "expedited removal" at the border—no hearing and removal within one day, if apprehended within two weeks of entry and one hundred miles of the border.[26] And, of course, Trump counted on building the wall to keep out future entries from Mexico. The more novel aspect of the Trump enforcement agenda lay in its campaign against undocumented immigrants living in the nation's interior. This population overwhelmingly comprises long-term residents: in 2017 two-thirds of unauthorized adult migrants had been in the United States for ten years or more.[27]

Trump canceled the policies of the Obama administration, which had shifted emphasis of enforcement from the interior to the border and prioritized for enforcement "aliens who pose a danger to national security or a risk to public safety"—namely, suspected terrorists and those convicted of violent crimes, felons, and repeat offenders.[28] Under Obama the number of removals increased, owing in part to the law Congress passed in 1996 for "expedited removal" and "mandatory removal" in criminal cases. Immigrant advocates criticized Obama as "deporter in chief" and for reproducing an unethical good immigrant / bad immigrant divide. Nevertheless, interior removals fell from 224,000 in fiscal year (FY) 2011 to 65,000 in FY 2016.[29]

By canceling priorities and prosecutorial discretion, the Trump administration made any and all immigrants in the country without authorization "equal priorities" for removal. It made special note of those convicted of any crime, including minor offenses such as traffic violations; those charged with (but not convicted of) any crime; and even those who "committed acts that constitute a chargeable criminal office" (neither charged nor convicted), as well as those who abused welfare benefits and committed fraud in any dealing with any government agency.[30]

ICE agents raided workplaces from meatpacking plants in the Midwest to garment factories in Los Angeles. They mounted pop-up road checks in Queens, New York, and Los Angeles, California, and boarded Greyhound buses from Vermont to Ohio demanding to see passengers' proof of citizenship, a violation of Fourth Amendment protection against unreasonable search. ICE agents apprehended parents dropping their children at school and witnesses leaving courthouses. A climate of fear and terror descended on immigrant communities as ICE agents celebrated their "unshackling." Anyone could be picked up for any or no reason.[31] Interior removals under Trump rose by 30–40 percent per year compared with the last year of the Obama administration.[32]

From another angle, however, the targets could be seen as low-hanging fruit; ICE could not possibly round up and deport the ten million undocumented persons estimated to be living in the United States. The gap between mass deportation as aspiration and as practicality played out in the controversy over the so-called detainer policy and sanctuary cities. ICE relied on a provision in the immigration law that sought cooperation from local law enforcement authorities to check all persons apprehended for a crime through the federal databases to see if they were wanted for an immigration violation, and to detain them until ICE could take them into custody. But under the

Tenth Amendment to the Constitution, states and localities cannot be coerced to enforce federal laws, and many states and localities declined to participate in the program. Trump denounced "sanctuary jurisdictions" for violating the law, but the opposite was in fact the case. More generally, the problem revealed that restrictionist immigration policies will always confront the problem of federal capacity. In fact, there were actually fewer removals under Trump than under Obama.[33]

## Family Separation

At the southern border, where the wall was slow to be built, Trump and Miller deemed expedited removal to be insufficiently "tough" against unauthorized entry. In fact, the volume of migration across the southern border had plateaued over the course of the past decade. But the nature of it had shifted, from being predominantly Mexican to Central American in origin. After Mexican migration registered at a net-negative during the 2008 economic recession, it settled at net-zero during the 2010s, the result of an ongoing soft labor market in the United States and trends in Mexico, including a general rise in prosperity (albeit uneven) and a declining birth rate.[34] But during the past decade, migrants from the northern triangle—El Salvador, Honduras, and Guatemala—were fleeing extreme violence and economic hardship; since 2014 they had increasingly been asking for asylum. They included women, families with children, and unaccompanied teenagers, many of whom were fleeing gang violence.[35]

Throughout 2017 and early 2018 Trump raged about the "invasion" advancing across the southern border and the government's long-established practice of releasing families from detention, usually to relatives already in the United States, while they awaited their court hearings.[36] Trump vowed to end what he derisively called "catch and release." DHS began discussing family separation as a deterrence strategy as early as February 2017—a month after Trump took office—and piloted a program in Texas during the summer, with minors handed off to the Department of Health and Human Service's Office of Refugee Resettlement.[37] In April 2018 Attorney General Jeff Sessions issued a formal "zero tolerance" directive, mandating criminal prosecution of all alleged unlawful entrants, including first-time offenders (a misdemeanor) and asylum seekers; and President Trump directed the Departments of Justice, Homeland Security, and Health and Human Services to end "catch and release."[38] These formalized and extended the practice already taking place of separating families, both to enable prolonged detention of adults and to deter future migrants. Sessions announced, "If you are smuggling a child, we will prosecute you. And that child may be separated from you as required by law."[39]

Between October 2017 and mid-April 2018, the border patrol separated more than seven hundred children from their parents, including more than one hundred under the age of four.[40] In the six weeks after Sessions announced "zero tolerance," U.S. Customs and Border Protection (CBP) separated an additional two thousand children from their families.[41] In addition to suffering from the trauma of separation, children were held in caged and unsanitary conditions, often without mattresses, adequate clothing, proper nourishment, diapers, bathing, or medical attention. Once "processed," the children were "put into foster care or whatever," sometimes in facilities thousands of miles from the border.[42] Two medical doctors contracted by the DHS to investigate the effects of the policy declared that zero tolerance was "an act of state sponsored child abuse." They, along with the professional associations of pediatricians, physicians, and psychiatrists, condemned both child detention and family detention for causing lasting harms to children, potentially for "an individual's entire life span."[43]

In June 2018 a U.S. district court judge issued a preliminary injunction against the administration and ordered it to reunite children under the age of five with their parents within two weeks and all others within a month.[44] In the face of public horror and widespread condemnation, Trump announced his commitment to family unification. But there were children whose parents could not be found because there was faulty or no information on their identities or whereabouts; in some cases, the parent had already been deported.[45] DHS also skirted the court's directive by continuing to take children who arrived with relatives who were not their parents, such as uncles or grandparents, and justified taking children from parents whom they deemed to be "criminals."[46] By the time Trump left office, more than 5,500 children had been separated from their parents and 628 children still had not been reunited with their families.[47]

On January 13, 2021, the Justice Department's Office of the Inspector General issued a report criticizing the planning and implementation of the Zero Tolerance policy.[48] On January 26, 2021, Acting Attorney General Monty Wilkinson formally rescinded the policy.[49]

## Asylum

The separation of families at the border meant that children were not included in their parents' asylum claims. That problem, however, diminished in importance as the Departments of Justice and Homeland Security made denial of asylum to all comers their general operating policy at the southern border. Sessions cynically called asylum a "loophole" in the immigration laws and treated asylum seekers as though they were "illegal" entrants. Accordingly, the administration crafted various policies, each more extreme than the last. First, it simply refused to honor the legal standard by which any person could present himself or herself at a port of entry to an immigration officer and declare that they were seeking asylum, a right under both domestic and international law. When asylum seekers entered at unauthorized points along the border, the border patrol detained those that it apprehended; if children were present, they were separated from the adults. Those asking for asylum were given a preliminary interview to determine whether there was a "credible fear" that they would face persecution, violence, or other harm if returned to their country. DHS scheduled those passing the credible fear bar for a hearing before an asylum officer, which could be months later, and deported the others. Because the administration now detained all asylum seekers until their hearing, detention facilities rapidly filled.

The administration then added two programs, each of dubious legality. First, it turned back migrants arriving at southern ports of entry to the Mexican side of the border, where they were made to wait until allowed to cross under a program of "metering." By November 2019, some twenty-one thousand people were waiting in border cities across Mexico for the opportunity to begin the asylum process. Depending on the location, the wait could be a few days or up to six months.[50]

In December 2018 DHS created a separate program, Migrant Protection Protocols (MPP), also called the "Remain in Mexico" policy.

Under MPP, asylum seekers who asked for asylum at the border were given a notice to appear in immigration court and returned to Mexico to wait for their appointment. Between January 2019 and January 2020, the CBP returned over sixty-eight thousand people to Mexico under MPP.[51] The United States took no responsibility for the welfare of migrants it returned to Mexico. While the Mexican government and private charities provided shelter for some, thousands of others lived in tent camps without electricity or running water. Human Rights Watch reported thirteen hundred publicly documented incidents of rape, assault, kidnap, and other crimes against migrants in MPP.[52]

The CBP also used "pre-screening" interviews (which did not inquire whether migrants feared returning to Mexico) that often preempted the required interview before an asylum officer. Those who received an official interview were often rushed through hearings held in "tent courts" via videoconference. Migrants had legal counsel in only 7.5 percent of MPP cases. Of 42,012 MPP cases heard through the end of December 2020, only 638 were granted relief in immigration court (1.5 percent).[53] Asylum officers complained that CBP pressured them to deny asylum cases; its union filed a brief in the Ninth Circuit calling MPP a policy "fundamentally contrary to the moral fabric of our nation and our international and domestic obligations."[54]

On March 23, 2020, the DHS suspended MPP hearings across the border, in response to the global coronavirus pandemic. The program remained suspended throughout the end of Trump's term, even as DHS sent an additional fifty-five hundred people to Mexico to wait. Many people, including those with appointments for asylum hearings, gave up and returned home.[55]

Other policies further restricting the right to asylum included banning asylum for persons entering the United States at the U.S.-Mexico border after "transiting" from another country and an expedited process at border detention centers for making a credible fear claim (in which asylum seekers were given only thirty minutes to contact a lawyer or family members).[56] In the final months of the Trump presidency, the Departments of Justice and Homeland Security established expansive new rules that gutted the asylum system by codifying the transit ban, rewriting the definition of "persecution," allowing judges to deny requests without a hearing, and other rules. On January 8, 2021, a federal judge in California blocked the rule just a few days before it was scheduled to take effect.[57]

Upon taking office, President Biden ended the MPP program and began to process the more than twenty-five thousand people in MPP camps, even as the border remained officially closed owing to COVID-19. But the number of new asylum seekers arriving at the border also dramatically increased, including many teenagers traveling alone, overwhelming border facilities and creating a new humanitarian crisis. A deployment of federal workers to the border expedited processing so arrivals could be released to family members or to child welfare facilities, and Vice President Kamala Harris began meeting with officials in Central America to address problems in origin countries that have impelled so many people to leave. But the problems resulting from the Trump years—and longer-term problems in Central America—will not be quickly or easily solved.[58]

## Public Charge Rule

Donald Trump and Stephen Miller made no secret of their disdain for immigrants from "shithole" countries and their preference for skilled and professional northern Europeans. Numerical quotas and preferences (family and employer sponsored green cards) are set by Congress, however, and cannot be changed by executive order or administrative rule change. The administration's work-around was to expand the meaning of "liable to become a public charge" in order to exclude poor people from getting green cards.[59] Throughout four hundred years of American history, dating to the British colonial era, a noncitizen "public charge" for purposes of exclusion or removal was defined as someone who was wholly dependent on the government for subsistence (poor relief, institutionalization, or full-time welfare). DHS added food stamps, Medicaid, housing vouchers, and other public benefits that assist working families earning poverty-level wages, including noncitizen legal residents. (Undocumented immigrants are already excluded from nearly all benefits.) Although a federal district court struck down the rule, the Second Circuit allowed the rule to be implemented in most of the country while the Trump administration appealed. Upon taking office, Biden withdrew the appeals and rescinded the rule change.[60]

---

Extreme nativist politics and restrictionist immigration policies were signature features of Donald Trump's presidency. The Trump administration sought nothing less than the mass expulsion of unauthorized migrants and closing the United States to immigrants, refugees, and asylees. Because the administration relied on executive orders and administrative rules, and not legislation, President Joe Biden was able to rescind most of them, through either executive order or new rule changes. But the damage to hundreds of thousands of migrants was done. Some of it is irreparable.

A full accounting of Trump's immigration policy must reckon with the relative ease with which it was implemented. The doctrine of the plenary power provided the legal zone that permits racial profiling, denial of constitutional rights, and summary expulsion of noncitizens. But the use of plenary power is also subject to public opinion. That's why the nativist rhetorical campaign was so crucial to Trump's ability to implement restrictionist policies.

To be sure, not all Americans support the view that paints Latinos, Muslims, Asians, and others from the global south as racialized "others." Tens of thousands of people went to JFK, LAX, and other airports on the day Trump issued the Muslim ban to demand that they be let in. Activists formed "rapid response teams" to thwart ICE raids and to protect DACA holders. Protesters demonstrated against detention and family separation, including Japanese Americans who had themselves been unjustly incarcerated during World War II. Lawyers and law students defended migrants and litigated every Trump policy. In 2018 the cruelty of child separation may have cost the Republican Party control of the House of Representatives. Polling data consistently show that a majority of Americans oppose mass deportations and support legalizing the undocumented.[61]

The political struggle over immigrant inclusion and exclusion is part of the larger struggle against the authoritarianism of the Trump era and will likely continue to be part of the post-Trump political landscape. Nativism not only harms migrants; it corrodes democracy. It is the handmaiden of authoritarianism. The right wing opposes legalization of undocumented immigrants not just because the undocumented are vulnerable to exploitation; legalization creates the potential for more citizens and hence more voters. Latinos and Asian Americans are not monolithic ethnic voting blocs. Not all consider immigration to be the most important policy issue; some supported Trump in 2020 because they identified with business interests or oppose the alleged "socialism" of the Democratic Party. Nevertheless, these communities remain consistently majority (if not overwhelmingly) Democratic.[62]

Casting foreign-born Americans outside the circle of national belonging, along with African Americans, long the nation's domestic "other," paves the way to restrict the democratic rights of all Americans. Trump's unfounded claim that the presidential election was stolen from him rested on the allegation that Black urban voters in the swing states committed fraud; but it was, in fact, an attack against all voters, against the sanctity of the vote, and the system of elected government itself.

# 9

# The Rhetoric and Reality of Infrastructure during the Trump Presidency

*Jason Scott Smith*

Donald Trump's appeal and effectiveness, both as politician and as president, can be clearly seen through the rhetoric and reality of his infrastructure policy. The relationship among the issue of infrastructure, the debt that Trump's politics owed to white nationalism and racism, and the powerful capacity of the federal government to detain and inflict harm on undocumented immigrants and citizens alike is crucial to apprehending the impact and consequential nature of Trump's presidency.

Trump's pledge to rebuild the nation's infrastructure was by far his most popular campaign promise, but it was one that went seemingly unfulfilled during his four years as president. Indeed, if one considered only the amount of money spent, miles of roads paved, number of bridges repaired, range of airports modernized, or amount of broadband fiber cable laid during Trump's presidency, it is easy to conclude that he appeared to be more talk than action. Some observers, such as conservative *New York Times* opinion columnist Ross Douthat, went so far as to point to the gap between Trump's words and his deeds as confirmation that Trump could never be considered a consequential president, since the scale of his incompetence and seeming inability to govern effectively outweighed, as Douthat put it, even his malevolence.

This superficial focus, however, misses a deeper connection between political language and public policy: Trump's rhetorical commitments to infrastructure in fact underwrote a sea change in the legal mechanisms and policing capacities of the federal government, changes with profound consequences, particularly for immigrants, asylum seekers, and people of color. Trump's use of the political vocabulary of infrastructure captures the ways that his administration combined and recast the physical, ideational, and legal networks and systems that facilitate—and inhibit—the circulation of people. In this way, Trump used the language of infrastructure as a strategic weapon, as historian of rhetoric Jennifer Mercieca has perceptively observed: to unite his supporters, divide his opponents, and avoid accountability for his words and deeds. The potent combination of rhetoric and infrastructure policy was nowhere more evident than in Trump's divisive pledge to build a wall along the U.S.-Mexico border.[1]

Throughout his campaign for the presidency and his time in office, Trump was singularly absorbed with advancing this particular infrastructure project. In focusing on the ways his presidential campaign and term in office engaged these issues, I argue that in many respects Trump's presidency can be interpreted as a strikingly successful one. When Trump announced he was running for president at his eponymous tower in New York City, he made opposition to immigrants and illegal immigration a cornerstone of his campaign. "When Mexico sends its people, they're not sending their best," he declared. "They're sending people that have lots of problems, and they're bringing those problems with us. They're bringing drugs. They're bringing crime. They're rapists," adding as an afterthought, "And some, I assume, are good people." Trump's remarks, along with his proposal to build a wall along the U.S.-Mexico border—and to have Mexico pay for it, no less—captured media attention and generated immediate controversy. Arturo Vargas, the executive director of the National Association of Latino Elected and Appointed Officials, commented, "It appears Mr. Trump is having a difficult time separating fact from fiction." And as he further observed, "Developing a sound foreign policy with the United States' most important trade partner and neighbor is not a reality TV show." Facing pressure to disavow Trump from a coalition of Latino organizations (including the National Council of La Raza and the United States Hispanic Chamber of Commerce), NBC and the Spanish-language network Univision quickly announced they would no longer broadcast the Miss USA and Miss Universe pageants, events co-owned by Trump and NBCUniversal.[2]

The controversy over Trump's racist pronouncements and border wall proposal overshadowed another aspect of the reality television star's campaign launch: to make the nation's infrastructure great again. "Rebuild the country's infrastructure," the candidate proclaimed. "Nobody can do that like me. Believe me. It will be done on time, on budget, way below cost, way below what anyone ever thought. I look at these roads being built all over the country, and I say I can build those things for one-third." Trump continued, "So we have to redo our infrastructure, our bridges, our roads, our airports," adding "You come into LaGuardia Airport, it's like we're in a third world country."[3] Trump's image as a high-profile and successful real estate developer had been broadcast for years to the millions of people who watched his top-rated NBC television show, *The Apprentice*. This reinforced the impression that Trump was running for president as a professional builder who understood how to get things done, an impression that transcended the six times his businesses had filed for bankruptcy protection between 1991 and 2009. Trump ultimately promised to spend twice as much as what his opponent, Hillary Clinton, proposed, outlining a $1 trillion commitment to create an infrastructure fund, supported by the sale of federally issued bonds. "We're going to go out with a fund," Trump said. "We'll get a fund, make a phenomenal deal with low interest rates and rebuild our infrastructure."[4]

Trump's infrastructure plan, while vague, turned out to be easily the most popular of his 2016 campaign promises, with 69 percent of those polled rating it "very important" that it be fulfilled. In contrast, cutting income taxes finished second (54%), and establishing tariffs on foreign imports (51%) and deporting more than two million illegal immigrants who had committed crimes (51%) were tied at third. Trump's commitment to build a border wall with Mexico finished twelfth with the general public, with 26 percent of those polled stating that it was "very important" that it be accomplished.[5] Infrastructure—as outlined in Trump's proposal to rebuild the nation's network of roads, bridges, and airports—represents an area of policy that, alongside his positions on taxes, trade, and immigration, demonstrates Trump's optimistic appeal to an earlier era of plentiful industrial jobs for white men and for a global economic system where U.S. firms and factory workers held an advantageous position. Trump's border wall proposal, however, signaled the ways in which infrastructure served to mark a turning away from America's founding myth of the open frontier, embracing instead reactionary populism and racist nationalism. This mix of nostalgia and fear in turn inflected Trump's affection for authoritarian governance and functioned to give right-wing extremists license to pursue extralegal violence against minorities. Viewed in this context, infrastructure is thus an issue where we might then measure the extent to which Trump was a "normal Republican," something more extreme, or something else entirely.[6]

In his campaign, Trump's speeches laid the groundwork for how his presidency would engage the issue of infrastructure, consistently linking nostalgia for midcentury industrial employment with the ideal of masculine independence and the need to rebuild the nation's infrastructure network, using this combination to attack Clinton and rally support. In accepting the Republican nomination in Cleveland, Ohio, in July 2016—a speech noteworthy for Trump's proclamation, "Nobody knows the system better than me, which is why I alone can fix it"—Trump charged that Clinton "wants to put the great miners and steelworkers of our country out of work and out of business." He promised, "That will never happen with Donald J. Trump as president. Our steelworkers and our miners are going back to work again. With these new economic policies, trillions of dollars will start flowing into our country. This new wealth will improve the quality of life for all Americans. We will build the roads, highways, bridges, tunnels, airports, and the railways of our tomorrow. This, in turn, will create millions of more jobs."[7]

In the 2016 presidential debates, both candidates discussed the importance of the nation's infrastructure in their first meeting. Clinton presented her view that infrastructure helped drive economic growth and employment. "First, we have to build an economy that works for everyone, not just those at the top," she declared. "That means we need new jobs, good jobs with rising incomes." Turning to the audience, she continued, "I want us to invest in you. I want us to invest in your future. That means jobs in infrastructure and advanced manufacturing, innovation and technology, clean renewable energy and small business because most of the new jobs will come from small business." Trump treated infrastructure differently, turning to the issue in order to deflect a question from moderator Lester Holt about why he had not released his tax returns. Trump instead redirected attention to the "third world" quality of America's airports. Using the infrastructure issue like a club, he went on the attack. Trump reminded the audience of Clinton's support for the U.S. invasion of Iraq when she was in the Senate, linking these two points to the consequences for the state of the nation's infrastructure in 2016. Asserting that the United States had spent $6 trillion in the Middle East, Trump claimed that with that amount of money "we could've rebuilt our country twice. And it's really a shame." Trump continued, "Our country has tremendous problems. We are a debtor nation. We're a serious debtor nation. And we have a country that needs new roads and tunnels, new bridges, new airports, new schools, new hospitals, and we don't have the money because it has been squandered on so many of your ideas," he said of his opponent.[8]

Trump's narrow but clear victory in the 2016 presidential election left many observers scrambling to explain how he managed to become the first person ever elected president without having held political office or served in the military. In victory remarks made around three o'clock in the morning following Election Day, Trump thanked Hillary Clinton for her service to the nation and called for national unity, pledging "to every citizen of our land that I will be president for all Americans, and this is so important to me." Trump did not mention his divisive plans for immigration, his desire to ban all Muslims from entering the United States, or his border wall proposal at all. Rather, his remarks focused not on fear of outsiders but instead on his popular infrastructure plans. "The forgotten men and women of our country will be forgotten no longer. We are going to fix our inner cities and rebuild our highways, bridges, tunnels, airports, schools, hospitals. We're going to rebuild our infrastructure, which will become, by the way, second to none. And we will put millions of our people to work as we rebuild it," Trump pledged. Trump also promised to help veterans and to double the rate of economic growth.[9]

In the aftermath of a divisive election, Trump's pledge held great potential for helping him expand his political base and build a larger coalition of supporters. For example, of the forty-nine measures relating to public transportation and infrastructure on local and state ballots in November 2016, voters approved at least thirty-three, calling for billions of dollars in public funds to be spent on a range of bus, rail, and transit projects. Atlanta, Seattle, and Los Angeles residents, for example, voted to raise sales taxes and dedicate the funds to infrastructure. New Jersey voters gave their approval to a constitutional amendment that would restrict all of the state's gas tax revenue to spending on transportation, following on the heels of the deal Republican governor Chris Christie struck with the state legislature to raise New Jersey's gas tax by twenty-three cents per gallon to improve the state's infrastructure and public transit. As the executive director of the Center for Transportation Excellence summarized, "We expected a historic year going into Election Day, and we got it in terms of the largest number of measures we've ever tracked and the largest dollar amount invested" in infrastructure measures on the ballot. Infrastructure was a policy area where Trump's presidency could have departed from Republican orthodoxy and reached across the aisle to address an issue that was important to Democratic voters and a key aspect of Trump's own political appeal.[10]

In his inaugural address, infrastructure thus took center stage, as Trump pledged to halt what he called the "American carnage" that had been created for years by a bipartisan establishment that had failed to stop the decline of industrial jobs, to provide a strong educational system, or to thwart the spread of crime and drugs. *Politico*, in its coverage, termed infrastructure a central theme of Trump's address, adding that this seemed a strange choice since Republican leaders in Congress had indicated this was not a central priority for them. Infrastructure was indeed a major focus for Trump, however, in that it allowed him to connect the key ideas that motivated his campaign to make America great again: Trump linked the nation's recent interventions in foreign conflicts with the poor health of the nation's infrastructure network, underscoring a clear link between investing in infrastructure and the need to secure the nation's boundaries from incursions from abroad. "We defended other nation's borders while refusing to defend our own. And spent trillions and trillions of dollars overseas while America's infrastructure has fallen into disrepair and decay," Trump asserted. As a result, he continued, "we've made other countries rich while the wealth, strength, and confidence of our country has dissipated over the horizon. One by one, the factories shuttered and left our shores with not even a thought about the millions and millions of American workers that were left behind." Trump's pledge—"America first"—combined his plan to rebuild the nation's infrastructure with repeated appeals to masculine independence, border security, and economic prosperity. "We will bring back our jobs. We will bring back our borders. We will bring back our wealth, and we will bring back our dreams. We will build new roads and highways and bridges and airports and tunnels and railways all across our wonderful nation. We will get our people off of welfare and back to work rebuilding our country with American hands and American labor." Many commentators noted the bleak tone of Trump's speech, with former president George W. Bush reported to have observed, "That was some weird shit."[11]

Setting aside Trump's tone and imagery, the speech's text, taken together with its continuities with Trump's rhetoric on infrastructure throughout the 2016 campaign that I've outlined above, underscores the crucial role the issue played in making America great again: nostalgia for an age of industrial employment for white men, a global economic system that kept nonwhites out of the country, and a robust commitment to transforming the nation's landscape and economy with highways, roads, bridges, hydroelectric projects, and airports. This language reflected infrastructure's central place in Trump's rhetoric, but it also clearly operated alongside other issues at the core of his appeal: a politics based on grievance, rage, white nationalism, and racism that consistently shaped his presidency. As it turns out, many of the occasions when the administration attempted to focus on infrastructure, writ large, were primarily exercises in public relations, attempts to distract the press and public from bad news by repeatedly bringing forward the most popular proposal from Trump's presidential campaign. The administration's first attempt to highlight its infrastructure plans, in June 2017, was undone when Trump turned a Rose Garden press conference into a forum to accuse James Comey, the FBI director he had fired, of committing perjury while giving congressional testimony about the Trump campaign's ties to Russia. "Yesterday showed no collusion, no obstruction" had been committed by Trump and his associates, he claimed, reacting to Comey's testimony. An unnamed administration official told the *New York Times* that what became known as "infrastructure week" had "gone horribly wrong, spinning out of control."[12]

The phrase "infrastructure week" soon became a kind of running joke, encapsulating the apparent lack of organization and floundering inconsistency of Trump's presidency. The administration's many failed attempts to mount a coherent infrastructure proposal and move policy forward seemed to underscore an inability to focus or govern competently. On a number of occasions, instead of pivoting to the political center and moving to fulfill the pledge of a multibillion-dollar effort to rebuild America's ports, airports, bridges, and highways, Trump instead recommitted to the politics of division. At a press conference held at Trump Tower on August 15, 2017—nominally called to promote the administration's efforts to streamline permitting processes and promote the building of infrastructure—the president and his advisers tried to divert public attention from his poorly received remarks that had followed the deadly extralegal violence committed by neo-Nazis and Ku Klux Klan members at a white nationalist "Unite the Right" rally held in Charlottesville, Virginia. In the wake of these remarks, a wide range of prominent Republicans criticized Trump for not taking a strong stand against white nationalists. The African American CEO of the pharmaceutical company Merck, Ken Frazier, resigned from the administration's council of manufacturing executives in protest, announcing "as a matter of personal conscience, I feel a responsibility to take a stand against intolerance and extremism."[13] The press conference went off the rails, however, as Trump's angry exchange with reporters became the story of the day. The uproar and criticism directed at Trump in the wake of his defense of violent white nationalists made clear the debt that his politics owed to racist extremism while simultaneously reinforcing a view of his presidency as one that could not deliver on his promise to rebuild the nation's infrastructure.

When Trump did deliver on infrastructure, however, he did so in dramatically effective fashion. In fulfilling his divisive campaign pledge to build a barrier along the U.S.-Mexico boundary, Trump's border wall stands as the signature piece of public infrastructure built during his presidency. Here, the president's rhetoric functioned alongside a broader transformation of immigration policy, spurring the construction of a barrier explicitly designed to frighten and deter foreigners from entering the United States. During Trump's term in office, the federal government allocated funds for approximately 738 miles of wall along the 1,952-mile border with Mexico. (About 700 miles of the border is on land and around 1,300 miles follow the winding course of the Rio Grande River in Texas.) By the time Trump left office, the federal government had supervised the construction of 453 miles of new primary and secondary wall, a further 211 miles of new primary and secondary wall were under construction, and approximately 74 miles of border wall were at the pre-construction stage. According to the Department of Homeland Security and the Army Corps of Engineers, as of January 8, 2021, U.S. Customs and Border Protection controlled a total of about 701 miles of primary barriers and around 70 miles of secondary barriers along the Southwest border. Trump's wall took the form of steel and metal barriers that rose from eighteen to thirty feet in height, anchored by concrete poured into the earth to form foundations six feet deep. Under Trump, the federal government transformed the infrastructure of the border, marking a striking departure from the approximately 650 miles of fencing that had been built during the presidencies of George W. Bush and Barack Obama, as part of their unsuccessful efforts to secure the passage of comprehensive immigration reform through Congress. At some points along the border, to be sure, urban sections continued to rely on tall "pedestrian fences," while in remote areas the federal government relied on vehicle roadblocks or the natural barrier formed by harsh mountainous terrain or the Rio Grande's water to secure the nation's boundary. Although relatively less of the wall's infrastructure was built in Texas, compared with other sections of the border, this was in part because of the legal obstacles the federal government encountered from private landowners along the boundary with Mexico. In contrast, construction on federally controlled lands in other sections of the U.S.-Mexico

FIGURE 4. U.S. Customs and Border Patrol map of the Border Wall System, January 25, 2021. Source: Archived U.S. Customs and Border Patrol webpage, at https://www.cbp.gov/border-security/along-us-borders/border-wall-system.

border, as was the case in California, Arizona, and New Mexico, was more straightforward.[14]

At an estimated cost of $15 billion, the wall was one of the most expensive public works projects ever built in the nation's history. The wall's construction involved the waiver of eighty-four federal laws intended to protect the environment and provide for public input and comment, including the National Environmental Policy Act, the Endangered Species Act, and the Clean Water Act. The Trump administration declared that a state of national emergency justified ignoring these laws. "We're going to confront the national security crisis on our southern border, and we're going to do it one way or the other," Trump said. "We have an invasion of drugs and criminals coming into our country," he warned.[15]

The construction of the border wall violated the tribal sovereignty of the Tohono O'odham Nation in Arizona, as well as causing substantial—and in many cases, irreversible—environmental damage in the Southwest and elsewhere along the border. Construction firms destroyed ancient burial sites and spiritual trails of the Tohono O'odham in clearing the way for the wall. The O'odham, whose ancestral homelands originally stretched from Phoenix and Tucson into the

Mexican state of Sonora, protested on multiple fronts, from the construction sites that encroached on their homelands to the fabrication plants that manufactured the thirty-foot-high metal bollard panels that make up the structure of the wall. "You did not have permission to demolition our sacred sites," one protester said. "You did not have permission to disturb our ancestors' bones. You did not have permission to take our water." Indigenous leaders pointed to the federal laws that govern Native lands, insisting that they be consulted before any construction took place. "We've historically lived in this area from time immemorial," Tohono O'odham Nation chairman Ned Norris Jr. explained. "We feel very strongly that this particular wall will desecrate this area forever. I would compare it to building a wall over your parents' graveyards. It would have the same effect." Decrying the treatment of protesters by the U.S. Customs and Border Patrol, Norris said, "The use of tear gas on O'odham and fellow American citizens exercising their sacred constitutional right to protest is utterly appalling, and not something that should be tolerated in our democracy."[16]

In terms of environmental damage, the consequences of the border wall's construction were wide ranging: the habitats of more than 114 species were fragmented, degraded, and in some cases eliminated; construction in the Organ Pipe Cactus National Monument destroyed centuries-old sixty-foot-high saguaro cacti; the San Pedro River (the last free-flowing river in Arizona) was dammed; contractors drained natural springs in the Coronado National Memorial and the San Bernardino National Wildlife Refuge to mix concrete; and the Sky Islands mountain ranges in the Coronado National Forest were dynamited to clear access to the border. More than fourteen hundred U.S. scientists were joined by over six hundred of their counterparts from Mexico and twenty-five hundred scientists from forty-three other countries in signing a statement protesting the border wall's threats to biodiversity and binational conservation. They noted the multiple impacts of its construction to the six ecoregions that compose the U.S.-Mexico borderlands. "Like any large-scale development," they observed, "construction of the wall and associated infrastructure, such as roads, lights, and operating bases, eliminates or degrades natural vegetation, kills animals directly or through habitat loss, fragments habitats (thereby subdividing populations into smaller, more vulnerable units), reduces habitat connectivity, erodes soils, changes fire regimes, and alters hydrological processes (e.g., by causing floods)." As the scientists noted, "the wall" was far more than simply the barrier itself, involving the construction of an entire support system of primary and secondary barriers, access and patrol roads, high-intensity light towers, and other associated infrastructure necessary to produce and maintain the actual division along the border.[17]

The federal government turned to a range of contractors, from smaller companies to large conglomerates, in undertaking the building of such a large structure over such a long distance. Twelve firms carried out twenty-nine different projects in building the wall, following the border from San Diego, California, to Brownsville, Texas, erecting barriers, creating patrol and access roads, building lighting, access gates, drainage improvements, and levee walls, and executing the other improvements, alterations, and repairs necessary for placing a wall on challenging terrain. Firms selected to bid on the contracts included large construction firms from Montana (BFBC), Texas (Sterling Construction Company and SLS Ltd.), Alaska (Bristol Construction Services LLC), New Mexico (Burgos Group LLC and Southwest Valley Constructors Company, an affiliate of the large Kiewit Infrastructure firm), Alabama (Gibraltar-Caddell JV), North Dakota (Fisher Sand & Gravel), Missouri (Randy Kinder Excavating Inc.), California (Martin Brothers Construction and CJW JV), and New York (Posillico Civil Inc. / Coastal Environmental Group JV).[18]

North Dakota's Fisher Sand & Gravel attracted Trump's personal support in its bids for government contracts, as its CEO, Tommy Fisher, was a prominent donor to the Republican Party. Fisher also frequently appeared as a guest on Fox News programming, in part with the goal of attracting the attention of the president, an avid viewer of cable television news coverage. Fisher claimed that his firm's new weathered steel fabrication process and pioneering building methods would speed up construction and lower costs. Fisher worked with former White House adviser Steve Bannon, Blackwater USA founder Erik Prince, Kansas Republican Kris Kobach, and others who had formed We Build the Wall, a private nonprofit organization designed to support Trump's border wall project. Fisher built some sections of wall as a demonstration project in Sunland Park, New Mexico, for Bannon's organization, in order to generate publicity for his firm. Donald Trump Jr. addressed Bannon and his comrades to congratulate them on their efforts. "This is what capitalism is all about. This is private enterprise at its finest. Doing it better, faster, cheaper than anything else. What you guys are doing is amazing," Trump Jr. declared. Fisher Sand & Gravel ultimately won a $1.3 billion federal contract to build forty-two miles of wall through the mountains of southern Arizona, with strong backing from Trump. Trump personally requested that the wall be painted black, to increase the heat and pain experienced by anyone who might touch it, adding about $1.2 million to the cost of each mile constructed.[19]

Bannon and three of his collaborators were subsequently indicted by federal prosecutors for fraud relating to their nonprofit organization. While We Build the Wall raised over $25 million in donations, much of the money was funneled to pay for the personal expenses of the board members, including private home renovations, boat payments, hotel and travel bills, luxury cars, jewelry, and cosmetic surgery. Bannon pleaded not guilty to federal charges that he had used more than $1 million improperly. He subsequently received a pardon from Trump just hours before his presidential term ended, before the case could proceed to trial.[20]

While Mexico did not pay for the wall's construction as Trump had repeatedly promised, the Trump administration took advantage of different pools of federal funds in order to bypass congressional authority and find the money it needed. Repeated refusals from Congress to appropriate funding for the wall led to the longest shutdown of the federal government in history, stretching over thirty-five days in December 2018 and January 2019. Trump responded with a declaration of national emergency, using this claim to justify unilaterally repurposing $3.6 billion that had been allocated to military construction projects and combining it with $2.5 billion from counternarcotics programs and $600 million from a Treasury Department asset forfeiture program in order to fund the wall's construction. Trump and his son-in-law, Jared Kushner, were in agreement that fulfilling the commitment to build the border wall was crucial to securing Trump's reelection, and thus a top priority for his presidency. Although Trump had made little progress on the wall during the first two years of his presidency, when Republicans controlled Congress, he made up for lost time during the last half of his term in office, demonstrating a striking degree of focus on the project.[21]

The significance of the wall encompassed more than the physical infrastructure erected at the border. Indeed, the infrastructure and the rhetoric of the border wall together underwrote a cruel expansion of the state's capacity to police society, demonstrating Trump's ability to deploy a "political vocabulary of infrastructure" across a range of his administration's activities. Infrastructure provided Trump with an ideologically flexible set of terms, with the ability to stimulate legal regulations, expand state capacities, and reshape the landscape over a variety of registers, including politics, the built environment, the economy, and society. Many politicians, in different historical moments, have deployed rhetorical commitments to building infrastructure to strengthen and expand their political support. Franklin Roosevelt, for example, had used the New Deal's public works programs during the Great Depression of the 1930s to create infrastructure that provided jobs and invested in long-run economic growth. This, in turn, helped solidify the political strength of the Democratic Party for generations, from FDR's presidency to the 1980 election. Trump, in his border wall, possessed an infrastructure project that effectively underwrote the darkest and most compelling aspects of his political appeal, helping to lock in the support of his political base. The wall, along with the specious claim that Mexico would pay for it, functioned akin to the "big lie" often deployed by fascist demagogues in the past. For Trump, this claim helped him marshal hatred and fear of immigrants from Mexico and Central and South America, serving as a foundational element in his appeals to white nationalism and racism throughout his campaign and his presidency.[22]

The Trump administration relied on a number of federal agencies to transform the treatment of immigrants and asylum seekers, both at the border and within the nation's boundaries. Historically, federal agencies such as the Immigration and Naturalization Service (INS) and the U.S. Border Patrol played a key role in constructing the different infrastructural networks required to police the nation's borders, employing the personnel necessary to regulate trade and enforce immigration and customs regulations. In 2003, many of the INS's functions were reassigned to three new bureaucracies—U.S. Immigration and Customs

Enforcement (ICE), U.S. Customs and Border Protection (CBP), and U.S. Citizenship and Immigration Services (USCIS)—housed within the newly created Department of Homeland Security (DHS). As S. Deborah Kang has pointed out in her brilliant history of the INS, the processes involved in securing the U.S.-Mexico border have long taken place at the intersection of law, physical infrastructure (including inspection stations and checkpoints), and the bureaucratic capacities to enforce (and adapt) administrative regulations. These bureaucracies not only enforced federal regulations but also functioned to generate policy as well. As Kang argues, "While outsiders often construed the work of the INS in narrow enforcement terms, the agency on the U.S.-Mexico border defined itself not only as a law enforcement agency, but also as a lawmaking body. As such, the agency played a profound role in shaping our conceptions of immigration law and policy, immigrant rights, and the border."[23]

The bureaucratic heirs to the INS, especially DHS, ICE, and CBP, continued in this vein. During the Trump presidency they played a key role in the formulation and enforcement of Migrant Protection Protocols (MPP). First implemented at the San Ysidro port of entry in January 2019, the MPP were then rolled out across the southern border and applied to people seeking asylum in the United States (including many people from Cuba, Venezuela, and Nicaragua). As a result, sixteen thousand asylum seekers under the age of eighteen, including about five hundred infants and forty-three hundred children under the age of five, were ordered by the federal government to remain in Mexico while they waited for U.S. immigration court hearings. All told, approximately fifty thousand people were forced to live in tents, on the streets, or in crowded shelters on the Mexico side of the border.[24]

With his first attorney general, Jeff Sessions, and White House adviser Stephen Miller leading the way, the Trump administration pursued multiple avenues to strengthen control over the nation's borders, including a ban restricting travel from predominantly Muslim nations, restrictions on refugees, increased immigration enforcement and unannounced raids carried out by ICE agents, and restrictions on asylum seekers looking to come to the United States. Trump even posited that Islamic terrorists could sneak into the United States at its southern border, at one point commanding his aides to investigate the feasibility of adding a trench filled with water to the wall, stocked with alligators or snakes. (The president also wanted to know if the border wall could be electrified, with flesh-piercing spikes added to the top.) In public and in private, Trump asked if soldiers could be stationed at the border and ordered to shoot migrants to keep them from even approaching the border wall.[25]

While these proposals were obviously impractical—and, in the case of shooting migrants, illegal—their cruelty is revealing. As David Blackbourn has pointed out, in his discussion of the different plans considered by Nazi Germany to drain the marshes along the border between Poland and the Soviet Union, the rhetoric of infrastructure can reveal the intersection between control of the physical landscape and ideologies of racism. In each case, the connection between dominating the built environment and advancing racial purity is clear. For the Nazis, as Blackbourn writes, "Even more than road construction, marshlands seemed to draw the National Socialist gaze as places where Jews could be worked to exhaustion or beyond."[26] For Trump, the border wall served as a manifestation of the multiple ways that his administration could marshal and deploy the legal and enforcement capacities of the federal government to police immigrants and peoples of color in order to secure the nation's borders. As the *New Republic* reported, ICE and CBP used funding authorized by Congress to carry out "some of the standout horrors of the president's border and immigration agenda: separating migrant families, allowing children to die in filthy, disease-ridden cages at CBP 'processing centers,' and staging shock-and-awe raids to detain and deport immigrant workers throughout the country." One prominent international observer described these policies as "pre-fascism," a kind of "test marketing" to see if the American people were willing to accept the dehumanization of migrants. In Portland, Oregon, unidentified federal agents roamed the streets in camouflage, in the wake of protests following the killing of George Floyd by Minneapolis police in May 2020, arresting protesters and throwing them into unmarked vans. Tom Ridge, who had run DHS during George W. Bush's presidency, declared that the agency's officials should not serve as "the president's personal militia." These sorts of events mark what historian Gary Gerstle and political scientist Desmond King have termed "spaces of exception," places where state-enforced "subordination and exclusion have often been imposed on citizens or aspirant citizens or involuntary residents on grounds of national origins and ethnicity, race, and gender."[27]

The policing carried out in these spaces of exception also inspired extralegal violence against immigrants and people of color. For example, on August 3, 2019, in El Paso, Texas, a city that shares the border with Ciudad Juárez, Mexico, an armed white nationalist shot and killed twenty-three people at a Walmart store, many of them Latino, and injured twenty-three others. In advance of this attack, the killer posted an anti-Hispanic and anti-immigrant manifesto on the online message network 8chan. His manifesto cited as inspiration a 2019 mass shooting at a New Zealand mosque in Christchurch, where fifty-one people were killed, and echoed the conspiracy theories advanced by far-right white nationalists at Charlottesville, who feared that white people would be outnumbered and "replaced" by people of color, declaring "this attack is a response to the Hispanic invasion of Texas." Although the perpetrator wrote that his beliefs "predate Trump," many observers noted that the manifesto's language resembled ideas that Trump often advanced. In the run-up to the 2018 midterm elections, for example, Trump had regularly warned that migrants were traveling in a caravan to attack the United States. "You look at what is marching up, that is an invasion!" he announced at one political rally. "That is an invasion!" Analyzing the connections between Trump's rhetoric and the El Paso manifesto, *New York Times* reporters Peter Baker and Michael Shear wrote, "If Mr. Trump did not originally inspire the gunman, he has brought into the mainstream polarizing ideas and people once consigned to the fringes of American society," reminding readers that Trump for years had repeated the "birtherism" lie that President Barack Obama was not born in the United States, had described immigrant gang members as "animals," and reinforced his calls for a border wall in order to stop the "invaders" who were coming over the border.[28]

Interpreting the Trump presidency through the lens of infrastructure reinforces the insights of historian George Mosse, who observed that the power of political violence could activate spectators, transforming them from bystanders into participants in fascist movements. Individuals such as the Charlottesville and El Paso killers were not only inspired by a domestic network of racist nationalism; they are emblematic of a broader transnational set of connections as well. Right-wing organizations also played an active role in promoting extralegal violence, at times inspired directly by the president. For example, the *New York Times* reported a link between the White House and the members of the Proud Boys, who participated in the assault on the U.S. Capitol on January 6, 2021, in their effort to thwart Congress's certification of Joe Biden's victory over Trump in the 2020 presidential election. The attempted insurrection resulted in 5 deaths and over 140 injuries. In the speech that preceded the assault on the Capitol, at the "Save America" rally held to "stop the steal," Trump concluded his attack on the integrity of the election by reflecting on his presidency's achievements. "We are the greatest country on Earth and we are headed and were headed in the right direction," he told the crowd.

> You know, the wall is built. We're doing record numbers at the wall. Now, they want to take down the wall. Let's let everyone flow in. Let's let everybody flow in. We did a great job in the wall. Remember, the wall, they said it could never be done. One of the largest infrastructure projects we've ever had in this country, and it's had a tremendous impact, that we got rid of catch and release. We got rid of all of this stuff that we had to live with. But now, the caravans, I think Biden's getting in, the caravans are forming again. They want to come in again and rip off our country. Can't let it happen.[29]

This link between infrastructure and the threat posed by a potential invasion of immigrants was further reinforced in Trump's last days in office, when he traveled to the U.S.-Mexico border near Alamo, Texas, on January 12, 2021, to personally inspect sections of the new border wall construction. Before an audience largely made up of agents from ICE, CBP, and the border patrol, Trump touted the border wall's excellent construction, praised the implementation of rules that forced asylum seekers to remain in Mexico, and autographed a plaque commemorating the 450th mile of wall built during his presidency. The next day, Trump became the first president of the United States to be impeached twice, this time for inciting the January 6 insurrection against the U.S. government at the Capitol.[30]

In this chapter, I have argued that a view of Trump's border wall with Mexico—and his infrastructure policy, more generally—as evidence of an inability to govern is profoundly mistaken. Rather, Trump's mastery of the political vocabulary of infrastructure demonstrates his administration's ability to move from a popular campaign promise to rebuild the nation's bridges, roads, and airports, to a focus on building the border wall and restricting immigration. The rhetoric of Trump's infrastructure policy activated and empowered white nationalists and racist extremists while strengthening the capacity of the federal government to detain and inflict harm on undocumented migrants and citizens alike. In many respects, this consistent, focused, and deep commitment to the infrastructure of the border helps explain Trump's political successes, from solidifying his base of political support and capturing the Republican Party to creating fear and terror among communities of immigrants and people of color. The fiasco of "infrastructure week" should not distract from recognition of the Trump administration's real achievements in mobilizing the legal, political, and physical networks of immigration enforcement at, as well as within, the nation's boundaries. The border wall stands as the signature piece of infrastructure built during the Trump presidency, a powerful example of how rhetoric successfully transformed reality.

# 10

# Against the Tide

## THE TRUMP ADMINISTRATION AND CLIMATE CHANGE

*Bathsheba Demuth*

In 2014, two years before Hillary Rodham Clinton and Donald J. Trump vied for the U.S. presidency, the United Nations Intergovernmental Panel on Climate Change (IPCC), the body that assesses and summarizes climate science, issued its most unequivocal and alarming report to date: evidence of "human influence on the climate system is clear and growing, with impacts observed across all continents and oceans." The primary cause, the report's scientific authors made clear, was greenhouse gasses emitted by burning fossil fuels. Industrial nations—the United States and China foremost among them—had energy policies that risked "severe, pervasive and irreversible impacts for people and ecosystems." The report called for "urgent and fundamental departure from business as usual" as delay would be expensive and unequal and would incur greater "technological, economic, social and institutional challenges."[1]

Yet climate change had a relatively small role in the 2016 presidential campaign. Clinton and Trump spent a mere five minutes on the issue during their three debates. Clinton framed policies to reduce fossil fuel emissions as one element in an energy plan that anticipated expanding natural gas production. Trump denied being a climate-change denier, despite a history of statements and tweets calling global warming a hoax.[2] Despite a thorough, if unrevolutionary, climate policy, Clinton addressed the issue less frequently as the election neared, preferring general statements about making the United States a "clean energy superpower."[3] Trump mocked wind turbines in his campaign speeches and promised to "bring the coal industry back and we're going to bring every industry. We're going to bring our energy industry back. We're going to bring it back."[4]

Climate change was harder to avoid in daily life. The year 2016 was the warmest recorded to date, 0.94 degrees Celsius above the twentieth-century average. *Homo sapiens* had never lived in an atmosphere containing more carbon dioxide. The Climate Mobilization, a grassroots advocacy group, sponsored the Climate Emergency Caucus in Iowa ahead of 2016's first presidential contest; by the late summer, protests against the Dakota Access Pipeline put the long practice of Indigenous activism against the unequal tolls of fossil fuel extraction on their land in national headlines.[5] Fifteen domestic weather events—floods, tornadoes, wildfires, droughts, hail, Hurricane Matthew—caused over a billion dollars in damage each.[6] Across the country, Americans experienced an increasingly turbulent climate. But such experiences did not make 2016 a climate election. On November 8, Americans chose, in the electoral college if not the popular vote, a vision of the future that explicitly endorsed the fossil fuel consumption of decades past. Over the next four years, Trump's climate policies—particularly his enthusiastic embrace of a Republican deregulatory agenda crafted late in the previous century—would fall increasingly out of step with Americans' experience of the climate crisis and their sense of appropriate political responses.

## Climate Change in Presidential Politics

The past that Trump campaigned on "bringing back" was, in terms of energy policy, a time before Barack Obama. This was not due to particularly radical climate policy during the Obama years. While a "Green New Deal" was part of his 2008 campaign proposals, the American

Clean Energy and Security Act (ACESA) that Democrats offered during Obama's first term focused on reducing emissions through cap-and-trade, not a comprehensive rethinking of how energy policy might be linked to employment. To craft the ACESA, Democratic lawmakers worked with environmental groups and fossil fuel corporations. The result was critiqued on efficacy grounds, as similar market solutions had failed to curb emissions in Europe, but narrowly passed the House. It became a primary flashpoint in 2010, when Tea Party candidates—many funded by Charles and David Koch's fossil-fuel-derived fortune—ran against potential Republican ACESA supporters. Yet the legislation's eventual failure in the Senate was also partly due to a long-standing Democratic inability to link climate stability to voters' present needs. Cap-and-trade was no New Deal; it made the climate an abstract problem fixed by "inter-organizational deals among corporations, unions, advocates, and industrial sectors," as Theda Skocpol has argued, with no indication of what "concrete benefits that new legislation could bring to ordinary families."[7] As a result, the legislation was easily painted by critics as a threat to employment in a country still reeling from the Great Recession.

After ACESA's failure, the Obama administration did not attempt further climate legislation. Instead, Obama's second-term Clean Power Plan used the regulatory power of the Environmental Protection Agency (EPA) to lower the acceptable level of greenhouse gas pollution from coal-fired power plants. It went into effect in 2015. A year later, the United States joined the Paris Climate Accords, a nontreaty international agreement with the goal of limiting global warming to as close to 1.5 degrees Celsius—the threshold many scientists consider manageable for ecosystems and societies—as possible, primarily through large-scale reductions in fossil fuel production and consumption. Joining the Paris Accords marked the end of the United States' almost twenty-year absence from major international climate change policy.[8]

The United States had not always looked so recalcitrant. Following James Hansen's 1988 testimony to Congress that "the greenhouse effect is here," George H. W. Bush campaigned on climate policy and made the United States a signatory to the 1992 United Nations Framework Convention on Climate Change.[9] Yet five years later, when the Clinton administration needed congressional support to join the binding emissions targets set out in the Kyoto Protocol, lawmakers balked, leaving Clinton to reduce emissions via agency policies. By George W. Bush's presidency, U.S. energy independence—seen as domestic oil and gas production rather than investment in alternative energy sources—was the administration's priority. Bush never tried to ratify Kyoto or involve Congress in climate legislation, but he did speak openly about the reality and risks of climate change. His cabinet implemented a variety of emissions reduction programs, despite the generally pro-oil extraction position of his administration.[10]

The difficulty of ratifying international climate agreements or legislating domestic climate policy stemmed in part from a cultivated sense, particularly among Republican politicians, that climate science was uncertain and that climate policy would require "the most expensive attack on jobs and the economy" in U.S. history, as Senator Mitch McConnell put it in 1992.[11] The jobs line was a well-worn objection to industrial regulations. In ideal form, regulations demand that businesses internalize the social costs of production—such as pollution, dangerous products, or preventable worker injury—rather than pushing them onto individuals, governments, and ecologies. Environmental regulations, where the harms are often diffuse and not immediately visible, particularly in wealthy, majority white communities where political power concentrates, were easy to attack as needlessly cutting into wages and profits. Thus, despite the fact that the Clean Air Act alone prevents hundreds of thousands of deaths and trillions of dollars in health expenses each year, industry has fought such outcomes for decades by rhetorically aligning short-term elite profits with middle-class employment.[12]

Pushing antiregulatory policies was a good way to attract campaign funding and, during the Cold War and its immediate aftermath, was ideologically palatable to both parties. But since the New Deal, Republican politicians in particular have rallied around the idea that legislated requirements on businesses to reduce or pay for what their industry costs society was antithetical to "free enterprise" and inefficient, putting a damper on economic growth.[13] Ronald Reagan made clear how Republicans could be useful to industry; actions like his Executive Order 12291 allowed companies to avoid regulations set by the Clean

Air and Clean Water Acts by arguing that the need for near-term profit outweighed future mortality due to pollution or environmental damage.[14] Since Reagan, fossil fuel developers seeking fewer limitations or extractive access to federal lands saw Republicans as better antiregulatory allies than Democrats. After 1990, two-thirds of donations from companies, lobby groups, and individuals enriched by fossil fuels—notably the Kochs, ExxonMobil, and other companies—have funded Republican candidates.[15] Carbon wealth also financed think tanks like the Heartland and Competitive Enterprise Institutes, organizations that, among other activities, promoted disinformation about climate science.[16] In the case of Exxon (now ExxonMobil), funding disinformation was not curtailed by internal research warning company leaders about the risks of climate change as early as the 1970s.[17]

Policy briefs and white papers from Heartland, the American Petroleum Institute, and others helped harden the ideological line against regulation by associating environmental protections with a dangerous slide toward communist authoritarianism, a move that united several disparate constituencies of the Republican Party.[18] As a collective problem, climate change requires the kind of society-wide solutions branded as socialist by libertarian-leaning conservatives. For right-wing evangelical voters, who associated socialism with a collapsed separation between church and state, climate legislation was a step toward religious persecution. Some evangelicals also saw human dominion over nature as a doctrinal requirement; limiting fossil fuel extraction was thus an affront to godly behavior. For others, climate change was irrelevant, given Christ's imminent resurrection.[19] For career government workers, as Naomi Oreskes and Erik Conway have argued, a Cold War–inflected resistance to environmental regulation inclined some to downplay or dispute basic climate science, or fully deny the consensus linking greenhouse gas emissions to a dangerously altered climate system.[20] It certainly impeded the consensus necessary to make climate change regulations into law. By 2016, U.S. climate policy was, regardless of party, an issue addressed via executive orders and agency powers.

The simmering tendency in right-leaning circles to link climate policy with leftist radicalism also made for a ready Republican talking point when Obama took up the issue, both in Congress and via executive order. And climate policy had all the advantages of speaking against environmental regulations—particularly alluding to job losses due to coal or fracking rules—without alienating Republican hunters, anglers, or other recreational outdoorspeople, who did see a place for some conservation policy. As a result, the 2012 Republican Party platform broke with its 2008 position of taking "reasonable steps today to reduce any impact on the environment" in order to oppose any greenhouse gas regulation and critique climate models.[21] By the 2016 Republican primary, the candidates ranged from Rick Santorum's religiously inspired frank climate denial to Chris Christie's acknowledgment that climate change was real but did not require federal attention. Some, like Marco Rubio, changed their positions; once a proponent of solar energy in his home state of Florida, he argued that only maximal fossil fuel extraction would prevent the destruction of "our economy the way the left-wing government that we are under now wants to do."[22]

Trump offered no concrete energy or climate policy during the primaries. But his known beliefs—flirting with denial while championing fracking and coal—were hardly fringe. By the time Trump accepted the Republican nomination, the party wanted out of the Paris Accords and an end to Obama's "war on coal" and development restrictions on public lands. Climate legislation was "a triumph of extremism over common sense."[23] It was a list designed to appease fossil fuel interests. Yet during the 2016 campaign, concerned by Trump's lack of a clear energy policy and assuming a Clinton victory, the fossil fuel industry broke with tradition and gave the bulk of its presidential donations to the Democratic candidate.[24]

Industry fears proved misguided. Within weeks of his victory on November 8, Trump signaled a radical openness to not just increasing U.S. fossil fuel production and consumption but bringing industry advocates and leaders into his administration. He named Rex Tillerson, a past chief executive at ExxonMobil, as secretary of state. Former Texas governor Rick Perry led the Department of Energy (DoE), an agency he once vowed to eliminate. Scott Pruitt, who spent years attacking the EPA as Oklahoma's attorney general, accepted Trump's nomination to be its leader. And Ryan Zinke, a Republican representative from Montana who became Trump's secretary of the interior, had a history of promoting U.S. "energy dominance" particularly through fossil fuel production.[25] Trump made clear, even before taking the oath of office, that his campaign slogan of "Make America Great Again" would be powered by petroleum and coal.

## The Rollback Years

Within days of Trump's inauguration, all mentions of climate change had been removed from the White House website. Inside the building, the president's staff began a project that lasted until the final hours of Trump's single term: the diminution or elimination of environmental regulations. The commitment carried on through scandals, protests, impeachment, and the COVID-19 pandemic, eventually gutting or eliminating over one hundred environmental rules. Many had a direct impact on fossil fuel emissions. Others enabled the expansion of oil, gas, and coal extraction, particularly on public lands and in coastal waters. The Trump administration's changes were broad in scale, but continued the trend of enacting environmental policy without environmental legislation: Trump's rollbacks on air quality, water safety, land protections, fuel efficiency standards, and wildlife habitat were primary done by executive order and agency rules.

The administration's first year of environmental actions checked off the Republican wish list with marked effectiveness. As with judicial appointments and other areas where the administration worked competently, Perry, Pruitt, and Zinke had clear remits developed by conservative leaders and think tanks long before Trump's election. Environmental policy was also an arena where Trump could appease Republican politicians distressed by the administration's shambolic approach elsewhere. And, primed by the Tea Party's attacks on Obama climate policy almost a decade before, rolling back regulations played well with core Trump voters, if not with a majority of the public. On March 27, 2017, an executive order dismantled Obama's Clean Power Plan.[26] Trump approved the Keystone XL Pipeline—designed to haul oil from Alberta, Canada, to the Texas gulf, and which, following years of environmentalist pressure, Obama rejected shortly before leaving office—and increased permits for offshore oil exploration. Zinke recommended shrinking the Bear's Ears National Monument, a particularly controversial part of a larger move by the Department of the

Interior to lease public lands to extractive industry. This action opened up 12.8 million acres to oil and gas development alone.

In June, Trump announced that the United States would leave the Paris Accords, effective in November 2020, timing that essentially put the accords back on the presidential ballot. Senate Majority Leader Mitch McConnell called the move a "significant blow to the Obama administration's assault on domestic energy production and jobs."[27] And in November, the signature piece of Trump legislation—the Tax Cuts and Jobs Act—contained an authorization to sell oil and gas leases in the Arctic National Wildlife Refuge (ANWR), opening land that had been the site of almost four decades of political, and increasingly partisan, contest over drilling.

The impact of Trump's policies did not go unnoticed. Following the removal of climate change data from government websites and changes to agency function seen as overt political interference in research, scientists organized the March for Science, which occurred on Earth Day, 2017, and on subsequent Earth Days. Agencies saw high-profile resignations, including that of Michael Cox, a twenty-five-year veteran of the EPA, who quit via a letter that described Scott Pruitt mocking the agency's mandate and planning to dismantle EPA effectiveness, and called his questioning of the "basic science of climate change" corrosive, as "we are seeing the effects of climate change on the landscape right now."[28] Senate Minority Leader Chuck Schumer refused to work on Trump's oft-discussed infrastructure plans unless a bill included "policies and funding that help transition our country to a clean-energy economy and mitigate the risks the United States already faces from climate change."[29] And environmental groups filed lawsuits challenging changes to EPA and other agency rules.

Some of the political pressure and legal actions were effective. Early in Trump's administration, the Senate rejected a repeal of an Obama-era rule that reduced greenhouse gas emissions by restricting methane emissions at oil and gas facilities; Senators John McCain, Susan Collins, and Lindsey O. Graham joined the Democrats in voting nay. Most of Trump's defeats were in court, initially due to a shaky grasp of the Administrative Procedures Act. The DC Circuit overturned an EPA rule that had legalized the use of hydrofluorocarbons, a potent greenhouse gas once common in refrigeration. Other rulings were openly critical of the factual basis for policy changes. In 2018, Trump's Keystone XL pipeline authorization was blocked by U.S. district judge Brian Morris, who found the administration's rationale "simply discarded prior factual findings related to climate change."[30] Even Trump's early executive order to eliminate Obama's Clean Power Plan did not last his entire presidency; it was overturned by a federal appellate court a few days before he left office.

## Urgency and Protest

In the months surrounding the 2018 midterm elections, a wave of corruption allegations showed Trump's environmental appointees to be as good at undermining their own public standing as at eroding capacity within their agencies. Scott Pruitt tenured his resignation at the EPA in July 2018, after repeated ethics violations drew congressional attention. Rick Perry resigned his position that October, following his naming in the whistleblower complaint that would lead to Trump's first impeachment. Ryan Zinke resigned in December 2018, dogged by multiple investigations into inappropriate use of government funds and conflicts of interest.

The exit of Trump's core climate appointees was not the only reason environmental policy was part of public discussion in the lead-up to the midterms. California was in the midst of its most catastrophic fire season to date. Hurricanes Florence and Matthew caused billions in damages across the Southeast. Climate activism, building on the momentum of the Dakota Access Pipeline protests and outrage at Trump policy, was on the rise; the youth-led Sunrise Movement and other left-wing activists proved effective at backing Democratic candidates with progressive climate politics. And in October, the IPCC issued a forcibly urgent report, warning that unless global emissions met the most ambitious Paris Accord targets by 2030, the world would likely warm more than 1.5 degrees Celsius. Media coverage turned the report into a kind of global deadline, one requiring rapid and unprecedented changes to industrial economies. As Debra Roberts, an IPCC cochair, stated, the report was "a line in the sand and what it says to our species is that this is the moment and we must act now."[31]

Trump did not respond to the IPCC report beyond asking "Who drew it?"[32] Voters offered up a mixed response to its dire climate prediction, and to Trump policies—and corruption—in November 2018. Clean energy and regulatory state ballot initiatives lost in Arizona, Colorado, and Washington State, after fossil fuel companies spent millions on ads dismissive of the measures. But the Democrats, including a group of young candidates who campaigned on the need for sweeping climate action, retook control of the House. Using the Tea Party's tactic of creating new policy goals outside mainstream parties and publicly shaming politicians who failed to meet them, several hundred Sunrise Movement activists held a sit-in in House Majority Leader Nancy Pelosi's office shortly after the midterms, calling for the Democratic Party to renounce fossil fuel campaign donations. Joined by newly elected House member Alexandria Ocasio-Cortez of New York, the activists also called for a Green New Deal (GND). Unlike past Democratic climate policy, the GND argued explicitly that emissions-reducing climate policy was also job-producing employment policy. The sit-in moved the idea from its longtime home in left-wing think tank and academic circles to the nightly news.

For the Trump administration, losses in the midterms did not change the approach to climate policy. In 2019, the major environmental agencies were under new leadership—former coal lobbyist Andrew Wheeler at EPA, ex–oil lobbyist David Barnhardt at the Interior, and George W. Bush energy staffer Dan Brouillette at DoE—who carried on the deregulatory work of their predecessors. New polices included Trump ordering a 30 percent increase in logging on public lands; changes to conservation policy enabling more oil and gas extraction in Colorado, Idaho, Nevada, Oregon, Utah, Wyoming, and parts of California; rollbacks to offshore drilling safety rules; and executive orders consolidating presidential power to authorize oil and gas pipelines.[33] At the EPA, criminal enforcement of pollution violations hit a thirty-year low.[34] Federal agencies continued scrubbing references to climate change from their websites and press releases.[35] Under Secretary for Energy Mark W. Menezes even tried rebranding natural gas as "molecules of U.S. freedom" or "freedom gas."[36]

The Trump administration's obfuscation met increasingly ambitious, if legislatively doomed, climate proposals from Democrats. In

FIGURE 5. Sunrise Movement rally in support of Alexandria Ocasio-Cortez's proposed Green New Deal, 2018. Photo by Jim Lo Scalzo/Shutterstock.

early 2019, Ocasio-Cortez and Senator Edward J. Markey of Massachusetts kept up climate momentum by introducing House and Senate resolutions calling for a GND. Instead of treating climate change as a narrow environmental or energy policy issue, the Ocasio-Cortez and Markey resolution took the scale of the climate crisis as an opportunity to rethink the relationship between citizens and government. By emphasizing how "climate change, pollution, and environmental destruction have exacerbated systemic racial, regional, social, environmental, and economic injustices," the GND linked a zero-emission plan to a robust welfare state and employment programs.[37] The proposal met with a good deal of centrist Democratic skepticism and immediate Republican denunciations. Myron Ebell, director of the Center for Energy and Environment at the Competitive Enterprise Institute, named it the "green leap backwards."[38] Trump called it "unthinkable" and "unaffordable even in the best of times" in a speech meant to highlight his record of delivering on his energy-related campaign promises.[39]

It was a message that Trump also emphasized in his choice of foreign guests. In 2019, the White House hosted Australian prime minister

Scott Morrison, a noted coal booster, and Brazilian foreign minister Ernesto Araujo. In statements that echoed the talking points of U.S. fossil fuel lobbyists, Araujo defended the climate policies of his president, Jair Bolsonaro, by calling climate change a conspiracy and "a pretext for dictatorship" by the Left.[40] Both visitors were striking choices in a year featuring a massive international wave of climate protest. Beginning with small-scale Friday school walkouts led by Greta Thunberg, a sixteen-year-old Swedish activist, by fall the climate strikes encompassed millions of people in 150 countries, including in many U.S. cities and towns. Trump's response to the protests was to mock Thunberg on Twitter.

Trump's ridicule made for good media fracas but could not obscure the volatility of the climate. In the Midwest alone, 2019 saw devastating spring floods stretching from South Dakota to Michigan and costing $10.8 billion in damages. Thirteen other disasters, from fires to hailstorms and tornadoes, cost more than a billion dollars each. It was the fifth consecutive year that the United States experienced more than ten billion-dollar weather-related events, many of which could be tied to a warmed climate.[41] Nor could Twitter spats and campaign speeches realize Trump's promise to "bring our energy industry back." Despite EPA attempts to make burning coal cheaper by increasing legal pollution levels and subsidizing coal plants at the expense of consumers' electrical bills, coal demand continued to decline: in 2007, U.S. coal companies supplied more than a billion short tons, a number that fell to less than six hundred in 2019.[42] The cause was not regulation but the competitive prices of natural gas and renewable energy sources.

Coal was not the only part of the fossil fuel sector experiencing slowdowns in 2019. Hydraulic fracturing, or "fracking," the technology that enabled a massive petroleum boom during the Obama administration and Trump's first two years, had made the United States the largest oil-producing country in the world. The industry was buoyed by a pool of easy credit after the 2008 housing crisis but was consistently unprofitable. In 2019, investors began demanding returns. It was a prelude to 2020, when the COVID-19 pandemic reduced fuel consumption in an already glutted oil market. In April of that year, oil prices were negative, as companies struggled to pay to store their product. ExxonMobil alone had to write down $20 billion in natural gas investments.

## Out of Step

COVID-19, climate change, and the role of the government in supporting citizens harmed by both were all part of the 2020 campaign. In the Democratic primary, two years of activism and organizing around the GND pushed left and liberal candidates to embrace climate change polices more comprehensively than in any previous presidential election. Candidates were also more forthright about the inequities of climate change, tying their proposals to ideas of environmental justice in ways resonant even before the summer 2020 protests over the extrajudicial police killings of Black Americans. As Lauren Maunus, the Sunrise Movement's legislative and advocacy manager, explained, the policies of, base voters of, and donors to the Trump administration made the "inextricable tie between the GOP, fossil fuel profiteers, and white supremacy. Those who benefit from white supremacy and are trying to maintain it at all costs are those who have created the planetary crisis we are in today."[43]

The climate policies initially offered by Joseph Robinette Biden Jr. were comparatively moderate compared with those of competitors Bernie Sanders or Elizabeth Warren. But once he secured the Democratic nomination, Biden brought key aspects of a GND into his proposed $2 trillion plan to "build back better," which linked COVID recovery, infrastructure, job creation, and climate change policies. It was a marked change in Democratic messaging about the climate crisis, making it not an abstract issue external to politics or economics but one deeply linked with the prosperity and safety of individuals and communities.

Biden's plan showed both a change in mainstream economic thought—away from concern about inflation and deficits, and toward industrial policy and social spending—and a generational shift. The charge that environmental regulations were socialist, still voiced by many on the right, was less threatening to voters who came of age amid capitalist instability, from the 2008 financial crisis to rising student debt and income inequality. Young activists, according to Maunus, wanted a new relationship with the government, one leading with "bold and populist policies—along the lines of the Green New Deal—that match the scale of the crises we're facing."[44]

The desire for more robust climate action by voters under forty was, by the end of the Trump administration, not just a position of the Democratic Party or left-wing activists. In 2019, 67 percent of registered Republicans between the ages of eighteen and thirty-four described themselves as worried about climate change, an eighteen-point increase over five years.[45] While many evangelical congregations retained their hostility to environmental regulation along with their unwavering support of Trump, younger members also expressed more climate worry.[46] In response, some elected Republicans quietly began working on their own climate legislation in 2020. As House Minority Leader Kevin McCarthy put it, his party had to "actually do something different than we've done to date. For a 28-year-old, the environment is the No. 1 and No. 2 issue."[47]

It was a break, if a quiet one, with the president. In a year when a quarter of U.S. households reported job losses due to the COVID-19 pandemic, and 400,000 people died from the virus, Trump's campaign messaging painted climate policies as more of an imminent, existential threat. "At stake in this election is the survival of our nation," he stated. Democrats are "going to waste the money on the Green New Deal. You know what you'd get out of that? Nothing. Nothing except debt and death."[48]

It was not a winning message: Trump did not earn reelection. Amid the conspiracy theories and court cases Trump marshaled to try to hold office in late 2020 and early 2021, the EPA, the DoE, and the Interior held the deregulatory course. On January 6, the same day that Trump loyalists attempted an insurrection at the U.S. Capitol in protest of their candidate's defeat, the Department of the Interior rushed through a final piece of the Republican wish list: the sale of oil and gas leases in the ANWR.

The sale was supposed to demonstrate the importance of fossil fuel development to the nation, not just by supplying petroleum but in paying for some of the 2017 tax cuts. The anticipated payout would be almost a billion dollars. At auction, however, only half the lots sold, and for less than $15 million. No major oil company participated. Pressure from Indigenous Gwich'in activists on behalf of their homelands meant no large bank would finance ANWR exploration. Reluctance from the financial sector was also part of a growing, if still new, investor trend of moving assets out of fossil fuels, and not just fracked gas or coal. BlackRock, the world's largest asset management firm, was one of the most explicit in this; as CEO Larry Fink argued, climate change was both causing and necessitating "a significant reallocation of capital" away from carbon-emitting industry and into more sustainable alternatives.[49]

The sale, in many ways, was a fitting summation of Trump's climate change stance: hasty, unpopular, a policy relic from a different century, if one that delighted the Republican Party. It was emblematic of how out of sync Trump, and many in his party, had become. Where the urgency of climate change was concerned, organizations as different as BlackRock, Bank of America, the Sunrise Movement, and the Gwich'in Steering Committee had more in common with each other than with the president of the United States.

## Conclusion

The 2016 election might prove the last presidential contest where climate change was not a first-order concern. With the repeated crises experienced by Americans in 2020, from wildfires across the West, tropical storms and hurricanes in the South, and flood damage across the Midwest, the majority of Americans thought the federal government was not doing enough to address climate change.[50] Sixty-eight percent of Democratic voters considered the climate a "very important" issue, up twelve points from 2016.[51] For the first time, climate change was a featured debate question. Four years of Trump "didn't slow down the shift in the zeitgeist," longtime environmental activist and journalist Bill McKibben argued. "By the end of his term, far more people were concerned about climate change."[52]

Trump left office out of step with climate science, climate reality, markets, and public opinion. He also left a legacy of climate pollution: by 2035, up to 1.8 billion metric tons more of greenhouse gases will be in the atmosphere than if Obama's polices had stayed in effect, the equivalent of Germany's, Britain's, and Canada's annual emissions combined. Biden's election will lower this total but not erase it.[53] As emissions researcher Hannah Pitt explained, the rollback of Obama-era rules builds in excess pollution, since "cars purchased in that period will be less efficient and burn more fossil fuels than they would have otherwise. And those cars can stick around on the road for 10 or 12 years. And once those greenhouse gases are in the atmosphere, they trap heat for decades."[54] Leaving the Paris Accords further undermined the United States' status as a legitimate partner in international decarbonization efforts, despite a historically outsize role in global greenhouse gas pollution. Mostly, as McKibben put it, Trump cost time: "It delayed the transition to renewable energy by four years. And given that time is the thing we're shortest on, that is a huge, huge cost."[55]

Trump also reinforced climate disinterest, if not outright climate denial, in his party: despite increased urgency among young Republican voters, only 11 percent of registered party members indicated climate was a very important issue in 2020, down 4 points from 2016.[56] The fossil fuel industry still overwhelmingly donates to Republican candidates, showing a continued desire to reap short-term profits at the expense of long-term planetary livability.[57] Given the financial incentives and base voter support, climate seems likely to be another arena, like gun control or abortion, where the Republican Party is willing to flout public opinion for an electoral strategy dependent on gerrymandered districts, advantages in the Electoral College, and increasingly bald voter suppression.

Thus, while Trump's leadership cost the Republican Party its majorities in the House in 2018 and the Senate in 2020, the Democratic lead is slim. The Biden administration needs bipartisan support—or must eliminate the Senate filibuster—to pass the kind of enduring climate legislation that has eluded American presidents for thirty years, and make a coherent case to the American public that reduced carbon pollution is not antithetical to employment or a decent quality of life. Even then, climate policy may run into legal challenges, given the more than two hundred Trump-appointed federal judges filling seats from the district level to the Supreme Court. Justices Neil Gorsuch and Brett Kavanaugh, Trump's first two appointees to the high court, are not climate-change deniers but both take a narrow view of federal environmental regulatory power. Justice Amy Coney Barrett, meanwhile, refused to acknowledge the reality of climate change at her confirmation hearings.[58]

Biden began overturning Trump's executive orders on climate change on his first day as the forty-sixth president. How much he will push for legislative change, despite ongoing pressure from the Sunrise Movement and other activists, is an open question. And some of the Trumpian influence in American politics cannot be quickly signed away. Trump left a legacy of greenhouse gas pollution and an open question for the Republican Party, American citizens, and the globe: Will the few—the minority of a country that is itself a minority in the world—further impede effective climate policies? Or, more than thirty years after James Hansen explained the threats of a warmed planet to Congress, will U.S. politicians take up the difficult work of ensuring a just and livable future for the many?

# 11

# From Color-Blind to Black Lives Matter

## RACE, CLASS, AND POLITICS UNDER TRUMP

*Keeanga-Yamahtta Taylor*

On June 16, 2015, Donald Trump announced his run for president of the United States. In unsettling ways, the speech forecast his presidency: rambling, racist, and truculent. He claimed that "thousands" attended his announcement. He lamented that the United States doesn't win wars anymore. He described the country as a "dumping ground for everybody else's problems." And he infamously said of Mexico, "They're sending people that have lots of problems, and they're bringing those problems with us. They're bringing drugs. They're bringing crime. They're rapists." But it wasn't just Mexico that was the problem. Trump described the "it" as coming from "all over South and Latin America . . . from the Middle East."[1] The idea that the United States is victimized by foreigners, including undocumented immigrants, and the responding efforts to drive them out to "make America great again" formed a central tenet of Trump's political thought, a building block of "Trumpism."

Scarcely more than twenty-four hours later in Charleston, South Carolina, twenty-one-year-old Dylann Roof, a self-avowed white supremacist, walked into the Mother Bethel African Methodist Episcopal Church and shot to death nine Black parishioners during their Bible study. As the shots rang out, Roof declared, "I have to do it. You're raping our women and taking over the country. You have to go."[2] The invocation of rape, by Roof and Trump, was a graphic and brutal envisioning of white men as the feminized victims of rogue outsiders who have taken advantage of a flaccid state ill equipped for war, unable to protect its borders, soft on crime, and generally weak and unable to function effectively, the result being white Americans shoved from the security of their position in the social hierarchy, cast about, and unsure of what the future holds. The road to making America great again was one that would correct those malfunctions in American society. And according to Trump, during his quest for the office, only he could restore the United States to greatness. Inferred within this promise was his singular ability to return white men to a position of superiority.

Trump was not the catalyst for Roof's rampage at Mother Bethel, but throughout his term his xenophobia and racism would inspire and rationalize other rampages that expressed pent-up rage directed at those outsiders and other perceived threats to the nation. Trump, of course, denies his racism, incredulously claiming that he is the "least racist person in the world."[3] But that was news to the white supremacist fringe in the United States and globally that celebrated his rise to the presidency. Richard Spenser, an avowed racist, led other white racists in celebration of Trump's victory, chanting, "Hail Trump! Hail our people! Hail victory!"

A year into his presidency, Trump inquired in an internal meeting why the United States had to accept immigrants from Haiti, El Salvador, and African nations that he described as "shithole countries." He had said of Haitian immigrants that they "all have AIDS."[4] While decrying immigration from nations with dark-skinned individuals, Trump asked why the United States could not have more people coming from Norway. Tweeting in response to the controversy created by his comments, Trump wrote, "The Democrats seem intent on having people and drugs pour into our country from the Southern Border, risking thousands of lives in the process. It is my duty to protect the lives and safety of all Americans. We must build a Great Wall, think Merit and end Lottery & Chain. USA!"[5]

The manifesto of a white supremacist who shot and killed fifty people at two mosques in New Zealand in the spring of 2019 lauded Trump as a "symbol of renewed identity and common purpose."[6] Five months later, a white man walked into a Walmart in El Paso, Texas, and murdered twenty people, most of whom were Latinx, injuring dozens more. In his published manifesto, the killer did not praise Trump, but he used language similar to Trump's in describing Latinx people as "invaders."[7] The Trump administration worked to shift the focus toward the mental health of the killer and away from his espoused racism and xenophobia.

From the wall along the southern border of the United States, rationalized by his characterization of Mexicans as rapists and criminals, to his equivocation about how or whether to condemn Nazis and white nationalists who, in 2017, rampaged through Charlottesville, Virginia, resulting in the murder of antiracist activist Heather Heyer, Trump deflected questions about the existence of white supremacy as a dangerous phenomenon even as federal agencies have continued to describe it as a persisting and growing threat within the country.[8] Trump's rise to the top of the Republican Party, along with his noxious cocktail of racism, xenophobia, nationalism, and misogyny, has been branded by some as that of a political outlier whose presidency constituted a breach with existing political norms.[9] The notion of Trump as the consummate outsider had dual functions within the Republican Party: it validated Trump's claims of being outside the political establishment, and it allowed the Republican Party establishment, early on, to distance itself from Trump's antics. But for some time now, it has been impossible to argue that Trump is anything but at the center of the Republican Party. Its key leaders, with rare exception, are enthralled and exalted by the former president. The fascination may have little to do with his actual ideas, but instead reflects his popularity with the Republican base.

Mainstream appeals to racism from the president of the United States seem appalling, regressive, if not confusing in a country that professes a formal commitment to color-blind neutrality and equal rights for all. But Trump has been able to transform what was once politically poisonous into political gain. His willingness to break political norms to embrace racism and xenophobia authenticated his claims that he was not a politician but an outsider coming to "drain the swamp." In a crowded Republican field of elected officials, Trump could carve out his own audience on his own terms. His formula for success included casting racist screeds as hard truths, honest assessments freed from the chains of political correctness, in the service of restoring American power. It was a way of showcasing his authenticity and validating his claims that he was not a typical politician, that, in fact, he was not a politician at all. In 2015 while on the campaign trail, he claimed, "I'm not a politician, thank goodness. Politicians are all talk and no action."[10] Just days before the 2020 presidential election, Trump told voters in Omaha, Nebraska, "In 2016 . . . you elected an outsider as president who finally put America first. And if I don't sound like a typical Washington politician, it's because I'm not a politician."[11] Republicans who once reviled Trump, like South Carolina senator Lindsey Graham, became ardent supporters because Trump's formula ultimately worked.

Trump's formula may have been cast as outside the norms of even Republican politics, but the tenor and trajectory of conservative politics over the past generation would confirm Trump as in sync, not out of order. But this evolution is not only about Trump's political calculation or gamble but also about how the United States has changed. From Nixon through Reagan and George H. W. Bush, conservative politics pushed the bounds of racist innuendo, framed as color blindness, to contain institutional civil rights action, antiracist activist mobilizations, and, in the shadow of the civil rights movement, the power of the accusation of racism. In the post-civil-rights period, conservatives honed the art of powerful political metaphor, allusion, and subterfuge, even when it was clear what was being averted. Consider Reagan's "welfare queen" and even the "war on drugs" and eventually "super predators" as examples of the kind of thinly veiled misdirection that allowed for talking about race and policy without mentioning race.

These interventions were never only about the invective they activated; they were connected to a larger political project that intended to upend the social contract originally connected to the New Deal state and then its expansion with the Great Society state, while growing other powers of the state, including those of police and prisons. These were bare-knuckle efforts to sully the idea of the social contract as social welfare by painting it as "something for nothing" for undeserving Black women and their children. Beyond an attack on the American version of the welfare state that could also impact poor and working-class white people, these ideological attacks were intended to undermine popularized notions of "institutional racism" and its prescribed remedies, including affirmative action but also the social welfare state itself, which had been legitimized in the wake of the civil rights movement. The appeal of these arguments among the white public and the adaptation to them by the leading lights of the Democratic Party succeeded in undermining the idea of social welfare, including public services, as necessary in a society racked by many manifestations of inequality.

In 1996 when Democratic president Bill Clinton signed into law his signature welfare reform bill titled the Personal Responsibility and Work Opportunity Reconciliation Act, it marked the extent to which the ideological gears of American politics were in bipartisan hands. It marked the realization of a bipartisan political goal of ending welfare "as we knew it" and the triumph of the politics of "personal responsibility." These kinds of changes fulfilled certain political objectives but also narrowed the field upon which those kinds of opaque politics of resentment could be played. In other words, it would be difficult to continue to assail "welfare" when there was none or a very thin shadow of itself. It would be difficult to condemn "big government" when it had been shrunk to its bare necessities. These well-honed ideological interventions would become even more abstract as government grew to feed the post–September 11 wars and the evolving criminal justice system. But when the economy collapsed as part of an international financial crisis in 2008, that space upon which blaming the poor for their condition shrunk further as the freefall of the economy was blamed on the reckless and corrupt activities permeating the world of finance and real estate. From Bush's Middle Eastern wars to the disastrous incompetence of the federal response to Hurricane Katrina to the feckless response to the newest catastrophe, now in the form of financial crisis, the long neglect of a federal safety net and the impaired state of the federal government opened new possibilities for the resurrection of an expanded social welfare state.

The ideological break with conservatism as representative of a kind of Washington consensus and the emergence of Obama liberalism in the 2008 presidential election represented among a portion of the electorate the desire for a different set of explanations for the condition of the country, one that went beyond the conservative framing that had dominated mainstream American politics for four decades. But the shortcomings of Obama liberalism combined with a racist backlash in reaction to his presidency undermined notions of the possibility of incremental progressive change by way of electoral politics, opening up the door to two different alternatives. One was the return of conservative politics but on different terms than had been established in the 1980s and afterward. The successes of the political Right in undermining the social welfare state, while ingratiating big government with robust military spending and the growth of the criminal justice system, meant that scapegoating the poor for the problems in the country had less resonance. This was especially true because of a relatively new dynamic created by the perceived limitations or failures of liberalism: the emergence of Black Lives Matter (BLM). Not only did this new movement serve to challenge long-held, lightly challenged assumptions about Black life in the United States. It also sharpened the political polarization in the country when many of its organizers and organizations made political demands that challenged basic presumptions about contemporary governance: anathema to government investment in social welfare and more broadly the public sector and the reverence of law enforcement and the larger criminal justice system.

Between Occupy Wall Street and Black Lives Matter, both of which grew from disillusionment with the Obama administration, a new Left emerged, creating new pressures not only on liberalism but also on the Right to more sharply rebuke new demands for expanding government after years of neglect. Moreover, the fresh wave of financial crisis and the showcased role of banks and big business at its core created risks in rolling out the old, banal scripts blaming welfare, especially when it had been gnawed down to the bone. A space beyond the color-blind innuendo of the post-civil-rights era emerged for more direct and racist attacks on entire groups of people, cultures, and religion as a way for the Right to more clearly distinguish itself. This was not necessarily in reaction to these new movements, but developed in reaction to the Obama presidency, which became a dress rehearsal for a later brand of Trumpism. Indeed, Trump made his leap into national politics by questioning Obama's citizenship and thus his qualifications for the presidency. Republicans impugned Obama's politics and religion with claims that he was a Muslim socialist, but ultimately those efforts failed when he was elected president. New pathways were opened for more virulent and direct racism that Trump would ultimately deliver. Meanwhile, Black activists mobilized in response to a perception of deepening racism evidenced by publicized incidents of police brutality, deep disparities in engagement with the criminal justice system, and long-standing patterns of racial inequality in housing, education, employment, debt accumulation, and all other quarters of American life. Policing and the excesses of the criminal justice system were an entry point into a much larger critique of systemic inequalities that made poor and working-class African Americans increasingly vulnerable to encounters with the police. The BLM analysis linking abusive policing to other patterns of inequality is the context within which we can understand the emergence of "defund the police" as a popular slogan and movement demand. Though the demand was not widely embraced and was deemed as generally alienating, it marked the ways that the failure to successfully respond to the issues of police brutality had the potential to unravel Democratic Party loyalties. It also showed how liberalism's concessions to the Right did not mean a lessening impact of conservatism in mainstream politics; instead, they opened the space for sharper polarization as the Right was encouraged and the Left became more cynical and alienated from the electoral arena.

This chapter examines how Trump's ascendance was rooted in the popularity and dominance of conservative politics in the mainstream in the aftermath of the Black movement in the 1960s. The particular brand of Trump conservatism was a departure from earlier iterations that relied on subterfuge and elusive coded racism infamously described by Republican strategist Lee Atwater.[12] The success of those methods seemed to have run its course, opening up new possibilities for an escalation in tactics, as Trump's eventual victory appeared to validate. But I also wish to examine the ways that the successes of the Right and its destabilization of Democratic Party liberalism also laid a foundation for the reemergence of a new Left embodied by the rise of Occupy Wall

Street, Black Lives Matter, and Bernie Sanders's successive presidential campaigns. The rising fortunes of both the Right and the Left underlie a deepening political polarization that finally unraveled in the explosion of riots and rebellions in the summer of 2020.

## The End of Racism

When Richard Nixon accepted the Republican Party's nomination for the presidency in Miami in 1968, he pledged that he could unite a country that was unraveling. He would do so as the mouthpiece for the "quiet voice," amid "the tumult and the shouting. It is the voice of the great majority of Americans, the forgotten Americans—the non-shouters, the non-demonstrators. They are not racists or sick; they are not guilty of the crime that plagues the land. They are Black and they are white, they're native born and foreign born, they're young and they're old. . . . They are good people, they are decent people; they work, and they save, and they pay their taxes, and they care."[13]

In his quest for the presidency, Nixon argued not only that reestablishing order in the tumultuous streets of the United States required a new respect for the office of the presidency and the laws of the country, both of which had been targets of relentless protest throughout the decade, but also that a renewed commitment to stability also required a different approach to governing. Nixon called for a new approach:

> Just as we cannot have progress without order, we cannot have order without progress, and so, as we commit to order tonight, let us commit to progress. . . . And this brings me to the clearest choice among the great issues of this campaign. For the past five years we have been deluged by government programs for the unemployed, programs for the cities, programs for the poor. And we have reaped from these programs an ugly harvest of frustration, violence and failure across the land. And now our opponents will be offering more of the same—more billions for government jobs, government housing, government welfare. I say it is time to quit pouring billions of dollars into programs that have failed in the United States of America. To put it bluntly, we are on the wrong road—and it's

> time to take a new road, to progress. America is a great nation today not because of what government did for people but because of what people did for themselves over a hundred-ninety years in this country.[14]

Nixon did not, in one fell swoop, dismantle Lyndon Johnson's Great Society, but his administration helped crack the ideological underpinnings that sustained it. The Nixon administration was a pivotal one between the high liberalism of Johnson and the conservative consolidation offered by the Reagan administration in the 1980s.[15] On the way to the Reagan Revolution, Nixon's policies and public speech helped establish color blindness as the new status quo in public policy. When discussing low-income housing, Nixon vowed that his administration would fight "outright racism," but that without the smoking gun of racism the government was limited in its ability to act. In this post-civil-rights era, this simply meant that evading the language of race was good enough to evade the charge of racism. Nixon was speaking narrowly of housing and busing, but his administration was creating a new script to circumvent the host of new civil rights protections created as a result of the civil rights movement and Black insurgency.[16]

Attenuating federal power also motivated Nixon's turn to what he described as "new federalism," where decision-making power over the distribution of social welfare funds and the placement of low-income housing could be devolved to state and local authorities. In a televised speech about the meaning of new federalism, Nixon argued, "Nowhere has the failure of government been more tragically apparent than in efforts to help the poor, and especially in its system of public welfare."[17] This overhaul was mainly framed as a reform of Johnson's War on Poverty in an effort to make "government more effective as well as more efficient and to bring an end to its chronic failure to deliver the services that it promises."[18] While this approach to governance could tap into "common sense" intuition that those closest to the problems would be best equipped to deal with them, it ignored the local movements of African Americans demanding federal intervention because of the ways that racial discrimination had been ignored by local officials.

The Nixon pretext for new federalism was not only that federal "bureaucrats" were out of touch but also that federal programs were bloated and ineffective, while local officials were touted as having superior insight into local problems and were thus more capable and efficient with taxpayers' money. In his speech introducing the concept of new federalism, he tied it to a need to revamp the country's welfare state. In doing so, he crafted racialized and gendered characterizations of welfare recipients that would take hold for a generation. Nixon described welfare as a "quagmire" that "often penalizes work. It robs recipients of dignity." Historian Julilly Kohler-Hausmann has argued about the 1970s, "Welfare became a terrain to articulate a host of frustrations, particularly about hard economic times and changing racial, gender and sexual relations."[19]

Thin appropriations for social welfare could be rationalized in the downwardly mobile economy of the 1970s. Dim financial horizons mapped onto the politics of blame that not only described poor and working-class African Americans as undeserving but saw them as responsible for the deteriorating conditions in cities; they were both cause and effect. The persistence of poverty in the aftermath of federal interventions that had been framed as particularly geared toward African Americans, combined with high-profile scandals in the distribution of social welfare dollars, helped to mar assistance programs along with the people who relied on them.[20]

Ronald Reagan, a former governor of California, thrived on these politics of blame and resentment and mobilized them during his successful run for the U.S. presidency in 1980. Reagan pinned the hopes of "Let's Make America Great Again," his campaign slogan, on reaching back to the prelapsarian period before the Black insurgency and Left renewal of the 1960s. Building on the foundation laid by Nixon, Reagan castigated social welfare spending and its recipients, linking American greatness to moralistic self-sufficiency and the glorification of free market capitalism. Rejecting social-scientific interventions that linked poverty and social marginalization to crime rates, Reagan echoed Nixon's calls for law and order alongside the retrenchment of the American welfare state. These were seen as mutually reinforcing: liberals' emphasis on "root causes" amounted to excuses for bad behavior, resulting in a socially permissive atmosphere that created the conditions for crime to flourish. In a wide-ranging speech made to police chiefs, nearly nine months after his inauguration as president, Reagan connected his critique of government largesse to a social permissiveness that encouraged crime, arguing that

> a tendency to downplay the permanent moral values has helped make crime the enormous problem that it is today, one that this administration has, as I've told you, made one of its top domestic priorities. But it has occurred to me that the root causes of our other major domestic problem, the growth of government and the decay of the economy, can be traced to many of the same sources of the crime problem. This is because the same utopian presumptions about human nature that hinder the swift administration of justice have also helped fuel the expansion of government. Many of the social thinkers of the 1950s and '60s who discussed crime only in the context of disadvantaged childhoods and poverty-stricken neighborhoods were the same people who thought that massive government spending could wipe away our social ills. The underlying premise in both cases was a belief that there was nothing permanent or absolute about any man's nature, that he was a product of his material environment, and that by changing that environment—with government as the chief vehicle of change through educational, health, housing and other programs—we could permanently change man and usher in a great new era.
>
> Well, we've learned the price of too much government: runaway inflation, soaring unemployment, impossible interest rates. We've learned that federal subsidies and government bureaucrats not only fail to solve social problems but frequently make them worse. It's time, too, that we acknowledge the solution to the crime problem will not be found in the social worker's files, the psychiatrist's notes or the bureaucrat's budgets. It's a problem of the human heart, and it's there we must look for the answer. We can begin by acknowledging some of those permanent things, those absolute truths I mentioned before. Two of those truths are that men are basically good but prone to evil, and society has a right to be protected from them.[21]

Reagan matched his rhetoric with acute political action, as his first budget voted on in 1981 knocked more than 400,000 families off the welfare rolls while reducing the benefits of 258,000 families. Nearly one million families were kicked off food stamps, and more than a million had their benefits reduced.[22] And Reagan was just getting started. Eventually he would cut taxes by about 30 percent across the board. This combined with regulatory rollbacks marked a stark transition in American economic policy and approach.[23]

Reagan's political success provoked imitation. Casting about as their electoral fortunes continued to diminish, the leadership of the Democratic Party began adapting to the prevailing antiwelfare and pro–criminal justice system and policing logics. Senator Joe Biden of Delaware led Democratic Party efforts in criminal justice and welfare reform. He cosponsored three bills that were key pieces of the architecture that came to be known as "mass incarceration." Biden teamed up with former segregationist and Republican senator Strom Thurmond to write the Comprehensive Crime Control Act of 1984, which introduced mandatory minimum sentencing for drug offenses and curtailed access to bail, among many other things. Biden is more well known for cosponsoring the 1994 crime bill, which expanded the death penalty and pledged millions of dollars to put more police on the streets.[24] As was the hallmark of postwar conservative politics, expanding the reach of law enforcement accompanied attacks on the welfare state. In a 1988 column for *The Post* of Newark, Delaware, titled "Welfare System about to Change," Senator Biden, echoing Nixon and Reagan, wrote, "We are all too familiar with the stories of welfare mothers driving luxury cars and leading lifestyles that mirror the rich and famous. Whether they are exaggerated or not, these stories underlie a broad social concern that the welfare system has broken down—that it only parcels out welfare checks and does nothing to help the poor find productive jobs."[25] This pull to the right in Democratic politics continued through the 1990s, perhaps culminating with Bill Clinton enacting welfare reform in 1996, ending welfare as an entitlement to poor families in the United States.

## The End of Color Blindness

The effects of the forty-year war on welfare bolstered by clamors for law and order included a massive redistribution of wealth, the erosion of safety nets for the poor, and an expansion of the criminal justice system.

Typically, these conditions remain hidden from the general public even as they cause enormous pain in the communities in which they are concentrated. But two events sharply focused the nation's attention on the multiplying manifestations of inequality in the country: the perpetual war and occupation in Iraq and Afghanistan, respectively, which helped train the public's attention on the enormous costs of those military actions in contrast to much slimmer budgets at home. Nearly a year after a contentious presidential election in 2004 pitting John Kerry against President George W. Bush, Hurricane Katrina dramatically unearthed poverty in the United States. It was mostly poor and working-class African Americans from New Orleans and elsewhere across the Gulf Coast who suffered its consequences, and the underwhelming response of the federal government was clear for all to see. As was the enormous poverty in New Orleans that was an obstacle to the evacuation of the city. As the Black actor Danny Glover said of Katrina, "[It] did not turn the region into a Third World country. . . . It revealed one."[26]

Even as the old tropes about culture and irresponsibility shrouded the discussion about Katrina, when the financial crisis of 2008 led to the greatest global economic calamity since the Great Depression, the propensity to blame individuals, including Black individuals, for their own hardship was increasingly difficult to rationalize. Within this context, Barack Obama's presidential campaign constituted a revival of Democratic Party liberalism, but mostly in terms of its rhetoric and orchestrated optimism rather than a substantive shift in public policy making. There were important differences between the Obama administration and the bipartisan conservative frameworks that came before it. This was most clear in Obama's commitment to extricate the United States from its Iraq War while drawing down its troops in Afghanistan. In domestic politics, Obama's Affordable Care Act was evidence that Democrats might have been regaining their stomach for big-government policies. But the deep erosion in the social welfare state over the previous thirty years was exposed and strained beyond its capacity as a result of the catastrophic fallout from the 2008 financial crisis. In real terms, it meant that the federal government had very few resources to offer families in the face of crisis. This was most pronounced when it came to the foreclosure crisis spawned by the financial collapse. By the end, more than 240,000 Black families lost their homes to foreclosure, which had devastating and lasting impacts on the wealth inequality separating African Americans from their white peers.

These structural deficiencies exposed by a historic financial crisis prompted the Occupy Wall Street movement in 2011, which captured the imagination of the country with the slogan "We are the 99 percent!" The movement highlighted how widening class inequality was not created by lazy poor people but was the result of the reckless, fraudulent, and corrupt practices running unchecked on Wall Street. Occupy helped resuscitate the street protests that had become popular with the emergent antiglobalization movement in the late 1990s but had ultimately been sidelined by the events of September 11. It sharpened the focus on systemic crisis, pivoting away from the fixation of the political class on the behavior and morality of the poor and the working class.

The same was true, in a different way, with the publication of legal scholar Michelle Alexander's book *The New Jim Crow: Mass Incarceration in the Age of Colorblindness*, which also drew the public's attention to the systemic factors fueling young Black men's disproportionate arrests and incarceration. These were issues that Black communities were long aware of, but Alexander's book helped pierce the wall of segregation that typically shrouds the ways that racism impacts Black communities. The increasing popularity of social media platforms combined with the growing use of cell phone video cameras to capture police brutality—and worse—in real time. The filmed murder of Oscar Grant in 2009 in Oakland inaugurated this new era of filmed encounters with police. As Elizabeth Hinton has argued, the videos provided "proof" to a broader white public that police brutality went beyond bad apples.[27] The growing publicity surrounding police brutality as well as the disproportionate effects of the financial crisis in Black communities, evidenced by historically high unemployment rates, growing poverty rates, and a crisis of foreclosures, helped establish the structural dimensions of racial inequality.

## Black Lives Matter

The social movement Black Lives Matter grew out of this ferment of glaring social inequality buttressed by police brutality. Perhaps the most consequential factor, though, was the deep disappointment that came with the shortcomings or failure of the Obama administration to address the crises afflicting Black communities. Instead, by 2012, in the heat of his bid for reelection, Obama insisted that he was not the president of Black America.[28] Given the historic mobilization of Black America to elect Obama president, there was an expectation among African Americans that Obama would pursue policies that could effectively attend to the particular crises impacting them. By 2012, Black unemployment had fallen to 13.9 percent from a high of 15.9 percent in 2011, but it was still more than twice the rate of unemployment among white people.[29] Obama's pronouncement came mere months after young Black people had mobilized to demand the arrest of George Zimmerman for the death of Trayvon Martin in Florida. Nearly two years after Obama's statement disavowing any particular commitment to Black Americans, the suburb of Ferguson, Missouri, boiled over after a white police officer killed a young and unarmed Black man, eighteen-year-old Michael Brown Jr. The killing of Brown along with the publicized deaths of other young Black people in the fall of 2014 helped mobilize the largest and most prolonged Black protests in more than a generation.

Obama had been responsive to protesters and their demands for changes to policing. He convened a task force on policing that included the participation of activists. But by the spring of 2015, when an initial draft of the report was released, the pace of police killings had hardly abated. Almost one month after the report was published, on April 4, video of a Black man being shot to death by a white cop as he ran away in North Charleston, South Carolina, emerged. The murder of Walter Scott took the wind out of any perception that progress was being made.

And then three weeks later to the day, a Black rebellion exploded in Baltimore, fewer than fifty miles from the White House, where the nation's first Black president resided. This uprising signaled not only tragic continuities but also bewildering political changes. The impotence of Black elected officials in containing the rise of Black Lives Matter pointed to deep disillusionment among young African Americans with formal politics in addressing the array of problems affecting Black communities. If the uprising in Baltimore was evidence of disillusionment with mainstream politics on the left, then Dylann Roof's vicious murder of nine Black parishioners was proof of the same phenomenon on the right.

Black Lives Matter was more than just protests. It marked the emergence of a new Black Left led by such groups as the Dream Defenders, Black Youth Project, #BlackLivesMatter, and eventually the Movement for Black Lives. The protests had highlighted not only abusive and deadly policing but also the ways that poverty and inequality made Black people vulnerable to encounters with the police. It was not enough to address policing; the larger conditions that exposed African Americans to the police had to be addressed as well. By the fall of 2016, just as the presidential race was building, the Movement for Black Lives released a wide-ranging policy platform built around the concept of "divest-invest." While "defund the police" was popularized through the 2020 uprising, the idea is an old one, stretching back even to the Black Panther Party's Ten Point Program, which called for an end to police brutality, a release of political prisoners, and an investment in jobs and housing in Black communities. The 2016 document described the divest-invest model as a demand for "investments in the education, health and safety of Black people, instead of investments in the criminalizing, caging, and harming of Black people. We want investments in Black communities, determined by Black communities, and divestment from exploitative forces including prisons, fossil fuels, police, surveillance and exploitative corporations."[30]

Black protests and demands came into sharp conflict with the forty-year consensus on small government interventions with an underlying hostility to poor and working-class Black communities. They introduced new pressures to the Democratic Party and its establishment presidential candidate Hillary Clinton. Moreover, the dynamics introduced by the Occupy movement had not gone away but intensified as economic inequality continued to reach historic levels. From almost out of nowhere a democratic-socialist Vermont senator, Bernie Sanders, captured the imagination of young voters in the Democratic primary, where he posed a surprising challenge to Clinton's assumed nomination. The relentless pace of events through the summer of 2016 made it impossible for Clinton to pivot away from the narrowing focus on police abuse and violence, topics on which she was politically vulnerable. Within the first seven days of July a spate of shootings would leave the country on edge. On July 6, Philando Castile was shot and killed by police outside Saint Paul, Minnesota, while in a car with his girlfriend and her four-year-old daughter. The next day, Alton Sterling, who was unarmed, was shot and killed by police in Baton Rouge, Louisiana, reigniting dramatic street protests and confrontations with the police. On the evening of July 7, in Dallas, Texas, five police officers were killed and twelve were injured by a Black Army Reserve veteran, Micah Xavier Johnson, who was reported to be angry about white police killing Black men.[31] More critically for Clinton, her shared history with Bill Clinton as champions of law-and-order politics made her a target of BLM activists. In 1996, the same year Bill Clinton ended welfare as an entitlement, Hillary Clinton had described some young people as "super predators," as a particular variety of super criminals. While she did not describe them as Black, she didn't have to. In response to the surprising pressure exerted by the Sanders campaign and the unrelenting skepticism of Black activists, Clinton broke new ground for mainstream Democratic Party politicians. In February 2016 she said,

> Ending systemic racism requires contributions from all of us—especially those of us who haven't experienced it ourselves. White Americans need to do a better job of listening when African Americans talk about the seen and unseen barriers that you face every day. . . . We need to recognize our privilege and practice humility, rather than assume that our experiences are everyone's experiences. . . . If we're serious about our commitment to the poor, to those who need some help, including African Americans, if we continue to ask Black people to vote for us, we cannot minimize the realities of the lives they lead or take their concerns for granted.[32]

It was a long way from the race baiting with law-and-order rhetoric but also from the demonization of poverty that allowed for the dismantling of the social welfare state.

## Trumpism

As Democrats were pushed to move uncomfortably to the left, Republicans felt the need to distinguish themselves and their program. They were in their own disarray with the rising popularity of Obama in the political mainstream and with a crowded field of candidates who seemed driven by antics and sideshows rather than serious politics. Republican talking points were stale and lacked resonance in the new realities created by the 2008 financial crisis. In 2014, Wisconsin representative and former Speaker of the House, Republican Paul Ryan, appeared on a program hosted by the archconservative William Bennett and said that there was a "tailspin of culture, in our inner cities in particular, of men not working and just generations of men not even thinking about working or learning the value and the culture of work." A generation earlier, this would have been a banal and bipartisan observation. But in the age of Black Lives Matter, this was political dynamite and Ryan had to walk it back. He clarified, "After reading the transcript of yesterday morning's interview, it is clear that I was inarticulate about the point I was trying to make."[33]

The growing Black Lives Matter movement and the continuation of police abuse pushed both the mainstream media and Democratic political figures to engage with the "root causes" that Reagan had denounced earlier. It forced the Democratic Party to shift its political message, and it even complicated the political terrain for Republicans. The Left-led social movements and the popularity of Bernie Sanders raised questions about systemic inequality across the board, making attacks on the welfare state seem inconsequential given its minimal imprint in society, especially as banks and other corporate titans were beneficiaries of generous government bailouts.

Trump stepped into this political void with xenophobic attacks on those perceived as outsiders whether they were Black or brown immigrants or descendants of them. He promised to exclude Muslims from entry into the United States. When accepting the Republican Party's nomination as its candidate for president, he painted a bleak picture of American life. He blamed the political establishment, Muslim and Mexican immigrants, and protests against police brutality, which he dismissed as a crime. He said,

> Together, we will lead our party back to the White House, and we will lead our country back to safety, prosperity and peace. We will be a country of generosity and warmth. But we will also be a country of law and order. Our convention occurs at a moment of

> crisis for our nation. The attacks on our police, and the terrorism in our cities, threaten our very way of life. It is finally time for a straightforward assessment of the state of our nation.
>
> I will present the facts plainly and honestly. We cannot afford to be so politically correct anymore. So if you want to hear the corporate spin, the carefully crafted lies and the media myths, the Democrats are holding their convention next week. My plan will begin with safety at home—which means safe neighborhoods, secure borders and protection from terrorism. There can be no prosperity without law and order. On the economy, I will outline reforms to add millions of new jobs and trillions in new wealth that can be used to rebuild America.[34]

Trump posed as a populist also assailing job loss and poverty, and identifying with ordinary people whose jobs had been sacrificed in the global economy. He didn't attack rapacious capitalism, but he did attack immigrants and politicians sympathetic to them as the main problem in the United States. Trump even made appeals to African Americans to join his crusade against the outsiders who would destroy our way of life:

> Every action I take, I will ask myself: Does this make life better for young Americans in Baltimore, Chicago, Detroit, Ferguson, who have as much of a right to live out their dreams as any other child in America? To make life safe in America, we must also address the growing threats we face from outside America: We are going to defeat the barbarians of ISIS.

This along with more traditional promises to create jobs and rebuild infrastructure marked Trump's unconventional route into mainstream electoral politics. But his unfiltered racist characterization of Muslims and immigrants created the aura of authenticity and a rejection of "political correctness" when contrasted with the careful curation of most presidential campaigns. Even as Hillary Clinton was forced to pivot left and make statements against "systemic racism," Trump could dismiss it all as political spin from an elected official willing to say anything for votes. In the end, Trump did not need Black supporters more than he needed Black people to stay home on election day. If Clinton represented Obama's third term, then what did it mean that Black turnout fell to a twenty-year low for a presidential election? Donald Trump shocked the world and won the presidency in the 2016 election.

## Conclusion

As president, Trump acted on the reactionary tone of a historic campaign. Within days of his inauguration, he signed an executive order banning Muslims from seven countries entry into the United States.[35] On his fifth day in office he ordered the construction of his "big, beautiful wall" to be built along the southern border of the country.[36] Eventually he would successfully implement draconian and cruel policies along the border that encouraged the separation of families and their placement in detention camps. Within the United States, Trump's election unleashed a wave of dangerous hate crimes. The aftermath of his election was accompanied by a large spike in hate crimes, second only to the aftermath of the September 11 attacks.[37] Hate crimes against Latinx people and Jews or Jewish institutions rose between 2018 and 2019. African Americans remained the most likely to be targeted by hate crimes. In 2017, anti-Black hate crimes were among the most common in the ten largest American cities.[38] Trump's casual insertion of a racial epithet or thinly coded racism—as when he described in tweets Congressman Elijah Cummings's district in Baltimore as a "very dangerous [and] filthy place . . . a disgusting, rat and rodent infested mess"[39]—revealed the hollow core of "color blindness" in Republican politics. But beyond rhetoric, when the novel coronavirus pandemic swept the United States, the material consequences of deprivation and vulnerabilities created by decades of insufficient public policies and the practices of private enterprise were shown to be the real and lasting consequence of racial discrimination.

Trump's explicit race talk in combination with the effects of the pandemic would boil over when the recorded police murder of a Black man in Minneapolis, Minnesota, became public on Memorial Day in 2020. The killing of George Floyd touched off unprecedented protests against racism in the United States, leading to a resurgence of the BLM movement. The racism of the Trump administration left little doubt among African Americans that their complaints about police treatment would not be taken seriously on a federal level. This was even clearer as COVID-19 cut a path through Black communities where working from home was an impossibility for most and the cramped and crowded nature of poor and working-class life amplified the effects of the virus. The massive protests harked back to the late 1960s, a period of riots and rebellions, but also where new alignments within the Republican Party had become viable as the Democrats fractured over Vietnam and civil rights. But history doesn't repeat itself. These were new protests largely rising out of the catastrophic consequences of nearly five decades of denying the materiality of racial discrimination through the steady erosion of the infrastructure to oversee the implementation of civil rights legislation and the undoing of the social welfare state. While a robust Black middle class emerged during this time, a Black majority of ordinary people have felt stuck in place, dogged by debt, locked out of homeownership, and harassed by the police. Trump was certainly not the cause of any of this, but the lightly varnished racism of his administration laid bare the structures of Black inequality and pressured the political and financial establishments to denounce what they also described as "systemic racism." These developments reflect the ways political polarization clarifies that which is being fought over for both the political Left and Right.

# 12

# The Gilded Elevator

## TECH IN THE TIME OF TRUMP

*Margaret O'Mara*

On a crisp afternoon in mid-December 2016, the leaders of America's largest computer hardware and software companies stepped into the gilded and mirrored elevators of Trump Tower in Manhattan, ascending to its upper floors to meet the real estate developer and reality-television personality who had just been elected president.

It was a familiar transition-season tableau: chiefs of a key American industry, eager to press its case and maintain good political relationships, sitting down with an incoming president for a carefully choreographed conversation. But, as with much about the Trump enterprise, it wasn't clear how things were going to go. The new president-elect had spent much of the campaign bashing tech companies and their billionaire moguls as prime examples of the excess and hubris of the American liberal elite. A particular target was Amazon founder and CEO Jeff Bezos, who among his other offenses owned a flagship of what Trump scorned as "the Fake News Media," the *Washington Post*. "Believe me," Trump declared of Amazon and Bezos at one primary-season stop, "if I become president, oh do they have problems, they are going to have such problems."[1]

The feeling was mutual. The technology industry had enjoyed a stunning decade of growth, and the executives were among the wealthiest people in the world, used to glowing press coverage, starstruck political support, and generally getting what they wanted. After eight years of cozy relations with the Obama administration, what most of them had wanted in 2016 was another Democratic presidency: the industry's campaign donations and votes went overwhelmingly to Hillary Clinton, as they did in the regions where tech flourished. On Election Day 2016, over 70 percent of Silicon Valley voters chose Clinton over Trump. In San Francisco, nearly 85 percent voted for her; in Seattle, 87 percent.[2]

That December day, however, as journalists' camera shutters clicked and television cameras panned the power players—Bezos included—seated uneasily around the table, Trump cast aside his antitech stump speech and showered the group with praise. "This is a truly amazing group of people," he declared. "I'm here to help you folks do well." Trump might have delighted in roasting tech's billionaire class in public, but in truth he saw himself as one of them—an innovative, celebrity business leader—and he had little issue with their having accreted so much wealth and market power. "I was very proud of Google, Amazon, all of them," he remarked after leaving office, "even though they were not fans of mine."[3]

The executives were similarly polite. Candidate Trump's harsh stance on immigration had horrified tech leaders—some of whom were immigrants and refugees, and all whom ran companies heavily reliant on foreign-born talent—but it was mentioned only briefly. Conversation instead shifted to lowering corporate tax burdens, an issue beloved to business interests and especially to tech companies, which had proved themselves particularly adept at working the loopholes of the tax code in order to pay as little as possible. America's high-tech regions may have been some of the most Left leaning in the country, but the industry itself was built by Reaganomics, growing large in a four-decade era of tax cuts, deregulation, pro-employer labor laws, and a laissez-faire approach to antitrust enforcement.

These companies had long branded themselves as a nobler strain of capitalism, able to make money and do good at the same time. "Think different" was Apple's onetime slogan; "don't be evil" was Google's

FIGURE 6. One month after being elected, President-Elect Donald J. Trump and Vice President Elect Mike Pence met with leaders of large U.S. technology companies, including (*left to right*) Jeff Bezos of Amazon, Larry Page of Google, and Sheryl Sandberg of Facebook.

unofficial company motto. But the people in that conference room had become so stunningly successful in good part by playing the game pretty much like any other company might, and that included working cooperatively with the president, no matter who he might be. As Apple CEO Tim Cook explained, "The way that you influence these issues is to be in the arena." Plus, some reasoned, Trump might surprise them.[4]

The following four years indeed were full of surprises. By the end of Donald Trump's presidency, the group was known simply as "Big Tech": the biggest story in business, ubiquitous and inescapable, simultaneously glorified for their staggering business success and vilified as latter-day robber barons. Because of their market-gobbling business models and the fractious politics of Trump's America, these moguls and their companies faced stiff political headwinds from both the progressive Left and populist Right.

Yet, thanks to pro-corporate policies, frothy global markets, and a soaring demand for tech products and platforms that spiked further amid the pandemic ruination of 2020, Big Tech exited Trump's term richer and more entrenched in American life than ever. How and why the industry did so speaks to broader shifts in national politics and modern capitalism that preceded—and most likely will long outlast—the Trump era.

## The Rage Machine

Donald Trump's use of social media, and his relationship with the Silicon Valley companies behind these platforms, became a defining feature of his presidency. Just as presidents before him deftly employed new forms of media to amplify the power and persuasiveness of presidential communication—Franklin Roosevelt and radio, John Kennedy and television—Trump used social media to make an end-run around Washington's traditional policy-making processes and appeal directly to voters. But the design, speed, and scale of social media turned Trump's use of it into a political megaphone like no other.

Other parts of the media ecosystem (notably the robustly pro-Trump Fox News) played a critical role in amplifying White House talking points and solidifying Trump's relationship with his base. Yet the design and scope of social media platforms like Twitter, Facebook, and YouTube made them perfectly suited to do something their youthful, liberal-to-libertarian creators never expected: advance the message and momentum of Trump and Right-populist voices like him, even—and especially—those on the Trump movement's radical and sometimes violent fringe.

Timing was everything: Trump's campaign and presidency occurred in the wake of an extraordinary shift in the information ecosystem. In the early years of the twenty-first century, newspaper readership had declined precipitously and ad revenue that once had sustained print journalism drained away to online platforms. Local newspapers merged and folded by the hundreds, leaving vast swaths of the country without any local news source other than internet forums and social media sites. Cable news remained a primary source of political news for most Americans, but social media surged forward in ways it had not in earlier election cycles. In one survey early in 2016, over half of respondents reported that they learned about the election from a social media site; 37 percent got this news from Facebook.[5]

The political power of the internet's network effects had first grabbed headlines during the 2004 presidential run of Howard Dean. The former Vermont governor became an early Democratic front-runner by rallying supporters on one of the first social networking platforms, Meetup.com, and raising a record-setting $15 million in small-dollar donations in one quarter via online fund-raising. Dean's online triumphs failed to translate into primary victories, however, and he was out of the race by late February.[6]

But a seed had been planted. At the same time campaign staff were coding a "donate here" button into the Dean for President website, a Harvard freshman named Mark Zuckerberg was pulling all-nighters in his dorm room to build a network for fellow students he called thefacebook.com. By the spring of 2004, John Kerry was on his way to becoming the Democratic nominee and Zuckerberg's website had become the buzziest new thing on campus at Harvard and Stanford. The nineteen-year-old soon dropped out of school and moved to Silicon Valley.[7]

When Barack Obama launched his 2008 presidential bid, Facebook had been in business four years. Twitter, a microblogging site, less than two. Both were youthful and fast-growing hubs, known for college party photos and "what I had for breakfast" status updates rather than political organizing. Obama changed that, picking up where Dean left off to focus early and aggressively on internet fund-raising and voter mobilization through Facebook and other online platforms beloved by young voters. His campaign recruited one of the first members of Facebook's youthful founding team, Mark Zuckerberg's former college roommate Chris Hughes, to lead the effort.[8]

Obama's election victory that year, followed by his tech-heavy and successful reelection effort in 2012, was celebrated by campaign operatives and tech executives alike as proof that social media could make voters better informed and elections more democratic. While political advertising was only a tiny fraction of Facebook's revenue, the company had embraced its role as twenty-first-century electioneer by 2016, providing dedicated staff and resources to both the Trump and Clinton campaigns.

By 2016, the ad-based businesses of Facebook, Twitter, and YouTube had made great leaps in the scope and sophistication with which they gathered user data, and in deploying it to increase "engagement"—that is, the time users spent on a platform reading content and being exposed to tightly targeted ads. The sheer volume of content also was far greater than it had been a few years earlier, making it harder to capture and sustain users' attention, and making meaningful moderation by the platforms nearly impossible.[9]

The surest path to "engagement," it turned out, was *enragement*: tapping into users' fear, sense of outrage, and negative emotions in order to be heard in a crowded and already cacophonous online room. This was ideally suited to Trump, a candidate who had sucked in most of the attention of conventional media outlets through extreme rhetoric and disregard for typical political niceties. In his reality-television heyday, Trump had built an enormous Twitter following with his prolific and unfiltered posting on everything from the appearance of female celebrities to the shortcomings of Barack Obama as man and president. He continued this apace as a presidential candidate.[10]

The landscape was further upended by the reality that the usual rules governing political advertisements did not apply to ads on social media. Political advertising in print and on the regulated airwaves of television and radio had long been required by the Federal Election Commission (FEC) to include disclaimers about who paid for an ad and was responsible for its message. As political advertising spread to social media, Google and Facebook successfully petitioned the FEC in 2010 and 2011 for exemptions from disclaimer requirements, arguing that complying with such requirements would require fundamental product changes that would undermine other, much larger parts of their businesses.

As a result, by 2016 anyone—campaign, political action committee, or enterprising hackers from Macedonia—could buy social media ads in support of a particular candidate or issue without disclosing the ad's source. U.S. laws prohibiting foreigners from donating to or otherwise influencing American elections also proved hard to enforce on platforms that had been designed to, as Facebook's onetime motto declared, "make the world more open and connected." Yet advertising on these platforms was anything but open and was instead informed by the companies' spectacularly detailed (and closely held) troves of demographic data that allowed advertisers to tightly target messages to specific voters.[11]

Well before Election Day it was clear that the combination of scale, opacity, microtargeting, and possible exploitation by foreign actors had turned social media into a hotbed of overheated political speech and disinformation. In the wake of Trump's victory, furious Democrats and their allies immediately singled out the platforms as agents of destruction, allegations that tech executives immediately—and not so convincingly—denied. The notion that disinformation on Facebook influenced the election "is a pretty crazy idea," Mark Zuckerberg scoffed a few days after the election. "Voters make decisions based on their lived experience." Brad Parscale, who led Trump's digital campaign, had a different post-hoc assessment. "I understood early that Facebook was how Donald Trump was going to win," Parscale told CBS's *60 Minutes* in 2017. "It was the highway which his car drove on."[12]

## The Social Media President

Trump's victory in 2016 proved a turning point for the social media platforms and the other companies that dominated the consumer-facing internet. Academics had long been pointing out the dangers of an ad-based internet business model in which consumers were surrendering vast amounts of personal data in exchange for use of "free" software and services. But such warnings had been muted under a wave of largely uncritical media celebrations of software-industry innovation.

In the age of Trump, the tone of tech coverage markedly shifted. For the first time in their relatively young lives, companies like Google and Facebook were being treated by many journalists as if they were latter-day Standard Oils: predatory capitalists, relentless in their gobbling up of competition and deceptive in their treatment of customers, helmed by greedy billionaires who refused to see the damage their products had wrought. No longer rule-busting upstarts, large tech companies became shorthand for the excesses and inequities of modern capitalism.

Meanwhile, Donald Trump continued to take full advantage of social media's rage machine. Those who had hoped he might be tamed once in the Oval Office looked on with dismay as he became tweeter in chief, using his personal Twitter handle, @RealDonaldTrump, to issue a daily blizzard of tweets on matters of state, policy, and self-promotion. By November 2020, he had tweeted nearly twenty-four thousand times as president. Trump and his allies used Facebook just as intensively.[13]

Journalists, freshly tech-skeptical and both fascinated and alarmed by the president's deployment of social media, kept digging deeper into the workings of the tech platforms. Silicon Valley executive suites reeled from one public-relations crisis after another. In 2017, Google-owned YouTube came under fire for letting disturbingly violent videos slip past its filters into the feeds of videos recommended to very young children. In 2018, Facebook faced scandals around the role its platform played in inciting genocide in Myanmar, boosting the fortunes of dictatorial Philippines president Rodrigo Duterte, and continuing to divide and conquer the American electorate.[14]

In March 2018, news broke that Cambridge Analytica, a data firm bankrolled by Trump donors Robert and Rebekah Mercer and his adviser Steve Bannon, had improperly harvested Facebook user data to target voters with misleading advertising during the 2016 campaign. The resultant scandal dragged Mark Zuckerberg before a Senate committee, where his stilted performance was overshadowed by the seeming cluelessness of elderly lawmakers about how the internet economy actually worked. "How do you sustain a business model in which users don't pay for your service?" Utah Republican senator Orrin Hatch demanded of the thirty-three-year-old Facebook founder. "Senator, we run ads," Zuckerberg replied evenly.[15]

The political headwinds were not improved by the companies' efforts to moderate the content on its platforms. When Facebook attempted to push users to more authoritative news sources and crack down on extremism, conservative activists and Trump seized on its actions as censorship of right-wing views. Worried about alienating users and a Washington, DC, in which Republicans controlled the White House (and, until the 2018 midterms, both houses of Congress), tech executives held listening sessions with conservatives and staffed up their lobbying and corporate communications offices with savvy veterans of Republican politics.

Despite this, Trump and other Republicans continued to hurl accusations of anticonservative bias at the social media companies throughout the Trump years, further escalating during the 2020 campaign. That summer, Trump held a conference at the White House to which some of the biggest—and most outrageous—right-wing online personalities were invited. Later that fall, as Trump's reelection effort reached its crescendo, Senate Republicans led a messy, shouty hearing on social media in which Zuckerberg and other CEOs were called to account for alleged anticonservative bias. In reality, the enraging and engaging content delivered by conservative voices attracted some of the platforms' biggest audiences.

## Build the Wall

Another showdown between Trump and the technology industry resulted from the president's sharp turn away from U.S. policies that for five decades had aided the movement of people and capital across national borders. In contrast to the old-line manufacturing giants that had foundered in the modern era of economic globalization, Silicon Valley had thrived. Its semiconductor manufacturers were among the first U.S. companies to outsource production to the cheaper, high-skilled labor markets of East Asia in the 1960s; its workforce had been transformed and inestimably enriched by post-1965 immigration liberalization and skilled-worker visa programs. By 2020, Silicon Valley's tech workforce was more than 70 percent foreign-born. Seattle was nearly 40 percent; Boston and Washington, D.C., were both over 30 percent.[16]

Thus, the aggressive immigration and trade restrictions the Trump administration enacted from its first days in office were not only a moral affront but also a serious business threat to the tech industry. First came the "Muslim ban" on refugees from a series of majority-Muslim nations ordered by Trump one week after taking office, a move that unleashed a wave of unusually heated statements from Silicon Valley C-suites.[17]

Among the thousands flooding the terminals of American airports in protest of this extraordinary travel restriction was Google cofounder Sergey Brin, who had come to the United States from Russia at the age of six. This was personal, Brin admitted to a reporter who caught sight of him among the crowd at San Francisco International. "I'm here because I'm a refugee."[18]

Although activists aghast by Trump's move hoped that Silicon Valley moguls would bring their full influence to bear on the immigration issue, the sound and fury of their early statements had little bearing on the White House's anti-immigrant trajectory. It was lawyers and judges, not tech billionaires, who blunted the impact of some, but not all, of the Trump administration's most extreme measures.

A further layer of complexity came from the national security state's increasing reliance on these same companies for platforms and software to support the Trump administration's increasingly draconian immigration enforcement measures. One Silicon Valley company specializing from the start in delivering such services to national security agencies was the secretive and fast-growing Palantir, cofounded by Peter Thiel, a techno-libertarian iconoclast who had been one of the few Silicon Valley moguls to endorse Trump. These political ties made it perhaps unsurprising that Thiel's company would have large contracts with the U.S. Department of Homeland Security, the CIA, and other federal law enforcement and national security units, providing data analysis services that promised to aid these agencies in tasks such as tracking and deporting immigrants with criminal records.[19]

More discomfiting to activists and tech workers alike was the news that Microsoft and Amazon were also doing business with these agencies, even though the companies averred that they were simply providing support to core administrative functions, not directly aiding surveillance or enforcement. Indeed, providing such support for border enforcement agencies was now only one piece of a quickly widening market of government contracting for Silicon Valley companies.

But in dollar figures, such contracts were far outflanked by work these firms were doing—often with little public fanfare—for the Pentagon. It was in many respects a return to form for a region and industry that owed much of its existence to the military-industrial complex. By the start of the Trump years, national security work had become a significant book of business for tech's largest companies as the U.S. national security establishment embraced cloud computing platforms and sought Silicon Valley know-how for advanced weapons systems.

Many who worked in Silicon Valley had little inkling of this longer history, nor did they have any interest in being part of the new defense establishment, especially after Trump became the nation's commander in chief. This tension burst into the open in 2018, when Google employees discovered that their "don't be evil" employer was working with the Pentagon on an artificial-intelligence-enabled surveillance drone project, code-named Maven. Thousands signed an open letter to Sundar Pichai, Google CEO, an act of white-collar protest at a scale and visibility unprecedented in Silicon Valley history. "We believe that Google should not be in the business of war," the letter began, with almost charming naïveté about the company's roots in a graduate research project sponsored in part by the Pentagon's Defense Advanced Research Projects Agency. "Therefore we ask that Project Maven be cancelled and that Google draft, publicize and enforce a clear policy stating that neither Google nor its contractors will ever build warfare technology." The letter worked; Google cut its ties to the project and Pichai promised that the company would not bid on future work of its kind.[20]

Similar protests bubbled up at Microsoft and Amazon, but their CEOs were not as easily swayed. "If big tech companies are going to turn their back on the U.S. Department of Defense, this country is going to be in trouble," Jeff Bezos retorted. "This is a great country and it needs to be defended." What's more, the business had become too lucrative to give up.[21]

## Trade War

Tech was also at the center of another nationalist element of Trump's economic agenda: his trade war with China. Tariffs had long been a staple of U.S. trade and economic policy through the nineteenth century and into the twentieth, but Trump's enthusiastic embrace of them and bellicose rhetoric about Chinese competition felt like a throwback to a much earlier age. To tech executives and financiers, it also seemed to be operating largely in ignorance of how computer hardware and software industries actually worked.

By the time Trump arrived in the White House, five decades of experience in global markets had turned technology companies into some of the most sophisticated users of transnational labor and supply chains. Most of the blue-collar work of computer hardware manufacture had long been offshored to Asia, where it was outsourced to a web of contractors and subcontractors who sourced the raw materials, ran the factories, and employed the workers on the assembly line.

While tech companies had originally outsourced in search of cheaper labor, they now relied on overseas contractors for many phases of design and manufacture, as well as counted on non-U.S. customers as major buyers of their consumer and business products. The southern Chinese city of Shenzhen, first opened to foreign trade in 1979, had become a major hub of low-cost manufacturing and had turned into a major center of tech manufacturing and industrial design as well as becoming the hometown of Chinese internet giant Tencent and the hardware manufacturers ZTE and Huawei.

Apple had perfected the made-in-Shenzhen business model, something that for many years American buyers were reminded of as they opened a new iPhone or iPad and were greeted by the words "Designed by Apple in California. Assembled in China." Thus, when the Trump administration announced in May 2019 that it would impose up to a 25 percent tariff on Chinese-made laptops and smartphones, Apple suddenly faced a major threat to its exceedingly lucrative supply chain.

Joined by fellow hardware makers Microsoft and Intel, Apple asked the United States to make an exception. But, for a president who took nearly everything personally, the most powerful influence was the relationship Trump had forged with Tim Cook. With his even manner and southern accent, the Apple CEO stood out from the Silicon Valley crowd, and he had pleased the president when he called with congratulations shortly after the election. Cook sustained his outreach once Trump took office, dining at the White House, regularly speaking with Trump's daughter and son-in-law Ivanka Trump and Jared Kushner, and calling Trump's personal cell phone, as the president preferred. "The only one who calls me is Tim Cook," Trump declared. Once the tariff boom was lowered, Cook pumped up the charm offensive even further.

The result was a dance of public and private only possible in the Trump era: a major manufacturer making a great show of moving some jobs back to the country (and giving the president photo opportunities he craved as reelection loomed), while still assiduously maintaining the

FIGURE 7. Apple CEO Tim Cook and President Donald Trump during a tour of an Apple assembly facility in Texas, November 2019.

global web of suppliers and customers on which it greatly depended. Trump toured a factory run by an Apple contractor in Texas, boasting about the jobs repatriated to the United States. Apple, meanwhile, scrambled to move some of its manufacturing to Vietnam and Korea instead of China. Cook praised, cajoled, and ultimately convinced Trump that lowering or delaying tariffs would be better for American business, and that Apple was as American as apple pie.[22]

For software-driven internet platforms—whose business interests lay chiefly in capturing overseas markets rather than retaining the ability to manufacture in them—the Trump trade policies ultimately became less of a challenge than an opportunity to solidify their global dominance. Trump took foreign heads of state to task for attempting to levy an internet tax on global giants like Facebook and Google: "these are our companies," he recounted telling French president Emmanuel Macron, "and if anyone is going to tax our companies it's going to be us." Even as antitrust sentiment surged on Capitol Hill (including among some staunchly conservative allies), "I didn't want to break them up," said Trump, for "then China will take over the whole industry."[23]

Ultimately for tech, Trump's trade war had more bark than bite. This could not have been clearer in one of the closing trade salvos of his presidency, the attempted ban of TikTok, which had by 2020 replaced Facebook as the favored social app of America's young. TikTok's short videos were turning teens into celebrities, minting new pop stars, and proving a useful tool for mass organizing, including a prank pulled by thousands of users who signed up for a Trump campaign rally in Oklahoma that spring but didn't show up, leaving the president speaking to a mostly empty arena. (The likely reason for the feeble turnout was not TikTok but the still-raging coronavirus pandemic, but teenaged America claimed victory anyway.)

Like the other social platforms, TikTok relied on huge streams of detailed user data and sophisticated artificial intelligence to deliver its addictive product. Unlike the others, it was Chinese owned. For that reason, TikTok was a security threat, Trump declared that August. He first announced that he would prohibit it from operating in the United States altogether, then said he'd allow its continued operation if it were bought by a "very American" company, signing an executive order to that effect with his customary Sharpie-assisted flourish. Microsoft expressed interest. But the deal ultimately went to two very unlikely owners of a trendsetting social media app: Arkansas-based retail giant Walmart, and enterprise software company Oracle, whose founder and former CEO, Larry Ellison, was a Trump supporter and large donor.[24]

The deal didn't get far. "Ownership" consisted of Oracle and Walmart buying a stake in TikTok and keeping an eye on its data collection practices. Even then, TikTok's parent company challenged the deal in court, and the handover remained unfinished by the time Trump left office. In February 2021 the Biden administration halted the sale; in June, Biden reversed Trump's executive order. The saga was over, and TikTok cruised on, its U.S. customer base soaring to over 100 million daily users.[25]

Trump's campaign to curb China's rising economic power was compromised by his pugilistic words, snap decisions, and personal feelings, whether it be pleasure at a courtly tech CEO or annoyance with teenaged pranksters on a Chinese-owned app. But even Trump critics who decried his blunt tactics and xenophobic nationalism could not ignore the economic and political problems that had resulted from the bipartisan embrace of free trade.

The tech industry was enmeshed with China in ways that no trade war or presidential decree could untangle. Unlike the Cold War, when U.S. and Soviet computing ecosystems were separate and self-contained, the international entanglements of this new economic cold war were deep in the machine, in routers built in Shenzhen and software designed in Shanghai, in the artificial intelligence delivering up dance videos to teenagers and the data-harvesting smartphones nestled in back pockets, in perpetual Pacific crossings of people and capital. What's more, China was now investing in advanced research and higher education much in the way the United States had done during the mid-twentieth century but no longer did. How to remedy that imbalance, and reckon with this new high-tech rival, would be a task for the next president to tackle.

## Break 'Em Up

As social media raged, border walls rose, and employees revolted, the biggest technology companies kept growing at a staggering rate. One of the many boosts of the Trump years came with the massive tax reform package passed by Congress in 2017, which slashed the corporate tax rate from 35 percent to a record low 21 percent. The law also included a deal to discourage the offshoring of corporate revenue—one of tech's favorite tax-avoidance strategies—by lowering the tax on repatriated profits to 15.5 percent.

Big Tech worked hard and spent heavily to make this happen, increasing already considerable D.C. lobbying budgets as the bill made its way through Congress. It paid off, handsomely. In 2018, for example, Amazon made more than $11 billion in profit but paid $0 in U.S. federal income tax thanks to lower corporate rates, tax credits for research and development, and employee stock awards.[26]

In the wake of the tax cuts and amid a Trump-era Wall Street bull market, tech stock prices soared. In 2005, only one of the eight wealthiest companies by market capitalization in the world was a tech company, Microsoft. By 2020, seven of the eight were tech companies, including the five American giants: Apple, Amazon, Google/Alphabet,

Facebook, and Microsoft. The combined valuation of the five companies made up more than 20 percent of the entire S&P 500.[27]

As in earlier eras of American history, the companies' size and wealth—not to mention the personal wealth of their founders, who now ranked among the richest people in American history—spurred new momentum for antitrust enforcement and regulation that would place guardrails on their growth or break them up entirely. This was a sharp departure from recent political history. From Reagan through Clinton and Bush, federal antitrust enforcement had taken a laissez-faire turn, with neither federal regulators nor Congress exacting strong oversight over the growth of industrial giants, including and especially in tech.

The one exception was Microsoft, sued by the Department of Justice in the late 1990s after Silicon Valley competitors complained of the software giant's aggressive, market-gobbling practices. The case ended in a mistrial, however, helping bolster the industry's case that federal regulators should not bother with antitrust enforcement. The fast-moving tech market would take care of unfair competition all on its own.

In the decade before Trump took office, federal regulators mostly sat back while the industry's largest embarked on a frenzy of mergers and acquisitions that vastly expanded market share and allowed entry into new lines of business altogether. The number of initial public offerings of tech companies on Wall Street dropped sharply, as established companies acquired young start-ups before they could grow large enough to become a competitive threat.

Over the course of the Trump years, attitudes shifted markedly across the political spectrum. Senator Elizabeth Warren of Massachusetts, a progressive Democrat, became one of the fiercest critics of the new American monopolism. A new crop of Democratic lawmakers elected to Congress in 2018 pushed the House back into Democratic control and prompted fresh legislative scrutiny of the industry's data-gathering practices and market control. By the summer of 2020, the House investigation reached a crescendo with a hearing at which CEOs Bezos, Pichai, and Zuckerberg were subjected to a barrage of questions about their business practices.[28]

The progressive fervor on the left was matched by a rising Republican populism on the right, led by President Trump, although his take was a little more personal. "Well, I can tell you they discriminate against me," Trump retorted when asked whether he thought tech companies behaved unfairly. "You know, people talk about collusion. The real collusion is between the Democrats and these companies." In October 2020, the Trump Justice Department hit Google with an antitrust suit; two months later, Facebook was sued by the Federal Trade Commission along with fifty state attorneys general—a bipartisan group whose politics ranged from ultraconservative to progressive liberal. In fractured and fractious Trump-era America, the only thing on which all could agree was that the nation's largest technology companies had become too big and too rich for their own good.[29]

## The Great Disruption

The COVID-19 pandemic that upended American society in 2020 cost Donald Trump reelection and propelled a tech boom greater than any before it. As the nation and world shut down and stayed at home, tech usage spiked. Consumers who had deleted their Facebook accounts reactivated them, Amazon Prime membership spiked by 50 million new customers, apps delivered everything, and Zoom became a verb. Americans who had in 2019 been fretting about screen time now found themselves thrust into a total-tech-immersion environment. It did not seem that tech could have become even more ubiquitous and essential. The pandemic made it so.

As working-from-home professionals busily clicked up orders delivered by a COVID-vulnerable working class, the role tech had played in the yawning inequality gap became impossible to ignore. The rumblings of employee discontent within tech continued in its privileged white-collar ranks but now extended to the enormous submerged iceberg of blue-collar labor that made the app-fueled, just-in-time internet economy possible. Unionization campaigns bubbled up from tech's lower ranks, met with swift, full-court opposition from tech employers. The sector had been notoriously antiunion since the days when Silicon Valley was filled with semiconductor fabrication plants, and large companies proved unafraid to use their cash and political clout to prevent any changes that might compromise speed and profits. Gig-economy giants Uber, Lyft, and DoorDash spent mightily to defeat a 2020 California ballot initiative that would have reclassified gig workers as employees. Amazon launched an aggressive (and ultimately successful) campaign to counter a union drive in its warehouse in Bessemer, Alabama.[30]

It was clear by the end of Trump's time in office that the tech industry occupied a more central place in American life, and American politics, than it had before he arrived. But it was also clear that the industry faced political threats—of regulation, antitrust enforcement, and labor activism—that would very likely challenge and compromise its neoliberal business model in the Biden era to come. High market capitalization and net worth could not insulate tech's wealthy from criticism and challenge. The old rules that had allowed it to grow so astoundingly successful were now under threat. As Trump exited the scene, it became clearer that far greater forces had made the digital economy what it was, and other leaders would be responsible for making it fairer.

One last collision was left before the president left the stage. On January 6, 2021, a group of Trump supporters—angered about the election results and fed two months of falsehoods about a stolen election by Trump and the right-wing media ecosystem—marched from a Trump rally near the White House to the U.S. Capitol, storming it by force in an attack that left both House and Senate on the run and both Capitol Police officers and protesters dead.

Once again, it was impossible to escape the reach of Big Tech. Nearly all of the insurrectionists held in their pockets smartphones capable of pinpointing their precise location and broadcasting sound and video to the world. While some of the rioters turned off location tracking, and others chose not to livestream or post about their experiences, many others did, documenting their crimes as they were being committed. More than five hundred videos were posted on the right-wing platform Parler, but much of the organizing and posting related to the events of that day happened on mainstream social media platforms like Facebook. This was political history in the making unlike any before it, with nearly every participant carrying their own camera and broadcast network, proudly streaming and curating and interpreting the events on their own terms. It was information overload at its most intense, where all had emptied from the room except the loudest and angriest voices.[31]

Insurrection Day was a gut-wrenching coda to a one-term presidency full of online bombast and internet-fueled falsehoods, an era in which American lives were ever more defined by a relatively small set of digital platforms and products. Leading up to January 6 were more than seven decades of debate over the meaning of American institutions, of revolt against the establishment, of a corrosion of trust, of seizing power—especially digital power—from "The Man" and putting it in the hands of the people.

Silicon Valley technologists had long celebrated the idea of "neutrality": platforms that didn't take a side, didn't privilege some voices over others, and didn't stand in the way of free speech. "We are creating a world where anyone, anywhere may express his or her beliefs, no matter how singular, without fear of being coerced into silence or conformity," wrote John Perry Barlow in the urtext of this Silicon Valley ideology, 1996's *A Declaration of Independence of Cyberspace*. That the financiers and founders of social media platforms embraced this philosophy with little hesitation for a quarter century speaks both to Silicon Valley's abiding faith in the power of well-designed code and to their astounding political naïveté.

The Trump presidency tested both the Silicon Valley belief that more technology was, in essence, good for the world, and the faith that growth—of platforms, of markets, of networks—should be its singular goal. The tech world long celebrated and was celebrated for its "disruption." But that notion felt particularly problematic in the wake of one of the most disruptive presidents in American history, and in a turbulent four years that culminated in the greatest virus-fueled disruption of them all.

# 13

# No More Mulligans

## DONALD TRUMP AND INTERNATIONAL ALLIANCES

*Jeffrey A. Engel*

Donald Trump's was an unusual presidency. That was its point: to break away from the tired and worn in order to "make America great again." The word "great" naturally draws the eye. Nouns matter and verbs do the work, but adjectives typically get the glory, prompting in this case questions of how greatness might be measured, and for whom? More enlightening is the phrase's adverb—"again"—especially for understanding Trump's foreign policy. This word is temporal, narrative, and prescriptive all at once. America was great before; it is no longer; his policies would restore the country to the pinnacle of global power experienced in his youth. The "late '40s and '50s" were ideal, he said in 2016, particularly for the country's global standing. "We were not pushed around, we were respected by everybody, we had just won a war, we were pretty much doing what we had to do."[1]

Greatness in Trump's formulation required thinking "America First," prioritizing the country's needs rather than the welfare of others, be they allies, adversaries, or merely coparticipants in the global commons policed, for too long in his view, at America's expense. Unilateralism—or at least the absence of foreign constraint and diminished concern for others—thus lay its at core, putting Trump's vision at odds with the broad trend of American foreign policy since World War II.[2] He did not mind sailing against the tide, but rather embraced the challenge. "It's time to shake the rust off America's foreign policy," he campaigned. "It's time to invite new voices and new visions into the fold."[3]

Turning the ship of state proved easier said than done. The Constitution provides executives great leeway in foreign affairs, giving Trump opportunity to change the country's course in ways easily undone by his successor, whose own course corrections made Trump's long-term impact on America's relations with the world and with international alliances in particular appear superficial at best. "This is the message I want the world to hear today," President Joe Biden declared soon after firing off a series of executive actions, including the rejoining of multiple international accords and agreements, in his first days in office. "America's back," he said, and ready to rebuild "the muscle of democratic alliances that have atrophied over the past few years of neglect and, I would argue, abuse."[4]

Superficial wounds are not always so easily healed. Trump's emphasis on independence misread American history, and thus the true nature of its post-1945 strength. He idealized unrestrained leadership and unparalleled power, and thus weakened the country's connections to its traditional global partners. The United States succeeded best after World War II not when it went alone but when it led broad coalitions of willing allies and followers, especially during the idealized 1940s and 1950s. Trump's approach toward international alliances and international organizations, therefore, eroded the very cooperative ethos that made the America of Trump's youth the world's greatest power in the first place. Put simply, he wanted to feast on greatness, but failed to follow the recipe.

Across four years in office, Trump's management of the nation's vast network of international alliances reinforced the disruption he hoped to make at home, though ultimately by the close of his single term the ledger of the country's international alliances had hardly changed. By some measures, American engagement with its allies even increased. More American troops were stationed within European allies, for example, at the end of Trump's term than at its start. Numbers do not tell the whole story, however. Donald Trump left the country's relations with its closest allies, especially those in Europe, more frayed than at any point since the onset of the short-lived "American Century" proclaimed in 1941. A majority of European Union citizens polled at the close of his single term believed that the American political system was broken and that Europe could no longer rely on the United States in matters of national security and defense.[5] More directly, a majority thought Americans untrustworthy.[6] Trump's disruptive presidency on its own didn't break global trust in American leadership. Fraying had long predated him. However, his diplomatic approach seems to have been enough to cause its final demise, the proverbial straw that broke the American Century's back.

Greatness used to be the American standard, Trump claimed throughout his unorthodox campaign for the White House, assailing a political system he deemed too sclerotic and corrupt to keep pace with a competitive modern world, and too beholden to elites—from both sides of the nation's partisan divide—to keep the country from faltering militarily, economically, culturally, religiously, and even racially. Convinced for decades that the country had been led into steady decline by "stupid" and "predictable" bureaucrats who failed to leverage the nation's economic and especially military might into sustainable prosperity, and equally convinced of his own prowess as both a strategist and master negotiator, Trump offered voters a radical shift from even the most fundamental consensus planks of American foreign policy developed since 1945. Why? Because since winning the Cold War in particular, American leaders had been "a complete and total disaster. No vision. No purpose. No direction. No strategy."[7]

His crusade against orthodoxy continued throughout his presidency. "We inherited a foreign policy marked by one disaster after another," he explained a month after taking office. Frankly, he had a point. The war in Afghanistan had officially become the country's longest, with no sign of victory in sight. The 2003 invasion of Iraq, meanwhile, ranked atop any list of major American strategic debacles.[8] American combat troops formally left the war-torn country in 2011 after suffering more than five thousand dead and tens of thousands more scarred for life, to say nothing of the trillions of dollars it cost.

For $8,000 per capita, U.S. taxpayers produced a country they could not even safely visit, not that they would have expected a warm welcome from radical groups like the Islamic State of Iraq and the Levant (ISIS) that did not even exist before the war.[9] "We don't win anymore," Trump lamented. More accurately, "We don't fight to win. We fight politically correct wars. We don't win at trade. We don't win in any capacity. We don't win anymore."[10]

Everything would be different, Trump claimed, now that he was in charge. "We're going to start winning again, believe me," he told supporters soon after taking office. This meant winning at international relations, too. Enthralled by globalism, corrupted by personal gain, incompetent, or perhaps never too patriotic in the first place, Republicans and Democrats alike had forgotten the fundamental purpose of all foreign policy, Trump said, which was to put "America first." The challenges he'd "inherited . . . really showed what previous mistakes were made over many years—and even decades—by other administrations." But "the one common thread behind all these problems was a failure to protect and promote the interests of the American people and American workers."[11]

This was a more provocative charge than might appear at first blush. One might expect diplomats and foreign policy strategists to prioritize their own nation's needs. Self-preservation alone suggests as much, and Trump embraced this innately competitive, even zero-sum, view of the world. "It is the right of all nations to put their own interests first," he explained in his inaugural, codifying the sentiment in his first National Security Strategy published at the close of 2017.[12] The problem was, he further explained, that previous American leaders hadn't. "I promised that my Administration would put the safety, interests, and well-being of our citizens first," he thus formally pledged, and would "revitalize the American economy, rebuild our military, defend our borders, protect our sovereignty, and advance our values." The world still needed American leadership, he (and his 2017 National Security Strategy) argued. But leadership of a different kind, the kind that did not cripple the United States and allow others to profit at its expense. "We will pursue this beautiful vision—a world of strong, sovereign, and independent nations, each with its own cultures and dreams, thriving side-by-side in prosperity, freedom, and peace."[13]

This was a fundamental break from the way American presidents had conceived of their country's global role for generations. That is remarkable on two levels, both in Trump's vowing of a break with well-established precedent and in the precedent's strength. There are remarkably few substantive ideas every president from Franklin D. Roosevelt to Barack Obama endorsed. They all loved baseball, apple pie, and their mothers, or at least knew it was politically wise to say as much if queried. They all claimed to strive for "freedom," though no single definition of the word would include them all. Since 1945, they all also believed their nation the undisputed champion of the self-styled "free world," and indispensable to global peace and prosperity.[14]

They'd disagree on the details, of course, but not the premise. "Responsibility for political conditions thousands of miles away can no longer be avoided by this great Nation," Franklin Roosevelt told Americans as World War II neared its end.[15] References to the United States as the "leader of the free world" multiplied under Harry Truman and spiked under Dwight Eisenhower. Once Americans "established as our goals a lasting world peace with justice and the security of freedom on this earth," Ike explained, "we must be prepared to make whatever sacrifices are demanded as we pursue this path."[16] John Kennedy promised Americans would "bear any burden" and "pay any price" in the struggle against global communism.[17] Rather than list each of their successors in turn, let us merely stipulate that each not only made the same point while president but largely believed it as well. Moreover, the world believed it too, friends and foes alike. From 1945 until 2017, however uncomfortable or immodest the mantle, there was no doubt that the president of the United States came to mind when one spoke of the "leader of the free world," and no question that presidents considered themselves as such.

Even presidents who governed during moments of declining American power—power, of course, being a relative and not an absolute quality—believed in this orthodoxy of American leadership and, more critically, that global as well as American security depended on it. "The United States is and remains the one indispensable nation," Barack Obama told graduating West Point cadets in 2014. American leadership had, Obama said in a sentiment none of his immediate predecessors would have denied, largely built the post-1945 world. "From NATO and the United Nations, to the World Bank and the IMF." Hardly perfect, these institutions were in Obama's words nonetheless "force multipliers" where American leadership catalyzed international consensus. The "point is this is American leadership," he said. "This is American strength. In each case, we built coalitions."[18] Coalitions that, on the whole, accepted American leadership. "We know that as leaders of the free world you will get plenty of criticism," Britain's prime minister illustratively offered in 1977. "But you also need support and encouragement, too."[19] In sum, Trump's predecessors never renounced unilateral action when necessary, but their tone always placed the United States within a larger family of like-minded nations, the lead boat if you will at the head of a massive flotilla of nations collectively navigating the world's seas and rocky shores.

Trump thought it time for the United States to do more traveling alone. Leadership had been a bad investment, siphoning blood and especially treasure from American to foreign shores. "For many decades, we've enriched foreign industry at the expense of American industry," he said at his inaugural. "Subsidized the armies of other countries while allowing the very sad depletion of our military . . . defended other nations' borders while refusing to defend our own; and spent trillions of dollars overseas while America's infrastructure has fallen into disrepair and decay."[20] These weren't just words from speechwriters. Trump said the same both unprompted and unscripted. "We are spread out all over the world. We are in countries most people haven't even heard of," he told troops stationed in Iraq at the midpoint of his administration. "Frankly, it's ridiculous." More importantly, it wasn't a good deal. "It's not fair when the burden is all on us, the United States," Trump explained. No more. "We're no longer the suckers, folks. People aren't looking at us as suckers anymore. . . . We're respected again as a nation."[21]

Beyond overseeing its decline and selling out its prosperity, Trump claimed, his predecessors had even sullied the nation's very image. Their foreign policy had become lazy, predictable, and even "boring," which ranks among the worst insults in his vocabulary. "Our rivals no longer respect us," Trump said, weighting the word to include agreement, obedience, and no small element of fear. "In fact, they're just as confused as our allies, but an even bigger problem is they don't take us seriously anymore. The truth is they don't respect us." For example, "when President Obama landed in Cuba on Air Force One, no leader was there, nobody, to greet him. Perhaps an incident without precedent in the long and prestigious history of Air Force One."[22]

Accuracy was never Trump's forte. Even his own White House communications director advised, "Don't take him literally, take him symbolically," and Trump's retelling of Obama's 2016 reception in Cuba was a prime example of a rhetorical strategy repeatedly, even incessantly, employed during his sole term in office.[23] Like so many of his statements as candidate and then as president, the charge that Obama was snubbed was factually incorrect yet layered with meaning. President Obama's March 20 tarmac reception by Cuba's foreign minister, in advance of an official welcoming ceremony with the country's highest leaders, was entirely normal as a matter of diplomatic protocol. There was also plenty of precedent. Most famously, China's foreign minister Zhou Enlai met President Richard Nixon on the tarmac in Beijing in 1972, before Mao Zedong offered the country's formal welcome after nearly a quarter century of mutual diplomatic isolation. Indeed, Trump did not meet Chinese president Xi Jinping upon arrival when he visited Florida in 2017 for a mini-summit, detailing instead Secretary of State Rex Tillerson to the Palm Beach International Airport in advance of the official welcome hours later at the president's Mar-a-Lago estate.[24] Details like these mattered less than effect whenever Trump spoke, however, and his message couldn't be clearer. America had fallen. "It's called no respect," he said of his country's global standing after eight years of Obama. "Absolutely no respect."[25]

Words were malleable tools in Trump's rhetorical arsenal, yet carry particular meaning in the world of international diplomacy. Quite a lot of meaning, in fact, especially when constructing and maintaining alliances. Diplomacy at its essence is persuasion, which often requires explanation, extortion, encouragement, and most important of all, trust. To threaten or to bribe, at least to do so effectively, one's words must be credible.[26] Words build trust, which actions subsequently test, making trust what one leading international relations scholar recently called the "central concept and major concern" of international politics.[27]

This is nowhere truer than when negotiating with one's international allies and friends. Coalitions of any kind, even those of temporary convenience, require confidence that each player will do its promised part. The confidence need not be complete, just sufficient. Every nation ultimately prioritizes its own needs above any previous commitment, and as Ronald Reagan repeatedly intoned, it was only prudent to "trust, but verify."[28] But confidence in an ally's words must be more than merely possible for any international alliance, let alone broad coalitions, to survive over time. "Patience, tolerance, frankness, absolute honesty in all dealings, particularly with all persons of the opposite nationality, and firmness are absolutely essential" for any allied effort to succeed, Dwight Eisenhower said.[29] He knew a thing or two about coalitions, after all.

Trump did not agree. "I don't trust people," he bluntly stated. "I'm a non-trusting person."[30] For one thing he largely didn't consider other people, and by extension other nations, particularly necessary when it came to defining America's national interest. "I'm speaking with myself, number one," he replied when asked in 2016 whom he consulted on foreign policy, "because I have a very good brain and I've said a lot of things."[31] Neither did he expect others to trust or rely on him. His was a transactional world, and each transaction stood only until it was no longer worthwhile. This was especially the case if he'd not been an accord's main negotiator. "Who made the deal? Obama? This is a stupid deal. This deal will make me look terrible," he complained to Australia's prime minister only days after taking office, refusing to honor an agreement to accept refugees negotiated by his predecessor.[32]

The impact of Trump's dismissal of Obama's efforts reverberated far beyond the question of refugees. Curiously, in international affairs the implicit penalties and dishonor of breaking a bilateral accord far exceeds the price that nations typically pay for rejecting or departing from a broader accord. The former appears more personal, and thus more revealing of an actor's integrity. "There is nothing more important in business or in politics than a deal's a deal," Prime Minister Malcolm Turnbull therefore replied when Trump sought to back out of Obama's deal, but the president did not feel beholden to agreements the "stupid people" before him had negotiated. "I do not know how you got them [the Obama administration] to sign a deal like this, but this is how they lost the election. . . . That is why they lost the election, because of stupid deals like this. You have brokered many a stupid deal in business and I respect you," the new president continued to berate the prime minister, "but I guarantee that you broke many a stupid deal. This is a stupid deal. The deal will make me look terrible."[33]

"Mr. President, I think this will make you look like a man who stands by the commitments of the United States," Turnbull tried to respond. "It shows that you are a committed . . ."

Trump cut him off. "This shows me to be a dope. . . . It was a rotten deal. I say that it was a stupid deal like all the other deals that this country signed. You have to see what I am doing. I am unlocking deals that were made by people, these people were incompetent. . . . We never get anything out of it—Start Treaty, the Iran Deal. I do not know where they find these people to make these stupid deals."[34]

Trump refused to be bound by the actions of his predecessor, in foreign as well as domestic affairs. As longtime Washington insider Philip Zelikow put it, his goal was to "bust things up," and thus he refused to act as expected once in office.[35] "I can be more presidential than any president ever," he told a crowd, "except for the possible exception of Abraham Lincoln when he's wearing a hat." Presidential norms bored him, Trump explained, and boring was bad for ratings. "This got us elected," he told a rally. "If I came like a stiff, you guys wouldn't be out here tonight."[36]

It wasn't just norms; American strategy required wholesale busting as well. Predictability, Trump said time and again, was no virtue, whether it was following presidential precedents or engaging the world. Predictable players were easily thwarted, in business, sports, politics, or international affairs. Predictability was to his mind partly why previous administrations had failed. In Trump's view, the United States trusted its allies, and they routinely betrayed that trust, confident that dependable and predictable Americans wouldn't raise a fuss. "Our allies take advantage of us far greater than our enemies and someday I'm going to explain that to a lot of people," Trump explained in 2019.[37] Yes, we'd (previously) been governed by "stupid" leaders, but the other side was smart enough to take advantage of Washington's weakness. "We must as a nation be more unpredictable," he intoned. "We are totally predictable," leaving our enemies too well prepared to thwart our plans, and our allies too confident that we would never, in fact, break an alliance no matter how much the scales turned a previously good deal for America into a poor one. “We have to be unpredictable,” he said. “And we have to be unpredictable starting now.”[38]

Trump’s penchant for unpredictability played out along utterly predictable lines once he assumed office. Having long derided one of Obama’s signature diplomatic achievements, development of a twelve-nation Transpacific Partnership as an economic counterweight to growing Chinese influence, for example, Trump signed an executive order only three days into his tenure withdrawing the United States from the agreement. Later that week, equating Islam with terrorism, he subsequently made good on his promise to ban nationals from six Muslim-majority nations from entering the United States.

Lawsuits flowed in the wake of this “travel ban,” as Mae Ngai explains in this volume, but when this perceived retreat from the country’s long history of religious tolerance coupled with ensuing reductions in the overall number of refugees his administration agreed to accept, the ban’s impact on America’s standing with many of its closest allies long outlived the travel prohibitions. The United States of course had the right to control its own borders, Britain’s prime minister Theresa May explained, though her own government “did not agree with this kind of approach.”[39] Germany’s Angela Merkel agreed on both counts. “She is convinced that even the necessary, decisive battle against terrorism does not justify putting people of a specific background or faith under general suspicion,” her spokesman explained.[40] British foreign secretary (and ensuing prime minister) Boris Johnson was characteristically blunter. The ban was “divisive and wrong,” Johnson said.[41]

Trump’s rejection of previous treaties and accords continued as his first year unfolded. In May his White House announced plans to “modernize” the North American Free Trade Agreement (NAFTA) with Canada and Mexico. It was eventually replaced by the United States–Mexico–Canada Agreement, negotiated and signed in 2018, whose most significant break with the prior accord was the significant decline in acronym quality (NAFTA vs. USMCA). By the close of his first year the president had additionally authorized his country’s withdrawal from the 2015 Paris Climate Agreement and from another of Obama’s signature diplomatic achievements, the Joint Comprehensive Plan of Action (JCPOA) to limit Iranian nuclear development, known more colloquially as the “Iran Deal.”

This, too, was expected. "This was a horrible one-sided deal that should never, ever have been made," Trump exclaimed when renouncing further American participation in the seven-country deal. "It didn't bring calm, it didn't bring peace, and it never will." Signatories to the agreement included all the permanent members of the United Nations Security Council, plus Germany and the European Union, and thereby represented not only the world's most powerful nations but several of Washington's closest allies.[42] "Any nation deserves the right to correct a past mistake," National Security Advisor John Bolton explained, noting that other American allies (Saudi Arabia and Israel in particular) applauded Trump's decision.[43]

Withdrawal nonetheless produced a cooler response from the accord's other signatories. "France, Germany, and the UK regret the US decision to leave the JCPOA," France's president wrote on Twitter, demonstrating that the new communications medium could still employ diplomacy's traditional understatement. We are "deeply concerned," the United Nations secretary-general similarly intoned.[44] Before his term was up, Trump had similarly withdrawn the United States from such significant agreements and international organizations as the United Nations Human Rights Council, the World Health Organization (WHO), the United Nations Educational, Scientific and Cultural Organization (UNESCO), and the Intermediate-Range Nuclear Forces Treaty. He'd also questioned American membership in the World Trade Organization and North Atlantic Treaty Organization (NATO) itself.

Very little of which mattered the day Trump left office. Within his first two weeks in office, President Joseph Biden announced executive orders rejoining the country to the Paris Climate Accords and the WHO, ending the Muslim travel ban, and extending the New Strategic Arms Reduction Treaty with Russia. Biden vowed a new era of cooperation with the country's allies and renewed respect for both international agreements and organizations. "Diplomacy is back at the center of our foreign policy," he said.[45]

Why, then, should we even care what Trump did, if his signature foreign policy achievements were so easily undone? The answer might have been quite different given a second term. Trump had only begun the process of unmooring the country from its long-term commitments by the time he left office. Eight years of executive orders would have been far more difficult to reverse for his successor (should he or she even so desire). Yet he had only four years in office, and in part because of his aversion to foreign entanglements, no major crises arose on his watch other than the global pandemic of COVID-19. It is therefore difficult to measure the consequences of his presidency. There were no new wars, for example, and neither did the cast of America's foes increase or decrease on his watch. For all of his blustery rhetoric on trade, the country and indeed the global economy chugged along largely at the same clip during his presidency as before—until COVID. Moreover, for all of his departures from international organizations such as the WHO and multilateral deals such as the JCPOA, the United States remained at his presidency's end as formally embedded within the web of its international security alliances (NATO, most visibly) as when he began. One might therefore be tempted to disregard his tenure in office entirely (at least when considering the country's international alliances) as an anomaly—curious but ultimately inconsequential.

We should care because the damage he inflicted in fact reopened old wounds. Trump didn't just strain American credibility abroad by his dismissive and caustic treatment of allies and alliances; he restrained it. Recall Barack Obama's somewhat controversial and no-doubt surprising receipt of the Nobel Peace Prize in 2009. What had the new president, and as Obama readily pointed out, the commander in chief of *two* simultaneous wars, done to advance the cause of peace that could possibly warrant such an honor? He'd been in office little more than eight months. Even his own staff was perplexed. The news was "more of a surreal challenge" to explain "than a cause for celebration," White House adviser David Axelrod explained. Staffers even investigated whether any winner capable of making the trip had ever declined to attend the ceremony, which given his obvious dearth of accomplishment seemed as likely to be awkward as celebratory.[46]

In reality, Obama won arguably the world's most prestigious award in 2009 less for what he did than for whom he was not. He was not George W. Bush, whose administration was widely perceived in Europe as disdainful of longtime democratic allies and corrosive of international alliances. Obama vowed a different course, a return to pre-9/11 normalcy, and this is what the Nobel Committee endorsed. The award "was because we would like to support what he is trying to achieve," Prize Committee chairman Thorbjoern Jagland explained in 2009, an assessment confirmed five years later by a rare published peek inside the committee's negotiations.[47] "It is true, Obama did not do much before winning," a member of the selection committee (and a noted scholar of American foreign relations) explained in 2014. "But he represented the ideals of the committee. And when we have an American president who supports that message, we like to strengthen him." After all, Geir Lundestad (director of the Norweigan Nobel Institute from 1990 until 2014) continued, "to Norwegians, it is almost as if the USA is split in two. A liberal and a democratic country with which we feel solidarity and a conservative country for which we have little respect."[48]

There is little doubt into which camp similarly minded Europeans placed Trump. "I will probably never get it," he said in 2019. "I think I'll get a Nobel Prize for a lot of things—if they ever gave it out fairly, which they don't."[49] Fair or not, unilateralism rarely appealed to the Nobel Prize Committee, including the aforementioned Lundestad, who rose to international prominence not just by extolling the virtues of multilateral cooperation but by arguing that Europeans had willingly ceded leadership—an "empire by invitation," he called it—to the United States after World War II precisely because of Washington's charitable benevolence.[50] Trump took the opposite tact, doing little to win friends in Western Europe during his four years in office, instead undermining what has been, and remains, arguably the most significant pillar of his country's entire system of international security. As a lens for appreciating the real long-term damage Trump did even beyond reminding allies that they'd questioned American leadership before, no better example exists than focus on his treatment of NATO.

Trump loathed NATO, considering it emblematic of his country's mismanaged foreign policies and misused resources, and wasted few opportunities to voice his displeasure. Designed in 1949 to thwart Soviet designs on Western Europe, Trump considered the organization "obsolete" a full generation after communism's collapse.[51] To be fair, NATO's continuation, let alone its post–Cold War expansion, was a live question even for its supporters in the years since the Cold War's close. More than once the organization searched for a mission, or even for meaning. Holding fast to transatlantic ties appeared sufficient to most. NATO was "the cornerstone of the West's defence," British prime minister May contended, and the alliance undergirded the entire rules-based international system the United States helped construct after World War II. "We must turn towards these multinational institutions like the UN and NATO that encourage international cooperation and partnership," she argued.[52] Both Presidents George W. Bush and Barack Obama agreed, to cite only Trump's two immediate predecessors. "Since NATO's founding, the assurance of mutual defense has been a safeguard for peace," Bush said in 2008.[53] Its existence exemplified, indeed codified, the trust upon which strong international relations rested. "NATO is sending a clear message that we will defend every ally," Obama said in 2016.[54]

The mutual defense pledge was explicit, in fact, codified in the fifth article of the organization's founding charter: an attack upon any would be perceived, and treated, as an attack against all. A strike against original member Turkey, Poland (which joined in 1999), or Latvia (which was among the group given NATO membership in 2004) was by both treaty and custom considered no different than an attack on Toledo, Pittsburgh, or Los Angeles. "If our common approach to the East over the years has given coherence to our message of peace and world freedom," Ronald Reagan said of NATO in 1988, "it has been our unwavering commitment to defend ourselves that has given it credibility."[55]

Trump disagreed. NATO's only contemporary use, he charged in 2016, was the opportunity it offered member states to attain security on the cheap, so long as the United States was willing to foot the bill. "We are protecting them, giving them military protection and other things, and they're ripping off the United States," he railed from the campaign trail. "Either they have to pay up for past deficiencies," not only investing in military spending commensurate with their treaty commitments but also paying some manner of arrears, "or they have to get out."[56] If they didn't, the United States would. Trump's logic was simple: membership in any club requires dues, and failure to pay invalidated one's place. Most NATO allies were in arrears, he argued. Known for his rhetorical flights of fancy and the impermanence of his positions throughout his presidency, Trump remained consistent on the issue of nonpayment from his candidacy until the end of his administration.

Little in his frustration was new. Previous presidents had railed against the military frugality of member states. Criticism of European defense spending is another of the few universal views of postwar presidents. "Blackmailing bastards! Damn them!" Eisenhower ranted early in his first term when French forces bogged down in their reconquest of Indochina.[57] "Every time I ask the sons of bitches to put more troops into NATO they kiss me off unless I promise to bail them out," Ike said. John Kennedy similarly vented his spleen over European allies living off "the fat of the land" that America's nuclear umbrella secured.[58] Similar rebukes were heard in every ensuing Oval Office. Fast-forwarding to the twenty-first century, both George W. Bush and Obama found NATO spending frustrating, and said so publicly. "America believes if Europeans invest in their own defense, they will also get stronger and more capable when we deploy together," Bush said at his last NATO summit.[59] Obama privately called them "free riders," publicly noting that "if we've got collective defense, it means that everybody's got to chip in, and I've had some concerns about a diminished level of defense spending among some of our partners in NATO."[60] Lamenting lethargic European defense spending was indeed bipartisan sport in 2016 when Trump ran for president. "It is important to ask for our NATO allies to pay more of the cost," Hillary Clinton said. "There is a requirement that they should be doing so, and I believe that needs to be enforced."[61]

Complaining about NATO spending is one thing; blackmailing members with the threat of American withdrawal, or more accurately American defense aid only for allies who'd paid in full, was something else entirely. Trump did the latter. "They're ripping off the United States. And you know what we do? Nothing," Trump said in 2016. "Either they have to pay up for past deficiencies or they have to get out. And if that breaks up NATO, it breaks up NATO."[62] He said much the same once sworn in. "Twenty-three of the 28 member nations are still not paying what they should be paying and what they're supposed to be paying for their defense," Trump said on his first visit as president to NATO headquarters in Brussels. It "is not fair to the people and the taxpayers of the United States and many of these nations owe massive amounts of money from the last years."[63] Rectifying the accounting imbalance was one of his top presidential priorities.

Trump's hard bargaining appeared to have worked. "No President has ever achieved so much in so little time," he said three years later while celebrating his successful renegotiation of the organization's contributions and finances after a NATO summit. "Without a U.S. increase, other countries have already increased by $130 billion—with $400 billion soon. Such a thing has never been done before."[64]

Actually it had, and as before, Trump's rhetoric did not wholly match reality or the issues' complexity. In this instance, Trump conflated NATO's two major forms of funding: direct funds for the organization's upkeep and operations, which member countries pay on a sliding scale based on the size of their gross national product (GNP), and indirect funds distinguished by the total amount each nation spent on its own military, again in proportion to its GNP. The United States has historically paid the largest sum for NATO's indirect funding, which should not be surprising given that it has the largest GNP.

More galling to Trump, however, was the failure of most NATO countries to reach the mutually agreed upon target for military spending of 2 percent of each country's GNP. In total, the organization's other twenty-nine member states annually spend less than half of what the United States alone spends on its military, an imbalance largely present since its 1949 inception but exacerbated by the surge in American military spending in the years since 2001. In 2019, nearly the end of Trump's time in office, only seven of the thirty member states spent this much. In 2015, before he took office, only the United States and the United Kingdom met that threshold.[65]

Most members increased their military spending during Trump's tenure, for which he took credit. Indeed, overall non-U.S. military spending within the organization bottomed out at 1.42 percent of overall GDP in 2015 and had reached 1.55 percent by 2019. Trump simultaneously reduced his country's share of direct spending from roughly 22 percent to 16 percent, placing American spending at the same level as Germany's. Collectively, therefore, Trump claimed to have negotiated and pressured his allies into an annual difference of $530 billion in the American and non-American shares of NATO spending between 2016 and 2020. "NATO was suffering very badly from depletion of funds, and it was going down like a roller coaster goes down," he said. "Not up, but down. And I was able to, over the last couple of years, increase their contribution."[66]

It is curious math. For starters, American direct payments to NATO totaled approximately $500 million a year, or 0.0008 percent of the country's overall defense budget.[67] Reducing America's contribution to Germany's level therefore saves little more than a rounding error in the overall defense bill, suggesting the issue mattered more for Trump as a matter of principle, or potential political gain, than as a cool assessment of return on investment. More significantly, the $400 billion Trump claimed to have wrung from NATO is actually its cumulative projected spending through 2024, not per year. There can be no doubt that Trump's bluster contributed to the rise in military spending for non-U.S. members of NATO, though significantly the 2 percent threshold itself was reaffirmed in 2014—before Trump even declared himself a candidate for office—in response to Russian aggression. Spending had already begun to rise before Trump took office, in other words, with an overall non-U.S. growth of 1.4 percent in 2015 and 3 percent in 2016.

To add one more level of complexity, the 2 percent target equation itself is not particularly helpful when attempting to fairly evaluate burden sharing. American GNP in 2018 was nearly 1,500 times larger than Albania's (the smallest NATO GNP), thus even large percentage boosts for most states did little to enhance the organization's overall military might. Bulgaria crossed the 2 percent threshold in 2019 when it purchased eight F-16 fighter jets from the United States, for example, while Greece joined the above 2 percent club not by virtue of increasing its military spending but because the overall size of its economy shrank dramatically amid financial crisis.[68]

A better metric for evaluating contributions to NATO is the share of spending devoted to European and Atlantic defense. Here the numbers get really interesting. The United States, of course, has global responsibilities—too many, Trump repeatedly said. It consequently spent approximately $31 billion on European defense in 2018, or 5 percent of its total defense spending. The rest of NATO, meanwhile, contributed $239 billion to defending Europe, or nearly eight times as much.[69] This should not be a surprise. Albania's global footprint being expectedly small, one would think the vast majority of its own spending to be spent closer to home, and nearly 100 percent of its military budget contributes to European defense, which includes of course defense against one of the foes singled out in Trump's 2017 National Security Strategy as a present and looming threat to U.S. security: Russia. By this metric, therefore, one might think NATO is a bargain for American taxpayers: for 5 percent of their defense spending, they get to deter a principal foe and secure one of the country's second-largest trading zones with a defense program underwritten eight times over by their allies.[70]

The truth is that many of Europe's leaders did not necessarily mind the nudge from Trump to spend more, finding his threats and bluster quite useful when negotiating with their own parliaments and legislatures for greater defense spending. Previous presidents had asked for more, after all. Few blinked, therefore, when Trump explained that "it will be increasingly difficult to justify to American citizens why some countries do not share NATO's collective security burden while American soldiers continue to sacrifice their lives overseas or come home gravely wounded."[71] What they did mind was his open suggestion both that the United States might not live up to its mutual-defense promises for nations in arrears and, more fundamentally, that perhaps it might not respond as promised even for nations in good financial standing. "If they fulfill their obligations to us," Trump responded when asked if he intended to protect NATO's smallest (and predominantly furthest east) states from Russian aggression, "the answer is yes."[72] The conditionality, as noted before, was new for an American president.

And words, indeed, matter. The history of NATO is one of strife, angst, jealousy, and competition.[73] In other words, it functions like a typical extended family. Yet family dysfunction reaches a new level entirely when excommunication becomes a possibility or a reality. No previous American president since NATO's founding in 1949 had given Europeans significant reason to doubt their fidelity to Article Five. More importantly, no American president gave foes, the Soviet Union or Russia especially, reason to think Washington's decision to respond to an attack against a fellow member state might be calculated with a cash register. American presidents before him consistently saw NATO as a conduit of American influence in Europe and abroad, but many questioned the investment. Obama in particular considered himself more a Pacific-minded than Atlantic leader. Yet considering a rebalance of investments rang differently to European ears than presidential consideration of foreclosure. Trump thus left Europeans to wonder if the side they naturally preferred within American politics, the liberal democratic forces that more closely aligned with their own—and, of course, with the type of governments the United States had once help establish and prosper after World War II—might not be irretrievably weakened by the nation's basic divisions.

We return in closing to George W. Bush and Barack Obama. Europeans, or at least the Norwegians at the Nobel Institute, found Bush so distasteful and damaging a president that they lauded his successor merely for charting a different course. Many Americans, of course, thought the same. "The Bush administration's hubris and relentless disregard for our allies abroad shredded the fabric of multilateralism," the *Los Angeles Times* editorialized in 2009. Bush's tenure but also his legacy, they said, "must be brought to a swift close with a renewed emphasis on diplomacy, consultation, and the forging of broad international coalitions."[74]

But Bush never crossed the Rubicon of disparaging mutual defense. Quite the contrary, he endorsed NATO solidarity even as most member states criticized his global agenda and methods. Donald Trump did much over the course of his single term in office to actually strengthen the alliance. As mentioned above, spending is up, as is acquisition of new equipment. More is on the way, including new initiatives designed to bolster the credibility of NATO's deterrence of Russian influence and overreach, which see NATO's easternmost states increasingly home to exercises, military development, and coordination within the multilateral system. It is wrong, therefore, to say blithely that Trump weakened NATO or any of the other bilateral and multilateral alliances he oversaw for four years. Nuance is required to understand the damage he wrought. As Robert Blackwill, a renowned American diplomat, noted from the safety of the Council on Foreign Relations, "NATO is stronger in all respects but one: its members' confidence that the others, in particular the United States, will uphold their Article 5 commitments in the event of a war."[75] If one prefers a view from a more pro-Trump analyst, consider the remarkably similar words from conservative classicist Victor Davis Hanson. "The point, then, is that the Trump administration did not reduce U.S. material commitments to either its own security forces, its allies' security, or the security of the international community—in terms of either manpower or money."[76] Rather, Trump's tone, and its effect on the psychology of allies and adversaries alike, mattered more.

FIGURE 8. President Trump meets with world leaders and negotiates on trade, Iran, and national security.

And of course, the past is never quite past. Trump's volatility made allies question American credibility and the worth of American promises for the past four years, but there is little sense in NATO circles or beyond that the fundamental divisions within American society he exposed and exploited have receded with his exit from the White House. Previous changes in administration brought different policies but not wholesale different strategic commitments. That consistency appears a thing of the past, forcing America's allies to question their own reciprocal commitment. "If you know that whatever you're doing will at most last until the next election," the head of the European Council on Foreign Relations explained in the wake of Trump's term, "you look at everything in a more contingent way." The change in American attitude toward the world he embodied, the desire to "bust things up," could be found within the Democratic Party as well in 2016 and 2020. Fatigue from foreign wars, dismay over America's relative decline, and disparagement of international trade pacts in particular know no partisan bounds in contemporary America. The key foreign policy planks of a Bernie Sanders administration might not ultimately have appeared that different from Trump's, even if the accent and tone would likely have differed widely. "By producing a Trump presidency and calling attention to the underlying domestic dysfunction that allowed a previously inconceivable development to occur," specifically a questioning of the very basis of mutual security between the United States and its key allies, "the United States is now looked at quite differently than it once was," a senior foreign policy analyst confirmed.[77]

One need not take his American view as gospel. Consider the words of Portugal's defense minister, offered not coincidentally soon after Joe Biden's inauguration. The Trump years had "devastating effects in terms of the credibility of the United States and its strength internationally."[78] Ultimately this is Trump's legacy, and while we should not have been surprised that Biden stressed the "sacred" nature of America's Article Five commitment in the first NATO meetings of his presidency, we should not expect him to garner the Nobel Prize merely for not being his predecessor.[79] The world might have been willing to give the United States a new chance to revert back to the mean in 2009. It is unlikely to so fluidly offer a new chance this time around.

# 14

# Trump's China Policy

## THE CHAOTIC END TO THE ERA OF ENGAGEMENT

*James Mann*

As an introduction to Donald Trump's impact on American policy toward China, consider two disparate events during Trump's final week in office. First: On January 19, 2021, Trump's last full day as president, Anthony Blinken, who was about to become the secretary of state for Trump's successor, Joe Biden, testified at his confirmation hearing that he had largely agreed with the overall direction of Trump's China policy. "President Trump was right in taking a tougher approach to China," Blinken said. "I disagree very much with the way he went about it in a number of areas, but the basic principle was the right one." As one example, Blinken said he concurred with the Trump administration's declaration that China's policy toward Uighurs in Xinjiang province amounted to genocide.[1]

Second: The next day, during the inauguration ceremonies that marked the final moments of Trump's presidency, American television viewers could see that an unidentified man of Asian descent was always standing behind Biden or at his side. His name was David Cho, a Korean American Secret Service agent, who had been placed in charge of Biden's presidential security detail (after having previously protected Trump). American social media soon lit up with speculation that this man with an Asian face was a Chinese agent, assigned by Beijing to control the new president. "I just asked why has [Biden] got a Chinese handler," said one typical tweet.[2]

Those two episodes serve to illustrate the legacy of Trump's China policy, with its many underlying forces and currents. During Trump's administration, China policy was steered onto a new course, different in tone and in policy from that of the previous eight American presidents. On policy questions, Trump often operated with bipartisan support, because American views on China were changing. Yet Trump's pronouncements on China also set loose some of the darker forces that he displayed elsewhere: demonization, conspiratorial thinking, and a strain of racism, along with some self-dealing for the family businesses. It would be wrong to focus solely on either one of these two aspects of Trump's diplomacy with China to the exclusion of the other.

Trump's approach to China was beset with ironies and contradictions. For example, during his presidential campaign in 2016, Trump had focused on two particular aspects of America's relationship with Beijing: the outflow of American manufacturing jobs to China and the large trade imbalance between the two countries. In particular, his focus on job losses to China during that campaign can be said to have helped propel his victory over Hillary Clinton, as decisive numbers of workers in industrial states switched parties and voted for Trump. Yet during his four years in office, Trump did little to bring American manufacturing jobs back to the United States, nor did he have much impact on the continuing trade imbalance with China. Trump did have a substantial impact on trade in high-technology and communications equipment, imposing ever-stricter limits on Chinese companies like Huawei and ZTE.

In fact, Trump's greatest impact on America's approach to China lay not in any one particular policy area. Rather, it was more abstract: during the Trump administration, America's conception of China, its long-term strategy toward it, and its assumptions about China's future all changed dramatically, although sometimes in ways that Trump himself probably could not have articulated.

In becoming ever tougher in dealing with China, Trump was generally aligned with American public opinion; he was certainly helping to shape it and was also perhaps following it on occasion as well. A Gallup poll taken a few weeks after Trump left office showed that American views of China had dropped to the lowest levels in at least forty years. Only 20 percent of Americans had a favorable view of China, down 13 percent in a year, and 79 percent of Americans viewed China unfavorably, up 12 percent over the previous year.[3]

## The End of Engagement

Let us return to Blinken's statement at his confirmation hearing that Trump was correct to have taken a "tougher approach" with China. Blinken was not attempting to say something new or different. At the time, and throughout much of Trump's presidency, other leaders in the mainstream of American public life had been offering various versions of this same idea. Henry Paulson, the treasury secretary for former president George W. Bush, asserted that Trump had been "largely right" to take a tougher line on China. Richard Haass, the president of the Council on Foreign Relations, said that Trump had "reset the conversation" with China. Thomas Friedman, the *New York Times* columnist, said Trump had dealt with China "with I would say more grit and toughness than any of his predecessors. I give him credit for that."[4]

But what did this mean, this vague invocation to be "tougher"? These commentators were not referring to any specific action. What their comments indicated was that America's previous policy of "engagement," which had dominated American thinking about China over the previous quarter century, essentially came to an end during the Trump administration.

The idea of engagement was first set forth by President George H. W. Bush in the aftermath of China's crackdown on demonstrations in Tiananmen Square.[5] There were calls at the time for Bush to freeze all contacts with Chinese leaders. Instead, Bush said he wanted to pursue a "comprehensive policy of engagement" with China.[6] (The Reagan administration had previously used the word "engagement" in its policy toward South Africa.) Following Bush's lead, the Clinton administration then picked up the idea of engagement to describe its rationale for continuing to trade with China and approving its entry into the World Trade Organization (WTO), and the phrase continued to be used until the Trump administration. At the time, the policy enjoyed particularly strong support from the American business community, which was eager for trade and investment with China.

Under the policy of engagement, America pursued conciliatory policies toward Beijing in hopes that over the long run, the Chinese regime might ease its repressive policies at home and eventually become a member in good standing of the international system that America had created after World War II. The United States backed away from direct challenges to China and, in particular, avoided taking concrete actions to retaliate against broken promises or other bad behavior. Continuing dialogue became an end in itself, overriding any short-term conflicts.

The ideas behind engagement with China were closely linked to the optimistic views that accompanied the end of the Cold War—in particular, Francis Fukuyama's famous essay, "The End of History?"[7] The underlying assumption was that eventually trade, growing prosperity, and interaction with the outside world would cause the Chinese leaders to liberalize the country's political system. Clinton told President Jiang Zemin that Chinese policy was "on the wrong side of history" and predicted that an increase in the spirit of liberty in China was "inevitable, just as inevitably the Berlin Wall fell." As he was running for the presidency, President George W. Bush said in 1999, "Trade freely with China, and time is on our side."[8]

Donald Trump began to run for president in 2015, roughly a quarter century after George H. W. Bush set forth the policy of engagement. Over the intervening years, a series of events had caused the support for engagement with China inside the United States to erode. After becoming a member of the WTO in 2001, China was able to dramatically increase its exports to the United States. By one formal study, America lost 2.4 million manufacturing jobs to Chinese competition between 1999 and 2011—many of them in politically important states like Michigan, Pennsylvania, Wisconsin, and North Carolina.[9]

Meanwhile, as American companies began operating in China, both to take advantage of cheap labor and in hopes of selling to its large market, they found themselves with ever less leverage in dealing with their Chinese partners and with the Chinese government itself. Increasingly, foreign companies were subjected to demands to transfer their technology to China. Complaints of theft of intellectual property became commonplace. Chinese firms were emerging as serious competition. By the mid-2010s, the American business community was no longer the bedrock of support it had once been for strong relations with China. To be sure, there was a noticeable divide: financial firms, still hoping to make inroads in China, continued to lobby in Washington on China's behalf.[10] However, manufacturing firms across the United States had shifted their outlook: whereas in the 1990s they had been urging Washington to avoid conflict with China, by the mid-2010s many of them were pleading with Washington to take stronger action against China. While Wall Street looked favorably on Beijing, Main Street was becoming ever more disenchanted.

This shift in attitude in the business community helped contribute to a noticeable change in Congress. During the trade debates of the 1990s, China could count on being able to win support from local businesses in congressional districts across the country. Two decades later, this was no longer true. As a result, when Trump proposed tougher actions against China, there was remarkably little pushback from Capitol Hill.

The increasing disaffection with the engagement policy extended beyond the business community to the field of national security. When the elder Bush had first set down the policy of engagement, the United States was still seeking to collaborate with China in dealing with the Soviet Union—and for fifteen years after the Soviet collapse, America enjoyed virtually unchallenged supremacy in the world. But following America's intervention in Iraq in 2003 and particularly after the financial crisis of 2008, America's power seemed on the wane, and China meanwhile became increasingly assertive in international affairs. It began to build artificial islands and military structures in the South China Sea and was willing to challenge the United States at international forums like the Copenhagen climate summit of 2009. Above all, the United States found that China's growing economic and industrial strength was turning it into an increasingly powerful competitor. In this respect, economics and national security were interrelated: American leaders worried that China's growing economic power would prompt it to build up its military strength, and they were also concerned that China's pursuit of military power would spur on economic advances, particularly in high-tech sectors of the economy. Meanwhile, China's economic advances also meant that it was less responsive to American concerns on issues such as human rights.

All these factors were already in play before Trump ran for president in 2016. Indeed, they raise the counterfactual question: Would the policy of engagement with China have come to an end even under a Democratic president, without the rise of Trump? That seems conceivable, but if so, the engagement policy would have been changed in a different, slower, less dramatic way.

President Barack Obama voiced occasional unhappiness with the China policy he had inherited. At one point, he complained to veterans of the Clinton administration serving in his administration that they had allowed China to enter the WTO under loose terms that had left him with little leverage on trade issues.[11] However, Obama took little concrete action in response to China's more assertive behavior. As Obama's first-term secretary of state, Hillary Clinton was generally more hawkish on China than he was. Clinton's top adviser on China, Kurt Campbell, later wrote an article for *Foreign Affairs* arguing that America's policy toward China had long been based on false assumptions that China would change.[12] Still, despite the Democrats' own growing uneasiness with America's long-standing China policy, it is impossible to imagine a President Hillary Clinton upending that policy in the fashion that Donald Trump did—relying heavily on tariffs, using incendiary language mixed occasionally with flattery, all the while forsaking efforts at multilateralism.

China was ambivalent about Trump, both during the 2016 campaign and during his early years in the White House. Over the years, the Chinese regime had tended to prefer Republican administrations to Democratic ones. The Republicans were after all the party of Richard Nixon and Henry Kissinger, and in the years that followed, Republican leaders had been eager to maintain strong relations with Beijing. From the Chinese perspective, the Democrats were the party of labor unions, and China feared American protectionism. In 1988, Deng Xiaoping had even proclaimed openly that he hoped George H. W. Bush would win the presidency over Michael Dukakis, the Democratic candidate.[13]

The rise of Trump had shaken up China's long-standing assumptions about the American political parties. On the one hand, Trump was a different sort of Republican who attacked China regularly and favored protectionism, and in those ways he seemed harmful to China. On the other hand, Trump also frequently disparaged America's alliances and sought to erode them in ways quite unlike any previous modern president, whether Republican or Democratic. Because of Trump's unilateralism, Chinese leaders, particularly those responsible for foreign and military strategy, could see Trump's presidency as potentially beneficial to China's long-term strategic interests.

## Phases and Factions

The Trump administration's approach to China can be divided into three distinct phases: first, an initial year of tentative maneuvering; second, the trade negotiations of 2018–2019; and third, the tumultuous final year amid the COVID pandemic. Over these phases, different factions and personnel emerged within the administration, struggling for Trump's approval of their different points of view.

One faction was composed of economic officials who generally favored free trade with China and sought to prevent or limit punitive actions against it, such as tariffs. Treasury Secretary Steven Mnuchin led this group, and he was joined during Trump's first two years by Gary Cohn, director of the National Economic Council. Both men had backgrounds in finance and on Wall Street. In essence, these men were the successors on China policy to business-oriented officials such as Robert Rubin in the Clinton administration and Henry Paulson in the George W. Bush administration. (In particular, Mnuchin saw Paulson as a mentor and spoke regularly with him throughout his time as treasury secretary.) Their views also enjoyed the support of some of Trump's closest friends in the business community, such as Sheldon Adelson and Steve Wynn, both of whom had extensive casino interests in Macao, and Steven Schwartzman of the Blackstone Group, who had both business interests in China and close ties to Chinese leaders.

It was a staple of newspaper commentary to refer to "the hawks" within the Trump administration, but in fact the hawks were themselves a coalition of different forces and people. One group was the "trade hawks," who focused on getting China to take concrete, policy-oriented steps to give up its restrictive trade practices and theft of intellectual property. Their leader was U.S. trade representative Robert Lighthizer, a veteran trade lawyer who had for years sought to protect the American steel industry from growing Chinese imports. Another group, who could be called the "political hawks," focused less on specific policy actions than on nativist rhetoric that would convey to the public that China was a malign force in the world, and that Trump's political opponents were too soft on China. For the first eighteen months of the administration, Steve Bannon, Trump's former campaign manager and White House counselor, served as leader of the political hawks; and through the four years, Peter Navarro served as a key player within this grouping.

There was another faction of China hawks within the Trump administration, which received vastly less public attention than the trade hawks or the political hawks, but which often proved more influential than either of the others: the national security hawks. They were, largely, hidden within the bureaucracy, and they didn't appear on Sunday news shows in the fashion that, for example, Lighthizer, Bannon, or Navarro did. This third group of hawks included officials in the Pentagon, who were concerned about China's growing military power and its effort to dominate high-tech industries; officials in the FBI, worried about Chinese efforts at espionage, technology theft, and influence operations; and other officials at the CIA and the Commerce Department with comparable complaints about Chinese behavior. One principal focus for such officials was Beijing's "Made in China 2025" plan, which called for China to dominate high-technology fields such as artificial intelligence, 5G communications, and robotics.

There was no single public face for the national security hawks, but the driving force for them inside the administration was a young official on the National Security Council named Matthew Pottinger. He served as the NSC's point man on China policy under four consecutive national security advisors. Pottinger had an unusual background: he was for a time a *Wall Street Journal* correspondent in Beijing, then joined the Marines to serve overseas as an intelligence officer. Under Trump, he drafted some of the Trump administration's leading strategy documents for China, and he coordinated other such documents within the government; he also delivered some innovative speeches aimed at worldwide Chinese audiences, which he proceeded to deliver in Mandarin.

A final faction inside the administration was the Trump family itself. The family was particularly significant during the early days, when China sought to forge personal connections to the new administration. As Trump was preparing to take office, China sought to work with and through Henry Kissinger (as Beijing had sometimes done with earlier presidents); and Kissinger, in turn, sought to emerge as the adviser to Trump with and through Jared Kushner and Ivanka Trump, the president's son-in-law and daughter. The Kushners were a frequent presence during Trump's first meeting with Chinese president Xi Jinping at Mar-a-Lago in the spring of 2017; their daughter Arabella and son Joseph were brought out to sing a Chinese song for Xi.

Over time the Kushners' role and influence on China policy waned, after reports were published of some of their business dealings in China. (In 2017, Kushner's family was for a time seeking Chinese financing for their building at 666 Fifth Avenue.[14]) Ivanka Trump sought trademarks for some of her fashion lines in China, and more than once, Chinese authorities approved some of these trademarks just before important meetings between the two governments. Eventually, Kushner devoted most of his attention to the Middle East, while on China issues, he came to support Lighthizer's hawkish positions on trade.

Standing above all the factions was Trump himself. Sometimes, in his rhetoric and tweets, he reflected the views of the political hawks beneath him, like Navarro. On other occasions, such as when trade tensions caused the stock market to drop, he embraced the views of his advisers and friends from the business community. Above all, Trump sought to influence events through his own personalized diplomacy. Throughout the first three years of his administration, Trump sometimes suggested, and appeared to believe, that his own personal relationship with Xi Jinping would be the key factor in settling disputes between America and China. In his tweets and public comments, Trump referred to Xi as a "friend"—or, in one formulation, "a very, very good friend of mine."[15]

In this respect, Trump was seeking to do with China what he also attempted with North Korea: to try to resolve complex, long-standing problems by somehow persuading the top leader of another country to reverse course through personal contact with Trump himself. In the case of North Korea, Trump held three highly publicized meetings in Asia with the country's top leader, Kim Jong Un, in an effort to try to induce Kim to abandon his country's nuclear weapons program. Trump even acknowledged that early in his presidency he delayed trade negotiations with China because he wanted to concentrate on North Korea. "For the first year, I was focused—I was doing North Korea, and I didn't want negotiations [with China] to come in the way."[16] These summits gave some new legitimacy to Kim, since no previous American president had been willing to meet with any North Korean leader. However, in the end, Trump's diplomacy broke down because, no matter how much friendship Trump offered, Kim viewed nuclear weapons as essential to his country's (and his own) survival, and he would not give them up.

With China, too, Trump for a time sought to build a personal relationship with Xi as a way of getting China to change course, but he found that many of China's policies—its mercantilist trade practices, its subsidized state economy, its increasingly assertive foreign policy—had roots and support that extended well beyond Xi himself. After a couple of years in the White House, Trump began to acknowledge occasionally the limits of personalized diplomacy. "We're probably not as close now," Trump said of Xi Jinping at one event in 2019. "But I have to be for our country. He's for China and I'm for USA, and that's the way it's got to be."[17]

## Trade Negotiations

Trump's trade negotiations with China went on for two years and brought forth the sorts of mini-dramas that characterized many other aspects of his years in the White House. Members of his administration—Lighthizer, Navarro, Mnuchin, Commerce Secretary Wilbur Ross—sometimes openly skirmished with one another during talks in Beijing and Washington. Trump intervened with tweets that threatened earthshaking retaliation. At one point, Trump appeared to be ordering a total decoupling of the American and Chinese economies. "Our great American companies are hereby ordered to immediately start looking for an alternative to China, including bringing your companies HOME and making your products in the USA," Trump tweeted on August 23, 2019.[18] (The complete decoupling never came close to happening, although the prolonged trade upheavals did, over time, spur a gradual transfer of low-cost manufacturing away from China to countries such as Vietnam.)

Above all, Trump relied on the most sweeping use of tariffs since the Smoot-Hawley tariffs of the early 1930s. When China countered with tariffs of its own, Trump retaliated with additional tariffs. The American tariffs were as much as 25 percent of the value of the goods China exported to the United States, though Trump later reduced some of the tariffs. The tariffs served to give American trade negotiators new leverage: part of China's effort in the talks was devoted to getting the United States to lift the tariffs. But Trump's tariffs imposed penalties on the American economy too, as American consumers paid higher prices for Chinese imports and as the Chinese tariffs harmed American exporters to China.

What Trump and his negotiators were originally seeking throughout these trade talks were structural changes in the nature of China's mercantilist economy; these included steps such as phasing out state subsidies to favored industries, ending the practice of forcing American companies to transfer their technology to China, and ending the theft of intellectual property. Chinese officials countered that these American complaints about structure amounted to an improper attempt to alter China's economic system. "We are very clear that we cannot make concessions on matters of principle," China's senior trade negotiator Liu He observed at one point.[19] At the same time, Trump was also seeking large increases in Chinese purchases of American products, especially agricultural products ("So I've become a soybean salesman," Mnuchin, Trump's treasury secretary, explained in one television interview).

In December 2019, the two sides reached agreement on a partial deal that was, at the time, called Phase One of the trade negotiations. Under it, China agreed to purchase an additional $200 billion in American exports, including at least $40–$50 billion in agricultural products. There was, however, no broad agreement on the larger structural issues; China offered some promises of change but refused to change its laws or add the sorts of tough enforcement mechanisms that Lighthizer had been seeking. At the time, most of the structural issues were put off for what was said to be a prospective Phase Two agreement—but as it turned out, there never was a Phase Two deal. Overall, Trump's effort at obtaining structural changes in China's support for its state-controlled industries resulted in failure. At the same time, China did not get what it most wanted in the Phase One deal, either: the United States made only modest cuts in its tariffs, and thus most of Trump's tariffs remained in place at the end of his administration.

Trump's promises to reduce the trade deficit with China did not have far-reaching results. In 2016, the year when Trump as a presidential candidate was inveighing against the trade imbalance with China, the deficit amounted to $310 billion. In 2019, the figure came to $308 billion, only a little less. (The figures for 2020, Trump's final year, were all skewed downward by the impact of the pandemic first on China and then on the United States.) Meanwhile, overall American investment in China increased during Trump's presidency.[20]

Although Trump made little headway in his larger trade goals, he did succeed in bringing about some far-reaching changes when it came to high-technology trade, particularly in regard to items with implications for national security. This strand of trade policy enjoyed the strong support of the Pentagon, the intelligence agencies, and America's high-tech community. Most notably, his administration carried out campaigns against the Chinese telecommunications firms Huawei and ZTE. At one point in 2018, the Commerce Department prohibited American firms from any exports to ZTE—a move that could have effectively killed the company, which relied on American semiconductors. But Trump reversed himself weeks later, after a phone call with Xi Jinping. Other administration officials complained that Trump had been merely using ZTE as a bargaining chip in the larger trade negotiations.[21]

The administration's efforts against Huawei were more prolonged and determined. The Huawei campaign galvanized strong support from Washington's national security agencies, which maintained that Huawei had ties to China's People's Liberation Army and that it represented a cybersecurity risk. American officials urged other countries not to buy Huawei equipment. The effort was made more difficult by Trump's frequent denigration of America's allies and of the value of alliances: for example, while Britain agreed to a prohibition on Huawei equipment, Germany did not, opting instead for milder restrictions. As a further complication, Trump administration officials in 2018 charged

Huawei's deputy chairman, Meng Wanzhou, with violating U.S. sanctions against Iran and issued an extradition warrant for her; Canadian officials detained her and kept her under house arrest in Vancouver, while Beijing imprisoned two Canadians in China in response. The issue remained at an impasse throughout the end of the administration.

Thus, while ordinary American workers in manufacturing jobs failed to obtain much change from Trump's trade policies, America's high-tech industries did reap some benefits. The idea of America decoupling from China came much closer to reality in the realm of advanced technology. Indeed, when it came to high-technology production, China was moving toward decoupling from America, too. In the summer of 2019, China's Communist Party leadership decided to create a task force to examine how to carry out decoupling in technology.[22]

## Ideas and Rhetoric

America's thinking about China shifted profoundly under Trump, and in many different ways. These ranged from the formulations within American strategy documents, to the terminology with which American officials spoke of the Chinese Communist Party, to the base prejudices and demonization of the Trump political campaigns. Overall, these amounted to the biggest changes in American views of China since the Nixon administration; even the Tiananmen Square crackdown of 1989 led to fewer changes than the Trump era. This chapter can highlight only a few of the most important strands in America's changing idiom about China under Trump.

The first change lay in the conception of China as America's principal adversary in the world. During the Cold War, of course, America had viewed China as a partner in countering the Soviet Union. Later, in the George W. Bush and Obama administrations, American officials increasingly came to describe China as a strategic competitor at the same time that they were focusing American foreign policy above all on the task of stopping terrorism from the Middle East. From its first days and in its earliest policy documents, the Trump administration shifted toward the task of combating two "great power" rivals, China and Russia—but because China had vastly greater economic power than Russia, this effort increasingly boiled down to China as the main rival.

In early 2018, the Trump White House issued a strategy statement, originally classified, in which it asserted that the principal challenge for American policy in Asia was "how to maintain U.S. strategic primacy . . . and promote a liberal economic order while preventing China from establishing new illiberal spheres of influence."[23] Such formulations would endure past the Trump administration: William J. Burns, the career diplomat who became President Biden's CIA director, testified at his confirmation hearing that "an adversarial, predatory Chinese leadership poses our biggest geopolitical threat."[24] The notion of engaging China in order to integrate it into the international community all but disappeared from American strategy statements.

Second, the efforts to counteract growing Chinese power led to changes in the way American officials thought of and spoke about Asia as well. For decades, American policy statements and, indeed, the U.S. government itself had viewed China as part of the "East Asia and Pacific" region. But under Trump, the ideas and terminology changed: the United States began increasingly to speak of the "Indo-Pacific" region; White House statements regularly spoke of American policy toward the "Indo-Pacific," and the military changed the name of its Pacific Command (Pacom) to the Indo-Pacific Command.

This appeared at first glance to be merely a change in terminology, but it reflected a larger change in American strategy and thinking that was prompted by China's growing strength. In the decades after the Nixon opening, American officials had wavered between a China-centered approach to Asia and an alternative approach that gave priority to America's East Asian military allies, notably Japan and South Korea. The national security advisors Henry Kissinger and Zbigniew Brzezinski, for example, had pursued Sinocentric policies, while President Reagan's secretary of state George Shultz placed less stress on relations with China and more on deepening ties with the East Asian allies. But by the time of the Trump administration, this East Asia focus was itself deemed insufficient, and American officials sought broader and more distant support, pursuing ever-closer cooperation with India (as well as other nations like Australia) in helping the United States offset China's growing military power.

During Trump's term in office, the policies of Chinese president Xi Jinping grew ever more repressive. China's security apparatus all but eliminated dissent inside the country and established an extensive system of camps to house and indoctrinate Uighurs in Xinjiang province; it also eliminated the last vestiges of political autonomy in Hong Kong. These changes in Chinese domestic policy served as a backdrop to the third strand of changes in the way Trump administration officials talked about China: they tried, in ways without precedent since the Nixon opening, to draw a distinction in public statements between China or the Chinese people, on the one hand, and the Chinese Communist Party, on the other—thus implicitly challenging the ruling party's right to speak for China's population of 1.4 billion. This was also to some extent a defense against allegations by the Chinese regime that American policy was "anti-China" or "anti-Chinese": the response by Trump administration officials was that the actions were being taken against the Chinese regime and the Communist Party, not against the country or its people.

The Trump administration's verbal campaign against the Chinese Communist Party ranged from the sophisticated to the crude. On the more intellectual level, Matt Pottinger, the deputy national security advisor, took a novel approach by delivering a series of speeches in Mandarin, aimed at Chinese-speaking audiences both inside and outside China. The first of these commemorated the traditions of China's May 4 Movement, which erupted in 1919 when Chinese students marched to Tiananmen Square to protest China's treatment at the Versailles peace conference. Choosing that date sent a message that there exist traditions of Chinese nationalism and patriotism separate from the narratives of the current regime.

"Will the [May 4] movement's democratic aspirations remain unfulfilled for another century?" Pottinger asked in the speech. "Will its core ideas be deleted or distorted through official censorship and disinformation? Will its champions be slandered as 'unpatriotic,' 'pro-American,' 'subversive'? We know the Communist Party will do its best to make it so."[25] (Unsurprisingly, Pottinger's address was immediately blocked inside China.)

Other Trump administration efforts along these lines were much blunter. Secretary of State Mike Pompeo, considerably more prominent than Pottinger, simply substituted "Chinese Communist Party" for "China" in public statements whenever he was referring to the

Chinese regime or government. (In a way, this was reminiscent of the era when Secretary of States John Foster Dulles and Dean Rusk had referred to "Red China.")

Thus, the Trump administration tended to couch its rhetoric about the Chinese leadership in the idiom of anticommunism—but *not* in terms of violations of human rights. Indeed, when it came to classic human rights violations such as the Chinese camps in Xinjiang, Trump himself, throughout most of his term, made few objections and even signaled agreement with Chinese policies. At one point, aides reported, Xi Jinping told Trump in a meeting why the Chinese regime was building camps in Xinjiang, and Trump said it was the right thing to do. On Hong Kong, where the Chinese regime was in the process of eliminating first protest demonstrations and then democracy itself, Trump offered few objections to China's conduct, though he once tweeted, "I have ZERO doubt that if President Xi wants to quickly and humanely solve the Hong Kong problem, he can do it."[26] In this respect, there was nothing unique about China: Trump tended to minimize the importance of human rights issues in other countries around the world, like Saudi Arabia, too.

Beyond these various strands of thinking about China policy, Trump and some of his politically oriented advisers sometimes added appeals that were simply racist or demonizing. Many of these came during the COVID-19 pandemic that dominated Trump's final year in office. During one 2020 campaign appearance, Trump told a cheering rally that he called the disease the "kung flu," while on many other occasions he referred to it as the "Chinese flu" or "Chinese virus"—spurning quiet appeals from some of his advisers on China policy to stop doing so.

In an interview in the spring of 2020, Stephen Bannon (who by then no longer served in the Trump administration but remained an informal adviser) laid bare the political motivations underlying Trump's "kung flu" China rhetoric: in the presidential campaign, Bannon said, "China is the only thing that matters, the only thing that works."[27]

## The Pandemic and 2020

On January 15, 2020, at the beginning of Trump's final year as president, he hosted a festive event in the White House East Room to commemorate the signing of his Phase One trade agreement. With a standing-room-only audience in attendance, Trump effusively praised his own agreement, his trade advisers, and the American business leaders who were in the room.

In the years since the Nixon opening, the signing of a long-negotiated deal between Washington and Beijing had usually ushered in a period of smooth relations with China or, at a minimum, a year or two in which the remaining conflicts between the two countries would be temporarily shelved and ignored. This time, the dynamics moved in the opposite direction: the trade ceremonies marked only a fleeting moment of harmony between America and China, and the rest of the year 2020 saw the Trump administration take an unprecedented array of actions aimed at imposing various sorts of restrictions and penalties on the Chinese regime. These actions involved a range of the leading agencies of the U.S. government, from the FBI to the U.S. Navy, from the State Department and Pentagon to the Treasury and Commerce Departments.

There were several underlying factors behind this wave of measures against China. One was simply that the trade talks were over: Trump had sought to maintain amicable relations with Xi Jinping in hopes that he could inveigle him into a good deal. Once the talks were completed, and there was no hope of a second deal covering the more difficult structural issues anytime soon, Trump no longer had the same incentive to placate Xi. Instead, a second factor came into play: the forthcoming 2020 election, in which Trump was hoping to make China policy an issue, gave him an incentive to look ever tougher in dealing with China.

Finally, the wave of sterner actions against China stemmed from a third factor: the COVID-19 epidemic, which burst forth in Wuhan, China, and throughout 2020 spread throughout the world, hitting the United States with particular force. By January, Trump's own aides were beginning to warn him about the epidemic, whose significance and severity he minimized for several months. However, early on Trump did impose a ban on flights from China to the United States, angering the Chinese regime. Trump also began to emphasize in public statements that the virus had come from China, and other American officials questioned China's explanation that the virus originated from animals at a Wuhan open market. Some of them argued that the virus may have come from a mistake inside the Wuhan Institute of Virology.[28]

Angered by the travel ban and by Trump's frequent efforts to blame China for the virus, Chinese officials responded with a massive disinformation campaign suggesting that although the virus broke out in Wuhan, it nevertheless had American origins. One story China pushed in its propaganda was that the virus was introduced to Wuhan when members of the U.S. Army visited Wuhan in the fall of 2019. (There was no evidence to support this claim.[29]) For a time, China also held up the export of ventilators, surgical masks, and other sorts of personal protective equipment (PPE) made in its factories, at one point saying it would not send out the equipment unless other countries changed what they said about China and the virus; this action, in turn, infuriated White House officials trying to obtain the PPE.[30]

The combination of all these factors—the disputes over the virus, the conclusion of the trade talks, the ongoing presidential campaign—meant that any previous restraints came off when it came to U.S. government action against China. During the era of engagement, it was commonplace for the White House to intervene to prevent various individual departments and agencies of the federal government from taking too many actions of their own against China. In contrast, the Trump administration in 2020 gave the green light to a proliferation of new restrictions.

The Justice Department launched a series of new cases aimed at preventing theft of American technology at leading American institutions, such as university campuses and medical research facilities. In January, the chairman of Harvard University's chemistry department was charged with taking money to help China. In May, a former employee of the Cleveland Clinic was arrested. FBI counterintelligence sought to clamp down on China's Thousand Talents program, which seeks to recruit scientists to China from overseas. In July, the Trump administration ordered the closure of the Chinese consulate in Houston, saying it had become a hub for spying and for the theft of intellectual property. During the FBI's ongoing campaign against technology theft, more than a thousand Chinese researchers left the United States, in many cases because their visas were revoked.[31]

The Defense Department opened the way for repeated naval operations in the waters near China. U.S. Navy ships carried out ten freedom-of-navigation operations in the South China Sea, more than ever in the past, and at least twelve transit voyages through the Taiwan Straits as well. The Pentagon banned any contracts with companies that use Chinese equipment from Huawei or ZTE. Meanwhile, four of the Trump administration's senior officials (Pompeo, National Security Advisor Robert O'Brien, FBI Director Christopher Wray, and Attorney General William Barr) gave a coordinated series of speeches calling attention to various threats from China.

This wave of actions continued during the weeks after Trump lost the election. In January 2021, the U.S. government issued a sweeping ban on all imports of cotton from Xinjiang, the Chinese province where the reeducation camps for Uighurs are located. And, ten days before Trump left the White House, Pompeo lifted the series of restrictions on contacts between American officials and Taiwan, many of which had been in effect since the United States had established diplomatic relations with China and broken off ties with Taiwan's Nationalist government in 1979.

## Conclusion

Overall, Donald Trump presided over a historic redirection of American policy that marked an end to the era of engagement with China. Over the course of Trump's four years, American officials increasingly came to view and speak of China as an adversary. Some of the new policies that originated with Trump are likely to endure beyond his presidency. In its first weeks in office, for example, the successor Biden administration announced that it would use tariffs and other tools to combat unfair trade practices with China.[32] At the same time, Trump also conducted China policy in the chaotic fashion he displayed elsewhere: it was personalized and mercurial, characterized by short-term changes in direction, and punctuated by frequent tweets and off-the-cuff remarks.

After his four years in the White House, Chinese officials were thoroughly disenchanted with Trump. Wang Huiyao, an adviser to China's State Council, commented the day after Biden was sworn in that "the contradictions [between the United States and China] will continue to exist, and they will not disappear, but the Biden administration will not be as crazy and irrationally play cards like Trump."[33]

It is difficult to say what might have happened if Trump had won the votes to stay in the White House for a second term. Even some of the officials who worked most closely under him on China policy are in disagreement about this. John Bolton, who served as the third of Trump's four national security advisors, wrote that if Trump had won reelection, "he might have careened back to bromance and a disastrous trade deal, just for starters."[34] On the other hand, Pottinger, who coordinated China policy for nearly four years (until he resigned and hurriedly left the White House hours after the insurrection of January 6, 2021) had a different forecast: "In a second term, he (Trump) would have moved towards a wholesale decoupling from China."[35] Based on Trump's performance during his four years as president, it is possible that either—or even both—of these predictions would have been borne out.

# 15

# Trump's Middle East Legacy

## ARMS, AUTOCRATS, AND ANNEXATIONS

*Daniel C. Kurtzer*

Donald Trump left office on January 20, 2021, with a Middle East legacy as incoherent as many other areas of his presidency.[1] Despite suggestions to the contrary (including by Secretary of State Mike Pompeo), there was no Trump doctrine; Trump's version of "America first" prompted one analyst to define the administration's strategy as "primacy without a purpose."[2] As with other aspects of his foreign policy, Trump used a bully pulpit to declare America's predominance in a region from which he otherwise wanted to withdraw.

Trump had no strategic vision or sense of American national interests. He cared only about himself, his own needs and vanities, satisfying his political base, and enhancing the prospects for his reelection. While some of his advisers had an agenda, for the president it was "Trump first" much more than "America First." Virtually all of his policy actions and statements can be explained only in this context.

Trump's pronouncements and actions on the Middle East reflected a strong desire to reverse the policies of his predecessors. Under Presidents George W. Bush and Barack Obama, the Middle East presented significantly more problems than opportunities for U.S. interests. After 9/11, U.S. engagement in the region became heavily militarized with extended wars and extended troop deployments in Afghanistan and Iraq. The Israeli-Palestinian conflict never really recovered from the second Intifada, despite serious negotiating efforts by the Israelis and Palestinians in 2008 and by Secretary of State John Kerry in 2013–2014. The Arab uprisings in 2011 gave way to a modicum of hope for democracy in Tunisia, but also a plethora of crises and wars in Syria, Libya, and Yemen. In the geopolitical vacuums created by these crises, transnational terrorist groups flourished, especially al-Qaeda and the Islamic State (or ISIS). Iran's nuclear program had been constrained in 2015 by a nuclear accord strongly criticized by Republicans and many Democrats as deficient in both substance and scope.

The Middle East had also become increasingly dysfunctional internally over several decades. Weak or failed states, corruption and crony capitalism, increasing gaps between rich and poor, out-of-control population growth, food insecurity, lack of employment opportunities, protracted conflicts, increasing authoritarianism and human rights abuses—all these factors and more made the Middle East a headache for U.S. presidents going back decades.

Trump inherited a mess. Apart from Tunisia, the 2011 Arab Spring failed to change the politics of authoritarianism in the region. In Egypt, following a brief governing audition of the Muslim Brotherhood, the Egyptian military staged a "coup" in 2013 and installed yet another general as president. A broad crackdown against both the Brotherhood and the leftists ensued. Civil war broke out in Libya, Syria, and Yemen, resulting in severe humanitarian crises and significant flows of refugees and internally displaced persons. After decades of calling for democracy and freedom in the region, the United States offered little to help nascent democrats deal with powerful entrenched autocrats.

There is one sense in which Trump's predispositions and vanities actually reflected a new Middle East reality: whereas the Middle East had been critically important for decades because of its oil and gas reserves, this was changing rapidly as Trump took office. Domestic fracking and oil/gas discoveries in the United States had dramatically reduced U.S. reliance on Middle East supplies. The region's fossil fuels remained important to U.S. allies, but that meant Trump could try to exact a price for the U.S. role as guaranteeing the security of oil and gas exports.

Trump's break with long-standing U.S. policy across the board in the Middle East could have made sense, therefore, had it focused on root causes and been guided by an underlying sense of purpose and strategy. In reaction to decades of U.S. support for autocrats who backed American aims in the region, Trump could have reoriented American policy in support of freedom and democracy, traditional Republican (and American) values. That was not the case, however.

Trump launched a set of discrete actions that failed to achieve their stated purpose. He and his supporters believed that by withdrawing from the Iran nuclear deal, the Joint Comprehensive Plan of Action (JCPOA), America and its allies would have a freer hand to constrain Iran's nuclear ambitions. Iran's nuclear program resumed, however, after the U.S. withdrawal in 2018, and massive economic sanctions imposed by the administration did not change Iranian policy.

Trump and his advisers believed Israel to be the only reliable ally in the region, and thus the administration shaped U.S. policy to an unprecedented degree to the interests of Israel's governing party. The U.S.-Israel alliance prospered, and progress was made in Israeli-Arab state relations; but the underlying Israeli-Palestinian conflict festered. Trump sought to wind down U.S. military commitments in the region, in particular after the successes of the international coalition in the fight against ISIS; but he left office with U.S. forces—albeit in reduced numbers—in the same places they had been in 2016.

Trump's ambitions and motivations notwithstanding, his legacy in the Middle East might best be characterized as tactical maneuvers and strategic incoherence.[3] Trump's actions and tweets left the Middle East in worse shape than what he had inherited, as his policy unorthodoxy created a great deal of uncertainty.

As with his infatuation with powerful autocrats elsewhere in the world, Trump expressed a particular affinity for Middle East strongmen—kings, princes, and authoritarian leaders. They welcomed his unwillingness to criticize their actions and his bluster against the shared enemy, Iran. His approach toward Israel was largely a function of his seeing Israel through the lens of domestic politics and his prospects for reelection. Another area where Trump threatened action but failed to achieve policy success was in Iran, whose nuclear program advanced significantly after Trump withdrew from the JCPOA, even as the massive U.S.-imposed sanctions against Iran took a serious economic toll on the country's population.

A key focus for Trump was trying to broker deals that favored America's fortunes, without much regard for their impact on regional stability or respect for human rights. The administration promoted arms sales to Saudi Arabia, in part for the public relations effect of the lucrative deals, and as sweeteners to secure normalization agreements between Israel and several Arab states. While he presided over a boom in America's arms exports, virtually all of the arms sales transacted during Trump's administration made little strategic sense.[4] The security importance, or lack of it, appeared to be far less important to Trump than the billions of dollars of sales he was able to announce.

Trump's policy reflected his particular brand of transactionalism, driven by securing short-term wins (often based on questionable objectives) at the expense of long-term strategy. For example, the president flouted decades of American policy and international law to extend recognition to the annexation of disputed territory in protracted conflicts. Trump recognized Israel's sovereignty over the Golan Heights, an area of land seized from Syria in 1967. Trump's State Department decided that Israeli settlements in the occupied territories were not illegal.[5] In a parting assault on respect for international legality, Trump recognized Morocco's sovereignty over the disputed territory of Western Sahara.[6]

In December 2017, Trump announced he would move the American embassy from Tel Aviv to Jerusalem, declared Jerusalem to be the capital of Israel, and said Jerusalem was "off the table," ignoring previous agreements between Israel and the Palestine Liberation Organization to the effect that Jerusalem's status would be subject to negotiations and agreement.[7] For Trump's action on Jerusalem, the United States received nothing from Israel in return.

A cadre of unprofessional, inexperienced, and ideologically driven advisers formulated Trump's policy toward Israel and the peace process. Each entered the administration with strong right-wing views regarding Israel's policies in the occupied territories; one of them, Trump's son-in-law Jared Kushner, had a long-standing family friendship with Prime Minister Benjamin Netanyahu.

Trump's succession of national security advisors did not help much, as they proved unable to discipline the president's actions or thinking—including his reputed uninterest in intelligence and policy briefings[8]—and thus saw their roles in terms of merely curbing the president's worst instincts. Indeed, it is this apparent bumper-car approach that best characterized Trump's Middle East policies: make bold or inflammatory announcements on Twitter, make policy decisions impulsively, ignore European allies, coddle Middle East autocrats, sell weapons, encourage Israel's annexationist agenda, appeal to the domestic political base, and wander aimlessly through four years of foreign policy chaos.

Trump's legacy in the Middle East will be seen, therefore, as a series of tactical maneuvers without an underlying strategy. He touted his prowess as a deal maker, but most of the deals he promoted either never materialized or involved unilateral concessions with no discernible return for the United States. Trump abandoned orthodoxy in the Middle East, embarking on policy pathways that, for the most part, complicated rather than advanced U.S. interests.

## Trump, the Region, and Domestic Politics

Given Trump's laser focus on his domestic base and reelection prospects, it is no surprise how much domestic politics factored into his policies. This was evident in the degree to which he translated his arms deals with Arab states into employment and profit increases for American business. In this respect, Trump was no different from his predecessors.

The most pronounced connection between Trump's domestic and foreign policies related to Israel and the president's relationship with Netanyahu, the Israeli prime minister. For more than a decade, Netanyahu had courted the Republican Party and avoided the Democrats. He resented American pressure on settlements and practices in the occupied territories. The advent of the Trump administration was therefore a godsend. Netanyahu expected and received no criticism of Israeli policies in the occupied territories, and he expected and received U.S. support for his political agenda, in particular cementing Israel's grip on the occupied territories. Netanyahu not only was not disappointed but also received from the Trump administration even more than he asked for—for example, U.S. recognition of Israeli sovereignty in the Golan Heights.

All of this translated well for Trump's domestic political agenda. A significant part of his political base consisted of pro-Israel evangelical Christians and right-wing Jews who had been pushing for U.S. support—even encouragement—of Israeli control over the occupied territories. The appointment of David Friedman as ambassador reflected this intersection of domestic and foreign policies: Friedman, Trump's bankruptcy lawyer, headed a U.S. organization that channeled funds to an Israeli settlement in the West Bank. Trump paid his domestic supporters not only in the actions he took, such as relocating the embassy to Jerusalem, but also in concrete measures. Two prominent evangelical pastors—Robert Jeffress and John Hagee—were invited as guest speakers at the embassy's ribbon-cutting ceremony.[9]

## Iran: Nuclear and Conventional Threats

No other issue in the Middle East consumed more of Trump's attention and scorn than the Iran nuclear deal, the Joint Comprehensive Plan of Action, or JCPOA, which had been negotiated and agreed upon during Obama's presidency in 2015. Well before the 2016 election, Trump railed against the deal and promised to pull the United States out of it.[10] It's not clear what accounted for Trump's unyielding opposition to the JCPOA. He clearly opposed any deals entered into by predecessors, especially Barack Obama, believing that no one was as adept as he at deal making. He also tuned into the Republicans' wall-to-wall opposition to the deal, prompting him to be louder and more definitive in his views—always terming it the worst deal ever made.

Opposition to the JCPOA also aligned his policies with those of Israel's prime minister, an added benefit for what Trump wanted to accomplish on the Israeli-Palestinian issue. For all his rhetoric, he did not make clear the substantive shortcomings of the deal that he wanted to fix, simply promising that he would pull the United States out and negotiate a better deal. He made good on the promise of pulling out in May 2018 when the United States formally exited the JCPOA. He did not produce a better deal, however.

The JCPOA was controversial even before Trump entered the debate. A majority of the U.S. Senate opposed it, but the Senate could not muster the sixty votes needed to block it. Several issues dominated the debate: the fact that the JCPOA contained several "sunset clauses" (that is, dates after which Iran could resume some nuclear activities); concerns about international inspection and verification of a program that Iran had grown clandestinely for many years; and the absence of any agreements to curb Iran's missile program, support for terrorism, or aggressive action in places like Syria and Yemen. JCPOA advocates emphasized the importance of international consensus to effectively restrain Iran's nuclear ambitions (France, Germany, the United Kingdom, China, Russia, and the European Union were also party to the agreement) and the fact that the JCPOA successfully brought the Iranian program to a halt soon after it went into effect. Between 2015 when it was agreed upon and 2018 when Trump pulled the United States out, the JCPOA was working as envisioned by its framers.

The Trump administration did not hide its real interest vis-à-vis Iran—trying to ensure that no avenues existed through which a new or revised agreement could be reached with Iran, and tacitly promoting regime change in Tehran. On May 21, 2018, just two weeks after the U.S. withdrawal, Secretary of State Pompeo delivered a major address in which he listed twelve demands that Iran must meet before the United States would consider a new agreement. Among the conditions on Pompeo's list were a full accounting of the prior military dimensions of Iran's program; a complete halt to uranium enrichment and a commitment never to pursue plutonium reprocessing; an end to Iran's proliferation of ballistic missiles; permitting the disarming, demobilization, and reintegration of Iraqi Shia militias; ending military support for the Yemeni Houthi militia; withdrawal of all forces under its command from Syria; and ending threatening behavior against its neighbors. Pompeo later added improvement in human rights as a thirteenth demand.[11] These extensive requirements put the onus squarely on Iran to radically change its policies.

The administration systematically began reimposing sanctions against Iran, which had a surprisingly strong impact on the Iranian economy, and attempted to create a "sanctions wall" to deter businesses from trading with Iran.[12] Iran's daily oil exports in early 2020 were just 3 percent of 2018 levels, the local currency lost 85 percent of its value against the dollar, and the cost of consumer goods doubled.[13] Trump also tried to trigger the "snapback" provisions of the JCPOA, which would have reimposed multilateral sanctions against Iran, but he could find no support among either the original JCPOA signatories or the UN Security Council. In the meantime, Iran resumed some of its nuclear activities, including enriching uranium to 20 percent concentration, well above the 3.67 percent agreed to under the original deal (but still far below the 90 percent required for a nuclear weapon).[14]

Trump's "maximum pressure" strategy toward Iran had little lasting impact. Iran's ability to project power may have been hampered somewhat, but the real effect of the massive sanctions was to impose severe hardships on the Iranian people. Trump's Iran policy failed in all respects, except in making it more difficult for his successor to deal with Iran's nuclear program and other malign activities. Trump was unable to negotiate a better deal with Iran, and he was unable to force Iran to capitulate to his demands. Trump instead left a vacuum in which uncertainty flourished and tensions rose, creating much higher stakes and a more likely prospect of conflict. The only argument in Trump's favor, offered by one of his appointees: "Although Trump did not solve the Iranian nuclear challenge, neither did Obama."[15]

## Israel, the Palestinians, and Normalization with the Arabs

Like every president who preceded him, Trump avowed strong support for Israel's security and well-being, reflected in generous security assistance[16] and political support in international forums like the United Nations. Trump, also like his predecessors, did not subject the U.S.-Israel relationship to any litmus tests of continued relevance, for example, by asking whether Israel really needed U.S. security assistance given its economic strength, or whether Israel should be exempt from criticism over its treatment of Palestinians in the occupied territories. Unlike his predecessors, however, Trump took support of Israel to a different level, characterized by no daylight between their positions, no criticism, and no differences of view. Secretary of State Pompeo tweeted, "America has no greater friend than Israel, and the people of Israel."[17] The net effect was to encourage some of Israel's most egregious behaviors, such as continuing settlement activity and its human rights violations in the occupied territories.

Trump seemed to have no hard views on Israel before deciding to run for president. Rather, his appointees who formulated and executed U.S. policy toward Israel played an outsize role in defining Trump's approach. Trump's son-in-law, Jared Kushner, and Trump's pick for U.S. ambassador to Israel, David Friedman, were not only pro-Israel activists but also specifically right-wing pro-Israel policy activists. Less than a week before the 2016 election, Friedman and a Trump Corporation lawyer, Jason Greenblatt (later to be appointed as a Middle East negotiator), published a position paper on Israel that foreshadowed many of the administration's actions. Acting on behalf of a president who paid little attention to detail on any issue, these staunchly pro-Israel figures were able to lead American policy down a rabbit hole of unprecedented one-sided policies related to the Israeli-Palestinian conflict. Trump's policies commanded significant support and encouragement from key segments of his political base—especially the pro-Israel evangelical Christian community and a majority of those on the right wing of the American Jewish community.[18]

When Trump's long-awaited Middle East peace plan finally came together in a 181-page paper unveiled in January 2020, it proved to be a one-sided proposal designed to secure Israeli interests in the occupied territories at the expense of the Palestinians.[19] This plan, constructed in close collaboration with the Israeli government but with virtually no input from the Palestinians, came on the heels of a succession of administration decisions that distanced the Palestinians from the administration: closing the Palestine Liberation Organization (PLO) office in Washington; shuttering the American consulate in Jerusalem; cutting aid to the Palestinian Authority and to the UN agency responsible for Palestinian refugees; and moving the U.S. embassy to Jerusalem, accompanied by Trump's declaring that Jerusalem was "off the table of negotiations."[20]

Kushner and his colleagues argued that new thinking was necessary to solve a long-standing stalemate, and they placed responsibility for previous failures squarely on the Palestinians.[21] In their view, the Palestinians were at fault for refusing to accept or negotiate previous peace proposals, and thus it was time for a new paradigm. They believed their view to be confirmed when the Palestinians categorically rejected the December 2017 decision to move the embassy to Jerusalem. At that time, Palestinian president Mahmoud Abbas told a meeting of the PLO Central Committee, "We will not accept for the U.S. to be a mediator, because after what they have done to us—a believer shall not be stung twice in the same place. . . . The deal of the century is the slap of the century."[22]

The Trump plan was a mixture of wishful thinking in support of right-wing Israeli preferences and outright bias against the Palestinians. For example, Trump asked the Palestinians to accept a state in about 18 percent of Palestine. That state would be composed of six noncontiguous cantons, surrounded by Israel. All Israeli settlements and settlers would be permitted to remain in place, on top of which Israel would be permitted to annex 30 percent of the West Bank, while handing over to Palestine the equivalent of 16 percent of territory inside Israel. Palestine's capital would be in the village of Abu Dis, not Jerusalem, an affront to Palestinians' long-standing view of Jerusalem as their capital. Perhaps most insultingly, Israel would control the decision as to when the Palestinians had met the plan's conditions for their statehood. As should have been expected, the Palestinians rejected the plan outright.

The already-moribund peace process ground to a complete halt in late spring 2020 as even the Israeli government, the primary beneficiary of its provisions, could not decide whether Trump's plan went far enough to satisfy the demands of the settler leadership and right-wing members of Netanyahu's government. They balked at the idea that Israel would be permitted to annex "only" 30 percent of the West Bank, and they opposed the plan's support for a Palestinian state. During the run-up to July, when annexation would have been permitted under Trump's plan, international pressure mounted against the prospect of annexation. In an unprecedented op-ed in an Israeli newspaper, the United Arab Emirates (UAE) ambassador to the United States, Yousef Al Otaiba, warned Israel that it could achieve either annexation or normalization with the Arabs, but not both.[23]

Recognizing that the prospects for success of its peace plan were fading rapidly, the administration pivoted and started working behind the scenes to test the waters for Israel-Arab state normalization as a way to demonstrate Trump's effectiveness as a foreign policy deal maker. A breakthrough occurred in August when Israel put the question of annexation on the back burner, and the UAE and Israel announced their intention to establish diplomatic relations. This was followed in September by the signing of a treaty between the two countries. Soon after, Bahrain agreed to normalize relations with Israel, as did Sudan (the three agreements were announced collectively as the "Abraham Accords") and later Morocco. The administration backed into a strategy: to salvage something from Trump's disastrous pursuit of peace in the Middle East and to build regional consensus for a tougher approach vis-à-vis Iran.

To be sure, the normalization accords had far less to do with the Arabs embracing Israel publicly than did two important strategic factors. First, the two Gulf states that normalized—the UAE and Bahrain—increasingly feared that a U.S. "pivot" from the region would weaken the American "security umbrella" on which they relied. Israel, they believed, might prove to be a more reliable security partner. Also, each of the normalizers, except Bahrain, received a tangible benefit from Washington for bringing their relations with Israel out of the shadows.

The United States paid a high price to incentivize the Arab states to enter into these normalization agreements, with the only discernible benefit to America being the possibility of additional arms sales to the UAE and Morocco. Trump promised to sell the UAE advanced fighter aircraft and attack drones; promised to remove Sudan from the list of state sponsors of terrorism and to provide it with "sovereign immunity" for future terrorism emanating from Sudanese territory; and recognized Morocco's claim to sovereignty in the disputed territory of Western Sahara, bucking the near-unanimous international consensus against such a move. Commenting on these U.S. actions, a prominent American conservative journal noted, "Washington is strengthening repression in Bahrain, underwriting aggression by UAE, sacrificing the Sahrawi people [of Western Sahara], undermining reform in Sudan, and even abandoning justice for Americans harmed by Sudan. The administration calls this an 'America first' policy."[24]

While many American politicians and policy analysts welcomed the establishment of relations between Israel and Arab states, the

Palestinians reacted with strong criticism, arguing that the UAE and others had abandoned them and the consensus of Arab support for Palestine embodied in the Arab Peace Initiative of 2002. The agreements in fact achieved nothing for Palestinians.

Trump's policy on the Palestinian-Israeli conflict exacerbated the polarization of American politics on the issue. Some mainstream Democrats joined Trump's base and most Republicans in supporting most of Trump's policies vis-a-vis Israel, while progressive Democrats increasingly opposed the administration's actions. The debate about America's support for Israel was also waged vocally in Congress and among some state legislatures related to the Boycott, Divest, and Sanctions (BDS) movement.[25] Legislation was adopted both nationally and at the state level characterizing BDS as anti-Zionist and anti-Israel, equating these views with antisemitism, and outlawing support for BDS in some forms of employment, including in state government positions.

Trump's legacy on the Israeli-Palestinian conflict will remain solid among his most ardent American supporters and the Israeli right wing, but will be seen by almost all international players as having set back the prospects for peace. Trump's real objective could not have been a workable peace initiative, as even casual observers of the history of the conflict would have told him the plan was an absolute nonstarter for the Palestinians. Rather, he and his advisers sought to fundamentally alter the starting point of any future peace talks.[26] Guided by ideologically driven advisers, Trump tried to "ring bells Biden can't un-ring." Trump's ambassador to Israel summed it up, smugly and perhaps prematurely: "There's no going back on what we've been able to do. . . . I'm frankly somewhere between addicted and intoxicated with what I've been able to do, and how much joy it gives me. . . . We've changed the narrative dramatically."[27]

## A Poor Choice of Friends—the Autocratic Attraction

Trump clearly had an affinity for autocratic leaders, in the Middle East and elsewhere. Trump admired both their strength and the near absence of constraints on their policies and actions. His deference to Vladimir Putin,[28] Kim Jong-Un, the Saudi and Gulf monarchs, Turkey's

Erdogan, and Egypt's Sisi (anointed by Trump as his "favorite dictator")[29] stood in stark contrast with the disdain or uninterest he displayed for most democratic leaders, including long-standing allies.

Trump sought immediate gratification from these relationships with autocrats, in the form of either public statements that he could use to promote his policies at home or announcements of large arms sales as a boon to American manufacturers. Many of these defense deals were dubious in nature and overblown. For example, he boasted that Saudi Arabia agreed to pay $1 billion to receive additional American troops; officials reported the figure was actually $500 million.[30] He used executive powers to push through an $8.1 billion arms deal with the Saudis that sparked serious humanitarian concerns.[31] And the administration announced two huge arms deals with the Saudis and the Kuwaitis just weeks before Trump left office, with neither deal certain of acceptance by the Senate.[32]

## Damn the Torpedoes: Bring Home the Troops

Trump acted as though asserting America's primacy in the Middle East—absorbing no costs or responsibilities—was tantamount to actually being the primary outside actor.[33] Echoing this, Secretary of State Pompeo advocated for bold American leadership but also emphasized the need to put America's own security interests first.[34] Trump was not alone in wanting to bring U.S. troops home from their protracted commitments in the Middle East; this had been one of President Obama's priorities as well. Trump thought the wars in the Middle East were too costly, but he showed little understanding of the strategic context of why the troops were there at all. Thus, his approach contained no cost-benefit calculation: he simply wanted to bring them home.[35]

He was the first U.S. leader to seek direct talks with the Taliban in Afghanistan, but proved more interested in securing a deal with them than stabilizing the Afghan government for the long term.[36] The negotiations with the Taliban were both more nuanced and more challenging than Trump likely expected. On the one hand, the negotiations conducted by U.S. special envoy Zalmay Khalilzad recognized the power dynamics within Afghanistan and the potential for diplomacy to resolve a conflict that had roots in the 9/11 attacks. On the other hand, Trump accepted the Taliban's demand to exclude the Afghanistan government from the negotiations and thus lowered prospects of a durable power-sharing solution. In February 2020, the United States and the Taliban reached a tentative agreement, but subsequent negotiations between the Taliban and the Afghanistan government stalled.[37]

The Taliban believed it could outlast the United States and the North Atlantic Treaty Organization (NATO) in its pursuit of control of Afghanistan—"NATO has the watches, but we have the time"—and it was confident that it was winning and did not need to compromise.[38] Trump's self-proclaimed deal-making prowess was supposed to free the United States from costly foreign entanglements but instead threatened to undercut efforts to leave behind a stable Afghanistan once the United States finally withdrew.[39]

The Trump administration advanced a proposal in 2017 to create a Middle East Strategic Alliance, which envisioned a Riyadh-based alliance, dubbed the "Arab NATO," designed to counter Iran and other regional security threats and to limit the role of Russia and China in the region.[40] This initiative went nowhere, as differences between prospective members and competing plans proposed by Russia and Iran resulted in a stalemate on the issue of regional security architecture.

Trump celebrated American military actions against ISIS in Syria as a major achievement and symbol of U.S. military primacy.[41] His assertion that ISIS had been defeated led him to order the withdrawal of U.S. troops from Iraq and Syria; this was widely seen as a gesture to Turkish president Erdogan, who took advantage of the announcement to intensify Turkey's assault on the Kurds in northern Syria. However, Trump's generals (many of whom did not support the exit) stalled by being deliberately vague on troop numbers, and the United States did not fully withdraw.[42]

Notably, Trump presided over a period of U.S. history in which no foreign terrorist attacks were successfully launched on American soil. The Trump administration also started no new wars. Trump's signature military achievements included the 2017 and 2018 strikes against targets in Syria in response to Syrian chemical weapons use, the 2019 assassination of ISIS leader Abu Bakr al-Baghdadi, and the 2020 assassination of Iranian general Qassem Soleimani. The White House took credit for destroying ISIS; in fact, ISIS was degraded and lost its territorial base in Syria/Iraq, but it was far from defeated.

## Russia and China—Asleep at the Switch

The key source of concern in the national security establishment about the possible withdrawal of U.S. troops from the region and repeated calls for the United States to "pivot" to Asia was the power vacuum it would create and the opportunity for Russia and China to play a larger role in the region. Russia (along with Iran) helped Syrian president Bashar al-Assad prevail over domestic opposition in the lengthy Syrian civil war. Russia used its direct military involvement after 2015 to showcase new weaponry and resolve. For example, Egypt signed a $3.5 billion arms deal with Moscow. Russia's sovereign wealth fund established deals in Bahrain, Kuwait, Qatar, Saudi Arabia, and the UAE for investments in Russia's economy. Russia also proved to be one of the most powerful external actors in Libya. Russian naval activity in the Eastern Mediterranean came to be seen as a threat to U.S./NATO dominance in the region.[43]

China, as well as Russia, took advantage of the vacuum resulting from Trump's strategic uninterest in the region. China focused primarily on strengthening economic ties, as part of its Belt and Road Initiative, and ensuring the supply of energy. China and Iran reportedly began working on an economic and security partnership.[44] As of mid-2019, China had thirteen partnership agreements of various levels with Middle Eastern countries.[45] China also started some smaller-scale military activities, such as maintaining a base in Djibouti, and antipiracy and maritime security operations in the Arabian Sea and Gulf of Aden.[46]

## Human Rights? Not on Trump's Watch

Trump's first overseas trip (widely regarded as having symbolic importance) was to Saudi Arabia, where his objective was to elevate the relationship into a "strategic partnership." In one sense, Trump was recognizing the historical underpinning of U.S.-Saudi relations: Saudi oil in exchange for an American security umbrella. Trump appeared to have no strategic plan for this trip, however, other than the prospect of a quick arms deal; Saudi energy was far less important to the United States since U.S. dependency on foreign hydrocarbons had decreased substantially. Trump also evinced no concerns about Saudi Arabia's abysmal human rights record or its military involvement in Yemen. The absence of a strategy resulted over time in the administration's turning a blind eye to the Saudi regime's repressive tactics, including human rights abuses at home, the war in Yemen, and the brutal murder of journalist Jamal Khashoggi.

In general, the Trump administration's record on human rights and democratization was abysmal. Regarding the occupied Palestinian territories, the administration developed a legal position that effectively took no position on the legality of Israeli settlements, thereby flouting international law and previous U.S. policy.[47] The annual State Department Human Rights Report stopped referring to the occupied territories as "occupied."[48] The United Nations expressed serious concern over the implications of Trump's peace vision on human rights in the occupied territories.[49]

It is evident that Trump adopted a selective approach to human rights—criticizing Iran while remaining silent about abuses in countries friendlier to the United States.[50] For Trump, investment in human rights and democratization cost money, required sustained effort, and would only yield results in the distant future. Unlike his predecessors, Trump did not see human rights as a moral responsibility or an important part of promoting a liberal international order.[51]

## Scorched Earth: The Final Months

Following his defeat on November 3, 2020, Trump spent nearly all his time denying the election results and plotting ways to overturn it. However, his administration, especially Secretary of State Pompeo, filled this period with a number of decisions and actions designed to burnish his own political credentials and complicate the incoming Biden administration's policies.

The administration decided to designate the Houthis in Yemen as a terrorist organization, effective on January 19, 2021, the day before Biden's inauguration.[52] During the course of the Yemen civil war, the administration had lent support to Saudi Arabia, and this action against the Houthis was a parting gift to the Saudis, who were likely to face pressure from Biden to end their involvement in Yemen and to improve their human rights record. Many U.S. and international human rights organizations castigated the administration for its action, arguing that it would worsen the already dire humanitarian crisis in Yemen.

During the interregnum between administrations, Pompeo visited a West Bank settlement and the Golan Heights territory claimed by Israel, the first such official visits by a secretary of state. Pompeo's visit underscored the administration's support for Israeli settlements and its flouting of international law. Ahead of the visit, Pompeo announced the administration's intention to equate the BDS movement with antisemitism, but State Department foot-dragging prevented this from happening before Trump left office.[53] Following Pompeo's visit, he announced that products made in settlements could be labeled "Made in Israel."

Pompeo added Iran to his last-minute hit list, announcing sanctions on seven companies and two individuals involved in shipping steel to or from Iran.[54] Without presenting any evidence, Pompeo also declared Iran to be the new "home base" of al-Qaeda, a charge disputed by counterterrorism experts.[55] Finally, Pompeo added a parting shot at U.S. ally and NATO member Turkey, criticizing Turkey for its purchase of weapons systems from Russia and for paying Syrian soldiers to fight in Libya.[56]

## Conclusions

Donald Trump's approach to the Middle East oscillated between emotional, uninformed, uncaring, and impulsive statements and actions, on the one hand, and a sustained effort to undermine the policies that had defined American interests and informed decades of American diplomacy in the region, on the other. That said, his record is not without some achievements.

Trump can claim credit for bringing to fruition the normalization agreements between Israel and the UAE, Bahrain, Sudan, and Morocco—relationships that had been building behind closed doors for many years. The normalization agreements and several discrete actions, such as the relocation of the American embassy to Jerusalem, proved very popular among his political base but failed to advance the prospects of Israeli-Palestinian peace.

Trump can also boast of not starting a war during his tenure, as well as continuing the process of extricating American forces from long-standing conflicts in the Middle East. Trump was not a pacifist—witness the one-off missile attacks against Syria and the high-profile assassinations. But he proved to be highly risk-averse, even in response to the reported entreaties of some advisers for more active military measures against Iran.

Trump's defenders promote the idea that his disruptive nature actually advanced long-term American interests in the Middle East:[57]

> "Trump has been a disrupter, and his policies, informed by his heterodox perspective, have set in motion a series of long-overdue corrections. Many of these necessary adjustments have been misrepresented or misunderstood in today's vitriolic, partisan debates. But the changes Trump has initiated will help ensure that the international order remains favorable to U.S. interests and values and to those of other free and open societies."

This view rests on an assessment that America's "unipolar moment" in world affairs has ended, along with the so-called liberal international order that arose after World War II. Emerging powers, such as China and Russia, have no interest in adhering to the norms of liberal internationalism, while at the same time globalization has proved to be a chimera. Instead, according to this view, world politics is characterized by competition between states and disruptions by nonstate actors. In the Middle East, this has meant promoting strong allies (regardless of their actions) and abjuring efforts to decide how states should be governed or how they treat their own citizens. Trump believed that America should not expend resources to play "global cop" and thus stepped back from long-established norms such as promoting peace, stability, human rights, and democracy.

Some will argue that Trump's policies brought Israel, Saudi Arabia, and some other Arab states into an effective alliance to pursue a campaign designed to destabilize Iran and bring about policy change, if not regime change. Trump believed Iran would renounce its nuclear ambitions only under the pressure of economic sanctions. However, this coercive diplomacy approach offered nothing to the Iranians for their compliance, and thus Trump left office with a defiant Iran expanding uranium enrichment and restarting elements of its nuclear program that had been stopped when the JCPOA was in effect.[58] Trump proved able to punish the Islamic Republic and its people, but unable to deal effectively with its nuclear ambitions, missile program, support for terrorism, or malign activities in the region.

Contrary to the views of his defenders, Trump left behind a more dangerous Middle East, in much worse shape than what he inherited. Without a strategy, Trump did nothing to deal with the deep problems and fissures within Arab societies, which have proved to be a potent breeding ground for radicalism. Trump's boast that he "defeated" ISIS had no meaning, as the movement and its ideological/religious attraction survived a military loss in Syria but continued to operate elsewhere.

Trump also did nothing to advance the prospect of Israeli-Palestinian peace. His so-called vision of peace and its one-sided support for positions advanced by Israel's right-wing governing coalition gave up any pretense of the United States as an honest broker in negotiation. His support for Israeli settlement activity and Israel's creeping annexation of the occupied territories made it more challenging for the parties themselves and outside players to revive even the prospect of serious negotiations.

With problems abounding at home—COVID, the economy, race relations, immigration, infrastructure degradation, and increased political polarization—and a foreign policy that appeared to value the immediate gratification of Twitter over reasoned analysis and judgment, and with his infatuation with autocrats over traditional allies, Donald Trump's legacy ended up as an empty, purposeless assertion of American primacy, but with little likely lasting effect.

# 16

## "Nut Job," "Scumbag," and "Fool"

### HOW TRUMP TRIED TO DECONSTRUCT THE FBI AND THE ADMINISTRATIVE STATE—AND ALMOST SUCCEEDED

*Beverly Gage*

In late January 2017, a week after his inauguration, President Donald Trump invited FBI director James Comey to the White House for dinner. Comey thought—hoped, really—that it would be a group event, perhaps a gathering of law-enforcement or intelligence officials. Instead, he showed up to a table set for two: just the president and the FBI director, their names rendered in calligraphy on place cards. They dined on shrimp scampi. But as Comey later reflected, it was really "my job security" that was "on the menu." Within minutes, Trump asked whether Comey wanted to stay on as FBI director, then laid out the conditions for doing so. "I need loyalty," the president said. "I expect loyalty."[1]

If Comey had been a political appointee—one of the thousands who move in and out of the White House at moments of presidential transition—the demand might have been merely tacky, more mafioso than statesman. The FBI director occupies an unusual place in the federal system, however. Though appointed by the president, the head of the FBI is tasked with standing apart from politics, a civil servant loyal to the truth and the law rather than to any individual politician. The director's term of office lasts for ten years, longer than any single presidency. The reason is simple: as the country's leading federal law enforcement agency, the FBI is frequently called on to conduct politically sensitive inquiries. In order for such investigations to be credible, the bureau must be seen as a nonpartisan force composed of objective fact-finders and trained professionals, not as the tool of any party or president.

Trump gave little credence to that idea, just as he hated the idea that government experts—from health officials to diplomats to military leaders—might be in a position to render judgments and affirm truths at odds with his political priorities. His efforts to denigrate, undermine, ignore, and weaken the so-called administrative state began long before his dinner with Comey and lasted well beyond his final day in office. As a term, the "administrative state" encompasses most of the federal bureaucracy, shorthand for the two million career public servants who work for the government but whose jobs persist outside of election cycles.[2] In February 2017, just weeks after Comey's awkward dinner at the White House, Trump aide and chief strategist Stephen Bannon identified "the deconstruction of the administrative state" as one of the top priorities of the Trump White House.[3] According to Trump, federal employees acted as a drag on American capitalism—part of "the steady creep of government bureaucracy that drains the vitality and wealth of the people," as he complained during a speech in Warsaw, Poland, in the summer of 2017.[4] Nonpartisan government employees also posed a more direct threat to his political power: charged with uncovering facts and enforcing the law, they had the ability to challenge Trump's claims about the state of the world—and about the questionable activities of his own administration.

National security agencies, especially the FBI, bore the brunt of Trump's hostilities. Trump launched an open and unabashed political war against his own intelligence agencies, railing against them as "Deep State" conspirators out to undermine the public good and destroy his presidency. In doing so, he radically altered their status within American political culture. Before Trump, most Republicans and conservatives professed great admiration for the FBI, CIA, and other intelligence agencies, describing them as patriotic bulwarks vital to national security. Democrats and progressives tended to view them with greater skepticism, cognizant of national security imperatives but also aware of the potential for excessive secrecy and abuse of civil liberties. Trump flipped that equation, sending Republicans scrambling to condemn a disloyal and invasive "Deep State" while Democrats looked to the FBI and other intelligence services to hold the White House accountable.[5]

---

Trump's fear that career federal employees did not especially like him had at least some grounding in truth. According to an October 2016 poll by *Government Executive* magazine, a slim majority of federal employees said they were likely to vote for Democratic candidate Hillary Clinton, while just 34 percent favored Trump.[6] This was hardly a surprising finding, given Trump's open contempt for government work. But such partisan preferences should have been irrelevant. As members of the "administrative state," federal employees are supposed to set aside their political views when carrying out their official duties—to be as objective, nonpartisan, and professional as possible.

Congress codified this idea in law in 1883, spurred to action by a national crisis. Two years earlier, a deranged federal office-seeker had shot and killed President James Garfield, claiming that the president denied him the diplomatic job he deserved in exchange for supporting Garfield in the 1880 election. Congress soon passed the Pendleton Act, the nation's first major civil-service law, creating a system of exams to award federal jobs by merit rather than party patronage and establishing protections to prevent employees from being fired during shifts in administration. Since that moment, the federal bureaucracy has expanded far beyond anything imagined in the nineteenth century. The FBI alone—not even a figment of the imagination in the 1880s—now employs thirty-five thousand people. But the principles of that original vision still apply. In its modern incarnation, the federal civil service is supposed to be guided by merit, expertise, and professionalism rather than by partisan politics.

Things have never been so simple in practice, however—especially in the case of the FBI. In 1907, when the attorney general Charles Bonaparte first proposed an investigative bureau within the Justice Department, Congress resisted for fear that the detective force would be used for partisan ends. Bonaparte went ahead and created his bureau, but soon ran into accusations that he was deploying his new employees to spy on his political enemies.[7] Such accusations continued under longtime FBI director J. Edgar Hoover, who ran the bureau from 1924 through 1972. Throughout his career, Hoover insisted that the FBI was a bastion of professionalism and objectivity, a model of administrative expertise. At the same time, he was a deft political operator, sometimes supporting and sometimes undermining the current occupant of the White House and other politicians.

Hoover benefited from being in the right place at the right time. The FBI's most significant growth occurred during the New Deal and World War II, periods that gave birth to both the modern welfare state and the modern security state. As political scientists Stephen Skowronek, John A. Dearborn, and Desmond King point out, the bureaus and agencies created during that era were meant to be "deep"—to have roots and structures that would extend beyond the life of any presidency, thus giving the government forms of continuity and expertise that election-driven appointments could not. Trump's definition of the Deep State was far more negative: a conspiratorial vision in which career bureaucrats and intelligence officials were actively colluding with his political enemies to bring down the presidency.[8]

Republicans and Democrats alike participated in the expansion of the administrative state, voting for new laws and programs and agencies (most of them situated in the executive branch) that required the employment of an ever-growing number of Americans. Still, the two parties never saw eye to eye on the desirability of this expansion. In 1964, speaking on behalf of Republican candidate Barry Goldwater, the budding conservative star Ronald Reagan complained that a "little intellectual elite," embedded within agencies "in a far-distant capital," was abusing its authority to undermine individual citizens' autonomy.[9] Since that moment, attacking the federal bureaucracy and its allegedly arrogant, out-of-touch experts has been a staple of Republican politics. In his 1981 inaugural address as president, Reagan declared that "government is not the solution to our problem; government is the problem," perhaps the most famous indictment of the administrative state ever uttered.[10] Two decades later, President George W. Bush carried on the tradition of "politicizing and terrorizing the bureaucracy," in the words of one critic, attacking the federal civil service in both word and deed.[11]

Even the most conservative Republicans usually carved out a key exception to this critique, however. While they railed against the "do-gooders" of the welfare state and the diplomatic corps, they usually championed the men and women of the security state, the realm of government composed of the intelligence agencies, military branches, and related national-defense services. The FBI fell into this category. Its employees are bound by many of the same rules that govern other parts of the federal bureaucracy: distance from politics, hiring by merit, the cultivation of impartial expertise. But Republican presidents have traditionally viewed them as a far more congenial constituency than, say, the employees of the Social Security Administration. Even as a lifetime federal bureaucrat, FBI director Hoover became known as a "patron saint" of modern conservatives, who admired him for his outspoken right-wing views on race and religion and for his hostility to the American Left.[12] Hoover built the FBI in his image, giving it a reputation as both a professional law-enforcement agency and a bastion of conservatism.

This basic sympathy of outlook did not always prevent clashes between the FBI and Republican occupants of the White House. Though close friends with Hoover, Richard Nixon came to office in 1969 determined to bring the federal bureaucracy under White House control and to use agencies such as the FBI to serve his political interests. Within months, he found himself embroiled in clashes with Hoover, who sometimes accommodated and sometimes resisted Nixon's requests that the FBI surveil and investigate the president's political enemies. At one point, Nixon thought about firing Hoover but backed off for fear of a national scandal. When Hoover died conveniently in May 1972, Nixon appointed a political loyalist to head the FBI. That move exacerbated rather than contained the growing tensions, however. After the Watergate burglary that June, the FBI's second-in-command, a career civil servant named Mark Felt, began leaking to the press about the progress of the investigation as the top-secret source "Deep Throat"—the beginning of the end for Nixon.[13]

But even Nixon rarely denounced the FBI in public, preferring backroom maneuvering to any sort of open clash. Trump broke decisively from this tradition. Over the course of his presidency, Trump accused the FBI of collusion, corruption, incompetence, and even criminal activity, depicting the agency as the leading edge of a Deep State conspiracy out to discredit his administration. He attacked the FBI's leadership with demeaning names: "nut job," "phony," "ignorant fool," "major sleazebag."[14] His most aggressive assaults often came in response to specific investigations, acts of retaliation and intimidation aimed at undermining FBI inquiries into his administration's ties to Russia. To Trump, anyone who was not with him was against him, including a vast array of government employees who were supposed to be loyal to the facts and the truth and the law—and not to the Trump White House.

---

Comey was no stranger to political controversy when he showed up for dinner with Trump in January 2017. A lifelong Republican, Comey had spent much of his career as a federal prosecutor, first as a U.S. attorney in New York, then as a top official in the Department of Justice, followed by stints at two major defense contractors. Despite his partisan affiliations, Comey prided himself on his professional independence throughout his government employment. In 2004, as acting attorney general, he opposed renewal of a controversial domestic surveillance program initiated by President George W. Bush, arguing that it was unconstitutional. When Bush administration officials showed up at the hospital bedside of Attorney General John Ashcroft, hoping for a quick sign-off to renew the program, Comey rushed to the hospital as well, threatening to resign if the renewal went through. This reputation for independence made him appealing to President Barack Obama, who, unlike Trump, believed in the FBI's nonpartisan mission. Obama appointed Comey for a ten-year term as FBI director in May 2013.[15]

For his first few years, Comey focused on keeping the FBI humming along, attempting to expand the numbers of women and people of color in the bureau's ranks while steering clear of partisan politics.

Before 2016, his most controversial public statement concerned crime and policing. In response to the emerging Black Lives Matter movement, Comey argued that criticism of the police led to higher crime rates and more gun violence in embattled urban neighborhoods. "I don't know whether that explains it entirely," he told an audience at the University of Chicago Law School, "but I do have a strong sense that some part of the explanation is a chill wind blowing through American law enforcement over the last year." The statement sparked pushback among criminal-justice activists and even some members of his own Justice Department, who rejected the so-called Ferguson effect as a racist myth. But Comey's remarks had few repercussions in the rest of Washington, where most Republicans agreed with him and most Democrats seemed inclined to steer clear of the issue.[16]

Partisan politics caught up with him in March 2015. That month, as part of a fractious Republican-led inquiry into a fatal attack on U.S. diplomatic facilities in Benghazi, Libya, congressional investigators discovered that Hillary Clinton had used a private email server during her time as secretary of state. Over the summer, the FBI opened "Midyear Exam," an investigation into whether Clinton had transmitted classified information on her private server—and, if so, whether she had ill intent. The investigation hung over Clinton's presidential campaign throughout 2015 and into 2016, as she jousted with socialist rival Bernie Sanders for the Democratic nomination. Then, on July 5, 2016, Comey announced in a press conference that the FBI had found no evidence of criminal wrongdoing. Though Clinton had been "extremely careless" in handling classified information, he explained, she showed no malevolent purpose and therefore should not be subject to prosecution.

Comey praised FBI employees for their "remarkable work in this case," emphasizing that it had been careful, thorough, and above all objective. The press conference itself was hopelessly enmeshed in politics nonetheless. The previous week, Attorney General Loretta Lynch had met with former president Bill Clinton (Hillary's husband) aboard a plane on the Phoenix airport tarmac. Ostensibly just a meet-and-greet, the encounter had provoked a furor, since Lynch, as attorney general, was supervising the investigation into Hillary Clinton's email server. It was at that point that Comey made the unusual decision to release the results of the investigation during a press conference—without consulting Lynch or coordinating with the Department of Justice. He argued that his go-it-alone strategy stood the best chance of preserving the FBI's reputation as a nonpartisan, professional investigative agency in the midst of so much political turmoil.

It did anything but. Trump ran a "law and order" campaign, championing the police while vilifying immigrants and people of color as criminals out to undermine public safety and the American way of life. His message should have placed him in sympathy with the FBI, especially given Comey's statements about policing and crime. Instead, Trump seized on Comey's exoneration of Clinton as evidence that the FBI, like the Democratic Party, was scheming to destroy his candidacy. On the campaign trail, Trump had already called for Clinton to be thrown in jail for supposedly undermining national security, going so far as to lead chants of "Lock Her Up" at campaign rallies. After Comey's press conference, he transferred some of that fury onto Comey and the FBI. "FBI director said Crooked Hillary compromised our national security," Trump tweeted on July 5. "No charges. Wow! #RiggedSystem."[17]

Trump's attacks continued over the next several months as he and Clinton secured their parties' nominations and entered into the most divisive campaign in modern political history. On October 17, Trump retweeted an article from the far-right Daily Caller hinting that Comey deliberately "stood in the way" of the Clinton email investigation. "Crooked Hillary colluded w/FBI and DOJ and media is covering up to protect her," he declared in a follow-up tweet. "It's a #RiggedSystem!"[18] According to Trump, the FBI conspired to obscure massive criminal wrongdoing by Clinton in order to aid her election and thus provide a congenial environment for future machinations by the secretive and manipulative Deep State.

So Trump was as surprised as anyone by what happened on October 28, twelve days before the election, when Comey suddenly reversed course and announced that the FBI was reopening the Clinton email investigation. The impetus for this turn of events came from an unrelated inquiry into former Democratic congressman Anthony Weiner, who had been accused of inappropriate online sexual exchanges with an underage girl. In the course of that investigation, the FBI came across a laptop shared by Weiner and his wife Huma Abedin, a close adviser to Clinton. On the laptop were tens of thousands of "emails that appear to be pertinent" to the Clinton investigation, as Comey explained in a letter to Congress.[19]

Comey once again framed his decision to reopen the investigation—and to reveal the fact publicly—as the fulfillment of his duty as a federal civil servant. In truth, political pressures from within the FBI played a significant role in his decision-making. As Comey later acknowledged, the powerful New York field office contained a group of current and former officials who harbored a "deep and visceral hatred of Secretary Clinton"—the twenty-first-century extension of Hoover's conservative institutional culture. Under the circumstances, Comey feared that news of the Weiner email cache would be leaked to the press. He concluded that the FBI's reputation would be better served by a voluntary disclosure of the information, in keeping with its mission to follow the facts and to disregard politics.[20]

His announcement set off a political firestorm. Democrats were appalled at his decision to reveal inconclusive developments in an ongoing investigation—a highly unusual move in any case, much less in one involving a major-party candidate just days before a presidential election. Trump was delighted, tossing aside his previous grumbling about FBI collusion in favor of unmitigated praise. "I respect the fact that Director Comey was able to come back after what he did," Trump told a rally in Phoenix, absolving Comey of the earlier charge that the FBI had gone soft on Clinton. "I respect that very much."[21]

The admiration proved to be short-lived. On November 3, three days before the election, Comey sent another letter to Congress—this time declaring that the email investigation was closed once again, the FBI having found nothing of interest on the Weiner laptop. At that point, Trump resumed his attacks, going back to his old themes of FBI collusion with "Crooked Hillary." He could have saved his breath. Three days later, he won the election in a squeaker, with Democrats—including Clinton herself—convinced that he owed his margin of victory to Comey's October letter.

---

Had Clinton's email server been the only political investigation of significance that fall, Trump's struggle with the "Deep State" might have ended there, with the FBI receding in importance for Trump and Democrats resuming their traditional suspicions of the bureau. But another inquiry was also under way—one that Comey had failed to mention during the election. In July 2016, around the same time that Comey was closing the Clinton email investigation for the first time, the FBI received notice of strange contacts between Trump campaign operatives and representatives of the Russian government. Around the same time, the website WikiLeaks published thousands of private emails stolen from Democratic National Committee (DNC) servers. The FBI suspected that the two might be linked—that the Russians were attempting to influence the U.S. election in favor of Trump, largely through techniques of social media manipulation. In mid-July, Comey launched an investigation into Russian interference in the 2016 election and the Trump campaign's possible ties to Russia, code-named Crossfire Hurricane.

That inquiry continued from the summer into the fall, as Comey closed the Clinton email investigation, then reopened it, then closed it again. He said nothing in public about the Russia angle, on the logic that Crossfire Hurricane was a secret counterintelligence investigation and thus entirely different from the criminal inquiry into Clinton's email server. Not until December, several weeks after the election, did federal intelligence agencies publicly confirm that the Russian government was likely behind the DNC hack.

This was the context in which Trump made his bid for Comey's "loyalty" over dinner—not merely an attempt to secure the director's friendship but an overt bid to disrupt and interfere with the ongoing Russia investigation. Comey responded uneasily, explaining that he would give the president "honesty," in accordance with the FBI director's status as an independent, nonpartisan government employee. Trump wanted more, proposing the category of "honest loyalty" as a wink-and-nod alternative. Still concerned, Comey agreed that "you will get that from me," then retreated to make a written record of their disturbing conversation.[22]

What he got from Trump in return was an unceasing pressure campaign, fueled in part by advice from the president's top aides. Trump came to office surrounded by advisers suspicious of the Deep State machinations—not only Bannon but also Roger Stone, a longtime

Republican dirty-tricks operative whose 2013 book accused Lyndon Johnson of colluding with the FBI and other shadowy forces to murder JFK.[23] Right-wing publications similarly fed Trump's anxieties. In December 2016, a writer identified as "Virgil" published a four-thousand-word article on the right-wing *Breitbart* news site, warning that the "military-industrial complex" and the "establishment" were already out to get Trump. "The term 'Deep State' refers to the complex of bureaucrats, technocrats, and plutocrats that likes things just the way they are and wants to keep them like that—elections be damned," Virgil wrote. *Breitbart* titled the article "The Deep State vs. Donald Trump," a handy summary of the narrative that would guide the Trump administration's actions over the next four years.[24]

Comey continued to be a focus of Trump's ire and of White House efforts to shut down the Russia investigation. In mid-February, Trump asked Comey to stay behind after a group meeting with intelligence officials, in the hopes of persuading the FBI to go easy on National Security Advisor Michael Flynn, under investigation for lying about his conversations with Russian officials. The following day, Comey asked Attorney General Jeff Sessions to ensure that the FBI director and the president would never again be left alone together, fearing that Trump would continue to escalate his partisan demands and intimidation tactics. Deprived of direct occasions for influencing the FBI investigation, Trump once again turned to Twitter, accusing the FBI of leaking classified information and of harboring a vendetta against his fledgling administration. On May 9, in an act that stunned even his most diehard supporters, he took the aggressive step of firing Comey.

The firing occurred in true Trumpian fashion: it was sudden, personal, and calculated to be as embarrassing to Comey as possible. Rather than contact Comey directly, Trump released his letter of dismissal to the press, leaving Comey to discover what had happened when he heard it on the television news. At the time, Comey was in Los Angeles, preparing to deliver a speech at an FBI diversity-in-recruiting event. Upon learning that he had been fired, he wondered if he would have to drive back across the country or if he would be allowed to return on a government plane. Eventually acting FBI director Andrew McCabe approved one last flight, and Comey ventured back to Washington in both glory and disgrace, the first major casualty of Trump's war on the intelligence agencies and the administrative state.

---

By firing Comey, Trump hoped to shut down the Russia investigation. Instead, the opposite happened: what had been a routine counterintelligence investigation became a constitutional crisis, with much of the nation horrified at Trump's attempt to strong-arm an independent investigative agency into political submission. Concerned at the prospect of allowing a president to act with such impunity, Deputy Attorney General Rod Rosenstein appointed a special counsel to carry on the Russia investigation. For the position, he chose a man known around Washington as a paragon of the administrative state's by-the-books, nonpartisan ethos: former FBI director Robert Mueller.

Liberals and Democrats flocked to Mueller's side, predicting a report that would finally expose Trump's double-dealing with Russia as well as his attempts to obstruct investigators at home. So did at least a few Republicans, impressed with Mueller's reputation for probity and thoughtful public service (as well as his status as a lifelong Republican). Trump himself expressed outrage, not least because Mueller had worked closely for years with Comey. Trump labeled the Russia probe a "totally conflicted and discredited Mueller Witch Hunt" and boasted that "if I wanted to fire Robert Mueller . . . , as reported by the Failing New York Times, I would have fired him" (though most legal experts agree that the president does not have the authority to fire a special counsel).[25] Privately, though, Trump was worried about the consequences of the Mueller probe. "This is terrible," he fumed upon hearing of Mueller's appointment. "This is the end of my presidency."[26]

In the end, the Mueller report, like Comey's press conferences, satisfied almost nobody. The report showed that Russian operatives had interfered with the 2016 election in order to help Trump, and that Trump campaign staffers provided information to them that may have helped with the effort. It also showed that Trump repeatedly attempted to interfere with the Mueller investigation, an effort that proved "unsuccessful" mostly "because the persons who surrounded the President declined to carry out orders or accede to his requests."[27]

The report stopped short of accusing the president of direct collusion or obstruction of justice, however, in part because Mueller did not believe that criminal charges could be pursued against a sitting president. "While this report does not conclude that the President committed a crime, it also does not exonerate him," Mueller wrote, a wishy-washy statement that clarified nothing.[28]

Attorney General Bill Barr quickly spun the results to Trump's benefit, arguing that Mueller's inconclusive conclusions showed that Trump had been right to suspect a witch hunt. "President Trump faced an unprecedented situation," Barr declared two days after receiving the report. He explained that the president was justifiably "frustrated and angered by a sincere belief" that his "political opponents" were conspiring with career government officials to undermine his presidency.[29] By the time Barr released the report to the public three weeks later, the official White House narrative was set: just as Trump had suspected, a group of partisan Deep State officials had conspired to undo the will of the American people, only to find themselves thwarted by lack of evidence.

---

Trump himself wasted no time in declaring the report a "Complete and Total EXONERATION."[30] Despite the alleged victory, he did not let up on his campaign against Mueller and Comey or against the other federal civil servants who spoke out against him. In the fall of 2019, the Democratic-controlled House began impeachment inquiries on charges that Trump solicited foreign interference in the 2020 election during conversations with the president of Ukraine, a serious abuse of presidential power. The preliminary hearings brought an array of career diplomats and public servants to the witness table, many of them hailed by the press for their deep knowledge and seriousness of purpose. Among them was Lieutenant Colonel Alexander Vindman, a Ukrainian-born career army officer and Eurasia specialist. Vindman testified not only about his knowledge of Ukraine but also about his love for the United States, where government employees could tell the truth—even about the president—without fear of retaliation. Several months later, he was forced out of the army after more than two decades of service because of "bullying, intimidation and retaliation" from the Trump White House, in the words of his lawyer.[31]

Such stories of an angry and contemptuous president wreaking vengeance on career government employees resonated well beyond the impeachment hearings. Morale at the State Department fell precipitously under Trump, as the White House ignored, dismissed, and actively mocked diplomatic advice. "In my three and a half decades as a U.S. Foreign Service officer, proudly serving five presidents and ten secretaries of state from both parties, I've never seen an attack on diplomacy as damaging, to both the State Department as an institution and our international influence, as the one now underway," retired diplomat William Burns wrote in *Foreign Affairs* magazine in 2019.[32] By neglect as well as intent, Trump allowed key positions at State to go unfulfilled, gumming up the work of the bureaucracy. Meanwhile, many high-ranking career employees resigned, while an untold number of prospective recruits never bothered to apply, loath to serve under a president who evinced so little use for their work.

Those who stayed found that their advice often went unheeded—indeed, that they were not consulted in even basic matters of policy. When Trump announced a ban on travelers from predominantly Muslim countries in early 2017, he did so with little input from top Defense or Justice officials.[33] After the COVID-19 pandemic took hold in the spring of 2020, he was quick to dismiss public-health advice and to denounce infectious-disease expert Anthony Fauci as a "disaster" surrounded by "idiots."[34] When a hurricane failed to strike Alabama, in defiance of Trump's predictions, he pressured the National Weather Service to alter its maps to make his claims seem more plausible. "He is demoralizing and undermining one government department after another," *Washington Post* columnist Max Boot wrote in 2019, citing a state of dismay not only at the State Department and the National Weather Service but at the Department of Homeland Security, the National Security Council, the CIA, and the Defense Department.[35]

Some agencies went out of their way to anticipate possible objections from the White House. In preparation for an exhibit on women's suffrage, the National Archives altered photographs of the 2017 Women's March to obscure signs critical of Trump, explaining that "as a non-partisan, non-political federal agency, we blurred references to the President's name on some posters, so as not to engage in current political controversy."[36] Others held firm under pressure. In 2020, after Trump threatened to call out the army to suppress protests for racial justice, military leaders objected vociferously, citing the dangers of deploying the army on domestic soil.

One Trump appointee went so far as to compose an anonymous editorial in the *New York Times* assuring the country that there were still "adults" within the White House orbit prepared to stand up for the higher virtues of fact, truth, law, and democracy. "This isn't the work of the so-called deep state," wrote Homeland Security chief of staff Miles Taylor, later revealed to be the author of the essay. "It's the work of the steady state."[37]

---

Taylor's essay highlighted the conflicted loyalties of some Trump appointees, who believed in the political mission but also admired the work of career government employees. In popular politics, by contrast, the response to Trump's attacks fell mostly along partisan lines. As recently as 2003, the FBI's approval rating among Republicans had exceeded that of Democrats by a wide margin: 63 percent to 44 percent, respectively.[38] Under Trump, that equation was reversed. By the middle of 2018, according to a Pew survey, 77 percent of Democrats approved of the FBI, while only 49 percent of Republicans did. And the Republican decline came almost exclusively during the Trump presidency, with the FBI's approval rating falling from 65 to 49 percent in little more than a year.[39] The conservative magazine *National Review* noted the change, labeling the Democrats' "newfound faith" in the intelligence establishment "every bit as partisan as Republicans' newfound skepticism."[40]

The FBI remained a special target for Trump even as the focus on Midyear Exam and Crossfire Hurricane receded. By 2019 nearly every high-ranking official who had worked on those investigations had either been fired or stepped down. A few created their own scandals as they left, amid charges of political corruption, incompetence, and sexual indiscretions. The most dramatic was the revelation of August 2016 text exchanges between FBI officials Peter Strzok and Lisa Page (who were engaged in an extramarital affair at the time), who assured each other that Trump was never "going to become president" because "we'll stop it."[41] Trump made the most of those discoveries, attacking Strzok as a "sick loser" and both officials as "corrupt FBI lovers" riddled with bias and lack of professionalism.[42]

The ongoing tensions with the Trump White House left Comey's successor in a difficult situation. To replace Comey, Trump appointed a low-key Republican lawyer and Yale Law graduate named Christopher Wray, who promised at his nomination hearing that "I will never allow the FBI's work to be driven by anything other than the facts, the law, and the impartial pursuit of justice."[43] Perhaps for that reason, Trump soon turned on his own appointee. Among Trump's complaints was the fact that Wray failed to denounce Hunter Biden, son of Democratic presidential candidate Joe Biden. He also disliked that Wray considered the left-wing activist group Antifa more of an "ideology" than a concerted terrorist organization. As the 2020 election approached, Trump threatened to fire Wray just as he had fired Comey.[44]

On the campaign trail, Trump doubled down on his "law and order" politics, alleging that "Biden stands with the riots & looters" while "I stand with the HEROES of law enforcement."[45] That fondness for law enforcement still did not extend to the FBI or other federal agencies, however. Throughout the campaign, Trump accused the "Comey/Mueller inspired FBI" of going soft on the "ANARCHISTS & THUGS" protesting in support of racial justice and police reform. He blamed other members of "the deep state, or whoever" for a variety of ills, including the obstruction of COVID vaccine development.[46] After losing the election, Trump excoriated the "'Justice' Department and the FBI" for doing "nothing about the 2020 President Election Voter Fraud, the biggest SCAM in our nation's history," falsely claiming that he had actually won the election. In that same tweet, he called on those who agreed with him to assemble "in D.C. on January 6th."[47]

When January 6 came, hundreds of Trump supporters stormed the Capitol as Congress attempted to certify the Electoral College count. They terrorized members of Congress and rampaged through the building, causing extensive property damage. A police officer and several protesters died as a result of the confrontation. It fell to the FBI to investigate what many Democrats characterized as a vicious terrorist attack, putting its agents at the center of one last partisan controversy. Many Republicans responded by blaming the FBI for failing to anticipate the riot.[48]

On January 20, 2021, Trump left office. Meanwhile, the people he had spent years attacking—the career officials of the government—stayed behind to assess the damage and pick up the pieces. Large swaths of the administrative state remained unscathed, its employees still employed, its ethos of nonpartisan professional work powerfully resistant to "deconstruction." But as political scientists Lisa K. Parshall and Jim Twombly have noted, there are many ways to measure Trump's impact on administrative governance, most of which go beyond questions of budgetary size or mere survival.[49] Rhetorically, Trump's attacks on public servants were unsurpassed among American presidents for their denigrating and dismissive tone. And his policy agenda, whether in diplomacy or health policy or immigration, changed the inner workings of many government bureaucracies. As President Joseph Biden's new secretary of state Anthony Blinken remarked upon taking up his appointment, "The State Department I'm walking into today is not the same one I left four years ago." According to Blinken, its employees were demoralized, its career service hollowed out, and its mission under question throughout the world.

The FBI was not the same either. Thanks to support in Congress, its budget actually grew slightly under Trump, from $8.76 billion in 2017 to $9.25 billion in 2020, as did its number of employees.[50] But few would say that the FBI came out of the Trump era better off. Four years of battling the president left the bureau reeling from high executive turnover, internal scandals, and damage to its reputation, especially among the Republicans, who had once been its greatest supporters.

Attempting to set a new tone, President Biden signaled early on that he would seek stability and cooperation rather than an ongoing war with the intelligence community. On January 21, the president's first full day in office, the White House announced that Wray would be staying on as FBI director and that Biden "has confidence in the job he is doing."[51] They currently have no plans to meet for dinner.

# 17

# The 60/40 Problem

## TRUMP, CULPABILITY, AND COVID-19

*Merlin Chowkwanyun*

Regular readers of the *New England Journal of Medicine* (*NEJM*) expect case reports of unusual maladies, results of clinical trials, and breakdowns of new health policy developments. But in October 2020, they got something else: a lacerating editorial on the impending presidential election. Without mentioning Donald Trump by name, it blasted his handling of the COVID-19 pandemic, declaring that a "magnitude of this failurc is astonishing." It pointed to a lackluster testing program, insufficient personal protective equipment (PPE) for health-care workers, and unevenly implemented isolation measures.

It went on to state that the Trump administration had ignored scientific expertise and instead embraced "charlatans who obscure the truth and facilitate the promulgation of outright lies." The journal suggested that the actions might even be criminal, charging that "anyone else who recklessly squandered lives and money in this way would be suffering legal consequences." But the election was a chance for the public to "render judgment" on a year of incompetence and lost opportunity to prevent excess death.[1] "Dying in a Leadership Vacuum" deviated from two hundred years of journal precedent during which *NEJM* had never commented directly on electoral affairs.[2]

The October polemic was a stark tonal contrast from another *NEJM* editorial published six months earlier. Written by Harvey Fineberg, the former president of the National Academy of Medicine, it presented a six-step plan "to crush the curve" of rising coronavirus cases in just ten weeks.[3] The plan called for ramping up diagnostic testing—into the "millions"—and using hotels and convention centers to isolate mild cases and those exposed, all in two weeks. It proposed sending masks to every American and PPE to essential workers needing it. And it suggested creating a channel wherein emerging science would inform decisions like business reopenings. It would all be overseen by a "commander" who would exercise "every civilian and military asset needed." By June 6, 2020, Fineberg asserted, the country might declare a new "D-Day" and "victory over the coronavirus." Beneath the urgency was optimism. Yet months later, almost none of Fineberg's suggestions were implemented at the federal level, much less with the hyperdrive effort that he had pushed.

Public utterances by Trump instead reflected the president's erraticism, flouting of scientific expertise, undercutting of public health measures, and indifference to the gravity of COVID. For example, on March 24, as New York State reported more than 5,000 new confirmed cases—a rate that increased daily for the next few weeks—Trump mused about ending COVID restrictions by Easter so there could be "packed churches all over our country."[4] On April 17, as armed protesters swarmed the Michigan State Legislature to protest Governor Gretchen Whitmer's COVID restrictions, Trump tweeted, "LIBERATE MICHIGAN!"[5] A week later, at a press conference where the antiviral properties of UV light and bleach were discussed by other officials, Trump asked if a "disinfectant where it knocks it out in a minute" might be injected into someone, prompting public health officials across the country to warn people about ingesting cleansing products like bleach.[6] On May 18, Trump promoted hydroxychloroquine, a drug used to treat malaria and lupus, as a COVID therapeutic, claiming to have taken it himself along with zinc.[7] In mid-July, he characterized new cases in heretofore untouched areas of the country as mere "burning embers" that could be easily doused, even as the national death toll by month's end exceeded 140,000, almost double what had been forecast by the epidemiological model the White House was most fond of invoking.[8]

Things did not change, either, when Trump himself developed a serious case of COVID and was sent to Walter Reed Hospital. A week later, he described the experience as a "blessing from God," touted the cutting-edge monoclonal antibody treatment he had received, promised it would soon be available widely "for free," and suggested Americans "get out there" and not let COVID "dominate your lives."[9] After his loss to Joe Biden, Trump lost virtually all interest in COVID, fixating on an election he claimed had been stolen.

Fly-on-the-wall books by journalists, articles in *Axios*, *Politico*, and the *New York Times*, and round-the-clock cable news documented dozens more moments like these. It is not difficult to look at this record and pin blame heavily on Trump and his headless leadership. Trump-centrism, however, ignores critical dynamics that transcended him: at lower levels of government, in the broader political culture, and in public health infrastructure. It was the collision of these features with the unique incompetence of the Trump administration that resulted in the United States' disastrous COVID outcome: thirty million confirmed cases and half a million deaths by the spring of 2021. Here, I situate Trump's inaction in three contexts: state and local autonomy, cultures of antiexpertise, and resource misallocation and inequality. It leads to what one might call the 60/40 question: If you had to apportion culpability, how much would you lay at the feet of Trump and how much at the larger social forces in which he operated?

## Federal Inaction

Trump's executive authority gave him several tools to wield against a worsening pandemic. One was the Defense Production Act of 1950 (DPA). If invoked, the law compels corporations with manufacturing capacities to prioritize production of critical supplies for the federal government, which in turn provides capital and compensation. Though originally designed to ensure necessary production during wars, it has since been used for several other purposes, including natural disaster response and bioterrorism preparedness.[10]

In the early months of the pandemic, eighteen senators urged Trump to exercise DPA powers for federal production of PPE, ventilators, and tests that could be sent to states and municipalities. "To avoid a worst-case scenario," they wrote, required "massively scale[d] up production."[11] Joe Biden, still competing in the waning Democratic primary against Bernie Sanders, a signatory of the statement, echoed its call and faulted the administration for not setting up a strong testing program.[12] James E. Baker, a Syracuse University law professor and former National Security Council adviser, asserted that in the face of hospital equipment shortages and inadequate data about the very scope of COVID, it was time to press the DPA button. "The administration can and should move forward with the DPA's authority. There's no time to waste," he argued.[13]

One of the loudest voices was the Rockefeller Foundation, which in late April proposed a national action plan for COVID-19 testing. More testing was critical to reining in the pandemic. It would enable the quick isolation of those who tested positive and the quarantining of their close contacts. This kind of rapid testing and tracing was proving to be critical in countries that had so far controlled the pandemic, most notably South Korea and Taiwan. For the United States to do so, the foundation argued that within the next two months, the United States would have to increase from one million to three million tests per week, and within six months, from three million to thirty million. Because of the "inherent commercial uncertainties in this 10-fold production increase," the DPA could prove crucial.[14] The foundation's urgency was not surprising. When it came to care of severely ill COVID patients early in the pandemic, emergency physicians had to rely on trial and error to learn about when (and when not) to use ventilators, remdesivir, corticosteroids, monoclonal antibodies, and various methods of oxygenation. More methodical studies on efficacy would only arrive later in the year.[15] In the meantime, a test-trace edifice could preempt serious cases for which medicine could offer few certain answers; the DPA might help with that.

Trump had committed to the DPA—sort of. In March and April, he signed three executive orders "delegating authority" the law granted to his heads of Health and Human Services and Homeland Security.[16] In practice, however, the administration was slow to invoke its full

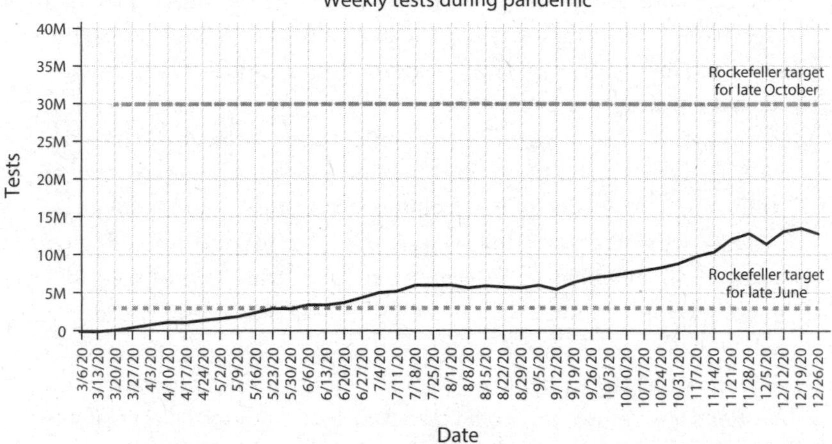


FIGURE 9. Weekly COVID diagnostic tests administered in 2020 and Rockefeller Foundation targets. Adapted from the Covid Tracking Project, https://covidtracking.com/data/download.

powers. In fact, in late March, officials boasted that they had found ways to procure tests without DPA assistance.[17] Trump endorsed a limited federal government role altogether, declaring at one press conference that it "is not supposed to be out there buying vast amounts of items and then shipping. You know, we're not a shipping clerk. The governors are supposed to be—as with testing, the governors are supposed—are supposed to be doing it." He continued: "This is really for the local governments, governors, and people within the state, depending on the way they divided it up."[18] One exception to this was Project Air Bridge, overseen by the president's son-in-law and adviser Jared Kushner. Initiated in March, Air Bridge shortened delivery times of supplies by subsidizing aerial, versus sea ship, transportation of PPE manufactured overseas. It spent $1.8 billion worth of mostly new, no-bid contracts, paying for flights and claiming the right to distribute up to half of the shipped goods through the Strategic National Stockpile. Air Bridge's efficacy remains hotly disputed. When it wound to a close in June 2020, the administration claimed it had "addressed the immediate shortfall" in PPE, pointing to 1.5 million N95 respirators, 2.5 million face shields, and 113.4 million surgical masks. Others painted a more critical picture. An investigation by three Democratic senators pointed out that 87 percent of the goods had been gloves and, further, that the total number of N95 respirators amounted to 0.04 percent of what the administration's own estimates had said was necessary.[19]

Whatever Air Bridge's merits, PPE shortages persisted into the year, and the facts on the ground were harrowing. Accounts spread of PPE shortages at constrained facilities across the country, with many health-care workers creating makeshift gear out of bandanas and other spare cloth, or worse, trash bags and swim goggles. One of the grimmest developments was a social media hashtag, #GetMePPE, through which exhausted hospital employees took photographs and videos documenting their plight, with some asking for direct donations on GoFundMe.com so they could purchase PPE themselves. Anecdotes were soon complemented by more systematic findings. An April survey of more than nine thousand ICU workers found that 55 percent ranked the need for adequate N95 respirators as their highest or second-highest concern; 75 percent put it in the top three.[20] Twenty percent of nursing homes surveyed between May and July reported "severe" PPE shortages, defined as only enough to last a week.[21] One in three nurses surveyed from July to August reported they were "out" or "short" of N95 respirators. Further, 68 percent said they had needed to reuse them "for at least five days."[22] Ad hoc consortiums sprang up to track PPE shortages and fulfill requests for equipment. But as valiant and impressive as these volunteer initiatives were, they were no substitute for more proactive federal purchasing and distribution needed to redirect a labyrinthine supply chain and web of economic incentives.[23]

The testing story was a bit more mixed. By the third week of June, the United States was conducting about a half million tests per day. This in fact exceeded the Rockefeller Foundation's goal of three million weekly tests by that time. But the overall progress masked challenges on the ground. Since the spring, the virus had spread geographically into suburbs and rural areas, many of which lacked tests or the capacity to administer them. And even regions that had increased testing still encountered logistic hurdles. It was not hard to find complaints of long lines or difficulty in locating testing sites. Speed of processing was also an issue. Many labs reported backlogs that prevented timely results, which were critical to any successful contact tracing effort. By one estimate, each day of delay decreased by 10–15 percent the likelihood of successfully tracing and isolating at least 80 percent of an infected person's recent contacts.[24]

The big picture also remained troubling. Increasingly, experts reflected soberly on the sluggish start—a little more than 10,000 daily tests in mid-March, a little less than 150,000 in mid-April—and concluded that a critical opportunity to squash outbreaks before they spread widely had now passed. Instead, wrote Eric Schneider in a July *NEJM* article, a more "narrow local testing strategy" had been adopted, one primarily "dedicated to managing the care of hospitalized patients and preventing health care workers from transmitting Covid-19" but not the population at large.[25] The overall testing curve six months later was not encouraging. In mid-October, a little more than one million daily tests were conducted. The weekly number of tests, then, was short—by more than twenty million—from the thirty million weekly benchmark to which the Rockefeller Foundation had aspired.

Without federal coordination, many states had taken it upon themselves to procure tests. Back in April, for instance, Maryland employees evaluated a number of options from Korean manufacturers, eventually purchasing half a million units from the firm LabGenomics (which later turned out to have too high a false-positive rate to be used, causing a minor scandal).[26] In the summer, a bipartisan group of seven governors banded together as a purchasing cooperative.[27] The closest the Trump administration came to providing strong federal help was the procurement, in August, of 150 million so-called rapid tests from Abbott Labs.[28] These tests had one advantage over the polymerase chain reaction (PCR) tests that detected genetic material: their results took as little as fifteen minutes to show. But they were also less accurate when it came to detecting asymptomatic cases, missing as many as two-thirds of them.[29]

For the most part, employers, hospital networks, and municipalities acquired diagnostic equipment with little federal help, leading the *New York Times* to lament, in September, "no coherent national testing strategy."[30] Lack of federal assistance meant forgoing ambitious ideas, like that of Harvard University epidemiologist Michael Mina, to test half the entire U.S. population weekly using rapid tests mailed to Americans. Those who tested positive would remain home until sufficient time had elapsed, and the sheer frequency of testing would make up for lower accuracy. "It would," Mina wrote in *Time*, "significantly reduce the spread of the virus without having to shut down the country again—and if we act today, could allow us to see our loved ones, go back to school and work, and travel—all before Christmas."[31] Instead, cases rose into and beyond Christmas, reaching a peak of three hundred thousand per day in the first week of January.

A rare bright spot was Operation Warp Speed (OWS), when the federal government, through the Department of Defense and Health and Human Services, incentivized rapid vaccine development. It did so by funding six pharmaceutical firms' various costs and committing to bulk purchasing of potential vaccines themselves.[32] In late 2020, two firms, Pfizer and Moderna, announced astonishing results in accelerated Phase 3 trials for their vaccines. In the study population, those who had been vaccinated exhibited 90–95 percent fewer COVID cases than those who had received a placebo. Thus, these vaccines were not only the most quickly produced but some of the most effective too.

Some of the success was due to developments before OWS itself. Because of previous viruses—Ebola, Zika, and SARS-1—the federal government and many of the firms had long been testing novel vaccine platforming technologies, in particular the use of messenger RNA (mRNA), which stimulated antibody production by producing proteins similar to those the coronavirus used for binding to cells.[33] Already tested for safety, these components were ready to be taken off the shelf and merged into the COVID vaccine process, saving years of time. Moreover, the process was insulated by strong traditions in the Food and Drug Administration (FDA) that made it impervious to top-down political interference. In the face of public pressure from Trump to speed up the review process, Peter Marks, head of the FDA's Center for Biologics Evaluation and Research, declared he would resign if a vaccine was approved without the usual checks for safety and efficacy.[34] The composition of the FDA's advisory committees was another check and balance. They were drawn from inside the FDA but also outside of it: a mix of scientists in academia, other federal agencies, and private industry.[35]

Still, OWS itself was critical to catalyzing the process. Given Trump's rejection of other scientific findings, one could easily have imagined him openly hostile to vaccine development. That he mostly got out of the way on this front must be acknowledged. Early vaccine rollout, however, was plagued by many of the same problems that had undermined PPE and test distribution: too much delegation and too little federal coordination. Governors and hospital care organizations soon complained publicly about receiving inaccurate information about quantities of doses and their arrival dates. In December, Brian Peters, the CEO of the Michigan Health & Hospital Association, decried poor communication from the Department of Health and Human Services, following a reduced allotment to his state. "Any delay in receipt of vaccine prolongs the vaccination process and puts healthcare workers at increased risk for contracting this deadly disease," Peters said.[36] By year's end, only two million people had been vaccinated, just 20 percent of the doses distributed and eighteen million fewer than a targeted twenty million by year's end.

## Governance Battles from Below

Lack of assertive federal action was not the full story, however. Outside Washington, developments at lower levels of governance were as determinative when it came to the country's COVID fortunes, and the Trump administration's outsize media imprint obscured tensions from below. This was most apparent with stay-at-home orders and mask mandates, which closed nonessential businesses, encouraged people to stay home as much as possible, and mandated facial coverings in public.

With these types of ordinances, the Trump administration legally could do the following: use the pulpit to encourage preventive behavior (it sometimes did), mandate masks on federal lands (it did not), or purchase them for governments (it also did not). Its chief effort was a two-week initiative in March called "15 Days to Stop the Spread," which sent out postcards and operated a website with basic advice: stay at home if you can, avoid going to work if symptomatic, wash hands and don't touch your face, and eschew social gatherings of more than ten people.[37]

Trump's reach, though, was in fact circumscribed by long-standing legal precedent, which affirmed the extraordinary powers of states and municipalities to craft their own policies regulating land and water use, noise, waste, and infectious disease control, among others.[38] In states like California, with strong public health traditions and needs, federalism was a boon. Since the 1970s, its Air Resources Board has regularly imposed more stringent standards than the federal Environmental Protection Agency itself.[39] This has enabled it to tailor air pollution control to the state's uniquely high emissions burden from automotive sources. Indeed, during the Trump administration, California initiated a lawsuit in 2018—subsequently joined by twenty-two other states—over whether it could impose its own gas mileage standards. (The protracted legal wrangling ended when the Biden administration withdrew the government's defense.[40])

States like Louisiana, on the other hand, were foils to California. For decades, state-level environmental regulators have imposed minimal standards allowed by federal law for petrochemical emissions, and when allowed to come up with their own rules, they have adopted some of the weakest in the nation.[41] As one recent report by *ProPublica* noted, Louisiana's benzene standard was "more than twice as lenient" as that of Texas, which in turn was "30 times looser than that of Massachusetts."[42] State-to-state differences in these and other matters point to one tension with twentieth-century public health and federalism. Circumscribed federal authority coexists alongside devolution to states. In and of itself, this is neither automatically antithetical nor beneficial to public health. What matters is what happens below.

COVID was a stage on which these tensions played out, as states rolled out stay-at-home orders in March and April. Those hit hardest by COVID responded with orders that were the most stringent, lasted the longest, and came earliest: Washington, Michigan, Connecticut, New Jersey, Pennsylvania, California, Massachusetts, and especially New York. California's contained blunt language, ordering "all individuals . . . to stay home or at their place of residence" unless they were critical to the state's day-to-day functioning.[43] New York's PAUSE program shut down all nonessential businesses—grocery stores, take-out restaurants, and social service and health institutions were the primary exceptions—and banned "non-essential gatherings of individuals of any size for any reason."[44] It lasted for two months, and as it ended, the state introduced strict benchmarks measuring COVID prevalence and sufficient contact tracing capacity, all of which a region needed to clear before reopening. Michigan's order was similar. Initially slated for two weeks, it was extended multiple times, and its most stringent provisions did not end until June 1, all while attracting terrifying misogynistic vitriol, an armed protest, and even a foiled kidnapping plot of Governor Gretchen Whitmer.[45] These states were also among the first to implement mask mandates, as growing scientific evidence showed that facial coverings not only reduced spread but reduced infection for wearers as well.

These states stood in contrast to states such as Texas, Florida, Iowa, and Georgia, where governors repeatedly flouted the seriousness of COVID, mirroring Trump. Iowa governor Kim Reynolds did not even implement a single blanket order, instead drawing up weekly lists of businesses throughout March that would be closed. By late April, most of the restrictions were lifted, though some were left at 50 percent capacity, with Reynolds remarking that "we must learn to live with COVID virus activity without letting it govern our lives."[46] Reynolds would not implement a mask mandate until a sudden surge in November 2020 that stretched many of the state's hospitals to the brink.[47] Similarly, Georgia governor Brian Kemp, one of the last of forty-two governors who had implemented stay-at-home orders, announced he would lift restrictions in less than a month, even as cases were rising elsewhere in the country. Kemp remarked, "I felt like the negative effects of not having our economy starting to open up was beginning to have the same weight as the virus itself."[48] Kemp, too, did not implement a mask mandate.

The most flagrant of the governors was Florida's Ron DeSantis. Like Kemp, he was one of the last to institute a stay-at-home order and business restrictions. And like Kemp, he lifted most of them in less than a month, though he kept on the books a capacity restriction at bars and restaurants. As he did so, DeSantis met with Trump at the White House, where he boasted, "You look at some of the most draconian orders that have been issued in some of these states and compare Florida . . . Florida's done better," before pointing to the state's low COVID mortality.[49] The situation looked markedly differently three months later in July, however, as Florida experienced a sudden COVID surge. Its total hospitalization numbers peaked in the third week of July at nearly ten thousand cases, half of New York's April apex but hardly anything to approach cavalierly. Still, in September, DeSantis lifted restrictions entirely. He allowed bars and restaurants to open at 100 percent capacity and, further, *prohibited* local governments from imposing restrictions of more than 50 percent.[50] Two months later, in the last week of October, Florida experienced a daily increase in cases that soon cascaded into a second surge that peaked in mid-January with the highest daily confirmed case count the state had yet experienced.

Local developments below the state level were consequential too. In Georgia, officials in a number of cities repudiated Governor Kemp, most prominently Atlanta mayor Keisha Lance Bottoms.[51] In addition to criticizing Kemp for a hasty reopening, Bottoms tested the powers of local government by issuing a series of executive orders that restricted large public gatherings and intermittently closed down dining rooms and restaurants, even after Kemp allowed them to operate at full capacity in June. Bottoms also implemented a mask mandate. Because these local actions ran counter to the state's, Kemp filed a lawsuit against Bottoms that was subsequently withdrawn. To observers' surprise, Kemp in August then allowed local mask ordinances, though the move came with caveats; they would apply mainly to government buildings and only private businesses "if the owner or occupant . . . consents to enforcement."[52] Still, Kemp's partial retrenchment affirmed Bottoms's assertion of local power. In Florida, local officials were less assertive than their mayoral colleague in Atlanta. But they also exercised as much autonomy as possible, with Miami-Dade County allowing restaurants to open at only 50 percent capacity and imposing a mask mandate that withstood a legal challenge filed by a travel agent.[53]

———

Resistant localities did not just defend public health measures, though. They could also undermine them. California, home of some of the strongest initial measures, saw a groundswell of resistance to them by May, especially in politically conservative Orange County. In Huntington Beach, fifteen hundred people gathered to protest ongoing business restrictions.[54] The county sheriff, Don Barnes, told its board of supervisors, "We are not the mask police—nor do I intend to be the mask police." "I think what we have seen repeatedly throughout the community is Orange County residents acting responsibly," he added.[55]

Perhaps bowing to pressure, Governor Gavin Newsom announced in mid-May, just two weeks after the first protests, that California would lift restrictions on restaurants. It was the start of California's divergence from northeast counterparts' early successes in mitigation. The anti-restriction effort would haunt Newsom throughout the year, culminating in a recall effort in early 2021. For those opposed to restrictions, he became a symbol of an overreaching state. (Newsom did himself no favors, of course, when he was photographed at a posh restaurant without a mask.) For those in favor of them, he earned derision for frequent changes in his position. Still, even in states that brought the virus under significant control, local cracks were constantly appearing. In New York, that included parts of Brooklyn, and later Staten Island, residents angrily resisted mask wearing, continued holding religious gatherings, and flouted bar and restaurant restrictions.[56]

These dynamics went beyond Trump and underscored how much public health action—far before COVID—was determined at the level of state and municipal government. Federalism was a mixed bag. In spite of Trump, many governors, county heads, and mayors were able to implement effective restrictions, even with a lack of federal assistance—material and rhetorical—that would have made the effort much more smooth. And conversely, because of Trump, many other elected officials were emboldened by a federal government and president whose approach was similarly hands-off and dismissive of the COVID threat. Throughout 2020, Trump regularly chimed in from afar with insults for states with restrictions and applause for those that accelerated economic reopening.

## The New Antiexpertise

Public opinion polls repeatedly showed majority support for restrictive measures and mask wearing.[57] But a sizable percentage of the population remained antagonistic. Casual internet browsing quickly uncovered rants about true hidden agendas behind COVID control or bizarre videotaped fights in shopping malls where unmasked protesters harassed staff and other patrons. They added up to rejection of COVID's seriousness and of the means required to combat it. It is not hard to view Trump as the major tailwind in this kind of thinking. Even before COVID, Trump had been fond of conspiracies and falsehoods; his presidential campaign, after all, had been rooted in pushing "birtherist" narratives about Barack Obama's true national origins. And more recently, his Twitter account had retweeted material associated with QAnon, a theory that alleged pedophilic government agents were actively undermining his presidency.[58] This is to say nothing of his podium antics throughout COVID.

Trump's proclivities explain some of his COVID rejectionism. But it also has roots in deeper cultural currents, datable to a larger 1960s and 1970s backlash against once-hallowed institutions, medicine and science among them. Much of this skepticism, of course, was welcome. The women's health movement, best exemplified by the book *Our Bodies, Ourselves*, overturned misogynistic assumptions in medical knowledge and spotlighted pervasive gender inequality in the profession itself.[59] HIV/AIDS activists self-educated and criticized the usual ways clinical trial membership was determined and the glacial approval process for experimental drugs on which their lives depended.[60] Groups like Science for the People and the environmental justice movement collaborated with nonprofessional citizen scientists both in framing overall questions—including ones scientists had missed—and in collecting data, leading to what the sociologist Phil Brown has dubbed "popular epidemiology."[61] In these cases, antiexpertise eventually made for better expertise.

Yet this democratizing impulse came with more than one underside. One was the rise of a billion-dollar alternative therapeutics industry, some of which lacked the oversight of traditional regulatory agencies.[62] Another was a plethora of unsubstantiated, if understandable, narratives about the dangers of products like genetically modified foods.[63] More dangerous medical conspiracism came in the form of HIV dissidence, which rejected the scientific consensus that AIDS was caused by the virus. Though it originated in the United States, dissident thought traveled and was embraced by South African president Thabo Mbeki, who from 2000 to 2005 banned distribution of antiretrovirals to expectant mothers, with disastrous consequences for HIV control.[64] Perhaps the most high-profile—and alarming—development was a renewed resistance to vaccination, propelled initially by a retracted 1998 study, based on false data, that purported to show links between vaccination and autism. Its author subsequently became a hero of the movement, which depicted him as a martyr muzzled by the medical establishment.[65] Infectious diseases long thought to be under control, like measles and whooping cough, instead resurfaced in periodic outbreaks as pockets of parents refused to vaccinate their children. Rejection of mainstream medicine grew alongside a rejection of mainstream science, especially that which showed the alarming rise of human carbon use and its effects on climate.[66]

Democratic currents were not the only contributor to the crisis of expertise of the past few decades. Unsettled disagreements within several public-facing expert fields—energy, economics, environmental risk, statistics, psychology, medicine, and public health—all chipped away at the notion of a united expert front, diminished public confidence, or at the very least, simply sowed confusion.[67] Within public health, nutritional research became an especially common (and well-deserved) target for jokes about contradictory advice on the harmfulness of salt, fats, and red meat, often issued in the public sphere by researchers wedded to defending their own pet paradigms.[68] But the problems extended into other areas. In breast cancer, fierce debates occurred over the need for mastectomies if BRCA genes were found in women, the wisdom of various aggressive treatments, and whether age forty or fifty was the right time for mammograms to start.[69] Various fields also confronted growing internal skepticism around the uncritical use of dominant statistical frameworks and the inability of researchers to replicate many common research findings.[70]

Whatever the sources, unified expertise frayed alongside the growth of a new internet-anchored media ecology. In the Trump era, there existed thousands of Facebook pages, Twitter accounts, Instagram feeds, YouTube channels, subreddits, and websites promoting beliefs like the above—and others. Many were well subsidized and had the aesthetic of professionally produced material. To the untrained eye, the popular National Vaccine Information Center website, run by an antivaccination group, looks as though it might be a university or even government site.[71] Not all of these digital materials were produced by uncredentialed amateurs, either. Many carried the imprimatur of heterodox physicians and scientists. The internet had made it possible for antiexperts to obtain data on their own, interpret the information the way they wanted, and easily shop for confirmatory experts and virtual communities that could reaffirm their a priori beliefs.

COVID was no exception, and the digital world spread a number of erroneous assertions, some of which the president actively repeated: that the virus was no worse than the flu; that in fact flu cases were being tabulated as COVID ones; that hydroxychloroquine could easily ward it off; that masks were ineffective; that an increase in testing in fact accounted for increases in confirmed cases; and that it was all a trojan horse for increasing political control. In the early days of the pandemic, a video titled "Plandemic," starring microbiologist Judy Mikovits, claimed that novel coronavirus was a laboratory-made virus and that hospitals and pharmaceutical companies (along with Bill Gates) had a stake in inflating severity to collect reimbursements and profiteer off vaccines. It was among the first, too, to float hydroxychloroquine as an effective COVID remedy and suggested that the annual flu vaccine increased one's COVID vulnerability. The video's reach was astounding. Before its removal from YouTube, it had been viewed, by one estimate, eight million times.[72]

Similar viral videos followed. In late April, two urgent care doctors from Bakersfield, California, distributed a recording of themselves. In it, they applied positivity rates from the five thousand COVID tests they had conducted locally to both Kern County and the entire state, and claimed COVID had already infected millions and in fact was not doing much harm. Because it was no worse than the flu, there was no reason to continue social distancing or stay-at-home orders. The video was tweeted by the celebrity entrepreneur and billionaire Elon Musk, who remarked, "Docs make good points." The dubious statistical analysis led to opprobrium from the two main emergency care organizations, though by then the video had been viewed millions of times before being yanked by YouTube.[73] In July, a group calling itself America's Frontline Doctors held a taped press conference in front of the Supreme Court to sound another message against stay-at-home orders while promoting hydroxychloroquine and zinc. It was viewed by an estimated fourteen million people.[74]

These were not just internet curiosities but seeped into White House statements and decision-making. Trump repeatedly promoted hydroxychloroquine throughout the summer, calling it a "game changer," even as evidence of its nonefficacy mounted. One of its biggest boosters on the White House's Coronavirus Task Force was an economist, Peter Navarro, who wrote a July 2020 *USA Today* op-ed denouncing Anthony Fauci for his refusal to endorse hydroxychloroquine use because of insufficient data.[75] The inflammatory piece was titled "Anthony Fauci Has Been Wrong about Everything I Have Interacted with Him On."

By fall, Trump had marginalized Fauci and Deborah Birx, the two infectious disease experts on the task force. He substituted instead Scott Atlas, a conservative radiologist whom he had first seen on Fox News. Atlas questioned mask use, discouraged testing of those with no symptoms, and endorsed accelerated reopening and laxer restrictions for all but the highest-risk populations, a strategy that had been deployed without success in Sweden.[76] Atlas's ideas hewed closely to those who pushed for reaching "herd immunity" via mass infection of lower-risk populations. In October, they gained additional currency when a group of epidemiologists and physicians signed what they called the Great Barrington Declaration. It advocated "Focused Protection"—that is, "allow[ing] those who are at minimal risk of death to live their lives normally to build up immunity to the virus through natural infection." The declaration closed by advocating the end of remote work and the opening of "restaurants and other businesses."[77] Unlike the viral videos that had circulated in the earlier phase of the pandemic, the declaration was spearheaded by three extremely accomplished scientists whose prestigious affiliations were prominently flagged: Martin Kulldorff (Harvard), Sunetra Gupta (Oxford), Jay Bhattacharya (Stanford). It was a notable variation on antiexpertise: experts invoking their expert reputations to bolster an antiexpert position.

These currents had their most damaging effect on the integrity of the Centers for Disease Control and Prevention (CDC). Documents obtained by a Democratic House subcommittee and *Politico* showed repeated meddling by deputies in Trump's Health and Human Services (HHS). Even before Atlas's arrival, Paul Alexander, a young "special assistant," advocated for HHS review of the CDC's *Morbidity and Mortality Weekly Report*, the agency's scientific journal, which he accused of "trying to hurt the President." Alexander declared, "The reports must be read by someone outside of CDC like myself, and we cannot allow the reporting to go on as it has been, for it is outrageous . . . Nothing to go out unless I read and agree with the findings how they CDC, wrote it and I tweak it to ensure it is fair and balanced and 'complete.'" He pushed herd immunity strategies aggressively, including the opening of on-campus colleges, though he ultimately did not succeed in getting them adopted. He did manage, however, to delay by one month a *Report* article that cast doubt on hydroxychloroquine's efficacy. Equally alarming was the CDC's August revision of a testing guidance, pushed by Atlas, which recommended that those without symptoms no longer needed to be tested, despite the now-accepted knowledge that asymptomatic people could easily spread the virus.[78] All the above actions raised the question of why somebody obsessed with highly visible "wins" like Trump would embrace policies almost certain to worsen COVID numbers. But it misses that the hands-off approach—and the flouting of scientific judgment undergirding it—was an end unto itself, one that roused a political base primed to cheer him on.[79] It did not help, either, that health officials were internally divided about various issues: early on, the helpfulness of masks; midway, whether protests might spread COVID; and later, if schools should be reopened.

At the same time, antiexpertise went beyond Trump. A culture of antiexpertise and tensions between scientific experts themselves had existed for decades before him. Trump may have rejected scientific expertise in a particularly flagrant way, but he was enabled by a milieu that long predated him.

## Resource Allocation and Deeper Inequality

There is a final context to consider: resource allocation and entrenched inequalities. COVID emerged after three decades of budgetary stringency, originating in the recessionary climate of the 1970s, which has long forced state and local health departments to do more with increasingly less. A CDC report published at the turn of the century surveyed three thousand health departments and found major infrastructural deficiencies: e-mail systems that did not work, outdated laboratory equipment, and heads without advanced degrees.[80] In 2004 and 2005, the Trust for America's Health (TFAH) conducted a similar examination of budgets. Its big takeaway was delivered by Shelley Hearne, its executive director, in a Congressional hearing where she stated bluntly that "the nation's public health system" was "being stretched to the breaking point."[81] The TFAH's report noted that more than a third of states had cut their budgets in the past year.[82]

These trends continued over the next decade. Budget windfalls, when they did come, were typically earmarked for very particular functions, like bioterrorism (shortly after 9/11), Medicaid, and tobacco control funds. A year before COVID, TFAH conducted another analysis. It found that the CDC's Prevention and Public Health Fund, created by the Affordable Care Act to fund on-the-ground initiatives, had its budget cut by between one-third and two-thirds each year "and used to pay for other legislation." Even more alarmingly, at the local level, a fifth of health departments reported cuts in 2017, and 23 percent in 2016.[83] In 2020, the Kaiser Family Foundation, working with the Associated Press, published a similarly sobering report that found spending for state and local public health departments, per capita, had declined by 16 percent and 18 percent, respectively, part of long-term trends that had left "a skeletal workforce for what was once viewed as one of the world's top public health systems."[84] The consequences were not hard to see. Throughout the pandemic, governments struggled to support testing sites, surveillance to monitor the outbreak, health education, and enforcement of COVID rules. Small health departments were particularly strapped. Many used dated cell phone technology and paper records and did not have epidemiologists on staff. While a more proactive federal effort would have surely blunted the worst of these infrastructural deficiencies, it would not have erased them entirely.

Perhaps the most sobering aspect of the COVID pandemic was patterns of disease that reflected durable fault lines of inequality. Although COVID could theoretically hit anybody, its distribution was decidedly nonrandom. The earliest evidence of this came just a month into the pandemic, when data showed disproportionate COVID prevalence among Black and Latinx Americans. It was likely the result of a few factors: pervasive residential segregation that concentrated respiratory hazards in minority neighborhoods; cohabitation in substandard housing; accumulated stress response effects from racial discrimination; and concentration at the lower rungs of the occupational ladder. Other preliminary analyses showed a similar effect for people of low income, with one analyst commenting that "those who because of the nature of their jobs and their financial circumstances have to work outside of the home, and their families, are more likely to become infected and die."[85]

Then in November, the journal *Nature* released one of the most systematic analyses to date of COVID inequalities using cell phone tracking data to trace the precise hourly movements of almost one hundred million people from their homes to various destinations. Overlaying these data with COVID rates, the researchers identified four overwhelming predictive factors for higher probability of COVID: racial minority status, socioeconomic disadvantage, frequent mobility, and movement to "places of interest" with high numbers of people, such as restaurants and grocery stores.[86] It was not hard to see that many of the anonymous statistical points in the study were low-wage service workers who regularly commuted to jobs where they were often underprotected and around many people. Another analysis by researchers at the University of California–San Francisco found that workers in the food and transportation sectors and those in "manufacturing" reported "excess deaths" during the pandemic period of 39 percent, 28 percent, and 23 percent, respectively, with increases for Black, Latinx, and Asian workers of 36 percent, 28 percent, and 18 percent.[87] Given how bound up occupational position and race were in areas with large nonwhite populations, these results painted a blunt picture of how race and class forces were working when it came to COVID risk. Alas, it was also an unsurprising one. It upheld two centuries of research that showed most diseases disproportionately hit society's most marginalized.[88] And it showed that underlying and entrenched inequalities, Trump or no Trump, still shaped much of the virus's fallout.

It was a reminder that future historians who narrate President Trump's COVID leadership will have to analyze his destructive habits of mind and his administration's abdication of duty at several junctures. But they will have to do so with an eye toward what happened in the states and localities below him, in the cultural milieu around him, and in the fractured society that preceded his political ascendance. They will have to confront, in other words, the 60/40 question.

# 18

# The Path of Most Resistance

## HOW DEMOCRATS BATTLED TRUMP AND MOVED LEFT

*Michael Kazin*

### Herbert Donald Trump?

Since the Democrats' nearly half-century reign as the majority party ended in the late 1970s, the election of a Republican president and large GOP gains in Congress had always persuaded party leaders to shift rightward. How else, ran the conventional Beltway wisdom, would they be able to win over swing voters who blamed liberals for fostering an overly permissive culture and creating an overbearing and inefficient "big government"—one allegedly more beholden to the rights of minorities than to the interests of the middle-class white majority?

Thus, Ronald Reagan's landslide victories in 1980 and 1984 inspired the birth of the centrist Democratic Leadership Council, and George H. W. Bush's win in 1988 gave Bill Clinton, the DLC chairman, a prime opportunity to grab the party's nomination in 1992. Although it took a 5–4 vote on the Supreme Court in 2000 to put George W. Bush in the White House, his popularity zoomed up nine months later after the terrorist attacks of September 11. Most Democrats backed the invasion of Iraq, despite doubts about the intelligence that justified it. The party regained a strong oppositional voice only after Bush's reelection when the war went badly, and when the GOP president fumbled vital aid to the mostly Black residents of New Orleans in the wake of a massive hurricane.

In this regard as in others, Donald Trump was a different kind of Republican. Unlike the three GOP chief executives who preceded him, the celebrity turned president did not seem genuinely interested in or capable of developing a coalition that could forge a new Republican majority. Instead, he devoted himself to inspiring a "Make America Great Again" movement loyal only to him and rife with racist, nativist conspiracy mongers, hundreds of whom staged a violent invasion of the Capitol as the electoral votes were counted on January 6, 2021. Alarmed by Trump's mendacious narcissism and his break with conservative orthodoxy on trade and foreign policy, such prominent disciples of Reaganism as John McCain's erstwhile campaign manager and Mitt Romney's former chief strategist broke with their party and endorsed Joe Biden in 2020. Because Trump's approval rating was mired in the mid-40s for nearly his entire tenure, he could not scare Democratic politicians into adopting his positions or echoing his belligerent rhetoric.

Instead, a good many Democrats openly identified themselves with "the Resistance." This uprising with a name borrowed, consciously or not, from the antifascist European partisans during World War II had no single organization, set of leaders, or common strategy. But its inchoate nature became a strength instead of a liability. It allowed any American who feared and despised Donald Trump as a man and/or as a president and was eager to block his policies and reelection to act in whatever way they felt appropriate.

The first mass act of the Resistance took place the day after the 2017 inauguration when some three million people packed the Washington Mall, and several million others thronged cities around the country in a Women's March animated by Trump's misogynistic words and actions. Its last big outpouring was the Black Lives Matter demonstrations during the summer of 2020, touched off by the outrage following the horrific killing of George Floyd by a white Minneapolis police officer, caught on a cell phone. Activism against similar murders of African Americans had been growing in size and public support since 2013, but Trump's unqualified defense of the police did much to attract more people to those demonstrations in 2020 than any other protests in U.S. history.

These and other Resistance events included both young leftists of all races and college-educated suburban white women shocked and angered that a man who bragged about being a sexual harasser had defeated the first woman to be nominated by a major party—and one who had bested him in the popular vote. Their sizable numbers and resolve helped embolden Nancy Pelosi, the Democratic leader in the House of Representatives, to call Trump out in a White House meeting and mock him during his 2020 State of the Union address.

The Resistance proved an electoral boon to the opposition party as well. In the 2018 midterm election, mass hostility toward Trump helped Democrats capture forty House seats, giving them control of the chamber they had lost in 2010. Pelosi identified herself with the grassroots insurgency and kept her own members united while supplying abundant funds to Democrats running against Republican congresspeople in competitive districts. Both as majority leader and as Speaker, she attended hundreds of events with potential donors every year. When a staff member questioned her exhausting pace, the tireless senior citizen responded, "I don't do downtime."[1]

Loathing of Trump also drove the massive turnout of eighty-one million for the Democratic presidential ticket two years later. In 2020, Joe Biden and Kamala Harris won over fifteen million more votes than had Hillary Clinton and Tim Kaine in the previous contest. It was the greatest such leap of support for a major party in American electoral history since 1932, when Franklin D. Roosevelt received nearly eight million more votes in his landslide victory than had Alfred E. Smith, his fellow Democrat, in his lopsided loss to Herbert Hoover four years before.[2]

The parallel with the 1932 contest that turned Hoover, another one-term president, out of the White House suggests a possible explanation for Trump's weakness. His tumultuous governance and defeat in 2020 fit rather neatly into a model of presidential regimes developed by the political scientist Stephen Skowronek. Each president, he argues, has governed during an era of "political time" during which one party or, at least, its ideology and program were either gaining or losing power and popularity. In Skowronek's view, just five presidents—Jefferson, Jackson, Lincoln, Franklin Roosevelt, and Reagan—were "reconstructive" figures who made a decisive break with what had been the dominant political ideas of their time. In the case of Lincoln and Hoover, it took a cataclysmic event—the Civil War and then the Great Depression—to reveal the inability of the old order to address or solve the crisis of the present.

Skowronek points out other similarities between Hoover and Trump. Both men rose to wealth and fame in private business, and neither had run for office before their initial campaigns for the presidency. Each also swore to shake up the status quo, although Hoover's stolid rhetorical style had nothing in common with Trump's self-aggrandizing bombast. More significantly, each faced and bungled a serious crisis—the economic slump for Hoover, the pandemic for Trump—that made many Americans condemn not just their leadership but the moral bankruptcy of the existing order. "Instead of fixing things up and giving the regime a new lease on life," writes Skowronek, such "presidents have consistently driven their parties to the breaking point and emboldened their opponents. Internal wrangling . . . has pushed the regime to indict itself and fomented its political implosion." Hoover and Trump also faced large and sustained protests that helped convince Democrats that voters would welcome a decisive break with their rule.[3]

If Trump does prove to be the last chief executive of a conservative era that began with Reagan's election in 1980, future historians may understand the debates among Democrats during his term as the birth pangs of a new regime. As FDR laid the cornerstone of a sizable federal welfare state, developed by his Democratic and Republican successors from Truman to Nixon, so Biden would have the opportunity to make such fundamental changes as dramatically decreasing economic and racial inequality and making serious progress toward stopping climate change. As Skowronek told *New York Times* columnist Michelle Goldberg just after Biden took office, "The old Reagan formulas have lost their purchase, there is new urgency in the moment, and the president has an insurgent left at his back."[4] Yet, with tiny majorities in both houses of Congress, Democrats could easily fail to achieve their ambitions.

## A Realistic Left

How did Joe Biden become the leader of a party that was moving steadily to the left of the stances he had taken throughout his half century in national politics? The story begins with how Democrats struggled to explain the shocking loss of the woman who, until late on election night in 2016, they assumed would be president. Some narratives of Hillary Clinton's narrow defeat blamed factors internal to her campaign, such as a failure to heed the advice of veteran Democrats "on the ground" in battleground states and a perception that the nominee had a condescending attitude to voters she might have won over. Other accounts stressed external influences, such as pervasive sexism or the reluctance of many Sanders's voters to cast a ballot for the woman who had defeated their hero. The widely read statistical pundit Nate Silver stated flatly that Hillary Clinton "probably" lost the election because of a blizzard of media attention given to a late October memo from FBI director James Comey about a private email account she had used while serving as secretary of state.[5]

What was striking about this debate was that most Democrats who took part in it seemed to care more about positioning the party to win subsequent contests than waging battle over their ideological commitments, strongly held as they were. In the summer of 2016, allies of Sanders persuaded backers of Hillary Clinton to create a Unity Reform Commission to revamp some of the party's nomination procedures, such as the power of superdelegates and how candidates could qualify for televised primary debates. Its report, released late the following year, did not satisfy everyone, of course. Members of the congressional Black Caucus, superdelegates all, were unhappy about relinquishing their influence "to assuage the concerns of mostly white progressives with little history in the party," as one analyst put it. But neither their complaint nor any other got widely reported. The Unity Commission, it appeared, had lived up to its name.[6]

To make headway, Democrats did take some comfort in the diversity of their base. All the hand-wringing about the party's steady loss of white working-class voters over the past half century could not obscure the fact that the Americans who had voted for Hillary Clinton represented a broader set of constituencies than the white Christians who were the mainstay of the GOP—and just 43 percent of the U.S. population. That potential Democratic majority included most people of color, most voters—of all races—either under thirty or who live in big cities or inner-ring suburbs, and most recent immigrants. If those constituencies begin to decline and the number of churchgoing whites surges, it would astonish every demographer in the nation.[7]

But demography is not, in fact, destiny. The breadth of the party's base can also be a weakness. In order to contain multitudes, Democrats have had to prevent their diverse rank-and-file supporters from waging bitter internal battles that weaken their party's image and power. Since party leaders decisively rejected their Jim Crow heritage in the 1960s and embraced feminism a decade later, they had often strained to satisfy the demands of nonwhites and women for appointments and a commitment to policies targeted to their specific economic and cultural interests. The white men who run the GOP don't have that problem: they seldom worry whether their cabinets contain enough African Americans or women or any LGBTQ people at all.

The ideological differences that had roiled the Democrats in 2016 had been around in one form or another since the days when Mayor Richard Daley's police smashed the heads of antiwar protesters in downtown Chicago during the party's national convention in 1968. The left-wing activists who worked to nominate Bernie Sanders both in 2016 and in 2020 were the heirs of the peace crusaders who sought to topple Hubert Humphrey half a century earlier, the followers of George McGovern in 1972, and the rainbow warriors who fought to nominate Jesse Jackson in the 1980s (one of whom was Sanders himself, then mayor of Vermont's largest city). In the past, the prime concern of party centrists was to gain power and retain it, while the Left burned to achieve transformative change. In the service of that bolder agenda, Left reformers were often willing to suffer a heroic defeat that built their movement and seemed to make a future triumph based on their ideals more possible.

But, in the long history of the party, only a broad coalition in which neither camp sought to vanquish the other has ever secured the victories needed to use the power of the state to make substantive reforms. The New Deal succeeded in the 1930s because it unified a party of vicious southern racists and Blacks who had fled an apartheid system to come north, Irish-Catholic bosses and socialist-minded union leaders, and white working-class evangelicals and bedhopping Hollywood stars. Three decades later, Lyndon B. Johnson pushed the Civil Rights Act, the Voting Rights Act, and Medicare through a Congress swollen with Democrats from big cities and farm towns, as well as moderate Republicans turned off by the Goldwater insurgency that had captured their party.

In 2008, during the Great Recession, the election of Barack Obama with enhanced majorities in both houses of Congress gave Democratic leaders an opportunity to initiate another wave of reform. Leftists and centrists united in the hope that big changes were likely. But the GOP's brutally effective opposition and Obama's clumsy, poorly communicated rollout of the Affordable Care Act soured voters on that promise and did much to reestablish Republican control on Capitol Hill and in many state legislatures. During Obama's time in office, Democrats lost over sixty seats in the House, eleven in the Senate, thirteen governorships, and nearly a thousand legislative seats. The president's lack of a strategy or much interest in building his party either nationally or in the states left the Democrats without a leader who might have put his own popularity on the line to help others win their races. In private, some White House aides even described his attitude as "benign neglect."[8]

Activists in such progressive movements as Black Lives Matter and Occupy criticized the administration quite harshly for failing to make far-reaching changes. In 2016, some backed Jill Stein, the Green Party candidate for president. While she received just over 1 percent of the national vote, the ballots Stein received in the three states that decided the election—Michigan, Wisconsin, and Pennsylvania—totaled more than the slim pluralities Donald Trump won there. After Hillary Clinton's narrow loss, most Left activists took that lesson to heart. With Donald Trump in the White House, the Democrats *were* a lesser evil. The old hope for a labor, socialist, or Green party that might awaken the dormant anticapitalist sentiments of the masses cracked, perhaps forever, against the wall of the adamantine major-party duopoly that had elected as president a man who all but declared himself to be the mortal enemy of every progressive. Over the past century, leftists had identified themselves with a variety of labels and ideological positions—socialist, anarchist, Communist, radical, and more. But Sanders's candidacy and fear of a second Trump term nudged most Americans on the left to become in fact, if not always in name, what most of the world calls social democrats: proponents of a larger and egalitarian welfare state that strictly regulates private business but makes no attempt to do away with the private ownership and control of most businesses. They agreed, however grudgingly, that the only electoral vehicle for achieving that end would be the sole major party that welcomed their participation.

On the eve of the 1960s, the social-democratic intellectual Irving Howe had acknowledged the same reality: "The decisive political struggles during the next few years will occur in the Democratic party," he wrote in *Dissent* magazine. "This may not be the ideal political arena—of course, it's not . . . but there it is: take it or leave it, a fact."[9] The triumph of Reaganism in the 1980s made his judgment seem dated, for a while. But nothing changed in the ensuing six decades to make the dream of a radical third party anything more than a sectarian fantasy.

By running two competitive races for the Democratic nomination, Sanders, who officially retained his status as an Independent, accomplished two things of substantial political consequence. First, he nudged other politicians to take stands to the left of where the center of the party was when Barack Obama moved out of the White House. Second, he inspired a number of his supporters to run for office as Democrats too. In the wake of Trump's victory, they launched such organizations as Brand New Congress and Justice Democrats to help them do it.

In the thick of the 2020 primaries for president, all the major Democratic contenders vied to present themselves as progressives of one shade or another. They endorsed either Medicare for All or a robust public option, doubling the minimum wage to fifteen dollars an hour, legislation to facilitate union organizing, and a transition to an economy based on renewable sources of energy. Sanders vowed to impose a heavy tax on billionaires, while Elizabeth Warren declared, "I support markets. . . . But markets without rules . . . that's corruption, that's capture of our government by the richest and most powerful around us." Joe Biden kept pace by declaring he would be the "most prounion president" and raise taxes on big corporations and the rich.[10]

However, Sanders was not able to reap the electoral benefits of this leftward move. In 2016, he had drawn 43 percent of the votes in the Democratic primaries and caucuses combined. But in 2020, he failed to win more than 40 percent in any contest, except that of his own state—even after he and Biden were the only major contenders left in the race. After the pandemic began in early March and every other serious candidate but he and Biden dropped out, even many voters who supported Sanders's core positions of Medicare for All and a Green New Deal opted for the more familiar figure who, they believed, had the best chance to beat Trump. Beginning with the South Carolina primary, older African American voters were particularly vital to Biden's triumph, although younger ones tended to back Sanders. For Black people born in Jim Crow America, the ideology and policy preferences, even the race of a candidate, meant less than who had the best chance to win a general election they believed Black people could not afford to lose. Biden won ten of the fourteen contests on Super Tuesday, and the race was essentially over.

But the grassroots fervor that Sanders had stoked over the past four years helped produce an impressive institutional gain for the Left. Democratic Socialists of America (DSA), founded in 1982 and long a minor bastion of veteran radicals, mushroomed from six thousand members to nearly one hundred thousand from Sanders's initial run for president through the election of 2020. There had not been so large a socialist organization in the United States since World War II, when the Communist Party boasted about eighty thousand members, before suffering a steep decline after the Cold War began in earnest. By 2021, some 101 DSA members held office, all in progressive districts, both federal and state. Four were members of the House of Representatives, double the number the old Socialist Party had managed to elect a century earlier.[11]

The wisest decision these freshly minted socialist politicians made came at the start of their political careers: to run as Democrats in primaries where the party's nominee was nearly certain to be elected. Abandoning the quixotic dream of a consequential third party made it possible to achieve something of unprecedented significance: they embedded a dynamic social democratic movement inside the heart of one of the two major parties. In the mid-1960s, the Black freedom movement and organized labor had worked together to compel politicians to enact the programs of the Great Society. But their leaders did not describe themselves as "democratic socialists"—although key actors like Martin Luther King Jr., Bayard Rustin, and Walter Reuther privately were. Lyndon Johnson's escalation of the Vietnam War tore that fragile alliance apart.

The standout figure among the new generation on the Democratic Left was Representative Alexandria Ocasio-Cortez, a charismatic activist from New York City who had interned for Senator Ted Kennedy while in college. Her family's Puerto Rican background and her fluency in Spanish, along with her knack for skewering conservatives on social media, helped make her a symbol of the multiracial "millennials" who had staged and marched in the massive protests during the Trump administration. The 2017 Women's March was the first national demonstration she had ever attended; naturally, she livestreamed it on her Facebook page. AOC, a nickname whose ubiquity signaled instant renown, organized for Sanders during the 2016 campaign. After upsetting a veteran Democratic congressman in the 2018 primary, she became one of the Vermont socialist's leading surrogates in the next one.[12]

## The Biden Non-surprise

That Joe Biden became the presidential nominee of a party moving closer to the views of his left-wing rivals seemed unlikely just a few weeks before it became inevitable. The longtime senator and erstwhile vice president finished fourth in the Iowa caucuses and a dismal fifth in the New Hampshire primary. In February, billionaire Michael Bloomberg's campaign ran through more money in a day than Biden's was able to spend in the entire month. If Black voters in South Carolina, where they composed a majority of Democratic voters, had not rallied to Barack Obama's former second in command at the end of that month, he may have had to drop out of the race.

However, as the year wore on, Biden revealed political strengths that were not apparent to many Democrats when he was struggling to escape from an image as a gaffe-prone centrist who inspired no one. Since Walter Mondale in 1984, every former vice president who later ran for the presidency has won the nomination of his party. And though Obama refrained from endorsing Biden until Sanders dropped out of the race, neither did he give any indication that he favored someone else. That Biden could claim the votes of most African Americans, the most loyal constituency in the party and one whose numbers were essential to carrying nearly every swing state, parried the Left charge that he was the candidate of the party "establishment." And his lack of ideological passion obscured the presence of what one Obama official called Biden's ability to be "a weathervane for what the center of the left is." When he saw where the party was moving, he quickly decided "I'm going to move."[13]

Biden also benefited from having a sincerely, if at times excessively, warm personality as well as a family history of untimely deaths, which he spoke about often and with feeling. His leading rivals for the nomination may not have admired him, but none disliked him. And that made it easier for them to drop out of the race and endorse him after his victories on Super Tuesday. Journalists often assume that personal relationships among politicians matter more than the exigencies of building a base and beating the opposition. But being a well-liked colleague can be an advantage if it helps unify a party and makes its victory more likely.

In the general election, Biden also had the good fortune to run against a president whose words and actions continually made a solid case against reelecting him. The Democrat told the media that he had resolved to join the race for the nomination in 2017 only after Trump's infamous remark that there were "very fine people on both sides" after neo-Nazis and other white supremacists attacked antiracist protesters in Charlottesville, Virginia. Whether or not that was Biden's true motive, it showed a keen recognition that abhorrence of Trump united Democrats across the ideological spectrum more than any single issue divided them.

By calling for the addition of a public option to the Affordable Care Act, Biden also managed to satisfy Democrats who wanted to strengthen "Obamacare" while embracing the principle of universal coverage dear to the Left. Since the first Black president left office, his signature achievement had become more popular. In 2018, Democrats turned the threat that Republicans might repeal it into a campaign weapon: candidates who ran on "strengthening Obamacare" won enough seats held by Republicans, most in white suburban districts, to enable their party to wrest back control of the House. Of course, protecting the health of Americans became the most urgent priority once the COVID pandemic battered the nation. Simply reminding voters of Trump's dismissive, erratic, and dishonest behavior as the death toll soared became the core of Biden's strategy for the general election campaign.

## The Blob and Beyond

As an institution, the Democratic Party could have equipped itself better to advance its goals during Trump's time in office. Without the state and municipal machines of old that dispensed patronage and rewarded loyalty, Democrats outside the national centers of power relied heavily on dedicated volunteers whose numbers and enthusiasm wax and wane with each election cycle. The ease with which individual candidates use technology to appeal directly to voters also weakens the party structures that remain. Candidates for state elections depend more on corporate money than their federal counterparts do, because small donors tend to know little and care less about issues that affect where they live in contrast to larger economic forces they hear about on cable news and read about online.[14]

At the national level, the DNC, despite the media visibility of its chairperson, devotes itself mostly to raising money and putting on a convention every four years. The task of winning or holding seats in Congress and the states falls largely to the Democratic Congressional Campaign Committee, the Democratic Senatorial Campaign Committee, and their counterparts who oversee races for governor and state legislatures—all driven by the labors of thousands of managers, consultants, publicists, programmers, and canvassers serving candidates whose ambitions can outstrip their political skills.

The cosmopolitan background of those who work in what political scientist Daniel Schlozman calls the party's "vast Washingtoncentric Blob" inclines them to give strong backing to abortion rights, marriage equality, and racial justice. But such professional Democrats often have less contact with those who live on meager paychecks and can feel less urgency about highlighting solutions to the economic inequality their candidates condemn in speeches.[15]

To battle Trump and the GOP, Democrats were not armed solely with the party's official apparatus. After the 2016 surprise, the reformist corners of civil society blossomed with a welter of grassroots organizations that vigorously performed many of the quotidian tasks of running campaigns and providing them with eager supporters. There was Indivisible, which boasted some five thousand local chapters with at least one in each congressional district. There was Fair Fight, the group created by Stacey Abrams to combat the voter suppression by Republicans who may have defeated her bid for governor of Georgia in 2018 and which educates new voters, particularly young ones of color. "Voting rights" may not be "the pinnacle of power in our country," as Abrams has asserted. But she understands they are indispensable in scaling the summits of American politics: making it easier for Democrats of all races to cast ballots expands the constituency demanding a program to meet their needs. There was also the Fairness Project, which spearheaded initiatives that raised the minimum wage in red states like Arkansas and Missouri and expanded Medicaid coverage in Idaho and Utah.

Older single-issue groups like the Sierra Club, Planned Parenthood, and the National Association for the Advancement of Colored People routinely donated to, and canvassed for, their favored candidates as well. But the fresh troops of the anti-Trump Resistance helped provide the Democrats with the élan of a social movement combined with a heightened zeal to carry out some of the practical duties ward bosses once performed—without the promise or reward of a patronage job as in the heyday of urban machines like Tammany Hall.

At the same time, however, the new generation of progressives did not attempt to turn the Democratic Party into something that might resemble a left-wing insurgency. The failure of Obama's presidency to live up to its exalted promise was a sober reminder of the difference between the ethos of a movement and the raison d'etre of a mass party. The job of the latter is to win elections and cajole enough officeholders to enact policies that voters want. Social movements exist to articulate bold alternatives and make convincing cases for them. Their task is not to capture a proximate majority but to mobilize a passionate minority to press for fundamental changes in how power works.

## Back to the Future

For Democrats, the election of 2020 spelled relief instead of deliverance from the dilemma of how to build an enduring new majority. In a contest that saw remarkably high turnout on both sides, Joe Biden won the presidency with over half the popular vote and took two states—Arizona and Georgia—that no nominee of his party had carried for over two decades. It represented the seventh time in the last eight presidential contests that more Americans favored a Democrat than his or her GOP rival.

However, the swing voters who rejected Donald Trump did not rush to embrace Biden's party. Democrats won the narrowest possible majority in the Senate, lost fourteen seats in the House, and failed to take a single state legislative chamber away from the GOP. The electorate remained as closely divided as it had since the decline of the New Deal order half a century earlier. If Republicans had won roughly ninety thousand more votes in key states and districts, Trump would have retained the presidency, and his party would have held the majority in the Senate and captured one in the House.[16]

The coalition that vanquished Donald Trump but scored few other notable victories was virtually the same one that had narrowly failed to defeat him four years earlier. Majorities of college-educated people of all races from large metropolitan areas and Black and Latino working people were enough to carry the popular vote and turn enough red states blue to win the presidency. Most Democrats inhabited thriving, if quite unequal, hubs of high-tech, health care, and finance that, since the 1990s, had fueled employment for the many and huge incomes for the few. But the white Americans who lived in rural areas and towns dependent on older industries like manufacturing, mining, and agriculture had become an equally faithful constituency of the opposition party; many viewed Democrat activists as an alien cultural force bent on taking away their jobs and destroying their culture.

Of course, the debate among Democrats about how to turn the support of more than half the nation's voters into consistent electoral victories did not cease. Would a vigorous advocacy of Left policies like Medicare for All and a Green New Deal enable progressives to bridge a racial and cultural chasm with an appeal to the economic self-interest of ordinary white people? Or would a disciplined focus on more modest, less controversial ideas like a higher minimum wage and a public health-care option be more likely to keep the party's existing coalition intact without incurring charges of "socialism" that could imperil the chances of winning at all? If left unresolved, the argument made it more difficult to express in vivid terms what Democrats actually stood for and how they planned to implement that vision.

In bygone days when Democrats ruled national politics, they robustly declared themselves to be on the side of anyone who earned a wage or ran a small business and against the moneyed elite seeking to deprive them of the rewards they deserved. In 1936, the party platform hailed the "right to collective bargaining and self-organization free from the interference of employers." To underline that message, FDR delivered a rousing acceptance speech blasting the "economic royalists" who loathed both him and the "organized power of government" that was challenging their "tyranny." In an explicit nod to labor, he announced, "Liberty requires opportunity to make a living—a living decent according to the standard of the time, a living which gives man not only enough to live by, but something to live for."[17]

This ethic drove the rationale for such landmark programs of the New Deal as public works jobs, the GI Bill, the Wagner Act, Social Security, and the Fair Labor Standards Act (which created the first national minimum wage and overtime pay rule). To win southern votes in Congress, the last three laws carved out exemptions for jobs held by millions of African Americans in agriculture and other people's homes. But they laid the foundation of a robust welfare state that, under popular pressure, could also provide greater security and income support to Black people and other minority groups. The kind of populist rhetoric employed by FDR and his allies had a long history in their party.

Democrats won national elections and were competitive in most states when they articulated a broadly egalitarian economic vision and advocated laws intended to fulfill it—for white Americans only until the middle of the twentieth century and then for everyone. A thread of ideological adherence to what I would call "moral capitalism" stretched from Andrew Jackson's war against the Second Bank of the United States to Grover Cleveland's attack on the protective tariff, and from William Jennings Bryan's crusade against the "money power" to FDR's assault on economic royalists to the full employment promise embedded in the Humphrey-Hawkins Act of 1978.[18]

In the 1990s, the pro-corporate centrism of the Democratic Leadership Council muted the traditional message, and Bill Clinton's two presidential wins made it seem outdated (although he never won a majority of the popular vote). But prominent Democrats picked up this thread again after the Great Recession. In 2011, Obama declared that crisis was "a make-or-break moment for the middle class, and for all those who are fighting to get into the middle class." But aside from signing the Affordable Care Act, he was unable or unwilling to back up that populist warning with any significant new program.[19]

The United States has lacked a dominant party since the downfall of the New Deal order more than forty years ago; the current partisan standoff that began with the election of 1980 has lasted longer than any such period in American history. If judged by the tiny majorities Democrats eked out in Congress in 2020, that stalemate shows no sign of ending. "I want to be the most progressive president since FDR," Joe Biden told Bernie Sanders when he asked for his endorsement after their primary battle had ended. To realize that ambition, the president needs a party with a coalition as broad and energized as that which Roosevelt used to govern the nation during its worst economic crisis and its bloodiest foreign war. By the time Biden leaves office, we will know if his administration created a new "reconstruction" or struggled even to adequately govern a bitterly divided, imperial power in decline.[20]

# 19

# Impeachment after Trump

*Gregory P. Downs*

On February 9, 2021, Senate chaplain Barry C. Black opened the second impeachment trial of Donald Trump with a prayer as extraordinary as the moment. Reverend Black quoted antislavery poet James Russell Lowell's "The Present Crisis," penned during the fierce 1845 debates over white southern planters' eagerness to expand slavery into territory they hoped to add in the U.S.-Mexico War: "Once to every man and nation comes the moment to decide, In the strife of Truth with Falsehood, for the good or evil side."[1]

"Could it really be just truth striving against falsehood and good striving against evil?" Black asked the Senate. The parts of the poem that Black did not quote recounted transgressive acts that saved a nation from collapse in a time of crisis, contrasting the Pilgrims' bravery with those who hoarded the Pilgrims' truths in "mouldy parchments, while our tender spirits flee / the rude grasp of that great Impulse which drove them across the sea." Lowell's lessons were stark: "They have rights who dare maintain them; we are traitors to our sires. / New occasions teach new duties." Americans must not "attempt the Future's portal with the Past's blood-rusted key."[2] While Black did not further explain his choice of poem, "The Present Crisis" presented a bleak but powerful vision for the nation at the end of the Trump administration: the country in a time of crisis could not be saved by reference to the past but could only be preserved by the boldness of the living.

The Trump impeachments presented a grave test not just of the senators' consciences but of the Constitution itself. The trials, particularly the second, suggested that the flaws were not only in some senators' judgment but also in the Constitution. Almost everyone in the Senate understood the close of the Trump administration as a time of present, even desperate, crisis for the country and its political system, but they differed sharply on where the crisis lay: in Trump's actions as president that led to two impeachments in a single year, or in the Democratic House that pursued them, even after Joe Biden's victory in the 2020 presidential election. Still, neither side quite captured the dire tone Black established with the Lowell poem. For all the disagreements about the impeachment, the Senate trials were, by and large, paeans to the Constitution, although often homages to quite different constitutional interpretations. Democrats voted for conviction to save the Constitution from abuse. Republicans claimed their acquittal honored the Constitution's high standard for impeachment. Few senators seemed to register the transgressive implications of Lowell's words and bleak judgment of "moudly parchments," which is fitting since Lowell in later writings mocked the way nineteenth-century conservatives used the term "Constitutional Obligations" to cover for "indifference," and derided the populace's "neglectful" belief that the Constitution was a "machine that would go of itself."[3]

The impeachment process was thought to be one of the most foundational elements of the Constitution. Other than elections, impeachment offered the only path for Congress to remove a political leader who abused his or her power in ways that were dangerous to the republic. So awesome was the power that it had rarely been used in American history. In the swirl of President Donald Trump's impeachments, it was not always clear what precisely remained solid about this crucial process and what melted into air. Until 2019, there were only two presidential impeachment trials since the nation's founding. In the twelve months between February 2020 and February 2021, that number doubled. Before 2020, no senator from the president's own political party had ever voted to convict a president. In 2020, Mitt Romney became the first; in the 2021 impeachment trial, six other Republican senators joined him. By those lights, a great deal had changed.

But the outcome remained the same as always in U.S. presidential impeachments: acquittal. Trump had tested the limits of presidential power in ways that very few, if any, predecessors had done, and still Congress was unable to remove him. Thus, Americans lived through a presidency when impeachment was being called the only way to save the republic, and also when it became evident that conviction might never be possible in what one scholar called a "tribal age." It was clear that impeachment talk was central to U.S. politics and that actual impeachment might never work.[4]

Beyond the Senate, this disjunction inspired outrage, cynicism, and panic about the limitations of the Constitution itself. The Trump presidency raised serious doubts about the system's stability or even survival. Whereas President Richard Nixon's resignation in 1974 gave rise to commentary that the "system worked," the Trump presidency left a large number of citizens wondering whether the constitutional system of politics was broken to the core.[5]

Trump, a baby boomer, had been the vehicle for severely weakening the post–World War II faith in constitutional institutions. This faith had been buttressed over the latter half of the twentieth century by the Supreme Court's actions on civil rights, the forced resignation of Nixon, and the period's general economic prosperity. While Americans had lost faith in most institutions since the 1960s, the Constitution—the overriding framework of the Constitution—still held sway. But by 2021, many Americans beyond Congress seemed to be looking past what Lowell called the "Past's blood-rusted key."

---

The role of impeachment in U.S. politics has never been clearly defined, even though the process is clearly outlined in the Constitution. In the Constitution, impeachment constitutes solely a political punishment, not a criminal charge. Once impeached and convicted, the officeholder is removed from the position and can be barred from holding future office, if so specified, but cannot be otherwise punished. While the framers debated different methods for trying impeachment, they settled on a majority vote of the House of Representatives for impeachment, then a two-thirds vote in the Senate for removal.

But what constituted impeachable conduct? The framers worried that Congress would dominate the president, and they also hoped elections, not impeachment, would be the normal way to replace an unpopular or unwise executive. But delegate George Mason reminded them that relying on elections could make the political system subject to more corruption if the unworthy president continued to abuse power to win reelection. "Shall the man who has practised corruption & by that means procured his appointment in the first instance, be suffered to escape punishment, by repeating his guilt?" he asked. English parliaments had used wide-ranging grounds for impeachment, but the constitutional framers sought to limit it to those charges that threatened the republic. They included "Treason" and "Bribery." Fearful that these words were too limiting, they looked for an addition, considering but then rejecting "maladministration" before settling on "high Crimes and Misdemeanors." This phrase was commonly used in English parliamentary impeachments but did not have a precise meaning, then or now. In his defense of the constitutional framework in *The Federalist Papers*, no. 65, Alexander Hamilton emphasized that impeachable offenses involved an "abuse or violation of some public trust" that "may with peculiar propriety be denominated political, as they relate chiefly to injuries done immediately to the society itself."[6]

For the first eighty years of the republic, presidential impeachment was rarely discussed. Although there were impeachments of a senator, a Supreme Court justice, and federal judges, it remained unclear whether those nonpresidential impeachments set a viable precedent for the president, or even if precedents mattered in political trials. The first impeachment of a president grew from the extraordinary political strife of the Civil War era. In 1864, President Abraham Lincoln selected loyal Tennessee Democrat Andrew Johnson as vice president for a unity ticket. After Lincoln's April 1865 assassination, Johnson became president, facing a Congress with massive Republican majorities. Although Johnson supported the Thirteenth Amendment, which abolished slavery, he worked to block other aspects of Reconstruction, pardoning thousands of ex-Confederates, returning their land, vetoing congressional civil rights bills, and denouncing congressional radicals as traitors. Over 1866 and 1867, House Republicans considered a range of impeachment charges but did not act, in part because of concerns that "high Crimes and Misdemeanors" required an actual criminal act. In 1868, after Johnson replaced more radical generals, undermined voter enfranchisement, and arguably violated a law that might have blocked him from removing his secretary of war, House Republicans impeached him. In the Senate, Johnson was acquitted by a single vote, as a handful of Republican senators feared the long-term consequences of impeachment without a clear crime, as well as the chance of a popular backlash with a presidential election only months away. The legacies of Johnson's impeachment were mixed. Impeachment did impact policy; fearful of conviction, Johnson pledged not to interfere with Reconstruction in the South. Republicans in turn won the 1868 presidential election, arguably validating moderate senators' concerns about backlash. For many legal scholars, however, the impeachment remains an error, since Republicans were obviously motivated by Johnson's policy positions more than any single bad act. But historians generally write supportively of this impeachment as an effort to defend congressional legitimacy, civil rights, and constitutional amendments. The revival of interest in Reconstruction during the Trump administration, owing to 150th anniversaries and the upsurge in attention to Black history after the police killing of George Floyd, helped press this supportive historical view of impeachment into popular consciousness, particularly among liberals.[7]

Johnson's acquittal seemed to quiet serious presidential impeachment talk for a century, though reactionaries called for the impeachment of Chief Justice Earl Warren in the 1960s after the Supreme Court's liberal desegregation rulings. Although not an impeachment, Richard Nixon's 1974 resignation under threat of impeachment and removal served as a reminder of the tool's power for saving the republic from a corrupt chief executive. Although Nixon was reelected handily in 1972, public disclosure of the administration's secret bombing campaign in Cambodia undermined some congressmen's faith in the administration. Then, newspapers began to report that the 1972 Nixon campaign paid burglars to ransack Democratic headquarters, while Nixon personally participated in the cover-up. At first many Republican congressmen resisted impeachment, but Nixon's ham-handed efforts to erase White House tapes, his damning words on those tapes, his firing of the attorney general, his campaign to stifle a special prosecutor, and the indictments of his closest aides led many to join the impeachment push, even though much of the Republican base resisted. In retrospect it is clear that this split between Republican popular opinion and Republican leadership reflected not an agreed-upon constitutional standard, but a particular set of Cold War contingencies, especially the power of network television and national newspapers to disseminate both information and calls for bipartisanship. Nixon resigned in August 1974, once he realized he could not prevail.[8]

Nixon's downfall reinforced the idea that impeachment was a rare and awesome tool. It did not prompt an upsurge of what scholars call "impeachment talk," the chatter about potential impeachments that has the power to shape political decision-making. Impeachment talk remained uncommon under the next four presidents, despite a small flurry during the Iran-Contra scandal in Ronald Reagan's last years in office. In 1987, congressional Democrats decided that attempting to impeach Reagan for his role in illegal assistance to the Nicaraguan Contras was not worth the political cost or the price the nation would pay for going through such a trauma for the second time in two decades. Since Reagan was at the end of his second term, and Congress could not find a smoking gun directly linking him to the wrongdoing of high-level national security officials, they didn't trigger the process despite controlling the House and Senate.

But the Nixon scandals did have a consequential institutional impact: the creation of an independent counsel to investigate allegations against the executive branch. In the infamous "Saturday Night Massacre," Nixon had removed the attorney general and his deputy for not firing the special prosecutor investigating the break-in and cover-up. In response, Congress in 1978 created a system of independent counsels who were to be appointed by the federal court of appeals when there was evidence of executive branch corruption. Under the law, the prosecutors were insulated from presidential oversight. After the Iran-Contra scandal, critics charged that the independent counsel act created unaccountable prosecutors who could pursue cases indefinitely. But in 1994, Congress nevertheless reauthorized the act, believing it essential to restraining the abuse of presidential power.

Meanwhile, politics was becoming increasingly polarized, as norms containing partisan warfare ebbed with the end of the Cold War, and conservative talk radio and then Fox News repeated extreme opinions in popular echo chambers.[9]

Over the eight years of Bill Clinton's presidency, these political and legal changes produced a new, and enduring, era of impeachment. In Clinton's second year in office, Attorney General Janet Reno asked the federal courts to appoint an independent counsel to investigate an alleged financial scandal involving the Clintons. Congressional Republicans, radicalizing under Newt Gingrich's leadership, had already been pushing for numerous investigations into Clinton over a number of issues, ranging from his and First Lady Hillary Clinton's prior role in an Arkansas land deal to trumped-up allegations about the firing of staff in the White House travel office. Some of the Far Right had gone so far as to outlandishly accuse Clinton of being involved in the death of his close friend and counsel, Vincent Foster.[10]

The intensity of the investigations increased after the 1994 Republican takeover of the House, but exploded as Clinton added fuel to the fire through his own sordid personal behavior. In 1997, the Supreme Court advanced a civil suit against Clinton by a former Arkansas public employee, Paula Jones, who charged that he sexually harassed her while he was governor. When the Jones lawyers learned that Clinton was having an affair with a young White House intern named Monica Lewinsky, they asked Clinton pointed questions in a sworn deposition. Under oath Clinton lied about his relationship, then allegedly began to act to conceal the relationship.[11]

Over 1998, the independent counsel investigation, Republican congressional extremism, and Clinton's misleading deposition intertwined. A court-appointed independent counsel, the fiercely partisan Kenneth Starr, turned from investigating alleged financial corruption to the relationship with an intern and subpoenaed Clinton to testify in front of a grand jury. As some Clinton aides falsely denigrated Lewinsky as a stalker, the president claimed in a finger-wagging televised statement to reporters that "I did not have sex with that woman, Miss Lewinsky." Once Clinton faced Starr's team in front of a federal grand jury in August, however, he admitted to an "improper relationship." Seeking to save himself, the president offered a number of inconsistent responses about the details. But the situation had changed. Clinton soon confessed on television, before shifting to a denunciation of the partisan witch hunt. On September 9, Starr submitted his report to the House, along with eighteen boxes of evidence filled with lurid detail about the president and Lewinsky. The House Judiciary Committee released 445 pages to the public, exposing the most intimate details. The committee also released the videotaped and jury testimony, which was broadcast on television and circulated through the internet.

House Republicans voted to start an impeachment in early October, claiming that President Clinton had perjured himself and attempted to obstruct the investigation. But Democrats gained five House seats in the November election, raising the question of whether the impeachment effort had backfired. Nevertheless, on December 19, the House of Representatives passed articles of impeachment largely by a party-line vote. Backed by five Democrats and most Republicans, two articles of impeachment progressed: one alleged lying to the federal grand jury and the other obstructing justice.[12] Clinton, whose popularity remained strong, refused to resign, even as a House Republican leader resigned amid stories of his own adulterous affair. Meanwhile, Democrats solidified their support for Clinton, arguing that even if his acts were disgraceful they did not meet the constitutional standard of "high crimes and misdemeanors." The Senate rejected the charges, with a number of Republicans crossing the aisle to vote with every Democratic senator for acquittal.[13]

For a moment, it seemed that the lesson of the Clinton impeachment was to avoid impeachments, and neither party's leadership wanted anything more to do with impeachment. Clinton ended his presidency with high approval ratings, and Hillary Clinton would win a seat in the U.S. Senate representing New York. In 1999, Congress allowed the law establishing the independent prosecutor to expire.

But predictions of impeachment's retreat were wrong. The bitter partisan wars of the 1990s incentivized elected officials to seek publicity by calling for the removal of the opposition party's president. Impeachment talk became normalized, especially during presidential second terms, as scandals were reported and personal popularity ebbed. Such talk swirled around President George W. Bush during his second-term struggles with the Iraq War, Hurricane Katrina, and newspaper revelations of torture and domestic surveillance in the war on terror. Between late 2005 and 2008, a number of Democratic House members publicly called for impeachment. Popular support polled between 33 and 36 percent, garnering majority favor among Democrats. Although Democrats carried the 2006 midterms, House Speaker Nancy Pelosi blocked impeachment consideration, wary of a popular backlash.[14]

Impeachment talk increased in volume and virulence during Barack Obama's administration, beginning in his first term. The new generation of Republicans—influenced by Gingrich and his allies—was willing to go to extreme lengths in pursuit of partisan power. Some allegations centered on absurd rumors that Obama had been born overseas, with Republicans implying that he was not a legitimate president or was a secret Muslim, and others on Obama's use of executive authority over immigration or his authorization of drone strikes or an attack on Libya. By 2014, 35 percent of Americans favored impeachment, including a majority of Republicans. But even after House Republicans gained control of Congress in 2010, party leaders feared that impeachment would backfire, especially since they could not find evidence of significant presidential wrongdoing.[15]

Still, impeachment's role in politics had changed over the early 2010s, and the 2016 campaign was shaped by impeachment in a way that had never happened in U.S. history. Much talk swirled around Donald Trump's public call for foreign actors to hack into and release information from Democratic email servers. But Trump was not the only source of impeachment talk. A good deal centered on the presumed front-runner, Democrat Hillary Clinton, and her use of a private email server while she was secretary of state. Although Republicans struggled to gin up controversy, they received an unexpected gift when Hillary Clinton's husband Bill summoned the incumbent attorney general to chat informally, even as the Justice Department was investigating Hillary Clinton's email servers. The appearance of impropriety led the attorney general to defer to FBI judgment, leading to a series of extraordinary public statements by Director James Comey that seem to have damaged Hillary Clinton's chances for victory even though the investigation cleared Hillary Clinton of personal legal wrongdoing. Just before the 2016 election, the *Washington Post* and *New York Times* each reported that leading Republican representatives were planning to impeach Hillary Clinton for her use of a private email server while secretary of state, should she be elected.[16]

Impeachment talk would have shaped Inauguration Day 2017 no matter who was taking the oath of office, but Donald Trump's surprise victory meant that impeachment talk centered on his wrongdoing. On January 20, 2017, two liberal advocacy groups launched a coordinated effort known as Impeach Donald Trump Now. This early campaign focused on Trump's potential violations of the Constitution's emoluments clause, which prohibits any U.S. official from receiving a "present, Emolument, Office, or Title, of any kind whatever, from any King, Prince, or foreign State." The president's refusal to create a clear firewall between his family-controlled international business and the White House obviously blurred the lines between his official actions and his personal economic interest. Foreign governments' payments for office space in Trump-owned buildings and rooms in Trump-affiliated hotels might constitute illegal payments or influence his policies toward Trump property clients like Saudi Arabia. Within two weeks of Trump's inauguration almost one-third of the public supported impeachment, a number that rose to 41 percent by the end of 2017.[17] Like many aspects of the Trump era, the surface issues were fleeting, but the fundamental crises remained solidly in place. Although lawsuits challenged Trump's apparent profiting, emoluments faded as a basis for impeachment. The movement, however, served notice that what scholars call "impeachment talk" would be prominent from day one.[18]

Still, talk was not action. One restraint was Republican control of the House of Representatives. The other was Democratic leaders' fears that taking action against Trump would lead to sympathy for a president who otherwise was historically unpopular. Democrats waited, also, for a much-anticipated report by former FBI director Robert Mueller on alleged collaboration between the Trump campaign and the Russian government during the 2016 campaign. Mueller had been appointed special prosecutor by Deputy Attorney General Rod Rosenstein after Attorney General Jeff Sessions had recused himself (over Trump's objections) from these decisions because of his own involvement in the scandal. Even after the 2018 midterm elections seated a Democratic majority in the House, Speaker Pelosi discouraged impeachment talk, although increasingly large numbers of Democratic members stated there was sufficient evidence to impeach. Pelosi's wariness seemed confirmed on March 22, 2019, when Mueller flubbed the unveiling of his team's report on Trump's ties to foreign governments. Although the report was devastating, Mueller's initial silence allowed Attorney General William Barr to issue misleading characterizations that overshadowed the report's details. Barr claimed that the report "exonerated" the president. The actual report documented a number of extremely problematic relationships between the president's campaign and Russian officials. Mueller, who did not believe he had the authority to call for impeachment since the independent counsel law had expired, then made things worse by faltering in congressional testimony.[19]

What finally broke this impasse between impeachment talk and impeachment action was the unprecedented behavior of President Trump and the concerted effort of government whistleblowers to expose his actions. The first impeachment of President Trump turned on U.S. aid to Ukraine, aid that aimed to protect that country from further aggression from Russia, which in 2014 annexed the previously Ukrainian peninsula of Crimea. Congress had allocated $391 million in military aid to Ukraine, but Trump ordered the State and Defense Departments to withhold the funding, in violation of government rules. At first, high-level officials responsible for these policies, such as National Security Council official Lt. Col. Alexander Vindman, were puzzled by the delay. Without their knowledge, a small group close to the president, including Ambassador of the United States to the European Union Gordon Sondland and the president's personal counsel Rudy Giuliani, were telling Ukrainian officials that the aid would be released only in exchange for favors that would help Trump's reelection campaign. Those favors were two extremely dubious investigations based on rumors and conspiracy theories: one of Democratic front-runner Joseph Biden's alleged family ties to a Ukrainian company, another of a discredited theory that Ukraine, not Russia, was the source of foreign manipulation of the 2016 election.[20]

The president exposed this effort to leverage foreign assistance to preserve his own power during a phone call with Ukrainian president Volodymyr Zelensky on July 25, 2019, the day after Mueller testified in front of Congress. When Zelensky inquired about the funds that

Congress had approved, Trump agreed to release them but then added, "I would like you to do us a favor though." The favor was those two investigations. After Zelensky pledged to "work on the investigation," Trump invited Zelensky to the White House, a further perk that U.S. diplomats had offered in trade. Vindman, who had written the talking points for the call, was stunned by the quid pro quo. As Zelensky tried to navigate this thicket, news of the hold on Ukrainian funds broke on August 28, 2019, in *Politico*.[21]

Meanwhile, on August 12, 2019, a whistleblower filed a report alleging that "the President of the United States is using the power of his office to solicit interference from a foreign country in the 2020 US election." During the subsequent impeachment trial, Pennsylvania Republican senator Pat Toomey would contest this interpretation, claiming that Trump had "legitimate national interests for seeking investigations into possible corruption." But Trump's own words seemed damning, even to members of his own administration, who took pains to suppress any record of them. Although required to inform congressional leaders of the complaint, Acting Director of National Intelligence Joseph Maguire did not do so. The White House further deleted the transcript of the phone call from the White House server. Under pressure, the Trump administration finally released the aid, hoping to defuse the growing controversy. But the die was cast.[22]

Five new congresswomen—Elissa Slotkin, Abigail Spanberger, Chrissy Houlahan, Mikie Sherrill, and Elaine Luria—and two male colleagues changed the political dynamics by writing an op-ed in the *Washington Post* calling for the impeachment process to begin. None of these legislators were considered to be from the left wing of the party, and all of them had impeccable national security credentials. Pelosi had come to believe that with backing such as this, and a clear-cut issue such as the president withholding public funds for his own interests, the Democrats had sufficient room to proceed without triggering a backlash. Democrats claimed that the president had engaged in the precise behavior that the founders had in mind when they designed the impeachment process. President Trump in turn tried to block the congressional investigation, citing executive privilege. Congressional Republicans mostly stood by the president; even those who condemned the president's actions denounced the inquiry as a partisan witch hunt and impeachment as unwarranted. The November 2020 election would allow the people to decide whether Trump was a fit president, they argued. Democrats responded that the president was already trying to use public funds to win the election, and would continue to do so, tainting the upcoming election with his corruption.[23]

In December 2019, the House impeached on two articles, with votes breaking almost entirely on partisan lines. The first article charged that Trump "abused the powers of the Presidency" by soliciting "the interference of a foreign government, Ukraine, in the 2020 United States Presidential elections" in a manner that "compromised the national security of the United States and undermined the integrity of the United States democratic process." The second article charged Trump with "obstruction of Congress" in defying subpoenas and directing Chief of Staff John Michael "Mick" Mulvaney and other officials not to cooperate with the impeachment inquiry. Trump's acquittal would "permanently alter the balance of power among the branches of government, inviting future Presidents to operate as if they are also beyond the reach of accountability, congressional oversight, and the law," House manager Adam Schiff (D-CA) argued to his colleagues.[24]

With Republicans in control of the Senate, the nature of the trial remained unclear. The first fight was over access to witnesses whom Trump had blocked from testifying. Senate Majority Leader Mitch McConnell, who had proved to be one of the most ruthless and effective partisan leaders in Washington, argued against seeking witnesses, claiming that the House had conducted "the least thorough and most unclear impeachment inquiry in American history." Thus the Senate did not need to bail out the House's investigation. Of course, most of the House limitations stemmed from the president's refusal to cooperate. Democratic senator Chris Murphy argued that a "show trial" made the Senate "complicit in the very attacks on democracy that this body is supposed to guard against. We have failed to protect the Republic." Republican senators voted to skip witnesses, aiming to put the impeachment behind them and prevent any unexpected revelations.[25]

More broadly, Senate Republicans argued that the charges were political, not criminal. Trump's legal team called the impeachment "a dangerous attack on the right of the American people to freely choose their President" and "a brazen and unlawful attempt to overturn the results of the 2016 election and interfere with the 2020 election." According to Senator Mitch McConnell, "This isn't really about Ukraine policy or military assistance money" but about "partisanship." Despite the fact that Republicans had been extraordinarily hawkish on Russia for many years, in this case they tolerated what the president had done. "We had a 230-year tradition of rejecting purely political impeachments, and it died last month," McConnell said. Conviction would "almost guarantee the impeachment of every future President of either party when the House doesn't like that President." Republicans looked to the phrasing of the impeachment clause—"Treason, Bribery, or other high Crimes and Misdemeanors"—reminding senators that the constitutional authors rejected the broader "maladministration." "House Democrats' novel theory of 'abuse of power' improperly supplants the standard of 'high Crimes and Misdemeanors' with a made-up theory that would permanently weaken the Presidency by effectively permitting impeachments based merely on policy disagreements," one Republican argued. While Tennessee Republican senator Lamar Alexander called Trump's acts "inappropriate," he agreed that they "don't meet the Constitution's . . . standard for impeachable offense." Others found novel ways to twist events. South Carolina senator Lindsey Graham later used the ultimate extension of aid, which the administration extended in response to the revelations of the call, to prove that there had been no abuse of power. "What you have done is impeached the President . . . because he suspended foreign aid for 40 days to leverage an investigation that never occurred." To 2020 Republicans, the lesson of Andrew Johnson remained clear: no crime, no conviction.[26]

Democrats responded that this was bad history and bad political theory. They quoted Alexander Hamilton's and George Mason's own words on the standards for impeachment and the political nature of the proceedings. They emphasized the absurdity of limiting impeachment to violations of federal laws, when the federal code was virtually nonexistent as the constitutional convention met, and they argued that the framers intended impeachment to save the country from corruption and abuse of power. Like virtually all reputable legal scholars and historians, Democratic managers argued that the founders adopted an English parliamentary standard of "high Crimes and Misdemeanors" that was not based on statute law but was "flexible enough to reach the full range of potential Presidential misconduct." Only one Republican was convinced by their argument, Utah senator Mitt Romney, the 2012 Republican nominee for president. Based on testimony about the "historic meaning of the words 'high crimes and misdemeanors,' the writings of the Founders, and my own reasoned judgment," Romney argued that "a President can indeed commit acts against the public trust that are so egregious that, while they are not statutory crimes, they would demand removal from office." It "defies reason" to think the constitutional authors expected Congress to pen a "comprehensive list of all the outrageous acts that a President might conceivably commit." Romney voted to convict on the abuse of power (though not on obstruction of Congress) because of Trump's "appalling abuse of public trust."[27]

As it became obvious that Senate Republicans had enough votes to acquit Trump, Democrats and Republicans argued about what this meant for the Constitution. For Democrats it suggested that the Constitution would lose its power if politicians and the populace did not commit themselves to enforcing it, even against partisan self-interest. If this action didn't rise to the level of warranting impeachment, what would? Had Republicans moved so far into their partisanship that a Republican president could do almost anything without having to fear being impeached? "While there is no greater privilege than living in a country whose constitution guarantees our rights, there is no greater burden than knowing that our actions could sap that very same Constitution of its power; that our inaction risks allowing it to wither like any other piece of parchment from some bygone era," Senator Tammy Duckworth said. Senate Republicans claimed that acquittal would vindicate the Constitution, both in upholding a high standard for impeachment and in defending the president's authority over the executive branch from congressional interference. Democrats sought to make the president "somehow subservient to the career civil servant bureaucratic class that has tended to manage agencies within the Federal Government," one Republican senator said. "The President is the executive branch."[28]

On February 6, 2020, just one month before the nation was in the full throes of the COVID-19 pandemic, the Senate acquitted Trump by a majority vote: 52–48 on abuse of power and 53–47 on obstruction. Romney was the only Republican to vote guilty and the only senator to shift his vote on the two counts. The other moderates in the GOP voted with the president. This solid Republican support for acquittal and unanimous Democratic support for guilt made impeachment seem at once necessary and impossible to achieve. Many Democrats were coming to believe that the fierce partisanship of the GOP rendered impeachment useless. The outcome prompted constitutional soul-searching by Democratic politicians and activists and questions about how a president like Trump could ever be held accountable.

Republican senator Susan Collins claimed that impeachment had taught Trump "a pretty big lesson," even without conviction. But her suggestion that Trump, like former president Andrew Johnson, might be restrained by impeachment proved grotesquely ungrounded as Trump behaved even more erratically over 2020. He cast the impeachment as an effort by radical Democrats and the "fake media" to remove him from office. Despite Collins's prediction, the president seemed to have learned a very different lesson from the failed impeachment. He could do what he wanted and get away with it—even in broad daylight.

As the November 3, 2020, election approached, Trump and his advisers sowed doubts about the validity of the election counting system and spread unfounded stories of voter fraud. Trump had been making these completely unfounded allegations since taking office. On election eve, Trump took the brazen step of going on air and charging that Democrats were trying to steal the election from him. In fact, the 2020 election *was* unlike any other. States scrambled to create safe ways for people to cast ballots during the COVID pandemic—in some cases expanding voting by mail and early voting. In battleground states of Georgia, Michigan, Wisconsin, Pennsylvania, and Arizona, Trump fared well in Election Day voting counts. As most experts had predicted, his early lead started to fade as mail-in ballots were counted, since Democrats disproportionately voted early and by mail. Over the days that followed the election, the count in each of the key swing states turned toward Biden. On November 7, virtually every news network called Biden the victor by a 306–232 electoral count. Biden and vice presidential nominee Kamala Harris gave victory speeches that evening.

But Trump did not concede. His campaign against the election results accelerated. He and his supporters focused on the creaky electoral count system and an 1887 law passed after the near-catastrophic

1876–77 electoral count crisis. That crisis had also raised grave fears about the nation's stability and the functionality of the Constitution. In November 1876, disputed returns from three former Confederate states, where white Democrats defrauded and intimidated Black Republican voters, and a single disputed elector from Oregon threw the presidential count into chaos, with Senate Republicans claiming the power to count the votes and House Democrats threatening to utilize their constitutional power to decide elections with no Electoral College majority. The Constitution offered no useful guidance on this issue, and the presidential race hung in the balance. As state governors called out militia and talk swirled of competing inaugurations, congressional leaders created a onetime solution in a commission to resolve the issue. Over the following years, the problems in the count led to a new law limiting each house's power to intervene in the electoral count. Both houses had to agree that a state's count was invalid before the votes were rejected. That was the window Trump tried to exploit.

Trump and his advisers used the time between the election tallies and the official count in Congress to pressure Georgia's secretary of state and other state officials to refuse to certify state election results. He took states to court challenging the results. Supporters unsuccessfully sued state governments. The president and top Republicans used their public platforms—including Twitter—to spread claims that the election had been stolen, including doctored videos of ballots for Trump being taken away. Meanwhile, militia members and followers of the QAnon online conspiracy movement discussed extraconstitutional remedies.[29] By the time that Congress was set to certify the results, the president, congressional Republicans, and prominent figures in the right-wing media had whipped up red state voters into a frenzy, convincing many that Biden's victory was based on a fraudulent process.

On January 6, 2021, Congress convened to officially count and certify the Electoral College ballots. Ordinarily, this has been a pro forma process. On rare occasion, symbolic votes have been cast in an act of protest, without any thought that the ballots could actually be blocked. On the several occasions when House members objected without a Senate pair, those objections were predictably dismissed. A technical joint objection to a single faithless elector in 1969 failed to carry and would not have affected the election. In 2005, one Democratic senator joined a House objection to Ohio's electoral vote but was the only senator to vote to overturn the state's outcome.

In January 2021, the situation was different. There were a group of Republicans attempting to complete the campaign that the president had begun. Some party leaders understood the danger of these actions. In 2021, Senate Republican Leader Mitch McConnell urged his colleagues not to join House Republican objections. But Republican Missouri senator Josh Hawley, a loyal foot soldier for the president, announced plans to object. More than ten Republican senators followed suit. Understanding that they didn't have the numbers needed in the House and Senate to overturn the result, conservative activists focused on Vice President Mike Pence, who would formally preside over the electoral count. Trump supporters and the president himself urged Pence to overturn the counts, even though he had no power to do so. Meanwhile, Trump supporters planned a mass "Save America" rally on the National Mall for the morning of January 6. QAnon followers, Proud Boys, and other militia members plotted to turn the rally into an attack mob.[30]

Addressing the early-morning rally at the Ellipse, Trump repeated his claims of a stolen election and told the crowd, "We will never give up." "If you don't fight like hell, you're not going to have a country anymore," he said. The crowd then proceeded to march to the Capitol to join those who had already gathered. What followed was one of the most shocking moments in U.S. history. Thousands of people marched forward, drove Capitol Police from barriers, beat officers to unconsciousness, and stormed into the nation's Capitol. Inside, Capitol Police officers feared for their lives, trying to hold back the mob and protect the legislators and vice president gathered inside. Congress recessed from counting the votes, and members fled for safety as the mob headed for their chambers. The crowd overwhelmed the police and broke into the Senate chamber and several members' offices. Some mobbers carried Confederate flags into the Capitol. Some chanted, "Hang Mike Pence." Outside, they built a mock gallows. While some mobbers were clearly going along with the crowd, others carried tactical gear and talked openly of kidnapping or murder. One rioter was shot dead by security as she tried to breach a doorway. One Capitol Police officer died after being pepper sprayed and assaulted. Many others were injured. Not since the War of 1812, when the British burned the Capitol and White House, had government buildings been under similar assault. For hours, Trump remained quiet. His administration provided little to no support to the U.S. Capitol Police. Only at 6:25 p.m., four hours into the riot, did Trump call on rioters to leave via a video, stating "these are things that happen when a sacred landslide election victory is so unceremoniously & viciously stripped away from great patriots who have been badly & unfairly treated for so long." "Remember this day forever!" Trump tweeted.[31]

After order was finally restored, and Congress certified the Electoral College results, Congress moved to impeach the president for a second time. This time there was no hesitation. On January 13, one week after the violent insurrection, the House of Representatives impeached Trump for "incitement of insurrection" by a 232–197 vote, with ten Republicans joining every Democrat. Pelosi and other Democratic leaders feared that if they didn't draw a line in the sand, the precedent would be set for future commanders in chief to literally do almost anything. House Democrats argued that the Constitution depended on clear, quick action. "American exceptionalism is not guaranteed," one Democrat said. "We must always work to grow it." Democratic congresswoman Pramila Jayapal asked, "What will our future look like? . . . This is an act toward preserving the integrity of our democracy." A prominent Republican defector, Congresswoman Liz Cheney, Republican Conference Committee chair and daughter of a former vice president, gave her reason for crossing party lines: "There has never been a greater betrayal by the President of the United States of his office and his oath to the Constitution."[32]

Although Cheney and a few other Republicans broke with the president and voted to impeach, most did not. Once again, party leaders drew on constitutional arguments to defend their position even as they condemned the president's actions. The GOP claimed the impeachment divided the country, impeded a peaceful transition of power, and criminalized political language. "If we impeached every politician who gave a fiery speech to a crowd of partisans, this Capitol would be deserted," Republican congressman Tom McClintock said. "That is all he did."[33]

What complicated the case was timing. Inauguration Day was January 20, 2021, a week after the impeachment. Could the Senate conduct a trial between January 13 and January 20? If so, a fast acquittal might empower Trump to resist the inauguration. The question of who controlled the Senate, and thus would set the terms for the trial, also caused delays. On January 5, the day before the insurrection, Georgians voted in runoff elections for both of their U.S. Senate seats. Democrats needed to win both to create a fifty-fifty tie in the Senate, which would be broken on Inauguration Day by new vice president Kamala Harris. As the mob was dispersed from the Capitol on the evening of January 6, networks had called the Georgia elections for Democrats. Still, Republicans remained in charge for the next two weeks.[34] Pulling one last procedural trick from his bag, McConnell delayed an impeachment trial in the Senate until after Biden assumed power, claiming Trump's team needed time to prepare.

On January 20, with Democrats in power and Biden in office, a new question emerged: Were impeachments of former officeholders legitimate? Conviction remained meaningful since it usually carries a disqualification from holding future office, and Trump already threatened to run again in 2024. After preventing the Senate trial when Trump was still in office, McConnell and other Republicans now argued that it was too late to do anything about the ex-president's actions.

There was a precedent Democrats could point to for impeaching a former office-holder: the long-forgotten 1876 impeachment of Secretary of War William Belknap for corruption. As the House in 1876 moved toward impeachment, Belknap resigned and claimed immunity from impeachment. Nevertheless, the House unanimously passed impeachment and the Senate voted by a majority (but not by two-thirds) that it still held jurisdiction. Then a majority, though not the necessary two-thirds, voted to convict Belknap. Thus, Belknap's case, like many impeachment cases, could be read both ways, as proof or refutation of the impeachment of former officeholders, and each party used Belknap to support their claims. Trump's defenders argued that Democrats were simply waging a political vendetta, not following the Constitution. "We are really here because the majority in the House of Representatives does not want to face Donald Trump as a political rival in the future," one of Trump's lawyers stated. Democratic congressman Jamie Raskin, a House impeachment manager, mocked the idea that "if you commit an impeachable offense in your last few weeks in office; you do it with constitutional impunity; you get away with it. . . . It is an invitation to the President to take his best shot at anything he may want to do on his way out the door, including using violent means to lock that door, to hang on to the Oval Office at all costs, and to block the peaceful transfer of power." Six Republicans joined all fifty Democrats in voting to proceed with the trial, enough to win the vote but not nearly enough to suggest the likelihood for conviction. Recognizing the unlikelihood of conviction, and pressed by the need to address economic problems, Senate Democrats moved to a quick vote. Fifty-seven senators voted to convict (against forty-three for acquittal), but not the constitutionally required two-thirds, or sixty-seven.[35]

Trump's second acquittal on February 13 raised serious questions about the future of impeachment. On the one hand, seven Republicans voted for conviction, a startling change from past history. On the other, the continuing power of partisanship, even in the face of what seemed to be an absolutely open-and-shut case of a president abusing his power, raised questions about whether conviction would ever be possible, no matter the crime. For a generation after Richard Nixon's resignation, law professors and commentators had articulated plausible arguments about standards of judgment, deploying various homespun phrases on the virtues of neutrality in assessing impeachment. Now those commentaries seemed almost touchingly naive, and also useless; impeachment was revealed as crude politics. Trump celebrated his acquittal, denouncing the trial as "yet another phase of the greatest witch hunt in the history of our Country. No president has ever gone through anything like it." He promised to continue to play a central role in public life, contemplating another run for office.[36] As in so many elements of the constitutional system, Trump had exposed previously unimagined space for illegitimate uses of power, and the impunity that went with partisan support.

The Trump era conclusively proved that impeachment is not a legal process and should not be discussed as one. Impeachment remains, as Hamilton said, a political process. If this clarity helps us dismiss confusing though sometimes appealing legal commentary on impeachment, it still leaves us in the dark about the future.

Some lessons seem clear: impeachment talk will surface quickly under new administrations. In an intensely partisan age, presidential impeachment will remain on the table. Indeed, one fringe Republican congresswoman submitted an impeachment resolution against President Biden on January 21, 2021, the day after his inauguration, for "abuse of power." Thus far Republican House leaders have not backed the measure, but it is likely that impeachment will surface as an issue during or after the 2022 midterms.[37]

But will impeachment action follow? Here, the lessons are mixed. The Trump presidency raised major questions about whether the process means anything at all. There is reason to doubt that an unsuccessful impeachment still has the capacity to restrain a president, as it did with Andrew Johnson. Trump's willingness to attack the 2020 election process even after being impeached a few months earlier suggests that we live in an era when confidence in presidential power and party loyalty seems greater than concerns about congressional oversight or public shame. A president willing to abuse power is most likely willing to live with the consequences of being impeached by the House, as long as they know they will remain in office. And conviction appears less likely than at any moment in U.S. history, barring a complete breakdown of the president's support from the base. Without much bipartisanship to speak of, it is extremely unlikely the Senate will ever achieve the votes needed to remove a president. And there is little evidence that senators will become more capable of acting against their party members' preferences.

If conviction is all but impossible, then the constitutional lessons of the Trump era are daunting ones. Impeachment was designed to empower Congress to save the Constitution. The failures of impeachment and conviction in the face of incontrovertible proof raise the specter that future political leaders will know that they have almost complete impunity as long as they retain the support of their base, no matter what the Constitution says. Can the long-standing popular veneration of the Constitution survive these strains?

In February 2021, the Senate chaplain invoked Lowell's poem "The Present Crisis." By a narrow reading of the word "present," that present crisis may have passed with Trump's departure from the White House. But ongoing problems in the nation's constitutional order loom. Perhaps not since the Civil War has the United States wrestled with such fundamental questions about its constitutional system, the "mouldy parchments" that govern it, and the challenges of attempting "Future's portal with the Past's blood-rusted key."

# NOTES

## Notes to Chapter 1

1. Jennifer Schuessler, "The Trump Presidency Is History. They're Writing the First Draft," *New York Times*, March 22, 2021.

2. Jason Miller, email to the author, April 14, 2021.

3. Jennifer Schuessler, "Historians Assess Obama's Legacy under Trump's Shadow," *New York Times*, November 13, 2016.

4. Mike Allen, "Trump Works Refs Ahead of Book Barrage," Axios Newsletter, June 21, 2021.

5. The Zoom recording of this meeting is in the possession of the author.

6. Gillian Brockwell, "Historians Just Ranked the Presidents, Trump Wasn't Last," *Washington Post*, June 30, 2021.

7. John Wagner, "Trump, after Agreeing to Sit for a Raft of Book Interviews, Declares Them a 'Total Waste of Time,'" *Washington Post*, July 9, 2021.

8. Arthur Schlesinger Jr., "On the Writing of Contemporary History," *The Atlantic*, March 1967, 69–74.

9. Schlesinger, "On the Writing of Contemporary History," 69–74.

10. Michael Wolff, *Fire and Fury: Inside the Trump White House* (New York: Henry Holt, 2018).

11. For examples of the first set of books out about the presidency, see Michael Wolff, *Landslide: The Final Days of the Trump Presidency* (New York: Henry Holt, 2021); Carol Lenning and Philip Rucker, *I Alone Can Fix It: Donald J. Trump's Catastrophic Final Year* (New York: Penguin, 2021); Michael C. Bender, *"Frankly, We Did Win This Election": The Inside Story of How Trump Lost* (New York: Twelve, 2021).

12. Julie Hirschfeld Davis and Michael D. Shear, *Border Wars: Inside Trump's Assault on Immigration* (New York: Simon & Schuster, 2019).

13. Elizabeth Hinton, *America on Fire: The Untold History of Police Violence and Black Rebellion since the 1960s* (New York: Liveright, 2021).

14. David Barstow, Susanne Craig, and Russ Buettner, "Trump Engaged in Suspect Tax Scheme as He Reaped Riches from His Father," *New York Times*, October 2, 2018.

15. William E. Geist, "The Expanding Empire of Donald Trump," *New York Times*, April 8, 1984.

16. Susan Mulchay, "Confessions of a Trump Tabloid Scribe," *Politico*, May/June 2016.

17. Judy Klemesrud, "Donald Trump, Real Estate Promoter, Builds Image as He Buys Buildings," *New York Times*, November 1, 1976.

18. Christopher Lehmann-Haupt, "Books of the Times," *New York Times*, December 7, 1987.

19. https://www.c-span.org/video/?297952-12/donald-trump-remarks, February 10, 2011.

20. Frank Rich, "He's Firing as Fast as He Can," *New York Times*, March 14, 2004.

21. Cited in Kevin Kruse and Julian E. Zelizer, *Fault Lines: A History of the United States since 1974* (New York: Norton, 2019), 332.

22. Patrick Radden Keefe, "How Mark Burnett Resurrected Donald Trump as an Icon of American Success," *New Yorker*, January 7, 2019, 34–49.

23. "Full Text: Donald Trump Announces a Presidential Bid," *Washington Post*, June 16, 2015.

24. Ali Vitali, "Donald Trump Goes Off on Ben Carson's 'Pathological Temper,'" *NBC News*, November 12, 2015, https://www.nbcnews.com/politics/2016-election/donald-trump-calls-ben-carson-s-pathological-temper-incurable-n462601; Ellen Uchimiya, "Donald Trump Insults Carly Fiorina's Appearance," *CBS News*, September 10, 2015, https://www.cbsnews.com/news/donald-trump-insults-carly-fiorinas-appearance/.

25. Douglas Ernst, "Ben Sasse Would Rather 'Watch Some Dumpster Fires' than Attend Trump Nomination: Spokesman," *Washington Times*, July 7, 2016.

26. Camila Domonoske, "Trump Fails to Condemn KKK on Television, Turns to Twitter to Clarify," *NPR.Org*, February 28, 2016.

27. Amie Parnes and Jonathan Allen, *Shattered: Inside Hillary Clinton's Doomed Campaign* (New York: Crown, 2017).

28. Julian E. Zelizer, *Jimmy Carter* (New York: Times Books, 2010).

29. Julian E. Zelizer, "America's Mirror on the Wall," *The Atlantic*, January 28, 2018.

30. Julian E. Zelizer, "How Conservatives Learned to Stop Worrying and Love Presidential Power," in *The Presidency of George W. Bush: A First Historical Assessment* (Princeton, NJ: Princeton University Press, 2010), 15–38.

31. Steve Fraser and Gary Gerstle, eds., *The Rise and Fall of the New Deal Order, 1930–1980* (Princeton, NJ: Princeton University Press, 1989).

32. For a look at the complex state of the New Deal Order after the 1970s, see the essays in Gary Gerstle, Nelson Lichtenstein, and Alice O'Connor, eds., *Beyond the New Deal Order: U.S. Politics from the Great Depression to the Great Recession* (Philadelphia: University of Pennsylvania Press, 2019).

## Notes to Chapter 2

1. Stuart Stevens, *It Was All a Lie: How the Republican Party Became Donald Trump* (New York: Knopf, 2020), 36.

2. Liz Cheney (@Liz_Cheney), Twitter, May 3, 2021, https://twitter.com/Liz_Cheney/status/1389225154639695881.

3. Rachel Janfaza, "Bush Says If GOP Stands for 'White Anglo-Saxon Protestantism, Then It's Not Going to Win Anything,'" *CNN*, May 3, 2021, https://www.cnn.com/2021/05/03/politics/bush-gop-white-anglo-saxon-protestantism/index.html.

4. For a long history of the GOP that emphasizes the competing ideological traditions, see Heather Cox Richardson, *To Make Men Free: A History of the Republican Party* (New York: Basic Books, 2014).

5. Thomas E. Mann, "Asymmetric Polarization Undermined? Thoughts on the New Pew Research Center's Report on Political Polarization," Brookings Institution, June 13, 2014, https://www.brookings.edu/blog/fixgov/2014/06/13/asymmetrical-polarization-undermined-thoughts-on-the-new-pew-research-centers-report-on-political-polarization/. For works on partisan polarization, see Julian E. Zelizer, *On Capitol Hill: The Struggle to Reform Congress and Its Consequences, 1948–2000* (New York: Cambridge University Press, 2004); Sam Rosenfeld, *The Polarizers: Postwar Architects of Our Partisan Era* (Chicago: University of Chicago Press, 2017); and Sean M. Theriault, *Party Polarization in Congress* (New York: Cambridge University Press, 2008).

6. Kevin Kruse and I trace this history in *Fault Lines: A History of the United States since 1974* (New York: Norton, 2019).

7. Matt Grossman and David A. Hopkins, *Asymmetric Politics: Ideological Republicans and Group Interest Democrats* (New York: Oxford University Press, 2016).

8. Thomas E. Mann and Norm Ornstein, "Let's Just Say It: The Republicans Are the Problem," *Washington Post*, April 27, 2012. See also Thomas E. Mann and Norm Ornstein, *The Broken Branch: How Congress Is Failing America and How to Get It Back* (New York: Oxford University Press, 2008); and Thomas Mann and Norm Ornstein, *It's Even Worse than It Looks: How the American Constitutional System Collided with the New Politics of Extremism* (New York: Basic Books, 2016).

9. William Henry Chamberlin, "Conservatism: A Test of Strength," *Wall Street Journal*, July 12, 1964.

10. Rick Perlstein, *Before the Storm: Barry Goldwater and the Unmaking of the American Consensus* (New York: Hill and Wang, 2001).

11. George F. Gilder and Bruce K. Chapman, *The Party That Lost Its Head: The Republican Collapse and Imperatives for Revival* (New York: Knopf, 1966), 6.

12. Geoffrey Kabaservice, *Rule and Ruin: The Downfall of Moderation and the Destruction of the Republican Party* (New York: Oxford University Press, 2012).

13. Julian E. Zelizer, *The Fierce Urgency of Now: Lyndon B. Johnson, Congress and the Battle for the Great Society* (New York: Penguin Press, 2015).

14. Earl Black and Merle Black, *The Rise of Southern Republicans* (Cambridge, MA: Belknap Press of Harvard University Press, 2003).

15. On the limits of Reagan's battle with liberalism, see Julian E. Zelizer, "The Unexpected Endurance of the New Deal Order: Liberalism in the Age of Reagan," in *Beyond the New Deal Order: U.S. Politics from the Great Depression to the Great Recession*,

ed. Gary Gerstle, Nelson Lichtenstein, and Alice O'Connor (Philadelphia: University of Pennsylvania Press, 2019), 71–92.

16. Julian E. Zelizer, *Burning Down the House: Newt Gingrich, the Fall of a Speaker, and the Rise of the New Republican Party* (New York: Penguin Press, 2020).

17. Cited in Rick Perlstein, *Reaganland: America's Right Turn, 1976–1980* (New York: Simon & Schuster, 2020), 233.

18. Mary McGrory, "Adding Aye of Newt," *Washington Post*, March 23, 1989.

19. Zelizer, *Burning Down the House*, 62.

20. Zelizer, *Burning Down the House*, 273.

21. McKay Coppins, "The Man Who Broke Politics," *The Atlantic*, October 17, 2018, https://www.theatlantic.com/magazine/archive/2018/11/newt-gingrich-says-youre-welcome/570832/.

22. Guy Gugliotta and Juliet Eilperin, "Gingrich Steps Down in the Face of Rebellion," *Washington Post*, November 7, 1998.

23. Rick Perlstein, "Lee Atwater's Infamous 1981 Interview on the Southern Strategy," *The Nation*, November 13, 2012, https://www.thenation.com/article/archive/exclusive-lee-atwaters-infamous-1981-interview-southern-strategy/.

24. John Brady, *Bad Boy: The Life and Politics of Lee Atwater* (New York: Addison-Wesley, 1996); Sidney Blumenthal, *Pledging Allegiance: The Last Campaign of the Cold War* (New York: Harper Collins, 1992).

25. Andrew Rosenthal, "Foes Accuse Bush Campaign of Inflaming Racial Tension," *New York Times*, October 24, 1988.

26. Nichole Hemmer, *Messengers of the Right: Conservative Media and the Transformation of American Politics* (Philadelphia: University of Pennsylvania Press, 2016); Brian Rosenwald, *Talk Radio's America: How an Industry Took Over a Political Party That Took Over the United States* (Cambridge, MA: Harvard University Press, 2019).

27. Patrick Buchanan, "Culture War Speech," August 17, 1992, *Voices of America*, The U.S. Oratory Project.

28. Robert G. Kaiser and Ira Chinoy, "Scaife: Funding Father of the Right," *Washington Post*, May 2, 1999.

29. Barney Frank, *A Life in Politics from the Great Society to Same-Sex Marriage* (New York: Macmillan, 2015), 180.

30. David Greenberg, "Creating Their Own Reality: The Bush Administration and Expertise in a Polarized Age," in *The Presidency of George W. Bush: A First Historical Assessment*, ed. Julian E. Zelizer (Princeton, NJ: Princeton University Press, 2010), 200.

31. For more, see Zelizer, *Presidency of George W. Bush*; and Peter Baker, *Days of Fire: Bush and Cheney in the White House* (New York: Doubleday, 2013).

32. "Bush Calls for Amendment to Bar Gay Marriage," *Baltimore Sun*, February 25, 2004.

33. Beverly Gage, "How 'Elites' Became One of the Nastiest Epithets in American Politics," *New York Times*, January 3, 2017.

34. "Anti-Obama Anger Erupts at McCain Events," *NBC News*, October 10, 2008, https://www.nbcnews.com/id/wbna27123224.

35. Dana Milbank, "Unleashed, Palin Makes a Pit Bull Look Tame," *Washington Post*, October 7, 2008.

36. Barack Obama, *A Promised Land* (New York: Crown, 2020), 195.

37. See essays in Julian E. Zelizer, ed., *President Barack Obama: A First Historical Assessment* (Princeton, NJ: Princeton University Press, 2018).

38. Charles M. Blow, "Liz Cheney, We Have a Memory. You're No Hero," *New York Times*, May 5, 2021.

39. Tim Alberta, "John Boehner Unchained," *Politico*, December 2017.

40. Julian E. Zelizer, "The Divided Mind and Politics of John Boehner," *New York Times*, April 8, 2021; John Boehner, *On the House: A Washington Memoir* (New York: St. Martin's Press, 2021).

41. Tim Murphy, "Mitt Romney Shifts His Position on Climate Change—Again," *Mother Jones*, January 20, 2015, https://www.motherjones.com/politics/2015/01/mitt-romney-climate-change-shift/.

42. Amy Sullivan, "Romney Meets with the Islamophobes," *New Republic*, August 10, 2012.

43. Paul Harris, "Republicans Will Rue Their Birther Backing," *The Guardian*, April 27, 2011.

44. Peter Wallsten and Krissah Thompson, "Top Republicans Try to Scotch Birther Theories," *Washington Post*, April 19, 2011.

45. David Daley, *Ratf**ked: The True Story of the Secret Plan to Steal America's Democracy* (New York: Liveright, 2016).

46. Ari Berman, *Give Us the Ballot: The Modern Struggle for Voting Rights in America* (New York: Farrar, Straus and Giroux, 2015); Carol Anderson, *One Person, No Vote: How Voter Suppression Is Destroying Our Democracy* (New York: Bloomsbury, 2018).

47. David Wiegel, "Southern Republican Senators Happy That Supreme Court Designated Their States Not Racist," *Slate*, January 25, 2013, https://slate.com/news-and-politics/2013/06/voting-rights-act-southern-republicans-contain-their-celebration.html; Amy Davidson Sorkin, "The Court Rejects the Voting Rights Act—and History," *New Yorker*, June 25, 2013, https://www.newyorker.com/news/amy-davidson/the-court-rejects-the-voting-rights-act-and-history.

48. "Trump Forces Didn't Just Beat the Establishment, They Overran It," *NBC News*, May 10, 2016, https://www.nbcnews.com/politics/2016-election/trump-forces-didn-t-just-beat-establishment-they-overran-it-n570851.

49. John Gramlich, "How Trump Compares with Other Recent Presidents in Appointing Federal Judges," Pew Research Center, January 13, 2021, https://www.pewresearch.org/fact-tank/2021/01/13/how-trump-compares-with-other-recent-presidents-in-appointing-federal-judges/.

50. Elizabeth Dias, "Most Conservative Christians Support Trump. Will They Help Him Win Again?" *New York Times*, November 3, 2020.

51. Meg Jacobs and Julian E. Zelizer, *Conservatives in Power: The Reagan Years, 1981–1989* (Boston: Bedford, 2010); Meg Jacobs, *Panic at the Pump: The Energy Crisis*

*and the Transformation of American Politics in the 1970s* (New York: Hill and Wang, 2016).

52. Lenny Bronner, "About Those Voters Who Left the GOP This Year? Things Have Now Normalized," *Washington Post*, May 7, 2021.

## Notes to Chapter 3

1. Nicole Hemmer, *Messengers of the Right: Conservative Media and the Transformation of American Politics* (Philadelphia: University of Pennsylvania Press, 2016), 42, 118.

2. Brian Rosenwald, *Talk Radio's America: How an Industry Took Over a Political Party That Took Over the United States* (Cambridge, MA: Harvard University Press), 167.

3. Quoted in Alessandra Stanley, "The Republican Primary Campaign in Iowa Is Right at Home on Fox News," *New York Times*, December 10, 2011, A16.

4. Nicole Hemmer, "The Boys Who Cried Fox," *New York Times*, April 19, 2012.

5. Brian Montopoli, "Donald Trump Gets Regular Fox News Spot," *CBS News*, April 1, 2011, https://www.cbsnews.com/news/donald-trump-gets-regular-fox-news-spot/.

6. Ashley Parker and Steve Eder, "Inside the Six Weeks Donald Trump Was a Nonstop 'Birther,'" *New York Times*, July 3, 2016, A1.

7. Quoted in Brian Stelter, *Hoax: Donald Trump, Fox News, and the Dangerous Distortion of the Truth* (New York: Simon & Schuster), 56.

8. Yochai Benkler, Robert Faris, Hal Roberts, and Ethan Zuckerman, "Study: Breitbart-Led Right-Wing Media Ecosystem Altered Broader Media Agenda," *Columbia Journalism Review*, March 3, 2017, https://www.cjr.org/analysis/breitbart-media-trump-harvard-study.php.

9. Sarah Posner, "How Donald Trump's New Campaign Chief Created an Online Haven for White Nationalists," *Mother Jones*, August 22, 2016, https://www.motherjones.com/politics/2016/08/stephen-bannon-donald-trump-alt-right-breitbart-news/.

10. Paul Gottfried, "The Decline and Rise of the Alternative Right," *Taki's Magazine*, December 1, 2008, https://www.takimag.com/article/the_decline_and_rise_of_the_alternative_right/.

11. Joshua Green, *The Devil's Bargain: Steve Bannon, Donald Trump, and the Storming of the Presidency* (New York: Penguin Press, 2017), 42–45.

12. Charlie Warzel and Lam Thuy Vo, "Here's Where Donald Trump Gets His News," *BuzzFeed News*, December 3, 2016, https://www.buzzfeednews.com/article/charliewarzel/trumps-information-universe.

13. Stelter, *Hoax*, 56.

14. Sarah Ellison, "Exclusive: Is Donald Trump's Endgame the Launch of Trump News?," *Vanity Fair*, June 16, 2016, https://www.vanityfair.com/news/2016/06/donald-trump-tv-network; Maggie Haberman and Emily Steel, "Jared Kushner Talks of a Trump TV Network with a Media Deal Maker," *New York Times*, October 18, 2016, A11.

15. Dave Schilling, "Trump TV Launches on Facebook," *The Guardian*, October 25, 2016, https://www.theguardian.com/us-news/2016/oct/24/trump-tv-facebook-live-us-election-media-tomi-lahren.

16. *Fox & Friends*, Fox News Channel, January 27, 2017, broadcast.

17. Maggie Haberman, Glenn Thrush, and Peter Baker, "Inside Trump's Hour-by-Hour Battle for Self-Preservation," *New York Times*, December 9, 2017, https://www.nytimes.com/2017/12/09/us/politics/donald-trump-president.html.

18. Asawin Suebsaeng, Sam Brodey, and Andrew Kirell, "Fox News Host Pete Hegseth Privately Lobbied Trump to Pardon Accused War Criminals," *Daily Beast*, May 21, 2019, https://www.thedailybeast.com/fox-and-friends-host-pete-hegseth-privately-lobbied-trump-to-pardon-accused-war-criminals.

19. Jeremy W. Peters, "The 'Never Trump' Coalition That Decided Eh, Never Mind, He's Fine," *New York Times*, October 5, 2019, https://www.nytimes.com/2019/10/05/us/politics/never-trumper-republicans.html.

20. Kevin Breuninger, "Glenn Beck's The Blaze and Mark Levin's CRTV Merge to Form Right-Wing Outlet Blaze Media, Which Could Rival the New Fox News Streaming Service," *CNBC*, December 3, 2018, https://www.cnbc.com/2018/12/03/glenn-becks-the-blaze-and-mark-levins-crtv-merge-to-form-blaze-media.html.

21. Lloyd Grove, "Glenn Beck Changes Sides Again. Does Anyone Believe Him?" *Daily Beast*, May 19, 2018, https://www.thedailybeast.com/glenn-beck-changes-sides-again-does-anyone-believe-him.

22. Jennifer Rubin, "A Bulwark against Trumpism," *Washington Post*, January 8, 2019, https://www.washingtonpost.com/opinions/2019/01/08/bulwark-against-trump-trumpianism/.

23. Matt Perez, "Death Toll Conspiracy: Why Conservative Media—and Soon, Possibly Trump—Are Doubting Coronavirus Mortality Figures," *Forbes*, May 10, 2020, https://www.forbes.com/sites/mattperez/2020/05/10/death-toll-conspiracy-why-conservative-media-and-soon-possibly-trump-are-doubting-coronavirus-mortality-figures/?sh=1af9953857d5.

24. Jeremy W. Peters, "Pro-Trump Media's Virus Pivot: From Alarm to Denial to Blame," *New York Times*, April 2, 2020, A1.

25. Michael M. Grynbaum, "Fox News on Malaria Drug: 'Very Safe' vs. 'Will Kill You,'" *New York Times*, May 20, 2020, B1.

26. Sarah Ellison and Elahe Izadi, "Coronavirus and Fox News Collide, and Chris Wallace Is at the Center of It," *Washington Post,* October 2, 2020, https://www.washingtonpost.com/lifestyle/media/trump-covid-fox-chris-wallace/2020/10/02/5f51a09e-04f1-11eb-a2db-417cddf4816a_story.html.

27. Lawrence Hamilton and Thomas Safford, "Conservative Media Consumers Less Likely to Wear Masks and Less Worried about COVID-19," September 1, 2020, https://carsey.unh.edu/publication/conservative-media-consumers-views-COVID-19.

28. Kathleen Hall Jamieson and Dolores Albarracin, "The Relation between Media Consumption and Misinformation at the Outset of the SARS-CoV-2 Pandemic in the US," in "Special Issue on COVID-19 and Misinformation," *Harvard Kennedy School (HKS) Misinformation Review* 1 (April 2020), http://nrs.harvard.edu/urn-3:HUL.InstRepos:42661740.

29. Quoted in Michael M. Grynbaum, Annie Karni, and Jeremy W. Peters, "What Top Conservatives Are Saying about George Floyd and Police Brutality," *New York Times*, May 30, 2020, https://www.nytimes.com/2020/05/30/us/politics/george-floyd-tucker-carlson-rush-limbaugh.html.

30. Sean Hannity Show, May 28, 2020.

31. Quoted in Oliver Darcy, "'You're Being Delusional': Rush Limbaugh Scolded by Hosts of 'The Breakfast Club' for Denying Existence of White Privilege," *CNN*, June 1, 2020.

32. Michael M. Grynbaum, Annie Karni, and Jeremy W. Peters, "What Top Conservatives Are Saying about George Floyd and Police Brutality," *New York Times*, May 30, 2020, https://www.nytimes.com/2020/05/30/us/politics/george-floyd-tucker-carlson-rush-limbaugh.html.

33. Caleb Ecarma, "Conservative Media Seizes on Portland-Is-Burning Narrative," *Vanity Fair*, July 20, 2020, https://www.vanityfair.com/news/2020/07/conservative-media-seizes-on-portland-burning-narrative.

34. Jane Mayer, "The Invention of the Conspiracy Theory on Biden and Ukraine," *New Yorker*, October 4, 2019, https://www.newyorker.com/news/news-desk/the-invention-of-the-conspiracy-theory-on-biden-and-ukraine; Jared Holt, "How Far-Right Conspiracy Theories Informed Trump's Ukraine Call," *Washington Post*, September 26, 2019, https://www.washingtonpost.com/outlook/2019/09/26/how-far-right-conspiracy-theories-informed-trumps-ukraine-call/.

35. Ken Dilanian and Tom Winter, "Here's What Happened When NBC News Tried to Report on the Alleged Hunter Biden Emails," *NBC News,* October 30, 2020, https://www.nbcnews.com/politics/2020-election/here-s-what-happened-when-nbc-news-tried-report-alleged-n1245533.

36. Zack Beauchamp, "Conservative Media Is Setting the Stage for Delegitimizing a Biden Victory," *Vox*, September 18, 2020, https://www.vox.com/policy-and-politics/21444007/biden-trump-2020-tucker-carlson-glenn-beck-coup.

37. Gabriel Sherman, *The Loudest Voice in the Room: How the Brilliant, Bombastic Roger Ailes Built Fox News—and Divided a Country* (New York: Random House, 2014), 244–251, 255–256.

38. Annie Karni and Maggie Haberman, "Fox's Arizona Call for Biden Flipped the Mood at Trump Headquarters," *New York Times*, November 16, 2020, https://www.nytimes.com/2020/11/04/us/politics/trump-fox-news-arizona.html.

39. Aaron Blake, "A Conservative Media in Flux Confronts a Troubling Phrase: 'President-Elect,'" *Washington Post*, December 17, 2020, https://www.washingtonpost.com/politics/2020/12/17/conservative-media-flux-confronts-troubling-phrase-president-elect/; Michael M. Grynbaum, "We've Got Nowhere to Go': After Trump, Fox Sticks with Message, If Not Messenger," *New York Times*, January 9, 2021, A20.

40. Lisa Richwine, "Fox News Lands Third in Cable News Ratings with Riot, Elections Coverage," Reuters, January 12, 2021, https://www.reuters.com/article/us-fox-ratings/fox-news-lands-third-in-cable-news-ratings-with-riot-elections-coverage-idUSKBN29H32L.

## Notes to Chapter 4

1. G. Kessler, S. Rizzo, and M. Kelly, *Donald Trump and His Assault on Truth: The President's Falsehoods, Misleading Claims and Flat-Out Lies* (New York: Scribner, 2020), 19, 27, 29, 34, 39; Lee McIntyre, *Post-Truth* (Cambridge, MA: MIT Press, 2018), 2.

2. Scott Horsley, "Fact Check: Who Gets Credit for the Booming U.S. Economy?," *NPR*, September 12, 2018, https://www.npr.org/2018/09/12/646708799/fact-check-who-gets-credit-for-the-booming-u-s-economy; "US Business Cycle Expansions and Contractions," National Bureau of Economic Research, June 8, 2020, https://www.nber.org/research/data/us-business-cycle-expansions-and-contractions; "Donald Trump's False Comments Connecting Mexican Immigrants and Crime," *Washington Post*, July 8, 2015; Jeffrey Passel and D'Vera Cohn, *U.S. Unauthorized Immigrant Total Dips to Lowest Level in a Decade*, Pew Research Center, November 27, 2018, https://www.pewresearch.org/hispanic/wp-content/uploads/sites/5/2019/03/Pew-Research-Center_2018-11-27_U-S-Unauthorized-Immigrants-Total-Dips_Updated-2019-06-25.pdf; McIntyre, *Post-Truth*, 2; German Lopez, "After Decades of Decline, the Murder Rate Went Up in 2016," *Vox*, September 25, 2017, https://www.vox.com/policy-and-politics/2017/9/25/16360606/murder-rate-2016-fbi.

3. Kessler, Rizzo, and Kelly, *Donald Trump and His Assault on Truth*, 2; Katie Rogers, "Trump on Releasing His Tax Returns: From 'Absolutely' to 'Political Prosecution,'" *New York Times*, July 9, 2020; Sheryl Gay Stolberg, "Trump's Secret Health Plan Is a Promise Voters Have Heard Before," *New York Times*, September 17, 2020; "All of the Times President Trump Said Covid-19 Will Disappear," *CNN*, October 31, 2020, https://www.cnn.com/interactive/2020/10/politics/covid-disappearing-trump-comment-tracker/.

4. Kessler, Rizzo, and Kelly, *Donald Trump and His Assault on Truth*, 8, 9, 38; "Tracking All of President Trump's False or Misleading Claims," *Washington Post*, September 11, 2020, https://www.washingtonpost.com/graphics/politics/trump-claims-database/.

5. Liz Spayd, "When to Call a Lie a Lie," *New York Times*, September 20, 2016.

6. Nicole Hemmer discusses conservative accusations of liberal media bias in her chapter in this volume, "Remade in His Image: How Trump Transformed Right-Wing Media."

7. Sophia Rosenfeld, *Democracy and Truth: A Short History* (Philadelphia: University of Pennsylvania Press, 2018), 12.

8. McIntyre, *Post-Truth*, 5.

9. Rosenfeld, *Democracy and Truth*, chap. 3.

10. Quoted in Michael J. Brown, *Hope & Scorn: Eggheads, Experts, & Elites in American Politics* (Chicago: University of Chicago Press, 2020), 254.

11. Kessler, Rizzo, and Kelly, *Donald Trump and His Assault on Truth*, xxiv.

12. Kessler, Rizzo, and Kelly, *Donald Trump and His Assault on Truth*, xvii.

13. Allison Graves and Linda Qiu, "Kellyanne Conway's Back and Forth with Chuck Todd on 'Alternative Facts,' Annotated," PolitiFact, January 23, 2017, https://www

.politifact.com/article/2017/jan/23/kellyanne-conways-back-and-forth-chuck-todd-alter/.

14. Quoted in Rebecca Morin and David Cohen, "Giuliani: 'Truth Isn't Truth,'" *Politico*, August 19, 2018, https://www.politico.com/story/2018/08/19/giuliani-truth-todd-trump-788161.

15. Shawn Lawrence Otto, *The War on Science: Who's Waging It, Why It Matters, What We Can Do about It* (Minneapolis, MN: Milkweed Editions, 2016); Matthew d'Ancona, *Post-Truth: The New War on Truth and How to Fight Back* (New York: Random House, 2017); Kessler, Rizzo, and Kelly, *Donald Trump and His Assault on Truth*; Thomas E. Patterson, *How America Lost Its Mind: The Assault on Reason That's Crippling Our Democracy* (Norman: University of Oklahoma Press, 2019).

16. Cailin O'Connor and James Owen Weatherall, *The Misinformation Age: How False Beliefs Spread* (New Haven, CT: Yale University Press, 2019); James W. Cortada and William Aspray, *Fake News Nation: The Long History of Lies and Misinterpretations in America* (Lanham, MD: Rowman & Littlefield, 2019); Julian Baggini, *A Short History of Truth: Consolations for a Post-Truth World* (London: Quercus Publishing, 2017); Gabriele Cosentino, *Social Media and the Post-Truth World Order: The Global Dynamics of Disinformation* (Cham, Switzerland: Palgrave Pivot, 2020).

17. Nancy L. Rosenblum and Russell Muirhead, *A Lot of People Are Saying: The New Conspiracism and the Assault on Democracy* (Princeton, NJ: Princeton University Press, 2020); Daniel J. Levitin, *Weaponized Lies: How to Think Critically in the Post-Truth Era* (New York: Penguin, 2017); Tom Nichols, *The Death of Expertise: The Campaign against Established Knowledge and Why It Matters* (New York: Oxford University Press, 2017).

18. Johan Farkas and Jannick Schou, *Post-Truth, Fake News and Democracy: Mapping the Politics of Falsehood* (New York: Routledge, 2019); Amanda Carpenter, *Gaslighting America: Why We Love It When Trump Lies to Us* (New York: HarperCollins, 2018); C. G. Prado, ed., *America's Post-Truth Phenomenon: When Feelings and Opinions Trump Facts and Evidence* (Santa Barbara, CA: Praeger, 2018).

19. James Ball, *Post-Truth: How Bullshit Conquered the World* (London: Biteback Publishing, 2017).

20. Patterson, *How America Lost Its Mind*, 14.

21. Thomas B. Edsall, "Is President Trump a Stealth Postmodernist or Just a Liar?," *New York Times*, January 25, 2018, https://www.nytimes.com/2018/01/25/opinion/trump-postmodernism-lies.html; David Ernst, "Donald Trump Is the First President to Turn Postmodernism against Itself," *The Federalist*, January 23, 2017, https://thefederalist.com/2017/01/23/donald-trump-first-president-turn-postmodernism/; Jeet Heer, "America's First Postmodern President," *New Republic*, July 8, 2017, https://newrepublic.com/article/143730/americas-first-postmodern-president.

22. McIntyre, *Post-Truth*, 123.

23. Casey Williams, "Has Trump Stolen Philosophy's Critical Tools?," *New York Times*, April 17, 2017, https://www.nytimes.com/2017/04/17/opinion/has-trump-stolen-philosophys-critical-tools.html.

24. Colin Wight, "Post-Truth, Postmodernism and Alternative Facts," *New Perspectives* 26, no. 3 (2018): 25.

25. Michiko Kakutani, *The Death of Truth: Notes on Falsehood in the Age of Trump* (New York: Tim Duggan Books, 2018), 45, 49, 55, 160–161.

26. For instance, see the quote from Mike Cernovic provided in Kakutani, *Death of Truth,* 46.

27. Bruno Latour, "Why Has Critique Run Out of Steam? From Matters of Fact to Matters of Concern," *Critical Inquiry* 30, no. 2 (January 1, 2004): 227. Emphasis Latour's.

28. See, for instance, Russell Jacoby, *The Last Intellectuals* (New York: Basic, 1985); Russell Jacoby, "Last Thoughts on *The Last Intellectuals,*" *Society* 46, no. 1 (January 1, 2009): 38–44.

29. Many of the problems with such claims are discussed in Rosenfeld, *Democracy and Truth,* 143–45.

30. Elaine Kamarck and Christine Stenglein, "Low Rates of Fraud in Vote-by-Mail States Show the Benefits Outweigh the Risks," Brookings, June 2, 2020, https://www.brookings.edu/blog/fixgov/2020/06/02/low-rates-of-fraud-in-vote-by-mail-states-show-the-benefits-outweigh-the-risks/.

31. Aspects of this story are covered, for instance, in Kakutani, *Death of Truth,* 105–117; McIntyre, *Post-Truth,* 86; and Patterson, *How America Lost Its Mind.* On the "Big Sort," see Bill Bishop, *The Big Sort: Why the Clustering of Like-Minded America Is Tearing Us Apart* (Boston: Mariner, 2009).

32. Naomi Oreskes and Erik M. Conway, *Merchants of Doubt: How a Handful of Scientists Obscured the Truth on Issues from Tobacco Smoke to Global Warming* (New York: Bloomsbury Publishing USA, 2011).

33. Robert N. Proctor and Londa Schiebinger, *Agnotology: The Making and Unmaking of Ignorance* (Stanford, CA: Stanford University Press, 2008), vii, 9.

34. On Trump in the context of critiques of scientific expertise, see Andrew Jewett, *Science under Fire: Challenges to Scientific Authority in Modern America* (Cambridge, MA: Harvard University Press, 2020).

35. Helier Cheung, "What Does Trump Actually Believe on Climate Change?," *BBC,* January 23, 2020, https://www.bbc.com/news/world-us-canada-51213003. See also the essay by Bathsheba Demuth in this volume.

36. David Foster Wallace, "Host," *Atlantic Monthly,* April 2005, 54.

37. Shanto Iyengar and Richard Morin, "Red Media, Blue Media," *Washington Post,* May 3, 2006, http://www.washingtonpost.com/wp-dyn/content/article/2006/05/03/AR2006050300865.html.

38. Farhad Manjoo, *True Enough: Learning to Live in a Post-Fact Society* (Hoboken, NJ: Wiley, 2008), 25, 193.

39. Marshall Van Alstyne and Erik Brynjolfsson, "Electronic Communities: Global Villages or Cyberbalkans?," March 1997, http://web.mit.edu/~marshall/www/papers/CyberBalkans.pdf.

40. Jonathan Haidt and Tobias Rose-Stockwell, "Why It Feels Like Everything Is Going Haywire," *The Atlantic,* December 2019, 56–60; Jonathan Haidt, *The Righteous Mind: Why Good People Are Divided by Politics and Religion* (New York: Pantheon, 2012).

41. Kimiko de Freytas-Tamura, "George Orwell's '1984' Is Suddenly a Best-Seller," *New York Times*, January 25, 2017.

42. Margaret Sullivan, "The Traditional Way of Reporting on a President Is Dead. And Trump's Press Secretary Killed It," *Washington Post*, January 22, 2017; Adam Gopnik, "Orwell's '1984' and Trump's America," *New Yorker*, January 27, 2017; Jean Seaton, D. J. Taylor, and Tim Crook, "Welcome to Dystopia—George Orwell Experts on Donald Trump," *The Guardian*, January 25, 2017.

43. Donald Trump Jr. (@DonaldJTrumpJr), Twitter, January 8, 2021, https://twitter.com/DonaldJTrumpJr/status/1347697226466828288.

44. "Misinformation Dropped Dramatically the Week after Twitter Banned Trump and Some Allies," *Washington Post*, January 16, 2021, https://www.washingtonpost.com/technology/2021/01/16/misinformation-trump-twitter/.

45. Farhad Manjoo, "How I Learned to Stop Worrying and Love Twitter's Trump Ban," *New York Times*, January 28, 2021, https://www.nytimes.com/2021/01/28/opinion/trump-twitter.html.

46. Jon Healey, "Opinion: It Took a Mob Riot for Twitter to Finally Ban Trump," *Los Angeles Times*, January 9, 2021, https://www.latimes.com/opinion/story/2021-01-08/twitter-fb-trump; Dean Obeidallah, "What If Twitter Had Banned Trump Sooner?," *CNN*, January 17, 2021, https://www.cnn.com/2021/01/17/opinions/social-media-ban-effect-trump-obeidallah/index.html.

47. Kevin Roose, "In Pulling Trump's Megaphone, Twitter Shows Where Power Now Lies," *New York Times*, January 9, 2021, updated January 11, 2021, https://www.nytimes.com/2021/01/09/technology/trump-twitter-ban.html.

48. Lincoln Caplan, "Should Facebook and Twitter Be Regulated under the First Amendment?," *Wired*, October 11, 2017, https://www.wired.com/story/should-facebook-and-twitter-be-regulated-under-the-first-amendment/.

49. Tim Wu, "Is the First Amendment Obsolete?," Knight First Amendment Institute, September 1, 2017, https://knightcolumbia.org/content/tim-wu-first-amendment-obsolete. Also see the related law review article: Tim Wu, "Is the First Amendment Obsolete?," *Michigan Law Review* 117 (2018): 547.

50. Rosenfeld, *Democracy and Truth*, 155.

51. Jürgen Habermas, *The Structural Transformation of the Public Sphere: An Inquiry into a Category of Bourgeois Society* (Cambridge, MA: MIT Press, 1991).

52. Borja Hermoso, "Jürgen Habermas: 'For God's Sake, Spare Us Governing Philosophers!,'" *El Pais*, May 25, 2018, https://english.elpais.com/elpais/2018/05/07/inenglish/1525683618_145760.html.

## Notes to Chapter 5

The author wishes to thank Alyssa Smith and Rachel Sass for research assistance on this chapter.

1. Kathleen Belew, *Bring the War Home: The White Power Movement and Paramilitary America* (Cambridge, MA: Harvard University Press, 2018).

2. See, for instance, Keeanga-Yamhatta Taylor, *Race for Profit: How Banks and the Real Estate Industry Undermined Black Homeownership* (Chapel Hill: University of North Carolina Press, 2019). For more on redlining, see Richard Rothstein, *The Color of Law: A Forgotten History of How Our Government Segregated America* (New York: Liveright, 2017). On mainstream opposition to integration and interracial sex and marriage, see Matthew Lassiter, *The Silent Majority: Suburban Politics in the Sunbelt South* (Princeton, NJ: Princeton University Press, 2005); and Natalia Petrzela, *Classroom Wars: Language, Sex, and the Making of Modern Political Culture* (New York: Oxford University Press, 2015). For an overview of how a system of racial capitalism has contributed to the maintenance of inequality in recent U.S. history, see *Histories of Racial Capitalism*, ed., Destin Jenkins and Justin Leroy (New York: Columbia University Press, 2021).

3. On coercion and forced confessions in the Central Park Five case, see Jim Dwyer, "The True Story of How a City in Fear Brutalized the Central Park Five," *New York Times*, May 30, 2019. For more on how misinformation in this case shaped discourses on race and crime during the 1980s and 1990s, see Kimberlé Crenshaw, "Mapping the Margins: Intersectionality, Identity Politics, and Violence against Women of Color" *Stanford Law Review* 42, no. 5 (July 1991): 1241–99.

4. NPR Staff, "Decades-Old Housing Discrimination Case Plagues Donald Trump," *All Things Considered*, September 29, 2016; Rebecca Morin, "'They Admitted Their Guilt': 30 Years of Trump's Comments about the Central Park Five," *USA Today*, June 19, 2019; Nicholas Wu, "Trump Doesn't Apologize to Central Park Five: 'You Have People on Both Sides of That,'" *USA Today*, June 19, 2019.

5. Kim LaCapria, "Was Donald Trump's Father Arrested at a KKK Rally?," Snopes, February 28, 2016, https://www.snopes.com/fact-check/donald-trump-father-kkk-1927/; "In 1927, Donald Trump's Father Was Arrested after a Klan Riot in Queens," *Washington Post*, February 29, 2016, https://www.washingtonpost.com/news/the-fix/wp/2016/02/28/in-1927-donald-trumps-father-was-arrested-after-a-klan-riot-in-queens/.

6. Washington Post Staff, "Full Text: Donald Trump Announces a Presidential Bid," *Washington Post*, June 16, 2015, https://www.washingtonpost.com/news/post-politics/wp/2015/06/16/full-text-donald-trump-announces-a-presidential-bid/.

7. "Build That Wall" was a common chant at Trump rallies. Los Angeles Times Staff, "Donald Trump's Full Immigration Speech, Annotated," *Los Angeles Times*, August 31, 2016, https://www.latimes.com/politics/la-na-pol-donald-trump-immigration-speech-transcript-20160831-snap-htmlstory.html; Michelle Moons, "Trump Gives Platform to 'Angel Moms' and Families on Immigration Speech Stage," *Breitbart*, August 31, 2016, https://www.breitbart.com/clips/2016/08/31/trump-gives-platform-to-angel-moms-and-families-on-immigration-speech-stage/.

8. See Belew, *Bring the War Home*; Kathleen M. Blee, *Inside Organized Racism: Women in the Hate Movement* (Berkeley: University of California Press, 2002); and Carly Goodman, "Unmaking the Nation of Immigrants: How John Tanton's Network of Organizations Transformed Policy and Politics," in *A Field Guide to White Supremacy*, ed. Kathleen Belew and Ramòn A. Gutiérrez (Berkeley: University of California, 2021), 203–19.

9. See, for instance, "The Trump Team," Southern Poverty Law Center, January 26, 2017, https://www.splcenter.org/news/2017/01/26/trump-team; Michelle Goldberg, "Stephen Miller Is a White Nationalist. Does it Matter?," *New York Times*, November 18, 2019, https://www.nytimes.com/2019/11/18/opinion/stephen-miller-white-nationalism.html.

10. Nicole M. Hemmer, "The Alt-Right in Charlottesville," in Belew and Gutiérrez, eds., *A Field Guide to White Supremacy*, 287–303.

11. Nausheen Husain, "Timeline: Legal Fight over Trump's 'Muslim Ban' and the Supreme Court Ruling," *Chicago Tribune*, June 26, 2018, https://www.chicagotribune.com/data/ct-travel-ban-ruling-timeline-htmlstory.html.

12. Adam Serwer, "The Cruelty Is the Point," *The Atlantic*, October 3, 2018, https://www.theatlantic.com/ideas/archive/2018/10/the-cruelty-is-the-point/572104/; Matt Stieb, "Everything We Know about the Inhumane Conditions at Migrant Detention Camps," *New York Magazine*, July 2, 2019, https://nymag.com/intelligencer/2019/07/the-inhumane-conditions-at-migrant-detention-camps.html; Special report, "The Wall," *USA Today*, accessed August 10, 2021, https://www.usatoday.com/border-wall/.

13. "Migrant Caravan" page, *Fox News*, accessed August 10, 2021, https://www.foxnews.com/category/world/migrant-caravan.

14. Michael D. Shear and Julie Hirschfeld Davis, "Shoot Migrants' Legs, Build Alligator Moat: Behind Trump's Ideas for Border," *New York Times*, October 1, 2019, A1, https://www.nytimes.com/2019/10/01/us/politics/trump-border-wars.html.

15. Mike Levine and Luke Barr, "Biden's Task Force Finds More than 3,900 Children Separated from Families at Border under Trump," *ABC News*, June 7, 2021, https://abcnews.go.com/Politics/bidens-task-force-finds-3900-children-separated-families/story?id=78134730; Jacob Soboroff, "More than 2,100 Children Separated at Border 'Have Not Yet Been Reunified,' Biden Task Force Says," *NBC News*, June 8, 2021, https://www.nbcnews.com/politics/immigration/more-2-100-children-separated-border-have-not-yet-been-n1269918; Associated Press, "US Watchdog Says Migrant Children Suffered Trauma after Family Separations," *CNBC*, September 4, 2019, https://www.cnbc.com/2019/09/04/migrant-children-suffered-trauma-after-family-separations-watchdog.html.

16. Michael Edison Hayden, "Stephen Miller: The Breitbart Emails," Southern Poverty Law Center, November 12–14, 2019, https://www.splcenter.org/stephen-miller-breitbart-emails; Lulu Garcia-Navarro, "Stephen Miller and 'The Camp of the Saints,' a White Nationalist Reference," *NPR*, November 19, 2019, https://www.npr.org/2019/11/19/780552636/stephen-miller-and-the-camp-of-the-saints-a-white-nationalist-reference.

17. Belew, *Bring the War Home.*

18. Hayden, "Stephen Miller."

19. Gregory Korte and Alan Gomez, "Trump Ramps Up Rhetoric on Undocumented Immigrants: 'These Aren't People. These Are Animals,'" *USA Today*, May 16,

2018, https://www.usatoday.com/story/news/politics/2018/05/16/trump-immigrants-animals-mexico-democrats-sanctuary-cities/617252002/.

20. See, for instance, Mae Ngai, *Impossible Subjects: Illegal Aliens and the Making of Modern America* (Princeton, NJ: Princeton University Press, 2004).

21. Anders Breivik, *2083: A European Declaration of Independence* (self-published 2011); Brandon Tarrant, *The Great Replacement: Toward a New Society* (self-published 2019); Dylann Roof, "Dylann Roof's Manifesto," reprinted in *New York Times*, December 13, 2016; Patrick Crusius, *The Inconvenient Truth* (self-published August 3, 2019).

22. Belew, *Bring the War Home*.

23. Belew, *Bring the War Home*.

24. See Belew, *Bring the War Home*; Cynthia Miller-Idriss, *Hate in the Homeland: The New Global Far Right* (Princeton, NJ: Princeton University Press, 2020).

25. Steve Contorno, "Memo Reveals a House Republican Strategy on Shootings: Downplay White Nationalism, Blame Left," *Tampa Bay Times*, August 16, 2019.

26. Simeon Man, "Anti-Asian Violence and U.S. Imperialism," in Belew and Gutiérrez, eds., *A Field Guide to White Supremacy*, 121–31. For more on recent violence against the Asian American Pacific Islander community, see Stop AAPI Hate, http://www.stopaapihate.org.

27. Louis Casiano, "Michigan Protesters Storm State Capitol in Fight over Coronavirus Rules: 'Men with Rifles Yelling at Us,'" *Fox News*, April 30, 2020, https://www.foxnews.com/us/michigan-lansing-coronavirus-protest-capitol-guns-rifles; Abigail Censky, "Heavily Armed Protesters Gather Again at Michigan Capitol to Decry Stay-at-Home Order," *NPR*, May 14, 2020, https://www.npr.org/2020/05/14/855918852/heavily-armed-protesters-gather-again-at-michigans-capitol-denouncing-home-order; Luke Mogelson, "The Militias against Masks," *New Yorker*, August 17, 2020, https://www.newyorker.com/magazine/2020/08/24/the-militias-against-masks.

28. Jason Wilson, "The Rightwing Groups behind Wave of Protests against Covid-19 Restrictions," *The Guardian*, April 17, 2020, https://www.theguardian.com/world/2020/apr/17/far-right-coronavirus-protests-restrictions; Ricardo Torres-Cortez, "Protesters Call for Sisolak to Reopen State, Stop Telling Them 'What to Do,'" *Las Vegas Sun*, April 18, 2020, https://lasvegassun.com/news/2020/apr/18/protestors-call-for-sisolak-reopen-state-stop-tell/; Andrew Solender, "Armed Protesters Storm Michigan State House over COVID-19 Lockdown," *Forbes*, April 30, 2020, https://www.forbes.com/sites/andrewsolender/2020/04/30/armed-protesters-storm-michigan-state-house-over-covid-19-lockdown/?sh=3b432d4369b5; Joshua Partlow, "Politics at the Point of a Gun," *Washington Post*, July 18, 2020, https://www.washingtonpost.com/politics/2020/07/28/conservative-armed-militias-protests-coronavirus/?arc404=true; Kirk Siegler, "Ammon Bundy Is Arrested and Wheeled Out of the Idaho Statehouse—Again," *NPR*, August 25, 2020, https://www.npr.org/2020/08/25/906046911/ammon-bundy-is-arrested-and-wheeled-out-of-the-idaho-statehouse; Erik Maulbetsch, "Conservative Group behind Deadly "Patriot Muster" Rally Working Closely with Colorado GOP," *Colorado Times Recorder*, October 12, 2020, https://coloradotimesrecorder.com/2020/10/conservative-group-behind-deadly-patriot

-muster-rally-working-closely-with-colorado-gop/31445/; Azmi Haroun, "Anti-lockdown Protesters Storm Oregon Capitol Building, Clashing with Police Officers," *Insider*, December 21, 2020, https://www.businessinsider.com/far-right-protestors-storm-oregon-state-capitol-building-2020-12; "Nationwide Freedom March," American Patriot Council, accessed March 15, 2021, https://www.americanpatriotcouncil.org/nationwide-freedom-march; Rachel Goldwasser and Hatewatch Staff, "The Year in Antigovernment Extremism, Part 1," Southern Poverty Law Center, February 8, 2021, https://www.splcenter.org/news/2021/02/08/year-antigovernment-extremism-part-1; Devin Burghart, "New Far-Right Groups Protesting COVID-19 Stay-at-Home Directives," Institute for Research & Education on Human Rights, updated May 6, 2020, https://www.irehr.org/2020/04/23/far-right-groups-protesting-covid-19-stay-at-home-directives/.

29. Larry Buchanan, Quoctrung Bui, and Jugal K. Patel, "Black Lives Matter May Be the Largest Movement in U.S. History," *New York Times*, July 3, 2020, https://www.nytimes.com/interactive/2020/07/03/us/george-floyd-protests-crowd-size.html.

30. "Police Brutality at the Black Lives Matter Protests," Forensic Architecture, 2020–present, https://forensic-architecture.org/investigation/police-brutality-at-the-black-lives-matter-protests. See also Robin D. G. Kelley, "What Kind of Society Values Property over Black Lives?," *New York Times*, June 18, 2020.

31. Tom Kertscher, "No Proof That Black Lives Matter Killed 36 People, Injured 1,000 Police Officers," Politifact, August 7, 2020, https://www.politifact.com/factchecks/2020/aug/07/facebook-posts/no-proof-black-lives-matter-killed-36-people-injur/.

32. Barbara Sprunt, "The History behind 'When the Looting Starts, the Shooting Starts,'" *NPR*, May 29, 2020, https://www.npr.org/2020/05/29/864818368/the-history-behind-when-the-looting-starts-the-shooting-starts.

33. Allan Smith, "Trump Promotes Video Showing Apparent Supporter Shouting 'White Power,'" *NBC News*, June 28, 2020, https://www.nbcnews.com/politics/donald-trump/trump-promotes-video-appearing-show-supporter-shouting-white-power-n1232356.

34. Associated Press, "Meet the Gun-Wielding St. Louis Couple Speaking at the RNC Monday Night," *Chicago Sun Times*, August 24, 2020.

35. Lancaster Online Staff, "How a Tattoo Helped Lancaster Police Identify White Agitators at the Protests for George Floyd," *Lancaster Online*, June 3, 2020, https://lancasteronline.com/news/local/how-a-tattoo-helped-lancaster-police-identify-white-agitators-at-the-protests-for-george-floyd/article_548a0408-a506-11ea-98b2-43d9993767e7.html; Katie Shepherd, "An Officer Was Gunned Down. The Killer Was a 'Boogaloo Boy' Using Nearby Peaceful Protests as Cover, Feds Say," *Washington Post*, June 17, 2020, https://www.washingtonpost.com/nation/2020/06/17/boogaloo-steven-carrillo/; Jim Carlton, "Black Lives Matter Protests Spread Quickly to White, Rural Areas," *Wall Street Journal*, June 22, 2020, https://www.wsj.com/articles/black-lives-matter-protests-spread-quickly-to-white-rural-areas-11592818201; Ruth Brown,

"Black Lives Matter Protesters Say They Were Attacked. Boise Police Investigate, Speak Out," *Idaho Statesman*, July 2, 2020, https://www.idahostatesman.com/news/local/community/boise/article243954757.html; "Police: Richmond Riots Instigated by White Supremacists Disguised as Black Lives Matter," *WSLS News*, updated July 28, 2020, https://www.wsls.com/news/virginia/2020/07/27/police-richmond-riots-instigated-by-white-supremacists-disguised-as-black-lives-matter/; Joel Shannon, "Far-Right Demonstrators, Counter-Protesters and Police Clash in Multiple States," *USA Today*, August 15, 2020, https://www.usatoday.com/story/news/nation/2020/08/15/proud-boys-blm-counter-protesters-police-clash-fights/5592437002/; Faiz Siddiqui and Isaac Stanley-Becker, "One Person Shot Dead in Portland Following Clashes between Pro-Trump Supporters, Counterprotesters; Far-Right Group Patriot Prayer Has Identified the Man Who Was Shot as a Member," *Washington Post*, August 30, 2020, https://www.washingtonpost.com/nation/2020/08/29/blm-activists-counterprotesters-clash-portland-leading-arrests/; Jenny Gathright and Margaret Barthel, "Black Lives Matter Protests Came with a Price for These Local Activists," *WAMU*, November 30, 2020, https://wamu.org/story/20/11/30/local-activists-say-blm-protests-have-taken-toll/; Carmel Delshad, Rachel Sadon, Debbie Truong, and Matt Blitz, "One Person Stabbed amid Violent Clashes in Downtown D.C. after Pro-Trump Rally," *WAMU*, November 15, 2020, https://wamu.org/story/20/11/15/stabbing-maga-protest-downtown-dc/; Mark Guarino, Mark Berman, Jaclyn Peiser, and Griff Witte, "17-Year-Old Charged with Homicide after Shooting during Kenosha Protests, Authorities Say," *Washington Post*, August 26, 2020, https://www.washingtonpost.com/nation/2020/08/26/jacob-blake-kenosha-police-protests/.

36. Miller-Idriss, *Hate in the Homeland*.

37. See, for instance, Jacob Shamsian, "Leaked Emails Reveal the Threat a Right-wing Extremist Group Posed to Biden's Inauguration Was Worse than We Realized," *Insider*, May 14, 2021, https://www.insider.com/leaked-police-memos-show-boogaloo-bois-planned-attacks-dc-landmarks-2021-5.

38. Lois Beckett, "White Supremacists behind Majority of US Domestic Terror Attacks in 2020: Data Stands in Stark Contrast to Claims by Donald Trump, Who Has Argued That Leftwing Violence Is a Major Threat," *The Guardian*, October 22, 2020, https://www.theguardian.com/world/2020/oct/22/white-supremacists-rightwing-domestic-terror-2020.

39. Adam Goldman, Katie Benner, and Zolan Kanno-Youngs, "How Trump's Focus on Antifa Distracted Attention from the Far-Right Threat," *New York Times*, January 30, 2021, https://www.nytimes.com/2021/01/30/us/politics/trump-right-wing-domestic-terrorism.html; Betsy Woodruff Swan, "They Tried to Get Trump to Care about Right-Wing Terrorism. He Ignored Them," *Politico*, August 26, 2020, https://www.politico.com/news/2020/08/26/trump-domestic-extemism-homeland-security-401926.

40. David D. Kirkpatrick and Alan Feuer, "Police Shrugged Off the Proud Boys, until They Attacked the Capitol," *New York Times*, March 14, 2021, A1, https://www.nytimes.com/2021/03/14/us/proud-boys-law-enforcement.html.

41. Sheera Frenkel and Annie Karni, "Proud Boys Celebrate Trump's 'Stand by' Remark about Them at the Debate," *New York Times*, September 29, 2020, https://www.nytimes.com/2020/09/29/us/trump-proud-boys-biden.html.

42. Kelly McLaughlin, "The Wolverine Watchmen Plot to Kidnap Michigan Gov. Whitmer Also Included a Plan to Burn Down the State Capitol Building, Officials Say," *Insider*, November 13, 2020, https://www.businessinsider.com/kidnap-plot-gov-whitmer-included-plan-burn-capitol-ag-says-2020-11; John Flesher, "6 Men Indicted in Alleged Plot to Kidnap Michigan Governor," AP News, December 17, 2020, https://apnews.com/article/gretchen-whitmer-michigan-indictments-coronavirus-pandemic-traverse-city-10f7e02c57004da9843f89650edd4510.

43. Department of Homeland Security, *Homeland Threat Assessment,* October 2020, https://www.dhs.gov/sites/default/files/publications/2020_10_06_homeland-threat-assessment.pdf.

44. David Shortell, "Pipe Bombs Found Near Capitol on January 6 Were Placed the Night Before, FBI Says," *CNN*, January 29, 2021, https://www.cnn.com/2021/01/29/politics/washington-pipe-bombs-dnc-rnc/index.html; Jordan Freiman, "2 Men Allegedly Seen in Viral Photos Carrying Zip Ties during Capitol Assault Arrested," *CBS News,* January 11, 2021, https://www.cbsnews.com/news/capitol-riots-zip-ties-larry-brock-eric-munchel-arrested/.

45. "Read: Former President Donald Trump's January 6 Speech," *CNN*, February 8, 2021, https://www.cnn.com/2021/02/08/politics/trump-january-6-speech-transcript/index.html; Tiffany Hsu and Katie Robertson, "Covering Pro-Trump Mobs, the News Media Became a Target," *New York Times*, January 6, 2021, https://www.nytimes.com/2021/01/06/business/media/media-murder-capitol-building.html.

46. Andrew Macdonald (pseud. for William Pierce), *The Turner Diaries* (Hillsboro, WV: National Vanguard Books, 1978).

47. Belew, *Bring the War Home*.

48. For more on white woman victimhood in service of white power organizing, see Belew, *Bring the War Home*; Seyward Darby, *Sisters in Hate: American Women on the Front Lines of White Nationalism* (New York: Little, Brown, 2020); Vera Bergengruen, "'Our First Martyr': How Ashli Babbitt Is Being Turned into a Far-Right Recruiting Tool," *Time Magazine*, January 10, 2021, https://time.com/5928249/ashli-babbitt-capitol-extremism/.

49. Larry Diamond, Lee Drutman, Tod Lindberg, Nathan P. Kalmoe, and Lilliana Mason, "Americans Increasingly Believe Violence Is Justified If the Other Side Wins," *Politico*, October 1, 2020, https://www.politico.com/news/magazine/2020/10/01/political-violence-424157.

50. Ivana Saric, "Poll: Nearly Half of Republicans Believe False Narratives about Jan. 6 Siege," *Axios*, April 5, 2021, https://www.axios.com/capitol-riot-siege-republicans-poll-false-narratives-221f1395-c314-41a7-8b76-2bc0a023bc79.html.

51. Chris Cillizza, "A Republican House Member Just Described January 6 as a 'Normal Tourist Visit,'" *CNN*, May 13, 2021, https://www.cnn.com/2021/05/13/politics/andrew-clyde-january-6-riot/index.html.

## Notes to Chapter 6

1. Geraldo Cadava, *The Hispanic Republican: The Shaping of an American Political Identity, from Nixon to Trump* (New York: Ecco, 2020), chapter 7.

2. Alfonso Aguilar, interview with author, November 20, 2020.

3. Rachel Campos-Duffy, interview with author, November 19, 2020.

4. Adam Gabbat, "Donald Trump Says He 'Will Win Latino Vote' Despite Calling Mexicans 'Rapists,'" *The Guardian*, July 8, 2015, https://www.theguardian.com/us-news/2015/jul/08/donald-trump-latino-vote-mexico-immigration.

5. "Transcript of Donald Trump's Immigration Speech," *New York Times*, September 1, 2016.

6. Aaron Blake and Jenna Johnson, "Hispanic Supporters Flee Donald Trump's Campaign after Fiery Immigration Speech," *Washington Post*, September 1, 2016.

7. Lionel Sosa, "Farewell, My Grand Old Party," *San Antonio Express-News*, June 22, 2016; and Linda Chavez, "Republicans Must Defeat Trump in November," *Chicago Sun-Times*, May 5, 2016.

8. Nick Valencia, "Meet the Man Leading the Group Border Hispanics for Trump," *CNN*, December 26, 2019, https://www.cnn.com/videos/tv/2019/12/26/lead-nick-valencia-pkg-live.cnn.

9. Monica De la Cruz, interview with author, September 2, 2020.

10. Zachary B. Wolf, "Yes, Obama Deported More People than Trump but Context Is Everything," *CNN*, July 13, 2019, https://www.cnn.com/2019/07/13/politics/obama-trump-deportations-illegal-immigration/index.html.

11. Aguilar, interview.

12. Jennifer Medina, "A Vexing Question for Democrats: What Drives Latino Men to Republicans," *New York Times*, March 5, 2021.

13. Jim Tankersley, "White Americans Gain the Most from Trump's Tax Cuts, a Report Finds," *New York Times*, October 11, 2018.

14. Galen Hendricks, "4 Ways Trump's Tax Bill Left Behind the Latino Community," Center for American Progress, October 29, 2020, https://www.americanprogress.org/issues/economy/news/2020/10/29/492566/4-ways-trumps-tax-bill-left-behind-latino-community/.

15. Christopher Scragg, "Trump Touts Economic Accomplishments to Receptive Latino Business Group," *Cronkite News, Arizona PBS*, March 4, 2020.

16. Cadava, *Hispanic Republican*, chapter 3.

17. "About Us," The LIBRE Initiative, https://thelibreinitiative.com/about-us/, accessed on August 20, 2021.

18. Stanford Latino Entrepreneurship Initiative, "The Impact of COVID-19 on Latino-Owned Businesses," 2020, https://www.gsb.stanford.edu/sites/gsb/files/2020_slei_first_covid_survey_results.pdf.

19. Geraldo Cadava, "Trump Appeared to Be Gaining with Latino Voters—but Coronavirus May Cost Him Crucial Support," *MarketWatch*, May 29, 2020, https://www.marketwatch.com/story/trump-appeared-to-be-gaining-with-latino-voters-and-then-coronavirus-hit-2020-05-27.

20. Cadava, *Hispanic Republican*, 234.

21. "National Hispanic Heritage Month, 2006," from the archived White House website of George W. Bush, https://georgewbush-whitehouse.archives.gov/history/hispanicheritage/, accessed on March 14, 2021.

22. US Truthwire, "President Trump Hosts the Hispanic Heritage Month Celebration," September 17, 2018, YouTube video, 3:45, https://www.youtube.com/watch?v=yZO5ec5fp3o.

23. McKay Coppins, "Trump Secretly Mocks His Christian Supporters," *The Atlantic*, September 29, 2020.

24. James Crump, "'Christians Don't Need Trump': Religious Group Leads Attack on President as Support Drops in Polls," *The Independent*, October 15, 2020, https://www.independent.co.uk/news/world/americas/us-election-2020/donald-trump-christian-not-our-faith-polls-2020-election-b1049740.html.

25. Manuel Madrid, "South Florida Pastor and Trump Ally Courts Latin America's Religious Right," *Miami New Times*, August 22, 2019; "Las Vegas Pastors among Latino Clergy Backing Trump on Border Wall," *American Renaissance*, November 27, 2019; Aaron E. Sanchez, "Who Are the Latino Evangelicals That Support Trump?," *Sojourners*, November 26, 2019.

26. Alejandra Molina, "Latino Evangelicals Narrowly Favor Trump," *Christianity Today*, October 6, 2020, https://www.christianitytoday.com/news/2020/october/latino-evangelical-christian-voters-survey-trump-biden.html.

27. Jennifer Medina, "Latino, Evangelical, and Politically Homeless," *New York Times*, October 11, 2020.

28. Seung Min Kim and Sarah Pulliam Bailey, "Trump Courts Latinos in Miami as Part of Launch of Evangelical Coalition," *Washington Post*, January 3, 2020.

29. Brooke Singman, "Trump Calls Biden 'Trojan Horse for Socialism' in Fiery Speech Ahead of Democratic Convention," *Fox News*, August 17, 2020, https://www.foxnews.com/politics/trump-biden-trojan-horse-socialism.

30. Catherine Garcia, "Venezuelan Opposition Leader Juan Guaidó Attends State of the Union," *Yahoo! News*, February 4, 2020, https://news.yahoo.com/venezuelan-opposition-leader-juan-guaido-024140821.html.

31. Jonathan Blitzer, "The Fight for the Latino Vote in Florida," *New Yorker*, September 23, 2019.

32. Cadava, *Hispanic Republican*, 265.

33. Ben Jacobs, "Why 'Socialism' Killed Democrats in Florida," *New York Magazine*, November 17, 2020, https://nymag.com/intelligencer/2020/11/republican-socialism-attacks-haunt-democrats-in-florida.html.

34. Debbie Mucarsel-Powell (@DebbieforFL), "Many have commented on Democratic losses in South Florida and with Latinos across the country," Twitter, November 18, 2020, https://twitter.com/DebbieforFL/status/1329091111734820866.

35. Jazmine Ulloa, "Trump's Improved Performance with Latino Voters in 2020 Was Powered by a Surprising Source: Women," *Boston Globe*, April 10, 2021, https://www.bostonglobe.com/2021/04/10/nation/trumps-improved-performance-with-latino-voters-2020-was-powered-by-surprising-source-women/.

36. "Trump to African Americans: 'What Do You Have to Lose' by Voting for Me?," *Washington Post*, August 19, 2016, https://www.washingtonpost.com/video/politics/trump-calls-for-votes-from-african-americans/2016/08/19/62c17a2a-6652-11e6-b4d8-33e931b5a26d_video.html.

37. "2016 Election Exit Polls," *Washington Post*, November 29, 2016; and "Exit Poll Results and Analysis for the 2020 Presidential Election," *Washington Post*, December 14, 2020.

38. Marco Rubio (@marcorubio), Twitter, November 4, 2020, https://twitter.com/marcorubio/status/1324038552292859906.

## Notes to Chapter 7

1. Signs quoted in *Why We March: Signs of Protest and Hope; Voices from the Women's March* (New York: Artisan, 2017). Women's March registers 673 sister marches of 4,814,000 people on its site, and most estimates range between two and five million. "Sister Marches," Women's March on Washington, accessed February 7, 2021, https://web.archive.org/web/20170123010344/https://www.womensmarch.com/sisters; Wikipedia, "List of 2017 Women's March Locations," accessed February 7, 2021, https://en.wikipedia.org/wiki/List_of_2017_Women%27s_March_locations.

2. Erica Chenoweth, Tommy Leung, Nathan Perkins, Jeremy Pressman, and Jay Ulfelder, "The Trump Years Launched the Biggest Sustained Protest Movement in U.S. History. It's Not Over," *Washington Post*, February 8, 2021.

3. Teresa Shook quoted in Carrie Scozzaro, "Women's March Founder Teresa Shook Shares Her Unlikely Path to Activism as She Visits Spokane," *Inlander*, March 7, 2019.

4. Shook quoted in Perry Stein, "The Woman Who Started the Women's March with a Facebook Post Reflects: 'It Was Mind-Boggling,'" *Washington Post*, January 31, 2017.

5. These leaders of the Women's March also faced criticism, accused of being antisemitic. Leah McSweeney and Jacob Siegel, "Is the Women's March Melting Down?," *Tablet*, December 10, 2018.

6. Marie Berry and Erica Chenoweth, "Who Made the Women's March?," in *The Resistance: The Dawn of the Anti-Trump Opposition Movement*, ed. David S. Meyer and Sidney Tarrow (New York: Oxford University Press, 2018), 75–89, 83; Jenée Desmond-Harris, "To Understand the Women's March on Washington, You Need to Understand Intersectional Feminism," *Vox*, January 21, 2017, https://www.vox.com/identities/2017/1/17/14267766/womens-march-on-washington-inauguration-trump-feminism-intersectionaltiy-race-class.

7. Nicole Eaton, "Tribute Politics: How Feminist History Became a Reference Point in the 2016 Election," in *Suffrage at 100: Women in American Politics since 1920*, ed. Stacie Taranto and Leandra Zarnow (Baltimore: Johns Hopkins University Press, 2000), 335–56, 338.

8. Donald J. Trump, "Transcript: Donald Trump's Taped Comments about Women," *New York Times*, October 8, 2016.

9. Sarah Huckabee Sanders quoted in Ali Vitali, "The White House Women Who've Got Trump's Back," *NBC News*, September 18, 2017.

10. Women for America First, accessed June 22, 2021, https://wfaf.org.

11. Trump quoted in Z. Byron Wolf, "Comparing Trump's Inauguration Crowd to the Women's March," *CNN*, January 21, 2017.

12. "Wilson Evades Vast Crowd: Goes by Side Streets to Hotel While Suffrage Parade Is On," *New York Times*, March 4, 1913, 2.

13. Celinda Lake and Kellyanne Conway with Catherine Whitney, *What Women Really Want: How American Women Are Quietly Erasing Political, Racial, Class, and Religious Lines to Change the Way We Live* (New York: Free Press, 2005).

14. Evgenia Peretz, "State of the Union," *Vanity Fair*, April 21, 2021.

15. Bob Dole and Elizabeth Dole quoted in Kathy Rudy, "Elizabeth Dole and Conservative Feminist Politics," *Genders* (August 1, 1999): 1–35, 32; Marisa Chappell, "Reagan's 'Gender Gap' Strategy and the Limitations of Free-Market Feminism," *Journal of Policy History* 24, no. 1 (January 2012): 115–34.

16. Donald T. Critchlow, "How Phyllis Schlafly Led America to Donald Trump," *Marketwatch*, September 8, 2016.

17. Kellyanne Conway (@KellyannePolls), Twitter, September 5, 2016, https://twitter.com/kellyannepolls/status/772954151567368192?lang=en.

18. Unnamed senior official, Conway, and Chris Christie quoted in Peretz, "State of the Union."

19. "An Examination of the 2016 Electorate, Based on Validated Voters," Pew Research Center, August 9, 2018, https://www.people-press.org/2018/08/09/an-examination-of-the-2016-electorate-based-on-validated-voters/.

20. Chuck Todd and Conway quoted on *Meet the Press*, January 22, 2017, YouTube video, 13:51, https://www.youtube.com/watch?v=MA1vD_L8Mjs.

21. Conway quoted in Nicki Rossoll, "Kellyanne Conway 'Didn't See the Point' to Women's March on Washington," *ABC News*, January 22, 2017.

22. Conway and Annette Saunders quoted in Jeremy W. Peters and Yamiche Alcindor, "Anti-Abortion Marchers Draw Inspiration from an Unlikely Source," *New York Times*, January 27, 2017.

23. Mercedes Schlapp quoted in Vitali, "White House Women Who've Got Trump's Back."

24. Elizabeth Williamson, "Meet the Schlapps, Washington's Trump-Era 'It Couple,'" *New York Times*, April 30, 2018.

25. Sarah Huckabee Sanders, *Speaking for Myself: Faith, Freedom, and the Fight of Our Lives Inside the Trump White House* (New York: St. Martin's Press, 2018); Elizabeth Williamson, "Stephanie Grisham's Turbulent Ascent to a Top White House Role," *New York Times*, August 22, 2019; Emma Green, "The Temptation of Kayleigh McEnany," *The Atlantic*, June 25, 2020.

26. Nancy Cook and Meredith McGraw, "Trump Looks to Hope Hicks as Coronavirus Crisis Spill Over," *Politico*, April 27, 2020.

27. Sarah Huckabee Sanders quoted in Vitali, "White House Women Who've Got Trump's Back."

28. Landon R. Y. Storrs draws this connection in "Rage against the Administrative State," *Modern American History* 1 (2018): 221–25.

29. Sean Spicer quoted in "Has the US Federal Workforce Really 'Dramatically Increased'?," *BBC News*, January 24, 2017.

30. U.S. Office of Personnel Management, "Women in the Federal Workforce," 2015, https://www.opm.gov/policy-data-oversight/diversity-and-inclusion/women-in-the-federal-workforce-infographics.pdf.

31. Annie Lowrey and Steven Johnson, "The Very Male Trump Administration," *The Atlantic*, March 28, 2018.

32. Kathryn Dunn Tenpas, "The President's Advisors: An Analysis of Women on the President's 'A' Team," Brookings Institute, June 2020, https://www.brookings.edu/essay/the-presidents-advisors-an-analysis-of-women-on-the-presidents-a-team/; Chabeli Carrazana, "Women in President Donald Trump's White House Earn 69 Cents for Every $1 Paid to Male Staffers," *USA Today*, September 23, 2020.

33. Margaret Weichert quoted in Lisa Rein and Damian Paletta, "If Trump Has His Way, This Major Federal Agency Is on the Way Out," *Washington Post*, April 10, 2019.

34. Derrick Clifton, "Why the Trump Administration Is Slashing Anti-discrimination Training," *NBC News*, September 11, 2020; Bryce Covert, "The Trump Administration Gutted the EEOC," *The Nation*, January 28, 2021.

35. Mike Allen and Jonathan Swan, "Trump 101: The Producer of His Own Epic Film," *Axios*, February 2, 2017, https://www.axios.com/trump-101-the-producer-of-his-own-epic-film-1513300239-d1cf23bd-7bf3-4dff-b0a1-d1ec970f6fc5.html.

36. Clare O'Connor, "Working Women Respond to White House Dress Code Report with #DressLikeAWoman Campaign," *Forbes*, February 3, 2017.

37. Trump quoted in Adam Withnall, "Donald Trump's Unsettling Record of Comments about His Daughter Ivanka," *The Independent*, October 10, 2016.

38. Kaitlin Holmes et al., "Ivanka Trump's Report Card on Women's and Working Families' Issues," Center for American Progress, October 3, 2017, https://www.americanprogress.org/issues/early-childhood/reports/2017/10/03/440171/ivanka-trumps-report-card-womens-working-families-issues/; Kevin Stankiewicz, "Ivanka Trump: 'Women Are Thriving in the Trump Economy," *CNBC*, February 12, 2020; Gina Adams, "A Historic Boost to Child Care Funding Means States Can Start to Realize the Potential of the Child Care and Development Block Grant," Urban Institute, February 15, 2018, https://www.urban.org/urban-wire/historic-boost-child-care-funding-means-states-can-start-realize-potential-child-care-and-development-block-grant.

39. Woman's Global Development and Prosperity Initiative, *Annual Report 2020–2021*, accessed February 20, 2021, https://2017-2021.state.gov/wp-content/uploads/2021/01/W-GDP-Annual-Report-2020-2021.pdf.

40. Valerie M. Hudson and Patricia Leidl, *The Hillary Doctrine: Sex and American Foreign Policy* (New York: Columbia University Press, 2015).

41. Nikki R. Haley, *With All Due Respect: Defending America with Grit and Grace* (New York: St. Martin's Press, 2019), 75.

42. Tim Alberta, "Nikki Haley's Time for Choosing," *Politico*, February 2021, https://www.politico.com/interactives/2021/magazine-nikki-haleys-choice/.

43. Haley quoted in Nick Bryant, "Nikki Haley: Aggressive Envoy Who Shook Up United Nations," *BBC News*, October 10, 2018.

44. Editorial Board, "Nikki Haley Will Be Missed: The U.N. Ambassador Has Managed to Represent President Trump and the United States," *New York Times*, October 9, 2018.

45. Dr. Susan Berry, "Trump Administration Expands Policy Ensuring No Taxpayer Funding for Overseas Abortions," *Breitbart*, March 26, 2019; "Crisis in Care: Year Two Impact of Trump's Global Gag Rule," International Women's Health Coalition, accessed February 20, 2021, https://iwhc.org/resources/crisis-care-year-two-impact-trumps-global-gag-rule/.

46. Eagle Forum mission statement, n.d., accessed February 20, 2021, https://moonvalley.guhsdaz.org/UserFiles/Servers/Server_758978/File/Boies%20files/The%20Eagle%20Forum%20info%20sheet%20for%20pba.pdf.

47. Trump quoted in Reena Flores, "Donald Trump: 'Anchor Babies' Aren't American Citizens," *CBS News*, August 19, 2015.

48. Jeff Sessions quoted in Tal Kopan, "Trump Admin Drops Asylum Protections for Domestic Violence Victims," *CNN*, June 11, 2018; Deborah Anker, "The History and Future of Gender Asylum Law and Recognition of Domestic Violence as a Basis for Protection in the United States," *ABA Human Rights* 45, no. 2 (April 27, 2020), https://www.americanbar.org/groups/crsj/publications/human_rights_magazine_home/immigration/the-history-and-future-of-gender-asylum-law/.

49. Secretary-General António Guterres quoted in Edith M. Lederer, "UN Chief Urges End to Domestic Violence, Citing Global Surge," Associated Press, April 5, 2020.

50. Kirstjen Nielsen quoted in Bill Chappell and Jessica Taylor, "Defiant Homeland Security Secretary Defends Family Separations," *NPR*, June 18, 2018.

51. Gus Bova, "'Treated Worse than Dogs': Immigrant Kids in Detention Give Firsthand Accounts of Squalid Conditions," *Texas Observer*, July 18, 2018.

52. Receiving 49,100 likes, Alyssa Milano (@Alyssa_Milano), Twitter, October 15, 2017, https://twitter.com/alyssa_milano/status/919659438700670976?lang=en.

53. "Tarana Burke, Founder," Me Too, accessed February 21, 2021, https://metoomvmt.org/get-to-know-us/tarana-burke-founder/; Sarah J. Jackson, Moya Bailey, and Brooke Foucault Welles, *#Hashtag Activism: Networks of Race and Gender Justice* (Cambridge, MA: MIT Press, 2020), 1–64.

54. Ronan Farrow, "From Aggressive Overtures to Sexual Assault: Harvey Weinstein's Accusers Tell Their Stories," *New Yorker*, October 10, 2017. See also Time's Up, https://timesupnow.org; Stephanie Zacharek, Eliana Dockterman, and Haley Sweetland Edwards, "Time Person of the Year: The Silence Breakers: The Voices That Launched a Movement," *Time*, December 18, 2017.

55. Brave New Films, "16 Women or Donald Trump—Whom Would You Believe?," *The Nation*, November 16, 2017, https://www.thenation.com/article/archive/16-women-or-donald-trump-who-would-you-believe/.

56. Woody Allen quoted in Andrew R. Chow, "Woody Allen Warns of 'Witch Hunt' over Weinstein, Then Tries to Clarify," *New York Times*, October 15, 2017.

57. Lindy West, "Yes, This Is a Witch Hunt. I'm a Witch and I'm Hunting You," *New York Times*, October 17, 2017; Race Hochdorf, "Garrison Keillor & the Dark Side of #MeToo," *Areo*, September 12, 2017.

58. Jess Bidgood, Miriam Jordan, and Adam Nagourney, "Sexual Misconduct in California's Capitol Is Difficult to Escape," *New York Times*, October 29, 2017.

59. Kirsten Gillibrand quoted in Shane Goldmacher, "On Sexual Misconduct, Gillibrand Keeps Herself at the Fore," *New York Times*, December 6, 2017; Jane Mayer, "The Case of Al Franken," *New Yorker*, July 22, 2019.

60. Katherine Tully-McManus, "Congress Mandated Harassment Training; Now They Have to Pay for It," *Roll Call*, December 19, 2017.

61. Clarence Thomas quoted in Michael S. Rosenwald, "'A High-Tech Lynching': How Brett Kavanaugh Took a Page from the Clarence Thomas Playbook," *Washington Post*, September 27, 2018.

62. Clyde Wilcox, "Why Was 1992 the 'Year of the Woman'? Explaining Women's Gains in 1992," in *The Year of the Woman: Myths and Realities*, ed. Elizabeth Adell Cook, Sue Thomas, and Clyde Wilcox (Boulder, CO: Westview Press, 1994), 1–24, 4.

63. Anita K. Blair, "Playing 'Trivia' with Sexual Harassment," Independent Women's Forum, October 2, 1998, https://www.iwf.org/1998/10/02/playing-trivia-with-sexual-harassment/.

64. Anita Hill, "How to Get the Kavanaugh Hearings Right," *New York Times*, September 18, 2018; Hill quoted in Amanda Holpuch, "Anita Hill: Kavanaugh Confirmation Hearing 'Disservice to the American Public,'" *The Guardian*, October 11, 2018.

65. Ann Coulter, "Cut the Theatrics in Kavanaugh Hearings," Associated Press, September 24, 2018; Chris Cillizza, "Amy Klobuchar's Moment in the Brett Kavanaugh Confirmation Hearings," *CNN Politics*, October 1, 2018.

66. Brett M. Kavanaugh, "I Am an Independent, Impartial Judge," *Wall Street Journal*, October 4, 2018; Jeffrey M. Jones, "Americans Still Closely Divided on Kavanaugh Confirmation," Gallup, October 3, 2018; Jason Breslow, "The Resistance at the Kavanaugh Hearings: More than 200 Arrests," *NPR*, September 8, 2018.

67. Ruth Bader Ginsburg quoted in Nina Totenberg, "Justice Ginsburg, Champion of Gender Equality, Dies at 87," *NPR*, September 18, 2020.

68. Carl Hulse, "'Kavanaugh's Revenge' Fell Short against Democrats in the Midterms," *New York Times*, November 25, 2018.

69. Tracking "moral shocks," Dana R. Fisher, *American Resistance: From the Women's March to the Blue Wave* (New York: Columbia University Press, 2019).

70. Emily Shugerman, "'Incredible Explosion': 40,000 US Women Interested in Running for Office since Trump's Election," Emily's List, 2018, https://www.emilyslist.org/news/entry/incredible-explosion-40000-us-women-interested-in-running-for-office-since-.

71. Jennifer L. Lawless and Richard L. Fox, "A Trump Effect? Women and the 2018 Midterm Elections," *The Forum* 16, no. 4 (2018): 665–86.

72. Susan Chira and Kate Zernike, "Women Lead Parade of Victories to Help Democrats Win House," *New York Times*, November 6, 2018.

73. Kelly Ditmar, *Unfinished Business: Women Running in 2018 and Beyond*, Center for American Women and Politics, Eagleton Institute of Politics (New Brunswick, NJ: Rutgers University, 2019); "Women in Congress: Statistics and Brief Overview," *CRS Reports*, April 9, 2019, https://www.everycrsreport.com/reports/R43244.html#_Toc5717364.

74. Julián Aguilar, "Texas Sending Its First Latinas to Congress: Veronica Escobar and Sylvia Garcia," *Texas Tribune*, November 6, 2018; Simon Romero, "Native Americans Score Historic Wins in Midterms after Years of Efforts," *New York Times*, November 7, 2018; Jennifer Steinhauer, *The Firsts: The Inside Story of the Women Reshaping Congress* (Chapel Hill, NC: Algonquin Books of Chapel Hill, 2020).

75. Patricia Schroeder quoted in Steinhauer, *The Firsts*, 35.

76. William Cummings and Deborah Barfield Berry, "Democratic Women Send Political Message by Wearing White to State of the Union," *USA Today*, February 5, 2019; Eleanor Mueller and Alice Miranda Ollstein, "House Passes Bill to Revive Equal Rights Amendment," *Politico*, February 13, 2020; German Lopez, "The House Just Passed a Sweeping LGBTQ Rights Bill," *Vox*, May 17, 2019, https://www.vox.com/policy-and-politics/2019/5/17/18627771/equality-act-house-congress-lgbtq-rights-discrimination; Molly Ball, *Pelosi* (New York: Henry Holt, 2020).

77. Emily Badger and Quoctrung Bui, "How the Suburbs Moved Away from Trump," *New York Times*, November 16, 2020.

78. Trump and Nancy Pelosi quoted in Ella Nilsen, "Trump Wants Everyone to Know He Is Extremely Calm and Pelosi Is the 'Crazy' One," *Vox*, May 23, 2019, https://www.vox.com/policy-and-politics/2019/5/23/18637729/donald-trump-nancy-pelosi-stable-genius; Paul Kane, "Trump and Pelosi Haven't Spoken in a Year as Grave Crises Grip the Nation," *Washington Post*, October 17, 2020.

79. Alexandria Ocasio-Cortez, "The Courage to Change," May 30, 2018, YouTube video, 2:08, https://www.youtube.com/watch?v=rq3QXIVR0bs; Shane Goldmacher and Jonathan Martin, "Alexandria Ocasio-Cortez Defeats Joseph Crowley in Major Democratic Upset," *New York Times*, June 26, 2018.

80. Ayanna Pressley quoted in Katharine Q. Seelye, "Ayanna Pressley Upsets Capuano in Massachusetts House Race," *New York Times*, September 4, 2018.

81. Trump tweet quoted in Bianca Quilantan and David Cohen, "Trump Tells Dem Congresswomen: Go Back Where You Came From," *Politico*, July 14, 2019; Ashley Parker, "How a Racist Tweet Became a Trump Rally Chant in Three Short Days," *Washington Post*, July 18, 2019.

82. Mark Walker quoted in Julie Hirschfeld Davis, Maggie Haberman, and Michael Crowley, "Trump Disavows 'Send Her Back' Chant after Pressure from G.O.P." *New York Times*, July 18, 2019.

83. Ilhan Omar quoted in Shane Croucher, "How 'The Squad' Have Responded to Trump Rally Chanting 'Send Her Back,'" *Newsweek*, July 18, 2019.

84. Maxine Waters quoted in Vanessa Williams, "'Auntie Maxine' and the Quest for Impeachment," *Washington Post*, May 1, 2017.

85. David Winston, "'Squad,' Impeachment Enthusiasts Leave Democrats in Trump Districts to Fend for Themselves," *Roll Call*, July 24, 2019.

86. Russell Berman, "Nancy Pelosi Has Had Enough," *The Atlantic*, September 24, 2019.

87. Gil Cisneros et al., "Seven Freshman Democrats: These Allegations Are a Threat to All We Have Sworn to Protect," *Washington Post*, September 23, 2019; Dana Bash and Bridget Nolan, "These Five Freshman Congresswomen Changed History by Becoming Unlikely Leaders on Impeachment," *CNN*, September 28, 2019; and critiquing, Tanya A. Christian, "Twitter Reacts to CNN Story Giving White Congresswomen Credit for Trump Impeachment Inquiry," *Essence*, September 30, 2019.

88. Trump quoted in Patrick Kelley, "Stefanik Seizes the Spotlight at Trump Impeachment Proceedings," *Roll Call*, November 18, 2019; Barbara Sprunt, "New York's Elise Stefanik Replaces Cheney in Republican Leadership Spot," *NPR*, May 14, 2021.

89. Nancy Pelosi quoted in Lisa Mascaro, "Pelosi: Power of Gavel Means Trump Is 'Impeached Forever,'" Associated Press, December 20, 2019.

90. Campbell Robertson and Robert Gebeloff, "How Millions of Women Became the Most Essential Workers in America," *New York Times*, April 18, 2020; Megan Cerullo, "Nearly 3 Million U.S. Women Have Dropped Out of the Labor Force in the Past Year," *Money Watch, CBS*, February 5, 2021; Angela Garbes, "The Numbers Don't Tell the Whole Story: Unemployment Statistics Can't Capture the Full Extent of What Women Have Lost," *The Cut, New York*, February 1, 2021.

91. Anna North, "6 Black Women Organizers on What Happened in Georgia—and What Comes Next," *Vox*, November 11, 2020, https://www.vox.com/21556742/georgia-votes-election-organizers-stacey-abrams; Nicquel Terry Ellis, "Black Women Helped Push Democrats to the Finish Line in Georgia. Here's How They Can Do It Again," *CNN*, November 21, 2020.

92. Ellen G. Rafshoon, "Pave It Blue: Georgia Women and Politics in the Trump Era," in Taranto and Zarnow, eds., *Suffrage at 100*, 377–94.

93. LaTosha Brown quoted in Robin Young and Allison Hagan, "'The Rise of the New South': Black Women Organizers Turn Georgia Bluish," *Here & Now, WBUR*, November 9, 2020.

94. Stacey Abrams quoted in Alan Blinder and Richard Fausset, "Stacey Abrams Ends Fight for Georgia Governor with Harsh Words for Her Rival," *New York Times*, November 16, 2018. See also Fair Fight, https://fairfight.com.

95. Angela Caputo, Geoff Hing, and Johnny Kauffman, "They Didn't Vote . . . Now They Can't," *APM Reports*, October 19, 2018, https://www.apmreports.org/story/2018/10/19/georgia-voter-purge.

96. Abrams quoted in Debbie Elliott, "Stacey Abrams Spearheads 'Fair Fight,' a Campaign against Voter Suppression," *NPR*, February 21, 2020.

97. Drew Desilver, "Turnout Soared in 2020 as Nearly Two-Thirds of Eligible U.S. Voters Cast Ballots for President," Pew Research Center, January 28, 2021, https://www.pewresearch.org/fact-tank/2021/01/28/turnout-soared-in-2020-as-nearly-two-thirds-of-eligible-u-s-voters-cast-ballots-for-president/; Sabrina Tavernise and John Eligon, "Voters Say Black Lives Matter Protests Were Important. They Disagree on Why," *New York Times*, November 7, 2020.

98. Amy Klobuchar (@amyklobuchar), Twitter, July 1, 2019, https://twitter.com/amyklobuchar/status/1145850403688501249?lang=en.

99. "Black Women Leaders Letter to Democratic Presidential Candidate Joseph Biden," letter from Katrina Adams et al. to Joe Biden, Action Network, April 24, 2020, https://actionnetwork.org/petitions/black-women-leaders-letter-to-support-black-women-for-vp/.

100. Kamala Harris, Acceptance Speech, Democratic National Convention, August 19, 2020, YouTube video, 19:14, https://www.youtube.com/watch?v=JijFLcbIqMs.

101. Samantha Schmidt, "The Gender Gap Was Expected to Be Historic. Instead, Women Voted Much as They Always Have," *Washington Post*, November 6, 2020.

102. Steven Shepard, "New Poll Shows How Trump Surged with Women and Hispanics—and Lost Anyway, *Politico,* June 30, 2021; Danielle Kurtzleben, "How a Record Number of Republican Women Got Elected to Congress," *NPR*, November 13, 2020.

103. Nicole Malliotakis quoted in Leigh Ann Caldwell, Haley Talbot, and Julie Tsirkin, "Freshman Republicans Look to Form a Conservative 'Squad,'" *Meet the Press Blog, NBC*, updated March 4, 2021, https://www.nbcnews.com/politics/meet-the-press/blog/meet-press-blog-latest-news-analysis-data-driving-political-discussion-n988541/ncrd1248407#blogHeader.

104. Trump quoted in Ben Nadler, "Georgia Republican Who Supports QAnon Wins US House Seat," *Breitbart (AP)*, November 3, 2020.

105. Kim Foxx quoted in Eugene Daniels and Christopher Cadelago, "The Hard Part for Kamala Harris Will Come after She Makes History," *Politico*, January 20, 2021.

## Notes to Chapter 8

1. "Proclamation on Ending Discriminatory Bans on Entry to the United States," White House, January 20, 2021, https://www.whitehouse.gov/briefing-room/presidential-actions/2021/01/20/proclamation-ending-discriminatory-bans-on-entry-to-the-united-states/; "Executive Order on the Revision of Civil Immigration Enforcement Policies and Priorities," White House, January 20, 2021, https://www.whitehouse.gov/briefing-room/presidential-actions/2021/01/20/executive-order-the-revision-of-civil-immigration-enforcement-policies-and-priorities/; "Proclamation on the Termination of Emergency with Respect to the Southern Border of the United States and Redirection of Funds Diverted to Border Wall Construction," White House, January 21, 2021, https://www.whitehouse.gov/briefing-room/presidential-actions/2021/01/20/proclamation-termination-of-emergency-with-respect-to-southern-border-of-united-states-and-redirection-of-funds-diverted-to-border-wall-construction/; "Fact Sheet: President Biden Sends Immigration Bill to Congress as Part of His Commitment to Modernize Our Immigration System," January 20, 2021, https://pennstatelaw.psu.edu/sites/default/files/documents/pdfs/Immigrants/Fact_Sheet__America_s_Citizenship_Act_of_2021.pdf. The bill—introduced into the Senate and House as the U.S. Citizenship Act of 2021, sponsored by Senator Bob

Menendez (D-NJ) and Representative Linda Sánchez (D-CA)—includes immediate legalization of the undocumented and an eight-year path to citizenship, with a fast track for DACA (Deferred Action for Childhood Arrivals) holders, a relaxation of the rigid country quotas that fuel unauthorized migration, and attention to improving conditions that drive migration from Central American countries. Notably, it unyokes legalization from border control, a trade-off that has characterized immigration legislative proposals since the 1980s. 117th Congress, 1st Session, U.S. Senate, "A Bill to Provide an Earned Path to Citizenship, to Address the Root Causes of Migration and Responsibly Manage the Southern Border, and to Reform the Immigrant Visa System, and for Other Purposes," https://www.menendez.senate.gov/imo/media/doc/USCitizenshipAct2021BillText.pdf.

2. John Higham, *Strangers in the Land: Patterns of American Nativism, 1860–1925* (1955; repr., New Brunswick, NJ: Rutgers University Press 2002), 4.

3. Higham, *Strangers in the Land*, 5–11. *Strangers in the Land* was published during the McCarthy era, when communism was defined, above all, as an "anti-American" ideology.

4. For a lengthier discussion comparing Chinese exclusion in the nineteenth century, immigration restriction in the early twentieth century, and contemporary nativism, see Mae Ngai, "Nativism, Past and Present," in *Immigration Matters: Movements, Visions, and Strategies for a Progressive Future*, ed. Ruth Milkman, Deepak Bhargava, and Penny Lewis (New York: New Press, 2021), 39–54. On the Reconstruction era in the American West, see Stacey Smith, *Freedom's Frontier: California's Struggle over Unfree Labor, Emancipation, and Reconstruction* (Chapel Hill: University of North Carolina Press, 2013).

5. David Koistinen, *Confronting Decline: The Political Economy of Deindustrialization in Twentieth-Century New England* (Gainesville: University Press of Florida, 2013); Lionel Fontagné and Ann Harrison, eds., *The Factory-Free Economy: Outsourcing, Servitization, and the Future of Industry* (Oxford: Oxford University Press, 2017); Robert Self, *American Babylon: Race and the Struggle for Postwar Oakland* (Princeton, NJ: Princeton University Press, 2003); Cary McClelland, *Silicon City: San Francisco in the Long Shadow of the Valley* (New York: W. W. Norton, 2019); Kate Clark and Alex Wilhelm, "The Cult of the Founder and Silicon Valley's Lack of Moral Authority," September 20, 2019, Tech Crunch, Equity podcast, episode 154, 31:25, https://techcrunch.com/2019/09/20/the-cult-of-the-founder-and-silicon-valleys-lack-of-moral-authority/; "National Exit Polls: How Different Groups Voted," *New York Times*, November 3, 2020, https://www.nytimes.com/interactive/2020/11/03/us/elections/exit-polls-president.html. See also Todd C. Frankel, "A Majority of the People Arrested at the Capitol Riot Had a History of Financial Trouble," *Washington Post*, February 10, 2021, https://www.washingtonpost.com/business/2021/02/10/capitol-insurrectionists-jenna-ryan-financial-problems/?outputType=amp, citing bankruptcies, tax liens, and other financial problems among the insurrectionists, including business owners, managers, and professionals.

6. According to the Pew Research Center, in 2019, 79 percent of Latinos in the United States were citizens. Luis Noe-Bustamante, "Key Facts about U.S. Hispanics

and Their Diverse Heritage," Pew Research Center Fact Tank, September 16, 2019, https://www.pewresearch.org/fact-tank/2019/09/16/key-facts-about-u-s-hispanics/. On undocumented workers, see Jeffrey S. Passel and D'Vera Cohen, "Size of US Unauthorized Immigrant Workforce Stable after the Great Recession," Pew Research Center Hispanic Trends, November 3, 2016, https://www.pewresearch.org/hispanic/2016/11/03/size-of-u-s-unauthorized-immigrant-workforce-stable-after-the-great-recession/.

7. FAIR, accessed May 29, 2020, https://www.fairus.org/?gclid=EAIaIQobChMI0LGT1_XZ6QIVw8DACh33Eg8zEAAYASAAEgLZ0_D_Bw.

8. FAIR has received funding from the Pioneer Fund, which underwrites studies on the alleged links between race and intelligence; and FAIR's executive director, Dan Stein, has "warned that certain immigrant groups are engaged in competitive breeding aimed at diminishing white power." "Anti-immigration Groups," Southern Poverty Law Center, March 21, 2001, https://www.splcenter.org/fighting-hate/intelligence-report/2001/anti-immigration-groups.

9. Cindy Carcamo, "These Latino Voters Are on a Mission to Persuade Other Latinos to Vote for Trump," *Los Angeles Times*, October 31, 2020, www.latimes.com/politics/story/2020-10-31/latinos-democratic-party-gop-trump-election.

10. Muzaffar Chishti and Faye Hipsman, "U.S. Immigration Didn't Happen in 2013; Will 2014 Be the Year?," Migration Policy Institute Policy Beat, January 9, 2014, https://www.migrationpolicy.org/article/us-immigration-reform-didnt-happen-2013-will-2014-be-year.

11. Jason DeParle, "How Stephen Miller Seized the Moment to Battle Immigration," *New York Times*, August 17, 2019. Recall that in 1985, Sessions's nomination to a federal judgeship was rejected on grounds of his racism. See also Katie Rogers, "Before Joining White House, Stephen Miller Pushed White Nationalist Theories," *New York Times*, November 13, 2019. On Trump and the Central Park Five, see Jan Ransom, "Trump Will Not Apologize for Calling for Death Penalty over Central Park Five," *New York Times*, June 18, 2019; on Trump and "birtherism," see Davis Richardson, "Former Trump Advisor Admits to 'Peddling Birtherism' about Obama," *The Observer*, August 3, 2018, https://observer.com/2018/08/former-trump-advisor-peddling-birtherism-about-obama/.

12. Exec. Order No. 13,767, Border Security and Immigration Enforcement Improvements (January 25, 2017); Exec. Order No. 13,768, Enhancing Public Safety in the Interior of the United States (January 25, 2017); Exec. Order No. 13,769, Protecting the Nation from Foreign Terrorist Entry into the United States (January 27, 2017).

13. Chae Chan Ping v. U.S., 130 U.S. 581 (1889). On the role of Chinese cases in refining the plenary power and shaping the administrative law with regard to immigration, see Lucy E. Salyer, *Laws Harsh as Tigers* (Chapel Hill: University of North Carolina Press, 1995).

14. Henderson v. Mayor of New York, 92 U.S. 259 (1875); Chy Lung v. Freeman, 92 U.S. 275 (1875); Mary Sarah Bilder, "The Struggle over Immigration: Indentured Servants, Slaves, and Articles of Commerce," *Missouri Law Review* 61, no. 4 (1996): 743–825.

15. 8 U.S.C. §1182(f). On "2-something-something," see Jason Zengerle, "How America Got to 'Zero Tolerance' on Immigration," *New York Times*, July 16, 2019.

16. The Fourth Circuit ruled on both First Amendment and statutory violations; the Ninth Circuit ruled more narrowly on the statute. International Refugee Assistance Project (IRAP) v. Trump, 857 F.3d 554 (C.A.4 2017); Hawaii v. Trump, 859 F.3d 741 (C.A.9 2017).

17. Trump v. Hawaii, 138 S. Ct. 2392 (2018). Travel ban 3.0 targeted Iran, North Korea, Syria, Libya, Yemen, Somalia, and Venezuela. Chad was originally on the list, but it was removed after meeting baseline security requirements. Linda Greenhouse, "The Supreme Court after Trump," *New York Times*, January 14, 2021.

18. Immigration Policy Tracking Project, https://immpolicytracking.org/. For more on the tracking project, see Sarah Stillman, "The Race to Dismantle Trump's Immigration Policies," *New Yorker*, February 2, 2021.

19. Nick Miroff, "Trump's Use of Military Funds for Border Wall Construction Is illegal, 9th Circuit Court Rules," *Washington Post*, June 26, 2020; Lucy Rodgers and Dominic Bailey, "Trump Wall: How Much Has He Actually Built?" *BBC News*, October 31, 2020, https://www.bbc.com/news/world-us-canada-46824649.

20. DHS rescinded DACA by memorandum in June 2017; the Supreme Court ruled that the DHS rescission order was arbitrary and capricious and violated the Administrative Procedures Act. DHS v. Regents of University of California (on certiorari from CAA 9), June 18, 2019. EO 13880, Collecting Information about Citizenship Status in the Decennial Census, July 11, 2019; Dept. of Commerce v. New York, June 27, 2019.

21. On refugee admissions, see "Asylum in the United States," Wikipedia, accessed September 3, 2021, https://en.wikipedia.org/wiki/Asylum_in_the_United_States. On asylum, see discussion below.

22. "How America Got to Zero Tolerance," Frontline interview with Nick Miroff, June 7, 2019, https://www.pbs.org/wgbh/frontline/interview/nick-miroff/.

23. Richard Gonzales, "America No Longer a 'Nation of Immigrants,' USCIS Says," *NPR*, February 22, 2018.

24. "President Derides Immigrants from 'Shithole' Countries," *Washington Post*, January 12, 2018.

25. Melendres. v. Arpaio, 784 F.3rd 1254, CAA (9th Cir. 2015).

26. Congress established the expedited removal procedure under the 1996 Illegal Immigration Reform and Immigrant Responsibility Act.

27. Jens Manuel Krogstad, Jeffrey S. Passel, and D'Vera Cohn, "Five Facts about Illegal Immigration in the U.S.," Pew Research Center, June 12, 2019, https://www.pewresearch.org/fact-tank/2019/06/12/5-facts-about-illegal-immigration-in-the-u-s/.

28. ICE Policy Directive, "Civil Immigration Enforcement: Priorities for the Apprehension, Detention, and Removal of Aliens," March 2, 2011, https://documentcloud.adobe.com/link/review?uri=urn:aaid:scds:US:c182bfa7-b569-440a-ab8e-d69b53941e56; Memorandum for All Field Office Directors, All Special Agents in Charge, All Chief Council from John Morton, Director, ICE, "Exercising Prosecutorial Discretion Consistent with the Civil Immigration Enforcement Priorities

of the Agency for the Apprehension, Detention, and Removal of Aliens," June 17, 2011, https://www.ice.gov/doclib/secure-communities/pdf/prosecutorial-discretion-memo.pdf.

29. Lazaro Zamora, "Comparing Trump and Obama's Deportation Priorities," Figure 1, Bipartisan Policy Center, February 27, 2017, https://bipartisanpolicy.org/blog/comparing-trump-and-obamas-deportation-priorities/.

30. Exec. Order No. 13768; DHS memorandum, Enforcement of the Immigration Laws to Serve the National Interest (February 27, 2017), implementing EO 13768, https://www.dhs.gov/sites/default/files/publications/17_0220_S1_Enforcement-of-the-Immigration-Laws-to-Serve-the-National-Interest.pdf.

31. On road blocks: "ICE and Border Patrol Abuses," American Civil Liberties Union, accessed September 3, 2021, https://www.aclu.org/issues/immigrants-rights/ice-and-border-patrol-abuses. On buses: Adiel Kaplan and Vanessa Swales, "Border Patrol Searches Have Increased on Greyhound, Other Buses Far from Border," *NBC*, June 5, 2019. On schools: Ray Sanchez, "ICE Arrests Undocumented Father Taking Daughter to California School," *CNN*, March 4, 2017. On courthouses: Tal Koppan, "Trump Administration Says ICE Courthouse Arrests Will Continue," *CNN*, March 31, 2017. On "unshackling": Nicholas Kulish, "Immigration Agents Discover New Freedom to Deport under Trump," *New York Times*, February 25, 2017.

32. There were 65,332 interior removals in 2016 (Obama); 81,603 in 2017; 95,360 in 2018; 85,958 in 2019; and 62,739 in 2020. DHS annual reports.

33. Detainer policy Sec. 287(g) of the Immigration and NationalityAct. As of 2020, 220 city and county jurisdictions signed up to cooperate with ICE under 287(g). "National Map of 287(g) Agreements," Immigrant Legal Resource Center, October 21, 2020, https://www.ilrc.org/national-map-287g-agreements. The Tenth Amendment, known as the noncommandeering amendment, protects states from being coerced into enforcing federal laws, usually in the form of federal sanctions, penalties, or withholding of funds. Most recently, the U.S. Supreme Court struck down the obligation of states to expand Medicaid provision under the Affordable Care Act. National Federation of Independent Business v. Sebelius, 567 U.S. 519 (2012). In 1997 the court struck down the provision of the Brady gun control law that required states to conduct background checks on prospective gun buyers. Printz v. United States, 521 U.S. 898 (1997).

34. D. Massey, J. Durand, and K. A. Pren, "Why Border Enforcement Backfired," *American Journal of Sociology* 121, no. 5 (2016): 1557–600.

35. Jeffrey Hallock, Ariel G. Ruiz Soto, and Michael Fix, "In Search of Safety, Growing Numbers of Women Flee Central America," Migration Policy Institute, May 30, 2018, https://www.migrationpolicy.org/article/search-safety-growing-numbers-women-flee-central-america.

36. The 1997 Flores agreement, a federal consent agreement, prohibits detention of children for more than twenty days.

37. Julia Edwards Ainsley, "Trump Administration Considering Family Separation at Border," Reuters, March 3, 2017, https://www.reuters.com/article/us-usa-immigration-children/exclusive-trump-administration-considering-separating-women-children-at-mexico-border-idUSKBN16A2ES.

38. AG Jeff Sessions, Memorandum to all Federal Prosecutors, "Zero Tolerance for Offenses under 8 U.S.C. Sec. 1325(a)," April 11, 2018, upgrading from the AG's "priorities" memorandum of April 6, 2017, "Renewed Commitment to Criminal Immigration Enforcement." Section 1325 of the INA allows prosecution for misdemeanor first-time unlawful entry and felony prosecution for subsequent entries, and section 1326 allows prosecution for reentry of formerly removed persons. U.S. Department of Justice, "Attorney General Announces Zero-Tolerance Policy for Criminal Illegal Entry," April 6, 2018, https://www.justice.gov/opa/pr/attorney-general-announces-zero-tolerance-policy-criminal-illegal-entry.

39. Jeff Daniels, "Trump Administration's 'Zero Tolerance' Border Enforcement Policy to Separate More Families," *CNBC*, May 7, 2018, https://www.cnbc.com/2018/05/07/tougher-us-border-enforcement-policy-to-separate-more-families.html.

40. "Hundreds of Children Taken at Border," *New York Times*, April 18, 2018.

41. "DHS: 2,000 Children Separated from Parents at Border," *CNN*, June 16, 2018.

42. "Foster Care or Whatever," John Kelly, White House Chief of Staff, interview with *NPR*, May 11, 2018, https://www.npr.org/2018/05/11/610116389/transcript-white-house-chief-of-staff-john-kellys-interview-with-npr.

43. Scott Allen, MD, and Pamela McPherson, MD, to Sen. Charles Grassley and Sen. Ron Wyden, Senate Whistleblowing Caucus, July 17, 2018, with appendix including statements and resolutions by the American Psychiatric Association (May 19, 2018), American Academy of Pediatrics (June 27, 2018), American Medical Association (June 12, 2018), American College of Physicians (July 5, 2018). https://www.wyden.senate.gov/imo/media/doc/Doctors%20Congressional%20Disclosure%20SWC.pdf.

44. Ms. L., et al. v. US ICE, Order Granting Plaintiff Motion for Classwide Preliminary Injunction, U.S. District Court for the Southern District of California, June 26, 2018.

45. Caitlin Dickerson, "Parents of 545 Children Separated at the Border Cannot Be Found," *New York Times*, October 21, 2020.

46. Camila Domonoske, "What We Know: Family Separation and 'Zero Tolerance' at the Border," *NPR*, June 19, 2018.

47. On the total number of children separated, see Colleen Long, "Watchdog: DOJ Bungled 'Zero Tolerance' Immigration Policy," Associated Press, January 14, 2021; Priscilla Alvarez, "Parents of 628 Migrant Children Separated at Border Still Have Not Been Found, Court Filing Says," *CNN*, December 2, 2020, https://www.cnn.com/2020/12/02/politics/family-separation-us-border-children/index.html.

48. Department of Justice, Office of the Inspector General, "DOJ OIG Releases Report on the Department of Justice's Planning and Implementation of Its Zero Tolerance Policy and Its Coordination with the Departments of Homeland Security and Health and Human Services," January 13, 2021, https://oig.justice.gov/sites/default/files/2021-01/2021-01-14.pdf.

49. "Justice Department Rescinds Trump's 'Zero Tolerance' Immigration Policy," *NPR*, January 27, 2021; Monty Wilkinson, "Rescinding the Zero Tolerance Policy for Offenses under 8 USC 1325(a)," http://cdn.cnn.com/cnn/2021/images/01/26/acting.attorney.general.memorandum.rescinding.zero-tolerance.policy.pdf.

50. Wait times were highest at Ciudad Juárez, across from El Paso. Mexicans and unaccompanied minors were not supposed to be subject to metering, but many were forced to wait or simply denied the right to apply for asylum and immediately turned back. "Policies Affecting Asylum Seekers at the Border," American Immigration Council, January 29, 2020, https://www.americanimmigrationcouncil.org/research/policies-affecting-asylum-seekers-border.

51. The CBP established MPP on the Mexico side of seven U.S. border towns: San Ysidro and Calexico, California; Nogales, Arizona; and El Paso, Eagle Pass, Laredo, and Brownsville, Texas. The CBP reported 59,241 MPP cases, but Mexico recorded 62,144 cases. The program was meant primarily for Spanish-speaking persons from Central America and excluded Mexicans and non–Spanish speakers (South Asia), though Brazil was later added. "Policies Affecting Asylum Seekers," 1–2; DHS, "Migrant Protection Protocol Metrics and Measures," accessed September 3, 2021, https://www.dhs.gov/sites/default/files/publications/migrant_protection_protocols_metrics_and_measures_3.pdf.

52. American Immigration Council, "Policies Affecting Asylum Seekers," 4.

53. American Immigration Council, "The Migrant Protection Protocols," January 2021, p. 1. The rate of positive determinations is far lower than that in recent years for Central Americans. Government estimates of the number of people who pass these interviews range from 1 to 13 percent, compared with the general rate of positive decisions in the United States of 13.5 percent. American Immigration Council, "Migrant Protection Protocols."

54. American Immigration Council, "Migrant Protection Protocols," 4.

55. American Immigration Council, "Migrant Protection Protocols," 4–5.

56. American Immigration Council, "Migrant Protection Protocols," 7–8.

57. DHS, 8 C.F.R. Parts 208 and 235 and DOJ, 8 C.F.R. Parts 1003, 1208, and 1235, "Procedures for Asylum and Withholding of Removal; Credible Fear and Reasonable Fear Review," Final Rule, Fed. Reg. V 85 no 239 (December 11, 2020), 80274–401; "New Rule Spells Death for the Asylum System," American Immigration Lawyers Association, December 10, 2020, https://www.aila.org/advo-media/press-releases/2020/new-rule-spells-death-for-the-asylum-system; Katie Shepherd, "Death to Asylum Rule Halted in the Last Days of the Trump Administration," Immigration Impact, January 14, 2021, https://immigrationimpact.com/2021/01/14/death-to-asylum-rule-blocked/?emci=2d44e20b-7457-eb11-a607-00155d43c992&emdi=e5938522-d758-eb11-a607-00155d43c992&ceid=7781354#.YBgWGoE8K-o.

58. "On Mexico's Border with U.S., Desperation as Migrant Traffic Piles Up," *New York Times*, March 14, 2021; Camila Montoya-Galvez, "FEMA Deployed to Help Process Migrant Children amid Overcrowding in Border Facilities," *CBS News*, March 14, 2021, https://www.cbsnews.com/news/immigration-migrant-children-border-facilities-overcrowding-fema/; "Biden Tasks Harris with Curbing Central American Migration," *New York Times*, March 24, 2021.

59. DHS, 8 C.F.R. Parts 103, 212, 213, 214, 245, and 248, "Inadmissibility on Public Charge Grounds," Final Rule, Fed. Reg. V 84 no. 157 (August 14, 2019), 41292–304,

comments and responses et seq. Denial of permanent residency was the first step. Observers believed removal of noncitizens who used public benefits would be next.

60. Torrie Hester, Mary E. Mendoza, Deirdre Molony, and Mae Ngai, "Now the Trump Administration Is Trying to Punish Legal Immigrants for Being Poor," *Washington Post*, August 9, 2018; Cybelle Fox, *Three Worlds of Relief: Race, Immigration, and the American Welfare State from the Progressive Era to the New Deal* (Princeton, NJ: Princeton University Press, 2013). Federal courts enjoined implementation of the new rule, but the Second Circuit allowed DHS to proceed in most of the country as the Trump administration appealed. Upon taking office, Biden withdrew the appeals and vacated the new rule. For judicial history, see U.S. Citizenship and Immigration Services, "Inadmissibility on Public Charge Grounds Final Rule: Litigation," April 23, 2021, https://www.uscis.gov/green-card/green-card-processes-and-procedures/public-charge/inadmissibility-on-public-charge-grounds-final-rule-litigation.

61. On the travel ban: "Travel Ban: Trump Defends Order as Dispute over UK Visit Deepens—as It Happened," *The Guardian*, January 30, 2017. On "rapid response teams": Randy Capps, Muzaffar Chishti, Julia Gelatt, Jessica Bolter, and Ariel G. Ruiz Soto, "Revving Up the Deportation Machinery: Enforcement under Trump and the Pushback," Migration Policy Institute, May 2018, https://www.migrationpolicy.org/research/revving-deportation-machinery-under-trump-and-pushback. On protests against family separation: Stacy Chen, "Coalition of WWII Japanese American Internment Camp Survivors Stage Peaceful Protest at Immigrant Detention Facility on Texas Border," *ABC News*, March 30, 2019. On lawyers and litigation: Kim Bellware, "Letter from 1,500 Attorneys Says Trump Campaign Lawyers Don't Have 'License to Lie,'" *Washington Post*, December 8, 2020. On polling and elections: Gallup, "Immigration," accessed September 3, 2021, https://news.gallup.com/poll/1660/immigration.aspx.

62. Comparing 2016 and 2020, Trump gained 4 percentage points with African Americans, 3 percentage points with Hispanics and Latinos, and 5 percentage points with Asian Americans. Musa al-Gharbi, "White Men Swung to Biden. Trump Made Gains with Black and Latino Voters. Why?," *The Guardian*, November 14, 2020, https://www.theguardian.com/commentisfree/2020/nov/14/joe-biden-trump-black-latino-republicans. Biden won 87 percent of the Black vote and 66 percent of the Latino vote. Robert Kuttner, "Why Did More People of Color Vote for Trump?," *American Prospect*, January 5, 2021, https://prospect.org/politics/why-did-more-people-of-color-vote-for-trump/. Sixty percent of Asian Americans supported Biden, according to a CNN survey. Li Zhou, "What We Know about Who Asian American Voters Supported in the Election," *Vox*, November 14, 2020, https://www.vox.com/21561408/asian-american-voters-presidential-election.

## Notes to Chapter 9

1. Ross Douthat, "Beltway Panic, Wall Street Zen," *New York Times*, February 18, 2017; Jeff Stein, "Trump's 2016 Campaign Pledges on Infrastructure Have Fallen Short, Creating Opening for Biden," *Washington Post*, October 18, 2020; Brian Larkin, "The

Politics and Poetics of Infrastructure," *Annual Review of Anthropology* 42 (2013): 327–43; for Trump's use of rhetoric, see Jennifer Mercieca, *Demagogue for President: The Rhetorical Genius of Donald Trump* (College Station: Texas A&M University Press, 2020); and Roderick P. Hart, *Trump and Us: What He Says and Why People Listen* (Cambridge: Cambridge University Press, 2020).

2. Brian Stelter, "Hispanic Leaders Urge NBC to Cut Ties to Donald Trump," *CNN*, June 27, 2015, https://money.cnn.com/2015/06/27/media/donald-trump-nbc-univision/?iid=EL; Brian Stelter and Frank Pallotta, "NBCUniversal Cuts Ties with Donald Trump," *CNN*, June 30, 2015, https://money.cnn.com/2015/06/29/media/donald-trump-nbc-ends-relationship/; and Janell Ross, "From Mexican Rapists to Bad Hombres, the Trump Campaign in Two Moments," *Washington Post*, October 20, 2016; Vargas quoted in Suzanne Gamboa, "Donald Trump Announces Presidential Bid by Trashing Mexico, Mexicans," *NBC News*, June 16, 2015, https://www.nbcnews.com/news/latino/donald-trump-announces-presidential-bid-trashing-mexico-mexicans-n376521.

3. "Donald Trump Presidential Campaign Announcement," *C-SPAN*, June 16, 2015, https://www.c-span.org/video/?326473-1/donald-trump-presidential-campaign-announcement.

4. Alan Rappeport, "Donald Trump Proposes to Double Hillary Clinton's Spending on Infrastructure," *New York Times*, August 2, 2016.

5. Ben Ryan, "Infrastructure Spending Deemed Most Important Trump Promise," Gallup, January 20, 2017, https://news.gallup.com/poll/202691/infrastructure-spending-deemed-important-trump-promise.aspx?g_source=link_newsv9&g_campaign=item_249161&g_medium=copy.

6. Jason Stanley, *How Fascism Works: The Politics of Us and Them* (New York: Random House, 2018); Sarah Churchwell, "American Fascism: It Has Happened Here," *New York Review of Books*, July 22, 2020; Federico Finchelstein, *A Brief History of Fascist Lies* (Berkeley: University of California Press, 2020); and Ruth Ben-Ghiat, *Strongmen: From Mussolini to the Present* (New York: W. W. Norton, 2020). For the consequences of deindustrialization for American politics, see Judith Stein, *Pivotal Decade: How the United States Traded Factories for Finance in the Seventies* (New Haven, CT: Yale University Press, 2011); and Gabriel Winant, *The Next Shift: The Fall of Industry and the Rise of Health Care in Rust Belt America* (Cambridge, MA: Harvard University Press, 2021). For the symbolic relationship between the border wall and the idea of the frontier, see Greg Grandin, *The End of the Myth: From the Frontier to the Border Wall in the Mind of America* (New York: Metropolitan Books, 2019).

7. Brad Plumer, "Full Transcript of Donald Trump's Acceptance Speech at the RNC," *Vox*, updated July 22, 2016, https://www.vox.com/2016/7/21/12253426/donald-trump-acceptance-speech-transcript-republican-nomination-transcript.

8. "September 26, 2016 Debate Transcript," The Commission on Presidential Debates, September 26, 2016, https://www.debates.org/voter-education/debate-transcripts/september-26-2016-debate-transcript/.

9. Emily Jane Fox, "Donald Trump Calls for Unity in Surprisingly Gracious Victory Speech," *Vanity Fair*, November 9, 2016, https://www.vanityfair.com/news/2016/11/donald-trump-victory-speech.

10. Emma G. Fitzsimmons, "What Trump, Clinton, and Voters Agreed On: Better Infrastructure," *New York Times*, November 9, 2016.

11. "President Trump's Inaugural Address, Annotated," *NPR*, January 20, 2017, https://www.npr.org/2017/01/20/510629447/watch-live-president-trumps-inauguration-ceremony.

12. Katie Rogers, "How 'Infrastructure Week' Became a Long-Running Joke," *New York Times*, May 22, 2019.

13. Rogers, "How 'Infrastructure Week' Became a Long-Running Joke"; and Tim Alberta, *American Carnage: On the Front Lines of the Republican Civil War and the Rise of President Trump* (New York: HarperCollins, 2019), 466–67.

14. Elaine Kamarck and Christine Stenglein, "What Do We Need to Know about the Border Wall?," Brookings, December 6, 2019, https://www.brookings.edu/policy2020/votervital/what-do-we-need-to-know-about-the-border-wall/; "Border Wall Status," U.S. Customs and Border Patrol, January 8, 2021, https://cdn.factcheck.org/UploadedFiles/CBP-Border-Wall-Status-Paper_as-of-01082021-002.pdf. For immigration policy during the Bush and Obama presidencies, see Gary Gerstle, "Minorities, Multiculturalism, and the Presidency of George W. Bush," in *The Presidency of George W. Bush: A First Historical Assessment*, ed. Julian E. Zelizer (Princeton, NJ: Princeton University Press, 2010), 252–81; and Sarah Coleman, "A Promise Unfulfilled, an Imperfect Legacy: Obama and Immigration Policy," in *The Presidency of Barack Obama: A First Historical Assessment*, ed. Julian E. Zelizer (Princeton, NJ: Princeton University Press 2018), 179–94.

15. Peter Baker, "Trump Declares a National Emergency, and Provokes a Constitutional Clash," *New York Times*, February 15, 2019.

16. Alisa Reznick, "Indigenous Activists Protest Wall Contractor in Coolidge," *Arizona Public Media*, August 27, 2020, https://news.azpm.org/s/79680-indigenous-activists-stage-demonstration-at-wall-contractor-subsidiary-in-coolidge/; Teo Armus, "'You Don't Control the Border': Indigenous Groups Protesting Wall Construction Clash with Federal Agents," *Washington Post*, September 23, 2020; "Tohono O'Odham Condemns Use of Tear Gas at Border Wall on Protesters," *Native News Online*, October 21, 2020, https://nativenewsonline.net/currents/tohono-o-odham-condemns-use-of-tear-gas-at-border-wall-on-protesters.

17. Robert Peters et al., "Nature Divided, Scientists United: US-Mexico Border Wall Threatens Biodiversity and Binational Conservation," *Bioscience* 68 (October 2018): 740–43.

18. Kim Slowey, "12 Contractors Shortlisted for $5B of Border Wall Contracts," Construction Dive, May 13, 2019, https://www.constructiondive.com/news/12-contractors-shortlisted-for-5b-of-border-wall-contracts/554600/; and Howard Altman, "A Dozen Companies Chosen to Work on Up to $5B in Construction Projects for Trump's Border Wall," *Military Times*, May 9, 2019, https://www.militarytimes.com/news/2019/05/09/a-dozen-companies-chosen-to-work-on-up-to-5-billion-in-construction-projects-for-trumps-border-wall/.

19. Nick Miroff, "Trump's Preferred Construction Firm Lands $1.3 Billion Border Wall Contract, the Biggest So Far," *Washington Post*, May 19, 2020; Trump Jr. quoted in

Andrew Kaczynski and Em Steck, "Fact Check: Trump Knows Most People Involved in Private Border Wall Project, Despite Claiming Not To," *CNN*, August 20, 2020, https://www.cnn.com/2020/08/20/politics/fact-check-trump-private-border-wall-project/index.html.

20. Zolan Kanno-Youngs, Eric Lipton, Stephanie Saul, and Scott Shane, "How Bannon and His Indicted Business Partners Cashed In on Trump," *New York Times*, August 20, 2020; and Maggie Haberman, Kenneth P. Vogel, Eric Lipton, and Michael S. Schmidt, "With Hours Left in Office, Trump Grants Clemency to Bannon and Other Allies," *New York Times*, January 20, 2021.

21. Peter Baker, "Trump Declares a National Emergency, and Provokes a Constitutional Clash," *New York Times*, February 15, 2019; Bob Woodward, *Rage* (New York: Simon & Schuster, 2020), 145.

22. Jason Scott Smith, *Building New Deal Liberalism: The Political Economy of Public Works, 1933–1956* (New York: Cambridge University Press, 2006); Steve Fraser and Gary Gerstle, *The Rise and Fall of the New Deal Order, 1933–1980* (Princeton, NJ: Princeton University Press, 1989); Stanley, *How Fascism Works*; Churchwell, "American Fascism"; Finchelstein, *Brief History of Fascist Lies*; Ben-Ghiat, *Strongmen*.

23. S. Deborah Kang, *The INS on the Line: Making Immigration Law on the U.S.-Mexico Border, 1917–1954* (New York: Oxford University Press, 2017), 3.

24. Kristina Cooke, Mica Rosenberg, and Reade Levinson, "Exclusive: U.S. Migrant Policy Sends Thousands of Children, Including Babies, back to Mexico," Reuters, October 11, 2019, https://www.reuters.com/article/us-usa-immigration-babies-exclusive/exclusive-u-s-migrant-policy-sends-thousands-of-babies-and-toddlers-back-to-mexico-idUSKBN1WQ1H1, cited in Krista Kshatriya and S. Deborah Kang, "Walls to Protection: The Grim Reality of Trump's 'Remain in Mexico' Policy," Policy Brief, U.S. Immigration Policy Center, La Jolla, 2019.

25. Michael D. Shear and Julie Hirschfeld Davis, "Shoot Migrants' Legs, Build Alligator Moat: Behind Trump's Ideas for Border," *New York Times*, October 1, 2019.

26. David Blackbourn, *The Conquest of Nature: Water, Landscape, and the Making of Modern Germany* (New York: W. W. Norton, 2006), 274.

27. Aaron Cantú, "How Democrats Abetted Trump's Bloated Border Regime," *New Republic*, January 7, 2020, https://newrepublic.com/article/156116/democrats-abetted-trumps-bloated-border-regime; Adam Serwer, "The Cruelty Is the Point," *The Atlantic*, October 3, 2018; Jacob Soboroff, *Separated: Inside an American Tragedy* (New York: Custom House/HarperCollins, 2020). The international observer is Fintan O'Toole; see his "Trial Runs for Fascism Are in Full Flow," *Irish Times*, June 26, 2018; Gary Gerstle and Desmond King, "Spaces of Exception in American History," in *States of Exception in American History*, ed. Gary Gerstle and Joel Isaac (Chicago: University of Chicago Press, 2020), 313.

28. Peter Baker and Michael D. Shear, "El Paso Shooting Suspect's Manifesto Echoes Trump's Language," *New York Times*, August 4, 2019.

29. George L. Mosse, "Toward a General Theory of Fascism," in *Masses and Man: Nationalist and Fascist Perceptions of Reality*, ed. George L. Mosse (Detroit, MI: Wayne

State University Press, 1967), 159–96; Daniel Geary, Camilla Schofield, and Jennifer Sutton, eds., *Global White Nationalism: From Apartheid to Trump* (Manchester: Manchester University Press, 2020); Timothy Snyder, "The American Abyss," *New York Times Magazine*, January 9, 2021; Katie Benner, Alan Feuer, and Adam Goldman, "F.B.I. Finds Contact Between Proud Boys Member and Trump Associate before Riot," *New York Times*, March 5, 2021; and Associated Press, "Transcript of Trump's Speech at Rally before US Capitol Riot," *U.S. News & World Report*, January 13, 2021, https://www.usnews.com/news/politics/articles/2021-01-13/transcript-of-trumps-speech-at-rally-before-us-capitol-riot.

30. James Dobbins and Simon Romero, "Trump Seeks Respite in Texas, Where G.O.P. Allies Face Pressure," *New York Times*, January 12, 2021.

## Notes to Chapter 10

I wish to thank Yara Doumani for her invaluable research assistance in preparing this chapter.

1. R. K. Pachauri and L. A. Meyer, eds., *Climate Change 2014: Synthesis Report. Contribution of Working Groups I, II and III to the Fifth Assessment Report of the Intergovernmental Panel on Climate Change* (Geneva, Switzerland: Intergovernmental Panel on Climate Change, 2014), v.

2. Donald J. Trump's tweets of December 6, 2013 and January 29, 2014, quoted in Jeremy Schulman, "Every Insane Thing Donald Trump Has Said about Global Warming," *Mother Jones*, December 12, 2018, https://www.motherjones.com/environment/2016/12/trump-climate-timeline/.

3. Clinton quoted in Karl Mathiesen, "Hillary 'Dropped Climate Change from Speeches after Bernie Sanders Endorsement,'" *The Guardian*, September 20, 2016, https://www.theguardian.com/environment/2016/sep/20/hillary-clinton-dropped-climate-change-from-speeches-after-bernie-sanders-endorsement.

4. Donald Trump, campaign speech (Las Vegas, Nevada, June 18, 2016).

5. On this history, see Nick Estes, *Our History Is the Future: Standing Rock versus the Dakota Access Pipeline, and the Long Tradition of Indigenous Resistance* (London: Verso, 2019).

6. Adam B. Smith, "2016: A Historic Year for Billion-Dollar Weather and Climate Disasters in U.S.," Climate.gov, January 9, 2017, https://www.climate.gov/news-features/blogs/beyond-data/2016-historic-year-billion-dollar-weather-and-climate-disasters-us.

7. Theda Skocpol, "Naming the Problem: What It Will Take to Counter Extremism and Engage Americans in the Fight against Global Warming," Paper presented at the Politics of America's Fight against Global Warming symposium, Harvard University, Cambridge, MA, January 2013, 52.

8. Joshua P. Howe, *Behind the Curve: Science and the Politics of Global Warming* (Seattle: University of Washington Press, 2014), 186.

9. Philip Shabecoff, "Global Warming Has Begun, Expert Tells Senate," *New York Times*, June 24, 1988.

10. See Meg Jacobs, "Wreaking Havoc from Within: George W. Bush's Energy Policy in Historical Perspective," in *The Presidency of George W. Bush: A First Historical Assessment,* ed. Julian Zelizer (Princeton, NJ: Princeton University Press, 2010), 139–68.

11. *U.N. Framework Convention on Climate Change*, hearings of the Senate Committee on Foreign Relations, 102nd Cong. (September 19, 1992), 19.

12. Environmental Protection Agency, *Benefits and Costs of the Clean Air Act 1990–2020, the Second Prospective Study*, 2011, https://www.epa.gov/clean-air-act-overview/benefits-and-costs-clean-air-act-1990-2020-second-prospective-study.

13. Lawrence B. Glickman, *Free Enterprise: An American History* (New Haven, CT: Yale University Press, 2019), chapter 5.

14. Kate Aronoff, *Overheated* (New York: PublicAffairs, 2021), 50–51

15. "Influence & Lobbying—Oil and Gas," Center for Responsive Politics, February 1, 2021, https://www.opensecrets.org/industries/indus.php?ind=e01.

16. Naomi Oreskes and Erik M. Conway, *Merchants of Doubt: How a Handful of Scientists Obscured the Truth on Issues from Tobacco Smoke to Climate Change* (New York: Bloomsbury Press, 2011), 233.

17. On Exxon and other oil companies' internal science, see Neela Banerjee, David Hasemyer, Lisa Song, and John H. Cushman, *Exxon: The Road Not Taken* (New York: InsideClimate News, 2015).

18. R. J. Brulle, "Institutionalizing Delay: Foundation Funding and the Creation of U.S. Climate Change Counter-Movement Organizations," *Climatic Change* 122 (2014): 681–94.

19. Naomi Klein, *This Changes Everything: Capitalism vs. the Climate* (New York: Simon & Schuster, 2014), 41–42; David C. Barker and David H. Bearce, "End-Times Theology, the Shadow of the Future, and Public Resistance to Addressing Global Climate Change," *Political Research Quarterly* 66 (June 2013): 267–79.

20. Oreskes and Conway, *Merchants of Doubt*, chapter 6.

21. "2008 Republican Party Platform," American Presidency Project, September 1, 2008, https://www.presidency.ucsb.edu/documents/2008-republican-party-platform; "2012 Republican Party Platform," American Presidency Project, August 27, 2012, https://www.presidency.ucsb.edu/documents/2012-republican-party-platform.

22. Marco Rubio, quoted in Emma Foehringer Merchant, "How the 2016 Presidential Candidates View Climate Change," *New Republic,* November 29, 2015, https://newrepublic.com/article/124381/2016-presidential-candidates-view-climate-change.

23. "2016 Republican Party Platform," American Presidency Project, July 18, 2016, https://www.presidency.ucsb.edu/documents/2016-republican-party-platform.

24. Trump was more popular with the coal industry than was Clinton, but Clinton generally outraised Trump from fossil fuel interests. Judy Fahys, "Surprises in Oil and Gas Campaign Spending," *Inside Energy*, November 4, 2016, http://insideenergy.org/2016/11/04/surprises-in-oil-and-gas-campaign-spending/.

25. Ryan Zinke, quoted in Juliet Eilperin, Josh Dawsey, and Darryl Fears, "Interior Secretary Zinke Resigns amid Investigations," *Washington Post*, December 15, 2018, https://www.washingtonpost.com/national/health-science/interior-secretary-zinke-resigns-amid-investigations/2018/12/15/481f9104-0077-11e9-ad40-cdfd0e0dd65a_story.html.

26. Exec. Order No. 13,783, Promoting Energy Independence and Economic Growth (March 28, 2017).

27. Mitch McConnell, quoted in Michael D. Shear, "Trump Will Withdraw from Paris Climate Agreement," *New York Times*, June 2, 2017, https://www.nytimes.com/2017/06/01/climate/trump-paris-climate-agreement.html.

28. Michael Cox to Director Pruitt, March 31, 2017, p. 1, https://www.documentcloud.org/documents/3538076-EPACoxlet.html.

29. Chuck Schumer, "No Deal on Infrastructure without Addressing Climate Change," *Washington Post*, December 6, 2018, https://www.washingtonpost.com/opinions/chuck-schumer-mr-president-lets-make-a-deal/2018/12/06/aeae0188-f99e-11e8-8c9a-860ce2a8148f_story.html.

30. The United States District Court for the District of Montana, Great Falls Division, Indigenous Environmental Network and North Coast River Alliance v. United States Department of State and Transcanada Keystone Pipeline and Transcanada Partners, Case 4:17-cv-00029-BMM, Document 218, Filed November 8, 2018, p. 35.

31. Debra Roberts, quoted in Matthew Taylor, Matthew Weaver, and Helen Davidson, "IPCC Climate Change Report Calls for Urgent Action to Phase Out Fossil Fuels—as It Happened," *The Guardian*, October 8, 2018, https://www.theguardian.com/environment/live/2018/oct/08/ipcc-climate-change-report-urgent-action-fossil-fuels-live.

32. Donald Trump, quoted in Bill McKibben, "How Extreme Weather Is Shrinking the Planet," *New Yorker*, November 26, 2018, https://www.newyorker.com/magazine/2018/11/26/how-extreme-weather-is-shrinking-the-planet.

33. Exec. Order No. 13,855, Issuance of Permits with Respect to Facilities and Land Transportation Crossings at the International Boundaries of the United States (December 21, 2018); Exec. Order No. 13,867, Promoting Active Management of America's Forests, Rangelands, and Other Federal Lands to Improve Conditions and Reduce Wildfire Risk (January 7, 2019); and Exec. Order No. 13,868, Promoting Energy Infrastructure and Economic Growth (April 10, 2019).

34. Public Employees for Environmental Responsibility, "Criminal Enforcement Collapse at EPA," press release, January 14, 2019, https://www.peer.org/criminal-enforcement-collapse-at-epa/.

35. Scott Waldman, "Trump Officials Deleting Mentions of 'Climate Change' from U.S. Geological Survey Press Releases," *Science Magazine*, July 8, 2019, doi:10.1126/science.aay6617.

36. Department of Energy, "Department of Energy Authorizes Additional LNG Exports from Freeport LNG," press release, May 28, 2019, https://www.energy.gov/articles/department-energy-authorizes-additional-lng-exports-freeport-lng.

37. Recognizing the Duty of the Federal Government to Create a Green New Deal, H.R. Res. 109, 116th Cong., 1st Sess. (February 7, 2019), 4.

38. Myron Ebell, "CON: Green New Deal Will Be All Pain and No Gain," Competitive Enterprise Institute, February 14, 2019, https://cei.org/opeds_articles/con-green-new-deal-will-be-all-pain-and-no-gain/.

39. Donald Trump, quoted in Joseph Zeballos-Roig, "President Donald Trump Used a Speech Aimed at Touting His Environmental Record to Declare War on Alexandria Ocasio-Cortez's 'Unthinkable' Green New Deal," *Business Insider*, July 8, 2019, https://www.businessinsider.com/president-trump-declares-war-on-aoc-green-new-deal-2019-7.

40. Quoted in Ishaan Tharoor, "Trump and His Ilk Clash with the Global Climate Movement," *Washington Post*, September 23, 2019, https://www.washingtonpost.com/world/2019/09/23/trump-his-ilk-clash-with-global-climate-movement/.

41. Adam B. Smith, "2010-2019: A Landmark Decade of U.S. Billion-Dollar Weather and Climate Events," Climate.gov, January 8, 2020, https://www.climate.gov/news-features/blogs/beyond-data/2010-2019-landmark-decade-us-billion-dollar-weather-and-climate.

42. "U.S. Coal Consumption Continues to Decline across All Sectors," U.S. Energy Information Administration, June 16, 2020, https://www.eia.gov/todayinenergy/detail.php?id=44115.

43. Lauren Maunus, personal communication with author, March 1, 2021.

44. Maunus, personal communication.

45. Anthony Deutsch, "Surge in Young Republicans Worried about the Environment: Survey," Reuters, August 29, 2019, https://www.reuters.com/article/us-environment-poll-republicans/surge-in-young-republicans-worried-about-the-environment-survey-idUSKCN1VJ17V.

46. James Bruggers, "What to Make of Some Young Evangelicals Abandoning Trump over Climate Change?," Inside Climate News, September 25, 2020, https://insideclimatenews.org/news/25092020/evangelical-christian-voting-climate-change-biden-trump-2020/.

47. Kevin McCarthy, quoted in Zack Colman, Anthony Adragna, and Eric Wolfe, "House Republicans Caught between Trump and Young Voters on Climate Change," *Politico*, January 26, 2020, https://www.politico.com/news/2020/01/26/climate-change-trump-republicans-104665.

48. Donald Trump, quoted in Scott Waldman, "Trump Platform Warns of Climate 'Extremism,'" *E&E News*, August 24, 2020, https://www.eenews.net/stories/1063712301.

49. Larry Fink's letter to CEOs, BlackRock, 2020, https://www.blackrock.com/uk/individual/larry-fink-ceo-letter.

50. Cary Funk and Brian Kennedy, "How Americans See Climate Change and the Environment in 7 Charts," Pew Research Center, April 21, 2020, https://www.pewresearch.org/fact-tank/2020/04/21/how-americans-see-climate-change-and-the-environment-in-7-charts/.

51. Brian Kennedy, "Clinton, Trump Supporters Worlds Apart on Views of Climate Change and Its Scientists," Pew Research Center, October 10, 2016, https://www.pewresearch.org/fact-tank/2016/10/10/clinton-trump-supporters-worlds-apart-on-views-of-climate-change-and-its-scientists/; Alec Tyson, "How Important Is Climate Change to Voters in the 2020 Election?," Pew Research Center, October 6, 2020, https://www.pewresearch.org/fact-tank/2020/10/06/how-important-is-climate-change-to-voters-in-the-2020-election/.

52. Bill McKibben, personal communication with author, February 22, 2021.

53. Hannah Pitt, Kate Larsen, and Maggie Young, "The Undoing of US Climate Policy: The Emissions Impact of Trump-Era Rollbacks," Rhodium Group, September 17, 2020, https://rhg.com/research/the-rollback-of-us-climate-policy/.

54. Hannah Pitt, quoted in Coral Davenport, "What Will Trump's Most Profound Legacy Be? Possibly Climate Damage," *New York Times*, December 3, 2020, https://www.nytimes.com/2020/11/09/climate/trump-legacy-climate-change.html.

55. McKibben, personal communication.

56. Funk and Kennedy, "How Americans See Climate Change and the Environment in 7 Charts."

57. Maunus, personal communication; Center for Responsive Politics, "Influence & Lobbying—Oil and Gas."

58. John Schwartz and Hiroko Tabuchi, "By Calling Climate Change 'Controversial,' Barrett Created Controversy," *New York Times*, October 22, 2020, https://www.nytimes.com/2020/10/15/climate/amy-coney-barrett-climate-change.html.

## Notes to Chapter 11

1. "Here's Donald Trump's Presidential Announcement Speech," *Time*, accessed March 4, 2021, https://time.com/3923128/donald-trump-announcement-speech/.

2. Katie Zavadaski, "Everything Known about Charleston Church Shooting Suspect Dylann Roof," *The Daily Beast*, accessed March 4, 2021, https://www.thedailybeast.com/cheats/2015/06/18/charleston-suspect-is-dylann-roof."

3. David Jackson, "Trump Claims He's Least Racist Person, Says Biden Is Democrat Favorite," *USA Today*, accessed June 18, 2021, https://www.usatoday.com/story/news/politics/2019/07/30/trump-claims-hes-least-racist-person-says-biden-democrat-favorite/1858853001/.

4. Ali Vitali, Kasie Hunt, Frank V. Thorp, "Trump Referred to Haiti and African Nations as 'Shithole' Countries," *NBC News*, accessed March 6, 2021, https://www.nbcnews.com/politics/white-house/trump-referred-haiti-african-countries-shithole-nations-n836946.

5. Tara Golshan, "Trump Uses Untruthful Tweets to Take a Hard Line against DACA Deal," *Vox*, January 12, 2018, https://www.vox.com/policy-and-politics/2018/1/12/16882482/trump-daca-tweets-hard-line-daca-deal.

6. Allan Smith, "Mulvaney after New Zealand Massacre: Trump 'Not a White Supremacist,'" *NBC News*, accessed March 6, 2021, https://www.nbcnews.com

/politics/donald-trump/mulvaney-after-new-zealand-massacre-trump-not-white-supremacist-n984191.

7. Lauren Villagran, "El Paso Shooting: Suspect's Writing Similar to Trump Facebook Ads," *El Paso Times*, accessed March 6, 2021, https://www.elpasotimes.com/story/news/2019/08/06/el-paso-shooting-patrick-crusius-manifesto-immigration-hispanics-trump-facebook-ads/1928238001/.

8. Zolan Kanno-Youngs, "Homeland Security Dept. Affirms Threat of White Supremacy after Years of Prodding," *New York Times*, accessed June 18, 2021, https://www.nytimes.com/2019/10/01/us/politics/white-supremacy-homeland-security.html.

9. Clare Foran, "An Erosion of Democratic Norms in America," *The Atlantic*, November 22, 2016, https://www.theatlantic.com/politics/archive/2016/11/donald-trump-democratic-norms/508469/. This article is only one example of a litany that point to the "norm erosion" that came to be identified with Trump's style of political intervention.

10. Morgan Chalfant, "Donald Trump: 'I'm Not a Politician, Thank Goodness,'" *Washington Examiner*, accessed June 18, 2021, https://www.washingtonexaminer.com/red-alert-politics/donald-trump-im-not-politician-thank-goodness.

11. KETV Staff Report, "'I'm Not a Politician': President Trump Speaks to 25,000 at Omaha Rally," KETV, October 28, 2020, https://www.ketv.com/article/president-trump-to-host-rally-in-omaha/34466020.

12. Rick Perlstein, "Exclusive: Lee Atwater's Infamous 1981 Interview on the Southern Strategy," *The Nation*, November 13, 2012, http://www.thenation.com/article/170841/exclusive-lee-atwaters-infamous-1981-interview-southern-strategy. "You start out in 1954 by saying, 'Nigger, nigger, nigger.' By 1968 you can't say 'nigger'—that hurts you, backfires. So you say stuff like, uh, forced busing, states' rights, and all that stuff, and you're getting so abstract. Now, you're talking about cutting taxes, and all these things you're talking about are totally economic things and a byproduct of them is, blacks get hurt worse than whites. . . . 'We want to cut this,' is much more abstract than even the busing thing, uh, and a hell of a lot more abstract than 'Nigger, nigger.'"

13. Richard Nixon, "Address Accepting the Presidential Nomination at the Republican National Convention in Miami Beach, Florida August 8, 1968" accessed June 4, 2013, http://www.presidency.ucsb.edu/ws/?pid=25968.

14. Nixon, "Address Accepting the Presidential Nomination."

15. Rick Perlstein, *The Invisible Bridge: The Fall of Nixon and the Rise of Reagan* (Simon and Schuster, 2014); Rick Perlstein, *Reaganland: America's Right Turn 1976–1980* (Simon and Schuster, 2020).

16. Richard Nixon, "Statement about Federal Policies Relative to Equal Housing Opportunity," accessed April 10, 2013, http://www.presidency.ucsb.edu/ws/?pid=3042; Keeanga-Yamahtta Taylor, *From #BlackLivesMatter to Black Liberation* (Chicago: Haymarket Books, 2016); Matthew D. Lassiter, *The Silent Majority: Suburban Politics in the Sunbelt South* (Princeton, NJ: Princeton University Press, 2007); Kevin M. Kruse, *White Flight: Atlanta and the Making of Modern Conservatism* (Princeton, NJ: Princeton University Press, 2007); Julilly Kohler-Hausmann, *Getting Tough: Welfare and Imprisonment in 1970s America* (Princeton, NJ: Princeton University Press, 2017).

17. "Address to the Nation on Domestic Programs August 8, 1969," The American Presidency Project, accessed June 18, 2021, https://www.presidency.ucsb.edu/documents/address-the-nation-domestic-programs.

18. Richard Nixon, "Address to the Nation on Domestic Programs," August 8, 1969, Online by Gerhard Peters and John T. Woolley, The American Presidency Project, https://www.presidency.ucsb.edu/node/239998.

19. Kohler-Hausmann, *Getting Tough*, 122.

20. Keeanga-Yamahtta Taylor, *Race for Profit: How Banks and the Real Estate Industry Undermined Black Homeownership* (Chapel Hill: University of North Carolina Press Books, 2019); Marisa Chappell, *The War on Welfare: Family, Poverty, and Politics in Modern America* (Philadelphia: University of Pennsylvania Press, 2010); Kohler-Hausmann, *Getting Tough*.

21. "Remarks at the Annual Meeting of the International Association of Chiefs of Police in New Orleans, Louisiana September 28, 1981," Ronald Reagan Presidential Library, accessed August 20, 2021, https://www.reaganlibrary.gov/archives/speech/remarks-annual-meeting-international-association-chiefs-police-new-orleans.

22. Fred Hiatt, "Oct. 1, 1981: That Day Is Finally Here—Reagan's Budget Cuts Begin," *Washington Post*, October 1, 1981, accessed June 18, 2021, https://www.washingtonpost.com/archive/politics/1981/10/01/oct-1-1981-that-day-is-finally-here-reagans-budget-cuts-begin/c4872e17-43c4-46a6-8d4e-6804027678c0/.

23. Kim Phillips-Fein, Gil Troy, and Vincent J. Cannato, "Reaganomics: The Rebirth of the Free Market," in *Living in the Eighties* (New York: Oxford University Press, 2009), 125–36.

24. Ed Kilgore, "On Crime Policy, Biden Worked Closely with His Segregationist Friends," *Intelligencer*, June 26, 2019, https://nymag.com/intelligencer/2019/06/on-crime-biden-worked-closely-with-his-segregationist-pals.html.

25. Sam Stein, "'A Racist Narrative': Biden Warned of Welfare Moms Driving Luxury Cars," *Daily Beast*, August 29, 2019, sec. politics, https://www.thedailybeast.com/when-joe-biden-worried-about-welfare-mothers-driving-luxury-cars.

26. Danny Glover and Harry Belafonte, "Belafonte and Glover Speak Out on Katrina," AlterNet, September 22, 2005, http://www.alternet.org/story/25862/belafonte_%26_glover_speak_out_on_katrina.

27. Elizabeth Kai Hinton, *America on Fire the Untold History of Police Violence and Black Rebellion since the 1960s* (New York: Liveright, a division of W.W. Norton, 2021), https://api.overdrive.com/v1/collections/v1L1BmUAAAA2X/products/9d8aeca5-39b2-44bb-b59e-8ce4adf2a730.

28. Byron Tau, "Obama: 'I'm Not the President of Black America,'" *Politico*, accessed March 28, 2015, http://www.politico.com/politico44/2012/08/obama-im-not-the-president-of-black-america-131351.html."

29. "Before the State of the Union, a Fact Check on Black Unemployment," Economic Policy Institute (blog), accessed June 13, 2021, https://www.epi.org/blog/before-the-state-of-the-union-a-fact-check-on-black-unemployment/.

30. Terence Ball, Richard Dagger, and Daniel I. O'Neill, "A Vision for Black Lives: Policy Demands for Black Power, Freedom, and Justice," in *Ideals and Ideologies*, 11th ed. (New York: Routledge, 2019), 391–99.

31. F. Brinley Bruton, Alexander Smith, Elizabeth Chuck, and Phil Helsel, "Dallas Police 'Ambush': 12 Officers Shot, 5 Killed during Protest," *NBC News*, July, 7, 2016, accessed June 14, 2021, https://www.nbcnews.com/storyline/dallas-police-ambush/protests-spawn-cities-across-u-s-over-police-shootings-black-n605686; Keeanga-Yamahtta Taylor, "After Dallas, Black Lives Matter Is More Important than Ever," *The Guardian*, July 11, 2016, http://www.theguardian.com/commentisfree/2016/jul/11/dallas-black-lives-matter-protests.

32. Hillary Clinton, "Breaking Down Barriers for African Americans," *Medium*, May 10, 2016, https://medium.com/hillary-for-america/breaking-down-barriers-for-african-americans-d444f1c568b6.

33. "Paul Ryan Clarifies 'Inarticulate' Remarks on Inner Cities," *BBC News*, March 13, 2014, sec. US and Canada, https://www.bbc.com/news/world-us-canada-26564949.

34. *Politico* staff, "Full Text: Donald Trump 2016 RNC Draft Speech Transcript," *Politico*, accessed June 14, 2021, http://politi.co/2ApcBDB.

35. "Full Text of Trump's Executive Order on 7-Nation Ban, Refugee Suspension," *CNN Politics*, accessed June 19, 2021, https://www.cnn.com/2017/01/28/politics/text-of-trump-executive-order-nation-ban-refugees/index.html.

36. Jane C. Timm, "What's Happening with Donald Trump's Border Wall?," *NBC News*, accessed June 19, 2021, https://www.nbcnews.com/politics/donald-trump/donald-trump-s-border-wall-progress-report-n764726.

37. Vanessa Williamson and Isabella Gelfand, "Trump and Racism: What Do the Data Say?," Brookings (blog), August 14, 2019, https://www.brookings.edu/blog/fixgov/2019/08/14/trump-and-racism-what-do-the-data-say/.

38. "Black Americans Still Are Victims of Hate Crimes More than Any Other Group," Center for Public Integrity, accessed June 19, 2021, https://publicintegrity.org/politics/black-americans-still-are-victims-of-hate-crimes-more-than-any-other-group/.

39. Wilborn Nobles, "Trump Calls Baltimore 'Disgusting . . . Rodent Infested Mess,' Rips Rep. Elijah Cummings over Border Criticism," *Baltimore Sun*, July 27, 2019, https://www.baltimoresun.com/politics/bs-md-pol-cummings-trump-20190727-chty2yovtvfzfcjkeaui7wm5zi-story.html.

## Notes to Chapter 12

1. Graham Ruddick, "Amazon v Donald Trump: Jeff Bezos May Soon Face His Biggest Challenge Yet," *The Guardian*, November 18, 2016, archived at https://perma.cc/4L32-4A2G; Ted Johnson, "Just Which Outlets Are Trump's 'Enemy'? By His Estimation, Many," *Variety*, October 29, 2018, archived at https://perma.cc/TEK5-YHCU.

2. "Here's How Seattle Voters' Support for Trump Compared to Other Cities'," *Seattle Times*, November 17, 2016, archived at https://perma.cc/9R47-EFCG.

3. David Streitfeld, "'I'm Here to Help,' Trump Tells Executives at Meeting," *New York Times*, December 14, 2016, archived at https://perma.cc/255A-FR3L; Donald J. Trump, interview with the author (via Zoom), July 1, 2021.

4. "Tim Cook Explains to Apple Employees Why He Met with President-Elect Trump," *TechCrunch*, December 19, 2016, archived at https://perma.cc/W4BU-N9ST.

5. Jeffrey Gottfried, Michael Barthel, Elisa Shearer, and Amy Mitchell, "The 2016 Presidential Campaign—a News Event That's Hard to Miss," Pew Research Center, February 4, 2016, archived at https://perma.cc/2TTS-A2LP.

6. "How the Internet Invented Howard Dean," *WIRED*, January 1, 2004, archived at https://perma.cc/29V5-RG8P.

7. Margaret O'Mara, *The Code: Silicon Valley and the Remaking of America* (New York: Penguin Press, 2019), 368–74.

8. Brian Stelter, "The Facebooker Who Friended Obama," *New York Times*, July 8, 2008, archived at https://perma.cc/9XHA-N3N7.

9. Social scientists and other media scholars were among the first to identify this transformation and its political and social consequences. See, for example, Zeynep Tufekci, *Twitter and Tear Gas: The Power and Fragility of Networked Protest* (New Haven, CT: Yale University Press, 2018); Siva Vaidhyanathan, *Antisocial Media: How Facebook Disconnects Us and Undermines Democracy* (New York: Oxford University Press, 2018); Ruha Benjamin, *Race after Technology: Abolitionist Tools for the New Jim Code* (Medford, MA: Polity, 2019); Meredith Broussard, *Artificial Unintelligence: How Computers Misunderstand the World* (Cambridge, MA: MIT, 2019); Sarah T. Roberts, *Behind the Screen: Content Moderation in the Shadows of Social Media* (New Haven, CT: Yale University Press, 2019).

10. Sara Polak, "'#Unpresidented': The Making of the First Twitter President," in *Violence and Trolling on Social Media: History, Affect, and Effects of Online Vitriol*, ed. Sara Polak and Daniel Trotter (Amsterdam: Amsterdam University Press, 2020), 65–84.

11. Katherine Haenschen and Jordan Wolf, "Disclaiming Responsibility: How Platforms Deadlocked the Federal Election Commission's Efforts to Regulate Digital Political Advertising," *Telecommunications Policy* 43, no. 8 (2019): 101824, https://doi.org/10.1016/j.telpol.2019.04.008; Anna Lauren Hoffman, Nicholas Proferes, and Michael Zimmer, "'Making the World More Open and Connected': Mark Zuckerberg and the Discursive Construction of Facebook and Its Users," *New Media & Society* 20, no. 1 (2018), https://doi.org/10.1177%2F1461444816660784. The full scope and content of 2016 campaign advertising on Facebook will never be known; until forced by public pressure to do so in 2018, the company maintained no archive of the ads that ran on its platform.

12. Casey Newton, "Zuckerberg: The Idea That Fake News on Facebook Influenced the Election Is 'Crazy,'" *The Verge*, November 10, 2016, https://www.theverge.com/2016/11/10/13594558/mark-zuckerberg-election-fake-news-trump. A year later,

Zuckerberg expressed regret for the statement. Parscale quote from Andrew Marantz, "#Winning," *New Yorker*, March 2, 2020, online edition archived at https://perma.cc/9YMX-ZHBK.

13. On numbers of tweets, see Adilbek Madaminov, "All the President's Tweets," *Medium*, November 24, 2020, archived at https://perma.cc/manage/create?folder=8288-46493. On Trump's media strategy, see Pablo J. Bockowski and Zizi Papacharissi, eds., *Trump and the Media* (Cambridge, MA: MIT Press, 2018). On the modern history of political communication and use of mass media, see David Greenberg, *Republic of Spin: An Inside History of the American Presidency* (New York: W. W. Norton, 2016). On Kennedy and television, see W. J. Rorabaugh, *The Real Making of the President: Kennedy, Nixon, and the 1960 Election* (Lawrence: University Press of Kansas, 2017).

14. Sapna Mahestwari, "On YouTube Kids, Startling Videos Slip Past Filters," *New York Times*, November 4, 2017, archived at https://perma.cc/M4UX-QFAH; Nicholas Thompson and Fred Vogelstein, "15 Months of Fresh Hell Inside Facebook," *WIRED*, April 16, 2019, archived at https://perma.cc/R2QQ-BQP2.

15. "Transcript of Mark Zuckerberg's Senate Hearing," *Washington Post*, April 10, 2018, archived at https://perma.cc/8GGL-EGE6.

16. Gene Balk, "More than Half of Seattle's Software Developers Were Born outside the U.S.," *Seattle Times*, January 19, 2018, archived at https://perma.cc/4GCM-98V9.

17. Exec. Order No. 13,769, Protecting the Nation from Foreign Terrorist Entry into the United States (January 27, 2017).

18. T. C. Sottek, "Google Co-founder Sergey Brin Joins Protest against Immigration Order at San Francisco Airport," *The Verge*, January 28, 2017, archived at https://perma.cc/NM4S-XJRH; Vauhini Vara, "The Tech Resistance to the Trump Refugee Ban," *New Yorker*, January 31, 2017, archived at https://perma.cc/JW38-M5MG.

19. Ina Fried, "Report Blasts Palantir for ICE Work, Trump Ties," *Axios*, August 8, 2019, archived at https://perma.cc/J3U4-48M2.

20. Letter to Sundar Pichai, April 4, 2018, archived at https://perma.cc/BJ98-D6Y6.

21. Nitasha Tiku, "Amazon's Jeff Bezos Says Tech Companies Should Work with the Pentagon," *WIRED*, October 15, 2018, archived at https://perma.cc/manage/create?folder=8288.

22. Kif Leswig and Andrea Miller, "How Apple CEO Tim Cook Charmed Donald Trump," *CNBC*, November 8, 2019, archived at https://perma.cc/NN5Q-K3XS; Russell Brandom, "Trump's Tariffs Are Aimed at China, but Apple Is in the Line of Fire," *The Verge*, June 25, 2019, archived at https://perma.cc/ECK2-ZDWP. Apple's use of global supply chains is explored further in Brian Merchant, *The One Device: The Secret History of the iPhone* (New York: Little, Brown, 2017).

23. Trump, interview with the author (via Zoom), July 1, 2021.

24. Ana Swanson and Mike Isaac, "Trump Reverses Course on TikTok, Opening Door to Microsoft Bid," *New York Times*, August 3, 2020, archived at https://perma.cc/L6YJ-23NP.

25. John D. McKinnon and Alex Leary, "TikTok Sale to Oracle, Walmart Shelved as Biden Reviews Security," *Wall Street Journal*, February 10, 2021, archived at https://perma.cc/P25U-323Q; Katie Rogers and Cecilia Kang, "Biden Revokes and Replaces Trump Order That Banned TikTok," *New York Times*, June 9, 2021, archived at https://perma.cc/8CWA-7N4N.

26. Monica Nickelsberg, "Tech Industry Cheers GOP Tax Overhaul," *Geekwire*, December 20, 2017, archived at https://perma.cc/R8LN-3U3R.

27. Matt Phillips, "Investors Bet Giant Companies Will Dominate after Crisis," *New York Times*, April 28, 2020, archived at https://perma.cc/EKE3-Q4BH.

28. Emily Birnbaum, "A Few of the Big Questions Big Tech CEOs Didn't Answer," *Protocol*, July 29, 2020, archived at https://perma.cc/C77Y-RH2T; Margaret O'Mara, "The Last Days of the Tech Emperors?," *New York Times*, July 30, 2020, archived at https://perma.cc/QE4C-4H89; U.S. House of Representatives, Subcommittee on Antitrust, Commercial and Administrative Law, Committee on the Judiciary, *Investigation of Competition in Digital Markets*, October 2020.

29. Trump on CNBC's *Squawk Box*, quoted in Aaron Rupar, "Trump's Interested in Breaking Up Big Tech for All the Wrong Reasons," *Vox*, June 10, 2019, archived at https://perma.cc/FT2X-AXPW.

30. On tech's antiunion history, see Margaret O'Mara, "The High-Tech Revolution and the Disruption of American Capitalism," in *Capitalism Contested: The New Deal and Its Legacies*, ed. Romain Huret, Nelson Lichtenstein, and Jean-Christian Vinel (Philadelphia: University of Pennsylvania Press, 2020), 199–223.

31. Lena V. Groeger, Jeff Kao, Al Shaw, Moiz Syed, Maya Eliahou, et al., "What Parler Saw during the Attack on the Capitol," *ProPublica*, January 17, 2021, archived at https://perma.cc/Q4HU-G8RD.

## Notes to Chapter 13

1. Maggie Haberman and David E. Sanger, "Transcript: Donald Trump Expounds on His Foreign Policy Views," *New York Times*, March 26, 2016.

2. Haberman and Sanger, "Transcript: Donald Trump Expounds on His Foreign Policy Views."

3. Presidential statements drawn from the University of California, Santa Barbara, The American Presidency Project (hereafter cited as TAPP with date). For "rust," see "Remarks on Foreign Policy," TAPP, April 27, 2016, https://www.presidency.ucsb.edu/documents/remarks-foreign-policy.

4. "Remarks by President Biden on America's Place in the World," White House, February 4, 2021, https://www.whitehouse.gov/briefing-room/speeches-remarks/2021/02/04/remarks-by-president-biden-on-americas-place-in-the-world/.

5. Carl Bildt, "After Trump, Can America Be Trusted Again?," *Project Syndicate*, January 20, 2021.

6. Ivan Krastev and Mark Leonard, "The Crisis of American Power," *European Council of Foreign Relations*, January 9, 2021.

7. "Remarks on Foreign Policy," TAPP.

8. "Remarks at the Conservative Political Action Conference in National Harbor, Maryland," TAPP, February 24, 2017, https://www.presidency.ucsb.edu/documents/remarks-the-conservative-political-action-conference-national-harbor-maryland.

9. Neta Crawford, "The Iraq War Has Cost the US Nearly $2 Trillion," *Defense One*, February 4, 2020.

10. "Remarks at a 'Make America Great Again' Rally in Melbourne, Florida," TAPP, February 18, 2017, https://www.presidency.ucsb.edu/documents/remarks-make-america-great-again-rally-melbourne-florida.

11. "Remarks on United States Relations with Asian Nations," TAPP, November 15, 2017, https://www.presidency.ucsb.edu/documents/remarks-united-states-relations-with-asian-nations.

12. "Inaugural Address," TAPP, January 20, 2017, https://www.presidency.ucsb.edu/documents/inaugural-address-14.

13. White House, National Security Strategy of the United States of America, December 2017, https://trumpwhitehouse.archives.gov/wp-content/uploads/2017/12/NSS-Final-12-18-2017-0905.pdf, 11.

14. On the concept of a "free world," see Dominic Tierney, "What Does It Mean That Trump Is 'Leader of the Free World,'?" *The Atlantic*, January 24, 2017.

15. "Address to Congress on the Yalta Conference," TAPP, March 1, 1945, https://www.presidency.ucsb.edu/documents/address-congress-the-yalta-conference.

16. "Remarks at the Fort Pitt Chapter, Association of the United States Army, May 3, 1961," Eisenhower Presidential Library, Museum, and Boyhood Home, accessed March 12, 2021, https://www.eisenhowerlibrary.gov/eisenhowers/quotes.

17. "Inaugural Address," TAPP, January 20, 1961, https://www.presidency.ucsb.edu/documents/inaugural-address-2.

18. For "indispensable nation" and Obama, see "Commencement Address at the United States Military Academy in West Point, New York," TAPP, May 28, 2014, https://www.presidency.ucsb.edu/documents/commencement-address-the-united-states-military-academy-west-point-new-york-3. Bill Clinton deployed the phrase "indispensable nation" frequently during his presidency. See, for example, "Remarks Announcing the Second Term National Security Team and an Exchange with Reporters," TAPP, December 5, 1996, https://www.presidency.ucsb.edu/documents/remarks-announcing-the-second-term-national-security-team-and-exchange-with-reporters.

19. "Visit of Prime Minister James Callaghan of Great Britain Remarks of the President and the Prime Minister at the Welcoming Ceremony," TAPP, March 10, 1977, https://www.presidency.ucsb.edu/documents/visit-prime-minister-james-callaghan-great-britain-remarks-the-president-and-the-prime.

20. "Inaugural Address," TAPP, January 20, 2017, https://www.presidency.ucsb.edu/documents/inaugural-address-14.

21. "Remarks to United States Troops at Al Asad Air Base in Al Anbar Province, Iraq," TAPP, December 26, 2018, https://www.presidency.ucsb.edu/documents/remarks-united-states-troops-al-asad-air-base-al-anbar-province-iraq.

22. "Remarks on Foreign Policy," TAPP, April 27, 2016, https://www.presidency.ucsb.edu/documents/remarks-foreign-policy.

23. Nolan McCaskill, "Trump Adviser: Don't Take Trump Literally, 'Take Him Symbolically,'" *Politico*, December 12, 2016.

24. Tom Phillips, "Chinese President Xi Jinping Arrives for First Meeting with Donald Trump," *The Guardian*, March 11, 2017.

25. "Remarks on Foreign Policy," TAPP, April 27, 2016, https://www.presidency.ucsb.edu/documents/remarks-foreign-policy.

26. "For diplomacy to be effective, words must be credible," President George W. Bush explained in words his predecessors, Democrats and Republicans alike, would have readily adopted. "And no one can doubt the word of America." "Address before a Joint Session of the Congress on the State of the Union," TAPP, January 20, 2004, https://www.presidency.ucsb.edu/documents/address-before-joint-session-the-congress-the-state-the-union-24.

27. For "central concept," see Richard Ned Lebow, "The Role of Trust in International Relations," *GlobalAsia* 8, no. 3 (September 2013): https://globalasia.org/v8no3/cover/the-role-of-trust-in-international-relations_richard-ned-lebow.

28. Reagan's overuse of the phrase "trust but verify," which his aides clumsily translated from a Russian proverb, annoyed the Soviet Union's Mikhail Gorbachev. See David E. Hoffman, *The Dead Hand* (New York: Doubleday, 2009), 261.

29. Robert H. Scales Jr., "Trust, Not Technology, Sustains Coalitions," *Parameters* 28, no. 3 (1998): 4–10.

30. Michael Kruse, "The Loneliest President," *Politico*, September 16, 2017.

31. Jesse Byrnes, "Trump's Top Foreign Policy Advisor? 'I'm Speaking with Myself,'" *The Hill*, March 6, 2016.

32. "Full Transcript of Trump's Phone Call with Australian Prime Minister Malcolm Turnbull on 28 January, 2017," *The Guardian*, August 3, 2017.

33. "Full Transcript of Trump's Phone Call with Australian Prime Minister Malcolm Turnbull on 28 January, 2017."

34. "Full Transcript of Trump's Phone Call with Australian Prime Minister Malcolm Turnbull on 28 January, 2017."

35. Robert D. Blackwill, "Trump's Foreign Policies Are Better than They Seem," *Council on Foreign Relations*, April 1, 2019, 2.

36. Trump offered his thoughts on being "presidential" numerous times in office, and as a standard element of his lengthy and (somewhat) unscripted public rallies. For the example above, see Jill Colvin, "Rally Shows Free-Wheeling, Media-Bashing Trump Here to Stay," Associated Press, March 11, 2018.

37. Doyle McManus, "The Trump Doctrine Is Simple: Allies Can't Trust Him," *Los Angeles Times*, October 9, 2019.

38. Michael Fuchs, "Donald Trump's Doctrine of Unpredictability Has the World on Edge," *The Guardian*, February 13, 2017.

39. "British PM May Says She Does Not Agree with Trump on Immigration," Reuters, January 28, 2017.

40. "Merkel Critical of US Immigration Ban, Spokesman Tells Spiegel," Reuters, January 29, 2017.

41. Anthony Bond, "Foreign Secretary Boris Johnson Calls Donald Trump's 'Muslim Ban' . . . ," *Daily Mirror*, January 29, 2017.

42. Mark Lander, "Trump Abandons Iran Nuclear Deal He Long Scorned," *New York Times*, May 8, 2018.

43. Lander, "Trump Abandons Iran Nuclear Deal He Long Scorned."

44. Emmanuel Macron, Twitter, May 8, 2018, @emmanuelmacron, https://twitter.com/EmmanuelMacron/status/993920765060878336. For "deeply concerned," see United Nations Meetings Coverage and Press Releases, "Secretary-General 'Deeply Concerned' by United States Announcement on Withdrawing from Iran Nuclear Agreement, Calls on Other Parties to Fulfil Commitments," May 8, 2018, https://www.un.org/press/en/2018/sgsmn19022.doc.htm.

45. Ishaan Tharoor, "Biden Faces a Relieved but Cautious Europe," *Washington Post*, February 4, 2021.

46. May Kay Linge, "Why Obama Got a Nobel Prize for Nothing—and Trump Never Will for Anything," *New York Post*, November 2, 2019.

47. Corney Flintoff, "Policy Experts: Obama's Potential Led to Peace Prize," *National Public Radio*, October 9, 2009.

48. Geir Lundestad, *The World's Most Prestigious Prize* (New York: Oxford University Press, 2019), 102.

49. Corazon Miller, "Trump Complains He Would Get Nobel Peace Prize 'If They Gave It out Fairly,'" *The Independent*, September 24, 2019.

50. Geir Lundestad, "Empire by Invitation? The United States and Western Europe, 1945-1952," *Journal of Peace Research* 23, no. 3 (1986): 263–77. See also Lundestad, *"Empire" by Integration: The United States and European Integration, 1945–1997* (New York: Oxford University Press, 1998).

51. "Trump Worries NATO with 'Obsolete' Comment," *BBC News*, January 16, 2017. Trump subsequently walked the statement back but then reinforced concern by "neglecting" a line in his prepared remarks at a NATO summit reaffirming his country's commitment to the organization. See Peter Baker, "Trump Commits United States to Defending NATO Nations," *New York Times*, June 9, 2017.

52. Adam Bienkov, "Theresa May's Speech to the Republican 'Congress of Tomorrow' Conference," *Business Insider*, January 26, 2017.

53. "President Bush Welcomes Seven Nations to NATO Alliance," TAPP, March 29, 2004, https://www.presidency.ucsb.edu/documents/remarks-ceremony-honoring-seven-nations-their-accession-the-north-atlantic-treaty.

54. "Press Conference by President Obama after NATO Summit," TAPP, July 9, 2016, https://www.presidency.ucsb.edu/documents/the-presidents-news-conference-warsaw-poland.

55. Julie Johnson, "At NATO Parley, Regan Reassures," *New York Times*, March 2, 1988.

56. Ashley Parker, "Trump Willing to Break Up NATO," *Atlantic Council*, April 4, 2016.

57. Michael Creswell and Victor Gavin, "A History of Vexation: Trump's Bashing of NATO Is Nothing New," *War on the Rocks*, August 22, 2017.

58. Creswell and Gavin, "A History of Vexation."

59. Stephen Collinson, "Trump Is Not the First US President to Bemoan NATO Spending . . . but No One Did It Like This," *CNN.com*, July 4, 2018, https://www.cnn.com/2018/07/04/politics/trump-us-presidents-nato-defense-spending/index.html.

60. "Transcript: Obama Addresses NATO Strength at March 26 News Conference in Brussels," *Washington Post*, March 26, 2014.

61. "Transcript: Democratic Presidential Debate in Brooklyn," *New York Times*, April 15, 2016.

62. Kevin Liptak, "Obama Huddles with NATO Leader as Trump Derides Alliance," *CNN.com*, April 4, 2016, https://www.cnn.com/2016/04/04/politics/obama-nato-jens-stoltenberg-trump/index.html.

63. Lorne Cooke and Angela Charlton, "NATO Leaders Meet under Intense Trump Pressure on Spending," Associated Press, May 25, 2017.

64. Michael Birnbaum, "After Trump Leaves NATO Summit . . . ," *Washington Post*, December 5, 2019.

65. Glenn Kessler, "Trump's NATO Parade of Falsehoods and Misstatements," *Washington Post*, December 10, 2019.

66. Kessler, "Trump's NATO Parade of Falsehoods and Misstatements."

67. Lucie Beraud-Sundreau and Nick Childs, "The US and Its NATO Allies: Costs and Value," International Institute for Strategic Studies, Military Balance Blog, July 9, 2018, https://www.iiss.org/blogs/military-balance/2018/07/us-and-nato-allies-costs-and-value.

68. Sundreau and Childs, "The US and its NATO Allies."

69. Lucie Beraud-Sundreau, "On the Up: Western Defence Spending in 2018," International Institute for Strategic Studies, Military Balance Blog, February 15, 2019, https://www.iiss.org/blogs/military-balance/2019/02/european-nato-defence-spending-up.

70. Beraud-Sundreau, "On the Up."

71. Julie Hirschfield Davis, "Trump Warns NATO Allies to Spend More on Defense, or Else," *New York Times*, July 2, 2018.

72. David E. Sanger and Maggie Haberman, "Donald Trump Sets Conditions for Defending NATO Allies against Attack," *New York Times*, July 20, 2016.

73. For an excellent overview of NATO relations across decades, see Timothy Andrews Sayle, *Enduring Alliance: A History of NATO and the Postwar Global Order* (Ithaca, NY: Cornell University Press, 2019).

74. Editorial Board, "Obama on Foreign Affairs," *Los Angeles Times*, January 17, 2009.

75. Blackwill, "Trump's Foreign Policies Are Better than They Seem," 31.

76. Victor Davis Hanson, "Is America to Be 1st, 2nd, or What?," *Telegraph Herald*, December 3, 2020.

77. Jonathan Kirshner, "Gone but Not Forgotten," *Foreign Affairs*, March/April 2021, 26.

78. Phil Stewart, "In NATO Debut, Biden's Pentagon Aims to Rebuild Trust Damaged by Trump," Reuters, February 15, 2021.

79. Stewart, "In NATO Debut."

## Notes to Chapter 14

1. Testimony of Anthony Blinken to Senate Foreign Relations Committee, January 19, 2021.

2. Quoted in Anthony Esquerra, "No, Biden Doesn't Have a Chinese Handler," *Vice*, January 22, 2021, https://www.vice.com/en/article/5dpjqk/no-biden-doesnt-have-a-chinese-handler-hes-a-us-secret-service-agent.

3. Mohamed Younis, "China, Russia Images in U.S. Hit Historic Lows," Gallup, March 1, 2021, https://news.gallup.com/poll/331082/china-russia-images-hit-historic-lows.aspx.

4. Paulson: David Ignatius, "The Global Establishment's Advice for Joe Biden," *Washington Post*, November 20, 2020, https://www.washingtonpost.com/opinions/the-global-establishments-advice-for-joe-biden/2020/11/12/4adfdede-2529-11eb-8672-c281c7a2c96e_story.html; Haass: appearance before Council on Foreign Relations, January 6, 2021 (author's notes); Friedman: Kevin Stankiewicz, "Trump Is the President That China Deserves, says New York Times' Thomas Friedman," *CNBC*, last updated September 1, 2020, https://www.cnbc.com/2020/09/01/new-york-times-columnist-thomas-friedman-donald-trump-is-us-president-china-deserves.html.

5. A few commentators have suggested that the notion of engagement began with Richard Nixon's opening to China. But Nixon and his immediate successors were preoccupied with keeping China as a partner in the Cold War with the Soviet Union, and at the time, China's domestic politics was of vastly lesser concern. It remained so until after the events of 1989.

6. See, for example, letter from President George H. W. Bush to House of Representatives, March 2, 1992, in Public Papers of the Presidents of the United States, George H. W. Bush, Book I, p. 363.

7. Francis Fukuyama, "The End of History?," *National Interest*, Summer 1989, 2–18.

8. Clinton press conference with Jiang Zemin, October 29, 1997; George W. Bush, "A Distinctly American Internationalism" (speech at Reagan Presidential Library, Simi Valley, California, November 19, 1999).

9. David H. Autor, David Dorn, and Gordon H. Hanson, "The China Syndrome: Local Labor Market Effects of Import Competition in the United States," *American Economic Review* 103, no. 6 (October 2013): 2121–68.

10. Lingling Wei, Bob Davis, and Dawn Lim, "China Has One Powerful Friend Left in the U.S.: Wall Street," *Wall Street Journal*, December 3, 2020, 1.

11. See David Wessel, "Free-Trade Winds May Be Picking Up Again," *Wall Street Journal*, July 1, 2010, A-2.

12. Kurt M. Campbell and Ely Ratner, "The China Reckoning: How Beijing Defied American Expectations," *Foreign Affairs*, March/April 2018.

13. James Mann, *About Face: A History of America's Curious Relationship with China* (New York: Alfred A. Knopf, 1999), 176.

14. See Suzanne Craig, Jo Becker, and Jesse Drucker, "Jared Kushner, a Trump In-law and Adviser, Chases a China Deal," *New York Times*, January 8, 2017, A-1.

15. "Remarks by President Trump at Signing of the U.S.-China Phase One Trade Agreement," White House, January 15, 2020, https://trumpwhitehouse.archives.gov/briefings-statements/remarks-president-trump-signing-u-s-china-phase-one-trade-agreement-2/.

16. Bob Davis and Lingling Wei, *Superpower Showdown* (New York: Harper Business, 2020), 181.

17. Doug Palmer, "Trump Says His Friendship with Xi Not as Good," *Politico*, July 15, 2019, https://www.politico.com/story/2019/07/15/trump-friendship-trade-china-1416131.

18. Trump's tweet: see Davis and Wei, *Superpower Showdown*, 358.

19. Wendy Wu, "Chinese Vice-Premier Liu He Says 'Small Setbacks Will Not Derail Trade War Talks," *South China Morning Post*, May 11, 2019, https://www.scmp.com/news/china/diplomacy/article/3009824/chinas-vice-premier-liu-he-says-small-setbacks-will-not-derail.

20. Derek Scissors, "The Trump Administration's Fake China Trade Policy," AEI, December 2020, https://www.aei.org/foreign-and-defense-policy/the-trump-administrations-fake-china-trade-policy/.

21. For ZTE, see John Bolton, *The Room Where It Happened* (New York: Simon and Schuster, 2020), 290–94.

22. Davis and Wei, *Superpower Showdown*, 392.

23. The strategy statement was later declassified and released. See "Page: U.S. Strategic Framework for the Indo-Pacific (February 2018)," Wikisource, last updated January 17, 2021, https://en.wikisource.org/wiki/Page: U.S._Strategic_Framework_for_the_Indo-Pacific_(February_2018).pdf/1.

24. See Shane Harris, "William Burns Gets a Warm Reception at Senate Hearing to Become Next CIA Director," *Washington Post*, February 25, 2021, A-8.

25. "Remarks by Deputy National Security Advisor Matt Pottinger to the Miller Center at the University of Virginia," White House, May 4, 2000, https://trumpwhitehouse.archives.gov/briefings-statements/remarks-deputy-national-security-advisor-matt-pottinger-london-based-policy-exchange/.

26. Quoted in Bolton, *Room Where It Happened*, 311–12.

27. David Barboza, "Steve Bannon on Hong Kong, Covid-19, and the War with China Already Underway," *The Wire*, May 24, 2020, https://www.thewirechina.com/2020/05/24/steve-bannon-on-hong-kong-covid-19-and-the-war-already-underway/.

28. See, for example, Mike Pompeo and Miles Yu, "China's Reckless Labs Put the World at Risk," *Wall Street Journal*, February 24, 2021, A-17.

29. Steven Lee Myers, "China Spins Tale That the U.S. Army Started the Coronavirus Epidemic," *New York Times*, March 13, 2020, https://www.nytimes.com/2020/03/13/world/asia/coronavirus-china-conspiracy-theory.html.

30. See Liza Lin, "China Tightens Customs Checks for Medical Equipment Exports," *Wall Street Journal*, April 10, 2020, https://www.wsj.com/articles/china-tightens-customs-checks-for-medical-equipment-exports-11586519333.

31. Reuters, "Over 1,000 Chinese Researchers Have Left US amid Tech Theft Crackdown," *Voice of America*, December 2, 2020, https://www.voanews.com/usa/official-over-1000-chinese-researchers-have-left-us-amid-tech-theft-crackdown.

32. Yuka Hayashi, "Biden Aims for Strong Posture on Trade," *Wall Street Journal*, March 9, 2021, A-2.

33. Gerry Shih, "China Fires Parting Shot at Trump," *Washington Post*, January 21, 2021, https://www.washingtonpost.com/world/asia_pacific/china-sanctions-pompeo-trump/2021/01/20/9c44ced4-5b92-11eb-a849-6f9423a75ffd_story.html.

34. John R. Bolton, "When It Comes to China, Biden Should Do What Trump Didn't," *Washington Post*, January 26, 2021, A-21.

35. Interview with Matt Pottinger, February 17, 2021.

## Notes to Chapter 15

1. Deep thanks to Iona Main, my research assistant at Princeton, and to friends and colleagues, especially Steven Bayme, Bernard Firestone, and Aaron Miller, for reviewing and improving various drafts.

2. Barry R. Posen, "The Rise of Illiberal Hegemony," *Foreign Affairs*, March/April 2018, https://www.foreignaffairs.com/articles/2018-02-13/rise-illiberal-hegemony.

3. Steven A. Cook, "Trump's Middle East Legacy Is Failure," *Foreign Policy*, October 28, 2020, https://foreignpolicy.com/2020/10/28/trumps-middle-east-legacy-is-failure/.

4. U.S. arms exports increased 23 percent between 2010–2014 and 2015–2019. About 25 percent of these arms went to Saudi Arabia, and a further 25 percent to other Middle Eastern countries. These sales ignored concerns regarding these countries' involvement in conflicts in Yemen, Libya, and elsewhere. SIPRE Arms Transfers Database, Stockholm International Peace Research Institute, March 15, 2021, https://sipri.org/databases/armstransfers.

5. "US Secretary of State Pompeo's Remarks to the Press on US Policy towards Israeli Settlements," United Nations, November 18, 2019, https://www.un.org/unispal/document/us-secretary-of-state-pompeos-remarks-to-the-press-on-us-policy-towards-israeli-settlements/.

6. James A. Baker III, "Trump's Recognition of Western Sahara Is a Serious Blow to Diplomacy and International Law," *Washington Post*, December 18, 2020, https://www.washingtonpost.com/opinions/2020/12/17/james-baker-trump-morocco-western-sahara-abraham-accords/.

7. Trump tweeted: "We pay the Palestinians HUNDRED OF MILLIONS OF DOLLARS a year and get no appreciation or respect. They don't even want to negotiate a long overdue peace treaty with Israel. We have taken Jerusalem, the toughest part

of the negotiation, off the table, but Israel, for that, would have had to pay more. But with the Palestinians no longer willing to talk peace, why should we make any of these massive future payments to them?" Donald J. Trump (@realDonaldTrump), January 2, 2018, https://twitter.com/realDonaldTrump/status/948322497602220032.

8. "Trump's relationship with intelligence was rocky from the beginning and has gone through four stages over the course of his tenure: 1. Ignorance during his business career and during his campaign. 2. Hostility when intelligence began documenting Russian meddling in the 2016 election. 3. Necessity when needing to determine things such as Syria's chemical weapons use and terrorist whereabouts. 4. Manipulation, most recently, with the clear intention of supporting his political objectives." John McLaughlin, "Biden's New Intel Chief Means Truth to Power Is Back," *Ozy*, December 1, 2020, https://www.ozy.com/news-and-politics/bidens-new-intel-chief-means-truth-to-power-is-back/407233/.

9. Matt Korade, Kevin Bohn, and Daniel Burke, "Controversial US Pastors Take Part in Jerusalem Embassy Opening," *CNN*, May 14, 2018, https://www.cnn.com/2018/05/13/politics/hagee-jeffress-us-embassy-jerusalem.

10. "My number one priority is to dismantle the disastrous deal with Iran. I have been in business a long time. I know deal-making and let me tell you, this deal is catastrophic—for America, for Israel, and for the whole of the Middle East." Ian Schwartz, "Full Speech: Donald Trump Addresses 2016 AIPAC," RealClear Politics, March 21, 2016, https://www.realclearpolitics.com/video/2016/03/21/full_speech_donald_trump_addresses_2016_aipac.html.

11. Mike Pompeo, "After the Deal: A New Iran Strategy" (speech at the Heritage Foundation, May 21, 2018), https://www.heritage.org/defense/event/after-the-deal-new-iran-strategy. Pompeo added the human rights demand on October 23, 2018.

12. Robert Malley and Philip H. Gordon, "Trump Still Has 70 Days to Wreak Havoc around the World," *New York Times*, November 11, 2020, https://www.nytimes.com/2020/11/11/opinion/biden-trump-foreign-policy.html.

13. As of April 2020, Iran's oil exports were 70,000 barrels per day compared with 2.5 million per day two years earlier. Iran's currency, the rial, lost 85 percent of its value against the dollar. "Donald Trump's Sanctions in the Middle East Have Had Little Effect," *The Economist*, November 26, 2020, https://www.economist.com/middle-east-and-africa/2020/11/26/donald-trumps-sanctions-in-the-middle-east-have-had-little-effect. Iran's GDP growth turned negative after sanctions were imposed, and its economy shrunk by between 2 and 6 percent each year from 2018 to 2020. Rick Noack, Armand Emamdjomeh, and Joe Fox, "How U.S. Sanctions Are Paralyzing the Iranian Economy," *Washington Post*, January 10, 2020, https://www.washingtonpost.com/world/2020/01/10/how-us-sanctions-are-paralyzing-iranian-economy/.

14. Erin Cunningham and Kareem Fahim, "Iran Begins Enriching Uranium to 20 Percent in New Breach of Nuclear Deal," *Washington Post*, January 5, 2021, https://www.washingtonpost.com/world/middle_east/iran-nuclear-uranium-enrichment/2021/01/04/588949be-4e76-11eb-a1f5-fdaf28cfca90_story.html.

15. James Jeffrey, "Biden Doesn't Need a New Middle East Policy," *Foreign Affairs*, January 15, 2021, https://www.foreignaffairs.com/articles/middle-east/2021-01-15/biden-doesnt-need-new-middle-east-policy.

16. Congressional Research Service reports this assistance was made up of $3.3 billion in foreign military financing for fiscal year 2021, plus $500 million in missile defense aid. Jeremy M. Sharp, "U.S. Foreign Aid to Israel," Congressional Research Service, November 16, 2020, https://fas.org/sgp/crs/mideast/RL33222.pdf.

17. Mike Pompeo (@SecPompeo), Twitter, January 14, 2021, https://twitter.com/SecPompeo/status/1349725459395858434.

18. A distinction should be drawn between those in the American Jewish community who voted for and supported Trump's policies generally—about 22 percent, according to a 2020 poll of the American Jewish Committee—and a larger number of American Jews who opposed Trump but applauded some of his policies vis-à-vis Israel. See "AJC 2020 Survey of American Jewish Opinion," American Jewish Committee, accessed August 4, 2021, https://www.ajc.org/news/survey2020.

19. The White House, *Peace to Prosperity*, January 2020, https://trumpwhitehouse.archives.gov/wp-content/uploads/2020/01/Peace-to-Prosperity-0120.pdf.

20. "By taking Jerusalem off the table I wanted to make it clear that Jerusalem is the capital of Israel and as for specific boundaries, I would support what both sides agreed to." "Donald Trump: Jerusalem Is off Negotiating Table," *Aljazeera*, February 12, 2018, quoting the *Israel Hayom* newspaper, https://www.aljazeera.com/news/2018/2/12/donald-trump-jerusalem-is-off-negotiating-table.

21. See, for example, Jared Kushner's interview with CNN's Christiane Amanpour, January 28, 2020: "They [the Palestinians] have a perfect track record of blowing every opportunity they have had in their past." https://www.cnn.com/videos/world/2020/01/28/amanpour-jared-kushner-intv-palestine-israel-middle-east-plan-vpx.cnn.

22. David Halbfinger, "Abbas Calls Oslo Accords Dead and Blasts U.S.: 'Damn Your Money!'" *New York Times*, January 14, 2018, https://www.nytimes.com/2018/01/14/world/middleeast/abbas-palestinians-trump.html.

23. Yousef Al Otaiba, "Annexation Will Be a Serious Setback for Better Relations with the Arab World," *Yediot Aharonot*, June 12, 2020, https://www.ynetnews.com/article/H1GulceTL.

24. Khaled Saffuri, "The Hidden Cost of the Abrahamic Accords," *American Conservative*, December 19, 2020, https://www.theamericanconservative.com/articles/the-hidden-cost-of-the-abrahamic-accords/.

25. See the website of the BDS movement at www.bdsmovement.net, accessed August 4, 2021.

26. See, for example, Murtaza Hussein, "Trump Destroyed Any Hope of Israeli-Palestinian Peace—and Biden Can't Rebuild It," *The Intercept*, November 14, 2020, https://theintercept.com/2020/11/13/trump-israel-palestine-biden/; and Mairav Zonszein, "Will Biden Undo Trump's Disastrous Legacy on Israel/Palestine?," *Jewish Currents*, November 24, 2020, https://jewishcurrents.org/will-biden-undo-trumps-disastrous-legacy-on-israel-palestine/.

27. David Halbfinger, "Strong Views and 'Close to the Boss': How U.S. Envoy Reshaped a Conflict," *New York Times*, January 10, 2020, https://www.nytimes.com/2021/01/10/world/middleeast/israel-friedman-ambassador-trump.html.

28. Trump tweeted: "The big Oil Deal with OPEC Plus is done. This will save hundreds of thousands of energy jobs in the United States. I would like to thank and congratulate President Putin of Russia and King Salman of Saudi Arabia. I just spoke to them from the Oval Office. Great deal for all!" Quoted in Jay Pandya, "Trump Hails 'Big Oil Deal' with OPEC+ after Top Oil Producers Agree on Record Output Cuts," *RepublicWorld*, April 13, 2020, https://www.republicworld.com/world-news/us-news/great-deal-for-all-donnald-trump-hails-oil-deal-with-opec.html.

29. Nancy A. Youssef, Vivian Salama, and Michael C. Bender, "Trump, Awaiting Egyptian Counterpart at Summit, Called Out for 'My Favorite Dictator,'" *Wall Street Journal*, September 13, 2019, https://www.wsj.com/articles/trump-awaiting-egyptian-counterpart-at-summit-called-out-for-my-favorite-dictator-11568403645.

30. Barbara Starr, "Saudi Arabia Has Paid $500m toward the Cost of US Troops in Country," *CNN*, January 16, 2020, https://edition.cnn.com/2020/01/16/politics/saudi-arabia-us-troops-payment/index.html.

31. Joe Gould, "Fired State Department IG Probed Trump's Saudi Arms Deals," *DefenseNews*, May 18, 2020, https://www.defensenews.com/congress/2020/05/18/fired-state-department-ig-probed-trumps-saudi-arms-deals/.

32. "Pentagon Notifies Congress of Plans to Sell Smart Bombs to Saudi Arabia," *Axios*, December 30, 2020, https://www.axios.com/pentagon-saudi-arms-sale-plans-congress-085d7eaa-e7cb-451c-8fa4-2fc71ec33d75.html?utm_source=twitter&utm_medium=social&utm_campaign=organic&utm_content=1100; and Tuqa Khalid, "US State Department Approves $4.2 Billion in Potential Arms Sales to Kuwait: Pentagon," *Al Arabiya*, December 30, 2020, https://english.alarabiya.net/en/News/gulf/2020/12/30/US-approves-4-2-billion-in-potential-arms-sales-to-Kuwait-Pentagon.

33. For example, see Trump's tweet: "The U.S. now has a very strong and powerful foreign policy, much different than proceeding [*sic*] administrations. It is called, quite simply, America First!" Quoted in "Live Coverage: Ex-Ukraine Ambassador Testifies in Public Impeachment Hearing," *The Hill*, November 15, 2019, https://thehill.com/homenews/house/470572-live-coverage-ex-ukraine-ambassador-testifies-in-public-impeachment-hearing. Also: "Thanks to REPUBLICAN LEADERSHIP, America is WINNING AGAIN - and America is being RESPECTED again all over the world. Because we are finally putting AMERICA FIRST!" Quoted in The American Presidency Project-UC Santa Barbara, July 6, 2018, https://www.presidency.ucsb.edu/documents/tweets-july-6-2018.

34. Michael R. Pompeo, "Confronting Iran: The Trump Administration's Strategy," *Foreign Affairs*, November/December 2018, https://www.foreignaffairs.com/articles/middle-east/2018-10-15/michael-pompeo-secretary-of-state-on-confronting-iran.

35. For details on troop levels, see "The U.S. War in Afghanistan, 1999–2021," Council on Foreign Relations, accessed August 4, 2021, https://www.cfr.org/timeline/us-war-afghanistan.

36. Barry R. Posen, "The Rise of Illiberal Hegemony: Trump's Surprising Grand Strategy," *Foreign Affairs*, March/April 2018, https://www.foreignaffairs.com/articles/2018-02-13/rise-illiberal-hegemony.

37. "Agreement for Bringing Peace to Afghanistan between the Islamic Emirate of Afghanistan which Is Not Recognized by the United States as a State and Is Known as the Taliban and the United States of America," U.S. Department of State, February 29, 2020, accessed August 4, 2021, https://www.state.gov/wp-content/uploads/2020/02/Agreement-For-Bringing-Peace-to-Afghanistan-02.29.20.pdf.

38. Steven Pressfield, *The Warrior Ethos* (New York: Black Irish Entertainment, 2011), cited in Robert D. Blackwill, *Trump's Foreign Policies Are Better than They Seem*, Council on Foreign Relations, Special Report number 84, April 2019, https://www.cfr.org/sites/default/files/report_pdf/CSR%2084_Blackwill_Trump.pdf.

39. Paul K. MacDonald and Joseph M. Parent, "Trump Didn't Shrink US Military Commitments Abroad—He Expanded Them: The President's False Promise of Retrenchment," *Foreign Affairs*, December 3, 2019, https://www.foreignaffairs.com/articles/2019-12-03/trump-didnt-shrink-us-military-commitments-abroad-he-expanded-them.

40. See Daniel Kurtzer, *The Middle East's Evolving Security Landscape: Prospects for Regional Cooperation and US Engagement*, Foundation for European Progressive Studies (FEPS) and Istituto Affari Internazionali (IAI), April 2020, https://www.iai.it/sites/default/files/iaip2010.pdf.

41. Trump tweeted: "After defeating 100% of the ISIS Caliphate, I largely moved our troops out of Syria. Let Syria and Assad protect the Kurds and fight Turkey for their own land. I said to my Generals, why should we be fighting for Syria. . . ." Quoted in John T. Bennett, "Trump Walks Back Claim of Defeating '100% of the ISIS Caliphate,'" *Roll Call*, October 28, 2019. Almost a year earlier, he had tweeted: "Getting out of Syria was no surprise. I've been campaigning on it for years, and six months ago, when I very publicly wanted to do it, I agreed to stay longer. Russia, Iran, Syria & others are the local enemy of ISIS. We were doing there [*sic*] work. Time to come home & rebuild." Quoted in Kyle Balluck and Michael Burke, "Trump Defends Withdrawal from Syria: 'Do We Want to Be There forever?'" *The Hill*, December 20, 2018, https://thehill.com/homenews/administration/422215-trump-getting-out-of-syria-no-surprise.

42. Katie Bo Williams, "Outgoing Syria Envoy Admits Hiding US Troop Numbers; Praises Trump's Mideast Record," *DefenseOne*, November 12, 2020, https://www.defenseone.com/threats/2020/11/outgoing-syria-envoy-admits-hiding-us-troop-numbers-praises-trumps-mideast-record/170012/.

43. Colin P. Clarke, William Courtney, Bradley Martin, and Bruce McClintock, "Russia Is Eyeing the Mediterranean. The U.S. and NATO Must Be Prepared," *The RAND Blog*, June 30, 2020, https://www.rand.org/blog/2020/06/russia-is-eyeing-the-mediterranean-the-us-and-nato.html.

44. Ali Wyne and Colin P. Clarke, "Assessing China and Russia's Moves in the Middle East," *Lawfare Blog*, September 17, 2020, https://www.lawfareblog.com/assessing-china-and-russias-moves-middle-east.

45. Jonathan Fulton, *China's Changing Role in the Middle East*, Atlantic Council, June 2019, https://www.atlanticcouncil.org/wp-content/uploads/2019/06/Chinas_Changing_Role_in_the_Middle_East.pdf.

46. Camille Lons, Jonathan Fulton, Degang Sun, and Naser Al-Tamimi, "China's Great Game in the Middle East," European Council on Foreign Relations, October 21, 2019, https://ecfr.eu/publication/china_great_game_middle_east/.

47. "Full Text of Pompeo's Statement on Settlements," *Times of Israel*, November 19, 2019, https://www.timesofisrael.com/full-text-of-pompeos-statement-on-settlements/.

48. Eric Cortellessa, "Trump's State Department No Longer Calls West Bank 'Occupied' in Annual Report," *Times of Israel*, April 21, 2018, https://www.timesofisrael.com/trumps-state-department-no-longer-calls-west-bank-occupied-in-annual-report/.

49. "Israel/OPT: UN Expert Alarmed by 'Lopsided' Trump Plan, Says Will Entrench Occupation," Office of the High Commissioner on Human Rights, January 31, 2020, https://www.ohchr.org/en/NewsEvents/Pages/DisplayNews.aspx?NewsID=25513&LangID=E.

50. Kathy Gilsinan, "It Was Never Just about Human Rights in Iran," *The Atlantic*, December 11, 2019, https://www.theatlantic.com/politics/archive/2019/12/iran-protests-trump-human-rights/603337/.

51. Rodger A. Payne and Kurt Mills, "How Donald Trump's 'America First' Agenda Has Damaged Global Human Rights," *The Conversation*, October 23, 2020, https://theconversation.com/how-donald-trumps-america-first-agenda-has-damaged-global-human-rights-148030.

52. "US 'Terrorist' Designation of Yemen's Houthis Comes into Effect," *Al Jazeera*, January 19, 2021, https://www.aljazeera.com/news/2021/1/19/us-houthi-terrorist-designation-comes-into-effect.

53. Judy Maltz and Ben Samuels, "Trump Plan to Label Pro-BDS Groups Antisemitic Is off the Table," *Haaretz*, January 24, 2021, https://www.haaretz.com/us-news/.premium-trump-plan-to-label-pro-bds-groups-antisemitic-is-off-the-table-sources-say-1.9477763.

54. "US Slaps More Sanctions on Iran in Final Days of Trump Presidency," *Al Jazeera*, January 16, 2021, https://www.aljazeera.com/news/2021/1/16/us-slaps-more-sanctions-on-iran-in-final-days-of-trump-presidency.

55. Julian Borger, "Mike Pompeo Claims without Evidence That Iran Is al-Qaida's New 'Home Base,'" *The Guardian*, January 13, 2021, https://www.theguardian.com/us-news/2021/jan/12/iran-al-qaida-mike-pompeo.

56. Robin Emmott, John Irish, and Tuvan Gumrukcu, "In Parting Shot, Pompeo Rebukes Turkey at NATO Meeting," Reuters, December 3, 2020, https://www.reuters.com/article/turkey-usa-nato-int/in-parting-shot-pompeo-rebukes-turkey-at-nato-meeting-idUSKBN28D1YJ.

57. Nadia Schadlow, "The End of American Illusion: Trump and the World as It Is," *Foreign Affairs*, September/October 2020, https://www.foreignaffairs.com/articles/americas/2020-08-11/end-american-illusion.

58. See, for example, Jackson Diehl, "Trump's Overarching Middle East Strategy Reaches a Disastrous Dead End," *Washington Post*, November 22, 2020, https://www.washingtonpost.com/opinions/global-opinions/trump-middle-east-legacy/2020/11/22/4563bec2-2a7d-11eb-8fa2-06e7cbb145c0_story.html.

## Notes to Chapter 16

1. James Comey, *A Higher Loyalty: Truth, Lies, and Leadership* (New York: Flatiron Books, 2018), 233–44.

2. Approximately two-thirds of those federal employees are members of the military or work for the Department of Defense. "Executive Branch Civilian Employment since 1940," U.S. Office of Personnel Management, accessed June 2021, https://www.opm.gov/policy-data-oversight/data-analysis-documentation/federal-employment-reports/historical-tables/executive-branch-civilian-employment-since-1940/.

3. Phillip Rucker and Robert Costa, "Bannon Vows a Daily Fight for 'Deconstruction of the Administrative State,'" *Washington Post*, February 23, 2017.

4. Gregory Korte, "In Poland, Trump Draws Battle Lines against Terror and Bureaucracy," *USA Today*, July 6, 2017; Charles S. Clark, "Deconstructing the Deep State," *Government Executive*, accessed August 2021, https://www.govexec.com/feature/gov-exec-deconstructing-deep-state/.

5. Trump's relationship with the administrative state is already the subject of a small but growing academic literature. See esp. Lisa K. Parshall and Jim Twombly, *Directing the Whirlwind: The Trump Presidency and the Deconstruction of the Administrative State* (New York: Peter Lang, 2020); Stephen Skowronek, John A. Dearborn, and Desmond King, *Phantoms of a Beleaguered Republic: The Deep State and the Unitary Executive* (New York: Oxford University Press, 2021).

6. Daniel Thomas, "Government Executive 2016 Presidential Poll," *Government Executive*, October 28, 2016.

7. Max Lowenthal, *The Federal Bureau of Investigation* (New York: William Sloane Associates, 1950), 4–13.

8. Skowronek, Dearborn, and King, *Phantoms of a Beleaguered Republic*, 4.

9. Ronald Reagan, "A Time for Choosing," Ronald Reagan Presidential Library and Museum, October 27, 1964, https://www.reaganlibrary.gov/reagans/ronald-reagan/time-choosing-speech-october-27-1964.

10. Ronald Reagan, "Inaugural Address," Ronald Reagan Presidential Foundation and Institute, January 20, 1981, https://www.reaganfoundation.org/ronald-reagan/reagan-quotes-speeches/inaugural-address-1/.

11. "Bush and the Bureaucracy: A Crusade for Control," *Government Executive*, March 25, 2005, https://www.govexec.com/management/2005/03/bush-and-the-bureaucracy-a-crusade-for-control/18859/.

12. Richard Dudman, *Men of the Far Right* (New York: Pyramid Books, 1962), 163.

13. Beverly Gage, "Deep Throat, Watergate, and the Bureaucratic Politics of the FBI," *Journal of Policy History* 24, no. 2 (2012): 157–83; Max Holland, *Leak: Why*

*Mark Felt Became Deep Throat* (Lawrence: University Press of Kansas, 2012); Stanley I. Kutler, *The Wars of Watergate: The Last Crisis of Richard Nixon* (New York: W. W. Norton, 1990).

14. Matt Apuzzo, Maggie Haberman, and Matthew Rosenberg, "Trump Told Russians That Firing 'Nut Job' Comey Eased Pressure from Investigation," *New York Times*, May 19, 2017; Donald Trump, Twitter posts: May 2, 2017; November 10, 2020; July 13, 2019, thetrumparchive.com (hereafter cited as TTA).

15. For an account of his early career, see Comey, *Higher Loyalty*, 5–115.

16. James Comey, "Law Enforcement and the Communities We Serve" (lecture, University of Chicago Law School, Chicago, IL, October 23, 2015); David A. Graham, "The FBI Director's Troubling Comments on the 'Ferguson Effect,'" *The Atlantic*, October 26, 2015; Will Femia, "FBI Director's 'All Lives Matter' Message Clashes with Obama," *MSNBC*, October 24, 2015; Laura Wager, "FBI Director Doubles Down on Linking Scrutiny of Police with Rise in Violent Crime," *NPR*, October 26, 2015.

17. Trump, Twitter post, July 5, 2016, TTA. For insider accounts of Midyear Exam and other FBI investigations during the Trump era, see Comey, *Higher Loyalty*; Andrew McCabe, *The Threat: How the FBI Protects America in the Age of Terror and Trump* (New York: St. Martin's, 2019), 160–206; Peter Strzok, *Compromised: Counterintelligence and the Threat of Donald J. Trump* (Boston: Houghton Mifflin Harcourt, 2019). For a useful journalistic overview, see David Rohde, *In Deep: The FBI, the CIA, and the Truth about America's "Deep State"* (New York: W. W. Norton, 2020). For an academic account, see Skowronek, Dearborn, and King, *Phantoms of a Beleaguered Republic*, 76–98. Where not otherwise cited, dates and events can be found in these sources.

18. Trump, Twitter post, October 17, 2016, TTA.

19. "Letter to Congress from F.B.I. Director on Clinton Email Case," *New York Times*, October 28, 2016.

20. Comey, *Higher Loyalty*, 188–210; Adam Serwer, "Trump Is Winning His War on the FBI," *The Atlantic*, June 17, 2018; Spencer Ackerman, "The FBI Is Trumpland,'" *The Guardian*, November 3, 2016. The New York office may already have been leaking to former New York mayor Rudy Giuliani, a Trump ally.

21. "Presidential Candidate Donald Trump Rally in Phoenix, Arizona," *C-SPAN*, October 29, 2016.

22. Comey, *Higher Loyalty*, 243.

23. Roger Stone with Mike Colapietro, *The Man Who Killed Kennedy: The Case against LBJ* (New York: MJF Books, 2013).

24. Virgil, "The Deep State vs. Donald Trump," *Breitbart*, December 12, 2016; Rohde, *In Deep*, 159–60.

25. Trump, Twitter posts: July 23, 2018; April 12, 2018, TTA.

26. Robert S. Mueller, *Report on the Investigation into Russian Interference in the 2016 Presidential Election* (Washington, DC: March 2019), 2:78, https://www.justice.gov/archives/sco/file/1373816/download.

27. Mueller, *Report*, 2:158.

28. Mueller, *Report*, 2:8.

29. William Barr, "Remarks on the Release of the Report on the Investigation into Russian Interference in the 2016 Presidential Election," United States Department of Justice, April 18, 2019, https://www.justice.gov/opa/speech/attorney-general-william-p-barr-delivers-remarks-release-report-investigation-russian.

30. Trump, Twitter post, March 24, 2019, TTA.

31. Tom Vanden Brook, Nicholas Wu, and Deirdre Shesgreen, "Alexander Vindman Retires from Army, Citing 'Bullying' from Trump for Impeachment Testimony," *USA Today*, July 8, 2020.

32. William J. Burns, "The Demolition of U.S. Diplomacy," *Foreign Affairs*, October 14, 2019, https://www.foreignaffairs.com/articles/2019-10-14/demolition-us-diplomacy. In 2021, President Joe Biden appointed Burns as director of the CIA.

33. Michael D. Shear and Ron Nixon, "How Trump's Rush to Enact an Immigration Ban Unleashed Global Chaos," *New York Times*, January 29, 2017.

34. Maggie Haberman and Michael Crowley, "Trump Calls Fauci 'a Disaster,'" *New York Times*, October 19, 2020.

35. Max Boot, "Trump Is Deconstructing the Government, One Agency at a Time," *Washington Post*, December 2, 2019.

36. Joe Helm, "National Archives Exhibit Blurs Images Critical of President Trump," *Washington Post*, January 17, 2020.

37. Anonymous [Miles Taylor], "I Am Part of the Resistance inside the Trump Administration," *New York Times*, September 5, 2018.

38. Amelia Thomson-DeVeaux, "Why Democrats and Republicans Did a Sudden 180 on the FBI," *FiveThirtyEight*, February 9, 2018, https://fivethirtyeight.com/features/why-democrats-and-republicans-did-a-sudden-180-on-the-fbi/.

39. "Growing Partisan Differences in Views of the FBI," Pew Research Center, July 24, 2018, https://www.pewresearch.org/politics/2018/07/24/growing-partisan-differences-in-views-of-the-fbi-stark-divide-over-ice/.

40. Jonathan S. Tobin, "Since When Are Liberals against Investigating the CIA and FBI?," *National Review*, June 17, 2019.

41. Office of the Inspector General, U.S. Department of Justice, *Report of Investigation: Recovery of Text Messages from Certain FBI Mobile Devices* (December 2018), https://oig.justice.gov/reports/2018/i-2018-003523.pdf.

42. Trump, Twitter posts, June 17, 2018, June 5, 2018, TTA.

43. Rohde, *In Deep*, 194.

44. Colby Itkowitz and Devlin Barrett, "Trump Suggests He'd Consider Removing FBI Director over Unfavorable Testimony," *Washington Post*, September 18, 2020; Devlin Barrett and Josh Dawsey, "Trump Weighs Firing FBI Director after Election as Frustration with Wray, Barr grows," *Washington Post*, October 21, 2020.

45. Trump, Twitter post, October 30, 2020, TTA.

46. Trump, Twitter posts: September 17, 2020; August 22, 2020, TTA.

47. Trump, Twitter post, December 26, 2020, TTA.

48. Luke Broadwater and Nicholas Fandos, "Senate Report Details Security Failures in Jan. 6 Capitol Riot," *New York Times*, June 8, 2021.

49. Parshall and Twombly, *Directing the Whirlwind*, 196–225.

50. "Federal Bureau of Investigation (FBI) FY 2020 Budget Request," accessed June 2021, https://www.justice.gov/jmd/page/file/1142426/download.

51. Eric Tucker, "White House: Biden Confident in FBI Head, Will Retain Him," Associated Press, January 21, 2021.

## Notes to Chapter 17

1. "Dying in a Leadership Vacuum," *New England Journal of Medicine* 383, no. 15 (October 8, 2020): 1479–80.

2. Gina Kolata, "In a First, New England Journal of Medicine Joins Never-Trumpers," *New York Times*, October 7, 2020.

3. Harvey Fineberg, "Ten Weeks to Crush the Curve," *New England Journal of Medicine* 382, no. 17 (April 23, 2020): e37.

4. "President Trump with Coronavirus Task Force Briefing," *C-SPAN*, March 24, 2020, https://www.c-span.org/video/?470667-1/white-house-recently-left-new-york-city-quarantine-14-days; "Interview: Bill Hemmer Interviews Donald Trump at the White House - March 24, 2020," *Fox News*, March 24, 2020, YouTube video, 8:38, https://www.youtube.com/watch?v=LCPHvxYjaHQ. All cited time-series data on COVID-19-confirmed cases and deaths is taken from "COVID-19 Data Repository by the Center for Systems Science and Engineering (CSSE) at Johns Hopkins University," GitHub, https://github.com/CSSEGISandData/COVID-19.

5. Although Trump's Twitter account, at the time of this writing, remains suspended, an archive of his tweets remains available at the Trump Twitter Archive V2, https://www.thetrumparchive.com/.

6. "President Trump with Coronavirus Task Force Briefing," *C-SPAN*, April 23, 2020, https://www.c-span.org/video/?471458-1/president-trump-coronavirus-task-force-briefing; Katie Rogers, Christine Hauser, Alan Yuhas, and Maggie Haberman, "Trump's Suggestion That Disinfectants Could Be Used to Treat Coronavirus Prompts Aggressive Pushback," *New York Times*, April 24, 2020.

7. "Restaurant Executives Meeting at the White House," *C-SPAN*, May 18, 2020, https://www.c-span.org/video/?472244-1/restaurant-executives-meeting-white-house.

8. "Transcript: 'Fox News Sunday' Interview with President Trump," *Fox News*, July 19, 2020, https://www.foxnews.com/politics/transcript-fox-news-sunday-interview-with-president-trump. The favored model was produced by the University of Washington's Institute for Health Metrics and Evaluation, which in March had forecast eighty-one thousand deaths by July. See "New COVID-19 Forecasts: US Hospitals Could Be Overwhelmed in the Second Week of April by Demand for ICU Beds, and US Deaths Could Total 81,000 by July," Institute for Health Metrics and Evaluation, March 26, 2020, http://www.healthdata.org/news-release/new-covid-19-forecasts-us-hospitals-could-be-overwhelmed-second-week-april-demand-icu.

9. Donald J. Trump, "Don't Let the Coronavirus Dominate Your Life!," October 5, 2020, YouTube video, 1:26, https://www.youtube.com/watch?v=OuhBF74ZD8E; Donald J. Trump, "A Message from the President!," October 7, 2020, YouTube video, 4:53, https://www.youtube.com/watch?v=lw78cZIAROU.

10. On the DPA, see *The Defense Production Act of 1950: History, Authorities, and Considerations for Congress* (Washington, DC: Congressional Research Service, 2020).

11. Letter from eighteen senators on DPA, March 20, 2020, https://www.markey.senate.gov/imo/media/doc/Trump%20DPA%20Follow-Up%20Letter.pdf.

12. Joe Biden, "Statement from Vice President Joe Biden on Immediate Actions the Trump Administration Must Take to Address the Public Health Crisis," Medium, March 18, 2020, https://medium.com/@JoeBiden/statement-from-vice-president-joe-biden-on-immediate-actions-the-trump-administration-must-take-to-57857de533b8.

13. James E. Baker, "Use the Defense Production Act to Flatten the Curve," Just Security, March 20, 2020, https://www.justsecurity.org/69275/use-the-defense-production-act-to-flatten-the-curve/.

14. *National Covid-19 Testing Action Plan: Pragmatic Steps to Reopen Our Workplaces and Our Communities* (New York: Rockefeller Foundation, 2020).

15. The National Institutes of Health regularly updated "treatment guidelines" based on information from new studies. See National Institutes of Health, *Coronavirus Disease 2019 (COVID-19) Treatment Guidelines*, 2021, https://files.covid19treatmentguidelines.nih.gov/guidelines/covid19treatmentguidelines.pdf.

16. Exec. Order No. 13,909, "Prioritizing and Allocating Health and Medical Resources to Respond to the Spread of COVID-19" (March 18, 2020); Exec. Order No. 13,910, "Preventing Hoarding of Health and Medical Resources To Respond to the Spread of COVID-19" (March 23, 2020); Exec. Order No. 13,917, "Delegating Authority Under the Defense Production Act With Respect to Food Supply Chain Resources During the National Emergency Caused by the Outbreak of COVID- 19" (April 28, 2020).

17. Quint Forgey, Sarah Owermohle, and Megan Cassela, "FEMA: Defense Production Act No Longer Needed to Secure Thousands of Test Kits," *Politico*, March 24, 2020.

18. "President Trump with Coronavirus Task Force Briefing," *C-SPAN*, March 19, 2020, https://www.c-span.org/video/?470503-1/president-trump-coronavirus-task-force-hold-briefing-white-house.

19. "FEMA Phasing Out Project Airbridge," Federal Emergency Management Authority Release Number HQ-20-161, June 18, 2020, https://www.fema.gov/press-release/20210318/fema-phasing-out-project-airbridge; Elizabeth Warren, Richard Blumenthal, and Charles Schumer to Michael Horowitz, June 8, 2020, https://www.warren.senate.gov/imo/media/doc/Letter%20to%20PRAC%20re%20project%20airbridge%202020.06.pdf.

20. Ruth Kleinpell, David Ferraro, Ryan C. Maves, et al., "Coronavirus Disease 2019 Pandemic Measures: Reports from a National Survey of 9,120 ICU Clinicians," *Critical Care Medicine* 48, no. 10 (October 2020): e846–55.

21. Brian McGarry, David Grabowski, and Michael Barnett, "Severe Staffing and Personal Protective Equipment Shortages Faced by Nursing Homes during the COVID-19 Pandemic," *Health Affairs* 39, no. 10 (August 20, 2020): 1812–21.

22. American Nurses Association, "Survey Reveals Alarming Conditions," September 1, 2020, https://www.nursingworld.org/~4a558d/globalassets/covid19/ana-ppe-survey-one-pager---final.pdf.

23. Preeti Mehrotra, Preeti Malani, and Prashant Yadav, "Personal Protective Equipment Shortages during COVID-19—Supply Chain–Related Causes and Mitigation Strategies," *JAMA Health Forum*, May 12, 2020; Suhas Gondi, Adam Beckman, Nicholas Deveau, et al., "Personal Protective Equipment Needs in the USA during the COVID-19 Pandemic," *The Lancet* 395, no. 10237 (May 23, 2020): e90–91.

24. Mirjam Kretzschmar, Ganna Rozhnova, Martin Bootsma, et al., "Impact of Delays on Effectiveness of Contact Tracing Strategies for COVID-19: A Modelling Study," *Lancet Public Health* 5, no. 8 (August 1, 2020): e457.

25. Eric Schneider, "Failing the Test—the Tragic Data Gap Undermining the U.S. Pandemic Response," *New England Journal of Medicine* 383, no. 4 (July 23, 2020): 299–302.

26. See "Ricci Messages and Documents Part 1," 2020, uploaded by Steve Thompson, https://www.documentcloud.org/documents/7338358-Ricci-messages-and-documents-Part-1.html; Steve Thompson, "Contradicting Hogan, Health Official Says First Batch of Korean Virus Tests Were Never Used," *Washington Post*, December 2, 2020.

27. Larry Hogan, Gretchen Whitmer, Mike DeWine, John Bel Edwards, Charlie Baker, and Ralph Northam to Richard Parson and Rajiv Shah, August 4, 2020, https://content.govdelivery.com/attachments/MIEOG/2020/08/04/file_attachments/1510778/Testing%20LOI.pdf. Later, North Carolina governor Roy Cooper was added to this initial group of six.

28. "Trump Administration Will Deploy 150 Million Rapid Tests in 2020," U.S. Department of Health & Human Services, August 27, 2020, https://www.hhs.gov/about/news/2020/08/27/trump-administration-will-deploy-150-million-rapid-tests-in-2020.html.

29. Jessica Prince-Guerra, Olivia Almendares, Leisha Nolen, et al., "Evaluation of Abbott BinaxNOW Rapid Antigen Test for SARS-CoV-2 Infection at Two Community-Based Testing Sites—Pima County, Arizona, November 3–17, 2020," *CDC Morbidity and Mortality Weekly Report* 70, no. 3 (January 22, 2021): 100–105.

30. Sharon LaFraniere and Katherine Wu, "Backed by Federal Funds, New Virus Tests Are Hitting the Market," *New York Times*, September 2, 2020.

31. Michael Mina, "How We Can Stop the Spread of COVID-19 by Christmas," *Time*, November 17, 2020, https://time.com/5912705/covid-19-stop-spread-christmas/; Michael Mina, Roy Parker, and Daniel Larremore, "Rethinking Covid-19 Test Sensitivity—a Strategy for Containment," *New England Journal of Medicine* 383, no. 22 (November 26, 2020): e120.

32. Moncef Slaoui and Matthew Hepburn, "Developing Safe and Effective Covid Vaccines—Operation Warp Speed's Strategy and Approach," *New England Journal of Medicine* 383, no. 18 (October 29, 2020): 1701–3.

33. Slaoui and Hepburn, "Developing Safe and Effective Covid Vaccines"; *Operation Warp Speed: Accelerated COVID-19 Vaccine Development Status and Efforts to Address Manufacturing Challenges*, GAO-21-319 (Washington, DC: United States Government Accountability Office, February 2021).

34. Dan Levine and Marisa Taylor, "Exclusive: Top FDA Official Says Would Resign If Agency Rubber-Stamps an Unproven COVID-19 Vaccine," Reuters, August 20, 2020.

35. On the organizational structures that help the FDA maintain independence and public esteem, see Daniel Carpenter, *Reputation and Power: Organizational Image and Pharmaceutical Regulation at the FDA* (Princeton, NJ: Princeton University Press, 2010).

36. "MHA Statement on Reduced COVID-19 Vaccine Allocation," Michigan Health & Hospital Association, December 18, 2020, https://mha.org/Newsroom/ID/2789/categoryId/14/MHA-Statement-on-Reduced-COVID-19-Vaccine-Allocation.

37. Centers for Disease Control and Prevention, "15 Days to Slow the Spread," March 2020.

38. On police powers and state and local autonomy, see Lawrence O. Gostin, *Public Health Law: Power, Duty, Restraint* (Berkeley: University of California Press, 2008), 91–98; Gostin, "*Jacobson v Massachusetts* at 100 Years: Police Power and Civil Liberties in Tension," *American Journal of Public Health* 95, no. 4 (April 2005): 576–81.

39. On the California Air Resources Board, see Ellyn Adrienne Hershman, "California Legislation on Air Contaminant Emissions from Stationary Sources," *California Law Review* 58, no. 6 (November 1970): 1474–98; Arie Haagen-Smit, "A Lesson from the Smog Capital of the World," *PNAS* 67, no. 2 (October 1970): 887–97.

40. Timothy Puko and Andrew Restuccia, "Biden Administration Moves to Unwind Trump Auto-Emissions Policy," *Wall Street Journal*, April 21, 2021.

41. For an overview of Louisiana's state-level environmental politics, see David Rosner and Gerald Markowitz, *Deceit and Denial: The Deadly Politics of Industrial Pollution* (Berkeley: University of California Press, 2002), ch. 9.

42. Lylla Younes, "Why Louisiana's Air Quality Is Going from Bad to Worse, in 3 Charts," *ProPublica*, October 30, 2019, https://www.propublica.org/article/why-louisianas-air-quality-is-going-from-bad-to-worse-in-3-charts.

43. State of California, Exec. Order, N-33-20, March 4, 2020.

44. State of New York, Exec. Order, No. 202.8, March 20, 2020; "New York State on PAUSE," March 20, 2020, https://coronavirus.health.ny.gov/new-york-state-pause.

45. State of Michigan, Exec. Order No. 2020-110, June 1, 2020.

46. Stephen Gruber-Miller and Kim Norvell, "Iowa Begins Easing Coronavirus Business Restrictions Starting Friday in 77 Counties with Low Cases," *Des Moines Register*, April 27, 2020.

47. State of Iowa, Proclamation of Disaster Emergency, November 16, 2020.

48. Alan Judd and Greg Bluestein, "Lifting Stay-at-Home Order, Kemp Shifts Focus to Economic Recovery," *Atlanta Journal-Constitution*, April 30, 2020.

49. "President Trump Meeting with Florida Governor DeSantis," *C-SPAN*, April 28, 2020, https://www.c-span.org/video/?471585-1/president-trump-meeting-florida-governor-desantis.

50. State of Florida, Exec. Order No. 20-244, September 25, 2020.

51. Eric Bradner, "Georgia Gov. Brian Kemp Faces Resistance over Move to Reopen Economy," *CNN*, April 21, 2020, https://www.cnn.com/2020/04/21/politics/georgia-governor-coronavirus-backlash/index.html.

52. "Providing Additional Guidance for Empowering a Healthy Georgia in Response to COVID-19," State of Georgia, Exec. Order No. 08.15.20.01, August 15, 2020.

53. Miami-Dade County, Emergency Order 30-20, September 26, 2020.

54. Andrew Turner, "Protesters in Huntington Beach Call for Full Reopen of State, Nation," *Los Angeles Times*, May 9, 2020.

55. Luke Money, "Orange County Authorities Won't Enforce Mask Requirement: 'We Are Not the Mask Police,'" *Los Angeles Times*, May 26, 2020.

56. Katie Honan and Paul Berger, "New York City's Ultra-Orthodox Jewish Leaders Decry New Lockdown Measures," *Wall Street Journal*, October 7, 2020; Emma Fitzsimmons and Alexandra Petri, "How N.Y.C.'s Conservative Bastion Became a Virus Hot Spot," *New York Times*, November 11, 2020.

57. Stephanie Kramer, "More Americans Say They Are Regularly Wearing Masks in Stores and Other Businesses," Pew Research Center, August 27, 2020, https://www.pewresearch.org/fact-tank/2020/08/27/more-americans-say-they-are-regularly-wearing-masks-in-stores-and-other-businesses/.

58. Tina Nguyen, "Trump Isn't Secretly Winking at QAnon. He's Retweeting Its Followers," *Politico*, July 12, 2020.

59. Wendy Kline, *Bodies of Knowledge: Sexuality, Reproduction, and Women's Health in the Second Wave* (Chicago: University of Chicago Press, 2010).

60. Steven Epstein, *Impure Science: AIDS, Activism, and the Politics of Knowledge* (Berkeley: University of California Press, 1998), 181–329; Epstein, "The Construction of Lay Expertise: AIDS Activism and the Forging of Credibility in the Reform of Clinical Trials," *Science, Technology & Human Values* 20, no. 4 (October 1995): 408–37.

61. Kelly Moore, *Disrupting Science: Social Movements, American Scientists, and the Politics of the Military, 1945–1975* (Princeton, NJ: Princeton University Press, 2008); Phil Brown, "Popular Epidemiology Revisited," *Current Sociology* 45, no. 3 (July 1997): 137–56.

62. Committee on the Use of Complementary and Alternative Medicine by the American Public, *Complementary and Alternative Medicine in the United States* (Washington, DC: National Academies Press, 2005).

63. Committee on Genetically Engineered Crops: Past Experiences and Future Prospects, *Genetically Engineered Crops: Experiences and Prospects* (Washington, DC: National Academies Press, 2016).

64. Pride Chigwedere, George Seage, and Sofia Gruskin, "Estimating the Lost Benefits of Antiretroviral Drug Use in South Africa," *Journal of Acquired Immune Deficiency Syndrome* 49, no. 4 (December 2008): 410–15.

65. Anna Kata, "Anti-vaccine Activists, Web 2.0, and the Postmodern Paradigm: An Overview of Tactics and Tropes used Online by the Anti-vaccination Movement," *Vaccine* 30, no. 25 (May 28, 2012): 3778–89.

66. On climate denialism, see Naomi Oreskes and Erik Conway, *Merchants of Doubt: How a Handful of Scientists Obscured the Truth on Issues from Tobacco Smoke to Climate Change* (New York: Bloomsbury, 2011), ch. 6.

67. For a sampling of this literature, see Brian Balogh, *Chain Reaction: Expert Debate and Public Participation in American Commercial Nuclear Power, 1945–1975* (New York: Cambridge University Press, 1991); Michael Bernstein, *A Perilous Progress: Economists and Public Purpose in Twentieth-Century America* (Princeton, NJ: Princeton University Press, 2001); Robert Collins, *More: The Politics of Economic Growth in Postwar America* (New York: Oxford University Press, 2000); Robert Proctor, *Cancer Wars: How Politics Shapes What We Know and Don't Know about Cancer* (New York: Basic Books, 1996); Joan Fujimura, *Crafting Science: A Sociohistory of the Quest for the Genetics of Cancer* (Cambridge, MA: Harvard University Press, 1997); Sharon Bertsch McGrayne, *The Theory That Would Not Die: How Bayes's Rule Cracked the Enigma Code, Hunted Down Russian Submarines, and Emerged Triumphant from Two Centuries of Controversy* (New Haven, CT: Yale University Press, 2011).

68. Ronald Bayer, David Johns, and Sandro Galea, "Salt and Public Health: Contested Science and the Challenge of Evidence-Based Decision Making," *Health Affairs* 31, no. 12 (December 2012): 2738–46; Ann La Berge, "How the Ideology of Low Fat Conquered America," *Journal of the History of Medicine and Allied Sciences* 63, no. 2 (April 2008): 139–77; Aaron Carroll and Tiffany Doherty, "Meat Consumption and Health: Food for Thought," *Annals of Internal Medicine* 171, no. 10 (November 19, 2019): 767–68.

69. For the broader context in which these periodic debates occurred, see Barron Lerner, *The Breast Cancer Wars: Hope, Fear, and the Pursuit of a Cure in Twentieth-Century America* (New York: Oxford University Press, 2003); and Robert Aronowitz, *Unnatural History: Breast Cancer and American Society* (New York: Cambridge University Press, 2007).

70. Ronald Wasserstein and Nicole Lazar, "The ASA Statement on p-Values: Context, Process, and Purpose," *American Statistician* 70, no. 2 (June 2016): 129–33.

71. National Vaccine Information Center, 2021, https://www.nvic.org/.

72. Casey Newton, "How the 'Plandemic' Video Hoax Went Viral," *The Verge*, May 12, 2020.

73. Elon Musk (@Elon Musk), Twitter, April 26, 2020, https://twitter.com/elonmusk/status/1254495050228260865; "ACEP-AAEM Joint Statement on Physician Misinformation," American College of Emergency Physicians, April 27, 2020, https://www.acep.org/corona/COVID-19-alert/covid-19-articles/acep-aaem-joint-statement-on-physician-misinformation/.

74. Jon Passantino and Oliver Darcy, "Social Media Giants Remove Viral Video with False Coronavirus Claims That Trump Retweeted," *CNN*, July 28, 2020.

75. Peter Navarro, "Anthony Fauci Has Been Wrong about Everything I Have Interacted with Him On," *USA Today*, July 15, 2020.

76. Atlas's views earned rebuke from many infectious disease specialists who criticized him in open letters. See, for example, "Open Letter from Stanford University Regarding Dr. Scott Atlas," Pediatric Infectious Diseases Society, October 8, 2020, https://pids.org/2020/10/08/open-letter-from-stanford-university-regarding-dr-scott-atlas/; Kaitlan Collins, "Trump Adds Coronavirus Adviser Who Echoes His Unscientific Claims," *CNN*, August 12, 2020.

77. "Great Barrington Declaration," October 4, 2020, https://gbdeclaration.org/.

78. Dan Diamond, "'We Want Them Infected': Trump Appointee Demanded 'Herd Immunity' Strategy, Emails Reveal," *Politico*, December 16, 2020; Susan Jaffe, "Media Reports Reveal Political Interference at the US CDC," *The Lancet* 396, no. 10255 (September 26, 2020): 875.

79. For an analysis of the forces that drove Trump—and to which he might have been pandering—see Rogers Brubaker, "Paradoxes of Populism during the Pandemic," *Thesis Eleven*, November 3, 2020, 1–15.

80. David Rosner and Gerald Markowitz, *Are We Ready?: Public Health since 9/11* (Berkeley: University of California Press, 2006), 67.

81. Rosner and Markowitz, *Are We Ready?*, 118.

82. Shelley Hearne, Laura Segal, Michael Earls, et al., *Ready or Not? Protecting the Public's Health in the Age of Bioterrorism* (Washington, DC: Trust for America's Health, 2004), 12.

83. Matt McKillop and Vinu Ilakkuvan, *The Impact of Chronic Underfunding on America's Public Health System: Trends, Risks, and Recommendations* (Washington, DC: Trust for America's Health, 2019).

84. Laura Weer, Laura Ungar, Michelle Smith, et al., "Hollowed-Out Public Health System Faces More Cuts amid Virus," Kaiser Health Network, July 1, 2020, https://khn.org/news/us-public-health-system-underfunded-under-threat-faces-more-cuts-amid-covid-pandemic/.

85. Les Leopold, "COVID-19's Class War," *American Prospect*, July 28, 2020.

86. Serina Chang, Emma Pierson, Pang Wei Koh, et al., "Mobility Network Models of COVID-19 Explain Inequities and Inform Reopening," *Nature* 589 (January 7, 2021): 82–87.

87. Yea-Hung Chen, Maria Glymour, Alicia Riley, et al., "Excess Mortality Associated with the COVID-19 Pandemic among Californians 18–65 Years of Age, by Occupational Sector and Occupation: March through October 2020," *medRxiv*, January 22, 2021.

88. Jo Phelan, Bruce Link, and Parisa Tehranifar, "Social Conditions as Fundamental Causes of Health Inequalities: Theory, Evidence, and Policy Implications," *Journal of Health and Social Behavior* 51, no. S1 (October 2010): S28–40.

## Notes to Chapter 18

1. Molly Ball, *Pelosi* (New York: Henry Holt, 2020), 93. On the amount raised during the 2020 cycle (in which the party lost seats), see Nicholas Fandos, "Leader of Impeachment Ponders Life after Trump," *New York Times*, November 19, 2020.

2. For an insightful analysis of suburban women in the Resistance that foreshadowed the 2018 and 2020 elections, see Lara Putnam and Theda Skocpol, "Middle America Reboots Democracy," *Democracy Journal*, February 20, 2018, https://democracyjournal.org/arguments/middle-america-reboots-democracy/.

3. Stephen Skowronek, *Presidential Leadership in Political Time: Reprise and Reappraisal*, 3rd ed., rev. and expanded (Lawrence: University of Kansas Press, 2020), 211.

4. Michelle Goldberg, "The First Post-Reagan Presidency," *New York Times*, January 28, 2021, https://www.nytimes.com/2021/01/28/opinion/biden-president-progressive.html?action=click&module=Opinion&pgtype=Homepage.

5. For an excellent discussion of how Democratic activists explained the defeat, see Seth Masket, *Learning from Loss: The Democrats, 2016–2020* (Cambridge: Cambridge University Press, 2020), especially 60–116; Nate Silver, *FiveThirtyEight*, "The Comey Letter Probably Cost Clinton the Election," May 3, 2017, https://fivethirtyeight.com/features/the-comey-letter-probably-cost-clinton-the-election/.

6. Masket, *Learning from Loss*, 145.

7. The next several paragraphs are adapted from my article "How Democrats Can Take Charge," published in the *New Republic*, March 2021, 20–25.

8. Edward-Isaac Dovere, *Battle for the Soul: Inside the Democrats' Campaigns to Defeat Trump* (New York: Viking, 2021), 15.

9. Irving Howe, "A New Political Atmosphere in America?," *Dissent*, Winter 1959, 7.

10. Warren quoted in "The Axe Files," *CNN*, March 2, 2019, accessed August 4, 2021, https://archive.org/details/CNNW_20190303_000000_The_Axe_Files/start/180/end/240.

11. Central Research Section of the FBI, "Membership of the Communist Party, USA, 1919–1954," 1955. Thanks to Harvey Klehr for sending me a copy of this document. On DSA members in Congress see Peter Dreier, "The Number of Democratic Socialists in the House Will Soon Double," accessed August 4, 2021, https://talkingpointsmemo.com/cafe/number-democratic-socialists-congress-soon-double-down-ballot-movement-scored-biggest-victories.

12. For a lively, entirely sympathetic report on the new Left Democrats, see David Freedlander, *The AOC Generation: How Millennials Are Seizing Power and Rewriting the Rules of American Politics* (Boston: Beacon Press, 2021).

13. Unnamed official quoted in Evan Osnos, *Joe Biden: The Life, the Run, and What Matters Now* (New York: Scribner, 2020), 65. Also see the postelection analysis of Biden's campaign in Alexander Burns, Jonathan Martin and Katie Glueck, "How Joe Biden Won the Presidency," *New York Times*, November 7, 2020, https://www.nytimes.com/2020/11/07/us/politics/joe-biden-president.html.

14. A point made by Democratic strategist David Shor: "And the reality is that state parties have to do some ethically questionable things to keep the lights on because small-dollar donors generally don't donate to their campaigns. So, in state and local politics, corporate money is absolutely a big driver." Eric Levitz, "David Shor's Unified Theory of American Politics," *New York Magazine*, July 17, 2020, https://nymag.com/intelligencer/2020/07/david-shor-cancel-culture-2020-election-theory-polls.html.

15. Daniel Schlozman, "Beltway Blues," *Dissent*, Summer 2018, https://www.dissentmagazine.org/article/beltway-blues-democrats-coalition-defining-party.

16. Aaron Blake, "Republicans Came within 90,000 Votes of Controlling All of Washington," *Washington Post*, February 9, 2020, https://www.washingtonpost.com/politics/2021/02/09/republicans-came-within-90000-votes-controlling-all-washington.

17. For the audio and transcript of the speech, see https://millercenter.org/the-presidency/presidential-speeches/june-27-1936-democratic-national-convention, accessed August 4, 2021.

18. I borrow the term from Lizabeth Cohen's splendid book, *Making a New Deal* (New York: Cambridge University Press, 1991).

19. Obama quoted in https://www.npr.org/sections/thetwo-way/2011/12/06/143215870/obama-this-is-a-make-or-break-moment-for-the-middle-class, accessed August 4, 2021.

20. Quoted in Osnos, *Joe Biden*, 13.

## Notes to Chapter 19

1. *Congressional Record*, February 9, 2021, S538; James Russell Lowell, The Present "Crisis," Poets.org, accessed August 17, 2021, https://poets.org/poem/present-crisis.

2. The poem is also the basis of a popular hymn "Once to Every Man and Nation," which diverges in interesting ways from the poem to emphasize personal, not national, salvation. *Congressional Record*, February 9, 2021, S538; Lowell, "Present Crisis"; James Russell Lowell, "Once to Every Man and Nation #538," Hymnary.org, 2008, https://hymnary.org/hymn/BH2008/538.

3. James Russell Lowell, "The Election in November," *Atlantic Monthly*, October 1860, https://www.theatlantic.com/magazine/archive/1860/10/the-election-in-november/306549/; Michael Kammen, *A Machine That Would Go of Itself: The Constitution in American Culture* (New York: Knopf, 1986).

4. Frank O. Bowman, *High Crimes and Misdemeanors: A History of Impeachment for the Age of Trump* (New York: Cambridge University Press, 2019), 311.

5. See, for example, the essays in "The Democracy Constitution," *Democracy*, Summer 2021, https://democracyjournal.org/magazine/61/the-democracy-constitution/; E. J. Dionne Jr., "Stacey Abrams Prods Our Constitutional Imagination," *Washington Post*, July 11, 2021, https://www.washingtonpost.com/opinions/2021/07/11/stacey-abrams-prods-our-constitutional-imagination/; and my own conclusion to Gregory P. Downs, *The Second American Revolution: The Civil War-Era Struggle over Cuba and the Rebirth of the American Republic* (Chapel Hill: University of North Carolina Press, 2019).

6. *Proceedings of the United States Senate in the Impeachment Trial of President Donald John Trump*, 116th Cong., 2d Sess., S. Doc. No. 116-18 (Washington, DC: Government Printing Office, 2020), I:415–16; *Congressional Record*, No. 166, No. 24, February 5, 2020, S897; "The Federalist Papers: No. 65," Avalon Project, accessed August 17, 2021, https://avalon.law.yale.edu/18th_century/fed65.asp.

7. *Proceedings of the United States Senate in the Impeachment Trial of President Donald John Trump*, I:478; Gregory P. Downs, "Impeachment Is the Right Call Even If the Senate Keeps President Trump in Office," *Washington Post*, October 7, 2019, https://www.washingtonpost.com/outlook/2019/10/07/impeachment-is-right-call-even-if-senate-keeps-president-trump-office/; Michael Les Benedict, *The Impeachment and Trial of Andrew Johnson* (New York: W. W. Norton, 1973).

A classic legal text on impeachment is the now-updated Charles L. Black Jr. and Philip Bobbitt, *Impeachment: A Handbook, New Edition* (New Haven, CT: Yale University Press, 2018), originally published in 1974. Some high-profile lawyers and professors attempt similarly high-minded, legalistic approaches now. Cass Sunstein, *Impeachment: A Citizen's Guide* (New York: Penguin, 2019); Jeffrey A. Engel, Jon Meacham, Timothy Naftali, and Peter Baker, *Impeachment: An American History* (New York: Modern Library, 2018).

8. Lawrence Tribe and Joshua Matz, *To End a Presidency: The Power of Impeachment* (New York: Basic Books, 2018), 169–72.

9. Bowman, *High Crimes and Misdemeanors*, 203, 217.

10. Russell Watson, "Vince Foster's Suicide: The Rumor Mill Churns," *Newsweek*, March 20, 1994, https://www.newsweek.com/vince-fosters-suicide-rumor-mill-churns-185900.

11. Bowman, *High Crimes and Misdemeanors*, 212–18.

12. Peter Baker, "Bill Clinton," in Engel et al., *Impeachment: An American History*, 155–204; Bowman, *High Crimes and Misdemeanors*, 216–26.

13. Mark Landler, "Meeting between Bill Clinton and Loretta Lynch Provokes Political Furor," *New York Times*, June 30, 2016, https://www.nytimes.com/2016/07/01/us/politics/meeting-between-bill-clinton-and-loretta-lynch-provokes-political-furor.html; Nate Silver, "The Comey Letter Probably Cost Clinton the Election," *FiveThirtyEight*, May 3, 2017, https://fivethirtyeight.com/features/the-comey-letter-probably-cost-clinton-the-election/.

14. Tribe and Matz, *To End a Presidency*, 178–81.

15. Tribe and Matz, *To End a Presidency*, 182–84.

16. Tribe and Matz, *To End a Presidency*, 186.

17. Matea Gold, "The Campaign to Impeach President Trump Has Begun," *Washington Post*, January 20, 2017; Tribe and Matz, *To End a Presidency*, 187.

18. Tribe and Matz, *To End a Presidency*, 151–96.

19. Sunstein, *Impeachment*, 178–87.

20. Neal Katyal with Sam Koppelman, *Impeach: The Case against Donald Trump* (Boston: Mariness Press, 2019), 76–87.

21. Katyal, *Impeach*, 76–87.

22. *Congressional Record*, No. 166, No. 24, February 5, 2020, S906, S909.

23. "Seven Freshman Democrats: These Allegations Are a Threat to All We Have Sworn to Protect," *Washington Post*, September 24, 2019, https://www.washingtonpost.com/opinions/2019/09/24/seven-freshman-democrats-these-allegations-are-threat-all-we-have-sworn-protect/.

24. *Proceedings of the United States Senate in the Impeachment Trial of President Donald John Trump*, I:23–25, 762; *Congressional Record*, No. 166, No. 24, S884.

25. *Proceedings of the United States Senate in the Impeachment Trial of President Donald John Trump*, I:16, 48; *Congressional Record*, No. 166, No. 24, February 5, 2020, S896.

26. *Proceedings of the United States Senate in the Impeachment Trial of President Donald John Trump*, I:16, 410, 463; *Congressional Record*, No. 166, No. 24, February 5, 2020, S874, S878, S902.

27. *Proceedings of the United States Senate in the Impeachment Trial of President Donald John Trump*, I:415–16; *Congressional Record*, No. 166, No. 24, February 5, 2020, S897; Avalon Project, "The Federalist Papers, No. 65."

28. *Congressional Record*, No. 166, No. 24, February 5, 2020, S885, S889.

29. Elise Viebeck and Daniela Santamariña, "Here's When Biden's Win Becomes Official—and How Trump Has Been Trying to Prevent That," *Washington Post*, December 8, 2020, https://www.washingtonpost.com/elections/2020/11/12/vote-certification-deadlines-ga-mi-wi-nv-az-pa/; John Bowden, "Collins: Trump Has Learned 'a Pretty Big Lesson' from Impeachment," *The Hill*, February 4, 2020, https://thehill.com/homenews/senate/481486-collins-trump-has-learned-a-pretty-big-lesson-from-impeachment.

30. "Counting Electoral Votes: An Overview of Procedures at the Joint Session, Including Objections by Members of Congress," Congressional Research Services RL32717, updated December 8, 2020, https://fas.org/sgp/crs/misc/RL32717.pdf.

31. Maggie Haberman and Jonathan Martin, "After the Speech: What Trump Did as the Capitol Was Attacked," *New York Times*, February 13, 2021, https://www.nytimes.com/2021/02/13/us/politics/trump-capitol-riot.html; Lauren Leatherby and Anjali Singhvi, "How Trump's Calls to G.O.P. Lawmakers Fit in the Timeline of the Capitol Riot," *New York Times*, February 13, 2021, https://www.nytimes.com/interactive/2021/01/15/us/trump-capitol-riot-timeline.html.

32. *Congressional Record*, January 13, 2021; H166-68, H179, H188; January 25, 2021, S125; February 13, 2021, S720.

33. "'It Is Never Too Late to Do the Right Thing': Read Key Quotes from Democrats and Republicans on Impeachment," *New York Times*, January 13, 2021, https://www.nytimes.com/live/2021/01/13/us/trump-impeachment#trump-impeachment-democrats-republicans-quotes.

34. Alex Rogers, "Democrats to Take Senate as Ossoff Wins Runoff, CNN Projects," *CNN*, January 6, 2021, https://www.cnn.com/2021/01/06/politics/ossoff-perdue-georgia-election-news/index.html; Barbara Sprunt, "With New Georgia Senators Sworn In, Democrats Officially Control the Senate," *NPR*, January 20, 2021, https://www.npr.org/sections/inauguration-day-live-updates/2021/01/20/958531015/new-georgia-senators-sworn-in-democrats-now-officially-control-the-senate.

35. *Congressional Record*, February 9, 2021, S538, S589, S598–600; Nicholas Fandos, "Senate Agrees Trial Is Constitutional, as Trump Consolidates Votes for an Acquittal," *New York Times*, February 9, 2021.

36. Lisa Kashinsky, "Full Text of Trump's Statement on Impeachment Acquittal," *Boston Herald*, February 13, 2021, https://www.bostonherald.com/2021/02/13/full-text-of-trumps-statement-on-impeachment-acquittal/; Katyal, *Impeach*; Engel et al., *Impeachment*; Black and Bobbitt, *Impeachment*.

37. Cristina Marcos, "Rep. Marjorie Greene Files Articles of Impeachment against Biden," *The Hill*, January 21, 2021, https://thehill.com/homenews/house/535317-rep-marjorie-taylor-greene-files-articles-of-impeachment-against-biden.

# INDEX